"It is both a pleasure and a privilege to provide this strong and unequivocal endorsement of so informative and consumer-friendly a book as this one. Grounded in the latest science of ADHD, filled with exceptionally detailed advice . . . parents and educators will find this book to be exceptionally useful in raising a successful ADHD child."

—Russell A. Barkley, Ph.D., professor of psychiatry, Medical University of South Carolina, and author of *Taking Charge of ADHD*

"For over a decade, Sandra Rief's *How to Reach and Teach Children with ADD/ADHD* has been the most definitive and user-friendly 'go-to' guide for teachers and parents eager to help children with ADHD succeed in school, home, and life overall. Now updated with the latest research findings from the last ten years, this book outstrips even the original. Unlike so many other volumes, this book is hands-on, well-organized, extremely readable, and full of the kind of wise, practical advice that only comes from someone who has been there (and continues to be there!) helping teachers, parents, children, and youth struggling with ADHD. I especially like the focus on different ages, school settings, and subjects. My highest recommendation for this book, and my greatest p̶ ̶ ̶ ̶ ̶ ̶Sandra making this invaluable resource available!"

—Peter S. Jensen, M.D., director, Center for the Advancement o̶ ̶U̶ ̶ ̶ ̶ ̶ ̶ ̶tal Health and Ruane Professor of Child Psychiatry at Columbia University

"Sandra Rief is one of the most astute as well as compassionate voices in the world about ADHD. She really gets it, and this book will give you what she gets. A wonderful contribution and valuable, practical resource for all teachers, parents, and clinicians."

—Edward Hallowell, M.D., author of *When You Worry About the Child You Love* and coauthor of *Driven by Distraction*

"This valuable resource should be at every teacher's fingertips! Sandra Rief offers current research-based strategies and information on ADHD that are a must read for every educator."

—Ellen Stantus, special education director, Davis School District, Farmington, Utah

"This book not only addresses the latest research on this neuro-biological difference, but goes further by offering creative strategies for home and school in order to help these students reach their full potential. As always, Sandra Rief fills her book with what to do about it."

—Jill Murphy, special educator, ADHD life skills and academic coach, ADD Resources Parent Support, and mother of two children with ADD/ADHD, Bonney Lake, Washington

Jossey-Bass Teacher

Jossey-Bass Teacher provides K–12 teachers with essential knowledge and tools to create a positive and lifelong impact on student learning. Trusted and experienced educational mentors offer practical classroom-tested and theory-based teaching resources for improving teaching practice in a broad range of grade levels and subject areas. From one educator to another, we want to be your first source to make every day your best day in teaching. *Jossey-Bass Teacher* resources serve two types of informational needs—essential knowledge and essential tools.

Essential knowledge resources provide the foundation, strategies, and methods from which teachers may design curriculum and instruction to challenge and excite their students. Connecting theory to practice, essential knowledge books rely on a solid research base and time-tested methods, offering the best ideas and guidance from many of the most experienced and well-respected experts in the field.

Essential tools save teachers time and effort by offering proven, ready-to-use materials for in-class use. Our publications include activities, assessments, exercises, instruments, games, ready reference, and more. They enhance an entire course of study, a weekly lesson, or a daily plan. These essential tools provide insightful, practical, and comprehensive materials on topics that matter most to K–12 teachers.

How to Reach and Teach Children with

ADD/ADHD

Practical Techniques, Strategies, and Interventions

SECOND EDITION

Sandra F. Rief

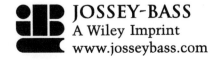

JOSSEY-BASS
A Wiley Imprint
www.josseybass.com

Published by Jossey-Bass
A Wiley Imprint
989 Market Street, San Francisco, CA 94103-1741   www.josseybass.com

Jossey-Bass books and products are available through most bookstores. To contact Jossey-Bass directly call our Customer Care Department within the U.S. at 800-956-7739, outside the U.S. at 317-572-3986, or fax 317-572-4002.

Jossey-Bass also publishes its books in a variety of electronic formats. Some content that appears in print may not be available in electronic books.

ISBN 0-7879-7295-9

Printed in the United States of America
SECOND EDITION
PB Printing   10 9 8 7 6 5 4 3 2 1

About the Author

Sandra F. Rief, M.A., is a leading educational consultant, author, and speaker on effective strategies and interventions for helping students with learning, attention, and behavioral challenges. Sandra presents seminars, workshops, and keynotes nationally and internationally on this topic. She received her B.A. and M.A. degrees from the University of Illinois. Sandra was formerly an award-winning teacher (1995 California Resource Specialist of the Year) with over twenty-three years' experience teaching in public schools.

Sandra is the author of several books and publications, including the following published by John Wiley & Sons: *The ADHD Book of Lists*; *How to Reach and Teach All Students in the Inclusive Classroom* (co-authored with Julie Heimburge); *The ADD/ADHD Checklist: An Easy Reference for Parents & Teachers*; and *Alphabet Learning Center Activities Kit* (co-authored with Nancy Fetzer).

Sandra also developed and presented the acclaimed educational videos *ADHD & LD: Powerful Teaching Strategies and Accommodations*; *How to Help Your Child Succeed in School: Strategies and Guidance for Parents of Children with ADHD and/or Learning Disabilities*; *ADHD: Inclusive Instruction & Collaborative Practices*, and together with Linda Fisher and Nancy Fetzer, the videos *Successful Classrooms: Effective Teaching Strategies for Raising Achievement in Reading and Writing* and *Successful Schools: How to Raise Achievement & Support "At-Risk" Students*.

Sandra is a past member of the CHADD National Professional Advisory Board and was on the faculty of NICHQ (National Initiative for Children's Healthcare Quality—Collaborative on ADHD). For more information, visit her website at www.sandrarief.com.

About This Book

This book offers comprehensive guidance to everyone engaged in the positive education of children who have been diagnosed with ADD/ADHD. Whether you are a classroom teacher or a parent; a special education teacher, counselor, or psychologist; or a school or district administrator, this book will be a valuable resource. You'll find information, techniques, and strategies to help these students succeed. While the book addresses the specific needs of students with ADD/ADHD, the strategies are also appropriate and recommended for all students who appear to have attention problems, learning disabilities, or are underachieving for any reason, including gifted children.

This second edition includes enhanced content in the following areas: medications, case studies, documentation, placement, model programs, and references, among others. For easy use, the information is organized into thirty-five sections that provide comprehensive, practical guidance on such topics as:

* Preventing behavioral problems in a classroom
* Learning styles: elements and interventions
* Cooperative learning techniques
* Q&A with a school nurse regarding medication and its management
* Techniques for relaxation and visualization
* Challenges and specific interventions for students of all ages
* Tips on communicating effectively with parents, physicians, and agencies

Dedication

This book is dedicated to the memory of my beloved son, Benjamin, and to all of the children who face obstacles in their young lives each day with loving, trusting hearts, determination, and extraordinary courage. I also wish to dedicate this book in loving memory of Levana Estline—dear friend, exceptional teacher, and a blessing to all who knew her.

Contents

PART 6: ADDITIONAL SUPPORTS AND STRATEGIES

Acknowledgments

My deepest thanks and appreciation to

- Itzik, Ariel, Jackie, Gil, Sharon, Jason, Mom, and Ben—for the joy you bring me, and your constant, loving support, encouragement, and good humor
- My girls (Jackie and Sharon), the new generation of teachers in the family—I am so proud of you and the enthusiasm, talent, and fresh ideas you bring to the profession
- All of the children who have touched my heart and inspired me throughout the years. It is because of you that I love what I do
- The special families who have shared with me their struggles and triumphs and allowed me to be part of their lives
- Mrs. Linda Haughey and the wonderful Haughey family, for courageously sharing their personal, powerful story in Section 4.1
- My dear friends, Lynda and Diana, for so generously sharing their precious sons' case studies, school histories, and intervention plans (last names omitted at their request to protect their privacy)
- All of the wonderful, dedicated educators I have had the great fortune to work with and meet over the years, thank you for sharing with me your creative strategies, ideas, and insights
- The extraordinary parents (especially the wonderful volunteers in CHADD and other organizations worldwide) whose tireless efforts have raised awareness about ADHD, and as a result, improved the care and education of our children
- All of the researchers and practitioners in the different fields dedicated to helping children and families with ADHD, LD, and other disabilities, from whom I have learned so much
- Steve Thompson, Ph.D., my editor at Jossey-Bass in San Francisco, for all of your help and guidance, and for making it such a pleasure to write this book
- Sandra Wright and Susie Horn, exceptional school nurses in the San Diego City Schools—my friends and role models—for all you have done to help children with ADHD and their families
- Karen Easter, one of the wonderful mothers I have been privileged to meet and befriend at one of my workshops, for sharing your original poems in this book

* My illustrators—Decker Forrest, an incredibly talented former student of mine, who was in the eighth grade at the time he drew these illustrations (first published in the 1993 edition), and Ariel Rief, my darling son, who provided some of the other illustrations in this book (as well as those in *The ADHD Book of Lists*)

* Joe, Spencer, Steve, Susan, Mike, Bruce, Amy, Joseph, John, Brita, Malinda, Bob, and Brad (teens and adults with ADHD), and the group of early childhood educators, who allowed me to interview them and share their insights in excerpts throughout this book

Introduction

When I first wrote *How to Reach and Teach ADD/ADHD Children* back in 1993, awareness of attention-deficit/hyperactivity disorder and information/resources available were minimal at best. Since that time, a tremendous amount of scientific research and education efforts have taken place. It would be rare to find anyone who has not heard of ADD or ADHD.

Reliable information is now easily accessible, and far more resources than ever before are available to parents/caregivers, educators, and those who work with and treat children with attention deficit disorders. However, there is still a great deal of misinformation, controversy, and myths surrounding this disorder. There are still countless children and teens who have ADHD and who have been suffering and experiencing school failure due to their lack of identification or treatment and misinterpretation of their behaviors by teachers and others, who don't understand or accept the reality of their disorder and its impact on school performance.

According to a Surgeon General's report, attention-deficit/hyperactivity disorder is the most common neurobehavioral disorder of childhood, affecting approximately 3 to 7 percent of school-aged children. Every teacher has at least one student with ADHD in his or her classroom. Educators need to be aware and knowledgeable about the nature of the disorder, as well as the strategies effective in reaching and teaching these students. Parents of children with ADHD also need to be well-informed and equipped with the skills and strategies that help in managing and coping with inattentive, hyperactive, and impulsive behaviors. It is often not easy to live with a child who has ADHD (either at home or at school). Knowledge about the disorder is very important, because when we understand what ADHD is and how it affects the child's behavior and performance, it helps us become more tolerant and empathetic.

Attention deficit/hyperactivity disorder is not something that we can "cure"; nor does a child with ADHD "outgrow" it in most cases (although behaviors are manifested differently as the child matures and symptoms may be less or more impairing at different times in their lives). We, the significant adults in their lives, play a major role in how well these children and teens succeed and how they feel about themselves. We are the ones who can help them manage with the challenges they face, cope with frustrations, and compensate for weaknesses. We are also the ones who can help them see and utilize their many strengths and value their uniqueness.

Many children with ADHD have grown up to be very successful adults. They have drawn on their strengths, creativity, and "survival skills" to their advantage.

On the other hand, there are many who have not fared well. There is a high correlation between ADHD and a number of negative outcomes. A significant percentage of individuals who drop out of school, are unable to keep a job, are stuck in work positions to which they have defaulted rather than aspired, fail in their interpersonal relationships, pack our prison system, have "self-medicated" with drugs and alcohol, and so on, had this disorder without the benefit of identification, intervention, and treatment. Many adolescents and adults with ADHD have painful memories of their childhoods, particularly of their experiences and frustrations in school. Many experienced years of failure and serious depression.

It is our responsibility in the schools to pull together as a team, doing everything we can to meet these students' needs effectively. This includes providing each child with the environment, engaging instruction, skills, tools, and confidence to learn and achieve. We need to be patient, positive, and understanding—and try to see past the behaviors to the whole child—as we provide support and remove the obstacles in their paths.

Much can be done to help those with ADHD. Most of this book focuses on specific strategies, supports, and interventions that have been found to be effective in minimizing the typical problems associated with ADHD and on helping these children/teens achieve success. I am very fortunate to have spent most of my twenty-three-year teaching career working at a school that was a model in "inclusive education." Our staff was firmly committed to reaching and teaching *all* students; and we were very successful in doing so. A number of strategies or recommendations in this book come from what I have learned from my many students with ADHD and/or learning disabilities, their families, and my colleagues.

In addition, I have had the privilege these past few years of observing hundreds of classrooms and working with scores of educators across the United States and internationally. I am grateful for the openness of these wonderful teachers (and parents), who so willingly shared their ideas, strategies, struggles, and successes. Their stories and insights have inspired and taught me so much.

For easy use, this resource is organized into six parts that provide comprehensive, practical guidance divided into sections. In essence, the content in much of this book comes from (1) a lot of "hands-on" experience working with students who have ADHD and (2) from many experts I have learned from—particularly in the fields of education and psychology. Although the book is designed and written to address the specific needs of students with ADHD, the suggested strategies are generally "good teaching practices" for *all* students (or "positive parenting practices" for any child). The techniques and suggestions are, however, of particular benefit for those who are experiencing behavior, attention, or learning difficulties. Be aware that many gifted, intelligent children fall within this category.

I urge all readers to read Section 4.1, A Parent's Story, the poignant account by the mother of six children, four of whom have been diagnosed with ADD/ADHD. The original story from the first edition is included, along with a follow-up about the family a decade later. In addition, be sure to read Section 4.2, the highly informative and insightful case studies of Adam and Vincent. One of the rewards I have gained in writing this book comes from the wonderful opportunity I had to interview teenagers and adults from across the country who have grown up with ADHD. Excerpts of these interviews are included throughout this book. By their openly sharing their experiences and insights, the parents' stories, the case studies, and the personal interviews reveal an important message about what makes a difference and the power we have as teachers.

It is always preferable to be able to identify children with ADHD or any special needs early and then initiate interventions and supports at a young age in order to avoid some of the frustration, failure, and subsequent loss of self-esteem. However, it is *never* too late to help a child. In many cases, the kind of help that makes a difference does not take a huge effort on our part. Sometimes even small changes (such as in the way we respond to our child or teen) can lead to significant improvements. If I am able to convey any single message with this book, I wish for it to be one of hope and optimism. When we work together—providing the necessary structure, guidance, encouragement, and support—each and every one of our children can succeed!

Sandra F. Rief

A Note from the Author

The most official term for the disorder at this time is Attention-Deficit/Hyperactivity Disorder (AD/HD). You may see it in print with or without the slash. In the past, the term ADD was commonly used. Many people still prefer to use ADD if the individual does not have the hyperactive characteristics. However, ADHD (with or without the slash) is the most current term or abbreviation, and it is inclusive of *all types* of the disorder:

* The predominantly inattentive type (those without hyperactivity)
* The predominantly hyperactive/impulsive type
* The combined type

I want to make clear to readers that, although I am maintaining the use of ADD/ADHD in the title (as in the first edition of 1993), I have chosen throughout this new book to refer to this disorder as ADHD. Please be aware that all references to ADHD also *include* those individuals who do not have the hyperactive behaviors.

Key Information for Understanding and Managing ADHD

Understanding Attention-Deficit/ Hyperactivity Disorder

As mentioned in this book's introduction as well, many people continue to use the two distinct terms of ADD (Attention-Deficit Disorder) and ADHD (Attention-Deficit/Hyperactivity Disorder). Some use the two terms interchangeably, and others specifically use ADD when referring to those who do not have the symptoms of hyperactivity. However, the most current and official term or acronym is ADHD (with or without the slash). This is the umbrella term or acronym under which all three types of the disorder are included:

* The *predominantly inattentive* type of ADHD (those without hyperactivity)
* The *predominantly hyperactive/impulsive* type of ADHD (those without a significant number of the inattentive symptoms)
* The *combined type* (the most common type of ADHD—those with a significant amount of symptoms in all three core areas—inattention, impulsivity, and hyperactivity)

In the first edition of this book (1993) I had used ADD/ADHD, and it remains as such in the title of this new edition. However, throughout the remainder of this text I choose to use the most current terminology of ADHD; and this will include all three types of attention-deficit disorders.

Definitions and Descriptions of ADHD

There are several descriptions or definitions of ADHD based on the most widely held belief of the scientific community at this time. The following are some of those provided by leading researchers and specialists in the field:

* ADHD is a neurobiological behavioral disorder characterized by chronic and developmentally inappropriate degrees of inattention, impulsivity, and, in some cases, hyperactivity (CHADD, 2001c).
* ADHD is a brain-based disorder that arises out of differences in the central nervous system (CNS)—both in structural and neurochemical areas.
* ADHD is a dimensional disorder of human behaviors that all people exhibit at times to certain degrees. Those with ADHD display the symptoms to a significant degree that is maladaptive and developmentally inappropriate compared to others that age.
* ADHD is a developmental disorder of self-control, consisting of problems with attention span, impulse control, and activity level (Barkley, 2000b).
* ADHD is a chronic physiological disorder that interferes with a person's capacity to

regulate and inhibit behavior and sustain attention to tasks in developmentally appropriate ways.

* ADHD is a neurobiological behavioral disorder causing a high degree of variability and inconsistency in performance, output, and production.
* ADHD refers to a family of related chronic neurobiological disorders that interfere with an individual's capacity to regulate activity level (hyperactivity), inhibit behavior (impulsivity), and attend to tasks (inattention) in developmentally appropriate ways (National Institute of Mental Health, 2000; National Resource Center on AD/HD, 2003a).
* Attention-deficit/hyperactivity disorder (ADHD) is the most common neurobehavioral disorder of childhood. ADHD is also among the most prevalent chronic health conditions affecting school-aged children (American Academy of Pediatrics, 2000).
* ADHD is a neurobehavioral disorder characterized by differences in brain structure and function that affect behavior, thoughts, and emotions (CHADD, 2001c).
* ADHD is characterized by a constellation of problems with inattention, hyperactivity, and impulsivity. These problems are developmentally inappropriate and cause difficulty in daily life (Goldstein, 1999).

Behavioral Characteristics of ADHD

The fourth edition of the *Diagnostic and Statistical Manual* (DSM-IV), published by the American Psychiatric Association [APA] in 1994, is the source of the official criteria for diagnosing attention-deficit/hyperactivity disorder. The DSM-IV and more recently the DSM-IV-TR (text revised) lists nine specific symptoms under the category of inattention and nine specific symptoms under the hyperactive/impulsive category. Part of the diagnostic criteria is that the child or

teen *often displays at least six of the nine* symptoms of either the inattentive or the hyperactive/impulsive categories. The lists below contain those symptoms or behaviors found in the DSM-IV (1994) and DSM-IV-TR (2000). Below are the symptoms specifically listed in the DSM *(which are indicated in italics),* as well as additional common and related behaviors (Rief, 2003).

The Predominantly Inattentive Type of ADHD

This type of ADHD (what many still call ADD), refers to those with a significant number of inattentive symptoms that occur frequently. They may have some, but not a significant number of the hyperactive/impulsive symptoms. Since they do not exhibit the disruptive behaviors that get our attention, it is easy to overlook these students and misinterpret their behaviors and symptoms (for example, as "not trying" or "being lazy").

It is common to display any of the following behaviors at times, in different situations, to a certain degree. Those who truly have an attention-deficit disorder have a history of showing many of these characteristics—far above the "normal" range developmentally—causing impairment in their functioning (at school, home, social situations, work). The nature of these inattentive symptoms tends to heavily impact academic performance and achievement. Those written in italics are the behaviors that are listed in the DSM-IV and DSM-IV-TR.

Characteristics and Symptoms of Inattention (That Occur Often)

* *Easily distracted by extraneous stimuli* (sights, sounds, movement in the environment)
* *Does not seem to listen when spoken to directly*
* Difficulty remembering and following directions
* *Difficulty sustaining attention in tasks and play activities*

DECKER
FORREST

* Difficulty sustaining level of alertness to tasks that are tedious, perceived as boring, or not of one's choosing
* *Forgetful in daily activities*
* *Does not follow through on instructions and fails to finish schoolwork, chores, or duties in the workplace (not due to oppositional behavior or failure to understand instructions)*
* Tunes out—may appear "spacey"
* Daydreams (thoughts are elsewhere)
* Appears confused
* Easily overwhelmed
* Difficulty initiating or getting started on tasks
* Does not complete work, resulting in many incomplete assignments
* *Avoids, dislikes, or is reluctant to engage in tasks requiring sustained mental effort (such as schoolwork or homework)*

* Difficulty working independently—needs high degree of refocusing attention to task
* Gets bored easily
* Sluggish or lethargic (may fall asleep easily in class)
* *Fails to pay attention to details and makes many careless mistakes (with math computation, spelling, written mechanics—capitalization, punctuation)*
* Poor study skills
* Inconsistent performance—one day is able to perform a task, the next day cannot; the student is "consistently inconsistent"
* *Loses things necessary for tasks or activities (toys, school assignments, pencils, books, or tools)*
* Disorganized—misplaces or loses belongings; desks, backpacks, lockers, and rooms may be total disaster areas

* *Difficulty organizing tasks and activities* (planning, scheduling, preparing)
* Little or no awareness of time—often underestimates length of time a task will require to complete
* Procrastinates
* Displays weak executive functions as described below in this section

Academic Difficulties Related to Inattention

Reading:

* Loses his or her place when reading
* Cannot stay focused on what he or she is reading (especially if text is difficult, lengthy, boring, not choice reading material), resulting in missing words, details, and spotty comprehension
* Forgets what he or she is reading (limited recall) and needs to reread frequently

Writing:

* Difficulty planning and organizing for the writing assignment
* Off topic as result of losing train of thought
* Minimal written output and production

* Slow speed of output/production—taking two or three times longer to execute on paper what is typical for the average child/teen that age or grade
* Poor spelling, use of capitalization/punctuation, and other mechanics, ability to edit written work (as a result of inattention to these boring details)

Math:

* Numerous computational errors because of inattention to operational signs ($+,-,\times,\div$), decimal points, and so forth
* Poor problem solving due to inability to sustain the focus to complete all steps of the problem with accuracy

The Predominantly Hyperactive-Impulsive Type of ADHD

Those individuals with this type of ADHD have a significant number of hyperactive/impulsive symptoms; they may have some, but not a significant number of inattentive symptoms. Children and teens with ADHD may exhibit many of the following characteristics (not all of them).

Even though each of these behaviors is normal in children at different ages to a certain degree, in those with ADHD, the behaviors *far exceed* that which is normal developmentally (in frequency, level, and intensity). Again, those written in italics are the behaviors that are listed in the DSM-IV and DSM-IV-TR.

Characteristics and Symptoms of Hyperactivity (That Occur Often)

* *"On the go" or acts as if "driven by a motor"*
* *Leaves seat in classroom or in other situations in which remaining seated is expected*
* Cannot sit still (jumping up and out of chair, falling out of chair, sitting on knees or standing by desk)
* Highly energetic—almost nonstop motion
* *Runs about or climbs excessively in situations in which it is inappropriate (in adolescents or adults, may be limited to subjective feelings of restlessness)*
* A high degree of unnecessary movement (pacing, tapping feet, drumming fingers)
* Restlessness
* Seems to need something in hands. Finds/reaches for nearby objects to play with and/or put in mouth
* *Fidgets with hands or feet or squirms in seat*
* Roams around the classroom—is not where he or she is supposed to be
* *Difficulty playing or engaging in leisure activities quietly*
* Intrudes in other people's space; difficulty staying within own boundaries
* Difficulty "settling down" or calming self

Characteristics and Symptoms of Impulsivity (That Occur Often)

* Much difficulty in situations requiring having to wait patiently
* *Talks excessively*
* Difficulty with raising hand and waiting to be called on
* *Interrupts or intrudes on others (butts into conversations or games)*
* *Blurts out answers before questions have been completed*
* *Has difficulty waiting for his or her turn in games and activities*
* Cannot keep hands/feet to self
* Cannot wait or delay gratification—wants things NOW
* Knows the rules and consequences, but repeatedly makes the same errors/ infractions of rules
* Gets in trouble because he or she cannot "stop and think" before acting (responds first/thinks later)
* Difficulty standing in lines
* Makes inappropriate or odd noises
* Does not think or worry about consequences, so tends to be fearless or gravitate to "high risk" behavior
* Engages in physically dangerous activities without considering the consequences (jumping from heights, riding bike into street without looking); hence, a high frequency of injuries
* Accident prone—breaks things
* Difficulty inhibiting what he or she says, making tactless comments—says whatever pops into head and talks back to authority figures
* Begins tasks without waiting for directions (before listening to the full direction or taking the time to read written directions)
* Hurries through tasks (particularly boring ones) to get finished—making numerous careless errors
* Gets easily bored and impatient
* Does not take time to correct/edit work
* Disrupts, bothers others

* Constantly drawn to something more interesting or stimulating in the environment
* Hits when upset or grabs things away from others (not inhibiting responses or thinking of consequences)

Other Common Characteristics in Children and Teens with ADHD

* A high degree of emotionality (temper outbursts, quick to anger, get upset, irritable, moody)
* Easily frustrated
* Overly reactive
* Difficulty with transitions and changes in routine/activity
* Displays aggressive behavior
* Difficult to discipline
* Cannot work for long-term goals or payoffs
* Low self-esteem

* Poor handwriting, fine motor skills, written expression, and output
* Overly sensitive to sounds, textures, or touch (tactile defensive)
* Motivational difficulties
* Receives a lot of negative attention/ interaction from peers and adults
* Learning, school performance difficulties— not achieving or performing to level that is expected (given his or her apparent ability)
* Language and communication problems (sticking to topic, verbal fluency)

Criteria for a Diagnosis of ADHD

It is not just the existence of symptoms that indicate ADHD. It must be proven that there is a history of those symptoms having been evident since before age seven and lasting for a while (at least the past six months). In addition, those symptoms must be (a) more severe than in other children that same age; (b) evident in at least two settings (for example, school and home); and (c) causing impairment in the child's function- ing (academically, socially).

Remember that each individual with ADHD is unique in the combination, amount, and degree of symptoms he or she exhibits, as well as that person's own set of strengths, tal- ents, interests, personality traits, and so forth.

Positive Traits and Characteristics Common in Many Children, Teens, and Adults with ADHD

Parents and teachers must recognize, appreci- ate, and nurture the many talents and positive qualities our children possess. To develop their self-esteem and enable them to become resilient, successful adults, we must help our children to value their areas of competency and strengths. The following are some common positive char- acteristics and traits that many of those with ADHD possess (Rief, 2003):

* Highly energetic
* Verbal
* Spontaneous
* Creative and inventive
* Artistic
* Persistent/tenacious
* Innovative
* Imaginative
* Warmhearted
* Compassionate/caring
* Accepting and forgiving
* Inquisitive
* Resilient
* Makes and creates fun
* Knows how to enjoy the present
* Empathetic
* Sensitive to needs of others
* Resourceful
* Gregarious
* Not boring
* Enthusiastic
* Intelligent/bright
* Humorous
* Outgoing
* Ready for action
* Willing to take a risk and try new things
* Good at improvising
* Enterprising
* Sees different aspects of a situation
* Able to find novel solutions
* Charismatic
* Observant
* Negotiator
* Full of ideas and spunk
* Can think on their feet
* Intuitive
* Good in crisis situations
* Passionate

Girls with Attention-Deficit Disorders

Many girls with ADHD have gone undiagnosed (or misdiagnosed) for years because they fre- quently do not have the typical hyperactive symptoms seen in boys that signal a problem and draw attention. In the past few years, much more attention has been given to girls with the disorder. Girls who do have the combined symptoms of ADHD are very recognizable because their behavior is so significantly out of norm for other girls. But on the whole, most girls have the predominantly inattentive type of the disorder and are often labeled or written off as being "space cadets," "ditzy," or "scattered" (Rief, 2003).

Much of what we are now aware of and beginning to understand about females with ADHD comes from the work of Dr. Kathleen Nadeau, Dr. Patricia Quinn, Dr. Ellen Littman, Sari Solden, and others who have strongly advocated on the behalf of this population. The scientific community has now been looking at gender issues in ADHD. Studies have recently begun to reveal the significance of gender differences and issues and will undoubtedly result in changes and improvements in the diagnosis and treatment for girls and women with this disorder.

According to Dr. Nadeau, Dr. Quinn, and Dr. Littman (1999), girls with ADHD:

* Have more internal and often less external (observable) symptoms
* Have greater likelihood of anxiety and depression
* Experience a lot of academic difficulties, peer rejection, and self-esteem issues
* Are more likely to be hyperverbal than hyperactive

In addition:

* Symptoms in girls tend to increase rather than decrease at puberty, with hormones having a great impact.
* PMS worsens ADHD symptoms by adding to disorganization and emotionality.
* Another reason girls are likely underdiagnosed is because the current diagnostic criteria require evidence of symptom onset before seven years of age; but in girls symptoms are likely to emerge later.

* Girls tend to try very hard to please teachers and parents. They often work exceptionally hard (compulsively so) to achieve academic success.
* Impulsivity in girls can lead to binge eating, engaging in high-risk/high-stimulation activities (smoking, drinking, drugs, sexual promiscuity, unprotected sex) (Nadeau, Littman, & Quinn, 1999).

Dr. Janet Giler (2001) also points out that female social rules place a greater value on cooperation, listening, caretaking, and relationship-maintaining activities, compromising girls with ADHD whose symptoms interfere with these social norms.

ADHD and the "Executive Functions"

When discussing difficulties associated with ADHD, many of them center on the ability to employ the "executive functions" of the brain. The following are some definitions/descriptions of what is referred to as "executive functioning."

Executive Functions Are

* The management functions ("overseers") of the brain
* The covert, self-directed actions individuals use to help maintain control of themselves and accomplish goal-directed behavior
* The range of central control processes in the brain that activate, organize, focus, integrate, and manage other brain functions—enabling us to perform both routine and creative work (Brown, 2000; National Resource Center on AD/HD, 2003b)
* Brain functions that have to do with self-regulation of behavior

Many specialists and researchers believe Dr. Russell Barkley's theory (2000a, May) that the deficit in inhibition (the core of ADHD) impairs the development of these executive functions. Apparently, in children with ADHD, the executive functions (at least some of them) are developmentally delayed compared to other children of the same age. The individual with ADHD, therefore, does not fully utilize his or her "executive functions" for self-management.

Executive Function Components

It has not as yet been determined exactly what constitutes the executive functions of the brain. However, some of those functions are believed to involve:

* Working memory (holding information in your head long enough to act on it)
* Organization of thoughts, time, and space
* Planning and prioritizing
* Arousal and activation
* Sustaining alertness and effort
* Self-regulation
* Emotional self-control
* Internalization of speech/language (using your inner speech to guide your behavior)
* Inhibiting verbal and nonverbal responding
* Quick retrieval and analysis of information
* Developing and following through on a plan of action
* Strategy monitoring and revising, which involves making decisions based on task analyses, planning, reflection, and goal-directed problem solving (Brown, 2000; Dendy & Ziegler, 2002)

It is important to realize that executive function weaknesses cause academic challenges (mild to severe) for most students with ADHD, irrespective of how intelligent, gifted, and capable they may be. Consequently, most children and teens with attention-deficit disorders will need some supportive strategies and/or accommodations to compensate for their deficit in executive functioning (whether they are part of a written plan or not).

ADHD "Look Alikes"

Not everyone who displays symptoms of ADHD has an attention-deficit disorder. There are a number of other conditions and factors (medical, psychological, learning, psychiatric, emotional, social, environmental) that can cause inattentive, hyperactive, and impulsive behaviors. The following can cause some of the symptoms that may look like or mimic ADHD:

* Learning disabilities
* Sensory impairments (hearing, vision, motor problems)
* Mood disorders (depression, dysthymia)
* Substance use and abuse (of alcohol and drugs)
* Oppositional defiant disorder (ODD)
* Conduct disorder (CD)
* Allergies
* Post-traumatic stress disorder (PTSD)
* Anxiety disorder
* Obsessive-compulsive disorder (OCD)
* Sleep disorders
* Bipolar disorder (manic/depressive)
* Thyroid problems
* Rare genetic disorders (for example, Fragile X syndrome)
* Seizure disorders
* Lead poisoning
* Hypoglycemia
* Anemia
* Fetal alcohol syndrome/fetal alcohol effects
* Chronic illness
* Language disorders
* Tourette's syndrome (Tourette's disorder)
* Pervasive developmental disorder
* Autism
* Asperger's syndrome
* Developmental delays
* Sensory integration dysfunction
* Low intellectual ability
* Very high intellectual ability
* Severe emotional disturbance
* Side effects of medications being taken (for example, anti-seizure medication, asthma medication)

Emotional and environmental factors that have nothing to do with ADHD can also cause a child or teen to be distracted, unable to concentrate, and have acting-out or aggressive behaviors. For example, if the child/teen is experiencing or witnessing physical/sexual abuse/violence or family stresses such as divorce and custody battles; a victim of bullying/peer pressure and other peer/social issues; or has a chaotic, unpredictable, unstable, and/or neglectful home life with inappropriate expectations placed on the child.

Inattention and disruptive classroom behaviors can be school-related (again without having anything to do with ADHD). Students may display those behaviors if they are in a school environment that has a pervasive negative climate, poor instruction and low academic expectations, nonstimulating and unmotivating curriculum, ineffective classroom management, and so forth.

ADHD and Co-Existing (or Associated) Disorders

Besides a condition that looks like ADHD, it is very possible that *in addition* to ADHD the child has some other co-existing conditions or disorders. ADHD may be only *part* of the diagnostic picture. It is important to be aware that there is a high rate of "co-morbidity" with ADHD, which means there are at least two co-occurring conditions. Studies show that approximately two-thirds of children with ADHD have (or will develop) at least one other co-existing condition (MTA Cooperative Group, 1999; Pierce, 2003). This, of course, makes treatment, intervention, and management more complicated.

Making an accurate and complete differential diagnosis requires a skilled, knowledgeable professional who is aware of conditions that produce symptoms similar to ADHD and who can identify and address other conditions or disorders that may co-exist.

The prevalence reported of individuals with ADHD who have additional co-existing disorders varies among sources. The following range is agreed on by most researchers (American Academy of Pediatrics, 2000; CHADD, 2001a):

Co-Existing Disorders in Those Diagnosed with ADHD

* Oppositional defiant disorder (ODD)—from 30 to 65 percent
* Anxiety disorder—from 20 to 35 percent of children and 25 to 40 percent of adults
* Conduct disorder (CD)—from 10 to 25 percent of children, 25 to 50 percent of adolescents, and 20 to 25 percent of adults
* Bipolar (manic/depressive illness)—from 1 to 20 percent
* Depression—from 10 to 30 percent in children and 10 to 47 percent in adolescents and adults
* Tics/Tourette's syndrome—about 7 percent of those with ADHD have tics or Tourette's syndrome, but 60 percent of Tourette's syndrome patients also have ADHD
* Learning disabilities—from 12 to 60 percent, with most estimating between one-third and one-half of children with ADHD having a co-existing learning disability
* Sleep problems—more than 50 percent of ADHD children need more time to fall asleep; nearly 40 percent may have problems with frequent night waking; and more than half have trouble waking in the morning
* Secondary behavioral complications—up to 65 percent of children with ADHD may display secondary behavioral complications such as noncompliance, argumentativeness, temper outbursts, lying, blaming others, being easily angered, and so forth

Keep the following points in mind:

* Most children with ADHD have some kind of school-related problems (achievement, performance, social).
* A high percentage of children with ADHD have co-existing learning disabilities. The multidisciplinary school team should always

evaluate students when there are signs of any learning problems.

* It is believed that having ADHD predisposes that person to these above-mentioned disorders. Therefore, the diagnostic process should include screening for possible co-morbidities through interview, questionnaires, and rating scales that may indicate or alert the diagnostician to symptoms of other co-existing disorders.

ADHD falls under the category of disruptive behavior disorder in the *Diagnostic and Statistical Manual of Mental Disorders* (4th ed.) (APA, 1994) and most current version, DSM-IV-TR (APA, 2000). Also in this category are the commonly co-occurring disorders of oppositional defiant disorder (ODD) and conduct disorder (CD). Children with ADHD are at a much higher risk than the average child of developing a more serious disruptive behavior disorder. It is important that we recognize the risk and implement early interventions.

The diagnosis of *oppositional defiant disorder* (ODD) requires a pattern of negative, hostile, and defiant behavior that has been evident for a while; occurs more frequently than is typical in individuals of comparable age and developmental level; and causes significant impairment. The child/teen with ODD often loses his or her temper, argues and actively defies adult requests or rules, deliberately annoys people, and blames others for his or her own mistakes or misbehavior. These children and teens also tend to be touchy or easily annoyed by others, angry and resentful, and spiteful or vindictive.

Conduct disorder (CD) is the most serious form of disruptive behavior disorders in children and teens, and involves a pattern of delinquent behavior. Some of the characteristics include aggression to people and animals, deliberate destruction of property, deceitfulness or theft, and serious violations of rules.

Parents, educators, and medical/mental-healthcare providers should be alert to signs of other disorders and issues that may exist or emerge (often in the adolescent years), especially when current strategies and treatments being used with the ADHD child/teen are no longer working effectively. This warrants further diagnostic assessment.

Formula ONE for Disaster
take ONE impulsive child
add ONE forbidden object
multiply by ONE minute
to equal
ONE predictable trip to the emergency
*   room. . . .*

Karen Easter ©1995

Statistics and Risk Factors

ADHD is associated with a number of risk factors. Compared to their peers of the same age, youth with ADHD (those untreated for their disorder) experience:

* More serious accidents, hospitalizations, and significantly higher medical costs than those children without ADHD (Centers for Disease Control and Prevention, 2003)
* More school failure and dropout
* More delinquency and altercations with the law
* More engagement in antisocial activities
* More teen pregnancy and sexually transmitted diseases
* Earlier experimentation and higher use of alcohol, tobacco, and illicit drugs
* More trouble socially and emotionally
* More rejection, ridicule, and punishment
* More underachievement, and under-performance at school/work (Barkley, Cook, Dulcan, et al., 2002; Barkley, 2000b)

Without early identification and appropriate treatment, ADHD can have serious consequences that include school failure and drop out, depression, conduct disorder, failed relationships, underachievement in the workplace, and substance abuse (CHADD, 2003b). Yet despite the serious consequences, studies indicate that less than half of those with the disorder are receiving treatment (Barkley, Cook, Dulcan, et al., 2002)

Prevalence of ADHD

* Approximately 3 to 5 percent of school-aged children have ADHD, according to much of the literature over the past several years, including the Surgeon General's Mental Health Report (1999, 2001).

* Current estimates, according to the American Academy of Pediatrics, indicate that as high as 4 to 12 percent of all school-aged children may be affected (American Academy of Pediatrics and National Initiative for Children's Healthcare Quality, 2002).

* Nearly 7 percent of elementary-aged children in the United States have been diagnosed with ADHD, according to the first nationwide survey conducted by the Centers for Disease Control and Prevention reported in May 2002. And ADHD is estimated to affect between 3 and 7 percent of school-aged children, according to the American Psychiatric Association (2000).

* ADHD affects approximately 2 to 4 percent of the adult population (Murphy & Barkley, 1996).

* ADHD is a lifelong disorder. Most children with ADHD (up to 80 percent) continue to have substantial symptoms into adolescence, and as many as 67 percent continue to exhibit symptoms into adulthood (CHADD, 2003a).

More risks associated with ADHD:

* Almost 35 percent of children with ADHD quit school before completion (Barkley, 2000b).

* Up to 58 percent have failed at least one grade in school, and at least three times as many teens with ADHD as those without

ADHD have failed a grade, been suspended, or been expelled from school (Barkley, 2000b).

* For at least half of children with ADHD, social relationships are seriously impaired (Barkley, 2000b).

* Within their first two years of independent driving, adolescents with a diagnosis of ADHD have nearly four times as many auto accidents and three times as many citations for speeding as young drivers without ADHD (Barkley, Murphy, & Kwasni, 1996).

* ADHD is diagnosed at least three times more frequently in boys than girls; although it is believed (and research is showing) that *many* more girls actually have ADHD. In fact, the actual number may be nearly equal (CHADD, 2003b).

What Is Currently Known About ADHD

There are degrees of ADHD ranging from mild to severe; types of ADHD with a variety of characteristics; and no one has all of the symptoms or displays the disorder in the exact same way. Symptoms vary in every child, and even within each child with ADHD the symptoms may look different from day to day.

ADHD is not new. It has been around, recognized by clinical science, and documented in the literature since 1902 (having been renamed several times). Some of the previous names for the disorder were "minimal brain damage," "minimal brain dysfunction," "hyperactive child syndrome," and ADD with or without "hyperactivity."

We know that ADHD is *not* a myth. It is *not* a result of poor parenting or lack of caring, effort, and discipline. ADHD is *not* laziness, willful behavior, or a character flaw. There is no "quick fix" or "cure" for ADHD.

Many children/teens with ADHD "slip through the cracks" without being identified and without receiving the intervention and treatment they need. This is particularly true of ethnic minorities and girls.

ADHD exists across all populations, regardless of race or ethnicity. There are racial and ethnic disparities in access to healthcare services. As such, ethnic minorities with ADHD are often underserved and do not receive adequate help and treatment (Satcher, 2001).

Children and teens with ADHD do much better when they are provided with activities that are interesting, novel, and motivating. Generally, the majority of students with ADHD can learn well in general education classrooms when teachers employ proper management, effective instructional strategies, and assistive supports/interventions.

Fortunately, we know a great deal about:

* Which behavior management techniques and strategies are effective in the home and school for children with ADHD
* The classroom interventions, accommodations, and teaching strategies that are most helpful for students with ADHD
* Specific "parenting strategies" that are most effective with children who have ADHD
* Treatments that have been proven effective in reducing the symptoms and improving functioning of children/teens with ADHD
* Many additional strategies that are helpful for individuals with ADHD, such as organization and time management, stress reduction/relaxation

We also know:

* ADHD can be managed best by a multimodal treatment and a team approach.
* It takes a team effort of parents, school personnel, and health/mental healthcare professionals to be most effective in helping children with ADHD.
* No single intervention will be effective for treating/managing ADHD. It takes vigilance and ongoing treatment/intervention plans, as well as revision of plans and going "back to the drawing board" frequently.
* The teaching techniques and strategies that are necessary for the success of children

with ADHD are good teaching practices and helpful to *all* students in the classroom.
* There is a lot of help out there, and resources are available for children, teens, and adults with ADHD, as well as those living with and working with individuals with ADHD.
* We are learning more and more each day due to the efforts of the many researchers and practitioners (educators, mental health professionals, physicians) committed to improving the lives of individuals with ADHD.

The extensive research into ADHD during the past several years has revealed a lot about the disorder. The following is a summary of the current evidence about ADHD, based on the research from metabolic, brain-imaging, and molecular genetic studies.

Differences in the Brain

Differences between those with ADHD and control groups have been identified using brain activity and imaging tests/scans (MRIs, SPECT, EEG, BEAMS, PET, and functional MRIs). Those brain differences include decreased activity level and lower metabolism levels in certain regions of the brain (mainly the frontal region and the basal ganglia); lower metabolism of glucose (the brain's energy source) in the frontal region; decreased blood flow to certain brain regions; and specific brain structures are smaller than in those unaffected by ADHD.

Note: *Imaging and other brain tests are NOT used in the diagnosis of ADHD. To date, a comprehensive history of the problem remains the best way to identify the disorder.*

There is very strong scientific evidence which supports that ADHD may be due to imbalances in various neurotransmitters or brain chemicals and/or reduced metabolic rates in certain regions of the brain. These chemicals are believed to travel across the synapses of the brain, affecting the braking mechanism or inhibitory circuits of the brain. Dopamine pathways in the brain, which link the basal ganglia and frontal cortex, for example, appear to play a major role in ADHD (Castellanos, 1997).

Genetic Research

Much of the recent research involves molecular genetic studies. One type is whole-genome scanning studies that genotype DNA in entire families to look for patterns and differences. Other genetic research involves "candidate-gene" studies seeking specific forms of genes, which show up more often in children with ADHD compared to those unaffected by ADHD.

Researchers have found at least two candidate genes associated with ADHD. One of those genes, the dopamine transporter gene (DAT1), is involved in regulating the amount of dopamine available in the brain. Researchers have found differences between the structure of the DAT1 gene in families with ADHD and "normal" control families. There is belief that the DAT1 gene in some individuals with ADHD may be causing an "overactive dopamine pump"—sucking up dopamine too fast and not leaving it in the synapse long enough (Barkley, 1998).

A second gene was found (DRD4) that may be involved with ADHD. It apparently makes specific nerve cells less sensitive to dopamine. It is suspected that, because ADHD is a complex disorder with multiple traits, that multiple genes are involved and will be discovered in the future. Researchers believe that variations in dopamine receptors or transporters, or both, may result in underactivity of brain regions that are involved in attention and behavior, according to James Swanson and others (Fine, 2001).

Landmark MTA Study

There has also been significant research with regard to treatments for ADHD and their relative effectiveness. The longest and most thorough study of the effects of ADHD interventions was the Multimodal Treatment Study

of Children with ADHD (MTA) by the National Institute of Mental Health. This study involved 579 children with ADHD ages seven to nine who were randomly assigned to one of four treatment groups, implemented over fourteen months. The groups were

* Medication alone (carefully managed and adjusted medication that was titrated for maximum benefit, with monthly office visits and phone contact with teachers)
* Behavioral therapy alone (very intensive training of parents and teachers on this approach, with an integrated program of specific psychosocial interventions and trained classroom paraprofessional)
* Combination of the above two treatments
* Routine care (treatment by physician in the community, which generally involved one or two office visits/year, no direct interaction with teachers, lower doses of medication prescribed) (MTA Steering Committee, 2003)

Researchers found that medication treatment alone and medication combined with behavior treatment worked significantly better than behavior treatment alone or community care alone at reducing the symptoms of ADHD. There was overwhelming evidence as to the effectiveness of well-managed use of stimulant medication in the treatment of ADHD. Stimulant medications have been proven to be very effective in improving the core symptoms of at least 70 to 80 percent of children and adults with ADHD (MTA Cooperative Group, 1999). Some estimates are even higher (up to 90 percent).

Combined treatments offered slightly greater benefits than medication management alone for symptom reduction as well as for other domains, such as peer relations, child-parent relations, and academic outcomes (MTA Steering Committee, 2003).

The MTA group continued to monitor (although not treat) all of the children and families and reevaluated the outcomes after twenty-four months. They generally found that the outcomes for the combined and medication only groups were still superior to the other groups, but the relative superiority was reduced by 50 percent. Those children who had received the MTA medication alone approach were still better off than children who received the intensive behavior therapy alone. This was particularly true for ADHD symptoms and oppositional/aggressive symptoms based on ratings by teachers (who were not part of the initial treatment component of the study) as well as by parents. Based on this, they concluded that the benefits of intensive medication management for ADHD extended ten months beyond the intensive treatment phase, although the effects appeared to diminish over time (MTA Steering Committee, 2003).

The investigators also observed "mild growth suppression" in the medication and combined medication/behavioral treatment group. The MTA researchers noted that medication appears to incur some risks in terms of slowing growth and weight. Children treated with medication did grow more slowly (by one-third inch) in the second study year (MTA Steering Committee, 2003).

What May Be the Causes of ADHD

ADHD has been researched extensively in the United States and a number of other countries. There have been hundreds of well-designed and controlled scientific studies trying to determine the causes and most effective treatments for children, teens, and more recently, adults. To date, the causes of ADHD are not fully known or understood. However, based on the enormous amount of research, there is a lot of consensus in the scientific community about most *probable causes,* which include the following.

Heredity

This is the most likely common cause of ADHD, based on the evidence:

* Heredity accounts for about 80 percent of children with ADHD, according to leading researchers (Barkley, 1998).

* ADHD is known to run in families, as found by numerous studies (especially twin studies with identical and fraternal twins, adopted children, family studies) (Lombroso, Scahill, & State, 1998).
* It is believed that a genetic predisposition to the disorder is inherited. Children with ADHD will frequently have a parent, sibling, grandparent, or other close relative with ADHD or whose history indicates he or she had similar problems and symptoms during childhood.

Prenatal, During Birth, or Postnatal Trauma/Injury

It has been found that trauma to the developing fetus during pregnancy or birth, which may cause brain injury or abnormal brain development, can cause ADHD.

According to Jenson (2001), trauma might include:

* Fetal exposure to alcohol and/or cigarettes
* Exposure to high levels of lead
* Complications during pregnancy and birth, such as toxemia
* Brain injury from disease or trauma

Illnesses and Brain Injury

Researchers say that no more than 5 percent of those with ADHD are believed to acquire the disorder through illness or postnatal brain damage. However, ADHD may be caused by trauma or head injury to the frontal part of the brain. Also, certain medical conditions such as thyroid disorder and illnesses that affect the brain (for example, encephalitis) may be a contributing cause.

Diminished Activity and Lower Metabolism in Certain Brain Regions

It has been found that, as a group, those with ADHD have less brain activity (compared to the non-ADHD population) taking place in certain regions of the brain (the frontal lobe, its connections to the basal ganglia, and their relationship to the cerebellum). These regions are known to be responsible for controlling activity level, impulsivity, and attention. Most neurological and neuro-imaging studies revealed that, as a group, those with ADHD have less blood flow, metabolism of glucose, electrical activity, and reactivity to stimulation in one or more of these brain regions (Barkley, Cook, Dulcan, et al., 2002).

Chemical Imbalance or Deficiency in Neurotransmitters

It is believed that those with ADHD have a deficiency, imbalance, or inefficiency in brain chemicals called neurotransmitters, affecting certain brain regions associated with ADHD. It is believed that stimulant medications affect the neurochemical signaling process of the dopamine and norepinephrine systems (the main ones thought to be involved in ADHD). It is believed that the medication works to increase the availability of these neurotransmitters—through facilitating their release and inhibiting their re-uptake (CHADD, 2001b).

Research is indicating that increases in dopamine levels that are associated with the stimulant medication methylphenidate (MPH) produces two therapeutic changes: an increase in the signal-to-noise ratio in the brain and an increase in the saliency (significance) of a task to an individual, making the task more interesting, and thus improving attention.

According to Volkow, a leading mental health and drug addiction researcher, random firing of nerve cells in the brain is normal. It allows the brain cells to react more quickly when there is an actual stimulus. However, if there is too much random firing, real signals can get lost in the noise. Increases in dopamine, like those associated with oral MPH, enhance task-specific signaling in the brain and decrease random firing and background noise (Imperio, 2004; Volkow, 2003).

Slight Structural Brain Differences

There is evidence of some structural differences in certain brain regions believed responsible for ADHD. Scientists have found through neuro-imaging studies that these specific brain regions are smaller and less asymmetrical than in individuals without ADHD (Barkley, 1998; Castellanos, 1997).

Follow-up studies of brain size in children with and without ADHD by renowned researcher Xavier Castellanos and his team of investigators found that the brain as a whole and cerebellum in particular were smaller in children with ADHD who had never taken medication. Although smaller, the ADHD brain followed a normal growth curve, indicating a normal growth process with a smaller base (Castellanos, 2003; Imperio, 2004). Their studies found that children with ADHD, both medicated and unmedicated, had less total gray matter (brain tissue containing nerve cells and blood vessels) than children without ADHD. Total white matter (brain tissue responsible for carrying information between nerve cells) was less in unmedicated children with ADHD. Medicated children with ADHD had the same volume of white matter as children without ADHD (Castellanos, 2003; Imperio, 2004).

Environmental Factors

It is also generally believed that factors in the environment (for example, the amount of structure versus chaos; the effective management techniques being used; the types of supports in place) affect the severity of the symptoms and behaviors displayed and the risk for developing more significant problems. However, these environmental factors are *not* found to be the *cause* of ADHD. Research has not supported many of the other suggested causes that are popular beliefs (diet, food additives, sugar).

Other environmental factors that may affect developing brains in very young children are being studied. One such study by researchers at the Department of Pediatrics, University of Washington, published in *Pediatrics,* the research publication of the American Academy of Pediatrics (2004), concluded that early exposure to television was associated with subsequent attention problems. The authors observe that "environmental exposures, including types and degrees of stimulation, affect the number and the density of neuronal synapses." The authors emphasize, "We cannot draw inferences from these associations. It could be that attentional problems lead to television viewing rather than vice versa" (CHADD, 2004b; Christakis, Zimmerman, DiGiuseppe, & McCarty, 2004). Replication of the study and more research needs to be conducted.

ADHD in Minority Populations

There is a greater likelihood that children of minority populations (for example, African American, Hispanic/Latino) are underserved and undertreated for their medical and mental health disorders, with less access to comprehensive assessment and to appropriate treatment options. The Executive Summary on Mental Health: Culture, Race and Ethnicity from the Report of the Surgeon General (2001) shows that African American youths are overrepresented in arrests, detentions, incarcerations, classes for emotional disturbance, and the child welfare system. However, African Americans do not appear to receive needed treatment for ADHD or for other mental health disorders (Ellison, 2003).

The vast majority of research on ADHD has been conducted with samples of white boys between the ages of six and eleven years with middle-class backgrounds. We have very little information on how ADHD symptoms might be expressed as a function of cultural background, or how to best account for diversity when evaluating children for this disorder (DuPaul & Barrett, 2003).

In the few studies exploring medication rates across races, ethnic minority children are two to two and a half times less likely to be medicated for ADHD compared to white children (Safer & Malever, 2000; Safer & Zito, 2000).

There is evidence that African Americans may be more mistrusting of medical research and treatment than individuals from other ethnic groups (Taylor-Crawford, Richardson, & Madison-Boyd, 2003).

A panel of experts voiced concerns to the Congressional Black Caucus about misperceptions of ADHD in the African American community during a Capitol Hill briefing in March 2004 (sponsored by CHADD). The panel presented scientific evidence that African Americans with ADHD are often undertreated and discussed the devastating implications for minority communities when denied appropriate access to care (CHADD, 2004a).

Although diagnostic interviews and rating scales appear "objective," these measures are only as accurate as the perceptions of the person completing them. The amount of subjectivity involved in assessing ADHD symptoms becomes even more of a concern when evaluating children from minority backgrounds, especially given the potential for over-identification and misdiagnosis when cultural differences are not taken into account (DuPaul & Barrett, 2003).

In Latino families it is common that, following a diagnosis of ADHD, many extended family members will be consulted on this diagnosis and their opinions will have considerable weight. Education and counseling of parents about ADHD needs to include extended family members to facilitate support and involvement in treatment (Bauermeister & Reina, 2003).

Educators and clinicians must be culturally sensitive and aware of barriers to ADHD diagnosis and treatment and take efforts in working with parents to bridge some of those barriers (language/communication issues, mistrust, stigma, fear, financial resources, access to healthcare).

It is important for schools and clinical practices to do what they can to bridge language and cultural barriers and support families. It helps to include in their team someone who is familiar with and who understands the family's culture (and language). Schools and clinicians should make every effort to provide materials/resources to families and contacts with whom parents can clearly and comfortably communicate, share concerns, and have their questions answered.

What Is Not Known About ADHD

There is still a great deal that we do not yet know about ADHD, including:

* How to prevent ADHD or specific symptoms that cause impairment in a person's functioning
* An easy, conclusive diagnosis for ADHD
* What may prove to be the best, most effective treatments and strategies for helping individuals with ADHD
* The causes (although there are more accepted theories supported by a growing body of scientific evidence)

Just in the past few years there has been a great deal of interest and focus on ADHD in adulthood. This has generated a lot of research, resulting in much more information and better treatment options for this population. ADHD in the early childhood years (prior to age six) is also an area that requires more research and understanding.

Gender issues and the differences between males and females with ADHD has gained considerable recognition, and consequently, has been the focus of various research studies in the past few years. Also, cultural variables and the effects of cultural factors on the diagnosis, treatment, and care of individuals with ADHD is another area that has only recently been a focus of research. These are very important topics that warrant much more research.

There is an overwhelming amount of evidence that ADHD is neurobiological in nature. Although much has been learned about this disorder over the past decade, there is still much to learn. Hopefully, with all of the research taking place about attention-deficit disorders, the scientific community will solve the puzzle of ADHD in the near future.

ADHD and the Impact on the Family

It is important to be aware of the challenges that exist in the home when one or more children (or a parent) have ADHD, as this disorder significantly impacts the entire family (Rief, 2003). Unfortunately, teachers are generally unaware or underestimate the struggles that families face. Typically, in homes of children with ADHD there is a much higher degree of stress than the average family has, along with depression or other pathology in one or more family members.

Note: *Remember, it is likely that more than one family member also has ADHD.*

Living with a child who has ADHD often takes a heavy toll on marriages. It is common for parents to be in different stages of a "grieving process" about having a child who struggles compared to other children, and whose differences may even be considered a disability. Parents frequently disagree about treatment, discipline, management, structure, and so forth. There are generally major issues surrounding the battle with homework as well as morning and evening routines (getting ready for school, bedtime).

Parents are also known to blame one another for the child's problems or to be highly critical of one another in their parenting or spousal roles. This causes a great deal of marital stress and a higher rate of divorce. Often it is the mother who must cope with the brunt of the issues throughout the day, which is physically and emotionally exhausting. In single parent homes it is even more challenging.

As any parent of a toddler knows, when your child needs constant supervision and monitoring, it is very time-consuming and interferes with one's ability to get things done as planned (housework, chores).

Parents of children who have ADHD are constantly faced with needing to defend their parenting choices as well as their child. They must listen to "negative press" about this disorder and reject popular opinion in order to provide the child with necessary interventions and treatment. Parents must deal with criticism and "well-meaning advice" from grandparents, other relatives, friends, and acquaintances regarding how they should be disciplining and parenting their child. This causes a lot of parental self-doubt and adds to the stress they are already living with day in and day out.

Frequently, the family must deal with social issues, such as the exclusion of the child from out-of-school activities and so forth. It is painful when your child is not invited to birthday parties or has difficulty finding someone to play with and keeping friends. Siblings are often resentful or jealous of the central role their ADHD sibling plays in the family's schedule, routines, and activities, as well as the extra time and special treatment he or she receives. In addition, siblings are acutely aware of and feel hurt and embarrassed when their brother or sister has acquired a negative reputation in the neighborhood and school.

Parents of children with ADHD have a much higher degree of responsibility in working with the school and being proactive in the management of their son or daughter. Further, it is crucial that they fully educate themselves about ADHD in order to successfully advocate for their child's needs.

Keep the following points in mind:

In many cases, other family members who have ADHD were never diagnosed and have been struggling to cope with their own difficulties without proper treatment and support. That is why the clinicians who specialize in treating children with ADHD say it is so important to view treatment in the context of the family. Learning about the family (communication, disciplinary practices, and so forth) helps in designing a treatment plan that is most effective for the child.

It is very common that a parent will recognize for the first time what he or she has been suffering with over the years (undiagnosed ADHD) when a son or daughter is diagnosed with the disorder. This can be most helpful and result in a positive change in the family dynamics. Without question, families of children with ADHD need support and understanding. Fortunately, there are far more supports available now than there were a decade ago.

Making the Diagnosis

A Comprehensive Evaluation for ADHD

*T*he diagnosis of ADHD is not a simple process. There is no laboratory test or single measure to determine whether a person has ADHD; nor can any particular piece of information alone confirm or deny the existence of ADHD. However, ADHD can be diagnosed reliably following the guidelines of the medical and psychiatric associations.

The cornerstone of an ADHD diagnosis is meeting the criteria for attention-deficit/hyperactivity disorder as described in the most current editions of the *Diagnostic and Statistical Manual of Mental Health Disorders,* published by the American Psychiatric Association (APA, 1994; APA, 2000). The diagnosis of ADHD is made by gathering and synthesizing information obtained from a variety of sources in order to determine whether there is enough evidence to conclude that the child meets *all* of the criteria for having ADHD.

The evaluator must collect and interpret data from multiple sources, settings, and methods and use his or her clinical judgment to determine whether the DSM-IV criteria have been met:

* There are a sufficient number of ADHD symptoms present (at least six out of the nine characteristics of inattention, hyperactivity/impulsivity, or both).

* The symptoms are to a degree that is "maladaptive and inconsistent with the child's developmental level."
* These symptoms are presently causing impairment in the child's life and affecting the child's successful functioning in more than one setting (at home, school, social situations in other environments).
* These symptoms have existed a significant amount of time (at least some since early childhood), and other factors, disorders, or conditions do not better account for these symptoms (APA, 1994, 2000).

It is *not sufficient* for a child to be seen by a community physician who has only seen the child for a brief office visit and has not gathered and analyzed the necessary diagnostic data from the parents, school, and other sources. An appropriate evaluation for ADHD takes substantial time and effort; and "the assessment will likely be completed only after two or three visits" (Baren, 2001).

Until recently, it would have been advised that a child only be evaluated by a specialist—a professional such as a child psychiatrist, developmental/behavioral pediatrician, or child neurologist—with much expertise in attention-deficit disorders. This is still highly recommended with more complex cases. Such specialists are among the professionals with the greatest expertise in being able to differentially diagnose and treat the range and variety of mental health and developmental disorders that may co-exist with ADHD.

However, since May 2000, when the American Academy of Pediatrics (AAP) published guidelines for the diagnosis of ADHD, far more pediatricians and primary care practitioners are now familiar with and capable of conducting the evaluation required to diagnose attention-deficit disorders—especially in average, uncomplicated cases of ADHD. As pediatricians and primary care doctors continue to receive more training in implementing these guidelines, there should be significantly more consistency in effective diagnostic practices for ADHD. Hopefully, children will benefit by receiving more appropriate evaluations, and consequently, effective treatment and management (Rief, 2003).

These American Academy of Pediatrics Guideline Recommendations (AAP, 2000) provide a framework for diagnostic decision making, and include the following:

1. If a child six to twelve years of age exhibits inattention, hyperactivity, impulsivity, academic underachievement, or behavior problems, primary care clinicians should initiate an evaluation for ADHD.

2. The diagnosis of ADHD requires that a child meet the criteria for ADHD in the DSM-IV.

3. The assessment of ADHD requires evidence directly obtained from parents or caregivers regarding the core symptoms of ADHD in various settings, the age of onset, duration of symptoms, and degree of functional impairment.

4. The assessment of ADHD also requires evidence *directly obtained from the classroom teacher (or other school professional)* regarding the core symptoms of ADHD, duration of symptoms, degree of functional impairment, and co-existing conditions. A physician should review any reports from a school-based multidisciplinary evaluation where they exist, which will include assessments from the teacher or other school-based professionals.

5. Evaluation of the child with ADHD should include assessment for co-existing conditions.

6. Other diagnostic tests are not routinely indicated to establish the diagnosis of ADHD but may be used for the assessment of co-existing conditions.

Note: *If a child is receiving an outside evaluation for ADHD and the school is NOT requested to send information, and no attempt is made to communicate with or obtain input from the school, it is an inappropriate evaluation for ADHD. The evaluator is NOT following recommended diagnostic guidelines by the American Academy of Pediatrics or acquiring sufficient evidence to meet ADHD diagnostic criteria as determined by the American Psychiatric Association.*

The Components of a Comprehensive Evaluation for ADHD

History

An evaluation for ADHD will require taking a thorough history (Rief, 1998, 2003). This is a critical part of the diagnostic process. The history is obtained through interviewing the parents, use of questionnaires (generally filled out by parents prior to office visits), and a review of previous medical and school records. By using these techniques and instruments, the evaluator obtains important data regarding: the child's medical history (prenatal, birth, illnesses, injuries), developmental history (milestones reached in various language, motor, adaptive, and learning skills), behavioral, and school history. This is a means of also obtaining from the parents the family medical and social history, any significant circumstances/stressors (serious illness in family, death, divorce, family moved), a sense of the parents' style of discipline and interactions with the child, and their perceptions of the child's strengths as well as difficulties.

Behavior Rating Scales

These are useful in determining the degree to which various ADHD-related behaviors/symptoms are observed in different key environments (home/school). In addition to teachers and parents, rating scales may be filled out by others who spend time with the child (school counselor, special education teacher, childcare provider, other relatives).

Rating scales list a number of items that the teacher or parent rates according to the frequency they observe the child exhibiting those specific behaviors or problems. Sometimes the ratings range from "never" to "almost always," or from "not at all" to "very much." Some rating scales are numerical (ranging from 1 to 5 or 0 to 4). The scales are standardized and enable the evaluator to compare a child's behavioral symptoms (activity level, distractibility, independent work habits, ability to interact and get along with others, display self-control, and inhibit behavior) to that of other children that age/developmental level. In some of the instruments used, various situations in the home or school are described, and the parent/teacher rates whether they see the child presenting difficulty in any of those situations and to what degree (mild to severe).

A variety of different rating scales and questionnaires are available for use by evaluators in obtaining information from parents and teachers. Examples of some of the more widely used scales and questionnaires include: Vanderbilt Assessment Scale, Conners' Parent and Teacher Rating Scales, ADD-H Comprehensive Teachers Rating Scale (ACTeRS), Child Behavior Checklist, Barkley Home and School Situations Questionnaires, The Snap Scale, Behavior Assessment System for Children (BASC-TRS), and Comprehensive Behavior Rating Scale for Children (CBRSC).

Gathering Current School Information

Another key part of the diagnostic process involves reviewing information supplied by the school that will indicate past and current student performance (academic, behavioral, social). No one is in a better position than the teacher to report on the child's school performance compared to other children of that age and grade. This includes the teacher's observations, perceptions, and objective information regarding the child's academic productivity and social/emotional/behavioral functioning, as well as the student's ability to exhibit self-control, stay focused and on-task, interact with peers and adults, initiate and follow through on assignments, and so forth.

Teachers may be asked to report their observations about the child through rating scales, questionnaires, narrative statements, phone interviews, or other measures. Teachers should be willing to speak and confer with whoever is conducting the evaluation. It is very beneficial for the physician (or other evaluator) and teacher to speak directly with each other (phone conference).

Review of School Records

Information indicating the existence of symptoms in previous school years is gathered in the history and review of school records. A great deal of useful data is located in the student's school records/cumulative file, including: past report cards, district/state achievement testing, any other school evaluations (psycho-educational, speech/language), past and current IEPs and/or Student Support Team (SST) referrals and intervention plans.

In addition, disciplinary referrals (which may be among the records of guidance counselors and/or administrators) and anecdotal records may provide information about the student's behavioral problems in school. Copies of work samples, particularly written samples and curriculum-based assessment, are also good indicators of a child's levels of performance and production. It is highly recommended that schools provide the information to the physician in a manner that takes into account the physician's limited time. A one- or two-page summary of the child's school history and current performance is helpful (Rief, 2003).

Observations

Directly observing the child's functioning in a variety of settings can provide helpful diagnostic information. Most useful are observations in natural settings where the child spends much of his or her time (for example, school). How a child behaves and performs in an office visit is often not indicative of how that same child performs and behaves in a classroom, playground, cafeteria, or other natural setting. As most clinicians do not have the time to make visits to observe the child in the school setting, school personnel can make some observations and provide those reports to the evaluating doctor.

Physical Exam

A clinical evaluation for ADHD generally includes a routine pediatric examination to rule out other possible medical conditions that could produce ADHD symptoms. Based on the child's physical exam, as well as medical history (through interview and questionnaire), a physician may look for evidence of other possible causes for the symptoms or additional issues that may need to be addressed (sleep disturbances, bedwetting, anxiety, depression).

The physical *may* include a neurological screening and/or other screening device. Most other medical tests (blood work, EEG, CT scans) are not done in an evaluation for ADHD. It is the physician's responsibility to determine the need for additional medical testing and/or referral to other specialists, if indicated.

Academic and Intelligence Testing

An evaluator should have at least a general indication of a child's academic achievement levels and performance, as well as a rough estimate of his or her cognitive (thinking/reasoning) ability. This can partly be determined through a review of the student's report cards, standardized test scores, classroom work samples, informal screening measures, and teacher/parent/student report.

If the child is exhibiting learning difficulties and struggles academically, a full psycho-educational evaluation needs to be done to more accurately determine ability, academic achievement levels, and information about how the child learns. Parents should request this evaluation from the school, which opens up the IEP process. (See Section 5.4, Educational Laws and Rights of Children with ADHD.)

Because of the high correlation between ADHD and learning disabilities, if the child is having significant difficulty academically (for example, learning to read), it should be suspected that the child may have a learning disability (often co-existing with ADHD). In order to determine whether the child has a learning disability, a psycho-educational assessment must be administered, which typically involves assessment of cognitive abilities, a battery of individualized achievement tests to determine academic strengths and weaknesses, and various processing tests (for example, measuring memory and sequencing skills, visual-motor integration). Often a communication assessment measuring language skills is needed as well.

Who Is Qualified to Evaluate a Child for ADHD?

ADHD is both a medical and behavioral disorder, and there are a number of professionals who can evaluate for attention-deficit disorders. This includes clinicians such as psychiatrists, clinical psychologists, neurologists, clinical social workers, pediatricians, family practitioners, and other qualified medical and mental health professionals. Many school psychologists are also qualified to evaluate for ADHD.

In selecting a professional to evaluate their child, parents are advised to do their homework and investigate before selecting a professional. It is important to find someone well qualified, and preferably recommended by others. Parents seeking professionals to evaluate (and treat) their child may wish to first speak with other parents of children/teens who have ADHD (for example, through the local chapter of CHADD) regarding recommended professionals in the community. School nurses and school psychologists are also excellent resources and very knowledgeable in most cases about healthcare providers in the community who have expertise in ADHD.

Parents should be proactive and question that individual about the methods he or she will be using in the diagnostic process. It is important that this professional:

* Adhere to recommended diagnostic guidelines for ADHD
* Conduct an evaluation that is comprehensive and multidimensional
* Be knowledgeable about ADHD and coexisting conditions
* Take adequate time to comfortably answer questions about assessment, treatment, and management to the parents' satisfaction (Rief, 2003)

Parents Seeking an Evaluation for Their Child (Rief, 1998, 2003)

At whatever stage, when parents are concerned about symptoms that are affecting the child's functioning and suspect that it may be the result of ADHD or another disorder/disability, they should pursue an evaluation. At any point, parents should communicate their concerns with their child's primary care physician and teachers.

Parents should set up an appointment to meet with the classroom teacher(s), asking for their input and observations regarding the child's academic achievement, performance/production, and behavior. Parents may ask the teacher(s) to implement a few reasonable interventions to help with any of the above concerns and find out how they can assist and support at home.

A school-based assessment can be done concurrent with, before, or after the clinical evaluation for ADHD. It is best to coordinate efforts. In pursuing a school evaluation, parents should let the teacher know why they want their child evaluated. Parents should speak with the school psychologist, school nurse, principal, special education teacher, or school counselor regarding this request for testing.

It is likely that the parent will be asked to first meet with the school's SST (Student Support Team). This is appropriate as long as the meeting is scheduled in a timely manner and parents agree to first meet with the school team. During the SST meeting, information and concerns are reviewed as a team (classroom teacher, support staff, administrator, and parents).

The SST meeting is recommended protocol, particularly if the child has never been referred before for a special education evaluation and there has not yet been an intervention plan developed to address the student's difficulties in the classroom. It is especially helpful to first have an SST meeting when considering an evaluation for ADHD for the following reasons:

* The school can share with parents its role in the assessment of ADHD and obtain parental permission (in writing) to begin gathering data (for example, child's school history and current functioning) and so forth.
* It is likely to ensure better coordination and communication if parents and school staff meet first prior to initiating the diagnostic process.

A school-based screening/evaluation may be initiated at the time of the SST meeting if review of information indicates it is appropriate. When a parent submits to the school a request for evaluation, which is their right under federal law, it formally opens an IEP timeline to begin the assessment and special education process.

As long as the school arranges to meet with the parents in a reasonable time frame, it is often best if parents channel their concerns and request for testing through the SST (if one exists at the school). However, parents may choose not to go through this process and request school testing at any time.

The school has the responsibility of initiating and following through with a comprehensive evaluation if the child is suspected of having ADHD or any other disability impairing educational performance. Then, if eligible, to provide supports and services under either of the two federal laws, IDEA or Section 504 of the Rehabilitation Act of 1973.

Teacher information that is valuable in an ADHD evaluation and potential treatments/interventions includes insights and observations regarding:

* The child's school performance difficulties (academic, social, behavioral)
* Most problematic times/environments (for example, transition times, playground)
* The child's strengths, interests, and motivators

* Environmental, instructional, and behavioral strategies/interventions that have been tried and seem to be most effective (Rief, 2003)

Parent information that is valuable in an ADHD evaluation, as well as for any potential intervention plans, includes insights and observations regarding:

* The child's difficulties in learning, behavior, health, and social interactions
* The child's strengths, interests, and motivators
* Responses to discipline and discipline techniques used in the home
* How the child responds when upset, angry, or frustrated
* How the child gets along with others (siblings, neighborhood children)
* The child's feelings (worries, fears)

1.3

Multimodal Treatments for ADHD

*O*nce a child is identified and diagnosed with ADHD, there are many ways to help the child and the family. It is important to realize that ADHD is not something that can be cured, but it can be treated and managed effectively. The best way of doing so in most cases is through a multifaceted approach—a "multimodal" plan of interventions, tailored to the needs of the individual child and family. (AAP, 2001a). This typically includes a combination of medical, behavioral/ psychosocial, and educational interventions, implemented *as needed* at different times in the child/teen's life. Children with ADHD often do best with a combination of structuring of their environment (home, school, and other settings), medication, behavior modification and specific behavior management strategies implemented at home and school, educational supports/ accommodations, and counseling of some kind (for example, parent counseling and training, family or individual counseling) (Goldstein, 1999; Rief, 2003).

Management Strategies

An effective multimodal management plan involves a collaborative partnership between parents, educators, and clinicians (medical and mental health professionals). All parties involved in the care and education of the child must communicate and work together in establishing target outcomes (goals), plans to reach the goals, and monitoring the effectiveness of any interventions.

According to the American Academy of Pediatrics (2001a), the focus of treatment should be on helping the child function as well as possible at home, at school, and in the community. Examples of target outcomes include:

* Improved relationships with parents, siblings, teachers, and friends
* Better schoolwork
* More independence in self-care or homework
* Improved self-esteem
* Fewer disruptive behaviors
* Safer behavior in the community (for example, when crossing streets)

There are a variety of medical and mental health professionals (physicians, psychologists, social workers) who may be involved. The school team also may involve a number of different school professionals (classroom teachers, guidance counselors, school nurse, administrator(s), special educators, and other special/related service providers). Parents may bring in to their team anyone who spends much time interacting with the child (extended family, baby-sitters, coaches).

A primary intervention is the education— particularly of parents and teachers (and the child when possible)—about ADHD. Parents, as their child's case manager, upon receiving the diagnosis must do everything they can to learn about ADHD, in order to put together an effective team of support. This is the start of the parents' journey on becoming "ADHD experts"—equipping themselves with the knowledge that will enable them to choose the most appropriate treatments and advocate for their child in the educational and healthcare systems.

Awareness and understanding (of significant adults in the child's life) with regard to how to structure and modify the environment and employ positive and proactive strategies to manage and respond to the ADHD-related behaviors is extremely important and comes with education and training.

ADHD is recognized as a chronic condition (such as asthma) and follows a chronic care plan of action (AAP & NICHQ, 2002). This means looking at the long-term picture. Various supports and treatments may be needed throughout one's lifetime or employed at different times in life as needed (assistance from educators, physicians, counselors/therapists, tutors, coaches). In addition, because of the long-term management involved, the treatment plan requires vigilance on the part of parents, educators, and health providers in monitoring and following up on the effectiveness of the plan.

A "multimodal" treatment program may include:

Medical/pharmacological intervention— Well-managed and monitored medication therapy (most commonly with stimulant medications). This has been proven by an abundance of research to be a highly effective intervention—the most effective as a single intervention—for managing symptoms and improving the functioning of children and teens with ADHD (Adesman, 2003; MTA, 1999). In fact, "Stimulants are highly effective for 75 to 90 percent of children with ADHD, according to a report of the Surgeon General (*Mental Health: A Report of the Surgeon General*, 2003).

Behavior modification and specific behavior management strategies implemented at home and school. Behavioral intervention has also been validated by research as effective intervention for children with ADHD and is generally another key component of the overall treatment plan (Hinshaw, 2000). It involves both parents and teachers learning how to provide the clear, consistent structure, follow-through, and effective use of rewards and consequences. It also includes specific techniques (for example, token economies, home/school communication systems, positive reinforcement, response cost) to help increase the child's positive, appropriate behaviors and reduce the undesirable, unwanted behaviors.

Counseling of various kinds is another type of treatment that can help the child and parents understand, cope with, and learn new skills to better manage the problems related to living with ADHD. There are several types of possible counseling (Rief, 2003):

* *Parent counseling/training*—This is a crucial part of any treatment plan, as parents must learn a new set of skills for managing their child's behaviors. This includes learning effective behavioral techniques and how to structure the home environment (and other aspects of their child's life). Parents must seek (and hopefully be provided with) accurate and reliable information about ADHD in order to understand the impact and developmental course of the disorder, the treatment options, and available resources.
* *Family counseling*—The whole family is often affected in the homes of children with ADHD. Family therapy can address issues that impact other family members (parents and siblings) and improve family relationships.
* *Individual counseling*—For the child to learn coping techniques, self-monitoring/self-regulation strategies, problem-solving strategies, and how to deal with stress, anger, and so forth.
* *Vocational counseling*—Often an important intervention for teens and adults.
* *Psychotherapy*—(for adolescents and adults) to talk about feelings, self-esteem issues, and self-defeating patterns of behavior.

* *Social skills training*—This training is usually provided in small groups with curriculum addressing specific skills that children with ADHD tend to have difficulties with (waiting for a turn, listening and responding, understanding body language and vocal tones, ignoring teasing, sharing and cooperating, resolving conflicts peacefully). Usually, social skills training teaches specific skills through discussion and role playing, but then the child must have many opportunities to practice the skills repeatedly in the natural setting where the skills are required. (See Section 1.7, ADHD and Social Skills Interventions.)

Educational Supports

A variety of possible school accommodations and interventions (for example, environmental, academic, instructional, behavioral) can be provided to enable the child to have better academic and social/behavioral success. Addressing the child's individual needs may involve classroom strategies/supports or other "safety nets" that may be available as part of the general education program at the school (for example, homework assistance, mentoring, academic tutorials, computer lab). It may also involve special education and/or related services (IEP) or a 504 Accommodation Plan for eligible students (Rief, 2003).

Teacher/school staff awareness training about ADHD, and effective educational and management strategies are very important as educational support.

Physical Outlets

These include activities such as swimming, martial arts, gymnastics, wrestling, track and field, bicycling, dance, hiking, etc.

Note: Team sports such as soccer or basketball are often better than team sports that require a lot of waiting for a chance to move and participate such as baseball.

Children with ADHD are often more successful in individual sports rather than team sports. Activities such as martial arts (aikido or karate) are often recommended because they increase the child's ability to focus and concentrate and teach the skills of self-control and self-restraint (Shapiro, 2002). Exercise provides individuals with ADHD an outlet to expend excess energy, while increasing the enzymes in the brain that are responsible for learning and memory (Putnam, 2002).

Recreation and enhancement of areas of strength and involving the child/teen in activities that build his or her strengths and interests (for example, arts/crafts, sports, scouts, dance, music, acting/performing arts) are especially helpful. (See Section 6.1, Stress Reduction, Relaxation Strategies, Leisure Activities, and Exercise.)

ADHD Coaching

This is a popular service for adolescents and adults with ADHD. Coaches work with clients to create structures, support, skills, and strategies. They assist their client in developing and following through on short- and long-term goals. They particularly assist with executive functioning difficulties related to their ADHD (planning, prioritizing, organization, time management). See www.add.org/content/coach for excellent information about coaching.

Support Organizations

Support groups are often very helpful for parents to interact with other parents who have children with ADHD. Parent support groups are excellent sources of information, assistance, and networking. The national organization CHADD (Children and Adults with Attention-Deficit Disorders) has local chapters throughout the United States and is a highly recommended source of information and support to families (and professionals). There are often other support groups, parenting classes, workshops/seminars, and various informational sources and resources in most communities. Parents can also find information and connections with other parents on the Internet (websites and chat rooms related to ADHD).

Note: Children/teens with ADHD may benefit from meeting and sharing with peers who also have ADHD and similar challenges.

AAP Guidelines and Additional Points

The American Academy of Pediatrics (2001) published guidelines for clinicians with the following recommendations for the treatment of ADHD in children aged six to twelve years:

1. Primary care clinicians should establish a treatment program that recognizes ADHD as a chronic condition.
2. The treating clinician, parents, and the child, in collaboration with school personnel, should specify appropriate target outcomes to guide management.
3. The clinician should recommend stimulant medication and/or behavioral therapy as appropriate to improve target outcomes in children with ADHD.
4. When the selected management for a child with ADHD has not met target outcomes, clinicians should evaluate the original diagnosis, use of all appropriate treatments, adherence to the treatment plan, and presence of co-existing conditions.
5. The clinician should periodically provide a systematic follow-up for the child with ADHD. Monitoring should be directed to target outcomes and adverse effects by obtaining specific information from parents, teachers, and the child.

Additional Points to Remember (Rief, 2003)

* When pursuing any treatment, parents should seek out doctors and therapists who are knowledgeable and experienced in the treatment of children with ADHD and willing to communicate closely with parents and the school.

* Parents and educators must learn how ADHD affects their child's school performance and how to work closely with each other in a positive, mutually supportive, and respectful relationship.
* Parents and teachers need to be familiar with the educational rights of children with disabilities and the types of school interventions and strategies that commonly help students with ADHD reduce their impairment in the school setting.
* Children, especially teens, should be included as active partners in the entire treatment program. They need to understand the reason for various interventions and how those treatments are intended to positively affect their daily lives. The child/teen must be respectfully included in this process and understand, so that he or she will be motivated to cooperate and participate in (not sabotage) the treatment.
* If ADHD-like symptoms are causing the child difficulty, classroom interventions should be implemented at once (regardless of whether or not the child has yet been diagnosed with ADHD). Parents should be encouraged to pursue an evaluation. A proper diagnosis is necessary to effectively address the child's needs.
* All professionals working with the child/family need to have a knowledge base about ADHD and focus on the issues from a positive, proactive approach. Interventions should be designed not only to address the child's areas of impairment but also to help the child recognize, develop, and draw on his or her strengths.

Dr. Sam Goldstein makes a very powerful point when he advises:

"Treatment planning must not only include identifying strategies to manage problematic symptoms and behaviors, but also finding strategies to build on what's right, to facilitate self-esteem, self-confidence, resilience, and a sense of self-efficacy. The discussion of treatment planning must equally focus on what is *right* with the child as upon what is wrong." (2003)

A Word About Alternative and Unproven Treatments

There are a number of alternative and unproven treatments that people claim are effective in treating ADHD. These include restricted diets, allergy treatments, megavitamins, biofeedback, anti-motion sickness medication, antioxidants, chiropractic adjustment and bone realignment, treatment for yeast infection, and so forth. There are also a variety of "natural" products advertised on the Internet and other places that claim to cure the symptoms of ADHD (CHADD, July 2001).

Parents must be cautious and informed consumers and be aware that these alternatives are not supported by controlled studies in the scientific literature that show that they work. In fact, many have been disproven. Others warrant further study, but for now remain unproven. Also, some products that are "natural" may actually be harmful, not having been through the scientific process to test for safety (CHADD, July 2001; Rief, 2003).

Medication Treatment and Management

An Optic View of ADD
If corrective lenses did not exist
No well-meaning parent could hope to resist
A pill that enabled their child to see
And increase that child's ability
For better sight and clear vision
No, this would not be a tough decision.
Then why wouldn't the same analogy
Apply to the problem of ADD?
For brains are a lot like eyes, I believe...
They both need to focus in order to see!
Medication as treatment might be prevented
If ADD lenses were someday invented.

Karen Easter, 1996

Note: *Parents should consult with their physician/medical professionals about any medication issues, questions, or concerns. This section is meant only as a general reference.*

*M*edications have been used for decades to treat symptoms of ADHD. Though none of them cure the disorder, they do temporarily control many of the symptoms. The most commonly used medications for treating ADHD are the stimulants (also called psychostimulants). A wide body of scientific evidence supports the use of medications in the treatment of ADHD (CHADD, 2001).

In the past years there has been much attention (media sensationalism and public controversy) regarding the use of stimulant medication in treating children with ADHD. A great deal of misinformation exists, which makes it difficult for parents trying to make an informed decision.

Psychostimulant (Stimulant) Medications

Stimulant medications have been used since the 1930s in the treatment of children with behavioral disorders. In fact, they are the most well-researched of all medications for children.

Stimulants have been proven to be highly effective for 75 to 90 percent of children with ADHD. (U.S. Public Health Service, 1999). These are, therefore, the most commonly prescribed medications for ADHD and are recommended as the first choice for treating children with ADHD. An abundance of data is available demonstrating the efficacy of stimulants across the lifespan (Sallee & Smirnov, 2003).

How Stimulants Are Believed to Work

Researchers suspect that stimulant medications, while they are in the child's blood system, act to normalize biochemistry in the parts of the brain involved in ADHD. Specifically, they enhance nerve-to-nerve communication by making more neurotransmitters available to boost the "signal" between neurons. The neurotransmitters that are released more effectively when a child takes stimulants are dopamine and, to a lesser extent, norepinephrine (Wilens, 1999). As a result, the child is able to better focus attention, regulate activity level and impulsive behaviors, and utilize executive functioning.

There are various kinds of stimulant medications at this time which include:

* *Methylphenidate* (Ritalin®, Ritalin SR®, Concerta®) Metadate CD®, Metadate ER®, Methylin®, Methylin ER, Methylin ER®, Focalin)
* *Dextroamphetamine* (Dexedrine®, Dexedrine Spansule®, DextroStat®)
* *Mixed amphetamine salts* (Adderall®, Adderall XR®)
* *Pemoline* (Cylert®)

However, Pemoline is not usually recommended for the management of ADHD symptoms due to the potential for very serious liver damage (CHADD, 2003).

Methylphenidates are among the most carefully studied drugs on the market. Hundreds of research studies and thousands of children have been involved in evaluating the use of these drugs in the treatment of ADHD. They are known to be highly effective and are considered safe (MTA, 1999).

Each of the stimulants has a high response rate. A child who does not respond well (in symptom improvement) with one stimulant medication will often respond well to another. There are now available a number of choices of stimulant medications that physicians can prescribe to treat children with ADHD. Choice of initial medication to be tried is a matter of physician and parent preference. The various types of stimulants have different onsets of action and drop-off slopes, duration of effects, and release systems into the body.

Some of the stimulants (for example, Ritalin®, Dexedrine®, Adderall®, and generic methylphenidate) come in short- and long-acting forms. The short-acting formulas of the stimulants:

* Start to work about twenty minutes from the time taken
* Metabolize quickly and are effective for approximately three or four hours
* Generally require an additional dosage to be administered at school
* May require a third dose (often a smaller one) to enable the child to function more successfully in the late afternoon/evening hours

The long-acting formulas of the medication have delivery systems that release the medication to give extended coverage throughout the day. Some deliver two doses from one pill at different times; others release some amount initially upon ingestion and then continue to release the medication over an extended period of time. One of the stimulants, Concerta®, has an osmotic release system, which releases some of the methylphenidate soon after ingested and then gradually the rest is pushed out—lasting for ten to twelve hours (CHADD, 2001; CHADD, 2003).

Long-acting formulas:

* Take longer for the effect to "kick in"
* Last for approximately six to eight hours for some of the medications, and others last as long as ten or twelve hours
* Provide a smoother, sustained level of the drug throughout the day
* Minimize fluctuations (peak and trough) in blood levels
* Minimize rebound phenomena
* Are very beneficial for those children and teens who are embarrassed, resistant, or forgetful about going to the school nurse/ office for a midday dose. These eliminate the need to receive medication during the school day and enhance compliance in taking the medication (Jensen, 2003)

Benefits of Stimulant Medications

In many cases, the improvement in symptoms and functioning is dramatic once the child starts taking a stimulant medication. Some children are fortunate to have this kind of dramatic response with the first prescription and dosage they receive. Many others will achieve this response after the medication is adjusted in dosage or on a different prescription for another one of the stimulant medications/formulas. The landmark Multimodal Treatment Approach study proved that, in and of itself, well-managed medication treatment of children with ADHD with a stimulant that has been titrated to a therapeutic level is the most effective of all treatments in improving the symptoms of ADHD (MTA, 1999).

The greatest effects of the stimulants are on the core symptoms of hyperactivity, impulsivity, inattention, and associated features of defiance, aggression, and oppositionality. They also improve classroom performance and behavior and promote increased interaction with teachers, parents, and peers (U.S. Public Health Service, 1999).

Adverse Side Effects from Stimulant Medications

The main side effects that occur with stimulant medications are initial headache, stomachache, delay of sleep onset, and reduction of appetite (Greenhill, 2001). Other possible side effects are irritability, dizziness, rebound phenomena, moodiness, and agitation. Most side effects from stimulant medications are mild, recede over time, and respond to dose changes (U.S. Public Health Service, 1999).

A relatively uncommon side effect of stimulant medications may be the unmasking of latent tics—involuntary motor movements, such as eye blinking, shrugging, and clearing of the throat. Psychostimulant medications can facilitate the emergence of a tic disorder in susceptible individuals. Often, but not always, the tic will disappear when the medication is stopped (CHADD, 2003).

Stimulant medication may incur some risks in slowing growth in height and weight. A twenty-four-month follow-up to the famous MTA study found that there was some growth suppression among the children studied who were receiving medication for the one- and two-year periods of time they were being measured and compared to children in the other ADHD treatment groups (Jensen, Abikoff, Arnold, et al., 2003).

Rebound Phenomenon

This is a worsening of ADHD symptoms (moodiness, irritability, less compliance, more activity) as the medication wears off. It usually lasts for about fifteen to forty-five minutes and can generally be altered by the physician adjusting the dosage or the times when medication is given, or prescribing a different medication.

It is noted that typically the time when the stimulant is wearing off and rebound is observed takes place when the child goes through a significant transition time of the day (with change of expectations and structure). Often the child is on the bus ride home from school, in an after-school childcare environment, or at home expected to do homework or other activities when ADHD symptoms take a turn for the worse. So it is not known whether the worsening of ADHD symptoms observed is entirely due to the drug wearing off or other factors (Greenhill, 2001).

Titration Phase

When a child begins medication treatment, it requires what is known as a titration phase. This is basically a trial period when the physician is trying to determine the appropriate medication and dosage (a therapeutic prescription). It involves:

* Close monitoring of symptoms and behavioral changes (at home and school) while progressively changing the doses and the timing of medication administered
* Starting typically with a very low dose and raising it every few days until a positive response is seen
* The attempt to achieve optimal effects from the medication with a minimum of side effects
* Parents and teachers communicating with the physician, and providing the feedback necessary for the doctor to determine the child's response to the medication and benefits that are being achieved at each dosage level

Many people have concerns about stimulant medications possibly leading to increased rates of drug use in adolescence or adulthood. The research shows the opposite to be true. Fifty years of research has shown that therapeutic use of stimulants does not cause drug addiction. Proper treatment of ADHD with stimulants can lead to a lower risk of the patient abusing alcohol and other drugs (Wilens, Faraone, Biederman, & Gunawardene, 2003).

Antidepressants

Another less frequently used group of medications are the antidepressants—which are also believed to work by acting on the neurotransmitters dopamine and norepinephrine in the brain (CHADD, 2003). These are used in the treatment of children with ADHD as a "second-line" choice. This class of medications is often prescribed for a child who is not responding to a stimulant medication or cannot tolerate the side effects (U.S. Public Health Service, 1999).

This category includes the tricyclic antidepressant medications:

* Imipramine (Tofranil®)
* Desipramine (Norpramin®)
* Amytriptyline (Elavil®)
* Nortriptyline (Pamelor®)

Antidepressants that only affect the serotonin system (Prozac®, Zoloft®, Celexa®) have not been shown to be effective for treating primary symptoms of ADHD but may be effective against co-existing conditions (CHADD, 2003).

Another drug is a novel class of antidepressant (not a tricyclic) called bupropion (Wellbutrin®), which has also been found in studies to be effective in treating ADHD.

The tricyclic antidepressants take some time to build up in the bloodstream and reach a therapeutic level. Their *benefits* include reduction in the symptoms of hyperactivity and impulsivity. In addition, they may also help with mood swings, emotionality, anxiety, depression, sleep disturbances, and tics.

Possible Short-Term Side Effects

Wilens (1999) and CHADD (2001) report that these are dry mouth, constipation, sedation, headaches, stomachaches, blurred vision, rash, nervousness, dizziness, and accelerated heart rate. The major side effects of bupropion are irritability, decreased appetite, insomnia, and worsening of tics (Wilens, 1999).

Atomoxetine (Strattera™)

There is *a new* class of medication that is a "selective norepinephrine reuptake inhibitor." This class of ADHD treatment works differently from the other ADHD medications available. This new drug is called Strattera™ and its generic name is atomoxetine. It was recently approved by the U.S. Federal Drug Administration (FDA) in the treatment of ADHD. Strattera™ is the first FDA-approved treatment for ADHD that is not a stimulant and is not a controlled substance (Sallee & Smirnov, 2003). Studies available in the literature at this time suggest that atomoxetine-related relief of ADHD symptoms is similar to the effect of methylphenidate (stimulants) when both are administered by clinical titration. Atomoxetine has demonstrated efficacy for ADHD symptoms irrespective of age and gender, and it appears to have advantages that include continuous coverage of symptoms throughout the work/school day, evening, and potentially for an entire twenty-four hours (Sallee & Smirnov, 2003).

According to the manufacturer of this product (www.strattera.com), Strattera™ is an oral capsule and can be taken once or twice a day to provide full-day relief from symptoms. It is believed that Strattera™ works by selectively blocking the reuptake of norepinephrine, a chemical messenger or neurotransmitter, by certain nerve cells in the brain. This action increases the availability of norepinephrine, which is thought to be another brain chemical essential in regulating impulse control, organization, and attention (Eli Lilly & Co., 2003).

The most common side effects in medical studies were upset stomach, decreased appetite, nausea and vomiting, dizziness, tiredness, and mood swings. As with the stimulants, most children who experienced side effects were not bothered enough to stop taking the medication (Eli Lilly & Co., 2003).

Atomoxetine is not a controlled substance like a stimulant. It does not start working as quickly as the stimulants do. Reports suggest that the full effects are often not seen until the person has been taking atomoxetine regularly for three or four weeks (CHADD, 2003).

Other Medical Treatments

In more complicated cases of ADHD, much less commonly used medications may be prescribed, such as Clonidine (Catapres®) and Guanfacine (Tenex®).

Also be aware that sometimes the child is best treated with a combination of medications. This is quite common practice for children with co-morbid (co-existing) conditions.

What Teachers and Parents Need to Know If a Child/Teen Is on Medication

Parents do not easily make the decision to medicate their child. Typically, parents agonize over the decision and many try avoiding the medical route for years (Rief, 2003). No parent wants to have their child take a "drug." They often are fearful of the long-term effects. Parents are frequently made to feel guilty by well-meaning relatives and friends who are uneducated about proven treatments, or biased against the use of medication from the misinformation that has been rampant in the media.

The school's role is to support any child receiving medication treatment. School personnel need to be aware of and sensitive to the issues involved with medicating children and fully cooperate as appropriate. Teachers must be involved with close observation of the child, and must communicate with parents, doctor, and the school nurse as to the effects of the medication. Remember:

* Medication(s), dosages, and times to be administered are often changed or adjusted until the right "recipe" or combination is found for the child.

* Children metabolize medication at different rates.
* Children may experience some side effects.

The teacher is an integral part of the therapeutic team because of his or her unique ability to observe the child's performance and functioning (academically, socially, behaviorally) on medication during most of the day. Teachers will need to monitor and observe students on medication carefully and report changes in

* Academic performance
* Work production
* Ability to stay on task
* Behavior
* Relationships
* Any possible side effects the child may be experiencing

These observations and feedback are necessary in helping the physician to regulate the dosage and/or to determine whether the medication has the desired positive effects on symptoms and functioning, with minimal adverse side effects. Teachers should feel free to contact the parent, school nurse, and (if parents provided the school written permission) the doctor directly—with input, observations, and any concerns they might have.

Generally it is the school nurse who acts as the liaison between the parent, physician, and teacher in helping to manage the medication at school. Coordination and communication between all parties involved is essential for optimal results.

Physicians (or their office personnel) should be initiating contact with the school for feedback on how the treatment plan is working. Some doctors may do so through direct contact (phone calls/email). Often teachers are given follow-up behavioral rating scales or simple forms of some type to fill out or are asked to share other observations or information (perhaps with work samples).

Teachers need to be aware that if a student is prescribed a short-acting stimulant medication requiring a dosage to be taken during school hours, it is important that the medication be given on time (generally during the lunch period or right after lunch). Many children/teens have a hard time remembering to go to the office at the designated time for medication because of the very nature of ADHD. It becomes the responsibility of the teacher, school nurse, counselor, and/or office staff to help with the administration of medication.

Ways to remind the student (or alert the teacher that the student needs to come to the office to take a midday dose) may include:

* A beeper watch or watch alarm for the student (or the teacher)
* "Coded" verbal reminders over the intercom
* Private signals from the teacher to the student
* Scheduling a natural transition of activities at that time and setting a clock, radio, or other signal to indicate that time of day
* A sticker chart kept where the medication is dispensed, rewarding the child for remembering
* Color-coded cards given to the child by the teacher or attached to his or her desk
* Post-it® Notes placed near the teacher's schedule or in a plan book reminding the teacher to quietly direct the student to leave the room for medication

It is very important to provide these reminders to students discreetly—without breaking confidentiality or discussing medication in front of other students. Pairing the medication time with a daily activity (perhaps on the way to the cafeteria) is also a common and effective technique because it helps establish a consistent schedule. In the nurse's absence, the office staff should be provided with a list of children who take medication and should send for the child if he or she does not come in to receive it.

With the long-acting formulas, the need for an afternoon dose can be eliminated altogether. For children/teens who are resistant or forgetful in taking their medication at school, a long-acting prescription is likely a better choice of medication.

Advice for Parents

If your child is on medication, it is important that you take responsibility for making sure he or she receives it as prescribed in the morning—on time and consistently. You will need to supervise that your child takes the medication and not leave it as your son's or daughter's responsibility to remember to do so. Close monitoring and management of the medication is crucial. If it is administered haphazardly and inconsistently, your child is better off without it.

Be responsive to calls from the school regarding medication. Be sure the school has the permission forms and filled prescriptions they need on hand, or consider using a long-acting formula.

Communicate with the school nurse and teacher(s). Obviously, the purpose for treating your child with medication is optimal school performance and functioning. This requires teamwork and close communication between the home, school, and physician. If your son or daughter is being treated medically for ADHD, do not keep it a secret from the school.

Be sure to take your child for all of the follow-up visits that are scheduled with his or her doctor. These are necessary for monitoring the effects of the treatment plan. It is very important to educate yourself about the medication treatment/intervention. There are many excellent resources available. Talk to your physician and ask all the questions you need to ask (Rief, 2003).

Most schools have specific policies and procedures for administering medication:

* A signed consent form on file
* Medication in the original, labeled prescription bottle/container

* Medication stored in a locked place
* Maintaining careful records of the dosage, time of dispensing, and person administering the medication
* Restricted administration (for example, may vary only by thirty minutes before or after the prescribed time on the doctor's written order)

Because the commonly prescribed stimulants are classified by the Drug Enforcement Administration as "Schedule 2" medications, there are strict laws regarding how they are prescribed and dispensed. The FDA has restrictions that pharmacists must follow. This makes it more difficult for refilling prescriptions. For example:

* The refill cannot be "called in."
* Doctors can only write a prescription for one month at a time.

It is important that parents pay close attention and communicate with the school nurse to make sure that the school has the medication needed. It helps if parents are reminded in advance if the school supply of medication is running out, so they have plenty of time to renew the prescription and deliver it to school. Again, the long-acting formulas of the medication have the advantage of eliminating the need to keep a prescription at school (Rief, 2003).

It is also recommended that children be counseled about their medication and why they are taking it. There are various resources available that can help children better understand ADHD and why they may be taking medication to treat it. Children need to know that the medication is not in control of their behavior—they are. But the medication helps them to put on the brakes, have better self-control and ability to focus, and therefore, enables them to make better choices.

INTERVIEW WITH MIKE
(Graduate Student in Colorado)

Mike was diagnosed in his twenties and treated for ADHD.

What are your memories of school?

"Grade school through high school, I rarely did my homework. I got through on my test scores. On all of my scholastic aptitude tests I scored above the 90th percentile. I was lucky to be an avid reader. I could get the course syllabus and do the reading without even attending class. But I had a very hard time coping in school. I was highly frustrated, and considered by most of my teachers as a 'problem child.' I wasn't shy about challenging teachers."

Which teachers did you do best with?

"Those who had interesting things to say, lectured well, would go with the flow, and had a sense of humor. I did well with teachers who appreciated an original or challenging thought, who gave latitude for originality, and who weren't rigid."

What is your advice to teachers?

"Kids with ADHD are going to need structure. When you find a kid is not making it, start lending a little structure and see if it will help. I still need a little more structure from my bosses than my co-workers do."

What was it like for you, beginning stimulant medication treatment at twenty-seven years of age?

"My chronic depression went away. I was in a hole and had a lot of problems. Economic: I couldn't hold a job. Relationship problems: My engagement was cut off, and it was devastating to me. Medication helped me to organize my perspective and make long-term plans. It was a revelation to me that I can start something and be able to accomplish it within a reasonable amount of time—even something like cleaning my apartment. If only I'd been caught at eighteen or even eight."

Do's and Don'ts for Teachers and Parents

Advice for Teachers

Assumptions, Attitudes, and Expectations

* Do not assume the student is deliberately not performing because you have observed that at times he or she is able to perform a particular task/assignment.
* Do remember that *inconsistency* is a hallmark characteristic of this disorder. Sometimes they can do the work; sometimes they cannot.
* Do not assume the student is lazy or apathetic.
* Do realize that students with ADHD are typically *not* lazy, but have neurobiological reasons for their poor performance and lack of productivity in the classroom.
* Do not give up on any student.
* Do know how much it matters that you believe in them, maintain high expectations, and give your best effort to help them succeed (no matter how difficult and frustrating it may be).
* Do not forget the quiet student in the background who can easily go through the school year unnoticed and anonymous.
* Do realize that these are students who are often in greatest need of support and intervention.
* Do not surround yourself with negative peers who are critical of students, not open to new techniques and strategies, and not updating their skills.
* Do keep a positive attitude and associate with colleagues who also have a positive mindset. Keep learning and growing. Take advantage of professional development opportunities.
* Do not listen to previous teachers who only want to pass on the negative traits and characteristics of certain students to you.
* Do assume the best of each child. Allow every student to start the year with a fresh, clean slate.
* Do not make assumptions about a child who is from a culture or ethnicity other than your own, based on your limited awareness or understanding of that culture.
* Do make every effort to be culturally sensitive, gain understanding of that culture and family's perspective, and try to bridge any cultural barriers that may exist. This is particularly important to be able to effectively discuss a student's learning, behavior, and need for evaluation or services.

Management

* Do not give up on using behavior modification techniques.
* Do realize that you will need to revamp, revise, and modify aspects of the behavioral plan (for example, incentives, reinforcement

schedule) to maintain the interest and motivation of ADHD students. It is well worth the time and effort!

* Do not tell children what you want them *not to do* ("Don't blurt out in class").
* Do tell children what you want them *to do* ("Raise your hand and wait to be called on").
* Do not focus an undue amount of your attention on a child's misbehaviors.
* Do attend to the student most of the time when he or she is behaving appropriately.
* Do not be afraid to make various accommodations or adjustments (instructional, behavioral, and environmental) as needed for certain students.
* Do choose to make the adaptations and special arrangements it takes for students to succeed in the classroom. It is *okay* and *fair* to make accommodations/modifications for students with ADHD and others with disabilities and special needs.

Communication and Collaboration

* Do not be afraid to ask questions or seek advice and support when you have concerns about a student.
* Do communicate with and involve your school support team for assistance. This multidisciplinary school team should support you in making observations, recommending or developing a plan of behavioral and instructional strategies, attending meetings with parents, providing information, suggesting any appropriate school-based interventions that may be available, and making necessary referrals.
* Do not neglect to do everything you can to forge a collaborative relationship with parents.
* Do remember and acknowledge that parents are the "experts" on their son or daughter. Invite their input, and welcome their involvement. Communicate with parents regularly, and make a plan for working together (for example, using a daily report card or other form of home/school communication) on specific goals. Let parents know

that your primary goal is to help their child achieve school success.

* Do not work alone.
* Do find buddies, share with colleagues, and collaborate!
* Do not make statements or imply to parents that their child has or likely has ADHD and should be evaluated and treated.
* Do share with parents your objective observations and concerns regarding the child's behavior and performance in the classroom and involve your school's multidisciplinary team to discuss further interventions or possible evaluation with parents. It is advised to inquire about procedures or protocol in your school/district regarding steps to take if you suspect a student may have ADHD. (See Section 5.2, The Role of the School's Multidisciplinary Team.)

Advice for Parents

Your Child and Family

* Do not be misled or fooled by your child's inconsistent performance.
* Do understand that variability of performance is a key symptom of ADHD, and it is to be expected. It can be frustrating and puzzling to see your child one day or minute be able to perform a task with ease, and be unable or struggle to perform that same task at a different time.
* Do not assume your child is lazy or apathetic.
* Do realize that your son or daughter may easily be working as hard or much harder than the average child of his or her age/grade. This neurobiologically based disorder causes difficulty activating and sustaining the attention and effort to do work that your child finds tedious, boring, or difficult.
* Do not forget the importance of time for your family to enjoy each other's company, laugh, and have fun together.
* Do play games and enjoy recreational activities together. Spend time listening and

talking to each other; and appreciate the joyful moments and memories that you build together.

* Do not focus on your child's weaknesses or overlook how essential it is to cultivate and nurture your son's or daughter's areas of strength.
* Do involve your child in opportunities to build on his or her talents, interests, and passions. Help your son or daughter gain confidence and competence through those activities in life that give them joy.

Behavioral Management

* Do not give up on using behavior modification techniques.
* Do know that an understanding of effective behavioral strategies is an important part of managing ADHD at home and school. It is worth the time and effort to learn how to incorporate behavior modification strategies into your parenting and disciplinary practices.
* Do not overly focus your attention and responses, setting your radar on your child's misbehaviors.
* Do consciously notice and pay attention frequently to your child when he or she is behaving appropriately. In other words, "catch them being good," and respond and interact at those times.
* Do not focus on what you cannot change or control—someone else's (your child's) behaviors.
* Do work on what you can take control over: your own responses to your child's behavior; your own education and knowledge about ADHD and ways to help; and the structuring, management, and discipline practices you choose to employ.
* Do not respond or dole out consequences when in an angry, emotional state.
* Do wait until you have had a chance to calm down, regain your composure, and ability to think through an appropriate response before acting.

Be Kind to Yourself

* Do not neglect yourself or your own needs for good physical/mental health, nurturing, respite, and support.
* Do take time for yourself, seek help, and find ways to recharge and fulfill your own personal needs. This is important for everyone—especially parents who live with the daily stress that is so common in families of children with ADHD. You are best able to parent and care for your family when you are happy and healthy.
* Do not doubt your parenting abilities or be hard on yourself for what might or might not have taken place so far.
* Do know that it is never too late to learn, make changes, and move ahead. You are not to blame for your child's ADHD, or for not acting on what you did not yet know.

Work with the School

* Do not be adversarial, accusatory, or hostile with school personnel.
* Do remain polite and diplomatic, and always try to build/maintain positive rapport with teachers and other school staff. Casting blame and being confrontational is almost always counterproductive.
* Do not bypass the classroom teacher by going directly to the administrator with issues or concerns.
* Do grant the teacher the courtesy and professional respect to first meet, share concerns, and try to resolve problems directly with the teacher.
* Do not be unrealistic or overly demanding of teachers with regard to the individual attention and degree of accommodations you expect for your child.
* Do understand the teacher's responsibility to *all* students in the classroom, and keep in mind what is "reasonable" when making requests of teachers.
* Do not enter meetings with school personnel with a closed mind, preconceived ideas, or the thought that the school does not have your child's best interest in mind.

* Do enter school meetings with an open mind and cooperative attitude. Be willing to share your opinions, feelings, observations, suggestions, and information about your child or family that may help with planning and intervention.
* Do not be afraid to ask questions and request that certain unclear language (educational jargon) be explained.
* Do ask for clarification on anything you do not understand.
* Do not feel you must accept the school's proposed plan of intervention if you are not comfortable with that plan or feel it is not addressing your child's needs.
* Do know that your input is welcome and generally requested by the school. No plans are set in stone; and they can always be reviewed and changed, if not working. Also, be assured that any plans or placement (for example, IEPs/special education programs) cannot go into effect without your agreement and written consent.

As Leader of Your Child's Team

* Do not use the services of professionals you do not feel comfortable with or whose knowledge and expertise about ADHD you doubt.
* Do choose professionals (physicians, psychologists, educational therapists, tutors) who have experience and training working with children and families with ADHD. Build a team with clinicians and other professionals who are committed to a multimodal treatment approach and are willing to communicate and collaborate closely with you and the school.
* Do not accept an evaluation or diagnosis by any clinician who does not adhere to the diagnostic and treatment guidelines for ADHD set forth by the American Academy of Pediatrics (AAP) and the American Psychiatric Association (APA).
* Do ask questions and make sure that whoever evaluates your child is qualified to do so and is familiar with accepted clinical diagnostic and treatment protocol.
* Do not act on advice from others (as well intentioned as they may be) who are not truly knowledgeable about ADHD.
* Do have the confidence to follow your own best judgment. After learning from expert sources, then make an informed decision on how to best treat and manage your child's ADHD.
* Do not isolate yourself or try to do it alone.
* Do know that there are many other parents in the same situation as you are. It helps to connect with those parents (for example, via organizations such as CHADD and other support groups). Build a team of support for your child and yourself.
* Do not keep your child's ADHD a secret from those who spend much time with your son or daughter (baby-sitters, teachers, coaches, relatives, close family friends).
* Do inform those people who will benefit from having a better understanding of ADHD and what is driving some of your child's behaviors that are difficult to understand and cope with. It is helpful to share, as well, some key strategies you find effective in preventing or minimizing some of the challenging behaviors.
* Do not believe everything you hear or read about ADHD (that is, the various myths and alternative treatments) if it's not coming from reputable, knowledgeable sources.
* Do ask for and seek out information that is based on evidence from the scientific research into ADHD and proven treatments.
* Do not stop learning all you can about ADHD.
* Do educate yourself through any number of avenues (for example, attending conferences and seminars, reading books and magazines, gaining information available on ADHD-related websites, attending parent support groups and organizations, receiving training from specialists in the field). Knowledge about ADHD and treatments

that are proven to work will empower you with confidence, hope, and the skills you need.

* Do not be daunted by your role as the leader and administrator of your child's care team.
* Do assume this parental responsibility by:
  — Knowing enough about the school and factors that make a difference for school success to help ensure the best placement for your son or daughter
  — Learning about your child's rights under the federal educational laws (IDEA and Section 504)
  — Maintaining frequent and regular communication with teachers
  — Facilitating communication between all parties involved in your child's education, treatment, and care
  — Keeping an updated and accessible file of your child's important records/data (health history, report cards, testing/reports, correspondence to and from the school, meeting summaries)

INTERVIEW WITH SPENCER'S MOTHER (Colorado)

What are some of the comments you remember from Spencer's teachers that were hurtful?

"One teacher told me, 'If he gets enough F's, he'll learn how to do what is expected of him in fifth grade,' referring to his homework. Another teacher said, 'He slipped a few times and has shown us how bright he is. He's just playing games with us.'"

Tell me about his best teacher.

"Spencer's third-grade teacher was wonderful. She read to the class with the lights off . . . made sure there wasn't a lot of clutter on the chalkboard or his desk. She seated him to reduce distractions . . . right up front near her. She spoke softly to him and every criticism was coupled with something positive."

INTERVIEW WITH STEVE (16 Years Old, California)

Steve has learning disabilities and ADHD.

What is your advice to teachers?

"Don't embarrass kids in front of the whole class. If you need to talk to them about something they did, the teachers should tell them in private. Otherwise, you just end up hating the teacher, and then you're not going to listen to what they say. . . . When somebody is frustrated, give them a couple of minutes to cool down before they get in trouble."

1.6

Critical Factors in the Success of Students with ADHD

Note: The following are listed alphabetically, not necessarily in order of importance. All of these topics will be discussed in more depth in sections throughout this book.

1. Belief in the Student—Doing What It Takes. Students with ADHD need teachers, parents, and other adults who are on their side, who believe in them and their ability to succeed. These supportive adults need to also realize that it takes vigilance and willingness to frequently come back to the "drawing board" and reexamine or revise our original plan. When Plans A, B, and C no longer seem to be working well, there are always Plans D, E, F, and so forth. These children are worth the extra time and effort, and we must never give up!

2. Clarity and Structure. Students with ADHD need to be placed in a classroom where teachers provide clarity of expectations and *structure*. Some people may have the misconception that a structured classroom is one that is "traditional" in room arrangement and teaching style (like adults remember from their school days). One may think that a structured classroom would certainly be very quiet most of the day. This may or may not be the case. The most creative, inviting, colorful, active, and stimulating classrooms (which are frequently the best placement for students with ADHD) are also sometimes the noisier classrooms in the building. What appears to an observer as a structured teacher and classroom may very well not be, and vice versa. It is important to understand the key structural components to be looking for in any classroom.

Students with ADHD need to have structure provided for them through clear communication, expectations, rules, consequences, and follow-up. They need to have academic tasks structured by breaking assignments into manageable increments and be provided with teacher modeling and guided instruction, clear directions, standards, and feedback. These students require assistance with structuring: their materials, workspace, group dynamics, handling of choices, and transitional times of the day. Their school day needs to be structured with altering of active and quiet periods. No matter what the particular teaching style or the physical environment of the classroom, any teacher can and should provide structure for student success.

3. Close Communication Between Home and School. It is very important for teachers to significantly increase communication with parents of students with ADHD. It is critical for teachers and parents to make every effort to establish a good working relationship and maintain open lines of communication. Early in the school year it is best to discuss which avenues of communication are preferred by both parties (for example, phone calls and voice mail, email correspondence, home/school notes, journals, daily/weekly reports). This population of students needs far more frequent and regular contact between home and school than the average student in the class. The success of students with ADHD is very much tied to the degree of mutual support, cooperation, and communication between home and school.

4. Collaboration and Teamwork. The partnership that is developed between parents, educators, and clinicians is a key element in the successful management of ADHD in any child or teen. ADHD is a chronic disorder that, similar to asthma, is long-term and has a lifetime course; it is not cured but managed. Various interventions will be needed in any given school year, and those interventions and treatments often change. ADHD affects many aspects of the child's life, and it takes a team approach to improve the performance of the child—not just at school, but at home and in other settings. Parents are truly the leaders of the team. They have the main role in seeking out and trying to assemble the optimal team for treating, caring for, and educating their son or daughter. The team may involve medical and mental health professionals, the teacher and other school personnel, before- and/or after-school caregivers, tutors, coaches, and so forth.

What about other teaming for school success? Many teachers find that team teaching is extremely helpful. Being able to switch or share students (particularly very challenging ones) for part of the school day may reduce the behavioral problems and preserve the teacher's sanity. It also provides for a different perspective on each child. Various student support services such as those provided by guidance/school counselors are often very helpful for students with ADHD. Some of those supports might include working with the teacher in the implementation of behavior modification techniques and positive reinforcement, time-out/time-away, training and practice in conflict resolution, social skills, anger management, and so forth.

Of course, if the student is receiving special education or related services, successful outcomes involve communication and collaboration between classroom teachers, special educators, and other service providers. The school's multidisciplinary team (the Student Support Team) can be a great resource and provider of direct and indirect assistance. The team often includes the school psychologist, school nurse, and other school-based support professionals. Administrators can be very instrumental in obtaining extra intervention and support for the student, as well. You are all part of the same team! Everyone's focus needs to be on the best interests of the student and on ways all parties can help that child or teen to experience school success. (See Section 5.1, Teaming for Success.)

5. Creative, Engaging, and Interactive Teaching Strategies. Instruction that enables students to be highly engaged, involved, and interacting with their peers is critical in the classroom—especially for students with ADHD. All students need and deserve a curriculum that is enriching, motivating, and employs a variety of approaches. In order for teachers to be successful in enabling all students to achieve and acquire the skills, standards, and content mastery for the grade level, they must be adept at differentiating instruction. Teachers need to be trained and skilled in use of strategies that provide for a high degree of active learning and student response opportunities. Teachers need a large repertoire of strategies and techniques that draw on the diverse learning styles and multiple intelligences of students in the classroom. All students need to be given the daily opportunity to work in a variety of formats (for example, with partners, small groups, individually, large group) and be instructed through a combination of methods involving multisensory strategies, student choices, and experiential learning. (See the several sections under Instructional Strategies and Supports that address these topics.)

6. Developing and Bringing Out Students' Strengths. We need to be very aware that many children with ADHD are highly gifted (intellectually, artistically, musically, athletically). Given the chance to nurture and develop their strengths, gifts, interests, and talents, they will be successful in life. Unfortunately, it becomes common knowledge in the classroom, and peers are acutely aware of the weaknesses and vulnerabilities of the child with ADHD. Teachers need to provide numerous opportunities for these students to showcase their strengths and demonstrate to their peers what they do well. Parents must provide as many opportunities as possible outside of school to help their children discover areas of interest, participate in activities that develop those skills, and give them joy and confidence in life.

7. Effective Classroom Management and Positive Discipline. All students deserve to be in classrooms in which there is a positive, respectful climate. Fundamental to school success is creating an environment in which everyone feels part of a caring, supportive community. Students with ADHD are in particular need of a classroom placement in which the teacher structures the classroom environment, procedures, routines, and instruction with a focus on *problem prevention*. Teachers must be aware of what may trigger behavioral problems and avoid it through careful planning. They need to teach and reinforce appropriate behavior, and employ positive, proactive discipline practices. (See Section 2.1, Classroom Management and Positive Discipline Practices, and Section 2.2, Preventing or Minimizing Behavior Problems During Transitions and Less Structured Times of the School Day.)

8. Environmental Modifications and Accommodations. Classroom environment is a very important factor in how students function. Due to a variety of learning styles, there should be environmental options for students as to where and how they work. Where the student sits can make a significant difference. Lighting, furniture, seating arrangements, visual displays, color, areas for relaxation, and provisions for blocking out distractions during seatwork should be carefully considered. Organize the classroom with the awareness that most students with ADHD need to be within close proximity to the teacher (to enable easy prompting and cueing) and be seated in less-distracting, low-traffic areas near and among well-focused students. There are many environmental factors that can be adjusted to improve the functioning and performance of students with attention-deficit disorders. (See Section 2.1, Classroom Management, and Section 3.3, Reaching Students Through Their Learning Styles and Multiple Intelligences.)

9. Flexibility and Willingness of Teacher to Accommodate. This is a key factor for success—placement with a teacher who has the commitment and belief that it is his or her responsibility to reach and teach *all* students in the classroom. This means being willing to put forth the extra time, energy, and effort necessary to work with an individual student (and the team) to help the child succeed. It also means having the flexibility to make changes and accommodations as needed.

10. Help and Training in Organization and Study Skills. Students with ADHD commonly have major problems with organization, time management, and study skills. They will need direct help and additional intervention to make sure assignments are recorded correctly, their work space and materials are organized, notebooks and desks are cleared of unnecessary collections of junk from time to time, and specific study skill strategies are taught to enable them to achieve academic success. There are numerous strategies and study skills that will improve the performance of children and teens with ADHD. These include what teachers and parents can do to help build these skills, which are so necessary for success (in school and in the workplace). (See Section 3.5, Organization, Time Management, and Study Skills Strategies.)

11. Knowledge and Understanding of ADHD. It is essential that teachers be aware that students with ADHD have a problem that is physiological and neurobiological in nature. Training about the disorder itself is very important so that adults working and interacting with these students every day at school understand what is underlying the challenging behaviors they often exhibit and realize that the behaviors are not deliberate in intent. In fact, most of the time children with ADHD are oblivious to how their behaviors are impacting those around them. A better understanding helps teachers, other school personnel, and parents maintain their patience, tolerance, sense of humor, and ability to deal with the child and his or her behaviors in a positive way. Every school (elementary, middle, and secondary) needs staff development devoted to educating all school personnel about ADHD (as well as LD and other neurobiological disorders). All educators need to understand how the disorder affects students' learning and school functioning and be trained in effective strategies and interventions. (See Section 1.1, Understanding ADHD.)

12. Limit the Amount of Homework. If the parent complains that an inordinate amount of time is spent on the homework, teachers should be flexible and reduce the homework to a manageable amount. Teachers need to be aware of the terrible homework hassles and stress in many homes of children with ADHD. This, of course, has to do with all the self-management issues, difficulty sustaining the attention and mental effort to get through work, such as the average homework assignment. It typically takes students with ADHD much longer than the average student to complete homework tasks, with need for more supervision and monitoring than most children of that age require to complete homework assignments.

In addition, students with ADHD, who may be medicated and more productive during the school hours, often are not receiving medication benefits in the evening hours. It depends on how long-acting the type of medication is, whether the child is on a type that continues to have a therapeutic effect during the late afternoon/evening hours, or if on a short-acting formula and whether parents are choosing to administer another dosage after school. Many teachers have the practice of sending home any incomplete class work. It is important for teachers to keep in mind that if the student was unable to complete the work during an entire school day, it is unlikely that he or she will be able to complete it that evening. *Instead of piling on all the incomplete work, teachers should prioritize, communicate closely with parents, set realistic goals, make accommodations, and find ways to modify without compromising the student's learning.*

13. Modifying Assignments and Written Workload. What takes an average child twenty or thirty minutes to do, may take a student with attention-deficit disorders *hours* to accomplish (particularly written assignments). There is no need to do every problem on the page to practice a skill or reinforce new learning. Teachers need to be open to making adaptations or modifications when needed for certain students. Remember that ADHD is a disorder that affects performance, production, and output. These students typically cannot produce the same amount of work at the same rate as the average child that age or grade. Teachers must be willing to make accommodations so that the amount of work assigned is reasonable for that particular student (for example, every other problem, half a page) to learn the material and demonstrate their knowledge. Accept alternative methods of demonstrating their learning through means other than in writing (for example, allowing student to answer questions orally, student dictates and a scribe writes or records, hands-on projects and demonstrations). Seek other more fun, creative, and artistic ways for them to practice skills and show their mastery of concepts. Ease up on handwriting requirements and demands for students if they struggle in the physical task of writing. Be sensitive to the extreme effort it often takes children with ADHD and/or learning disabilities to get down in writing what appears simple to you and what other students can do with ease. Typing/word processing skills are to be encouraged! (See the written language sections, 3.8 and 3.9.)

14. More Time, More Space. To compensate for the difficulty many students with ADHD have with speed of output, it is often a necessary accommodation to provide more time. This may mean extra time to complete assignments or exams. Also, many children with ADHD have co-existing learning disabilities and may have an auditory processing problem as well. If so, they may need extra time to process and think about a question before responding. Teachers who pose questions and provide at least five seconds of "wait time" before calling on students to respond help those with ADHD and others (for example, with LD, English language learners) who need extra time to think about a question and gather their thoughts before answering. Many elementary school teachers in the lower grades have experienced the benefits of class-size reduction. Having fewer students in the class has many clear benefits. One of them is less crowding and more space. Students with ADHD often have a tendency to intrude in others' space. They frequently need more room to themselves (for example, table top/desk space, more distance and buffer space sitting on the carpet) in order to stay better organized and reduce problems interacting with their peers. Of course, teachers in upper grades and crowded classrooms have fewer options in how to provide more space without getting very creative.

15. Support of Administration. It is critical that administrators also be aware of the characteristics and strategies for effectively managing and educating students with ADHD and support the teacher in dealing with disruptive children. Some students are extremely difficult to maintain in the classroom and require highly creative interventions. In these cases, administrative support is very much needed in providing the teacher with assistance. This may come in many forms (for example, student time away from the classroom—in other classrooms or settings, more push-in adult help at times of the day in the classroom, facilitating meetings with parents and other team members, helping with developing a proactive plan of behavioral intervention). Administrators need to be sensitive to and receptive of input from parents and teachers regarding classroom placement each year. As instructional leaders of their schools, they must help teachers to develop their skills and learn effective strategies for working with and instructing students with ADHD or LD, and others with diverse learning needs. This can be done by providing the necessary professional development and training. The school climate for academic and social/behavioral success is best established when the administrator takes the lead in setting, modeling, and reinforcing positive expectations in the building (for staff and students).

16. Valuing and Respecting Learning Styles/Differences, Privacy, Confidentiality, and Students' Feelings. Teachers who are going to be successful in reaching and teaching students with ADHD, and all the diverse learners in the classroom, must value and respect the different learning styles and differences each child possesses. This is part of what makes each student unique. Teachers and other school personnel must also be very conscious and respectful of privacy and confidentiality issues (evaluation results, medication issues, scores/ grades, family information). Self-esteem is fragile in students with ADHD (and many other children). Because of the high degree of negative feedback received over the years, many students with ADHD perceive themselves as failures. We must avoid ridicule, and never humiliate children or teens in front of their peers. Preservation of their self-esteem is critical in truly helping these children succeed in life.

INTERVIEW WITH JOE
(41 Years Old, California)

Joe was diagnosed as an adult with learning disabilities and ADHD.

"Watch Joseph. He's one of the most intelligent children I've ever seen." This was the comment made to Joe's parents when he and his siblings were tested at a young age by their neighbor, a professor of psychology in New York—Joe who never received higher than a D from sixth grade through high school. Joe, who was constantly ridiculed by his teachers and was a "big disappointment to his parents."

Joe was "left back" in the seventh grade while living in Connecticut. He remembers the trauma of all his friends moving on to another school when he repeated seventh. He flunked algebra four times. He graduated from high school "dead last" in his class. "After a while I had defaulted into a discipline problem. You gravitate toward those students who have absolutely no respect for the system. Otherwise you have to agree that the only other thing that could be wrong is YOU."

Junior (Community) College was an uphill battle all over again. He saw his classmates "cruise through all their subjects" to get their degrees. "The only difference between them and me was that I never knew what to do with numbers. Reading is extremely difficult for me. I have to do it very slowly and put everything into my own translator to assimilate the material and have it make sense." Joe's adult life has been "a patchwork of jobs." Up until a few years ago, the average time he stayed with a job was one year. "There were so many days I was beaten to a pulp, and completely down and out until I was thirty years old. I knew there was something wrong with me, but no one knew what it was."

One significant change came in his adult life when a friend took him "under his wing" and mentored him for three years in his business. "Now I have a good job as a technician in a good company. But it never lets up. I can't get a reprieve. In the real world of high tech, it requires constant training and schooling."

What would have made a difference for you growing up?

"No one saw or was interested in my strengths. The spoken word came easily to me, the written word was very difficult. I was able at a young age to take an engine apart and put it back together. I have an excellent understanding of mechanical things. I was always musically talented . . . and I knew everything there was to know about reptiles and amphibians.

"If one person would have interceded on my behalf. If one person would have said, 'This is not a stupid person we're dealing with. . . . There's something more involved here that we need to get to the bottom of,' the weight of the world would have been lifted from my shoulders."

ADHD and Social Skills Interventions

Children and teens with ADHD frequently have difficulty with interpersonal relationships—getting along with others at home and school, and in other settings. Social challenges can result in a lot of negative outcomes and low self-esteem, as well as be a source of great pain and frustration not just for the child, but for the entire family.

Some common struggles in children and teens with ADHD that negatively affect their interactions and social acceptance are

* Poor self-control and inhibition of their behavior
* Difficulty regulating their emotions and responses
* Poor problem-solving skills and over-reactivity—easily provoked to fighting, arguing, name calling, and inappropriate means of resolving conflicts
* Problems with anger management
* Poor self-awareness—often unaware of their own behaviors that others find annoying or intrusive
* Difficulty controlling and modulating their tone, volume, language
* Poor communication skills (for example, listening to others, refraining from interrupting others)
* Easily overaroused, overstimulated, having difficulty calming themselves down

In addition, children and teens with ADHD often miss important verbal and nonverbal cues that may alert them to regulate their emotional reactions and to modify their behaviors when things are not going well in social interchanges (Teeter & Goldstein, 2002).

Individuals with the predominantly inattentive type of ADHD may have social problems that are different from those who are impulsive and hyperactive. They tend to be unsure, anxious, initially withdrawn in social situations, and reluctant to take social risks. They may misinterpret tone in voice or nonverbal language, believing others are being more critical than they really are, and may lack the language skills to keep up verbally—remaining quiet or making inappropriate or out-of-context comments (Wallace, 2000).

Skill Deficits Versus Performance Deficits

Social skills problems can result from a skill deficit, in which the child does not know what to do in a social situation and needs to learn the skills to become socially competent. Social challenges can also have nothing to do with a lack of skills. According to a leading authority, Dr. Russell Barkley, children with ADHD typically do not have a skill deficit, but rather a *performance* deficit. They know what they are supposed to do

55

and the appropriate social skills, but fail to *apply* or *perform* those needed skills (Barkley, 1998).

When the child has difficulty acquiring or learning a skill, he or she may need a different intervention than a child who already knows the skill, but struggles to perform it. Children who have a deficit in specific social skills need direct, explicit teaching and frequent opportunities to practice those appropriate skills. Those children/teens who know the appropriate skills but do not perform them due to inhibition problems need a lot of external reinforcement (behavioral modification techniques) to help them exhibit better self-control in order to *use* the skills (Rief, 2003).

Children with social skill deficits will benefit from social skill training in which they learn age-appropriate social behavior, reading of social cues, and social perspective. Those with social performance deficits should be trained to develop control strategies (for example, anger management training) so they can apply what they already know (Zumpfe & Landau, 2002).

An important study and national survey, called I.M.P.A.C.T. (Investigating the Mindset of Parents about AD/HD and Children Today), conducted by New York University Child Study Clinic (2000), revealed some of the impact of having ADHD on the life of the child and the whole family. According to the survey results:

* 72 percent of parents of children with ADHD report that their child has trouble getting along with siblings or other family members (compared to 53 percent of parents of children without ADHD).
* Nearly one-quarter say their child has problems that limit their participation in after-school activities (compared to only 7 percent of parents of children without ADHD).

Parents of children with ADHD are nearly:

* Three times more likely to report that their child has difficulty getting along with neighborhood children

* More than twice as likely to say their child gets picked on
* Half as likely to believe their child has many good friends (Koplewicz, 2002)

Susan Sheridan, author of *The Tough Kid Social Skills Book,* explains that in any classroom, students can be classified into one of four groups:

1. *Popular students*—those who are highly rated or named frequently as those with whom others would like to play.
2. *Neglected students*—not many classmates report them as those with whom they would like to play, and not many report them as those with whom they would not like to play.
3. *Controversial students*—several students say they would like to play with them, but several say they would not like to play with them.
4. *Rejected students*—not named by many as those with whom they would like to play; and named by many of their classmates as those with whom they would not like to play (Sheridan, 1995).

Using sociometric methods of data collection (classmates identifying peers they would and would not like to work and play with), it has been repeatedly shown that many children with ADHD are the most rejected among their classmates (Zumpfe & Landau, 2002). This is of great significance to parents and teachers, as children with peer problems can experience a great deal of sadness, worry, anxiety, and pain—which affects all aspects of their lives and functioning.

Interventions for Social Skills Problems

Research indicates that the most effective interventions for addressing interpersonal/social skills difficulties in children and teens with ADHD are multimodal. These involve a combination of (a) psychosocial/behavioral interventions, (b) medication (if indicated), and (c) educational strategies/interventions involving teachers, parents, and, of course, the child.

According to Dr. William Pelham Jr., one of the foremost researchers in the study of psychosocial interventions for children with ADHD, the essential components of treatment for ADHD are the psychosocial approaches—behavioral parent training, classroom management interventions in school, and behavioral interventions with children that focus mainly on peer relationships (Pelham, 2002).

Although the Multimodal Treatment Approach Study (MTA, 1999) found that medication treatment for children with ADHD had the greatest effect on the reduction of symptoms and impairment, it also showed that appropriate use of behavioral interventions can reduce the dose of medication needed. Another finding from the MTA study was that, looking at parent measures of satisfaction, parents were twice as likely to report strong satisfaction with the behavioral interventions, either alone or in combination with the medication, compared to the medication alone group. As Dr. Pelham points out, the treatment of ADHD (as it is a chronic condition) requires that the intervention be palatable to families, because they have to do it over years, not over just weeks or months. In essence, parents were far more accepting of medication treatment when combined with behavioral treatments; and by far, the combined treatment (medication and behavioral) had the best combination of effectiveness and parent satisfaction (Pelham, 2002).

Note: *See Section 1.1 for more information about the landmark MTA study.*

School Interventions

School interventions that specifically model, teach, practice, and reinforce pro-social behaviors are often provided through school-wide approaches and classroom approaches. In addition, direct, targeted small-group social skills training may take place.

School-Wide Approaches

Many schools are implementing character education programs or social-emotional learning (SEL) programs. These programs focus on teaching and positively reinforcing pro-social values, virtues, and behaviors. All staff and students are involved in the efforts to create a positive school-wide climate and culture. Some of the character traits and values taught in SEL or character education programs include:

Trustworthiness	Fairness
Respect	Caring
Responsibility	Citizenship
Leadership	Courtesy
Honesty	Sharing
Dependability	Friendship
Moral Courage	Sportsmanship
Empathy	Persistence
Integrity	Initiative

There are numerous ways of teaching and positively reinforcing targeted pro-social traits/behaviors throughout the school. Besides classroom lessons and activities, there can be school-wide assemblies, messages over the intercom, and school-wide/community campaigns. There are many visuals (posters, banners, murals) in classrooms, hallways, and other environments of the building. There are also school-wide activities such as the following:

* All teachers spend time at the beginning of the week or month discussing a particular value or social skill with their students (for example, courtesy).
* All adults on campus wear a badge that has the social skill topic/word of the month printed on the badge.
* Staff members are given a certain amount of "I Got Caught" tickets that they are to distribute to any student they happen to

observe on campus exhibiting the targeted social skill behavior of the week or month (being respectful, courteous, fair, and so forth).

* Students who receive tickets write their names on them and place the ticket inside the school box designated for that purpose. Once a day or week there is a raffle with prizes going to students whose names are drawn.

Some middle schools are teaching social skills in their P.E. programs through various formats:

* The specific social skill (such as encouragement, giving/accepting compliments, sportsmanship) is taught in three- or four-week units.
* Skills are discussed in terms of what it looks and sounds like when you display those skills, as well as the rationale for using them. For example, the following can represent what *encouragement* looks like: thumbs up, pat on back, smile, high five, and so on. And the following can represent what *encouragement* sounds like: "Nice try," "You can do it," "Way to go."
* The skills are then practiced and reinforced through a number of entertaining and motivating cooperative games and activities.
* Students receive positive reinforcement in a variety of ways for exhibiting those skills.
* Students are responsible for processing and evaluating how well they and their group performed regarding the use of the specific social skill.

Classroom Approaches

Within the classroom there is no better place and structure for teaching and practicing appropriate social skills than in the context of cooperative learning groups. Research has proven cooperative learning structures are effective not only in increasing student learning, but also in building positive/supportive relationships, stu-

dent acceptance, and the ability to see others' points of view. See Section 3.4, which contains information on cooperative learning, as well as a social skills planning unit.

Some elementary schools provide social skill training through various lessons and units taught by the classroom teacher to the whole class, or in sessions facilitated and presented by the counselor (either in the classroom or small-group sessions outside of the classroom). There are some excellent programs and social skill curriculums on the market from which to choose, listed at the end of this section.

In any context or format that social skills are being taught, do the following:

* Explain the need or rationale for learning the skill. Define the skill clearly. Discuss and reinforce by visual displays (posters, photos).
* Demonstrate appropriate and inappropriate skills through positive and negative examples. Provide modeling of the skills (live demos, using puppets, through books).
* Have students role play the appropriate skill while you provide feedback during this rehearsal.
* Ask students to look for and observe the skill being displayed in different settings.
* The key is providing many opportunities to *practice* the skill being taught in authentic, real-world activities. In the context of these settings (or in debriefing afterward) provide coaching, positive reinforcement for appropriate use, and corrective feedback/consequences for inappropriate behavior.
* Reward appropriate use of the targeted social skill(s).

Every day teachers informally model and teach students pro-social behaviors. By setting behavioral standards and enforcing expectations for respectful, cooperative behavior and good manners, most students learn and practice good social skills daily. Teachers infuse social skills training into daily instruction when they explicitly model, coach, prompt, monitor, and positively reinforce such skills as: sharing, taking turns, problem solving, encouraging and complimenting others, disagreeing and expressing opinions appropriately.

Teaching Tips for Building Social Competencies in Students

* Increase student awareness of appropriate skills by modeling, giving positive attention, and reinforcing student displays of pro-social behavior(s) both in and out of the classroom setting.
* Provide corrective feedback in a manner that is neither judgmental nor embarrassing, but rather focuses on teaching positive social skills.
* Help children weak in social skills by carefully pairing them with positive role models and assigning them to groups that will be more supportive. You may need to facilitate friendships for certain students who tend to be socially isolated.
* Take photos of groups or individuals engaged in cooperative behavior and hang them in prominent places as visual cues (Rief, 2003).

Child Social Skills Interventions

Many children with ADHD are not socially accepted because they have poor skills in playing various games/sports. It helps to involve them in as many opportunities as possible to build their skills and competencies so that peers will want to include them in their play and sport activities. As Dr. Pelham points out, in their renown summer treatment programs for children with ADHD, there is a major focus on teaching sports skills to the children. "If you teach a child to be a better baseball player, and therefore make him more popular among children in the neighborhood, he'll be a better baseball player forever. Medication will help him pay attention when he's playing baseball, but it won't teach him to catch, throw, and hit. That's an example of where a child might have

an attention problem and a skills deficit, and both forms of treatment might be helpful" (Pelham, 2002).

Social Skills Training Programs

Training programs can be implemented in a variety of settings (for example, counseling groups during school hours, after-school programs, summer treatment programs, clinical settings, learning centers/recreation centers).

Social skills programs are designed to teach specific skills within a small group (children/teens generally in same age range). Best evidence indicates social skills training programs should be delivered in small groups (for example, four to eight same-gender classmates), not one-on-one. This will increase the chance for positive feedback from peers and successful transfer from the training group to the classroom or other school setting. In addition, in school settings some of the more popular children should also be included in these groups. Their presence may reduce the stigma of participating and help their less popular peers interact more positively with the other students (Zumpfe & Landau, 2002). The trainer (the guidance counselor, for example) uses social skills training curriculum.

Social skills programs commonly address some of the following:

* Greeting others
* Listening and responding (developing active listening skills)
* Showing interest by smiling and asking questions
* Respecting personal body space
* Working and playing cooperatively
* Reading social signals (others' body language, expressions)
* Learning to join an ongoing activity (a game in progress)
* Ignoring teasing
* Managing anger/using effective coping strategies (for example, understand and recognize triggers to anger, find appropriate

ways to express anger, use positive "self talk" and "I feel . . ." statements)
* Following instructions and rules
* Awareness of feelings (self and others)
* Giving and accepting positive feedback
* Giving and accepting negative feedback
* Coping with teasing
* Avoiding and dealing with bullies
* Solving problems peacefully/non-aggressively (negotiation, compromising)

Most effective programs have sessions involving:

* A *brief* introduction to the skill, including examples/non-examples, role play, and rehearsal.
* The bulk of the session involves actually playing an indoor or outdoor game/activity in a supervised setting.
* Children are prompted and coached on the use of the skill.
* There is a short debriefing with feedback and rewards/reinforcement for demonstrating the use of the targeted skill.
* Children are often provided homework assignments to actually practice the use of the skill before the next session.
* If the child reports failure on the homework assignment, the facilitator/trainer uses problem-solving strategies to help the child determine what went wrong and what he or she might try differently next time.

Use of the skill with feedback and contingent reinforcement applied in authentic situations (playing a game) is a critical component of effective social skills programs. Any social skill taught should be one that can be generalized across settings. This requires that the skill(s) be practiced and reinforced at school, home, and so forth.

Goal Setting

It is recommended that teachers, parents, and other adults help the child to set concrete, achievable social goals to work on. Goals should include the "who," "what," "when," and "where," and be as specific as possible. The following are some examples:

Goal: Sally will say hello (what) to Pam (who) tomorrow at lunch (when) in the cafeteria (where).
Goal: Jack will start a conversation with a child in school at least three times in one week (Cohen, 2000).
Goal: I will ask Sarah to play with me at recess tomorrow.
Goal: I will invite Jane to my house one day before Sunday (Sheridan, 1995).

Additional Social Interventions and Training for Children

Other important interventions involve teaching the child/teen some cognitive approaches and other methods to help improve interpersonal relationships/social skills and self-regulation of behavior. This includes training in

* Problem-solving techniques (for example, various strategies such as those in Shure's book, *I Can Problem Solve*)
* Conflict resolution
* Anger management and self-control strategies (for example, use of self-talk statements)
* Relaxation strategies

The following are examples of some cognitive approaches:

Strategy for Using Self-Control (Sheridan, 1995)

1. Stop, take a deep breath, and count to five.
2. Decide what the problem is and how you feel.
3. Think about your choices and their consequences:
   * Ignore the situation.
   * Tell yourself, "It's okay."
   * Tell yourself to relax.
   * Speak calmly.
   * Compromise.
   * Say how you feel, using I-statements.

4. Decide on your best choice.

5. Do it.

Examples of "Self-Talk" Statements to Help with Anger Management and Keeping Oneself in Control (Parker, 2002)

1. "I can handle this situation."

2. "I can work this out."

3. "Stay calm. Breathe easily. Just continue to relax."

4. "Relax and think this through."

5. "I'm not going to let this thing get the best of me."

6. "I can stay in control."

7. "Getting upset won't help anything."

Examples of Encouraging Positive Self-Talk (Cohen, 2000)

1. "Nobody is good at everything."

2. "I'll get better if I keep trying."

3. "I'll do better when I'm not so tired or frustrated."

4. "Maybe I'm not such a great speller, but I have lots of good ideas to write down."

5. "I can do this."

Note: See Section 2.5 for the shining light bulb strategy—a cognitive technique for helping children who struggle with listening and paying attention.

Preliminary research suggests that having a best friend may have a protective effect on children with difficulties in peer relations as they develop through childhood and into adolescence (Hoza, Mrug, Pelham, et al., 2001; Mrug, Hoza, & Gerdes, 2001). Researchers have developed programs that help children with ADHD build at least one close friendship. These programs always begin with other forms of intervention (for example, systematic teaching of social skills, social problem solving, teaching sports skills/board game rules, decreasing undesirable and antisocial behaviors) and then add having the families schedule monitored play dates and other activities for their child and another child

with whom they are attempting to foste friendship (CHADD, 2004).

Parent Interventions

Parents, of course, are their child's primary teachers throughout their childhood and adolescence. It is important that parents model and teach the social skills they want their child to exhibit, and effectively reinforce their child's use of those pro-social behaviors and positive interpersonal skills. Part of the multimodal intervention plan for the child with ADHD involves parent training in

* Behavior modification techniques and positive discipline
* Understanding and dealing with challenging behaviors
* Communicating effectively
* Avoiding problems (for example, by modifying the environment, providing more structure)

Note: These topics and strategies are covered in other sections of this book.

Parents must become educated about ADHD and aware of the resources and supports in their community. For children with social and interpersonal problems, parents can help by:

* Seeking counseling for their child, and/or a well-designed social skills training program for their child facilitated by someone who is knowledgeable and skilled working with children who have ADHD
* Orchestrating, when necessary, opportunities for their child to socialize and play with other children
* Reinforcing the pro-social skills being taught at school and any other social skills training in which the child may be participating

Parents may try bringing to their child's attention the inappropriateness of some of their social behaviors, the impact they have on maintaining friendships, and so forth. However, it is recommended to have such conversations at a time when it is calm at home (a more "teach-able moment")—not when emotions are running high. It is most important that parents be able to effectively model, enable their child to practice under supervision, and praise or otherwise reinforce the child when using the proper social skills.

In some communities there are centers or clinics specializing in multimodal treatment approaches for children/teens with ADHD. They may offer a variety of services and supports for both children and their parents. For example, children may be participating in a social skills training group in one room, while parents are in a different room in a parent training session with a facilitator and group of other parents.

Summer Treatment Programs

There are some highly effective summer treatment programs for children with ADHD that utilize a strong behavioral and social skills component, along with parent training and other aspects of a multimodal approach. For information about such programs in the United States and Canada, see the following website: http://summertreatmentprogram.com or contact CHADD at www.chadd.org.

A number of books and hands-on board games that foster the spirit of cooperation (not competition) are available through:

Co-Operative Games™
Family Pastimes™
RR 4 Perth, Ontario
Canada K7H 3C6
www.familypastimes.com
(613) 267-4819
Fax: (613) 264-0696
Email: fp@superaje.com

Players help each other climb a mountain, make a community, bring in the harvest,

complete a space exploration, or other such challenges. Players learn through the games that they will get better results learning how to get along and cooperate (with Time, Winter, Gravity, and Mountains) rather than fighting them. Games provide the opportunity to experience sharing and caring behavior. There are games for preschool children through adults. Some are suitable for two to four players; others for groups of up to eight, twelve, or eighteen players at a time.

Lunchtime / Trouble Time
Lunchtime is mostly trouble time
for an ADHD kid
it's a welcome break to a boring routine
(and prime time to flip teacher lids!)
This diversion gives time for some mingling
but to the teacher a job must be done
thirty kids through the line in five minutes
but the hyper kid thinks "time for fun"!
Every dessert in the case he handles,
every cookie his fingers must touch
at the end of the line teacher wrinkles her nose
barks "You just get into trouble too much!"
He carelessly strolls to the table
spilling most of the food on his tray
when he asks, "Can I sit down beside you?"
his friends say "I don't think you may."
So he sits at the end of the table, alone.
His dessert he wolfs down first
he drinks a whole carton of milk in one gulp
to drown his unquenchable thirst.
Next comes an enticing challenge
the hot dog lying there on his plate . . .
1–2–3 chops of karate it takes
to sentence predictable fate.
Now he's stuck at the table of outcasts
where the crew is always the same,
this table is watched by the Eyes of a Hawk
so no one can wrongly cast blame.
Sighing, he accepts his usual sentence,
it's the same as his classroom fate—
You see, lunchtime is not the only time
the ADHD kid can't seem to relate.
                                        Karen Easter, 1995

ADHD in Preschool and Kindergarten

*M*ost children with ADHD are not diagnosed until first grade or higher. However, those exhibiting significant core symptoms (hyperactivity, impulsivity, inattention) are often identified in kindergarten, preschool, or even earlier. With very young children it is often hard to distinguish between what is "normal" rambunctious, active, uninhibited early childhood behavior and what may be abnormal (maladaptive and outside the limits of what is developmentally appropriate behavior for that age).

There are children with ADHD diagnosed under the age of five and receiving various treatments (including medication) with great success. However, most children enter preschool and kindergarten programs without having been evaluated or diagnosed with the disorder. At this stage, most teachers and parents don't know whether or not the child has ADHD or any other developmental disorder. Typically, they are doing the best they know how in managing the child's challenging behaviors and may be wondering if there is cause for concern.

Many children—not just those with ADHD—have difficulty adjusting to a classroom environment, the hours away from home, the structure and expectations of their preschool/kindergarten teacher, and to the other children. Sometimes it just takes time to make the adjustment and feel comfortable in the new environment. It is often the case that some of the behaviors that were problematic at the beginning of the year diminish and are no longer an issue, once the children learn the routine and structure, bond with their teacher, and/or mature somewhat (Rief, 1998).

If a child has ADHD, the preschool/ kindergarten teacher will often notice that the behaviors (impulsivity, hyperactivity, inattention) continue to remain problematic and excessive in comparison to the other children. It is appropriate to share concerns with parents and support staff and to put into place strategies and interventions to address the needs of the child. Parents may communicate frustrations and worries and share that the child has always had a more "difficult temperament," been "demanding" or "hard to discipline."

It is important to be aware that children with ADHD often have co-existing learning disabilities. Commonly, a child with ADHD may have other developmental weaknesses or delays in some areas (for example, speech/language, motor skills—gross/fine, acquiring academic readiness skills—such as learning and remembering ABCs, numbers, shapes, and letter/sound association).

Here is a list of possible warning signs that may signal the possibility of learning disabilities in preschool children (if the behaviors have persisted over time). This list was prepared by the International Dyslexia Association (2003).

Language

* Slow development in speaking words or sentences
* Pronunciation problems
* Difficulty learning new words
* Difficulty following simple directions
* Difficulty understanding questions
* Difficulty expressing wants and desires
* Difficulty rhyming words
* Lack of interest in storytelling

Motor Skills

* Clumsiness
* Poor balance
* Difficulty manipulating small objects
* Awkwardness with running, jumping, or climbing
* Trouble learning to tie shoes, button shirts, or perform other self-help activities
* Avoidance of drawing or tracing

Cognition

* Trouble memorizing the alphabet or days of the week
* Poor memory for what should be routine (everyday procedures)
* Difficulty with cause and effect, sequencing, and counting
* Difficulty with basic concepts such as size, shape, and color

Attention

* High distractibility
* Impulsive behavior
* Unusual restlessness (hyperactivity)
* Difficulty staying on task
* Difficulty changing activities
* Constant repetition of an idea, inability to move on to a new idea (perseveration)

Social Behavior

* Trouble interacting with others, playing alone
* Prone to sudden and extreme mood changes

* Easily frustrated
* Hard to manage, has temper tantrums

Note: *Many of the above behaviors are also indicators of ADHD (as well as learning disabilities and some other developmental disorders).*

Parent Concerns and Recommendations

Parents should share concerns with their child's pediatrician and preschool or kindergarten teacher. The pediatrician should be informed about parents' observations and concerns regarding the child's ability to function or perform in developmental areas; and parents should ask the doctor if the child is in norm with what are considered appropriate developmental milestones for children that age. Parents should also ask the teacher and day-care provider(s) for their observations and input.

If there are indications of a disability or developmental delays, the child's vision and hearing should be screened, and an evaluation through the school district can be initiated regarding any of the areas of concern. It is recommended to pursue an evaluation when symptoms are problematic and impairing, as early intervention (for example, speech and language therapy, adapted physical education, parent training, behavior management at home and school, academic and learning supports, and medication in some cases) can greatly improve the child's ability to function successfully (Rief, 2001).

It is highly recommended for parents to start early in seeking help learning how to parent a child with ADHD. It can be exhausting and frustrating trying to cope with and manage the challenging behaviors and knowing how to best provide the necessary structure and support for the child. There are many resources available to help parents learn how to do so (for example, parenting classes, behavior management training, counseling, parent support groups such as CHADD, books/videos, and other materials).

It is difficult for many parents to decide whether or not their child (particularly if the child has a "late birthday") is ready to start kindergarten or wait another year. Parents should visit the kindergarten classes at the school, speak with teachers, ask to see the district's academic performance standards and expectations, seek advice from their pediatrician, and try to make the most informed decision they can—based on knowledge of their own child and his or her needs. There are many kinds of early childhood programs and, of course, teaching styles. Some are better suited for certain children than others.

When a child has ADHD and/or LD, behaviors that impact on social and academic performance generally do not improve by just providing more time to mature. Other interventions will be necessary to specifically target their areas of weakness and build their skills. Early intervention makes a significant difference—preventing for many children the devastating effects of failure, and often the need for special education in the future.

Because early intervention is so important, federal law requires that school districts provide early identification and intervention services. The special education department of the local school district can direct families to the agency that provides these services. Families may also want to consult the child's doctor, who should also be able to refer the family to appropriate resources (Wright, Wright, & Heath, 2004).

No Child Left Behind (NCLB) legislation lists these age-appropriate preschool language skills:

* Recognizes letters of the alphabet
* Knows letter sounds, sound blends; uses increasingly complex vocabulary
* Knows that written language is composed of phonemes and letters that make up syllables, words, and sentences
* Has spoken language, vocabulary, and oral comprehension
* Knows the purposes and conventions of print

Early Reading First (federal grants for early language, literacy, and pre-reading for preschool children) focuses on early identification and early intervention of reading problems. Early Reading First programs are required to

* Use instructional materials based on sound research about language acquisition, reading, and spoken vocabulary
* Identify and help children who have trouble with spoken language and early reading skills (Wright, Wright, & Heath, 2004)

There are numerous ways that parents can help their young child build these language-related skills (for example, through songs, nursery rhymes, reading to their child, various games). When a kindergarten student is developmentally behind in these language skills and is at-risk for difficulty learning how to read, early intervention is necessary.

Preschool and Kindergarten Classroom Strategies for Success

The remainder of this section will focus on classroom strategies to maximize the success of students in preschool and kindergarten. This includes children with ADHD and others who may be struggling in school. Many early childhood teachers are challenged by what seems to be a rising number of children who are more difficult to manage and have a host of special needs. This includes children who:

* Are simply immature, needing a little extra time to develop the social and emotional skills to handle the structure and expectations of "the classroom"
* Have neurobiological disorders, developmental disorders, medical conditions, or disabilities—who for a variety of physiological reasons have immature or fragile coping systems
* Live in environments that are unpredictable, unstable, and sometimes unsafe

✳ Are lacking nurturing and attention, appropriate boundaries and discipline, and physical/emotional security in their home lives

Early childhood teachers are on the front line to meet the challenge—to find ways to provide for each child the necessary structure, nurturing, and education (academic, social, and behavioral) that will build their foundation for a lifetime of learning and success.

Much of the information and content presented in the remainder of this section comes from the "experts": nineteen kindergarten teachers from several schools in the San Diego, California, area. These wonderful teachers collectively have had years and years of experience and expertise working with young children and their families. I thank them all for their willingness to be interviewed and to share their teaching strategies, management techniques, and insight as to what works . . . how to best reach and teach children with ADHD or any student who may be experiencing learning, social, or behavioral difficulties. The teachers interviewed taught in a variety of kindergarten classes (general education, special education, and bilingual). My thanks and appreciation to Sue Sward, Marcia Giafaglione, Betsy Arnold, Noreen Bruno, Allison Carpenter, Cindy Cook, Julia Croom, Levana Estline, Christina Evans, Ellen Fabricant, Brenda Ferich, Nancy Fetzer, Cathy O'Leary, Nancy Paznokas, Jill Prier, Adrienne Tedrow, Yael Estline, Leilani Vigil, and Peggy Walsh.

All of these early childhood educators had the following in common:

✳ Provided a loving, nurturing, comfortable, and safe classroom environment

✳ Built a "community" in which every child and his or her family, culture, and uniqueness was celebrated and respected

✳ Were generous with hugs, smiles, and praise/positive attention

✳ Worked to establish close contact and involvement with parents

✳ Were specific, clear, and firm in their expectations

✳ Provided structure, consistency, and follow-through

✳ Established predictable procedures, routines, and schedules

✳ Were flexible, kind, and tolerant—and clearly loved children

✳ Provided lots of music, movement, and hands-on activities

✳ Provided students the opportunity to make choices

✳ Allowed children the time and opportunity to explore and make discoveries

✳ Incorporated a great deal of multisensory techniques and developmentally appropriate activities and materials that were fun and engaging

✳ Used individualized behavior management approaches and supports

✳ Took into account students' diverse learning styles, developmental levels, temperaments, strengths, and interests

✳ Clearly labeled the environment in pictures (that made it easy for children to access materials and clean up independently)

✳ Created language-rich, literacy-rich environments and curriculum (lots of rhymes/verse, literature, stories, song, reading/writing)

Creating the Climate for Success

In kindergarten, everything—every behavioral expectation and social skill—has to be taught. You need to explain and model each desired behavior and practice until all students know precisely what is expected of them.

Rules and Behavioral Expectations

From the minute the children walk through the door on the first day of school, they must be taught the specifics of how you want them to behave throughout the day. A few simple rules are established (preferably with children's input). For example:

1. Follow directions.
2. Keep hands and feet to yourself.
3. Use quiet voices.

One teacher starts the year by reading a story about a monster who came to school. Using the book as a kickoff for discussion, and a monster puppet, she teaches about rules. The class discusses the monster's inappropriate behaviors and the problems those behaviors cause in the classroom. After a lot of discussion and feedback from the children, the teacher prompts: "Tell what Mr. Monster *is* supposed to do." The students make up three or four class rules, which are then posted in words and pictures.

Another teacher explains how she spends at least the first two weeks of the school year teaching, modeling, and having the children practice over and over every behavioral expectation and procedure important for her classroom, such as:

* How and where to line up
* How to stand in line
* How to walk in line
* How to move to groups
* How and where to move to any station or learning center
* How to get the teacher's attention
* How loudly to talk in different situations
* How to sit on the rug
* How to sit at the table
* How and when to raise hands

The teacher is specific and consistent with those expectations, and students keep practicing until they clearly understand what to do. For example, they will be asked: "Show me how we get our lunch boxes and line up." Rather than reprimanding, teachers "check" for specific behaviors:

* "Are you using your inside voice?"
* "Are your ears listening?"
* "Are your eyes watching?"
* "Are your legs folded?"
* "Are your hands in your laps?"
* "Where are you supposed to be sitting?"
* "What do you need to do when you want to talk?"
* "Where should you be sitting right now?"

One of the teachers shared that every year she teaches students the expectation: "When I talk, you listen." After stating this over and over, she prompts students, "When I talk, . . ."; and then students respond in unison, "We listen!" She does this every time someone interrupts. This technique is helpful because typically the same children repeatedly talk out and interrupt. She explained that she does not believe in singling out those children who are having difficulty, calling attention to their inappropriate behavior by saying their names, or correcting them in front of their classmates. This avoids focusing negative attention on the child, yet helps remind them of the rule by hearing and saying it.

Noise Level

Some teachers tolerate more noise than others. Teachers mentioned that many children are extremely reactive toward noise and hubbub. Classroom activities are fun and exciting. However, the climate in the classroom needs to be calm, with a moderate noise level, not excessive noise . . . and not chaotic.

One teacher shared that during work time, her students are taught that they may whisper to a neighbor. She spends time making a game out of teaching and practicing whispering. "Children enjoy it because they love secrets and it's like a game to them." For example, you can do the following: "What do you think whispering is? When you put your hand on your throat over the voice box and talk, you feel it vibrate." (Students put their hands over their vocal chords/voice box and feel the vibration.) "When you whisper, it doesn't vibrate." (Students do the same while whispering.)

Schedules and Consistency

Children want to know exactly what comes next. They need the security of knowing their schedule and daily routines. All early childhood teachers use pictures that graphically depict the flow of the day's activities for the children to refer to. Some teachers also include clock faces of the times of day for those activities. One teacher shared how she uses two charts—one for the schedule on regular days and the other for shortened/minimum days.

Children need the predictability of knowing what group they are in, where it works, what it does, and so on. They need the consistency of routines and schedules. One of the special education teachers shared her structure. She stressed the importance of establishing a predictable sequence of activities from the first day of school. Most everything in her class is structured in fifteen-minute increments, alternating between sitting and moving. Her sequence is as follows: Beginning at "rug time," after shared reading/writing, she goes over the rules and explains the activities for the literacy stations. She has a consistent routine of language arts activities with four activity stations related to the literacy skills, literature, and theme of the lesson being taught. Students rotate to four tables of literacy-related activities. Before math, children again come to the rug for an explanation of the day's math activities, which follow a consistent pattern:

* Mondays—Sorting activities
* Tuesdays—Patterns
* Wednesdays—Measurement/graphs
* Thursdays—Shapes
* Fridays—Numbers

The same four tables operate for math activity stations related to the day's concept being taught. For example, on Fridays:

* Table 1—Manipulatives and puzzles
* Table 2—Journals and number books
* Table 3—Writing and tracing numerals
* Table 4—Cutting and pasting number activities

Management Techniques in Kindergarten

Behavior management techniques for children with ADHD in kindergarten are basically the same as those in higher grades (for example, using a high degree of feedback; visual prompting/cueing; proximity control; group positive reinforcement systems; corrective consequences that are applied consistently; and individualized behavioral plans/supports). The following are recommendations and examples from the nineteen kindergarten teachers regarding what they have found to be successful in their classrooms.

The Best Way to Manage: With Positive Attention

All the teachers agreed that the best way to manage is through watching for positive behaviors and recognizing children for what they are doing right. They reinforce appropriate behavior through lots of smiles, hugs, and specific praise:

* "I like the way you came over here and sat down next to Marcus even though someone else took your chair."
* "I see Johnny has his eyes right up here. I can tell he is really paying attention."
* "I noticed the way Cathy is remembering to raise her hand. That helps me teach so everyone can learn. Thank you, Cathy."
* "I really appreciate how Coby has been waiting quietly for his turn. Thank you for being so patient, Coby."

Many teachers encourage and guide students in showing appreciation for each other's individual accomplishments:

* "Let's give a big round of applause to . . ." (Children clap finger-to-finger in a large circular movement.)
* "Let's give ourselves a pat on the back." (Children reach over and pat themselves on backs.)
* "Let's give the silent cheer for . . ." (Children make a "rah rah" hand motion in the air without using voices.)

One teacher uses praising words that correspond by letter-sound association with the letter being learned in class at the time.

I—incredible; W—wonderful; F—fabulous, fantastic

Heading Off Trouble with Diversionary Tactics

A key management technique is redirecting a child when he or she shows signs of beginning to escalate in behaviors. Young children are often easy to distract and involve in something else that will be a diversion, and thus prevent their problematic behaviors from spinning out of control. Most kindergarten children love to be the teacher's helper. Give the child a task such as straightening the library center, passing out materials, or turning the pages of the Big Book being read. When a child is starting to get restless, it helps when the teacher goes over to the child, looks directly into his or her eyes, and encourages the child to wait a short time more for something he or she looks forward to. For example: "Michael, in about four minutes it is snack time, and we'll be going to the snack table. We're almost there. You can do it."

Signals and Cues

Teachers use different signals and cues to get their students' attention and to focus them. One teacher rings a bell. Students are taught to quickly hug themselves and look up at her. She prompts, "I'm going to ring the bell. Who is going to be ready?" (She gently assists children who have difficulty.) She will not begin instruction until they all stop and look up at her. Another teacher uses the cue: "Stop, look, and listen." At this cue, the children stop, put their hands behind their backs, and look at the teacher.

Teachers use many nonverbal signals:

* Hand up in stop position (Stop)
* Pointing to or cupping behind teacher's ear (Listen)
* Pointing to and tapping teacher's chin (Look here at my face)

Teachers signal by playing a chord on the piano or keyboard, ringing a bell, or flashing the lights. Some follow this signal with the word "freeze." Teachers physically cue their students by touching a hand, shoulder, or arm.

Teachers also use private cues, signals, and reinforcers worked out between an individual child and the teacher. For example, one teacher had a system with a girl who was having real difficulty staying with the group. "I'm going to put three checkmarks on the corner of the chalkboard. Each time you get up and move away from the table, I will erase a checkmark. At the end of the period [about ten to fifteen minutes], I will give you a sticker for every checkmark still on the board." The behavior improved considerably. ***Note:*** *This is an example of a response cost technique that will be described in Sections 2.1 and 2.3.*

Transitions

Teachers use a variety of techniques, cues, and signals for transitions. In addition to those previously mentioned, the following techniques have proven helpful: One teacher sets a timer when her class breaks into language arts and math activities. A few minutes before the activity ends, she warns, "We have about three minutes left before the timer rings." When it rings, she says, "FREEZE." Then she gives directions to the class, usually to clean up.

Other teachers reward table groups for good transitions. Table numbers are listed on the board. Every time a group does something well, the teacher praises specifically and puts a star by the table number. Clean up time: "Table two cleaned up first. They get a star. Table three has the most stars—let's give them a round of applause. They will get to line up first."

Voice Control

Many teachers mentioned voice control as an effective management technique. Lower your voice and drop the pitch (rather than raise your voice) to get a child's attention.

Behavior Modification, Monitoring, and Reward Systems

Most teachers use some kind of whole group management incentive system (for example, marbles in the jar, colored card system). In addition, they use individualized behavior programs for certain children, as needed. (See Sections 2.1 and 2.3.) Teachers used variations of many of the techniques or behavioral charts described in these sections, such as charts broken into short time frames. If the child exhibits the target positive behaviors during that time period, he or she receives a sticker or stamp on the chart. X number of stickers/stamps earns the reward.

One teacher described her weekly chart she uses. On the chart she draws faces that correspond with point values: happy face = 3 points, straight face = 2 points, sad face = 0 points. Parents initial the chart and return it, as well as reward the child at home based on the number of points earned. This is an example of a daily report card.

It is important to identify what an individual child will find to be motivating and reinforcing. Some children have no interest whatsoever in earning a sticker or tangible reward, but would love to work hard for the chance to play with bubbles, use certain "special materials or equipment," or care for the class rabbit.

Giving the Child Space

Children who show signs of losing control or needing to leave the group are sometimes on "sensory overload." They often do better given the opportunity for some quiet time and space to remove themselves to that is calming. One teacher said she uses the library corner or the playhouse area for this purpose. She refers to this as a "cool down" area. It is important to allow the child some limited choices and be given time and space to settle, regroup, and get away from some of the overstimulation of the classroom.

For children showing this need, you may ask: "Do you need some time?" "Do you need to move to a different area?" "Is there a better place for you to do your work?" You may try redirecting to a quieter, calming area by whispering to the child, "Go to the pillow area and read a book/look at the pictures."

Children with ADHD often have difficulty knowing and understanding their physical boundaries. They tend to invade other people's space and react adversely to being crowded, bumped into, and so forth. They need concrete visual structuring of their space (for example, colored masking or duct tape on the floor or table, a carpet square, or other means) that reminds them about what is their "space." This includes the child's acceptable space on the rug, at tables, in line, and so on.

Time-Outs

Many teachers use some system of removing disruptive students briefly from the group's activity. The child must know what inappropriate behavior he or she did that resulted in the time-out. Some teachers reported that they don't have a designated spot or area in the classroom for a time-out (or "time away"). They just send the child over to any table, chair, or area away from the group. Teachers emphasized the power of the group and children's desire to participate.

One teacher has a system whereby she gives three warnings and then sends the student to the "Think-About-It Chair." This chair is for "Oops . . . I have to think about what I am supposed to do." Another teacher said she tries never to interrupt instruction when sending a child to time-out. She either points or walks over to the child, taps his or her shoulder, and walks the child to a time-out area without discussion.

It is important that the teacher clearly communicate his or her expectations and consequences. "I would like you to sit here. But if you do, you've got to keep your hands and feet to yourself. If you can't handle it, you will have to go back there (away from the group)." All teachers agreed that any time-out or time-away must be brief. Many pointed out how they welcome the child back to the group: "We are glad that you are ready to join us again. Welcome back."

What Else Is Important?

Making Learning Fun

All early childhood teachers stressed how they do everything possible to make learning fun for their students and give them opportunities to build developmental skills (language, motor) through creative means and expression. Many shared about the special programs that were built around holidays, multicultural themes, and student performances that the children and their families loved (involving singing, musical instruments, movement, dance, costumes, and so forth).

One teacher summarized her philosophy, which is consistent with all of the teachers I interviewed: "If my kids are happy and feel good about themselves, they will learn!"

Movement and Exercise

Children—particularly young ones—need numerous opportunities to move. Teachers build movement into the day at frequent intervals. Some teachers have a regular routine of stretching, warm-up, jogging, and cool-down every morning—as well as physical education and motor skills training. In the classroom there are songs and rhymes with motions (hand and whole body) that are integrated throughout the day. Early childhood programs need to provide children with many opportunities to build large and small muscle movements in fun ways throughout the curriculum.

Involving Parents

All teachers stressed the importance of close communication and collaboration with parents—particularly if the child is having difficulty. Parents are warmly welcomed in the classroom in any capacity—as a volunteer, a guest speaker, or to observe their child in the classroom setting. Specific activities and ways parents can support their child's learning and school success are shared by the teacher.

Many early childhood teachers see parents almost daily, dropping off or picking up their children. Most make great efforts to communicate regularly with their students' parents—doing what it takes to build a partnership at this important stage of schooling.

Keeping Them Engaged and Focused

Teachers try to keep children actively responding and participating. Some examples are

* "Put your thumb on your nose if you think . . ."
* "Put your finger on the __ as I walk around and check."
* "Show me with your fingers how many bears there were in the story."
* "I'm going to ask Table 1 to give me a word that starts with a *b,* but they all have to agree." (If they give the wrong answer, the teacher says, "Oh. This table didn't agree. Talk about it some more until you agree.")
* Give instructions and ask if there are any questions. Then ask one or two children to repeat the instructions—targeting one of the children who has difficulty.
* "Every time you hear me say [magic word] clap your hands/wiggle your fingers." This technique helps focusing and listening skills.

Building Trust and Connecting with the Child

Teachers need to give the child the most they can at the emotional level. One of the hardest things for a teacher to gain is a child's confidence. Children need to trust you and know that you are going to follow through. As one teacher put it, "You have to mean what you say. Never make a promise that you may not be able to keep. And never break a promise!" Building trust is a process that takes place over time and is different for each child.

It is important to find at least one other child for a student to attach to (someone accepting). For all children, especially those with special needs, having a friend makes all the difference in the world and can "save the day." Children with ADHD often have significant difficulty making and keeping friends. Teachers will find themselves in the role of facilitator, trying to find a friend for this child.

Resolving Conflicts Among Young Children

One teacher explained that many children have never been taught or shown how to handle problems in a positive way. They need to be taught and rewarded for this skill. She shared her technique: A child collides into another one or someone hits somebody else or gets elbowed (either deliberately or accidentally). They consequently get mad at each other and run to the teacher for a resolution.

* Teacher: "Can you tell Jason how you feel? I'll help you. I will say it, then you can say it after me. 'I don't like it when you hit me like that. It hurt.'"
* Student repeats.
* Teacher (prompt to Jason): "I'm sorry, Bobby."
* Student repeats.
* Teacher (prompt to Bobby): "That's okay."
* Student repeats.
* This is followed by students shaking hands and the entire class clapping loudly and enthusiastically, with the teacher starting the applause.

Noticing Patterns and Intervening

It is important for teachers to be observant, and to try to determine the conditions or antecedents that precede challenging behaviors. With many children who have ADHD, their behavior and performance might fluctuate greatly—depending on the day, situation, and even time of day. One teacher gave an example of a student who was "falling apart" and crying frequently. The teacher noticed that this was actually happening around 11:00 every day. Aware of the pattern and time factor, the teacher gave the child something she liked to do during this time (lead number rock music), which significantly helped the situation. She also shared with the parents and school nurse her observation about the child's deteriorating behavior at around this time. With this information, the physician changed the child's medication schedule, which completely eliminated the problem.

What to Do About . . .

The Impulsive Child Talking Out Disruptively in Class

* Teachers generally seat this child right near them—within arm's reach for cueing. One teacher explains to her students that everyone has to wait his or her turn, and why they have that rule. For example: "Samantha, I know you're really excited. The rule in class is that we raise our hands so that I and all of us can hear what you say. Wouldn't it be sad if we didn't hear what you said because it was too noisy in the room?"
* Acknowledge the child, but say, "Right now it's time for you to listen. It's Joshua's turn to talk. Raise you hand." Try to call on the child right away when raising his or her hand and waiting to be called on, and praise the child for remembering to do so.
* When the behavior persists disruptively, one teacher says in a matter-of-fact voice, "Mark, that's yelling out. You need to go to the 'think-about-it' chair [or some mild consequence]." It is important to catch the student showing improvement. Example: "Mark, I noticed that you are really catching yourself from yelling out in class. I am very proud of you."
* One special education teacher has her classroom aide sit near one of the highly disruptive children in her room and quietly prompt the child, reminding of the rules. "Hold that question." "Raise your hand. James is speaking now."

The Out-of-Control Child

* Teachers trying to calm an out-of-control child find rocking and a matter-of-fact, calm voice helpful. The child needs to feel "safe." One teacher shares how she might say to a child, "I will not allow you to do

that. Yes, I do love you, but I will not allow you to . . . ."

* Generally the child will be removed from the classroom with an adult, or the teacher summons assistance and she removes her class, while the counselor or administrator deals with this child in the classroom.

* One special education teacher on occasion has needed to wrap herself around an out-of-control child. She describes how she rocks the child and says over and over in a calm voice what will occur: "When you are ready to calm down, you will go to lunch. If not, you will stay with me. You let me know when you're ready."

Children Who Want Your Attention and Need to Wait

One teacher uses a cue with children who come up to her when she is busy with another group or individual child. She covers his or her hand gently with her hand and rubs it, as she continues with the student(s) she is engaged with. This acknowledges that she is aware that the child is there waiting to speak to her and eliminates the calling out, interrupting, and pulling on her. Then she gets back to those children in order.

Another teacher has a colored hat that she uses as a visual cue meaning, "Don't interrupt me now. I'm busy and off-limits." The children learn that when the teacher wears that hat, they may not approach her at that time.

Handling Disappointments

Kindergarten children can become very upset if they are not chosen for certain privileges or responsibilities. Many do not deal well with the disappointment of not being selected or having to wait their turn. One teacher taught her students an "Oh well" signal. With a snap of the fingers in a big, sweeping motion, she leads her children in saying, "Oh well . . . maybe next time." The class has practiced this technique repeatedly in response to disappointments. When students use the "Oh well" response, the teacher reinforces with much praise, telling them: "You are so grown up. I am very proud of you."

The Tactile-Defensive Child

There are some children, especially among those with neurobiological disorders, who have poor tolerance for being touched (the feel of anything rubbing or touching the body, such as certain textures, clothes, or being crowded in line). Many overreact to being bumped into or may refuse to wear socks because the seam across the toes is "bothering them." These children have what is called "tactile defensiveness." For some children this means that sitting on the carpet may be almost intolerable. One of the adults I interviewed for this book shared that he still prefers to wear silks and cannot wear many other fabrics. As a child he refused to wear anything but flannel shirts.

In one special education class the teacher does a lot to build tolerance and acceptance for some degree of touching through numerous sensory activities. For example, she has a box of items for children to play and experiment with—feather dusters, rolling pins, fabrics of different textures, sandpaper, and gloves of different textures. (Read Section 4.1, A Parent's Story, and the two case studies in Section 4.2 that describe some of the sensory issues their children had at young ages.)

Note: *It is highly recommended to consult with an occupational therapist if a child is showing signs of being tactile defensive or having unusual reactions to various sensory stimuli.*

The Child Who Has Trouble Sitting

Of course, most young children can only sit still a relatively short amount of time. Teachers and parents sometimes forget, and inadvertently place unreasonable expectations on the child (regarding the length of time being asked to sit quietly and pay attention).

* One special education teacher said that she finds having children sit with legs crossed on the carpet is the best place and position for paying attention because hands are down, they have a base of support, and bodies are centered. Children sometimes need help sitting in this position.

* Sometimes a child's inability to sit is blamed on behavior when in reality the child does not have the physical tone or ability to sit up on the carpet and listen. Again, an occupational therapist and/or adapted P.E. teacher should be consulted.

* One teacher said that she tries to have an adult sit down with the child, with a gentle hand on the shoulder or back—some physical contact to help keep the child seated and focused.

* It often helps when a child has trouble (for example, sitting on the rug listening to a story) to be given some object that he or she can hold while sitting.

* Allow leeway. Some children cannot sit for more than a few moments. Teachers may permit the child to get up, walk around quietly, and try to redirect when possible.

Sometimes it is necessary to provide the child space and ignore when he or she lies down or rolls around on the rug or other behaviors.

Other Students' Perception That a Certain Child Is Being "Bad"

One teacher shared that children have a real sense of understanding and compassion. They always take the teacher's lead. Sometimes there is one child who is so disruptive or aggressive that children think of him or her as "bad." The teacher always corrects and softens, for example, by saying: "There are no bad children. Sometimes Michael has trouble remembering the rules. It doesn't mean he is bad. Sometimes he can't help it. We need to help him. How do you think we can help Michael remember the rules?"

ADHD in Middle School and High School

*M*any of us recall with a shudder our middle school/junior high and high school experiences and are relieved that those years are far behind us. Children have a great deal to contend with during this time of their lives.

Challenges of Adolescence

* Transitioning and adjusting to a different school environment with many new adults and students (sometimes their first experience having classmates from diverse cultures and backgrounds)
* Learning their way around campus
* Getting to know and deal with several teachers, each with his or her own unique teaching styles, expectations, and requirements
* Sometimes the feeling of anonymity and being "alone"
* Enormous social and peer pressures
* The desire to feel accepted and "fit in"
* Physical changes, raging hormones
* Stress related to home life and out-of-school factors
* The pressure of high academic/cognitive demands and work load

Adolescents with ADHD have all the above "normal" stresses as their peers to cope with, in addition to several other ADHD-related factors that impact on their lives. Weaknesses in executive functions, which affect their class work and homework production, become more impairing in upper grades. Issues that tend to be problematic for middle school and high school students with ADHD include:

* Poor organization, planning, memory, and time management—causing difficulty

keeping track of and keeping up with assignments from several classes

* Poor study skills (work habits, note taking, test taking)
* Instruction that is not conducive to their learning styles (for example, lecture, little opportunity for hands-on, active learning)
* Multiple teachers' behavioral expectations, classroom procedures, and work requirements
* Teachers who frequently have little or no training in ADHD, resulting in less empathy and willingness to accommodate students' individual needs
* Being more difficult to discipline than the average student
* More likely to engage in activities that place them "at risk" than their non-ADHD peers

What All Adolescents Need

Adolescents need the feeling of "connection" and being valued. They are seeking a sense of community and belonging. Protection of their image and being treated with respect are of utmost importance. They need to feel safe and comfortable in their classroom environment, knowing that they will be treated with dignity, and not deliberately criticized or humiliated in front of their peers.

This is a critical time for students to learn *how to* learn—how to study and access information and have awareness of their own best learning styles. Adolescents often complain about school being boring, and they don't see the connection between what is being taught in school and their own lives. Instruction at this level must be meaningful, challenging, and relevant—eliciting active participation and student involvement. The curriculum and schedule at this level have to provide for options, variety, and choices. Teachers must be able to motivate and tap into the interests and strengths of their students. They must stimulate their students' curiosity and desire to think, work hard, challenge themselves, and take risks as learners.

The bulk of strategies throughout this book (instructional, environmental, organizational, behavioral) that are effective in the home and school for younger children are still effective and recommended for older children/adolescents, as well.

Adolescents still require structure and frequent monitoring both at home and school (even as they complain and resist). During the middle school and high school years many youngsters are vulnerable and insecure. Students of this age may appear mature enough to need less adult guidance. However, this is the stage when there is probably a greater need for guidance, interaction with caring adults, and open channels of communication than ever before. This is especially true with all of the outside pressures and influences to which our children are exposed. Parental involvement at school and presence on campus frequently declines during these years, but should be strongly encouraged. Schools must explore ways to make parents feel comfortable and welcome on campus.

The Value of Mentorship

A positive role model or mentor can make a significant impact on a child's life. Often a school employee (teacher or other staff member) will give his or her time to an individual student, and that connection and mentorship can make an enormous difference in the success of that student. Parents are also in the position of being able to facilitate finding a role model or mentor outside of school to develop their child's interests and skills, as well. Parents can connect their children with friends or relatives with a similar interest, take them to visit facilities that relate to the child's interests, or call professionals and ask if they would be willing to give fifteen or thirty minutes to share about their work or interest. These experiences can lead to ongoing mentoring, if both parties are willing to sustain the relationship. The following story illustrates the positive impact of a mentor on the life of one young man.

Dan's Story (First Published in 1993)

Dan was a child with ADHD. He had a history of physical and emotional distress, which centered around his experiences in school. His behavior was impulsive and his teachers frequently telephoned home to tell his parents that Dan would not stay in his seat, was disruptive, and that they should try to better control his behavior at school. By fifth grade, Dan had several interventions, including stimulant medication and counseling. Although he achieved fairly well, but not "up to his potential," he had been held back a grade due to emotional immaturity. Dan now had much difficulty with peer relationships. His parents pursued every avenue they could find in their search to help him, but not enough changed.

During sixth grade Dan learned to cook, an activity that really held his interest. At the beginning of seventh grade he learned about a restaurant with a sports theme that interested him. He asked if he could see it and eat there sometime. His mother, Marla, promised to take him there as soon as she could. One night, Dan's mother and father unexpectedly ended up at the restaurant. Marla mentioned to the hostess that her thirteen-year-old son really wanted to visit the restaurant. The hostess said that if Dan wanted to visit about 1:00 p.m. on a weekday, she would take him on a tour of the kitchen and he could watch the chef at work. The hostess gave Marla her card.

On their next mutual weekday off, Marla and Dan had lunch at the restaurant. When Marla made reservations, she reminded the hostess of their conversation. Dan not only enjoyed the meal, but he met the chef, Peter, and watched him work. Peter told Marla and Dan that he was impressed with Dan's mature behavior and interest. He said that Dan could come back and observe sometime during the summer.

As soon as school ended for summer vacation, Dan called Peter and asked if he could come in to visit. It was a thirty-minute drive from his home to the restaurant, but his parents agreed to transport him. Once each month Peter allowed Dan to come in. First Dan observed, but gradually Peter allowed him to assume certain tasks. Dan loved it! Peter and the rest of the cooking staff began to include Dan in their exchanges of music and in their friendship.

One day after about four months, Peter asked Marla for a "parent-chef conference." Peter asked if Dan was really learning anything and if he liked it. Marla's first thought was that Dan was "messing up," but she told Peter that Dan was baking desserts and showing her "meal presentation" tips. Peter said he was concerned about whether Dan was truly interested. Marla thought he was.

Months went by and Dan continued to help out. He got A's in cooking, and his organizational skills improved, as did his relationships with others, including his peers. Gradually as he began to perceive himself as competent in his work at the restaurant, Dan seemed to feel more competent in other areas.

Dan was really excited when Peter told him that he had "graduated" and could come in every other week. After over a year invested, Peter told Dan that he really needed him to help with preparation for Saturday nights. Dan was really "staff" now, and Peter gave him his own staff T-shirt. Soon after that, some of the young staff members asked Dan to go to a concert with them. Dan's confidence swelled.

Dan continues to work at the restaurant. Currently he is working on his driver's training, anxiously awaiting the time he can transport himself to the restaurant more often. Dan plans to graduate from high school in three years instead of the usual four and is taking effective steps toward that goal. When he graduates, he knows he wants to enroll in a four-year college hotel and restaurant management program. He has even selected colleges to apply to. So far, Marla reports that Dan has maintained the academic credentials that will help to ensure his college admission.

No one can be sure what contributed to Dan's personal growth—age, the neurochemical changes of puberty, and the attention Dan received at school and at home probably all helped. What seems pivotal, however, is the attention and skill Dan has gained from Peter. Dan knows what he enjoys and that he can become a competent professional one day. He also knows that Peter cares about him and believes in him. In terms of his education, and how he feels about what Peter has taught him, Dan told me the following:

> "Peter is such a good communicator. He takes his time and tells me how to do things. He taught me what it means to do 'teamwork.' Peter 'cultures me' and he has fun when he's mentoring me, too. Peter is my top learning experience!"

Follow-Up to Dan's Story

A number of years have passed since Dan's story was written and published in the first edition of this book (1993). It is included in this edition, as it remains highly relevant. Readers will be interested in knowing that Dan has successfully graduated from the college of his choice (while also working to help pay his living expenses). Currently Dan is independent—living in his own apartment. He has a lovely supportive fiancee, is the manager of a popular restaurant, and is happy with his life!

The Core Symptoms of ADHD During Adolescence

As children with ADHD mature and move to the adolescent years, some of the core symptoms of ADHD may diminish or manifest differently. For example, a hyperactive teen will most likely not be jumping out of his or her seat or running around the classroom, but will probably appear restless and antsy. Some of the issues that were of concern when they were younger may no longer appear to be problematic. However, for most adolescents with ADHD, the symptoms continue to persist to varying degrees. In fact, for many preadolescents and teens with ADHD, these years can be the most difficult and stressful for them and their families.

Impulsive behavior can be more problematic during these years than it was when they were younger. Lack of self-control, impulsivity, and poor planning in adolescence are associated with many high-risk behaviors that pose a danger to adolescents and others. Adolescents with ADHD have significantly more than average: traffic violations, accidents, teen pregnancies, and conduct resulting in conflict with school authorities, parents, and law enforcement. (See Section 1.1.)

How Parents Can Help

Many parents may not be aware that their children continue to need treatment or are in need of different kinds of intervention as they experience difficulty in middle school or high school. Many adolescents with ADHD are in great need of support from mental health professionals. As discussed in Section 1.1, ADHD is often accompanied by other co-existing disorders. It is important for parents and teachers to be aware of conditions that commonly co-occur with ADHD and may emerge or become apparent in the middle/high school years (for example, depression, anxiety, sleep disturbances, ODD, conduct disorder, LD).

Parents must have their child reevaluated when other conditions are suspected. Clinical evaluations should be done by medical/mental health professionals who are well aware of and have expertise in ADHD and other common comorbid conditions. Because of the tendency to gravitate toward high-risk behavior, parents of preteens/teens with ADHD need to be alert for any signs of substance use/abuse, and intervene immediately if suspected.

School evaluations may be needed to determine whether the student is eligible for an IEP or 504 Accommodation Plan. Parents must seek help and implement whatever interventions may be indicated at this time (academic assistance, medical treatment, psychosocial).

Parents of adolescents with ADHD still must be vigilant in monitoring their son's or daughter's progress. They can request updates from teachers at any time. Many schools send home computerized progress reports halfway through the grading period. Parents may request this feedback on a more frequent basis. At this level, many teachers keep students' daily grades and points on the computer and are able to print out updated grades without much inconvenience.

Older children need to understand about ADHD, the nature of the disorder, and how they can best manage to deal with the symptoms. There are some excellent resources on ADHD geared to the older child/adolescent. Parents and doctors should take the time to explain and educate the preadolescent/teen about ADHD. It is very important to acknowledge their feelings and solicit their input in decision making, monitoring, and management (Rief, 1998).

Middle and high school students with ADHD need to understand their learning differences and know how to approach teachers respectfully with requests for accommodations. Parents must still take an active role in their child's education and maintain communication with teachers. However, it is also appropriate for students to speak directly with their teachers. Parents should encourage their child to do so and help them to learn to self-advocate. It helps to role play with the youngster and practice how to approach teachers, politely explaining what makes it easier or harder to learn in their classrooms and the kind of supports/accommodations that help them (for example, preferential seating).

Critical to the success of adolescents with ADHD is parent:

* Structuring—with negotiable and non-negotiable rules, reasonable expectations, and follow-through
* Use of positive discipline approaches and proactive (not reactive) behavior management strategies
* Monitoring and supervision (although teen may complain bitterly)
* Efforts to listen, have open channels of communication, and involve the teen in decision making
* Time and attention
* Awareness of their child's friends and activities
* Encouragement, support, and belief (Rief, 2003b)

Why Can't They "Act Their Age"?

Adolescents with ADHD may appear mature physically and "grown up," but looks are deceiving. They are typically far less mature socially and emotionally than peers their own age, with a two- to four-year developmental delay in skills affecting their self-management. Parents and teachers need to be aware of this and not inadvertently place unrealistic expectations on them. Although they may be of an age when the expectation is to demonstrate more independence, responsibility, and self-control, the reality is that adolescents with ADHD take longer to exhibit those behaviors. They need more adult monitoring and direct support than their peers. These are years when it is very difficult for parents and teachers to find that proper balance: how to teach our children to assume responsibility for their own learning and behavioral choices, and how to intervene as we guide and support them to success.

School Supports

One of the advantages in middle and high school is the availability of more options in scheduling. Sometimes the best intervention is a change of classes or teachers. Other times, rescheduling the class with the same teacher but at a more optimal time of the day makes a difference. It is helpful when there is an adult at school who is willing to be a case manager (officially or unofficially)—someone who will be able to monitor progress, advise, and intervene in school situations. For students on IEPs, the special education teacher (for example, resource teacher) is generally that case manager. Sometimes it is a school counselor, one of the classroom teachers (for example, advisory or homeroom teacher), or a coach who serves this function. Some schools use upperclassmen as peer counselors or mentors, although they would not serve the same function as an adult case manager.

It also helps if middle and high schools have in place supportive interventions or "safety nets" available to students in need (for example, mentors, homework assistance, study skills/learning strategies classes, tutoring). Teens with ADHD would benefit from such school supports, as well as the opportunity to participate in clubs, sports, and electives to build on their interests and showcase their areas of strength.

Essential to the success of adolescents with ADHD is teacher:

* Training, awareness, and understanding of ADHD
* Use of effective classroom management strategies
* Monitoring of behavior and academic progress
* Willingness to work with the student and parents to provide extra support and follow-through (for example, daily or weekly report cards, contracts, checking assignment calendar, organizing materials)

Before Transitioning to Middle or High School

Chris Dendy (2000), a leading authority on teens with ADHD, suggests the following:

* Encourage parents to notify the new school about their child and his or her needs.
* Notify in May-June, or check with the guidance counselor at the new school to find out when student schedules are developed.
* Parents and the current school should provide input on the fall schedule.
* Develop an IEP or 504 Plan for eligible students before they transition to the next school.
* Schedule a Student Support Team (SST) meeting.
* Assign an upper-class mentor to help with the transition.
* Give parents an update on grades after two or three weeks in the new school.

Adolescents with ADHD still benefit from and typically need incentive systems, behavioral contracts, and home/school monitoring plans.

One of the best supports/interventions that can be provided by the school are programs that:

* Teach specific study skills and learning strategies

* Monitor how well students are keeping up in their classes, and help enable them to do so—especially on long-range projects
* Provide tutorial assistance to students in areas of weakness

Exemplary Model Program for Students with ADHD (The ADHD Zero Period Program)

The following is a model program for middle school students with ADHD. This exemplary program not only provides the above, but far more. It is called the ADHD "Zero Period" Middle School Program at James Rutter Middle School, Elk Grove Unified School District, Sacramento, California.

Linda Ramer, a speech therapist in Elk Grove Unified School District (EGUSD), a large and diverse school district, developed this unique model program for serving students with ADHD and their families. Linda Ramer and Deborah H. Gordon (a multi-published novelist) have co-authored a wonderful book that describes the program in depth. Their book, *How to Help Students with AD/HD Succeed—in School and in Life* (Gordon & Ramer, 2001), is highly recommended and contains all the details and information needed for anyone interested in replicating this program in his or her own school community. The following information is obtained from their book and shared with the authors' permission.

This program began in 1990 when Linda requested permission from her administrator to start working with a small group of her students with ADHD in the mornings before school started. Since then, the program has expanded and grown into the model innovative program it is today—one that provides intensive training in skills necessary for academic/social/behavioral success to middle school students with ADHD. This occurs during the "zero period"—before school hours. In addition, there is close collaboration among students, teachers, and parents. Additional supports are in place for students in the program and their parents.

Students enter the ADHD program via referrals from educators and parents. After the fifth year of the program's existence, enrollment procedures formalized to require that students obtain a medical diagnosis of ADHD before acceptance into the class. Where appropriate, a complete educational work-up is done, as well. Linda now has a regular classroom assigned to her. She uses it for her program, for classes throughout the day, for testing, and as a study place for her ADHD students whenever they need a time-out from their regular classroom.

The general goals of the ADHD Zero-Period Program are

1. To improve students' self-esteem by teaching them about their ADHD and what Linda refers to as the "hidden treasures" of ADHD. Along with providing students with general information about ADHD, Linda helps students discover their own "hidden treasures."

2. To empower students by teaching them they have control over their lives. Linda explains that all people develop in different ways and at different rates. Each student discovers how he or she learns most effectively, what educational accommodations to request, and how to advocate effectively with teachers.

3. To learn strategies to improve academic success, including study skills, organizational skills, time-management skills, and skills to structure the students' environment.

4. To learn strategies to improve citizenship and social success. Students with ADHD often have problems "fitting in." Linda helps them learn to succeed in the world outside school and home.

The Hidden Treasures of ADHD

* People with ADHD have heightened awareness. They are the eagle-eyed observers of the world.
* They are creative and innovative—the divergent thinkers of the world.

* They are persistent. They keep trying until they get it right. Despite setbacks, students with ADHD show up for school every single morning, ready to try again. They are determined. Once they make up their minds to do something, they will.
* They have high energy, which can be channeled for good use.
* They are resilient. They have a willingness to keep working to improve, to come back again and again, to take setbacks in stride and keep right on going.
* They have a desire to fit in and to be successful.
* They want to please their parents and teachers.
* They have a wonderful sense of humor, often on the delightfully devilish side.
* They live life with gusto. They have a capacity for huge enjoyment of their experiences and plunge into life with wonderful abandon.
* They are great fun to talk to (one-on-one).

The Structure of the Program

1. Individualizing the Program

Each year, Linda gives students a list of specific class goals and asks them to choose their own four or five top goals ("I would like to improve . . ."). She then tailors her work with individuals and the class as a whole to the students' needs and desires.

Zero-Period Goals

The student will:

* Learn about the nature of ADHD, including the treasures of ADHD
* Learn how to overcome the challenge of ADHD
* Improve listening/focusing skills and processing skills
* Improve study skills
* Improve grades
* Improve control of emotions such as anger and frustration
* Learn to recognize individual strengths

* Improve self-esteem
* Learn coping strategies for school success
* Learn vocational environments where people with ADHD survive and thrive
* Improve friendships at home and at school
* Hear success stories of people with ADHD
* Learn how to have fun and not get into trouble
* Learn appropriate ways to speak for different social settings

2. The System of Rewards and Consequences

Together with her students, Linda adopts "class rules" each year, and everyone signs a pledge to abide by them. The first rule is that students are to show up every day, and on time (a difficult task for children with ADHD)—an hour before the school day begins! Incentives are also built into the program for motivating students to achieve their goals.

3. Daily Routine

On the instructional days, Linda uses a high-interest, high-energy, multisensory approach so students can hear, see, touch, and relate to the information she presents. Students also practice extensive role playing to learn to get along with peers and advocate for themselves with teachers.

4. Weekly

On study hall day (Tuesday), Linda reviews students' assignments for other classes and helps them with their work.

5. Fun Time

On fun and games day (Friday), Linda monitors students' language, behavior, sharing, and choices as they learn to interact appropriately with their peers.

Curriculum of the Zero Program

* Students acquire general information about ADHD and learn to recognize and be cognizant of their own ADHD. They learn what type of ADHD they have (predominantly inattentive, predominantly

hyperactive-impulsive, combined type); what accommodations they should seek; and practice asking for them.

* Students are taught several specific study skill strategies: obtaining and remembering information; organizing information; using information.

* Even the most admirable human trait can have a negative side if carried too far. For example, too much honesty can lead to tactlessness, and too much energy can create havoc. Linda helps her students learn to use their positive traits in a beneficial way. She also uses ADHD success stories from real life (including kids who have passed through her program) to educate and motivate her students.

* The final unit of the program covers topics such as coping with impulsivity and dealing with feelings and frustrations; how to express yourself so you feel heard and understood; and how to speak and act appropriately in different settings. In this unit Linda works on effective communication (written, verbal, body language). She uses role playing and class discussions to help students learn to fit in and to control themselves in a variety of situations. She also teaches students to seek adult help when confronted by serious matters such as sexual harassment, physical assault, or racial slurs.

Linda very successfully builds partnerships with parents, and part of that teamwork is very close communication. Agenda books are the key mechanism, but Linda carries a beeper for emergencies and also gives parents her email address. She calls parents when their child does something great and when their child runs into serious trouble. In response to parents sharing that they needed expert advice and other parents to talk with, Linda founded the James Rutter Middle School Parent Support Group (which meets monthly). The parent support group meetings and regular contacts/conferences between home and school are an integral part of this program's success.

One of the final chapters of Linda's book provides guidance for parents or educators who wish to set up a similar program in their school. The authors talk about how to enlist the help of such people as counselors, speech therapists, special education personnel, and school administrators to get such a program off the ground and provide specific resources for tailoring a curriculum to fit the needs of the individual school and community.

For more information about their book or to contact the authors, visit their website: www.helpforadhd.com or DBHGordon@aol.com and LindaLRamer@aol.com.

Looping in Middle School

Many middle schools have had much success with what is called "looping" (multiyear teaching or placement). When grades are looped, the teacher is "promoted" along with his or her students to the next grade level and stays with the same group of students for two or three years. ("When Two Years Are Better Than One," 1998).

According to Crosby (1998), some of the many benefits to looping seventh and eighth grades include:

* Consistency and continuity—same adults and peers provide a safe, stable learning situation; and students know what to expect

* Teachers get to really know their individual students—differentiating instruction and providing supports accordingly

* Bridging the summer gap (may be assigned summer projects, much less "review" time needed the first couple of months of the school year)

* A caring, supportive environment is easier to build within context of a two-year team—with students having a stake in how their "team" does

* Mutual trust and sense of community (In one middle school, students within the "team" all were a part of some working committee for their team [field trip, newsletter,

tutoring, monthly breakfast]. They were in charge of planning and organizing the activities of the committee. The teacher held weekly team meetings to discuss issues and report on committee work.)

* Greater flexibility (for example, scheduling and pacing)
* Parents tend to become more involved
* Conducive to co-teaching/teaming situations

Student Support Teams

Most schools have some multidisciplinary team process, which goes by many different names depending on the district (for example, the Student Support Team or SST, the Instructional Support Team or IST). Typically, schools have one team per building that is comprised mostly of school support personnel (for example, counselor, school nurse, school psychologist) and includes the parent(s) and teacher(s) of the student being discussed at the time. Rather than have one SST per building (which is very limited in the number of students whose needs can be addressed through the process), establishing multiple teams or using a "tiered" SST process is recommended. Large schools that are divided into smaller academies or "mini-schools" can easily form more than one SST in the building. Each academy or "mini-school" can have its own SST, thereby having greater opportunities to strategize action plans for students "at risk" and ensuring the necessary follow-up to make sure the interventions of the plan are working.

Middle schools often have a core team of teachers who share the same students. They may have level one meetings in which the classroom teachers have time blocked in their schedules to meet and discuss individual students—deciding on strategies and interventions in support of those students. If interventions are not effective after a period of time of the teachers working together at this level, then the teachers move to the next level of requesting a school SST meeting for that student (Rief, 2003a).

Warning Signs of Trouble in Middle School and High School

It is important to try detecting a problem in its early stages and begin intervention as quickly as possible—increasing the chances for a better outcome. The following signs (Parker, 1999) may alert parents or teachers to the possibility of a problem warranting investigation. Minimally, parent-teacher conferences should be scheduled. A school team meeting with parents is recommended. If the student has an IEP or 504 Plan, the team (including parents and the student) may need to meet to review the plan and determine whether additional services or interventions are indicated. Watch for the following warning signs:

* Frequent complaints of boredom
* Excessive absenteeism from school
* Drop in grades
* Lack of interest in doing homework
* Frequent tardiness
* Talk about dropping out
* Resentment expressed toward teacher
* No books or papers brought to or from school
* Reports from teachers that student is not completing work
* Disorganization—books and papers not appropriately cared for
* Work done sloppily or incorrectly
* Doesn't seem to care about school attitude
* Low self-esteem
* Teacher complains of frequent inattention in class
* Hyperactivity
* Teacher reports student doesn't do in-class assignments
* Teacher notes student is hanging out with other students who are doing poorly in school
* Student doesn't seem to comprehend assignments when trying to do them
* School reports unauthorized absences from class

Warning Signs of Learning Disabilities in Secondary School Children

As co-existing learning disabilities are common in children with ADHD, parents and teachers should be aware of signs of learning disabilities (LD). Some children may have learning disabilities that have gone undetected to this point. They may have achieved well in earlier grades, especially if they are very bright children. Academic performance problems most likely had been attributed to their ADHD. To determine whether or not a student has learning disabilities requires a psycho-educational evaluation. Educational interventions must be provided, addressing the student's individual learning needs.

The following is a list of warning signs of possible LD in teens (Inland Empire Branch of the International Dyslexia Association, 2003).

Note: These would only be "red flags" if showing as a pattern of behaviors, to a significant degree, and over time.

Language/Mathematics/Social Studies

* Avoidance of reading and writing
* Tendency to misread information
* Difficulty summarizing information
* Poor reading comprehension

* Difficulty understanding subject area textbooks
* Trouble with open-ended questions
* Continued poor spelling
* Poor grasp of abstract concepts
* Poor skills in writing essays
* Difficulty in learning foreign language
* Poor ability to apply math skills
* Difficulty staying organized
* Trouble with test formats such as multiple choice
* Slow work pace in class and in testing situations
* Poor note-taking skills
* Poor ability to proofread or double check work

Social Behavior

* Difficulty accepting criticism
* Difficulty seeking or giving feedback
* Problems negotiating or advocating for oneself
* Difficulty resisting peer pressure
* Difficulty understanding another person's perspective

Note: The case studies and the interviews throughout this book of adults and teens with ADHD (who share their personal stories and accounts of what happened to them during these years) are also very revealing and highly recommended reading.

INTERVIEW WITH JOE (15 Years Old, Minnesota)

Joe was diagnosed at a young age with ADHD and LD.

Tell me about your favorite teacher in elementary school.

"My second grade teacher was my favorite. When I was held back a grade, she always checked on me and asked how I was doing. I still go back and visit her."

I understand you have seen many different doctors over the years. How do you feel about that?

"Yeah. I saw all kinds of doctors, including different psychologists and psychiatrists. I took those psychological tests so many times, but the doctors didn't really talk to me. I went to two doctors at the same time, one who took care of my medication, and one because of my psychological problem. I didn't like him. He talked down to me, and I didn't like that."

How did you get along with other kids?

"I'm really good with adults. It's kids who were kind of tough for me. I took offense at what they said. I tried to ignore it, but it took a while. I realize that those kids I had trouble with were just jerks. I'm getting much better now. I've learned that it doesn't happen overnight. It takes a while—everything takes time."

What do you want teachers to be aware of?

"Teachers should be as respectful of kids as kids are to be respectful of them. Class should not be stressful, but relaxed. Teachers shouldn't ever make fun of students. I like active things like research, projects, and reports (especially oral reports)."

What do you want to tell parents?

"Parents need to be aware that kids have a tough time, too, and don't need problems at home. Parents may have had a hard time at the office. Well, we have a hard time, too. My dad (a lawyer) does every day what he learned to do and likes to do. In school we're learning new things, and we have to do what we've never done before, and reach our teacher's expectations. It's tough. Parents have to be aware and know what their kid is doing in school . . . be involved and make teachers tell you more."

Part 1: General References

Section 1.1

American Academy of Pediatrics. (2000, May). Clinical Practice Guideline: Diagnosis and Evaluation of the Child with Attention-Deficit/Hyperactivity Disorder. *Pediatrics, 105,* 1158–1170. Also: www.aap.org/policy/acooo2.html.

American Academy of Pediatrics (AAP) & National Initiative for Children's Healthcare Quality (NICHQ). (2002). *Caring for Children with ADHD: A Resource Toolkit for Clinicians.* Chicago: American Academy of Pediatrics. www.aap.org and www.nichq.org.

American Psychiatric Association. (1994). *Diagnostic and Statistical Manual of Mental Disorders* (4th ed.). Washington, DC: APA.

American Psychiatric Association. (2000). *Diagnostic and Statistical Manual of Mental Disorders—IV-TR* (revised). Washington, DC: APA.

Barkley, R. A. (1998, September). Attention-Deficit Hyperactivity Disorder. *Scientific American,* pp. 66–71. www.sciam.com/1998/0998issuebarkley.html.

Barkley, Russell A. (2000a, May). Presentation at Schwab Foundation for Learning. Transcript retrieved August 10, 2002, from www.schwablearning.org/pdfs/2200_7-barktran.pdf.

Barkley, Russell A. (2000b). *Taking Charge of ADHD* (Revised). New York: The Guilford Press.

Barkley, R., Cook, E., Dulcan, M., Prior, M., Gillberg, C., Halperin, J., Pliszka, S., et al. (2002, January). International Consensus Statement on ADHD. *Clinical Child and Family Psychology Review, 5*(2), 89–111. Retrieved November 4, 2002, from www.additudemag.com/additude.asp?DEPT_NO=201&ARTICLE_NO=8&ARCV=1Full-Text:http://www.kluweronline.com/issn/1096–4037/contents.

Barkley, R. A., Murphy, K. R., & Kwasni, D. (1996). Motor Vehicle Driving Competencies and Risks in Teens and Young Adults with ADHD. *Pediatrics, 98*(6), Pt 1, 1089–1095.

Bauermeister, Jose J., & Reina, Graciela. (2003, October). *How Can I Understand and Manage More Effectively Latino/Hispanic Students with ADHD?* Presented at 15th Annual CHADD International Conference, Denver, Colorado, October 29-November 1, 2003; program book pp. 69–73.

Brown, Thomas. (2000). *Attention Deficit Disorders and Co-morbidities in Children, Adolescents, and Adults.* Washington, DC: American Psychiatric Press.

Castellanos, F. X. (1997). Approaching a Scientific Understanding of What Happens in the Brain of AD/HD. CHADD: *ATTENTION, 4*(1), 30–35.

Castellanos, F. X. (2003). *Research Symposium II.* Presentation at the 15th Annual CHADD International Conference, Denver, Colorado, October 31, 2003.

Centers for Disease Control and Prevention. *ADHD and Risk of Injuries.* Retrieved August 31, 2003, from www.cdc.gov/ncbddd/adhd/injury.htm.

CHADD. (2001a). *AD/HD and Co-Existing Disorders.* CHADD Fact Sheet #5. Retrieved September, 4, 2003, from www.chadd.org/fs/fs5.htm.

CHADD. (2001b). *AD/HD: Fact vs. Fiction.* Retrieved July 14, 2003, from www.chadd.org/factvsfiction.cfm.

CHADD. (2001c). *The Disorder Named AD/HD.* CHADD Fact Sheet #1. Retrieved August 30, 2003, from www.chadd.org/fs/fs1.htm.

CHADD. (2003a). *The Disorder Named AD/HD.* CHADD Fact Sheet #1. Retrieved November 6, 2003, from www.chadd.org/fs/fs1.htm.

CHADD. (2003b). *Evidence-Based Medication Management for Children and Adolescents with AD/HD.* CHADD Fact Sheet #3. Retrieved January 7, 2004, from www.chadd.org/fs/fs3.htm.

CHADD. (2004a, March). *Experts Assail Undertreatment of AD/HD in African American Youth.* Press release March 18, 2004. Retrieved April 20, 2004, from www/chadd.org.

CHADD. (2004b, April). *Three Pediatric Studies Emphasize Important Factors in Better Understanding AD/HD.* Press release April 5, 2004. Retrieved April 21, 2004, from www.chadd.org.

Christakis, D.A., Zimmerman, F. J., DiGiuseppe, D.L., & McCarty, C. A. (2004, April). Early Television Exposure and Subsequent Attentional Problems in Children. *Pediatrics, 113*(4), 708–713.

Dendy, Chris, & Ziegler, A. (2002). Five Components of Executive Function. CHADD: *ATTENTION, 4*(8), 26–31.

DuPaul, George, & Barrett, Charles. (2003, June). Diagnosing AD/HD in Minorities. CHADD: *ATTENTION, 9*(6), 34–37.

Ellison, P. A. Teeter. (2003, June). Science Over Cynicism: AD/HD Myths. CHADD: *ATTENTION, 9*(6), 27–33. Also at www.help4adhd.org/en/about/myths.

Fine, L. (2001, May 9). *Research: Paying Attention.* Retrieved June 12, 2001, from www.edweek.org/ew/ewstory/efm?slug=34adhd.h20.

Giler, Janet Z. (2001). Are Girls with AD/HD Socially Adept? CHADD: *ATTENTION, 7*(4), 28–31.

Goldman, L. S., Genel, M., Bezman, R., et al. (1998, April 8). Diagnosis and Treatment of Attention-Deficit/Hyperactivity Disorder in Children and Adolescents. *Journal of the American Medical Association, 279*(14), 1100–1107.

Goldstein, S. (1999). *The Facts About ADHD: An Overview of Attention-Deficit Hyperactivity Disorder.* Retrieved November 14, 2001, from www.samgoldste4in.com/articles/9907.html.

Imperio, Winnie Anne. (2004, February). AD/HD Through the Years: From Science to Practice. Highlights from the 15th annual conference, October 29-November 1, 2003, Denver, Colorado. CHADD: *ATTENTION, 10*(4), 25–30.

Jensen, P. M. (2001). AD/HD: What's Up, What's Next? CHADD: *ATTENTION, 7*(6), 24–27.

Lombroso, P., Scahill, L., & State, M. (1998). The Genetics of Attention Deficit Hyperactivity Disorder: An Update. CHADD: *ATTENTION, 4*(4), 25–28.

MTA Cooperative Group. (1999). A 14-Month Randomized Clinical Trial of Treatment Strategies for Attention Deficit Hyperactivity Disorder. *Archives of General Psychiatry, 56,* 1073–1086.

MTA 13-Member Steering Committee. (Jensen, P. S., Abikoff, H. B., Arnold, L. E., Epstein, J., Greenhill, L. L., Hechtman, L., Hinshaw, S. P., March, J. S., Newcorn, J. H., Swanson, J. M., Vitiello, B., Wells, K., & Wigal, T.). (2003, December). A 24-Month Follow-Up to the NIMH MTA Study. CHADD: *ATTENTION, 10*(2), 22–46.

Murphy, K. R., & Barkley, R. A. (1996). The Prevalence of DSM-IV Symptoms of AD/HD in Adult Licensed Drivers: Implications for Clinical Diagnosis. *Comprehensive Psychiatry, 37,* 393–401.

Nadeau, Kathleen, Littman, Ellen, & Quinn, Patricia. (1999). *Understanding Girls with AD/HD.* Silver Spring, MD: Advantage Books, pp. 25–26.

National Institute of Mental Health. (2000, March). *Attention Deficit Hyperactivity Disorder (ADHD)—Questions and Answers.* Retrieved November 14, 2001, from www.nimh.nih.gov/publicat/adhdqu.cfm.

National Resource Center on AD/HD. (2003a). *About AD/HD: The Science of AD/HD.* Retrieved August 31, 2003, from www.help4ahd.org/en/about/science.

National Resource Center on AD/HD. (2003b). *About AD/HD: Pathophysiology.* Retrieved August 31, 2003, from www.help4adhd.org/en/about/causes/pathophysiology.

National Resource Center on AD/HD. (2003c). *Statistical Prevalence.* Retrieved August 31, 2003, from www.help4adhd.org/en/about/science/statistics.

Pierce, Karen. (2003). Attention-Deficit/Hyperactivity Disorder and Comorbidity. *Primary Psychiatry, 10*(4), 69–76.

Rief, Sandra. (2003). *The ADHD Book of Lists.* San Francisco, CA: Jossey-Bass.

Safer, D. J., & Malever, M. (2000). Stimulant Treatment in Maryland Public Schools. *Pediatrics, 106,* 533–539.

Safer, D. J., & Zito, J. M. (2000). Pharmacoepidemiology of Methylphenidate and Other Stimulants for the Treatment of ADHD. In L. L. Greenhill & B. B. Osman (Eds.), *Ritalin: Theory and Practice* (2nd ed.) (pp. 7–26). Larchmont, NY: Mary Ann Liebert, Inc.

Satcher, D. (2001). *Mental Health: Culture, Race and Ethnicity.* Rockville, MD: U.S. Department of Health and Human Services.

Surgeon General of the United States. (1999, December). *Mental Health: A Report of the Surgeon General.* Full text: www.surgeongeneral.gov/library/mentalhealth/chapter3/sec4.html.

Surgeon General of the United States. (2001). *Report of the Surgeon General's Conference on Children's Mental Health. A National Action Agenda. Mental Health: Culture, Race and Ethnicity.* Rockville, MD: Department of Health and Human Services.

Taylor-Crawford, Karen, Richardson, Jerome, & Madison-Boyd, Sybil. (2003, June). AD/HD: Cultural Attitudes and Perceptions. CHADD: *ATTENTION, 9*(6), 38–45.

U.S. Department of Health and Human Services. (2001). *Mental Health: Culture, Race, and Ethnicity—A Supplement to Mental Health: A Report of the Surgeon General.* Rockville, MD: U.S. Department of Health and Human Services.

Volkow, Nora. (2003). *Stimulants: The Path to Treatment, Not Addiction.* Research Symposium I. 15th Annual CHADD International Conference, Denver, Colorado, October 31, 2003.

Section 1.2

American Academy of Pediatrics. (2000, May). Clinical Practice Guideline: Diagnosis and Evaluation of the Child with Attention-Deficit/Hyperactivity Disorder. *Pediatrics, 105*(5), 1158–70. Also at www.aap.org/policy/ac0002.html.

American Psychiatric Association. (1994). *Diagnostic and Statistical Manual of Mental Disorders* (4th ed.). Washington, DC: APA.

American Psychiatric Association. (2000). *Diagnostic and Statistical Manual of Mental Disorders* (4th ed.)(text revised). Washington, DC: APA.

Baren, Martin. (2001). The Assessment of ADHD in School-Aged Children. CME/CE Supplement to: *Drug Benefit Trends, 13,* 5–6.

Rief, Sandra. (2003). *The ADHD Book of Lists.* San Francisco: Jossey-Bass.

Rief, Sandra. (1998). *The ADD/ADHD Checklist.* San Francisco: Jossey-Bass.

Section 1.3

Adesman, A. (2003, April). Effective Treatment of Attention-Deficit/Hyperactivity Disorder: Behavior Therapy and Medication Management. *Primary Psychiatry, 10*(4), 55–60.

American Academy of Pediatrics. (2001a). *Understanding ADHD: Information for Parents About Attention-Deficit/Hyperactivity Disorder.* Elk Grove Village, IL: American Academy of Pediatrics.

American Academy of Pediatrics. (2001b). Clinical Practice Guidelines: Treatment of the School-Aged Child with Attention-Deficit/Hyperactivity Disorder. *Pediatrics, 108,* 1033–1044.

American Academy of Pediatrics and National Initiative for Children's Healthcare Quality. (2002). *Caring for Children with ADHD: A Resource Toolkit for Clinicians.* Chicago: American Academy of Pediatrics.

CHADD. (July, 2001). *Assessing Complementary and/or Controversial Interventions.* CHADD Fact Sheet #6. Retrieved September 7, 2003, from www.chadd.org/fs/fs6.htm.

Goldstein, S. (1999). *The Facts About ADHD: An Overview of Attention-Deficit Hyperactivity Disorder.* Retrieved November 14, 2001, from www.samgoldstein.com/articles/9907.html.

Goldstein, S. (2003). *Current Trends and the Diagnosis, Evaluation and Treatment of Attention-Deficit Hyperactivity Disorder.* Salt Lake City, UT: Neurology, Learning, and Behavior Center. Also: *From Assessment to Treatment: Developing a Comprehensive Plan to Help Your Child with ADHD.* Retrieved August 20, 2003, from www.samgoldstein.com/articles/0009.html.

Hinshaw, S. (2000). Psychosocial Interventions for ADHD: How Well Does It Work? CHADD: *ATTENTION, 6*(4), 30–34.

Mental Health: A Report of the Surgeon General. Chapter 3. Retrieved September 4, 2003, from www.surgeongeneral.gov/library/mentalhealth/chapter3/sec4.html.

MTA Cooperative Group. (1999). Fourteen-Month Randomized Clinical Trial of Treatment Strategies for Attention-Deficit Hyperactivity Disorder. *Archives of General Psychiatry, 56,* 1073–1086.

Putnam, Stephen C. (2002, June). Keeping Up the Motivation to Exercise. CHADD: *ATTENTION, 8*(6), 21–25. Attention@chadd.org.

Rief, Sandra. (2003). *The ADHD Book of Lists.* San Francisco: Jossey-Bass.

Shapiro, Michael S. (2002, August). Tae Kwon Do and AD/HD. CHADD: *ATTENTION, 9*(1), 36–39. Attention@chadd.org.

Section 1.4

CHADD. (2001, July). *Medical Management of Children and Adults with AD/HD.* CHADD Fact Sheet #3. Retrieved September 9, 2003, from www.chadd.org/fs/fs3.htm.

CHADD. (2003, December). Evidence-Based Medication Management for Children and Adolescents with AD/HD. CHADD Fact Sheet #3 (revised). Retrieved February 7, 2004, from www.chadd.org/fs/fs3.htm.

Eli Lilly and Company. (2003). *About Strattera.* Retrieved August 15, 2003, from www.strattera.com/1_1_about_strattera/1_1_about.jsp.

Faraone, Stephen. (2003, January 11). *ADHD Facts and Fiction.* Presentation in Atlanta, Georgia, at the TEAM Approach to ADHD Conference.

Greenhill, Laurence L. (2001, December). ADHD and Medication Management. *Drug Benefit Trends, 13* (Supplement C).

Jensen, Peter S. (2002, November 9). *Evidence-Based Treatment of ADHD.* Presentation in Orlando, Florida, National Initiative for Children's Healthcare Quality, 1st International Summit on Improving Care for Children with ADHD.

Jensen, P. S., Abikoff, H. B., Arnold, L. E., Epstein, J., Greenhill, L. L., Hechtman, L., Hinshaw, S. P., March, J. S., Newcorn, J. H., Swanson, J. M., Vitiello, B., Wells, K., & Wigal, T. (2003, December). A 24-Month Follow-Up to the NIMH MTA Study. CHADD: *ATTENTION, 10*(2), 22–46.

MTA Cooperative Group. (1999). Fourteen-Month Randomized Clinical Trial of Treatment Strategies for Attention-Deficit Hyperactivity Disorder. *Archives of General Psychiatry, 56,* 1073–1086.

Rief, Sandra. (2003). *The ADHD Book of Lists.* San Francisco: Jossey-Bass.

Sallee, Floyd R., & Smirnov, A. (2003, April). Atomoxetine: Novel Therapy for Attention-Deficit/Hyperactivity Disorder and Potential Therapeutic Implications. *Primary Psychiatry, 10*(4), 41–48.

U.S. Department of Health and Human Services. (1999). *Mental Health: A Report of the Surgeon General.* Chapter 3. Rockville, MD: Office of the Surgeon General, U.S. Public Health Service. Retrieved September 4, 2003, from www.surgeongeneral.gov/library/mentalhealth/chapter3/sec4.html.

Wilens, Timothy E. (1999). *Straight Talk About Psychiatric Medications for Kids.* New York: The Guilford Press.

Wilens, T. E., Faraone, S. V., Biederman, J., & Gunawardene, S. (2003). Does Stimulant Therapy of Attention-Deficit/Hyperactivity Disorder Beget Later Substance Abuse? A Meta-Analytic Review of the Literature. *Pediatrics, 111,* 179–185.

Section 1.7

Barkley, R. A. (1998*). Attention Deficit Hyperactivity Disorder: A Handbook for Diagnosis and Treatment* (2nd ed.). New York: The Guilford Press.

CHADD. (2003, October). One-on-One with William E. Pelham, Jr. CHADD: *ATTENTION, 10*(2), 33–37.

CHADD. (2004). *Evidence-Based Psychosocial Treatment for Children and Adolescents with ADHD.* CHADD Fact Sheet #9. Retrieved March 12, 2004, from www.chadd.org/fs/fs9.htm.

Cohen, C. (2000*). Raise Your Child's Social IQ: Stepping Stones to People Skills for Kids.* Silver Spring, MD: Advantage Books.

Cunningham, C. E., Bremner, R., & Secord-Gilbert, M. (2000). *The Community Parent Education Program (COPE Program): A School-Based Family Systems Oriented Course for Parents of Children with Disruptive Behavior Disorders.* Hamilton, Ontario: McMaster University and Chedoke-McMaster Hospitals. Available through Center for Children and Families, University at Buffalo. http://wings.buffalo.edu/psychology/adhd.

Fad, K. S., Ross, M., & Boston, J. (1995). We're Better Together: Using Cooperative Learning to Teach Social Skills to Young Children. *Teaching Exceptional Children, 27*(4), 28–34.

Giler, Janet Z. (2000). *Socially ADDept™—A Manual for Parents of Children with ADHD and / or Learning Disabilities.* Santa Barbara, CA: CES Publications.

Goldstein, A., Sprafkin, R. P., Gershaw, N. J., & Klein, P. (1980). *Skillstreaming the Adolescent—A Structured Learning Approach to Teaching Prosocial Skills.* Champaign, IL: Research Press.

Hoza, B., Mrug, S., Pelham, W. E., Jr., Greiner, A. R., & Gnagy, E. M. (2001). A Friendship Intervention for Children with Attention-Deficit/Hyperactivity Disorder: Preliminary Findings. *Journal of Attention Disorders, 6,* 87–98.

Jackson, J., Jackson, D., & Monroe, C. (1983). *Getting Along with Others.* Champaign, IL: Research Press.

Koplewicz, H. S. (2002, April). Managing Social Skills All Day, Every Day. CHADD: *ATTENTION, 8*(5),25–31. Attention@chadd.org.

McGinnis, G., & Goldstein, A. (1990). *Skillstreaming in Early Childhood—Teaching Prosocial Skills to the Preschool and Kindergarten Child.* Champaign, IL: Research Press.

McGinnis, E., & Goldstein, A. (1984). *Skillstreaming the Elementary School Child.* Champaign, IL: Research Press.

MTA Cooperative Group. (1999). Fourteen-Month Randomized Clinical Trial of Treatment Strategies for Attention-Deficit Hyperactivity Disorder. *Archives of General Psychiatry, 56,* 1073–1086.

Mrug, S., Hoza, B., & Gerdes, A. C. (2001). Children with Attention-Deficit/Hyperactivity Disorder: Peer Relationships and Peer-Oriented Interventions. In D. W. Nangle & C. A. Erdley (Eds.), *The Role of Friendship in Psychological Adjustment: New Directions for Child and Adolescent Development* (pp. 51–77). San Francisco: Jossey-Bass.

New York University Child Study Clinic. (2000). *I.M.P.A.C.T. Survey and Study: Investigating the Mindset of Parents About AD / HD and Children Today.* New York: NYU Child Study. www.AboutOurKids.org.

Novotni, M., & Peterson, R. (2001). *What Does Everybody Else Know That I Don't?—Social Skills Help for Adults with AD / HD.* Plantation, FL: Specialty Press.

Parker, H. (2002). *Problem Solver Guide for Students with ADHD.* Plantation, FL: Specialty Press.

Pelham, W. E., Jr. (2002). *ADHD: Diagnosis, Nature, Etiology, and Treatment.* Buffalo, NY: Center for Children and Families. http://wings.buffalo.edu/psychology/adhd.

Rief, Sandra. (2003). *The ADHD Book of Lists.* San Francisco: Jossey-Bass.

Rosenthal-Malek, A. (1997, January/February). Stop and Think! Using Metacognitive Strategies to Teach Students Social Skills. *Teaching Exceptional Children, 29*(3), 29–31.

Sheridan, S. (1995). *The Tough Kid Social Skills Book.* Longmont, CO: Sopris West.

Shure, M. B. (1992). *I Can Problem Solve—An Interpersonal Cognitive Problem-Solving Program.* Champaign, IL: Research Press.

Smith, C. A. (1993). *The Peaceful Classroom: 162 Easy Activities to Teach Preschoolers Compassion and Cooperation.* Beltsville, MD: Gryphon House, Inc.

Teeter Ellison, P. A., & Goldstein, S. (2002, April). Poor Self-Control and How It Impacts Relationships. CHADD: *ATTENTION, 8*(5), 19–23.

Walker, H. M., McConnell, S., Holmes, D., Todis, B., Walker, J., & Golden, N. (1983). *The Walker Social Skills Curriculum: The ACCEPTS Program.* Austin, TX: PRO-ED.

Wallace, Ian. (2000). *You and Your ADD Child.* Sydney, Australia: HarperCollins.

Zumpfe, H., & Landau, S. (2002, April) Peer Problems. CHADD: *ATTENTION, 8*(5), 32–35.

Section 1.8

International Dyslexia Association® (2003, Fall). The Warning Signs of Learning Disabilities. Inland Empire Branch of the International Dyslexia Association®. *The Resource, 18*(2). www.dyslexia-ca.org.

Rief, Sandra. (1998). *The ADD/ADHD Checklist.* San Francisco: Jossey-Bass.

Rief, Sandra. (2001). *Ready . . . Start . . . School—Nurturing and Guiding Your Child Through Preschool & Kindergarten.* New York: Penguin Group.

Wright, Peter, Wright, Pamela, & Heath, Suzanne. (2004). *Wrightslaw: No Child Left Behind.* Hartfield, VA: Harbor House Law Press, Inc. www.wrightslaw.com.

Section 1.9

Crosby, Patricia. (1998, November/December). Looping in Middle School: Why Do It? *Teaching PreK–8, 29*(3), 46–48. www.TeachingK-8.com.

Gordon, D., & Ramer, L. (2001). *How to Help Students with AD/HD Succeed in School and in Life.* Lincoln, NE: Choice Press.

IDA: Warning Symptoms of Adolescence and Adulthood. (2003, Fall). Riverside, CA: Inland Empire Branch of the International Dyslexia Association.

Parker, Harvey. (1999). *Put Yourself in Their Shoes—Understanding Teenagers with ADHD.* Plantation, FL: Specialty Press.

Rief, Sandra. (1998). *The ADD/ADHD Checklist.* San Francisco: Jossey-Bass.

Rief, Sandra. (2003a). *Instructional Support Team Manual.* www.sandrarief.com.

Rief, Sandra. (2003b). *The ADHD Book of Lists.* San Francisco: Jossey-Bass.

When Two Years Are Better Than One. (1998, November/December). *Teaching PreK–8, 29*(3), 38–41. www.TeachingK-8.com.

Part 1: Recommended Resources

Recommended Reading on ADHD in Adolescence

Dendy, Chris Zeigler. (2000). *Teaching Teens with ADD and ADHD*. Bethesda, MD: Woodbine House.

Dendy, Chris A. Zeigler. (1995). *Teenagers with ADD—A Parent's Guide*. Bethesda, MD: Woodbine House.

Ellison, Phyllis Anne Teeter. (2000). Strategies for Adolescents with AD/HD: Goal Setting and Increasing Independence. *The CHADD Information and Resource Guide to AD/HD*. Landover, MD: CHADD.

Flick, Grad L. (2000). *How to Reach & Teach Teenagers with ADHD*. Paramus, NJ: The Center for Applied Research in Education.

Fowler, Mary. (2001). *Maybe You Know My Teen*. New York: Broadway Books.

Ingersoll, Barbara, Pfeffer, Bruce, Weiss, Sharon, & Nadeau, Kathleen. (1998). *ADD Adolescents in the Classroom: An Educator's Survival Guide* (videos/guide). Fairfax, VA: CHADD of Northern Virginia.

Markel, G., & Greenbaum, H. (1996). *Performance Breakthroughs for Adolescents with Learning Disabilities or ADD*. Champaign, IL: Research Press.

Nadeau, Kathleen. (1998). *Help 4 ADD @ High School*. Silver Spring, MD: Advantage Books.

New York University Child Study Clinic. (2000). I.M.P.A.C.T.

Phelan, Thomas W. (1998). *Surviving Your Adolescents*. Glen Ellyn, IL: Child Management, Inc.

Phelan, Thomas. (2000). Lessons from the Trenches: "Managing" the Teen with AD/HD. *The CHADD Information and Resource Guide to AD/HD*. Landover, MD: CHADD.

Quinn, Patricia. (1995). *ADD and Adolescents*. New York: Magination Press.

Robin, Arthur L. (1998). *ADHD in Adolescence: Diagnosis and Treatment*. New York: The Guilford Press.

Snyder, Marlene, & Hamphill, Rae. (2000). Parents of Teen Drivers with AD/HD: Proceed with Caution. *The CHADD Information and Resource Guide to AD/HD*. Landover, MD: CHADD.

Teeter, Phyllis A., & Stewart, Paula. (1997). *Transitioning of the ADHD Child to Secondary School: A Multimodal Approach*. CHADD's Ninth Annual Conference.

Managing the Challenge of ADHD Behaviors

Classroom Management and Positive Discipline Practices

Children with ADHD are in particular need of a classroom that is well-structured—meaning they know precisely what the expectations are from the minute they enter the room until the time they are dismissed at the end of the day. The structure that is necessary comes from teachers who clearly teach what is acceptable and unacceptable behavior and who provide predictability, consistency, and follow-through. These are probably the most important steps teachers can take to prevent or minimize common behavioral problems in the classroom.

To establish good classroom management, teachers need to spend the majority of their time being proactive—with care and attention to: environmental factors (for example, furniture arrangement and student seating); the behavioral expectations/standards (class rules, routines, procedures); the positive reinforcement strategies and systems that will be used to encourage, motivate, and reinforce appropriate behavior; and the corrective consequences that will be employed when students misbehave.

Effective classroom management, of course, goes hand in hand with good teaching and instruction. Even students with the tendency for significant behavioral challenges generally demonstrate appropriate behavior when teachers provide:

* Engaging, meaningful, high-interest learning activities/instruction

* Differentiated instruction and pacing to avoid frustration and boredom
* Lessons that are well planned, and class periods that have little lag time (when students are unoccupied and waiting to find out what they are expected to do next)

The key to effective classroom management is building positive relationships and rapport with students and making a connection on a personal level. This requires teachers to be understanding, flexible, and patient. Children typically work hard and will want to cooperate and please adults whom they like, trust, and respect. It is important for teachers to make the time and effort to know their individual students and build a relationship, demonstrating that they truly and sincerely care about their lives and their success.

Ways for teachers to build this rapport (Rief, 2003) are through:

* Modeling respectful language, tone of voice, and body language
* Greeting and welcoming students with a smile every day
* Communicating an enjoyment and appreciation for the class
* Maintaining high expectations and supporting students in achieving those expectations
* Finding time to make personal connections with students

* Being sensitive, empathetic, and responsive to students' special needs
* Maintaining a sense of humor
* Making learning activities interesting and fun
* Providing requests, redirection, and corrective feedback in a way that respects students' feelings and dignity
* Building communication with the students' parents/families
* Avoiding lecturing, criticism, or embarrassment of students (addressing issues in private when possible, not in front of peers)

Common Triggers or Antecedents to Misbehavior

Students may misbehave for any number of reasons. Certain conditions, times of day, settings, activities, events, and people can be triggers to misbehavior. By teacher awareness of common triggers (or antecedents) to problematic behaviors, teachers can be proactive and make adjustments that can prevent or significantly reduce the chance of many behavioral problems from occurring. Again, the best management involves anticipating potential problems and avoiding them through careful planning.

Some of the antecedents to misbehavior are

A. Environmentally Based

* Uncomfortable conditions (too noisy, crowded, hot, or cold)
* Settings (hallways, cafeteria, playground)
* When there is a lack of structure, organization, predictability, interesting materials, clear schedule, visual supports

B. Physically Based

* When the child is not feeling well (ill, overly tired, hungry, thirsty)
* Medication related: short-acting medication is wearing off, change of prescription or dosage

C. Related to Specific Activity or Event

* Certain subject areas (math, science, reading, music)

* Change of routine without warning
* Large group discussions
* Seat work
* Cooperative learning groups and sharing of materials
* Tasks that student perceives as boring, lengthy, frustrating

D. Related to a Performance/Skill Demand

* To remain seated
* To read independently
* To write a paragraph
* Having to wait patiently for a turn
* To hurry and complete a task
* Any behavioral/performance expectation that is a struggle for that individual student

E. Related to a Specific Time

* First period of the day
* Before or after lunch
* Transition times of day
* After school (late afternoon)
* Mondays

F. Related to a Specific Person (in the Presence or Absence of . . .)

* Administrator(s)
* A particular teacher or staff member
* Peers (a particular classmate/peer, or group of students)
* Parent(s)

G. Other

* When given no choices/options
* When embarrassed in front of peers
* When having difficulty communicating
* When given no assistance or access to help on difficult tasks
* When teased by classmate(s)

When students misbehave, it helps to understand that there are motivators to behavior—functions, goals, or needs that are being met by demonstrating those undesirable behaviors. When able to determine which of the student's needs are being fulfilled as a result of the misbehavior, the teacher can make changes to reduce that inappropriate behavior from occurring.

The main functions or goals of student behavior are

* To obtain something (attention, power/revenge, stimulation)
* To avoid or escape something (failure, fear, embarrassment, effort, blame, punishment, pain)

Classroom Management Tips

The following are the key components and strategies for effective classroom management necessary for creating a positive, productive learning environment (Rief, 2003; Rief & Heimburge, 1996).

Classroom Environment

Establish a classroom environment that:

* Is structured and well-organized (for example, clear schedule, routines, rules, careful planning of seating and physical space)
* Is calm and predictable
* Has clear rules/behavioral guidelines
* Has clearly defined, taught, and practiced procedures that become automatic routines of classroom operation
* Focuses on the use of positive reinforcement for appropriate behavior
* Backs up behavioral limits/boundaries with fair corrective consequences that are enforced predictably and consistently
* Is respectful and mutually supportive
* Is warm, welcoming, and inclusive
* Builds a sense of "community," teamwork, and interdependence
* Is flexible enough to accommodate individual needs of students
* Has high academic and behavioral expectations
* Builds on students' skills of self-management (while supporting those who struggle in this area)

* Is emotionally, as well as physically, safe; students are not fearful of making a mistake or looking/sounding foolish and, consequently, are willing to take the risk of participation

Classroom Rules/Behavioral Standards

Some effective practices include:

* Limit to a few comprehensive rules/behavioral standards.
* Explain the rationale for the chosen rules.
* Have students discuss, provide input, and decide on the classroom rules to give more ownership and buy-in.
* Clearly and positively state the behaviors you want (rather than "Don't . . .").
* Make sure they are observable behaviors (for example, "Keep hands, feet, and objects to yourself." "Be on time and prepared for class.").
* Define concretely what the behaviors should "look like" and "sound like."
* Discuss, model, and practice those expectations.
* Role play the desired behaviors. This can be done by demonstrating "non-examples" as well, to help teach the appropriate behaviors.
* Post rules in words/pictures, and refer to them frequently.
* Remind students of rules/expectations before the start of activities.
* Ask individual students to repeat the rules/expectations.
* Clearly communicate your rules and expectations in writing to parents, as well as students.
* Reward students for rule-following behavior.

With every behavioral expectation you communicate: (1) explain, (2) write it down or show through illustrations, (3) demonstrate it in action, and (4) let students practice. As an example: Practice 12-inch voices. "What does it sound like? Is this a 12-inch voice?"

Example A: Classroom Rules/Standards

1. Come prepared to work.
2. Follow directions and stay on task.
3. Keep hands, feet, and objects to yourselves.
4. Be kind and courteous to others.

Example B: Classroom Rules/Standards

1. Follow directions.
2. Pay attention.
3. Work silently during quiet time.
4. Do your best work.

Example C: Classroom Rules/Standards (Contract)

We agree to
1. Practice safety.
2. Be respectful of others.
3. Follow directions and cooperate with each other.
4. Take responsibility for our learning.

Many schools have character education programs or building-wide standards for pro-social behavior that is taught and promoted in every class and environment throughout the school. Individual teachers should have their classroom rules/standards tied to the school-wide values being taught. For example, in one school (P.S. 396 in Region I of the Bronx, New York City), the school has developed the acronym of STARS to represent the expectations of:

STARS

Safety first

Teamwork

Always Respectful

Ready to learn

Sharing and caring

The Previous Example C rules incorporate the STARS school-wide values, so they compliment and reinforce what is being taught throughout the school in all classes and environments in the building.

Teach Procedures and Routines

Smooth classroom management is dependent on the teaching of very specific and consistent procedures and routines. Teachers need to think through and decide on their precise expectations for all classroom procedures throughout the day. Plan procedures for the start of the school day/class period (from entering class and morning routine) all the way through dismissal at the end of class/day. This includes such things as what students are expected to do when they don't have a sharpened pencil or other needed materials, finish work early, need to go to the restroom, have a question during independent seatwork, need a drink of water, have homework or papers to turn in, need to line up to leave the classroom, are moving to different learning centers/stations, and so forth.

All expectations must be clear, not vague or ambiguous, and then taught and well practiced. Smooth classroom management is dependent on procedures becoming so well established and automatic that they become routine. Teaching procedures and routines is like teaching other behavioral expectations—through modeling, role playing, practicing, reviewing, and re-teaching, as needed throughout the year.

Procedures and routines once taught are best prompted through visual cues and reminders, such as in the following example of a poster showing what students need to check before leaving at the end of the day.

End of Day

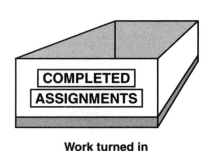

Work turned in

Papers in notebook

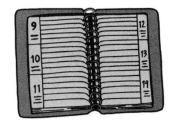

All homework recorded in planner

Pack all needed books and supplies

Shared Management and Responsibility

Assign to students any classroom management jobs and responsibilities that they are capable of doing themselves (for example, clean-up chores, passing out and collecting papers, gathering materials, taking attendance and lunch count).

Use Signals

Teachers should establish visual and auditory signals for getting students to stop what they are doing and pay attention. Visual signals include such techniques as flashing the lights, raising one's hand, or putting two fingers up in the air. Common classroom auditory signals are playing a bar of music (on a keyboard); ringing a bell, or using chimes, xylophone, or other instrument; starting a clapping pattern; calling out signal words (for example, "1, 2, 3,. . .eyes on me"). Auditory and visual signals in combination work best.

It also helps to devise nonverbal discrete signals for students to use in the classroom. For example, rather than raising their hands for help

when working independently, students can be given some other means of signaling the teacher, such as placing an upside-down colored plastic cup on the desk, or a sign of some sort. Student "help" signs or colored cards can be given to students to place or prop up on their desks.

Preventive Cueing and Visual Prompts

Nonverbal signals are very useful techniques in providing preventive cueing to individual students. Preventive cueing is a technique for stopping disruptive behavior before it begins and for avoiding confrontation or embarrassment of the student in front of peers. The teacher arranges privately with the student a predetermined hand signal or word signal to cue the student to calm down, pay attention, stop talking out, stop rocking in chair, and so forth. These are all quiet reminders.

Examples of cueing:

* Use traffic light or stop sign signal to indicate slow down/stop behavior.

* Go over to the student, look directly into his or her eyes, and tap your chin a few times to indicate that you want him or her to focus on you.
* Use the two-thumbs-up sign, indicating that the student can get up and move to another part of the room or outside the door.
* Students to whom you have taught relaxation, anger management, or other self-regulation strategies can be cued with a word or two or other signal to start using the specific strategies (for example, to relax and regain control). How effectively they will be able to use the strategy will depend on how much they practice and internalize the technique.

Provide Many Visual Prompts and Cues

Students with ADHD, but also many others (for example, English language learners, students with learning disabilities in auditory processing), respond better to visual cues and prompts as opposed to a lot of verbal reminders and directions. Teachers should always maintain a visual schedule, write on the board or other consistent location all class and homework assignments, and post all daily/weekly student responsibilities.

Using individual prompt cards with visual cues depicting expected behaviors (for example, in seat, focused and on-task, raising hand to speak) is highly recommended. These visual prompts can be illustrations/icons or actual photos of the student engaged in the appropriate behavior taken by the teacher. The visual cards/prompts can be placed on the student's desk, and the teacher can cue and remind the student (by some kind of a signal) to display the behavior(s) on the prompt card.

Classroom Transitions

Students with ADHD typically have the greatest behavioral difficulties during transitional times of the day in the classroom, as well as the school settings outside of the classroom that are less structured and less supervised (for example, playground, cafeteria, hallways, bathrooms).

Prevent problems during transitions in the classroom by doing the following:

* Talk about what will take place, role play, and teach the necessary behaviors.
* Clearly teach, model, and have students practice and rehearse all procedures that will occur during changes of activities. This includes such things as the students' quick and quiet movement from one area of the room to the next (for example, desks to carpet area), repositioning any chairs or furniture, putting away/taking out materials, and so forth.
* Primary grade teachers typically use songs or chants for transitions (for example, for cleaning up, moving to the rug, rotating to another learning center/station).
* Use auditory and visual signals to indicate that an activity is coming to an end and that students need to finish whatever they are doing to be ready for the next activity (for example, two-minute or three-minute warning). It is recommended to then set a timer for that amount of time. Many teachers then reward students if ready by the time the timer goes off.
* Reward smooth transitions. Many teachers use individual points or table points to reward students or table clusters/rows of students who are ready for the next activity.
* Some teachers use whole class incentives for transitions. One technique is to place a circle on the chalkboard. Prior to making the transition (for example, cleaning up after an activity and settling down before the next lesson), the teacher signals the students, tells them he or she will count to a certain number, and then proceeds to count. If everyone in the class manages to be ready with the cleanup by the time the teacher finishes counting, the teacher places a checkmark in the circle. If the

REMEMBER TO...

1	2	3
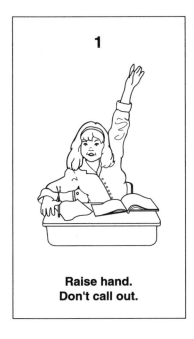		
Raise hand. Don't call out.	**Stay seated.**	**Keep on task.**

whole class is not ready, the teacher says, "Oh well, maybe next time." If the class earns a specified number of checks in the circle by the end of the week, there is a class reward.

* Avoid students being caught off guard. Prepare for any change in routine (for example, assemblies, guest speakers, field trips, substitute teachers) through discussion and modeling of expectations. When there are to be changes in the schedule or routine, point them out when possible in advance.

* Be organized in advance with prepared materials for the next activity. Planning well and beginning instruction promptly are good deterrents to behavior problems.

It is typical for misbehavior to occur when students have "down time" and are waiting without direction for instruction to begin. It is recommended that teachers position themselves at the door and greet students as they enter the room, immediately directing them to routine warm-up or "do-now" activities (journal entries, interpreting brief quotation on board, writing sentences using vocabulary words, two or three math problems). Besides being a deterrent to behavioral problems, it is also an excellent strategy for transitioning students mentally for the next lesson.

Teacher Proximity and Movement

One of the best management tools available to teachers is their use of physical proximity (their presence among students). Teachers with the best classroom management typically circulate and move around the room frequently. They create a floor plan of furniture/desk arrangement that enables easy access and pathways to all students in the room.

Most students tend to "shape up" behaviorally when their teacher is in close proximity. Teacher positioning is particularly important with students who have behavioral and/or attention problems. The teacher approaching and standing near those student(s), providing cues (for example, a hand on the shoulder or a tap on the desk) with quiet, discreet, but *clear* reminders about behavioral expectations is effective.

Organize the Physical Environment to Maximize Production and Management

Seating arrangement is important in any classroom. Many teachers prefer seating arrangements with desks in clusters (four to eight students per group and facing each other) to facilitate cooperative work. This is generally not the ideal arrangement for students with ADHD. If teachers use this arrangement, the desks need to be angled in such a way that all students can see the board or overhead screen, and students with ADHD would have to be carefully placed and positioned in the cluster (hopefully among tolerant, on-task, and supportive peers).

More optimal desk formations for students who struggle to maintain attention and productivity may be

* U-shaped/horseshoes
* E-shaped
* Straight rows
* Staggered rows (for example, groups of four students per row in the center and slanted groups of two students per row on the peripheries)

As mentioned above, furniture arrangement should enable the teacher to have easy access (with as few steps as possible) to each student without obstruction, which is an important consideration in crowded classrooms with little space.

One or two kidney-shaped tables are very useful in the classroom for small group work with students. Teachers are able to sit with a group of students, directly facing them, within arm's reach and cueing distance.

Whenever possible, students with ADHD should be seated close to the teacher and center of instruction, surrounded by and facing positive role models and well-focused classmates, and away from high traffic areas and distractors (for example, noisy heaters/air conditioners, doors, learning centers, windows, pencil sharpeners).

The room environment should be well organized, visually appealing, arranged for maximum use of space, and show student work/ownership. Efforts should be made, however, to reduce unnecessary clutter and visual overload in the classroom.

Comfortable lighting and room temperature are also very important environmental factors that affect students' energy level and productivity.

Whatever can be done to reduce unnecessary noise and auditory distractions in the classroom is helpful. This includes such strategies as inserting old tennis balls on the tips of each chair to reduce the noise level in uncarpeted rooms, minimizing use of pencil sharpeners during class time, and replacing or turning off buzzing fluorescent lights.

Desks should be adjusted (raised or lowered), or options provided so that each student can sit at a desk and chair of the appropriate height—in furniture that is stable, not wobbly.

A number of strategies address the needs of diverse learners and accommodate individual learning styles. (See Section 3.3, Reaching Students Through Their Learning Styles and Multiple Intelligences.)

Monitor Student Behavior

Teachers must be constantly monitoring students' behavior and alert to what students are engaged in at all times of the day and parts of the room. Good classroom managers learn to develop the skill of "having eyes in the backs of their heads."

Positively reinforce students engaged appropriately (for example, "I see Karen and Alicia busy on their assignment. Well done."). Address inappropriate behavior when scanning by techniques such as a gentle reminder, eye contact, and "the teacher look." When needing to redirect students, do so by mentioning their names, getting eye contact, and using a calm but firm voice.

Provide Positive Attention and Social Rewards for Desired Student Behaviors

One of the most effective strategies for motivating and rewarding desired student behaviors is the use of "social reinforcers" provided by the teacher, other school personnel, and/or classmates/peers. There is no substitute for teacher attention to students engaged in appropriate behaviors ("catching them being good"), and reinforcing those behaviors through recognition, acknowledgment, and praise that is specific, descriptive, and sincere. Here are some examples:

* "I like the way Brianna remembers to raise her hand and waits to be called on. Thank you, Brianna."
* "Adam, I appreciate how quietly you lined up."
* "Victor, you did such a good job paying attention and staying with the group."
* "I see that Marcus is in his chair facing forward with his book open to the right page. Nice job of following directions."
* "I appreciate the way Michael is standing in line quietly with his hands and feet to himself. Thank you, Michael."
* "Cynthia, I noticed the effort you put into that assignment."
* "Tamika, great job cooperating with your group and finishing the assignment on time."

It is common for students with ADHD to receive a high degree of teacher and peer attention for their misbehaviors and rule violations. Teachers need to be aware of this reality and make strong efforts to pay attention to the times when they are behaving appropriately. Strive to provide a *minimum* of three times more positive attention and comments to students than negative/corrective feedback.

Many older students would be humiliated if teachers praised them openly in front of peers. However, they still need and appreciate the positive feedback. Provide positive attention and recognition through thumbs-up signs, pats on the back, a smile, or other nonverbal acknowledgment. If verbal praise is embarrassing to students, provide positive feedback through notes and quiet statements before/after class. Try using a self-stick pad to jot down comments to students and place them on their desks while circulating throughout the room.

In addition to the teacher's recognition, it is a very powerful social reinforcer for classmates to provide the positive attention and recognition to their peers, such as giving each other compliments/praise, "high fives," "rounds of applause," or "silent cheers."

Additional social reinforcers that are effective in motivating and rewarding desired student behaviors include:

* Positive phone calls or emails directly to the student
* Positive notes, calls, emails to parents
* Earning a class privilege of social status (for example, team captain, class messenger)
* Recognition at awards assemblies
* Name being called on the school intercom recognizing something positive the student accomplished
* Choice of seating for the period, day, or week (near friends, in teacher's desk or chair)
* Being awarded "Star of the Day" or "Student of the Week"
* Sending the student to the administrator, counselor, or other staff member with a positive note about his or her performance so that the child receives positive attention and recognition from that other adult

Activity Rewards and Privileges for Students

The use of activity reinforcers is very effective in the classroom. In essence, students earn the time and opportunity to participate in activities or earn a privilege that they would like to do. Teachers often use the contingency: "When you finish ___, you'll get to do ___." "First, you need to ____. Then, you may _____." "When the class has ___, we will get to ___."

Teachers need to know their students and elicit their input to know what activities would be rewarding. This is also true in determining "privileges." Many students find classroom jobs or various responsibilities to be a privilege that they like to earn the chance to do. Inventory and brainstorm with the class to establish this list of possible privileges and activity rewards.

It is important to realize that students with ADHD need the opportunity to earn the reward of participation more frequently than the average child. It is often the case that they are penalized for their difficulties with work production by having to miss out on rewarding activities in order to complete unfinished assignments. When this is the case, teachers have to find ways to provide more support and accommodations to help ADHD students get caught up with their work, so that they can participate in rewarding activities along with their peers.

Examples of activity reinforcers for full-class or group rewards include:

* "Choice time" for fun, preferred activities can be awarded as frequently as needed by the developmental age of the group (for example, twice a day, daily, weekly—"Freaky Fun Friday")
* Participation in special events or activities (for example, field trip, party, assembly, movie, school performance)
* Lunchtime activities or privileges (choice of seating/eating in special location, special games)
* Earning time in class to catch up on work with teacher or peer assistance, if needed
* Listening to students' choice of music
* A special game of choice (in class or recess/P.E. time)
* Extra P.E., music, art, or computer time
* Breakfast or lunch with teacher, administrator, or other staff member
* Ice cream, popcorn, or pizza party for the class or group of students achieving a certain goal
* Earning a "Good for removing X items from assignment" coupon or "One late assignment accepted as on-time" coupon
* Free/earned time (individual or class) for activities of choice such as games, listening to music, drawing, working on special project, and accessing learning/interest centers
* Work on school projects (for example, painting school mural, gardening)

* Free reading (including books of choice, magazines, comic books)
* Cross-age tutoring or opportunity to read to younger grade students
* Early dismissal of one or two minutes for lunch/recess/passing to next class
* Opportunity to take a break and run a few laps, dance to a song, use playground equipment, or other physical activity
* Use of special materials, supplies, equipment

Material reinforcers are also used in the classroom. These include the following tangible things students may earn:

* School supplies (special pencils, pens, erasers, folders)
* Stickers, stars, badges, and certificates
* Food treats—preferably healthy snacks (for example, pretzels, popcorn, crackers, frozen ice sticks, trail mix, juice, fruit)
* Treasure-chest items (small toys, trinkets)
* Magazines/books
* Class money, tickets, or points redeemable at auctions/lotteries or class stores
* Free tickets awarded to school dances, concerts, plays, and sporting events
* Coupons from businesses in the community for discounts toward purchases or free items

Class (Group) Behavior Management Systems

Teachers use a variety of group positive reinforcement systems as a tool of classroom management. Such systems motivate and reward cooperative, rule-following behavior. There are various kinds of class (group) reinforcement systems teachers may choose to use to implement that may best fit their style of teaching, comfort level, and the interest of their students. The following are examples of some common group reinforcement systems (Rief, 2003):

Table/Team Points. Points are given for specific behaviors being demonstrated (for example, cooperation and teamwork, on-task, all assignments turned in, area cleaned up, transitioning on or before allotted time). Any tables/teams earning a target number (X amount) of points earns the reward or privilege. This is not table/team competition. Each table/team can earn the reward or privilege if meeting the goal.

Table/Team Competition. This is probably a more commonly used technique by teachers than what was described above. Here points are awarded to any table/team demonstrating the target behavior(s): "Table 4, good job of cooperating and helping your teammates. You just earned a point." At the end of the day/week, the table team with *the most* points earns the reward or privilege (or the top two teams win the reward).

Marbles in a Jar. Teachers (usually in primary grade classrooms) catch students engaged in appropriate behaviors. They call attention to the positive behavior (of an individual student, group of students, or something the whole class did well). Then the teacher reinforces the positive behavior by putting a marble (or other kind of object) in a jar.

Note: Many teachers use a scoop of dried beans or a scoop of uncooked kernels of popcorn. When the jar is filled, the class earns a reward (for example, popcorn party). This is a particularly effective technique for rewarding quick and smooth transitions.

Chart Moves. A chart is created for the class or group. The class is reinforced for meeting a set goal by advancing one space on the chart each time they meet the goal. When the chart is filled, the whole class earns the reward. There are numerous types of charts that can be made. It is recommended to change the chart frequently to maintain the novelty and students' interest. Dot-to-dot charts and any game-board type of charts will work.

A particular goal (or two) is set, such as all students are in their seats with materials ready by the morning bell or no observed incidents of a particular problematic behavior occurring in a certain time frame (for example, in the morning, after lunch). Each time the class meets that goal, a move is made on the chart, such as connecting to the next dot (on a dot-to-dot chart) or moving a Velcro-backed object to the next space on the chart (as in a race car moving along the track).

Token Economy System. Students have the chance to earn tokens, points, tickets, or class money. These are later redeemable at a

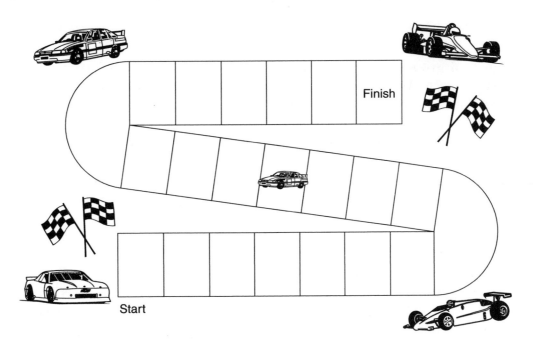

class store, auction, or raffle. A menu of rewards is developed with corresponding price values attached. Students can spend their earned tokens, points, or money at designated times during class auctions or shopping at the class store.

Token economy systems also allow a teacher to fine or charge students (for example, $10 class currency for forgetting book at home and needing to borrow another; $10 late to class).

Note: Teachers must be awarding generously and frequently for positive behaviors so that students (particularly those with ADHD) are not overly fined for rule infractions or forgetfulness. This would result in frustration, losing motivation, and the program not being effective.

Some teachers tie this system to teaching students how to balance a checkbook and have a whole "company payroll system." Typically, students receive their "paychecks," which have fines subtracted from earnings. They get to then spend their checks (on purchases of items or privileges).

Here is another example of a token system: Using plastic colored links (found in catalogs selling math materials), the teacher awards monetary value to the four colors of the links: yellow = penny, red = nickel, green = dime, blue = quarter. The teacher "pays" students for good behavior: (a) the whole class earns points and the teacher awards all students a certain value for their links; (b) individually, for on-task behavior; (c) groups, for cooperative work assignments/projects. The possibilities are limitless. Students are "fined" for offenses such as no homework, getting out of seat, and off-task behavior. Every week or every other week students get to "buy" small treats or privileges with their money (value of links).

Probability Reinforcers. Teachers who give raffle tickets for demonstrating target behaviors or meeting certain goals have students write their names on the tickets and place them in a container. Drawings are held (daily/weekly). Those students whose names are drawn receive prizes or privileges. Students understand the principle of probability—that the more tickets they have, the greater the chance of winning a reward.

Group Response Costs. Response cost techniques are an interesting means of improving and shaping behavior. It works differently from other positive reinforcement systems—in that instead of giving tokens/points for demonstrating the appropriate behavior, students work to keep the tokens/points that they are given up-front. If they have a certain number of tokens/points remaining at the end of the given time frame, that earns them a reward.

Basically, a target behavior that the whole class is working to improve is selected (for example, in seat/in place unless having permission to be elsewhere; appropriate language—no cursing/swearing; waiting to be called on to speak). A certain number of points or tokens (for example, stars written at the top of the board, paper or plastic links on a chain, sticks in a cup) are automatically given at the beginning of each day, class period, or other time frame. The number of tokens given up-front is determined after getting a baseline of how frequently the problematic behavior typically occurs. For example, if the target problem behavior (for example, talking out without raising hands) generally occurs at least ten times in a class period, initially the class may start with eight given tokens at the beginning of the period. Then a point or token is removed or crossed out every time the inappropriate behavior (talking out) occurs. If there is at least one of the points/tokens remaining at the end of the time frame, the class has met the goal successfully and earns a preselected reward (for example, a move on the class chart, minutes earned toward a rewarding activity). In this example, if they started with eight points at the beginning of the period and had one remaining by the end of the class period, the talking-out behavior was improved by 30 percent (from ten times down to seven).

The criteria for success is gradually raised. For example, next only seven tokens are given at the beginning of the class period, then six, five, and so on until the behavior has significantly improved to the point that the program can be discontinued or a different behavior may be selected.

There are many variations of response cost systems. The key is that students are working to keep what they have been given up-front. One variation is that at the beginning of the day, the teacher may automatically give fifteen minutes of free time or special activity time to the class to be used at the end of the day/week. Specific misbehaviors that occur during the day will result in one-minute losses of time from the free minutes given. The net positive balance will be awarded at the end of the day (or week). Of course, the teacher has the discretion to add bonus minutes during the day for exceptionally good behavior to increase the motivation. Section 2.3, Individualized Behavior Management, Interventions, and Supports, will describe the use of a response cost program/chart for an individual child.

Level Systems. Some classrooms (usually special education classes) find a level system effective. Each child in the class earns points for specified behaviors throughout the day such as for being in proper location (seat, desk), being on-task, appropriate language/verbal interactions, and so forth.

Depending on the number of points earned, the child has access to different levels of rewards at the end of the day (or at the end of the week). For example, earning 85 percent or higher of the possible points would enable that student access to the highest level of choices. During activity time, these students would have the choice of most desirable activities, materials, places to sit/play, and other privileges. Students earning lower percentages of possible points also have reinforcing activity time, but their choices are more limited.

Addressing Student Misbehavior

In addition to positive reinforcement to increase and maintain desirable, appropriate student behavior, teachers must also enforce rules/behavioral expectations with clear, fair, and reasonable corrective consequences (Rief,

2003). The following are recommendations for doing so:

* Enforce with predictability in a calm, non-emotional manner.
* Try to handle inappropriate behavior as simply and promptly as possible.
* Use a hierarchy of negative consequences or mild punishments. Address only the child's behavior, not the child himself or herself.
* Deliver consequences using as few words as possible. Act without lecturing. Discussions about behavior can occur later.

Punishment is a "reactive strategy"—it is a negative consequence that is occurring after the fact. A punishment is an aversive experience following misbehavior in an effort to reduce the behavior (in frequency, intensity, or duration). It is a response to misbehavior, but one that does not teach replacement behaviors. Many times punishment is delivered by the adult in anger and frustration and results in a child learning an unintended lesson (for example, be careful not to get caught) or emotionally not linking the consequence to their misbehavior, but instead blaming, feeling hostile towards, and wanting to avoid the adult.

That is why the use of punishment should be minimized, and the focus of positive classroom discipline should be on proactive efforts to (a) establish the structure and climate for success; (b) effectively *teach* appropriate behavioral expectations and acceptable ways of getting their needs met; and (c) motivate students to cooperate through the abundance of positive reinforcements available in the classroom.

Corrective consequences are actually mild punishments for misbehavior, and they are important. Not only are they a necessary component of classroom "management," but also provide students the safety and security of knowing there are behavioral boundaries, which will be respected and enforced. If, however, we want students to realize and accept the logical and natural connection between their behavior and the consequences of their actions, corrective consequences must be planned and delivered with care—in a respectful, non-emotional, and predictable manner.

Proactive teachers carefully plan a hierarchy of consequences for addressing misbehavior and inform students, parents, and administrators of the classroom behavioral plan. Students know in advance what kinds of consequences they can expect from misbehavior.

First, not every behavior warrants teacher intervention. Choose to ignore minor inappropriate behavior that is not intentional. For example, teachers will have to be tolerant and flexible with ADHD students, allowing extra movement, fiddling with objects, and behaviors they have significant physiological difficulty controlling.

Classroom management systems generally include an array of negative or corrective consequences, always beginning with mild and quiet interventions such as:

Nonverbal warnings and reminders that the student needs to correct his or her behavior. These include:

* Teacher positioning himself or herself near the student (close proximity)
* A gentle touch on the shoulder
* Whispering a reminder or directive to the student
* Private, pre-arranged signals
* Nonverbal cues (for example, making eye contact; giving "the teacher look" to convey disapproval of inappropriate behavior; pointing to or tapping on visual prompts)

Gentle, verbal reminders and warnings such as:

* "Steve, remember to raise your hand, please."
* "Anna, the rule is ____. That's a warning."
* "Vincent, where are you supposed to be right now?"
* "Jared, next time ask permission before you ____."
* Issuing a direct command (for example, "Susan, get busy doing problems one

through ten now." "Brianna, I need you in your seat and facing forward.")

After clear warnings, infractions of the rules need to result in a minor penalty of some type. Some teachers have an actual hierarchy of consequences they follow. Others may choose an appropriate consequence, considering first the situation, student, and other specific circumstances. The key is that students know the teacher means business and will enforce some kind of consequence.

Teachers who follow through consistently can often manage quite well by just asking a student, "Which do you prefer . . . paying me back the time you are wasting after school or getting busy now? It's your choice."

Possible Corrective Consequences

The following list is not intended to show a recommended sequence or hierarchy of corrective consequences, just an array of possibilities that teachers may wish to consider in responding to student misbehavior and in developing their own discipline plan:

Loss of something the student wants; for example, time from participating in a preferred activity, a privilege or responsibility, access or use of certain equipment/materials for a period of time.

Brief delay; for example, a minute or two of having to wait before participating in a desired activity or joining the group.

Owing time, which involves the student having to pay back a certain amount of time, generally as a consequence for disruptive behavior that takes away from class instructional time. It might mean having the student stay one minute to a few minutes after school/class or from their recess period; or it may be a longer "detention" period, generally after school. During such time the student is to pay back any time owed in a certain manner (for example, sitting quietly with desk cleared and nothing to do but wait).

Just one minute of time owed after class or from a preferred activity is a powerful consequence. "To an older student, one minute away from peers can seem like forever. Just one minute is enough to make a student miss walking to the next class with friends, be last in line at lunch, or unable to join a group after school" (Canter & Canter, 1993).

Positive practice/do-overs involve requiring the student to demonstrate the appropriate behavior one or more times. For example, if caught running in the hallway, send the child back to the room to walk appropriately.

Extra work or undesired task assigned. The consequences here are obvious.

Response costs were discussed earlier in the section. If tied to a token economy system, students can be fined for rule infractions and lose points or tokens they had already earned. One response cost method that teachers use is the *inverted stoplight system.* A stoplight is made (inverted with the green light on top and red on the bottom).

Each student has a clothespin with his or her name on it. Every day students start out "in the green." There are many variations to this system, but in most cases, students have their pins lowered to yellow for misbehavior (generally after a warning or two). Some teachers also provide a minor consequence (for example, sent back to seat for two or three minutes) if moved to yellow. Other teachers just use the yellow as a more visible warning to the student that they are in danger of moving down to red.

Most teachers allow students to redeem themselves and move back to green from yellow when behavior has improved. When misbehavior warrants moving down to red, there is a negative consequence attached (for example, note home, loss of privilege). Some teachers will provide a reward of some kind to students who are in the green at the end of the day. Another variation is to add colors on the light (an extra color and warning between yellow and red light) and even

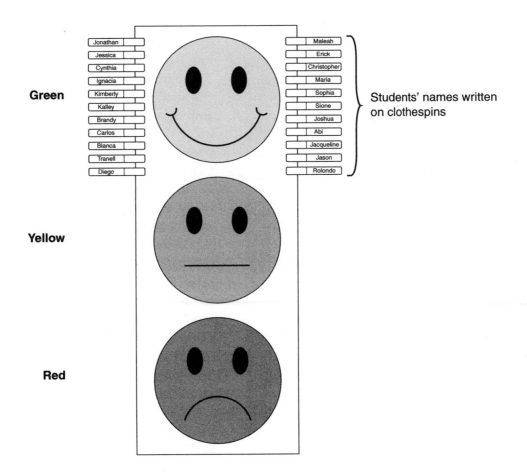

a colored light higher than green (for example, blue) for students showing exceptionally good behavior (tied to an extra privilege earned).

Color-coded cards is another graphic response cost system used in many classrooms that is similar to the stoplight. Again, there are many variations of this technique. It usually involves a pocket chart with an individual envelope or compartment for each student (identified by name or number). Each student has four or five colored cards in his or her envelope of the chart. All students start the day with one designated color (for example, pink card) visible in their envelopes. When there is an infraction of the rules—after a warning—that student's colored card is changed (for example, to yellow) resulting in a minor consequence (for example, two-minute time-out). With the next infraction, the card is changed to the next color (for example, orange) resulting in stronger consequence (five minutes of time-out and problem sheet to fill out). After another infraction, the red card appears, with another progression in the level of negative consequences (for example, loss of privilege, time owed, call or note home). Once again, most teachers using these strategies allow students to work their way back up for improved behavior. This is recommended; otherwise students such as those with ADHD, who change colors for misbehavior far more frequently than the average student, will likely become defeated and give up.

Time-out/time away is some form of brief time-out or time away from class participation or from the chance to earn positive reinforcement, such as:

* Head down at desk (could involve counting to a certain number)
* Being moved a few feet away from the group temporarily (for example, to sit in chair rather than on rug—still within the view of the group)
* Time-out location in classroom (away from view of the group—and without the opportunity for positive reinforcement)
* Time-out/time away location in a neighboring buddy class that has been pre-arranged to exchange students for this purpose

* Time-out in other school location that has supervision and is designed to be non-reinforcing for this purpose

If using time-out/time away, consider the following:

* Start with no more than a few minutes, with additional time added or a longer time-out period assigned for continued behavioral infractions.
* Try directing the student to time-out calmly and positively: "Michael, I would like for you to sit with your hands and feet to yourself. If you can't handle that, go back to the table. You can join us when you are ready to sit without touching others."
* Some teachers use a "think-about-it" chair for a specified amount of time, for example, three to five minutes to think about the inappropriate behavior. Other teachers have students sit away from the class until they feel ready to join the class again. The teacher might say something like: "I am glad you're ready to follow our rules. Please join us."
* If the student continues to be disruptive, the next step is often to be sent to a location outside of the classroom (for example, another classroom, counselor, office). However, whenever sending a student out of the room, be aware that you may be inadvertently rewarding rather than punishing the child by doing so. It must be a location that is boring and the student must prefer to be in the classroom rather than in the out-of-classroom location. Keep in mind that students often find it rewarding to leave the classroom because their goals/needs are being met by being sent out of the class (for example, getting attention, escaping a task they don't want to do, access to something fun or stimulating out of the room). Teachers must be careful not to overuse time-out as a consequence and be sure that the child is aware of the behavior that caused him or her to receive the time-out.

Behavioral logs/problem-solving sheets are used by many teachers. The strategy involves having students record behavioral infractions in a log or notebook. The student fills out a form of some type describing the behavior, requiring reflection on the behavioral choices made, and writing down what the child plans to do differently next time. Later, the teacher and student debrief with the problem-solving sheet that the student has filled out and discuss the plan (with one or two short-term goals to work on).

Teacher/student conferences occur along with many of the other consequences above—to discuss the behavior and ways to improve.

Restitution or fixing the problem is used, for example, if a student makes a mess. In this case, he or she has the responsibility of cleaning it up. If a student hurts someone's feelings or was disrespectful, he or she must apologize verbally or in writing.

Parental contact is used by many teachers when they haven't thought through an array of appropriate corrective consequences. They automatically threaten, "I'm going to call your parents." It is important to have close communication with parents, and they should be informed of behavioral concerns that are interfering with their child's school functioning.

However, not every incident warrants phone calls home to involve parents; and of course, when teachers call home, it should be to communicate about positive things regarding the student, not just problems.

When contacting parents for behavioral concerns, it might involve a phone call, email, or note home. Teachers who have access to a phone during the day may call the parent with the student, who must discuss the inappropriate behavior with parent(s) in the teacher's presence. A parent/teacher conference may need to be set up (with or without the student in attendance; with or without another staff member such as the counselor or administrator).

Suspensions are a more drastic measure. Teachers should always handle mild misbehaviors in the classroom. More serious infractions would, of course, require the involvement of the administrator. Some school code infractions might result in student suspensions (in school and out of school). Teachers and other school staff must be aware of students with disabilities—checking their IEPs and any behavioral intervention plans they may have, especially if suspensions are being considered. (See Section 5.4, Educational Laws and Rights of Students with ADHD—the section on disciplining students with disabilities.)

INTERVIEW WITH BRAD (34 Years Old)

Brad, a chaplain in the Navy, was diagnosed at twenty-eight as having ADHD and dyslexia.

Who helped you and made a difference?

"My mother was very supportive. She played an important role in my decision-making process. My mother would let me run things by her—like an article or things I was planning to do. She helped by acting like a filter, so I wouldn't make a lot of the mistakes that would come back and bite me. She gave me a lot of psychological approval.

"When I was diagnosed, I worked with a specialist for three years. She was excellent. She helped me improve my socialization skills and communication. With dyslexia, it's all tied together. The inconsistency in how you process language filters down on many levels. My mind skips from A to B to G to D to F. It was clear to me what I meant to say, but not necessarily to the listener. She helped me with my writing. I would run past her some of the writing assignments I was working on, and she would help me see when it wasn't linked together . . . it didn't flow. Through her help I developed an 'internal clock.'"

Tell me how you improved socially.

"I had no problems meeting people and getting dates. But after two or three dates, that was it. I knew when the dates were successful and the girl was interested, and I would ask to get together again. But I wanted to know then the date and time of the next date. It wasn't an issue of insecurity, but I was seeking clarification. Everything in my world was black and white. There was no gray area. One of the ways the specialist helped me was to deal with the gray area. I realized it was okay to ask a girl if I could give her a call later . . . no pressure."

How do you remember ADHD affecting you when growing up?

"Teachers attributed my problems to laziness or inattention to detail, even though I spent hours doing my work. I spent so many more hours than anyone else did. I always wondered why I didn't get an *A*. I would fall asleep during class. At school I would sit ten minutes and be ready to get up and move somewhere else. I always blurted things out in class and couldn't wait to talk. All the kids did that to an extent, but I was 'big time.' I didn't interact well socially. I had friends . . . I did the things everyone else did, only at the wrong time. Others got away with it, but I didn't. They knew when and when not to do something. I didn't realize there was a time and place for everything. I was doing things that were appropriate for kids maybe a few years younger.

"When we would get together and visit family, there were only two things I would talk about—the Navy and rabbinic school. Anything else . . . I was a wallflower. Looking back I can see that there were thirty people there and several separate conversations going on at the same time. I couldn't focus or follow any of them. By the time I got involved in a conversation, I was behind everyone else."

How has your life changed since you were diagnosed?

"Once I found out, I set my own agenda. You can say, 'Look. I can do this work, but I'll have to have extra time. Maybe I need to have an extra semester or year.' I had no problem with spending an extra year in rabbinic school—my ego was not on the line. Once I knew, I was able to ask questions . . . I wanted to find out everything. I started Ritalin at twenty-eight. It improved my ability to concentrate tremendously. I was able to sit down in front of the computer and write a paper. I was able to take notes in class and interact much more effectively. I didn't fall asleep in class. I only took (take) 25 mg. a day, which isn't much, but it has really helped my ADD. Some of my grades went from *C*'s to *A*'s, which is very gratifying when you're in an academic environment."

2.2

Preventing or Minimizing Behavior Problems During Transitions and Less Structured Times

Students with ADHD typically have the greatest behavioral difficulties during transitional times of the day in the classroom, as well as the school settings outside of the classroom that are less structured and less supervised (playground, cafeteria, hallways, bathrooms). In the average classroom, the time spent changing from one activity to the next cumulatively adds up to a significant number of minutes in the school day. Children with ADHD often have behavioral problems disengaging from or stopping one activity to move on to the next. The struggle they have with self-regulation and inhibition of their behavior frequently results in getting themselves in trouble during recess, riding the bus, waiting in the lunch line, on the way to the bathroom, in school assemblies, and so forth.

Some Ways to Help

Here are some ways to assist students to control their own behavior during unstructured time:

* Avoid catching students off-guard. Prepare for changes in routine (assemblies, substitute teachers, field trips) through discussion and modeling expectations. Talk about what will take place and teach the necessary behavior. Role play is helpful, especially for young students, in preparing for upcoming changes.
* Maintain a visual schedule that is reviewed and referred to frequently. When changes are to occur in the schedule, point them out in advance.

Classroom Transitions

* Communicate clearly when activities will begin and when they will end.
* Give specific instructions about how students are to switch to the next activity.
* Be sure to clearly teach, model, and have students practice and rehearse all procedures that will occur in changes of activities. This includes such things as the students' quick and quiet movement from their desks to the carpet area, putting away/taking out materials, and so forth.
* Use signals for transitions (playing a bar of music on a keyboard, flashing lights, ringing a bell or chimes, beginning a clapping pattern, using prompts such as "1, 2, 3 . . . eyes on me"). A signal indicates that an activity is coming to an end and children need to finish whatever they are doing.

Five-minute, three-minute, or one-minute warnings are often used. Such signals are helpful at all grade levels.

* Some teachers signal and tell students they will have a brief amount of time (three to five minutes) to finish what they are working on before the next activity or to clean up. They then set a timer for that amount of time.

* Primary grade teachers typically use songs or chants for transitions (for cleaning up, moving to the rug area, lining up).

* Build in stretch breaks and brief exercise between activities, particularly ones that require a lot of sitting or intense work and effort.

* Provide direct teacher guidance and prompting to those students who need it during transitions.

* Be organized in advance with prepared materials for the next activity.

* Reward smooth transitions. Many teachers use table points as an incentive to reward rows or table clusters of students who transitioned quickly and are ready for the next activity. As described in Section 2.1, some teachers use table points as a competition in the class (the one or two table groups with the most points at the end of the week earn the reward); other teachers reward every table of students when the group reaches a certain target number of points.

* Some teachers use whole class incentives for transitions. One technique is to place a circle on the chalkboard. Prior to making the transition (cleaning up after an activity that involved manipulatives or hands-on materials), the teacher signals the students, tells them that he or she will count to a certain number, and then proceeds to count. If everyone in the class manages to be ready with the cleanup by the time the teacher finishes counting, the teacher places a checkmark in the circle. If the whole class is not ready, the teacher says, "Oh well, maybe next time." If the class earns a specified number of checks in the circle by the end of the week, there is a class reward.

Transitions from Out-of-Classroom Activities Back to the Classroom

* It is helpful for teachers to meet their students after lunch, P.E., recess, and other activities outside of the classroom—and walk them quietly into the classroom.

* Set a goal for the class (everyone enters class after lunch/recess and is quiet and ready to work by a certain time). On successful days of meeting that goal, the class is rewarded by a move on a behavior chart.

* Use relaxation and imagery activities or exercises for calming after recess, lunch, and P.E. Playing music, singing, and/or reading to students at these times is also often effective.

Out-of-Classroom School Settings

* Teach, model, and practice appropriate behaviors and expectations for out-of-classroom activities (in the cafeteria, passing in hallways, during assemblies).

* Assign a buddy or peer helper to assist during these transitional periods and out-of-classroom times.

* It is important to have school-wide rules/behavioral expectations so that all staff members calmly and consistently enforce through positive and negative consequences. School-wide incentives and positive reinforcers (for example, "caught being good tickets" redeemable for school prizes) that are distributed by school staff to any student caught displaying targeted pro-social behaviors are helpful in teaching and motivating appropriate behaviors outside of the classroom.

* For students who have behavioral difficulty on the bus, an individual contract or monitoring form including the bus behavior on a daily report card should be arranged (with the cooperative efforts of the school, bus driver, and parent).

* Special contracts or some type of individualized behavior plan with incentives for appropriate behavior may need to be arranged for the playground, cafeteria, or

other such times of the day. If using a daily report card or monitoring form of some type, no reports of behavioral referrals in out-of-classroom settings for a specific period (for example, morning recess) can result in bonus points on the report card. (See Section 2.3 for information regarding daily report cards.)

* It is important that all staff be aware of the struggles children with ADHD often experience in non-structured environments. Awareness training of ADHD should be provided for personnel involved with supervision outside of the classroom.

* Staff members should identify and positively target those students in need of extra support, assistance, and careful monitoring outside of the classroom.

* Increase supervision during passing periods, lunch, recess, and school arrival/dismissal.

* Provide more choices of activities that children can engage in during recess and lunch periods (for example, hula hoops, jump rope, board games, library/computer, supervised games). It is helpful to have organized clubs and choices for students before and after school and during the break before/after lunch.

One of the biggest transitions students face is the move from one grade level to the next—particularly the changes from elementary to middle school, and middle school to high school. It is very helpful to prepare students (especially those with ADHD) by visiting the new school, meeting with counselors and/or teachers, practicing the locker combination, receiving the schedule of classes in advance, and practicing the walk from class to class.

2.3

Individualized Behavior Management, Interventions, and Supports

Teachers are often frustrated with the disruptive and challenging behaviors of many students with ADHD. It is important to build a large repertoire of strategies and skills to effectively address and manage those behaviors in the classroom. This section will provide tips for dealing with "challenging" or hard-to-manage students. It will focus on the individualized supports and interventions—the research-based approaches that work with this population of children and teens. These students typically need far closer monitoring, a higher rate and frequency of feedback, and more powerful incentives to modify their behavior than the average child.

Understanding the ABCs of Behavior

There are two fundamental principles of behavior: (1) challenging behavior occurs within the context of a child's interaction with his or her environment. As a result, changing the inappropriate behavior of a child requires educators first to identify, and second to change, relevant aspects of the environment that may contribute

to the problem (for example, instructional, curricular, or classroom variables). And (2) challenging behavior is meaningful, has a purpose, and serves a function for the child (Ryan, Halsey, & Matthews, 2003).

Behavior (B) is always something that can be *observed* and *measured*. For example, the number of times a child was out of his or her seat or how many times a student blurted out in class (during a certain time frame), the length of time it took to complete an in-class assignment, and so forth. With the ABCs of behavior, "B" stands for the behavior itself—what the child is actually doing that can be observed and measured objectively.

Prior to any behavior occurring, there are antecedents (A) to that behavior. The antecedents, as was discussed in Section 2.1, are typically the events or conditions that trigger the misbehavior. Teachers can prevent or minimize many undesired student behaviors by making adjustments to those antecedents. For example, making changes to the environment (change of seating, adding more structure or visual supports), to the instruction (providing more direct assistance, reducing the amount of time required to remain quiet by incorporating more partner talk opportunities during the lesson, modifying tasks/assignments), and so forth.

Following the misbehavior is some kind of consequence (C). The consequence may be either reinforcing or punishing to the child. It depends on an individual's needs and motivations. What could be perceived as a punishing consequence (for example, being sent out of the classroom) to the teacher, could actually be a reward for a student (who seeks to escape a task or enjoys the attention or stimulation received out of the classroom setting). Any time a problematic behavior repeatedly occurs, something is reinforcing or maintaining that behavior.

Often the functions or goals of target student behavior is to either *obtain* something (tangible item, attention, control, sensory stimulation) or to *avoid or escape* something (assigned tasks, activities, embarrassment, or negative emotions) (O'Neill, Horner, Albin, et al., 1997). Once the underlying motivation or function of a child's behavior is identified, that motivation may be used to determine the most logical and powerful behavioral consequences. For example, if the child is acting out in class to gain the attention of classmates, a behavioral program can be designed that rewards the child with peer attention for appropriate rather than inappropriate behavior (Illes, 2002).

In addition to classroom (group) behavior management systems (discussed in Section 2.1), students with ADHD will benefit greatly from individualized daily and/or weekly monitoring and reinforcement plans. When designing an individual behavior plan as an intervention for a student, it must be

* Tailored to address one or no more than a few specific, observable behaviors
* Tied to a reward or choice of rewards that is highly motivating for that individual student—a powerful enough incentive to motivate behavioral change
* Implemented consistently, reviewed frequently, and revised when it begins to lose its effectiveness

Target Behaviors

Examples of target behaviors (Rief, 2003) or goals selected for intervention in the individualized behavior plans of children with ADHD might include variations of

* On-task/effort (for example, turns in homework, on-task/working, starts seatwork right away, works quietly, uses class time effectively, pays attention, finishes/almost finishes assignments, shows good effort on tasks, participates)
* Cooperation and appropriate interactions with others (for example, uses appropriate language, refrains from fighting or arguing, gets along with peers, respects adults, works cooperatively, plays cooperatively, shares with classmates, solves problems peacefully)
* Following directions (for example, follows teacher instructions, obeys class rules, follows playground rules, listens to teacher, complies with adult requests without arguing)
* Showing preparedness, readiness to work, time management/organization skills (for example, brings all needed materials, arrives on time, is ready to work)
* Being in proper location (for example, stays in seat, participates and stays with group, remains in assigned area)
* Controlling impulsive verbal responses (for example, waits turn without interrupting, refrains from blurting, raises hand to speak)

Note: *Any of the target behaviors should be more specifically defined for the child, so it is clear what the criteria for success will be. For example, if any warnings will be given and, if so, how many; what each of the positive behaviors should look like and sound like, within what amount of time, the degree of accuracy expected, and so forth.*

The following are individualized interventions beneficial for students with ADHD.

Goal Sheets

With this technique, the child/teen identifies one goal to work on for the day or week (for example, organizing desk or locker; no fights; get caught up with incomplete math assignments). The student also plans the specific steps he or she will take to reach the goal. Some adult (for example, teacher or counselor) meets briefly in the morning with the student to discuss the goal and offer encouragement. At the end of the day, they meet again and reward success. Here are some sample statements:

* "I would like to improve _____."
* "This is my plan for reaching my goal _____."
* "If I am successful, I will earn _____."

STUDENT GOAL SHEET

My goal for the day/week is:

_____
_____
_____

This is my plan for reaching my goal:

1 _____
2 _____
3 _____

My reward for meeting the goal:

_____
_____

Student Name_____ Date _____

A+

Home Notes and Daily Report Cards

Home notes and daily report cards (DRCs) (Rief, 2003) are excellent tools for tracking and monitoring a student's social, academic, and/or behavioral progress at school. They are highly effective for communicating between home and school and for monitoring a child's daily performance. When parents are willing and able to consistently follow through with reinforcement at home for positive performance at school, it is a very powerful motivator for the student. Any means to forge a partnership between home and school and work together on improving specific behavioral goals is very beneficial for children with ADHD.

Basically, home notes and DRCs involve selecting and clearly defining one or more target behavior(s) to be the focus for improvement. The teacher is responsible for observing and rating daily how the child performed on the target behavior(s) and sending home the note or DRC at the end of the day with the student.

Parents are responsible for asking to see the note/DRC every day and reinforcing school behavior and performance at home. "Good days" in school (as indicated by the home/school note or DRC) will earn the child designated rewards at home on a nightly basis. Bonus rewards for a great week (for example, at least three out of five good days) may also earn the child or teen extra privileges on the weekend. It is recommended that parents back up the expectation that their son or daughter bring the note home daily by enforcing with some mild punishment (for example, being fined, losing some TV time) on those days the child "forgets" to bring the note home.

Home notes and DRCs can involve school rewards as well as home rewards. For example, a small school reward (for example, computer time, stickers, earned time for a preferred activity) can be given to the child at school on a "good day" and for a "good week" (for example, initially three days and later raise criteria to four days of successful performance out of the five), the student can earn a special activity reward at school on Fridays.

If the family is not able to follow through regularly with monitoring and reinforcement, it is best to do so at school. If the DRC is likely to get lost coming to and from school daily, then perhaps just a card that simply indicates "yes/no" or "met goal/didn't meet goal" can be sent home each day for parent notification of the student's performance, and the actual DRC remains at school. Parents can be asked to reward the child on the weekend if it was a "good week."

Creating a Daily Report Card

There are many variations of daily report cards. They basically require the following:

* Selecting the goals to be achieved and then defining those goals precisely
* Deciding on no more than three to five behaviors to work on improving and monitoring, and what will be the initial criteria for success (for example, at least five smileys out of eight possible, at least fifteen points out of a possible twenty for the day, 70 percent of possible points)
* Making a chart with time frames broken down (by periods of the day, subject areas, or whatever intervals fit the student's daily schedule and are reasonable for the teacher to monitor consistently)
* Putting designated target behaviors (for example, has all necessary materials, on-task, cooperating with classmates, following directions) on the other axis
* Marking at the end of each time frame a simple yes/no; +/–; thumbs up/thumbs down sign; smile/frown face
* Tallying the student's points at the end of the day to determine the net number of pluses (yeses, smiles) earned that day, and the student's overall performance (Did the student meet the criteria for success?)
* Informing parents of daily performance (preferably by the DRC coming home each day after school)
* Providing rewards accordingly (at home, school, and/or both), based on the child's performance on the DRC

Note: It is important that reinforcement be provided consistently and as promised. A well-coordinated system between home and school is the most effective.

Examples of DRCs and Other Monitoring Devices

Many middle schools use conduct sheets as a management tool. Teachers are asked to rate students, usually on a point scale (0 to 4) under "conduct" and "class work." For students with ADHD, those categories are too broad and must be defined precisely. These conduct sheets can be redesigned easily into DRCs by making the criteria very clear and awarding points objectively based on the specific behaviors listed under each category. Of course, to become a DRC, parents should be notified of the student's net points and successful days/weeks should be rewarded (at home and/or school). For example, on the student weekly progress report on page 125 there are four behaviors listed under conduct:

* Hands, feet, objects to yourself
* Respectful to adults and classmates
* Follows teacher directions
* Stays in your place unless you have permission (to move)

The teacher can now easily rate 0 to 4 based on how many of those four behaviors were observed during the class period. Also under class work are four specific behaviors:

* Participates in lessons and activities
* Comes to class prepared
* Gets started on assignments right away
* Stays on task and completes (or almost completes) assignments

Again, the student earns a 0 to 4 rating for the class period based on his or her performance of those four behaviors. To eliminate or reduce arguing about the teacher's rating, it is recommended that students on such a system know the rule: "Arguing about your score will result in an automatic 0 for that time frame."

WEEKLY BEHAVIOR REPORT

Name:_____ Teacher:_____ Week of:_____

BEHAVIOR	MONDAY		TUESDAY		WEDNESDAY		THURSDAY		FRIDAY	
	AM	PM	AM	PM	AM	PM	AM	PM	AM	PM
Stays in assigned place										
Uses class time effectively										
Respectful to adults & classmates										

Parent signature_____   ____ smiles per day earns_____

Yes, I did!   ____ smiles per week earns _____

One New York City middle school teacher using the above conduct/performance DRC took the system another step, which she found to be very effective. In her homeroom at the end of the day, those students on this DRC completed an entry in a daily log that included: name, date, total points earned, and corresponding rating (excellent, good, average, poor). In addition, they wrote a short reflection about their behavioral performance (what they need to work on, what they improved on). Any of the students who had at least three good or excellent days out of the week earned a special privilege or reward.

Here's one example of a student's log entries: "32 points—good. When kids talked to me, I did not talk back. I focused on my work. I am going to keep staying in the 'good or excellent.'" Another student's reflection entry was, "I was getting distracted a lot today and not getting my work done. I'm going to try harder tomorrow."

Daily report cards (DRCs) have been research-validated as an effective intervention for students with ADHD. They are highly recommended because they provide:

* Close monitoring of targeted behaviors
* The frequency and intensity of positive reinforcement that children/teens with ADHD need to maintain the motivation
* A means of measuring and determining improvement in functioning (for example, IEP goals)
* Increased communication with parents

✶ A means of reporting student performance throughout the day to parents and physicians, which is a useful tool in determining the effectiveness of medication on a child's daily functioning (Pelham, 2002)

For more detailed information about setting up a DRC, William Pelham Jr., Ph.D., a researcher and leader in the field of behavioral interventions for children with ADHD, has a packet of information entitled "How to Establish

_____'S DAILY REPORT

GOAL _____ DATE _____	stays seated		on task		follows directions	
	+	−	+	−	+	−
	+	−	+	−	+	−
	+	−	+	−	+	−
	+	−	+	−	+	−
	+	−	+	−	+	−
	+	−	+	−	+	−
	+	−	+	−	+	−
	+	−	+	−	+	−
	+	−	+	−	+	−
	+	−	+	−	+	−
	+	−	+	−	+	−
	+	−	+	−	+	−
	+	−	+	−	+	−
TOTAL						

a School-Home Daily Report Card," available and downloadable from his website at the Center for Children and Families, University of Buffalo, State University of New York—http://wings.buffalo.edu/psychology/adhd/. An adapted version can also be found on the website of National Initiative for Children's Healthcare Quality (www.nichq.org), as part of the "Caring for Children with ADHD: A Resource Toolkit for Clinicians" developed together with the American Academy of Pediatrics.

Options for Rewarding Successful Performance on Daily Report Cards

There are different options for rewarding students with a daily/weekly report card. Many DRCs use a leveled system of rewards as described by Pelham (2002). The greater the percentage of points earned, the higher the level of privileges or number of rewards that can be selected from the menu. For example, 75 to 89 percent of possible + marks (or yes marks) earns the child the privilege of choosing two things from the reward menu. Higher percentages earn more; lower percentages earn less. Another option for rewarding based on performance on the daily report card is having the reward contingent on the student successfully achieving a goal for the day or week (a target percentage of possible points).

When starting the program, it is important to make sure the child has immediate success. The target goal should be very much within the child's reach (depending on the baseline of

STUDENT WEEKLY PROGRESS REPORT

Name:_____ Class:_____ Teacher:_____ Week of:_____

| Daily Goal_____ | Weekly Goal_____ | Weekly Points Earned_____ | Reward_____ |

Period	MONDAY		TUESDAY		WEDNESDAY		THURSDAY		FRIDAY	
	Conduct	Classwork	Conduct	Classwork	Conduct	Classwork	Conduct	Classwork	Conduct	Classwork
1										
2										
3										
4										
5										
6										
7										
Earned points →										
	Student's Signature		*Student's Signature*		*Student's Signature*		*Student's Signature*		*Student's Signature*	
	Parent/Guardian Signature		*Parent/Guardian Signature*		*Parent/Guardian Signature*		*Parent/Guardian Signature*		*Parent/Guardian Signature*	

CONDUCT:
1. Hands, feet, objects to yourself + or –
2. Respectful to adults & classmates + or –
3. Follow teacher directions + or –
4. Stay in your place unless you have permission + or –

CLASSWORK:
1. Participates in lessons & activities + or –
2. Comes to class prepared + or –
3. Gets started on assignments right away + or –
4. Stays on task and completes or almost completes assignments + or –

I. The student will earn points based on the following: Unsatisfactory = 1 point, Fair = 2 points, Good = 3 points, Excellent = 4 points.
II. The number of points earned are based on the number of pluses: 4 pluses = 4 points, 3 pluses = 3 points, 2 pluses = 2 points, 1 plus = 1 point.
III. Indicate a goal for the day and for the week (e.g., 70% to 80% of daily goal and 70% to 80% of the weekly goal).
IV. The possible points per period are 8 (must meet 4 behavior & conduct criteria). Total points per day = 8 multiply by the number of class periods. Total points per week = Total per day multiply by number of days student is in attendance.

(Rief, 2003)

frequency of behaviors). For example, initially 60 or 70 percent of the possible number of points may be the goal, and if the child reaches the goal for the day, the pre-determined reward is delivered. Later, after a period of time successfully performing at 70 percent, the criteria can be raised slowly to 75 or 80 percent.

Chart Moves

As was described in Section 2.1, chart moves are effective strategies for reinforcing positive targeted behaviors. The examples in Section 2.1 are for whole class moves along a chart each time the class demonstrates a particular behavior. When the chart is completed, the class earns a reward. The same technique can be used successfully with individual students. Together with the child, a goal (target behavior) is selected and a chart of some kind is designed (for example, coloring in squares, placing stickers or stars in boxes, connecting dots). Whenever the target behavior is demonstrated or the goal is met, the child advances on his or her chart. When the entire chart is filled, a special reward is earned. It is recommended to have a few interim points along the way on charts that will take the child a while to complete. When reaching the interim points, a small reward is given, which will keep the reinforcement opportunities frequent enough to maintain the child's interest and effort.

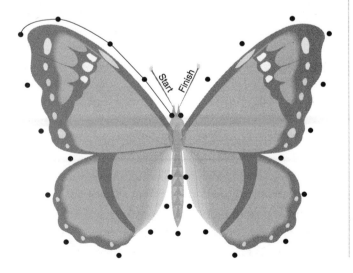

STUDENT CONTRACT

I, _____ , agree to do the following:
(Include criteria/standard for successful performance.)

_____

_____

_____

If I fulfill my part of this contract, I will receive the following reward(s):

_____

_____

This contract is in effect from (date) _____ to (date) _____.

It will be reviewed (daily___ weekly___ other_____).

Signed:

_____ _____ _____
   student   teacher   parent

Contracts

Contracts are another commonly used behavioral intervention. The contract is usually a two- or three-party agreement, which specifies the role each will perform in achieving a certain goal. It is tailored to address the individual student's areas of need. Together, the child and key adults identify and select one or more specific goals that the student agrees to work on improving. All parties then agree to the rewards (positive consequences) that will occur for meeting the goals; sometimes the contract includes a negative consequence that will occur for failure to do so. There is a place for signatures showing that all parties agree to the terms of the contract. The following is an example of such a contract:

Example: Charlie is a third-grade student with ADHD who is starting fights with peers during recess time. His teacher writes a contract in which Charlie agrees to stop fighting during recess. For each "fight-free day," Charlie will earn ten minutes of free time at the end of the school day. (Illes, 2002)

The terms of the contract should be perceived as fair, equitable, and reasonable. Individual contracts should be negotiated and discussed thoroughly. The child should not be overwhelmed with the terms of the contract. It is better to write a series of contracts than to construct one that is so complex it becomes unwieldy and possibly ineffectual (Walker, 1997).

Token Economy or Token Programs

Token programs use secondary reinforcers, or tokens, to provide students with immediate reinforcement for appropriate behavior. When the student earns a designated number of tokens, they may be exchanged for a primary reinforcement (such as a treat, small toy, or a highly valued activity). Thus, the tokens provide a reinforcement bridge during the time gap between the occurrence of the appropriate behavior and the provision of the primary reward. In this way, tokens may be used to provide students with ADHD the frequent and immediate reinforcement needed to sustain effort on low-interest tasks (Illes, 2002).

Token systems or programs are very effective at home and school. The tokens themselves, which are awarded easily and immediately in the form of points, poker chips, stickers, class money, punches on a card, and so forth, are later redeemed or cashed in for various privileges or rewards. Children with ADHD have significant difficulty delaying gratification. The immediate reward of the token helps students with ADHD maintain motivation in working towards the goal.

As with other behavioral programs, it is important that token programs focus on improving no more than a few clearly defined target behaviors and that expectations for improvement be realistic and achievable for that individual child. The program needs to be implemented consistently; and the rewards selected (or choice of rewards from a menu) must be valuable to the child in order to serve as an incentive for behavioral change.

Response Costs

Response costs were described in Section 2.1 for class (group) use. It is a particularly useful and effective method when used as an individualized behavioral program. Response cost techniques have been proven beneficial in modification of behavior in children with ADHD.

Similar to other reinforcement strategies, a reward is provided that is contingent on the child's behavior. However, unlike other reward programs, response cost focuses on the inappropriate rather than the appropriate behavior. Thus, it provides the ADHD child with a reward for reducing the frequency of an inappropriate behavior rather than for performing a specific appropriate behavior (Illes, 2002).

Token economy systems often include response cost as well. This means that, in addition to the child or teen earning tokens (for example, points, class money) for targeted desired behaviors, the child/teen can also lose or be deducted points/tokens for targeted misbehaviors. This method is a combination of positive reinforcement and response cost.

Response costs (penalties) are used all the time in daily life to discourage undesirable behavior, such as parking tickets, fines for traffic violations, yardage fines in football games assessed against the offending team for infractions such as clipping, interference, and so on (Walker, 1997). Strictly, a response cost system in the classroom would involve giving the child up-front a certain number of tokens determined by measuring roughly for an estimate of how often the inappropriate behavior typically occurs during certain time frames. To reduce the inappropriate targeted behavior, the number of tokens given up-front should be fewer (but not drastically less) than the baseline number of times the behavior typically occurs.

For example, if Leanne is physically aggressive (for example, hits, pushes, grabs things away from other children) approximately ten times every morning, then initially Leanne may be given six or seven tokens up-front. If Christopher uses profanity/obscene language at a rate of approximately fifteen times during P.E., he may be given ten tokens at the beginning of the period initially. Samantha, who blurts/talks out approximately ten times every math class, may be given seven tokens initially at the start of math class.

It is explained to the student on the response cost program that each incident of the inappropriate behavior results in losing a token. A reward is given if there are any remaining tokens at the end of the period. So initially a slight but reasonable reduction in the frequently occurring inappropriate behavior is rewarded; and then as the behavior begins to diminish, the number of tokens given at the beginning of each period (time frame) is gradually reduced. The program continues until the target inappropriate behavior has been reduced to a manageable level (not necessarily until it is totally extinguished).

The child does not have to be rewarded with a primary reinforcer. In fact, many would find it objectionable to reward a child with a prize for cussing or using obscene language nine times instead of the typical fifteen—or for still hitting classmates, even though it's only six instead of ten times. A secondary reinforcer can be used instead. For example, the reward for each response cost interval (in the cases above, morning, P.E. period, math class) in which the child successfully met the goal of having at least one remaining token can be to award the child a star or certain number of points, or allowing the child to make moves on his or her chart. The primary reinforcer (actual reward of a desired object, activity, or privilege) can be given when the chart is filled or when the student has accumulated a certain number of stars/points. Another method of rewarding the student can be that any remaining tokens at the end of a time interval can be tallied and cashed in later in the week as minutes toward a preferred activity.

Although emotionally fragile kids may become upset with fines, deductions, and such means, it is a technique known to be effective with ADHD children/teens. If using a token program that is a combination of positive reinforcement and response cost, it is very important that there be far more opportunities for points/tokens to be earned than taken away. Otherwise, the child will likely be frustrated and give up.

With any response cost program, the loss of the token should be implemented immediately after the behavior occurs and applied consistently. The child should never be allowed to accumulate negative points, and the subtraction of points should never be punitive or personalized (Walker, 1997). Also, if using secondary reinforcers as the immediate reward for there being any remaining tokens at the end of each interval, be careful not to make the long-term pay-off (when the child can actually receive the primary reward) too far down the road. This would result in the student with ADHD losing motivation to sustain the effort.

As with any behavioral program, the reward(s) the child may earn for successful performance must be powerful enough to be an incentive to change behavior. The rewards designated in the program must have meaning and value to that individual child or teen. It often helps to change the rewards frequently (or provide a menu of different reinforcers the child may choose from) in order to maintain interest in the program.

The following example is a behavior contract using a response cost technique that is developed and shared by Dr. Terry Illes, school psychologist in Utah's Jordan School District. Dr. Illes has several students using variations of these response cost charts. In this example, and others like it, first choose the problematic behavior to work on for the program (for example, talking at inappropriate times), then determine roughly how frequently the behavior occurs at certain times of the day. Monitoring times of the day are then established. The chart on page 129 shows every fifteen minutes throughout the day, but it could be half-hour periods or a few short intervals during only one or two subject areas or activities (for example, writing centers, whole class instruction on the carpet).

The numbers per time frame (1, 2, 3) are points that are crossed out for each occurrence of the inappropriate behavior. In this example, each time the student talks without waiting to be called on by her teacher, a point is removed (first 3, then 2 is crossed off). If there is one point remaining, a check mark is made under the column "great job" for that fifteen-minute period. If no points are remaining, then a check mark is placed under "try again." A daily treat is earned if she has six "great jobs" at the end of the day. Later, after experiencing success in reducing the talking-out behavior, the time frames can be lengthened (for example, to half-hour periods). Another option is to keep the fifteen-minute monitoring periods, but start with only two points instead of three—only one mistake allowed to be considered a "great job."

Self-Monitoring

Another behavioral technique that often helps reduce undesired behavior is self-monitoring of a specific behavior. This involves training the child in how to observe specific aspects of his or her behavior or academic performance, and to record those observations. For example, the student may be asked to observe whenever he or she calls out without raising his or her hand, is off-task when a signal is heard, is disruptive during a transition, and so forth (Parker, 2002). Other behaviors that can be self-monitored might include staying seated or in one's assigned place, completing work, keeping hands and feet to self, and working quietly.

Children typically record their behavior when self-monitoring on an index card or slip of paper at their desks. One popular self-monitoring program developed by Harvey Parker is called *The Listen, Look and Think* Program (Parker,

_____'S BEHAVIOR CHART

				Great Job	**Try Again**
10:45 – 11:00	1	2	3	_____	_____
11:00 – 11:15	1	2	3	_____	_____
11:15 – 11:30	1	2	3	_____	_____
11:30 – 11:45	1	2	3	_____	_____
1:30 – 1:45	1	2	3	_____	_____
1:45 – 2:00	1	2	3	_____	_____
2:00 – 2:15	1	2	3	_____	_____
2:15 – 2:30	1	2	3	_____	_____

Target Behavior: Raise hand and wait to be called on before talking
Consequences: 6 "Great Jobs" earn a daily treat

2000). It includes an endless cassette beep tape and self-monitoring forms. The tape runs during certain periods of the day (for example, independent seatwork). It is silent and at irregular intervals a beep is heard. Whenever the intermittent beep is heard on the tape, the child is to ask himself or herself, "Was I paying attention?" On the form, the child puts a checkmark indicating yes or no. Then the student is expected to immediately get back to work.

Rewards

The following are a few examples of possible rewards for school and home (Rief, 1998, 2003):

School Rewards/Privileges

* Breakfast or lunch with the teacher (or other staff member)
* Free/earned time (individual or class) for activities of choice, such as games, listening to music, drawing, working on special project, and accessing learning/interest centers
* Selecting items from class store or treasure chest
* Working with special materials/equipment
* Playing a special game or activity with friend(s)
* Responsibilities or privileges that are desirable (for example, taking care of class pet, assistant to other teacher or staff member, class messenger, operating AV equipment)
* Extra time/access to gym (for example, to shoot baskets), library/computer lab, music room
* Class money, tickets, or points redeemable at auctions/lotteries or class stores

Home Rewards/Privileges

* Special activity with parent/family
* Allowance/money
* Time for use on the computer/Internet, watching TV, or talking on the phone
* Purchase or rental of DVD or video
* Purchase of a desired item
* Friend for dinner or sleepover

* Playing special games
* Trips/outings
* Use of car
* Curfew extension
* Chore pass—doesn't have to do chore(s)
* Meal/dessert of choice
* Agreeing to drive child and friend(s) somewhere

Strategies to Aid Calming and Avoid Escalation of Problems

It is important that teachers and parents of children with ADHD be aware of strategies to prevent behavioral problems and how to intervene in a manner that helps the child/teen regain self-control, rather than trigger an escalation of problem behavior. Such strategies and interpersonal skills are particularly necessary with a child/teen who is emotionally fragile, overreactive, and/or has a tendency to be oppositional and confrontational. The following tips can be applied in school or home situations (Rief, 2003).

Watch for Signs and Intervene

Always watch for warning signs of a child or teen becoming frustrated, agitated, or overly stimulated. Be aware of triggers to misbehavior and make adjustments with regard to task-demand, environmental conditions, and so forth.

At the first signs of a child beginning to lose control, intervene at once by:

* Providing a cue or prompt (for example, standing near the student and placing a gentle hand on shoulder)
* Using a pre-arranged private signal (for example, nonverbal cue) as a reminder to settle down
* Diverting the child's attention, if possible
* Redirecting to a different location, situation, or activity (for example, run an errand/message to the office; bring a note to a neighboring class; ask to help pass out materials; sharpen a can of spare pencils).

* Cueing the child or teen to use relaxation techniques (for example, visualization, deep breathing, counting slowly, progressive muscle relaxation)
* Prompting the student to use self-talk that has first been taught as a self-regulation strategy (for example, "I am calm and in control." "I need to chill out." "I can handle this." "Just relax and stay calm.")
* Reminding the child about rewards and consequences
* Providing time and a means to regroup, regain control, and avoid the escalation of behaviors

Offer a Break

It is often helpful to encourage a child to take a break when there are warning signs of him or her beginning to lose control. In the classroom an area can be designated for this purpose. Many teachers (typically in primary grades and special education classes) set up an area for this purpose. It is not a punitive measure or "time-out," but is meant to be accessed by students briefly as a preventive strategy before behaviors escalate to a higher level. Such an area ("take-a-break" or "cool-down" spot) is equipped with something visually calming for the child to look at (for example, aquarium, lava lamp) and something to hold (for example, stuffed animal or Koosh® ball). A rocking chair in that location may be helpful, as rocking can also be a calming technique, or perhaps some soothing music (on a tape recorder with headset). Some teachers give these room locations names such as "Hawaii" (or some other name that the class agrees is a pleasant, relaxing reference).

Students are directed to or asked if they need to visit the cool-down area for a short amount of time when feeling agitated or angry ("Would you like to go to Hawaii for a few minutes?") The child may also request to go to that spot or signal for permission to do so for a short amount of time. This is an appropriate strategy the teacher may encourage the child to use to help him- or herself to regain better self-control and management of his or her behavior.

Note: *Again, this is NOT a "time-out," which is a negative, corrective consequence that must be time away from anything rewarding.*

Provide for Movement and Physical Activities

Physical activities (for example, brisk walking, jogging, swinging, pushing/pulling activities, pounding/manipulating clay) are also excellent means of calming and alleviating stress.

Watch Your Own Behavior and Communication Style

When communicating with a child or teen who is escalating in his or her behaviors and beginning to lose control:

* Speak softly and slowly.
* Watch your body language (relaxed).
* Visually prompt whenever possible (for example, pointing to visual cues depicting the expected behavior).
* Offer choices.
* Try to defuse a potential situation, and provide support.

It is *very important* to be composed and calm when interacting with a disruptive student. Take a few deep breaths before interacting with a student if you find yourself angry and upset. When responding to the student's disruptive/inappropriate behavior, try to do so away from an audience. It is best to communicate quietly and in a manner that is private between you and the student, not audible to the whole class.

In Section 2.1, it was pointed out that one of the best management tools teachers have is using their influence by moving toward, standing near, and positioning themselves close to a disruptive student and by communicating with eye contact to the student the need to discontinue disruptive behavior. However, teachers must be culturally sensitive to those students who have difficulty returning eye contact, as in some cultures it is disrespectful to do so. In such cases, never demand eye contact from the child.

Tips for Dealing with "Challenging" or "Difficult" Kids

The following suggestions are appropriate for both teachers and parents (Rief, 2003):

* Watch for triggers of misbehavior (for example, time of day, the activity/expectations), and try to prevent it by adjusting those triggers (antecedents)—beginning with a plan of early intervention.

* Plan a response and avoid "reacting" to challenging behavior (especially when you are in an emotional state). Do not feel compelled to give an immediate response in dealing with situations until you are in a calm, thinking state. Feel free to quietly and privately say to the child/teen, "We will deal with this after class (or after dinner)" or "I'm upset right now. I need time to think about this before we discuss the consequence of your behavior. I'll get back to you."

* It is okay to call for a break. Parents, go to a different room, take an exercise break or something away from each other. Teachers, provide the student with cooling-off options (time and space to regroup).

* Discuss, problem-solve, and negotiate solutions when both parties have had time to cool down and are in a calm, thinking mode.

* Realize that you cannot control anyone else's behavior. Change what you *can* control . . . yourself (for example, your attitude, body language, voice, strategies, expectations, and the nature of the interaction).

* Physically relax your body before dealing with situations. Take a few deep breaths. Unfold your arms and relax your jaw. Lower your voice. Cue yourself to be calm.

* Disengage from power struggles. Remember that you cannot be forced into an argument or power struggle. You only enter into one if you choose to do so (it takes two). Say, for example, "I am not willing to argue about this now. I will be free to discuss it later if you wish after class."

* Affirm and acknowledge the child/teen's feelings ("I see you're upset." "I understand that you are angry now." "I can see why you would be frustrated.").

* Express your confidence in his or her ability to make good choices. Communicate your hope that he or she will choose to cooperate. Provide choices: "I can't make you _____. But your choices are either _____ or _____."

* Avoid *"why"* questions (for example, "Why did you do this?" "Why did you do that?") Most kids cannot respond to that question—certainly not a child with ADHD. Instead, use *"what"* and *"how"* questions (for example, "What are you supposed to be doing right now?" "What do you want?" "What did we discuss?" "What would have been a better choice?" "How do you think that worked for you?" "What would you like to see happen?" "What is your plan to solve the problem?" "What can I do to help you?" "How would you like to handle that?" "How can I help you?").

* *Do not:* take the behavior personally, take the bait, demand, or threaten.

* Avoid nagging, scolding, lecturing, and any head-on battles or confrontations.

* Try to maintain your sense of humor.

* Send "I" messages ("I feel _____ when you _____ because _____." "I want/need you to _____.").

* Speak privately—away from an audience. Deal with behavior as discreetly as possible.

* Use the "broken record" technique. Respond by repeating your directions with the same words and calm, neutral voice.

* Use the words "however" and "nevertheless" (for example, "I understand you are feeling _____. However. . ." or "That may be _____. Nevertheless. . . ").

* Do all you can to build the relationship and take an active interest in the child/teen's life. The more challenging the child, the greater the need to make the effort to build

a positive relationship and more personal connection with that student. Increase one-on-one opportunities to meet with the student, conference, and establish a supportive relationship.

* Take time to actively listen to the child. Be attentive. Listen without interjecting your opinions. Ask a lot of open and clarifying questions. Rephrase and restate what was said. Avoid being judgmental in your interactions.

* Show caring and empathy.

* Try to determine whether there is another underlying problem (for example, poor reading skills; conflict with someone that needs to be resolved; or other reasons).

* Work together on establishing goals and identifying positive reinforcers that will be meaningful and motivating to the child/teen.

* Forge a strong home/school alliance with a positive behavioral plan in place.

* Teach problem-solving strategies (for example, identifying the problem, brainstorming possible solutions, evaluating pros and cons, choosing one and trying it, reviewing effectiveness, trying another if it wasn't working).

* If the child/teen appears on the verge of a "meltdown," try prompting the child to use self-calming, self-regulation techniques (for example, deep breathing, counting backwards, relaxation techniques).

* Seek opportunities for the student to feel more connected to the school as a positive contributor. For example, train and assign him or her as a peer tutor to a younger student, an assistant in the computer lab, or other school job that is valued by that student.

* Remember that children/teens with ADHD are typically not deliberately trying to aggravate you. Remind yourself that behaviors are stemming from their neurobiological disorder. However, those children with ADHD and the co-existing condition of oppositional defiant disorder (ODD) often do deliberately provoke a confrontation. Be aware, as well, that arguments are stimulating, and that children with ADHD do seek stimulation. So try to avoid getting pulled into an argument.

Dr. Ian Wallace suggests when a child or teen is oppositional to use language such as "Guess I can't talk to you," rather than "Don't you dare talk to me in that voice" or "I can't talk to you if you keep yelling. But then again you could calm a bit, and I can. It's up to you, not me." He recommends walking away from the situation briefly to a definite place in order to cool off for a second and avoid a head-on battle. "I'm just going to check my voice messages now [or some other brief activity], and then I'll be back. You decide what's going to happen next, and let me know when I come back" (Wallace, 1996).

What Is an FBA?

"A functional behavioral assessment (FBA) is a set of strategies for assessing the interaction between a behavior and the environment to form an educated guess about the function of that behavior. The goal of an FBA is to improve the effectiveness and efficiency of behavioral support for students, by linking intervention directly to the function of the behavior" (Sugai, Horner, & Gresham, 2002).

Since the reauthorization of IDEA in 1997, school districts have been required to conduct FBAs under some circumstances (for example, if a change of placement is to occur due to behavior for a student with an IEP). The information derived from the FBA is then utilized in the development of the behavioral intervention plan (BIP). These are typically done by school teams for students in special education whose behavior(s) are significantly impeding their school performance. However, FBAs and BIPs are very helpful in addressing the needs of any student with behavioral challenges impacting their school success.

An FBA is a multi-method problem-solving strategy. Standard components of an FBA include (Ryan, Halsey, & Matthews, 2003):

* Gathering descriptive information (for example, through interviews, informant rating scales, direct observation, record reviews) about the behavior and the environmental events that surround it.
* Forming hypotheses, or "informed guesses," about the function of the behavior, based on the descriptive data that teams collect.
* The hypotheses guide the team in developing the individually designed interventions, which teach socially appropriate alternative skills to replace problem behavior; the replacement behavior serves the same function for the student (for example, hand raising to access attention versus blurting out), in a manner that is more socially appropriate within that setting.
* The team then evaluates the accuracy of the hypothesis by monitoring the progress of the intervention.

The following are two case examples of hypotheses based on the ABCs determined from a functional behavioral assessment.

Amanda

Antecedents: During independent reading time of the day

Behavior(s): Amanda is likely to be out of her seat, wandering, and talking to students who are trying to do their reading (disturbing them); knocked her book off the table a couple times (deliberately).

Consequence(s): Teacher is frequently near her desk redirecting or reprimanding; classmates complain she is bothering them. Sent out of room to counselor.

Hypothesis Statement: Amanda is likely engaging in the above behaviors in order to protest and escape a frustrating task demand (independent reading), and to seek attention.

Joel

Antecedents: During cooperative group assignments (with three or four peers/group)

Behavior(s): Joel is likely to leave the group or engage in behaviors such as negative comments to peers, grabbing or hoarding materials.

Consequences: Group partners let Joel be in charge of the materials. Sometimes the teacher removes Joel from the group to sit and work by himself for not cooperating, but often he is not held accountable to do the group assignment.

Hypothesis Statement: Joel is likely engaging in the above behaviors in order to escape from the effort of the task or escape the group situation; to obtain power and control in the group situation; and perhaps to obtain attention.

FBAs involve gathering information in order to identify the following:

* Setting events (lack of sleep, forgetting to take medication, routine was disrupted, change of foster homes) or anything that makes the problem behavior or situation worse
* Triggering antecedents (specific situations, events, performance or activity demands, times, certain people) that precede and are likely to set off the occurrence of the problem behavior
* A clear description of the problem behavior, as well as how often it occurs and how long it lasts (frequency, intensity, duration)
* When and where the behavior is most likely and least likely to occur
* A desirable or acceptable alternative to the problem behavior
* The consequences that immediately follow the behavior and may be maintaining the problem behavior (for example, what usually happens after the behavior and the responses of peers and adults to the behavior)
* A hypothesis statement, prediction, or best guess about the function of the undesirable behavior or the basic need that is being met by the problem behavior (What does the child get/obtain or escape/avoid by that behavior?) The following are examples of some hypotheses: (a) The problem behavior occurs because Steven is trying to avoid paper/pencil tasks; (b) The problem behavior occurs because Yvette is trying to get attention and avoid feeling inadequate.
* A hypothesis or prediction about how the problem could be reduced. For example, Steven's problem behaviors may be reduced by providing writing accommodations such as reduced written demands, teaching him to ask for help appropriately when frustrated, and allowing Steven to access the computer/word processor. Amanda's problem behaviors may be reduced by providing

books for independent reading of her choice and level, providing remediation to build her skills, allowing her to read quietly with a partner instead of independently, or allowing her to follow along in the text while listening to the book on tape, or by providing the opportunity to visit the counselor as a reward at another time of the day (not as a consequence for misbehavior).

What Is a BIP?

After the FBA is conducted, the team uses that information to develop a proactive and positive behavioral intervention plan (BIP) for the student, which, according to Rankin, Dungan, Allison, et al. (2002), includes:

* Defining the target behavior and function the behavior serves the student
* Antecedent/setting event strategies— altering in some way any of the antecedent conditions that tend to trigger the problem behavior (for example, environmental, curricular, instructional factors)
* Identifying the replacement behaviors the team wants the child to exhibit (the behavioral goals and objectives stated on the IEP)
* Teaching any needed alternative skills (for example, social skills, conflict resolution/ anger management techniques)
* Skill building and reinforcement strategies (for example, use of specific behavioral programs/interventions as described throughout this section and identifying reinforcers that would be motivating and appropriate for this child)
* Reduction strategies—identifying appropriate corrective consequences for this specific child that takes into account the functions of his or her behavior
* Any additional accommodations or modifications to the student's program that would provide more positive ways of getting his or her needs met

Guiding Questions for Behavioral Issues

The special education team from Federal Way Public Schools in the state of Washington developed the following guiding questions that are very useful for school teams in obtaining background information/data for the FBA process. These guiding questions can also be used in the general education pre-referral and intervention process for any student exhibiting behavioral problems. School teams may wish to use these questions as a guide to learn more about what may be causing a student's behaviors, and determine the steps that should be taken to help that youngster.

After the guiding questions are answered, the school team then asks the processing questions on page 137 to determine next steps:

Federal Way Public Schools Guiding Questions for Behavioral Issues

To guide teams in efforts to develop a deeper understanding of problem behaviors so they can work together to identify and implement effective intervention strategies:

   I. Identify school staff who work with this student.
  II. Identify non-school agencies or persons working with this student. Is there a current release of information?
 III. Describe the family/home environment: Identify all people living in the home. Are there any environmental factors that may be impacting the student's success at school? Are there any times when the student is unsupervised? What is the student's typical weekend? What is parents' support network?
  IV. Describe the communication between home and school: Who initiated the communication, how often, and for what reasons?
   V. Student's general information: What are the strengths, interests, hobbies of student? Describe the student's support network. Are there any cultural issues that may impact student's school success or adjustment? Describe current health and medical concerns (for example, possible issues of attendance, hygiene, sleep patterns); previous health and/or medical concerns (for example, past surgeries, hospitalizations, medications). Medications being taken (name, dosage/frequency, where taken, prescribing doctor, procedure for administration). Are there any concerns regarding the medication/treatment plan? Are there any losses or traumatic situations which are significant?
  VI. Student's educational information: Currently on an IEP? Has student been retained? Number of schools attended? Current progress and modifications made in academic subjects. Describe the following for student: communication mode/needs/issues, learning style, opportunity to make choices, response to correction, rapport with staff/other students, feelings about school. Assessment data: Summarize pertinent information from cumulative file review, health record review, disciplinary review.
 VII. Student's social information: Plays best with (1 or 2 children, large group, alone); friends are usually (same age, older, younger, same sex, opposite sex, both). Does child fight with other children frequently? If yes, where? Anger management—if an issue, how often and severe?

* Do all school staff see the problem and issues the same way?
* Do additional referrals need to be made?
* Do we need any additional or more current information from people currently working with this student?
* Does the student and/or family need to be connected with additional services?
* What, if anything, can be done to enhance effective communication with the family?
* How do the student's communication needs impact behavior?
* How is the family/home environment impacting the student?
* How can the school better support the family?
* Does the student need further medical considerations?
* Does the student need a stronger support network?
* Does the student need further academic modifications?
* How can the classroom environment meet the student's needs and learning style?
* How can the student's self-esteem be enhanced? Does this student need more success/validation? Does student need more opportunities to be a leader? contribute to school? communicate his or her feelings? let off steam? make choices during the day? Does student need a mentor or buddy? help making friends? more individual attention? tangible rewards? conflict resolution training?
* What are the top three issues of concern?

Many children and teens with ADHD have significant behavioral challenges that are very impairing in their life—impacting heavily on their academic and social success. These children need a great deal of support and intervention, as well as the commitment and determination of significant adults to be by their sides and help them, as frustrating and difficult as that may be. It is imperative that educators, parents, and clinicians acquire as much knowledge as possible about the strategies/interventions proven effective for these children and work together in the implementation of these supports at home, at school, and in the community.

Strategies to Increase Listening, Following Directions, and Compliance

One of the key frustrations for teachers and parents of children with ADHD is getting the child to stop, listen, and comply with adult directions or "commands." There are a number of reasons children or teens with ADHD may have difficulty with compliance that have nothing to do with being deliberately defiant. These include (a) their struggle inhibiting and controlling their behavior; (b) being unable to readily stop and disengage from what they are doing (particularly if it is a fun activity or of high interest to the child); or (c) not being able to quickly switch gears at the adult's request to do something that is less motivating. In addition, (d) inattention reduces the likelihood that the child actually listened or heard the directions and (e) working memory weaknesses may also result in the child more easily forgetting the directions that were given.

Tips for Teachers and Parents

Here are some teaching strategies to help students with listening, attending to, and following directions:

* Wait until it is quiet and you have students' attention before giving instructions. Do not talk over students' voices, and be sure to face students when you give directions.

* You may need to walk over to touch or physically cue certain students for their focus prior to giving directions. If giving a specific direction to an individual child with ADHD, do so in close proximity, try to obtain eye contact, and state the child's name before giving directions.

* Train students that a specific auditory or visual signal (chimes, clap pattern, flickering lights) will indicate that students are to immediately stop what they are doing and focus on the teacher.

* Give concise, clear (to the point) verbal directions. Speak in simple, short sentences, avoiding a lot of unnecessary talk.

* Provide multisensory instructions—visual cues and graphics along with simple verbal explanations. Model what to do—show the class. Leave visual models in the classroom as a reference.

* Read written directions to the class and have students color highlight or circle/ underline key words in the directions.

* Write on the board a few key words, picture cues, phrases, and page numbers. Post directions needed for tasks in a consistent spot on the board, and leave them there for reference. Also provide, whenever possible, task cards with visual prompts and simple

written instructions at the student's desk, table, or work areas where the task is to be performed.

* Avoid multiple-step instructions—a string or chain of directions. Provide, whenever possible, one instruction at a time. If multi-step directions are used, always clearly delineate the steps and sequence (1, 2, 3) of the directions in writing. Break down multi-part tasks into smaller steps, simplifying directions for each phase of the task/assignment.

* Always check for understanding of directions by having individual students volunteer to repeat or rephrase your directions to the whole class.

* It is helpful to use a partner for clarification of directions: "Tell your partner what we are going to be doing on page 247." Use a buddy system for clarification and assistance with directions, as needed.

* Provide follow-up after you give directions. Give frequent praise and positive feedback when students are following directions and/or making a good attempt to do so.

* Make sure to give complete directions, including what you expect them to do (a) if they have any questions and (b) when they are finished with the task/assignment.

* Provide for a discreet means of clarifying directions without calling attention to and embarrassing individual students who need extra help (for example, use of private signals). Keep in mind that you may often need to provide more assistance and structure to enable students with ADHD to follow directions.

Compliance is a completion of a specific request and/or following previously taught rules. By around eight years old, most children comply with 60 to 80 percent of requests given by adults. A compliance rate of less than 60 percent indicates a problem with either ability (including attention/understanding) or motivation (Robinson, 2000).

Teachers may assume that a child or teen is deliberately being disobedient and ignoring or defying a teacher's direction or command. At times this is the case (especially if the child has oppositional defiant disorder). However, typically, this is not the reason for the child's noncompliance. Instead, it may be due to poorly issued or stated directives or commands on the part of the adult—and consequently, the message was not accurately conveyed or processed.

The following recommendations about how to state commands in an effective manner that increases compliance come from the works of Walker and Walker (1991), Forehand and McMahon (1981), Morgan and Jensen (1988), and Barkley (2000):

* Focus on the behavior you want the student(s) to *start,* rather than *stop,* and state the directive or command in the form of what you want them *to do.* For example: "Look at the chart," "Pick up your pencil," or "Turn to your assignment calendar."

* Be careful not to use vague language that is open to interpretation and lacks enough precise information ("Behave appropriately," "Clean up," "Get ready," "Be respectful," or "Do careful work"). Instead, be specific in what you expect to see (for example, "Eyes looking at me," "Bottoms in your chairs," "Book open to page 21," and "Desks cleared except for pencil").

* Avoid issuing a directive or command in the form of a question (for example, "Would you open your books to page. . .?" "Why don't you go back to your seat now?"). Clearly state the expectation ("Michael, go back to your seat now.") with authority.

* Adults have the tendency to keep on talking and elaborating after giving a direction or command. It is best to state the direction and remain silent (without additional verbalizing or restating), and then to wait approximately ten seconds to allow time for the child to comply. If the child does not begin the task within ten seconds, then

issue a "precision command." This technique involves (a) stating the child's name; (b) repeating the command but preceded by the words "You need to" ("Michael, you need to sit down right now.") (Morgan & Jensen, 1988).

* If the student complies at this point, praise and positively reinforce immediately after the child follows the direction. However, if the child does not comply after the precision command, provide a mild negative consequence.

Here are some parenting strategies to help children and teens with listening, attending to, and following directions:

* Get your child's attention directly before giving directions. This means in close proximity, face-to-face, and obtaining direct eye contact. You may need to walk over to touch or physically cue your child prior to giving directions.
* Do not attempt to give directions or instructions if competing with the distraction of TV, music, video games, and so forth. Before giving directions, you may need to turn those off or ask your child to do so (Barkley, 2000).
* Show your child what you want him or her to do. Model and walk through the steps. Always check for understanding of directions. Have your child repeat or rephrase what you asked him or her to do.
* Depending on the developmental level of your child, one direction at a time is often all your son or daughter is capable of remembering and following through on. Do not give a series of directions.
* Break down lengthy or complex tasks into smaller steps that you want done. Give one step at a time.
* Provide multisensory instructions by using a visual chart of tasks or chores your child is expected to do. A helpful technique for young children is to draw pictures on a chart hanging in the room that shows the sequence of morning or evening activities, for example (1) clothing (to get dressed); (2) cereal bowl (to show eating breakfast); (3) hairbrush and toothbrush. As your child completes the next task, he or she moves a clothespin down the chart next to that corresponding picture (Rief, 2003).

* Use color to get your child's attention with anything you put in writing (key words, pictures, and so forth).
* Write down the task you want done (words or pictures) and give that written direction or task card to your child for easy reference.
* Keep directions clear, brief, and to the point—reduce unnecessary talking and elaboration.
* Be sure to give frequent *praise* and *positive feedback* when your child follows directions and/or is making a good attempt to do so.
* Provide follow-up when you give directions (for example, inspect, check your child's work, and praise a job well done). Be sure to acknowledge and positively reinforce immediately after your child follows directions appropriately. Let your son or daughter know you notice and appreciate when he or she does so.
* Reward your child for following directions, as appropriate, for example: "You did a great job straightening up your room. You get to . . . (choose a game, have a snack, go outside and play)."
* Remember that children with ADHD have difficulty responding and following through without structuring, adult prompting, and cueing. If noncompliant, examine what you asked your son or daughter to do and see whether you provided enough structure and assistance to enable your child to follow through.
* It is easy to forget that, even though they are at an age where they *should* remember and be able to do a task independently, children and teens with ADHD developmentally may not be able to do so and require

some of the supports that a younger child would normally need.

* Try turning unpleasant chores and tasks into more pleasant or motivating experiences by making a game of it whenever possible. For example, try *Beat the Clock* challenges such as, "Let's see if you can finish putting all of your toys away while the commercials are still on (or before the alarm goes off, the song ends, and so forth)." (Rief, 2003)

* Timers are very effective tools for increasing your child's motivation and compliance in starting and completing tasks (for example, "It is now time to go upstairs and get in your pajamas. I'm setting the timer now for seven minutes. See if you can beat the clock.").

Here are some ideas of what parents can do to increase their child's compliance:

Note: The following recommendations about how to state commands in an effective manner that increases compliance come from the works of Walker and Walker (1991), Forehand and McMahon (1981), Morgan and Jensen (1988), and Barkley (2000).

Many times we adults request a particular behavior from a child—asking for the child's cooperation. Other times, there is the need to make a direct command—exerting one's authority when necessary for a situation. Whenever issuing a direct command, the adult must be prepared to follow through to ensure that compliance occurs.

* Use clear, well-stated commands. What you may interpret as your child's noncompliance may actually be the result of you not effectively communicating your directions.

* Focus on the behavior you want *started*, rather than *stopped*. Before issuing a directive or command to your son or daughter, think in terms of what you want to see your

child doing instead of what he or she is currently doing. Give your directions/commands as a direct statement and be specific, for example: "Lights off in fifteen minutes," "Sit with your bottom in the chair," "Hang up the wet towel, please."

* Do not use vague language that is open to interpretation and lacks enough precise information ("Clean your room," "Get ready," "Be nice to your brother"). Be precise in what you mean. For example, "Clean your room" means (1) clothes hung in closet or placed in drawers and (2) toys in storage bins.

* Do not continue to talk, explain, and elaborate after giving a direction or command. Instead, state what you want your child to do, and then stop talking to give your child the chance to comply without interruption.

* Commands should never be stated in the form of a question (for example, "Would you get in your pajamas, please?" "Isn't it time to get busy on your homework?" "Why don't you leave your brother alone?" "Are you ready to turn off the lights?"). If you do so, be prepared for your child responding with the word "no" to your appeal.

* Do not bark orders and demands or use an intimidating, wimpy, or emotional tone of voice. Instead, use a firm, matter-of-fact, and neutral tone of voice, but one that conveys that you mean business and will follow through.

* After issuing a directive or command, do not repeat, continue to verbalize, add on new directions, or intervene in any manner without waiting a minimum of five or ten seconds. It is important to wait a reasonable amount of time (depending on the situation) to enable your child to comply. If your child does not comply with the directive the first time given, give a "precision command." This time be sure to first say the child's name, followed by the words: "You need to . . ." For example, "Justin, you need to get in your pajamas now." Provide praise if your child follows the direction

this time, and provide a mild negative consequence (a response cost, brief time-out, loss of privilege such as TV time) if your child still does not comply. Then reissue the command and continue the process until your son or daughter does comply (Morgan & Jensen, 1988).

Compliance Training

School psychologist Dr. Terry Illes recommends the following procedure for training children to listen and comply with adult directions. It is a technique that parents and teachers of children with ADHD may wish to use with younger children (through third grade).

1. Give the command and wait ten seconds (counting silently or verbally) for the child to comply.

2. If he or she does not, provide the precision command, for example, "William, *you need to* open your book to page 12" or "Sarah, you need to turn around and face forward." Again, begin the counting and reward or punish accordingly for compliance. The task given as a directive should be something the child is able to start within ten seconds and to complete within a short amount of time (coming to the table, opening a book to a certain page, taking out a pencil, putting an item away). The situations chosen for compliance training need to be ones that the adult is able and willing to monitor and enforce.

3. Only a few situations per day should be used for compliance training. If the child complies with the command (begins the task before the adult counts to ten silently or aloud), a reward is provided. Besides praise, the child also immediately receives a token or gets to make a move on his or her chart. A certain number of tokens (stars, points) or reaching a target level on the chart earns the child a designated reward.

4. If the child does not begin to comply by ten seconds after the precision command is given, or if the task is not completed within a short but reasonable time limit, the child would receive a punishment (time-out, loss of privilege), for example, "Cherise, you need to put your pencil sharpener back in you desk before I count to ten." When the counting starts, there is no other interaction (discussion, arguing with the child). The child learns quickly that the only strategy available to stop the teacher or parent from counting is to comply.

5. After each act of appropriate compliance, the student moves up one square on his or her compliance chart (as shown on page 144).

6. Each day, the teacher (or parent) should color in the square that the child must reach to earn a daily reward. For example, a good starting point is square number 5 or 6 (representing a compliance rate of 50 or 60 percent). If the sixth square is selected, the child will earn a daily reward if that square is reached. When able to consistently comply at that level, then the expectations may be raised and the seventh square may be set as the daily goal. The program should be continued until the student is able to consistently comply at the rate of 90 percent (Illes, 2002).

Note: *Dr. Illes recommends that parents or primary grade teachers wishing to use this compliance training strategy with a child only give a few precision commands a day (perhaps ten) and restrict them to certain times of the day.*

"YES, I WILL" CHART

Week of_____

Monday	Tuesday	Wednesday	Thursday	Friday
10	10	10	10	10
9	9	9	9	9
8	8	8	8	8
7	7	7	7	7
6	6	6	6	6
5	5	5	5	5
4	4	4	4	4
3	3	3	3	3
2	2	2	2	2
1	1	1	1	1

TARGET BEHAVIOR

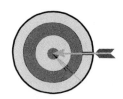

WHEN THE TEACHER GIVES ME A COMMAND, I WILL:

_____Say, "Yes, I will"
_____And, then I will do it before the count of ten

Attention!! Strategies for Engaging, Maintaining, and Regulating Students' Attention

*B*eing able to capture and hold our students' interest and attention is not always an easy task. Keeping a student with ADHD focused and on-task is a monumental challenge to teachers, and one that requires experimenting with a variety of approaches.

Getting and Focusing Students' Attention (Rief, 2003)

Following are a number of ideas for capturing students' attention in positive ways:

* Arouse students' curiosity and anticipation: ask an interesting, speculative question; show a picture; tell a little story; or read a related poem to generate discussion and interest in the upcoming lesson.
* Try "playfulness," silliness, humor, use of props, and a bit of theatrics to get attention and peek interest.
* Use storytelling, real-life examples, and anecdotes. Children of all ages love to hear stories (particularly personal ones, such as something that happened to the teacher when he or she was a child).
* Add a bit of mystery by bringing in one or more objects relevant to the upcoming lesson in a box, bag, or pillowcase. This is a wonderful way to generate predictions and

can lead to excellent discussions or writing activities.

* Model excitement and enthusiasm about the upcoming lesson.
* Explain the lesson's purpose and importance. Identify the objectives, content standards being addressed, and ultimate goals or outcomes to be achieved by the end of the session or unit.
* When giving examples, use students' names, experiences, and other means of helping students identify with the topic being discussed.
* Activate students' prior knowledge and draw on their past experiences. Elicit discussion and use strategies that enable students to see the relevance of the lesson you are about to teach, and make connections with past learning or experiences.
* Provide students with an overview of the major points they will be studying and their relationship to prior learning.
* Graphic organizers (of which there are numerous kinds) are excellent tools to focus attention, as well as in helping students organize and comprehend ideas/information.
* Post a few key points to be attentive to, listen for, and think about during the lesson.
* Students with ADHD are particularly drawn to novelty in their environment. Keep this in mind when planning lessons.

Auditory Techniques for Getting Students' Attention (Rief, 2003)

* Signal auditorily through the use of musical instruments (ringing a bell, chimes, or xylophone, playing a bar or chord on a keyboard or guitar).

* There are various toys that make a novel sound that may be an interesting auditory signal; and beepers or timers may be used.

* Use a clap pattern. You clap a particular pattern, and students repeat the clap pattern back to you.

* Use a clear verbal signal (for example, "Freeze. . . This is important. . ." "Everybody. . . Ready. . ." or "1, 2, 3, eyes on me").

* Use your voice to get attention, making use of effective pauses and tone variation (whispering also works).

* Be aware of competing sounds in your room environment (for example, noisy heaters or air conditioning units), and project your voice to ensure that you are heard by students.

Visual Techniques to Obtain Students' Attention

* Use visual signals such as flashing the lights or raising your hand (which signals the students to raise their hands and close their mouths until everyone is silent and attentive).

* Use visual prompts and cues. For example, point to a poster that has a visual depiction of the behavioral expectations for "Being a Good Listener" prior to giving instructions or beginning a class discussion.

* Use pictures, diagrams, gestures, manipulatives, and demonstrations to engage students' visual attention and interest. Write key words or pictures on the board or overhead projector while presenting.

* Illustrate, Illustrate, Illustrate: You do not have to draw well to illustrate throughout your presentation. Do so even if you lack the skill or talent. Drawings do not have to be sophisticated or accurate. In fact, often the sillier the better, and stick figures are fine. Any attempts to illustrate vocabulary, concepts, and so forth not only focuses students' attention, but helps in the retention of information.

* Point to written material you want students to focus on with a dowel, stick/pointer, or laser pointer.

* Cover or remove visual distractions. Erase unnecessary information from the board, and remove visual clutter.

* Call students up front and close to you for direct instruction (for example, seated on the carpet near the board or chart stand).

* Eye contact is important. Students should be facing you when you are speaking, especially while instructions are being given. Position all students so that they can see the board and/or overhead screen. Always allow students to readjust their seating and signal you if their visibility is blocked. Teach students (for example, those seated with desks in clusters who are not facing you) how to turn their chairs and bodies around quickly and quietly when signaled to do so.

* Try using a flashlight or laser pointer. Turn off the lights and get students to focus by illuminating objects or words with the laser/flashlight.

* Color is very effective in getting attention. Make use of colored dry-erase pens on whiteboards, colored overhead pens for transparencies, and colored highlighting tape or Post-it Notes. Write key words, phrases, steps to computation problems, tricky letters in spelling words, and so on in a different color.

* Frame visual material you want students to be focused on with your hands or with a colored box around it.

Overhead projectors are among the best tools for focusing students' attention in the classroom because they enable the teacher to (a) model and frame important information; (b) block unnecessary information by covering part of the transparency; (c) face students and not

BE A GOOD LISTENER

Eyes on speaker

Ears tuned in

Don't interrupt

ZIP

Respond with friendly words & body language

have to turn one's back on the students in order to write on the board; (d) avoid instructional lag time while writing on the board and erasing; (e) prepare transparencies in advance, saving instructional time (Rief, 1998, 2003).

In addition, teachers can place novel objects on the overhead (such as a variety of math manipulatives and other overhead tools). It is also motivating for students to write on the transparency. Cooperative groups, for example, can be given a transparency and colored pens and then share their work with the rest of the class on the projector. It is recommended that teachers who do not have access to an overhead projector try any available means to get one.

Note: With today's technology, more and more teachers will soon have the benefit of using Power-Point and other multimedia tools at their disposal for classroom instruction.

Maintaining Students' Attention Through Active Participation

Keeping or sustaining students' attention requires active, not passive learning. It also requires that teachers incorporate a variety of formats and activities that are woven throughout the lesson. Within a fifty-minute period of time, for example, the lesson may be formatted to include a mix of (a) whole group instruction and end of lesson closure (with engaging ways for students to respond and participate); (b) predominantly small group and partner structures for maximum involvement in learning activities; and (c) some time to work on a particular task independently.

Note: Section 3.1, Reaching Students Through Differentiated Instruction; Section 3.3, Reaching Students Through Their Learning Styles and Multiple Intelligences; and Section 3.4, The Advantages of Cooperative Learning for Students with ADHD, address in more depth how to engage and maintain students' attention and interest.

General Tips for Keeping Students Engaged

* Present at a lively pace with enthusiasm.
* Move around in the classroom, maintaining your visibility.

* Incorporate demonstrations and hands-on presentations into your teaching whenever possible, and use high-interest material.
* Build in "legitimate" movement opportunities during the lesson.
* Reduce lag time by being prepared.
* Monitor and vary your rate, volume, and tone of voice.
* Have students write down brief notes or illustrate key points during instruction.
* Make all efforts to greatly increase student responses (saying and doing something with the information being taught).
* Use a variety of graphic organizers and techniques such as webbing, graphing, clustering, mapping, and outlining.
* Increase the amount of teacher modeling, guided practice, and immediate feedback to students.
* Use study guides and partial outlines. While you are presenting a lesson or giving a lecture, students fill in the missing words based on what you are saying and/or writing on the board or overhead. Any kind of graphic tool for students to use accompanying verbal presentation is helpful. Jotting down a few words or filling in missing information in a guided format is helpful for maintaining attention.
* Create an environment where students feel "safe" to risk participation and make mistakes.
* Use questioning strategies that encourage student success without humiliation: probing techniques; providing clues; asking students if they would like more time to think about the question; and so forth.
* Ask questions that are open-ended, require reasoning, and stimulate critical thinking and discussion.
* Expand on students' partial answers ("Tell me more." "How did you arrive at that answer?").
* Format lessons to include a variety of questioning techniques that involve whole class, group, partner, and individual responses.

* Before asking for a verbal response to a question, have all students jot down their best-guess answers. Then call for volunteers to verbally answer the question.
* Structure the lesson so that it includes the opportunity to work in pairs or small groups for maximum student involvement and attention. Utilize alternatives to simply calling on students one at a time. Instead, have students respond by telling their partners, writing down or drawing their response, and so forth.
* Cooperative learning groups can be highly effective in keeping students engaged and participating during lessons. Teachers must follow the proper structure of cooperative learning groups (for example, assignment of roles, individual accountability). It is *not* just group work. Students with ADHD do not typically function well in groups without clearly defined structure and expectations.
* Use motivating computer programs for specific skill building and practice (programs that provide for frequent feedback and self-correction), and games for skill practice, whenever possible.
* Motivate all students to actively participate by differentiating instruction in the classroom. Provide many opportunities for student choices of activities/projects, and ways to demonstrate their learning. Provide student projects and assignments that have options, including music, drama, art, construction, designing, writing, speaking, use of technology, research, and any other means of creative expression.
* Differentiate instruction through use of learning centers, flexible grouping, interest groups, independent projects/study, and a variety of other instructional strategies, structures, and accommodations. (See Section 3.1, Reaching Students Through Differentiated Instruction.)

Questioning Techniques to Increase Student Response Opportunities

In all classrooms, teachers have students who are inattentive and easily distracted. There are also children who, for whatever reason, are reluctant to participate and are passively rather than actively involved in the lesson. One of the most effective ways of ensuring that all students are actively engaged is through specific questioning techniques that require a high rate of student response. The following are some methods to significantly increase student participation and response (Rief, 1998, 2003; Rief & Heimburge, 1996).

Whole Group and Unison Responses

Use choral responses. Have students recite poems or share reading of short passages or lines from the text chorally (in unison). Singing songs or chants, reviewing (for example, irregular/ sight words or math facts) with whole class response to flash cards or other such activities are examples of choral responses. During whole class instruction, make frequent use of choral or unison responses when there is one correct and short answer. While presenting, stop frequently and have all students repeat back a word or two. During choral responses, everyone in the group is actively involved and participating.

Direct Instruction Techniques

Special education teachers trained in direct instruction techniques are generally more familiar with this method than general educators are for eliciting unison responses from students. It is explained that there will be times when you will be asking questions that everyone will be answering at the same time (rather than raising their hands and waiting to be called on to respond). Students are trained (by modeling and practice) to respond to a teacher's question by calling out the answer in unison when signaled to do so. This method is used when there is only one correct answer and that answer is short.

Students are first focused to be looking directly at the stimulus (the teacher). The teacher holds out his or her hand as if stopping traffic (or arms up in the air), while presenting a question that has a short, single answer. The teacher continues to hold his or her hand still or arms in the air, pausing to give students time to think. Then the teacher gives a verbal signal (for example, "Everyone. . ." or "Ready. . ."), waits one second, and then immediately follows with a visual signal that has been previously shown to students (for example, a gesture of dropping the raised hand). At that signal, students respond by calling out the answer in unison (Archer, Gleason, & Vachon, 2000; Engelmann, Hanner, & Johnson, 1999). The types of questions can include providing examples and having students identify whether the example was a "simile" or "metaphor," a "proper" or "improper" fraction, and so forth. After students respond, a follow-up question for an individual response can be asked, "How do you know that?"

Another direct instruction method is used (the point-tap signal) when focusing on a visual stimulus (for example, reading a list of words on the board, reciting answers to math facts shown on the overhead projector). This method involves the teacher pointing to a stimulus (for example, a word on the list) and pausing for students to think and figure out the word. Then the teacher gives a verbal signal (for example, "What word?"), followed by a tap by a pointer next to the word. Students call out the word at this signal (Engelmann, Hanner, & Johnson, 1999). These direct instruction techniques greatly increase students' rate of response for these kinds of tasks. When incorrect answers are called out, the teacher can immediately correct the entire group and continue to practice as a group, without singling anyone out.

Note: A good technique for reducing impulsive student "blurt outs" and to build in more "think time" is to tell students that when they know (or think they know) the answer to visually signal by putting their thumbs up. Once a number of thumbs are up, call on students to respond in unison or individually. This is one of the techniques of educational leader Dr. Anita Archer (1997).

Hand Signals for Whole Group Responses

Unison responses can also be obtained by having students use various hand signals. For example, with thumbs up/thumbs down or open hand/closed hand responses from students indicating such things as "yes/no," "I agree/I disagree," or any other "either/or" response. Finger signals can be used as well. Teachers can pose questions, wait for students to think, and signal students to hold up a designated number of fingers to match their answers. For example, teachers can do quick assessments using multiple-choice questions in which students hold up the corresponding number of fingers rather than writing down their responses. The choices can be listed on the board. After posing the question, allowing for "wait time," and then signaling, students hold up the number of fingers that correspond with the choices on the board (Rief & Heimburge, 1996). Carolyn Chapman (2000) recommends a "Fist of 5" technique as a pre-assessment tool to find out what learners already know about a topic. Using a hand signal on a scale of 1 to 5, students self-assess: "How well do I know this?" Five fingers mean the student believes he or she has a high degree of understanding, and one finger means low.

Write-On Tools Other Than Paper

Most students (particularly those with ADHD, who often resist paper-and-pencil work) are motivated to work with colored pens and markers on dry-erase boards. Another way of eliciting unison responses is to ask the class a question, pause for "thinking time," and ask students to write their answers on individual dry-erase boards, individual chalkboards, or other write-on tools. Then, after a teacher signal (for example, "Boards up"), students hold up their boards for the teacher to see and quickly assess which students understand, and who needs extra help.

Students of all ages enjoy writing on the boards, and they can be used in any content area for short-answer responses (for example, solving individual math problems or equations, practicing spelling words). If used properly, they are also effective in checking for students' understanding and determining who needs extra help and practice. For dry-erase boards, a tissue serves as an eraser. For chalkboard use, it is very helpful to store a piece of chalk inside a baby bootie or sock, which serves as the eraser. Write-on tools can be kept in each student's desk or passed out as needed.

Pre-Made Response Cards

Another way to elicit unison responses is through pre-made response cards. Pre-printed response cards and fans are very effective in engaging students in lessons. They are a "hands-on" and motivating format for answering questions, involving *all* students, and significantly increasing active participation. Any pre-printed response card should be made easy for students to manipulate.

Examples of pre-made response cards include (a) cards with a single-hole punch that are held together by a metal ring; (b) cards that are held together by a brass fastener and opened up like a fan; and (c) single cards made of cardstock or construction paper that are divided into sections (halves, thirds, or quarters), pre-printed with a choice of responses. The answer is indicated on this card by placing a clothespin on the student's choice of correct answer.

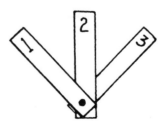

Note: When the teacher poses the question, students select their answers by holding up the card of choice, placing their clothespins, or similar method of indicating choices. Cards should be designed with words/symbols written on both sides of the card so both the teacher and student can see when holding it up. Pre-made response cards or fans are very useful at any grade level or content area to integrate into whole-class questioning strategies (Heward, Gardner, Cavanaugh, et al., 1996).

The following are examples of some uses for pre-made response cards. Students can review such things as:

* The vowel sound heard in different words (a, e, i, o, u choices)
* The part of speech of a particular word within a sentence (for example, noun, verb, adjective, adverb)
* The math process needed to solve a problem (add, subtract, multiply, divide)
* Final punctuation mark needed (period, question mark, exclamation point)
* Social studies terms or concepts (legislative, executive, judicial branch of government)
* Literary term that a given example demonstrates (alliteration, idiom, personification)
* Multiple choice (a, b, c)

Note: Teachers may wish to have the response card divided into three or four sections and laminated without anything written in the sections. These cards can then have multiple use by having students write in erasable marker the response choices for a particular lesson. A card, pen, and clothespin can be kept in each desk.

Vary the Method of Calling on Students

Students who perceive that they will be required to participate and respond to questions will remain more attentive. Sometimes teachers inadvertently neglect to call on certain students as frequently as others to contribute to class discussions or answer questions. One technique many teachers use to ensure they are giving all students in class an equal opportunity to respond is to write each student's name on either a deck of cards or on a tongue depressor stick. The cards or sticks are used to draw from when calling on students. Once a name is drawn, the name card or stick is put in a different stack (or container). When using this technique it is important that students not "tune out" and stop paying attention once they have had their turn. In order to prevent this from happening, it is good practice to draw names periodically from the discard pile of cards or sticks (those already called on). This way, students know they may be called on again at any time.

Students enjoy novel ways of being called on to respond, such as: "Everyone wearing earrings, stand up . . . this question is for you," "Everyone who has fewer than six letters in his or her last name, you may try to answer this question," "Anyone who has a birthday in January, February, or March may answer this one." Students from that group may answer or have the option to pass.

Build in Enough "Wait Time" to Increase Student Participation

Provide sufficient "wait time" (a period of teacher silence) from the time you pose a question until calling on the first student to answer that question. Studies first conducted by Mary Budd Rowe (1974) and others indicate the average amount of time teachers wait before calling on someone for a response is between one and three seconds (Sousa, 2001).

It is important to consciously allow *at least* five seconds of wait time. Many students need more time in order to process the question, gather their thoughts, and be able to express them. Partner strategies discussed below are excellent means of enabling all students to first share their thoughts and responses with another student, before asking individual students to answer questions in a whole class format. This automatically builds in extra "wait time" and opportunity to think about the question and formulate an answer. Try rephrasing, ask probing questions, and wait longer for a response. Ask students if they need more time to think about their answers. Tell students who cannot answer the question at that time that you will come back to them later—then do so.

Special Questioning Arrangements for Certain Students

Be sensitive to students who are often viewed by peers as poor students and who rarely know the answer to questions asked in class. Be open to making a special arrangement in private with a student to help bolster his or her self-esteem. You may try telling the student to go ahead and raise his or her hand with a closed fist, and agree that you will not call on him or her at that time. When the child raises an open hand, you will make every effort to call on the student at that time. This technique is reported to be helpful in changing peer perception of individuals who seldom raise their hands and often have fragile self-esteem. Other classmates are not aware of the fist or open hand signal, and only notice that the student appears to know the answer and wishes to contribute in class (Rief, 2003; Rief & Heimburge, 1996).

Methods for Small Group Responses

Much of classroom instruction involves small groups of students working together. Grouping patterns should be flexible, as discussed in Section 3.1, Reaching Students Through Differentiated Instruction. Small group active responses take place in any cooperative learning group structure. There are endless activities, learning tasks, and projects that are best accomplished in small groups such as creating a product together, solving a problem, brainstorming, analyzing, summarizing, conducting an experiment, studying and reviewing, reading and discussing, and so forth. Section 3.4, The Advantages of Cooperative Learning, describes in detail the components of effective small group formats that ensure all students in the group are active

participants, have an important role and contribution, and are held individually accountable.

Methods for Partner Responses

Use of partners (pair-shares) is perhaps the most effective method for maximizing student engagement—particularly students with ADHD (Rief, 2003; Rief & Heimburge, 1996). It involves turning to a partner for short interactions between two students. Pair-share formats are ideal for predicting, sharing ideas, clarifying directions, summarizing information, previewing information, drilling/practicing (vocabulary, spelling words, math facts), shared reading of text, discussing reading material, sharing writing assignments, and so forth. Some examples are

* "Pair up with your neighbor and share your ideas about . . ."
* "Turn to your partner/neighbor and . . ." After giving partners a chance to respond, ask for volunteers to share with the whole class: "Who would be willing to share what you or your partner thought about . . . ?"
* "Turn to your partner [or person across from you, behind you] and discuss for a few minutes . . ." or "Write down with your partner all the things you can think of that . . . ."
* "Help each other figure out how to do this."

Partner responses can be structured informally (turn to a neighbor) or with teachers more carefully assigning partners. Partners can be numbered 1's and 2's, or A's and B's, so the teacher can assign different partner tasks. For example, "A's tell your partner your prediction for the next page" (Archer, 1997).

Partners can be used to check over each other's work before turning it in, combine ideas and resources for a joint project, take turns reading aloud or questioning and discussing a reading passage together, listening to and providing feedback on each other's writing, working out math problems together, checking that others correctly recorded homework assignments in their daily planner, and numerous other tasks.

Consider allowing partners the opportunity to work together standing or moving to a location away from their desks. It is especially beneficial for students with ADHD to be able to get up and move, while still having the expectation to be on-task and working productively with their partners.

Keeping Students On-Task During Seatwork

Here are some ideas for keeping students focused while seated doing an assignment:

* Provide guided practice before having students work independently on seatwork activities.
* Check for clarity. Make sure directions are clear and understood before sending students back to their seats to work independently.
* Give a manageable amount of work that students are capable of doing *independently*.
* Make sure necessary supplies are available so students can work during independent time without excuses. Have extra (but less desirable) materials available for unprepared students.
* Send student(s) to their seat with a written task card or checklist. A task sheet (or "things to do" sheet) is also helpful. Have students cross out each task when completed.
* Provide desk examples (for example, math problems assigned) for reference.
* Study buddies or partners may be assigned for clarification purposes during seatwork, especially when the teacher is instructing another group of students while part of the class is doing seatwork. When part of the class has a seatwork assignment while you are instructing other students (for example, during a reading group), set the expectation that students who have a question during seatwork must ask their partners (or classmates in their group)

first. Only if no one in the group can answer the question may the teacher be interrupted. Some teachers assign one or more "experts" of the day for students in need of help to go to.

* Prepare some kind of signal to be used from the child's desk to indicate "I need help!" One method is to provide a colored card that students place or prop up on their desks when they want to alert the teacher (or any adult) scanning the room that they need assistance. Give other "fail proof" work that the student can do in the meantime if he or she is stumped on an assignment and needs to wait for teacher attention or assistance.
* Scan the classroom frequently, as all students need positive reinforcement. Frequently give positive comments, praising students specifically whom you observe to be on-task. This serves as a reminder to students who tend to have difficulty.
* If an assignment is difficult or lengthy, shorten or modify as needed. Don't give independent work that is very difficult if students haven't had sufficient guided practice.
* Try using a timer and "beat the clock" system to motivate completion of a reasonable amount of work (particularly for students who have ADHD). Reward for on-task behavior and work completed during short designated time segments.
* Provide study carrels and quiet areas for students who tend to be distracted during seatwork time.
* Block or mask some pages of assigned seatwork by covering up part of the page or folding the page under so lesser amounts are visible at one time.
* Actually cut (with scissors) assignments or work pages in half or smaller segments, and pass out one part at a time. Blocking or cutting apart pages of work may help reduce the frustration a student feels when seeing a paper that appears lengthy and overwhelming.

Tips for Helping Inattentive, Distractible Students

Some techniques I have recommended in other publications (1998, 2003) are listed below:

* Provide preferential seating—in front, within cueing distance of the teacher, and away from as many environmental distractions as possible (for example, doors, windows, high-traffic areas of the room, enticing learning centers, and visual displays). Make sure the child is seated among attentive, well-focused students.
* Increase teacher proximity (standing near or walking close by student). Use physical contact (for example, hand on shoulder or back) and eye contact to regain the attention of a student who appears to be mentally "drifting" and needs to refocus.
* Have student(s) clear desks of distracters, allowing only essential items for the current task on the desk.

Note: It is not uncommon for children with ADHD to have the need to touch or have some kind of object in their hands. For many children, this actually helps with self-regulation and staying alert. Consider providing certain students with something to hold and manipulate while seated and listening, such as a small squishy ball or a piece of Wikki Stix® (colored, non-toxic wax-covered twine). This should be permitted as long as it stays within the child's hand and is not bothering others. Another option is attaching something to a belt loop (for example, a key chain with small object attached) to accommodate this need to touch and fidget.

* Call positive attention to the student who is focused (for example, "I like the way Nick is following along and is on the right page." "See how nicely Sarah is sitting up and looking at the board.").
* Use behavior modification techniques with positive reinforcement/incentives for motivating and reinforcing attentive, on-task behavior (for example, table points, individual charts for teacher initials, stickers, points, contracts, and other means).
* Reward for a certain number of completed items that are done with accuracy.
* Include a target behavior such as "seatwork completed within the designated time" for monitoring and reinforcement of on-task behavior on a daily report card (or other form of monitoring/incentive plan). (See Section 2.3, Individualized Behavior Management, Interventions, and Supports.)
* Use contracts, charts, and other monitoring/reinforcement tools, rewarding for on-task behavior.
* Increase visual, auditory, and physical cues/prompts to gain attention and help refocus inattentive, distractible students.
* Use private signals and cues that have been pre-arranged with this student to help focus attention. For example, when the teacher points to his or her eyes, it means "look." Pointing to your ear means "listen." When you point to and tap your chin, it means "Watch my face and pay attention."
* Point to or tap next to a visual symbol/prompt (posted on wall chart or on a desk card) designating behaviors such as "Sit up." "Eyes forward (or on work)." "Busy working." (See example in Section 2.1, Classroom Management and Positive Discipline Practices.)
* Provide options for a less distracting work area through the use of study carrels, office areas, partitions, privacy boards, and so forth. These should not be used if they are viewed by the students in the class as punitive measures or as accommodations for students with special needs only.
* Allow the use of earphones or earplugs for distractible students during seatwork time and silent/independent reading times of the day. It is recommended that parents supply earphones for their own child for health reasons. If sharing earphones (for example, at a listening post or computer), sanitize them frequently. (See Section 3.3, Reaching

Students Through Their Learning Styles and Multiple Intelligences, for more information on tools and environmental supports to help children who have difficulties with paying attention.)

Self-Monitoring Attention and Listening Levels (Self-Regulatory Techniques)

It is very helpful for students with ADHD to employ self-monitoring strategies to become more aware of their behaviors. As was mentioned in Section 2.3, one such strategy is having the student(s) do seatwork while playing a cassette tape that has been pre-recorded with intermittent beeps, a ring of a bell, or other auditory signal. Children are trained to record on an index card or monitoring form whether or not they were on-task/paying attention whenever they hear the auditory signal. Students record either +/–, or yes/no at each signal. There is a commercial product of this self-monitoring strategy called *Listen, Look and Think—A Self-Regulation Program for Children* (Parker, 1990). It includes an endless cassette beep tape and self-monitoring forms. Whenever the intermittent beep is heard on the tape, the child is to ask himself or herself, "Was I paying attention?" On the form, the child puts a checkmark indicating yes or no. Then the student is expected to immediately get back to work.

Use picture prompts and cues at the student's desk. For example, a prompt card showing picture icons or words indicating behaviors such as sitting properly in seat, book open, pencil in hand, eyes on paper, and so forth. These are excellent visual reminders of expected behaviors. Besides the teacher (while circulating around the room during instruction) pointing to or tapping on the icons to cue the student about expected behavior, the child may also "check" himself or herself periodically, according to the behaviors indicated on the visual prompt card.

Teach students to self-monitor work production and to set individual short-term goals for improvement, for example, "I am going to write at least three more sentences by the time this work period is over" or "I will read to page 121 by the time the timer goes off." If meeting the mini-goal, the student self-rewards in some way (for example, giving self a star on a self-monitoring card).

The book *125 Ways to Be a Better Listener* (Graser, 1992) has lessons for teaching students to monitor and regulate their "listening attention levels" (LAL), the term the author uses in describing the amount of energy needed to pay attention in various situations. Some suggested strategies for raising one's LAL include:

* Changing posture
* Sitting up straight in the chair
* Putting both feet on the floor
* Raising head off shoulders
* Taking a quick, deep breath (to get a burst of oxygen)
* Tracking/observing closely the speaker's facial expressions and gestures
* Moving in closer to the speaker (if possible)

The following "shiny light bulb" strategy was developed by Terri Hilte, a speech-language pathologist in California, and is shared with her permission. This unique technique has been found to be very effective in increasing her students' awareness and ability to self-regulate their attention level. Terri uses the analogy of a light bulb which can be dark or unlit, dim (25 watts), semi-bright (50 watts), brighter (75 watts), and very bright (100 watts) to relate to degrees of attention level. Students learn to equate the visual of a dark light bulb (when off-task and inattentive) to a bright and shiny light bulb at 100 watts (when at full attention). Students are taught to STOP, self-check, and correct four behaviors that will enable them to pull themselves from a state of inattention back to attention. The four behaviors are

1. *Stop talking*—and the bulb is lit at 25 watts.
2. *Stop moving around*—and the bulb is lit at 50 watts.

3. *Stop looking around*—and the bulb is lit at 75 watts.

4. *Stop daydreaming*—and the bulb is shiny bright at 100 watts.

Students learn that "shiny light bulbs" enable them to learn best, and the technique is taught in either small or large group instruction. For example, working in collaboration with classroom teachers, Terri teaches full classes of elementary through secondary level students different lessons (which she refers to as "communication labs"). During the labs, each of the STOPS (the four behaviors above) are discussed and role played in various situations. As they learn and address each of the "STOP behaviors," students color in their individual light bulbs. One-quarter of the 25-watt bulb is colored in yellow marker. Half of the 50-watt bulb is colored and three-quarters of the 75-watt bulb. The 100-watt light bulb will be fully colored in yellow.

The children/teens use the expression "shiny light bulb" if they see another student off-task. Students with attention difficulties are given small versions of the five light bulbs on their desks (in their classrooms and in Terri's room when she works with them in speech-language therapy sessions). If they break a "STOP" rule, she (or their classroom teacher) use the visual prompt of touching the "black light bulb." Students have learned that means to check and self-correct their four STOP behaviors, and they do so automatically. It saves the need for verbal redirection.

The light bulb strategy is taught in "communication labs" that Terri has created. The first lab involves:

1. Introduction—Students are told the daily target which is to learn the STOPS so they can be 100-watt learners.

2. Sound Off—Students learn and practice the language, "shiny light bulbs—!!!" and

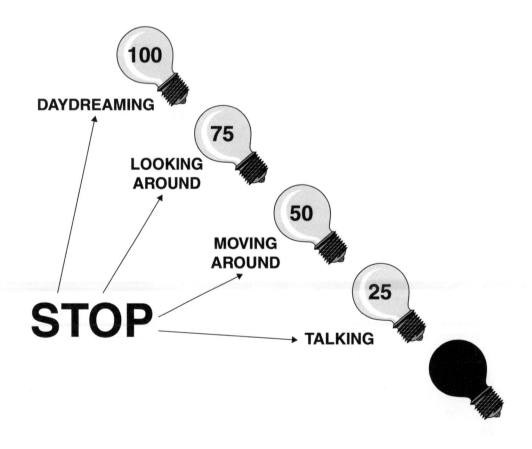

the four associated STOP behaviors in order of their "wattage." (Stop talking; stop moving around; stop looking around; stop daydreaming).

I NEED TO FOCUS MY ATTENTION!!!

"SHINY LIGHT BULBS HELP ME LEARN."

I HAVE TO <u>STOP</u>...

• **TALKING**

• **MOVING AROUND**

• **LOOKING AROUND**

• **DAYDREAMING**

3. Role Play—Students then are given an opportunity to act out "positive and negative" situations through role plays: (a) two people talking at the same time; (b) too much moving; (c) too much looking around; (d) too much daydreaming.
4. Wrap Up—Students orally interact in discussion about what "communication discovery" they made in that lab. For example, "Today I learned that to be an effective listener and learner I need to use shiny light bulb behavior."

5. Conclusion—Communication challenge is discussed.

In the second communication lab, students review and practice the strategy, as follows:

1. Introduction—Students are told the daily target.
2. Sound Off—Students practice asking, "What are the four STOPs?" and responding to the question by telling each other the four STOP behaviors.
3. Role Play—Different role-play situations are acted out, incorporating how to employ the shiny light bulb strategy.
4. Wrap Up—Students orally interact in discussion about the "communication discovery" they made in that lab/lesson.
5. Conclusion—The communication challenge is discussed in which Terri challenges students to check their attention five times during the day.

At the completion of these labs/lessons, once the rationale for and specifics of the strategy are clear to students, the strategy continues to be practiced and reinforced (by teachers, peers, and parents). The self-regulation technique can be employed when prompted or reminded by someone else or when the child/teen prompts himself or herself to activate the light bulb and make it shine at 100 volts.

Part 2: General References

Section 2.1

Canter, Lee, & Canter, Marlene. (1993) *Succeeding with Difficult Students.* Santa Monica, CA: Lee Canter & Associates.

Rief, Sandra. (2003). *The ADHD Book of Lists.* San Francisco: Jossey-Bass.

Rief, Sandra, & Heimburge, Julie. (1996). *How to Reach & Teach All Students in the Inclusive Classroom.* San Francisco: Jossey-Bass.

Section 2.3

Illes, T. (2002). *Positive Parenting Practices for Attention Deficit Disorder.* Salt Lake City, UT: Jordan School District.

O'Neill, R. E., Horner, R. H., Albin, R. W., Storey, K., Sprague, J. R., & Newton, J. S. (1997*). Functional Assessment of Problem Behavior: A Practical Assessment Guide.* Pacific Grove, CA: Brooks/Cole.

Parker, H. (2000). *Listen, Look and Think—A Self-Regulation Program for Children.* Plantation, FL: Impact Publications.

Parker, H. (2002). *Problem Solver Guide for Students with ADHD.* Plantation, FL: Specialty Press.

Pelham, W. E. (2002). *ADHD: Diagnosis, Assessment, Nature, Etiology, and Treatment.* Buffalo, NY: Center for Children and Families. http://wings.buffalo.edu/adhd.

Rankin, B., Dungan, S., Allison, R., Ikeda, M., Rahn, A., & Beener, T. (March, 2002). A Problem-Solving Approach to Functional Behavioral Assessment. NASP *Communique', 30*(6). Retrieved September 19, 2002, from www.nasponline.org/publications/cq306probsolve.html.

Rief, S. (2003). *The ADHD Book of Lists.* San Francisco: Jossey-Bass.

Ryan, A., Halsey, H., & Matthews, W. (2003). Using Functional Assessment to Promote Desirable Student Behavior in Schools. *Teaching Exceptional Children, 35*(5), 8–15.

Sugai, G., Horner, R. H., & Gresham, F. (2002). Behaviorally Effective School Environments. In M. Shinn, H. Walker, & G. Stoner (Eds*.), Interventions for Achievement and Behavior Problems II: Preventive and Remedial Approaches.* Bethesda, MD: National Association of School Psychologists, pp. 315–350.

Walker, H. M. (1997). *The Acting Out Child—Coping with Classroom Disruption* (2nd ed.). Longmont, CO: Sopris West.

Wallace, I. (1996). *You & Your ADD Child.* Pymble, Sydney, Australia: HarperCollins.

For more information on FBAs and BIPs, see:

http://cecp.air.org/fba/problembehavior/main.htm

http://ericec.org/digests/e580.html

http://mfba.net/multimodal

http://www.nasponline.org/publications/cq306probsolve.html

http://www.pbis.org

http://www.wrightslaw.com/info/discipl.fab.starin.htm

Section 2.4

Barkley, R. A. (1998). *Your Defiant Child.* New York: The Guilford Press.

Barkley, R. A. (2000). *Taking Charge of ADHD.* New York: The Guilford Press.

Forehand, R., & McMahon, R. (1981). *Helping the Noncompliant Child.* New York: The Guilford Press.

Illes, T. (2002). *Positive Parenting Practices for Attention Deficit Disorder.* Salt Lake City, UT: Jordan School District.

Morgan, D. P., & Jensen, W. R. (1988*). Teaching Behaviorally Disordered Students: Preferred Practices.* Columbus, OH: Merrill.

Rief, S. (2003). *The ADHD Book of Lists.* San Francisco: Jossey-Bass.

Robinson, K. (2000, July/August). Compliance—It's No Mystery. CHADD: *ATTENTION, 7*(1), 38–43.

Walker, H. M., & Walker, J. E. (1991). *Coping with Noncompliance in the Classroom.* Austin, TX: Pro-Ed Publishers.

Section 2.5

Archer, A. (1997). *Beginning Reading: A Strategic Start.* Santa Rosa, CA: The Sonoma County Office of Special Education and SELPA.

Archer, A., Gleason, M., & Vachon, V. (2000). *Rewards.* Longmont, CO: Sopris West.

Chapman, C. (2000). *Sail into Differentiated Instruction.* Thomson, GA: Creative Learning Connection.

Engelmann, S., Hanner, S., & Johnson, G. (1999). *Corrective Reading.* Worthington, OH: SRA/McGraw-Hill.

Graser, Nan Stutzman. (1992). *125 Ways to Be a Better Listener™.* East Moline, IL: LinguSystems.

Heward, W., Gardner, R., Cavanaugh, R., Courson, F., Grossi, T., & Barbetta, P. (1996, Winter). Everyone Participates in This Class. *CEC: Teaching Exceptional Children, 28*(2), 4–9.

Parker, Harvey. (2000). *Listen, Look and Think—A Self-Regulation Program for Children.* Plantation, FL: Impact Publications.

Rief, S. (2003). *The ADHD Book of Lists.* San Francisco: Jossey-Bass.

Rief, S. (1998). *The ADD/ADHD Checklist: An Easy Reference for Parents and Teachers.* San Francisco: Jossey-Bass.

Rief, S., & Heimburge, J. (1996). *How to Reach & Teach All Students in the Inclusive Classroom.* San Francisco: Jossey-Bass.

Rowe, M. B. (1974). Wait-Time and Rewards as Instructional Variables: Their Influence on Language, Logic, and Fate Control. *Journal of Research Science Teaching, 2,* 81–94.

Sousa, D. A. (2001). *How the Brain Learns.* Thousand Oaks, CA: Corwin Press.

Wikki Stix® are manufactured by Omnicor, Inc., in Phoenix, Arizona, and are available at 800-869-4554; www.wikkistix.com.

Part 2: Recommended Resources

*T*here are numerous books and resources that teachers and administrators will find useful in addressing the topic of classroom management and positive discipline practices in the school environment. We cannot possibly mention them all here. Some recommended resources include the following:

Bluestein, Jane. (1998). *21st Century Discipline—Teaching Students Responsibility and Self-Management.* Torrance, CA: Fearon Teacher Aids.

Fay, Jim, & Funk, David. (1995). *Teaching with Love and Logic: Taking Control of the Classroom.* Golden, CO: The Love & Logic Press.

Geddes, Betsy. (1995). *Handling Misbehavior in Your Classroom.* Portland, OR: Geddes Consulting.

Gootman, Marilyn E. (2001). *The Caring Teacher's Guide to Discipline: Helping Young Students Learn Self-Control, Responsibility, and Respect.* Thousand Oaks, CA: Corwin Press.

Jensen, William, Rhode, Ginger, & Reavis, Kenton. (1995). *The Tough Kid Tool Box.* Longmont, CO: Sopris West. (This is a book of forms, charts, and other aids to accompany *The Tough Kid Book.*)

Jones, Fred. (2000). *Tools for Teaching.* Santa Cruz, CA: Fredric H. Jones & Associates.

Mayer, G. Roy. (2000) *Classroom Management: A California Resource Guide.* Los Angeles: Los Angeles County Office of Education—Division of Student Support Services Safe Schools Division.

McEwan, Elane, & Damer, Mary. (2000). *Managing Unmanageable Students.* Thousand Oaks, CA: Corwin Press.

Nelsen, Jane, Lott, Lynn, & Glenn, H. Stephen. (1997). *Positive Discipline in the Classroom.* Rocklin, CA: Prima Publishing.

Rhode, Ginger, Jensen, William, & Reavis, H. Kenton. (1995). *The Tough Kid Book.* Longmont, CO: Sopris West.

Sprick, Randall, & Howard, Lisa. (1998). *The Teacher's Encyclopedia of Behavior Management.* Longmont, CO: Sopris West.

Walker, Hill M. (1997). *The Acting-Out Child: Coping with Classroom Disruption.* Longmont, CO: Sopris West.

Instructional and Academic Strategies and Supports

Reaching Students Through Differentiated Instruction

What Differentiation Means

To address the learning differences in all of our students and maximize their levels of performance and achievement, teachers need to "differentiate instruction" in the classroom. What does this mean? *Differentiated instruction* is a way of thinking about teaching and learning that recognizes the fact that "one size does not fit all learners." Some students are not successful in school because there is a misfit between how they learn and the way they are taught (ASCD, 2002). This concept or awareness certainly is not new for teachers (particularly special educators). But the term "differentiated instruction" is relatively new, and so is the recognition in the general education community that teaching must change in order to fulfill our responsibility to reach and teach *all* of the diverse learners in our classrooms. Students with ADHD are among those who most need teachers to embrace differentiated instruction in order to achieve school success.

Carol Ann Tomlinson, associate professor at the University of Virginia, Charlottesville, is one of the key educational leaders who has catapulted "differentiated instruction" throughout the educational community. She speaks and writes extensively about the subject. According to Tomlinson (2001), differentiated instruction is

* *Proactive*—Teachers proactively plan a variety of ways to get at and express learning that are planned to be robust enough to address the range of learner needs.
* *More qualitative than quantitative*—Adjusting the nature (not necessarily the length or quantity) of the assignment.
* *Student-centered*—Learning experiences that are engaging, relevant, and interesting.
* *Rooted in assessment*—Throughout the unit of study, in a variety of ways, teachers assess students' developing readiness levels, interests, and modes of learning, adjusting instruction accordingly.

For struggling learners, differentiated instruction means setting important goals of understanding, then figuring out how to build scaffolding leading to success in those goals—not diluting the goals. Scaffolds are supports needed for a student to succeed in challenging work; and "challenging" work means assignments or tasks that are slightly beyond the student's comfort zone—not overwhelming and frustrating assignments (Tomlinson, 2001). Scaffolds may include more modeling and structure, guided instruction and practice opportunities; re-teaching; provision of study guides, graphic organizers, and other learning tools; and any of

165

the numerous strategies and accommodations throughout this book that help make learning more accessible to students.

Some students need more time and opportunity to learn the basic content/material through various means (with additional explanation, review, and practice). Other students need less time on the core content and opportunities for extended, advanced learning. Adjusting time and degree of support provided are components of differentiated instruction.

Heacox (2002) further defines differentiated instruction as:

* Changing the pace, level, or kind of instruction you provide in response to individual learners' needs, styles, or interests
* Rigorous—providing challenging instruction to motivate students to push themselves, and basing learning goals on a student's particular capabilities
* Relevant—focused on essential learning, not on "side trips" or "fluff"
* Flexible and varied
* Complex—challenging students' thinking and actively engaging them in content that conveys depth and breadth

Differentiation is based upon the beliefs that:

* Students who are the same age differ in their: readiness to learn, interests, styles of learning, experiences, learning profiles, life circumstances, and levels of independence.
* The differences between students are significant enough to make a major impact on what students need to learn, the pace at which they need to learn it, and the support they need from teachers and others to learn it well.
* Students will learn best when supportive adults push them slightly beyond where they can work without assistance.
* Students will learn best when they can make a connection between the curriculum

and their interests and life experiences (Tomlinson, 2000).

Curriculum tells us *what* to teach. Differentiation tells us *how* to teach the same standard to a range of learners by employing a variety of teaching and learning modes (Tomlinson, 2000).

There are numerous ways to differentiate instruction, such as through provision of:

* Materials, tasks, and learning options at varied levels of difficulty
* Multiple and flexible groupings of students
* Multisensory instruction
* Lessons, assessments, projects, and so on that take into account students' varied learning styles and preferences, interests, talents, and multiple intelligences
* Varying degrees of supports and scaffolds
* Choices of where, how, and with whom students may work
* Choices about topics of study, ways of learning, and modes of expression
* Assignments, projects, student products, and so forth that draw on students' individual strengths and interests
* Adaptations, modifications, and multiple approaches to instruction
* A variety of assessments (portfolios, written/oral exams, learning logs, demonstrations)
* Tiered assignments

Note: *Tiered assignments are tasks focused on key concepts in the curriculum, differentiated by levels of complexity or challenge, process or product, and other factors. Tiering helps ensure appropriate challenge for all students.*

A number of the other sections in this book address various components of differentiated instruction. For example, see Section 3.2, Multisensory Instruction, Section 3.3, Reaching Students Through Their Learning Styles and Multiple Intelligences, and Section 3.4, The Advantages of Cooperative Learning for Students with ADHD.

What Can Be Differentiated?

We can differentiate content, presentation/instructional strategies, activities, performance tasks, and assessment tools (Chapman, 2000). Differentiated instruction typically involves multiple approaches and adaptations in the areas of content (what students learn), process (the ways students learn and how the content is taught), and product (how students present or demonstrate their learning).

Content can be differentiated by complexity based on readiness level. For example, if a writing lesson is focused on dialogue, one student might be ready to create a single dialogue exchange between two characters, whereas another may be ready to write four to five exchanges (Pettig, 2000). Students in a math class might be working problems of varying complexity, based on their readiness or skill level. For example, the class may be studying long division, but those students who are more advanced may be solving problems with two- or three-digit divisors, while others are solving problems with single-digit divisors.

It is important for teachers to pre-assess prior knowledge—what students already know and can do—through performance tasks, surveys, and interviews in order to be able to challenge all students at their appropriate readiness level. In addition, teachers should be assessing students' interests related to the topic (Chapman, 2000).

When teachers differentiate by readiness level, they can do so through varied texts or supplementary materials by reading level, varied scaffolding, tiered tasks or products, small group instruction, homework options, and negotiated criteria for quality. Content can also be differentiated by curriculum compacting, concept-based teaching, using varied resource materials, learning contracts, mini-lessons, reading partners and audiovisual recorders, note-taking organizers, highlighted print materials, digests of key ideas, peer and adult mentors, and so forth (Tomlinson, 2001).

Differentiating the process will include the wide array of engaging and motivating teaching and questioning strategies described in Section 2.5, Attention!! Strategies for Engaging, Maintaining, and Regulating Students' Attention. It also involves designing lessons and activities that utilize multisensory techniques—diversifying the teaching presentation by providing input that is auditory, visual, and tactile-kinesthetic. Differentiating the process includes incorporating the full range of Bloom's taxonomy (knowledge, comprehension, application, analysis, synthesis, and evaluation) levels of questions and learning activities, with an emphasis on developing students' higher-order thinking skills.

Flexible Grouping

Flexible grouping is another aspect involved in process differentiation. The teacher structures an array of grouping opportunities best suited for the activities (for example, whole-class, teams, cooperative groups, partners, independent, by interest, by preferred learning modality, by readiness level, heterogeneously, homogeneously, teacher-assigned, self-assigned).

Grouping formats for varying purposes may involve (Tomlinson, 2001):

* Whole class, for pre-assessment, introduction of concepts, planning, sharing, and wrap-up of explorations
* Small groups (pairs, triads, quads) for sense making, teaching skills, directed reading, planning, or investigation
* Individualized, for practice and application of skills, homework, interest centers, products, independent study, and testing
* Student-teacher conferences for: assessment, tailoring and planning, guidance, and evaluation

Multiple Intelligences

Dr. Howard Gardner, professor of education at Harvard University, developed the theory of "multiple intelligences." In his book *Frames of Mind* (1983), he posed the theory that there are at least seven distinct intelligences, or ways in which a person may be smart. Since then, Dr. Gardner identified a minimum of eight separate intelligences. This theory has had a tremendous impact over the years in the educational community. Teachers who embrace the theory recognize that our students differ in their relative strengths and areas of "smartness" and that it is our responsibility to enable students to learn best by building on, teaching through, and encouraging students to utilize their various aptitudes in all learning situations.

Intelligence (IQ) tests have typically measured verbal abilities (linguistic or word smartness) and logical/mathematical abilities (number smartness). However, educators are now more aware of the several other aptitudes that are very important in life and which need to be nurtured, developed, and displayed. In Section 3.3, Reaching Students Through Their Learning Styles and Multiple Intelligences, the diversity in individual learning preferences (modality preferences, environmental preferences, cognitive style preferences, and other factors that contribute to how each person learns best) will be discussed.

For the past several years, there has also been an awareness and understanding that individuals have their own unique learning style preferences. One aspect of learning style preferences is the modality (auditory, visual, or tactile-kinesthetic) or channel through which the person prefers to receive new information/learning. It also includes cognitive styles and other elements that make up the person's learning profile. Teachers take into account students' modality preferences for learning when they present through a variety of modes: verbally (through lecture, discussion, questioning, reading aloud); visually (through use of charts, graphics, video, illustrations); tactile-kinesthetically (through demonstrations, role play, hands-on materials).

Differentiated instruction (the process) can also be accomplished by tapping into students' diverse learning styles, strengths, and interests, and incorporating a variety of options in how students are able to access the curriculum. Teachers should present information through multiple modes and provide students with choices in how they learn the curriculum. There are countless ways of doing so. To name a few:

* Interest and/or instructional learning centers or stations
* Projects (individual, partner, or group)
* Technology
* Choices of or built within activities
* Mentorships/apprenticeships
* Exploration
* Cooperative learning strategies (for example, think-pair-share, jigsaw)
* Tiered assignments
* Books on tape

Note: *Our book,* How to Reach & Teach All Students in the Inclusive Classroom *(Rief & Heimburge, 1996) contains numerous lessons/activities developed around student interests and multiple intelligences and incorporates a wide array of student choices throughout the content areas—grades three through eight.*

Another key aspect of differentiating instruction is differentiating *the output or the product*—how students demonstrate mastery of the content and their learning that has taken place. Students with ADHD have their predominant weakness in this area of performance and output—particularly if the way they must demonstrate their understanding is through written language. Teachers who allow their students to draw on their strengths and have options in how and what they produce to show learning will have more motivated and successful students with ADHD.

Numerous ways can be used to differentiate the product, such as oral presentations, dramatic performances, demonstrations, designing a creative product, constructing or building something, analyzing something, and so forth. Section 3.3, Reaching Students Through Their Learning Styles and Multiple Intelligences, contains more on this topic.

When differentiating the product, teachers encourage all students to draw on their personal interests and strengths. At the same time, the teacher retains focus on those curricular components he or she deems essential to all learners (Tomlinson, 2001). Some teachers provide a project menu based on Bloom's taxonomy (Heacox, 2002). Other teachers design project menus based on multiple intelligences (Rief & Heimburge, 1996).

Note: Whenever providing a student with ADHD a project menu or any list of choice options, it is recommended to first limit the number of choices (among those of highest interest), or the student is likely to become overwhelmed.

Layered Curriculum

Layered Curriculum™ (Nunley, 2001) is an excellent source of practical ideas and ways to differentiate instruction based on a three-layered triangular-shaped learning model. Each layer represents a different depth of study of a topic or unit of learning; and students can choose how deep they wish to examine a topic—

thereby choosing their own grade as well. The bottom layer is the largest and covers general content designed around meeting the district's and state's core curriculum and standards. The middle layer is smaller and asks students to apply concepts learned in the bottom layer. The top layer is the smallest and requires higher critical thinking of students.

To earn, for example, a C in a biology class, students must select from a unit menu of learning activities for that topic of study. In this section there may be a choice of fifteen different activities, each worth approximately ten to fifteen points. Students can earn up to a maximum of sixty-five points through performance of activities at the C level. To be able to earn a B, students must also perform a lab. Labs are B-level activities. Students may choose one lab from a choice of three or four for fifteen points. In order to earn an A, students must also do one A-level activity. A few A-level choices are provided (each worth twenty points). In such an example, for this unit, a student may earn a D (forty to fifty-five points), C (fifty-six to seventy points), B (seventy-one to eighty-five points), or A (eighty-six or above). The author and creator of this model, Kathie Nunley, provides a wealth of strategies and guidance in layering curriculum in any subject or grade level to address the diverse range of learners in any classroom. Visit her website at www.Help4Teachers.com (Nunley, 2001).

INTERVIEW WITH BOB (49 Years Old)

Bob grew up in New England. He has a master of science degree, is retired from the Navy, and is currently a business consultant and government contractor. He was diagnosed as an adult with ADHD.

Tell me how your attention problems affected you in school.

"Reading was my biggest frustration. I would avoid it at all costs. I loved picture books and resources like *National Geographic,* but read the captions only. That was the extent of my attention span. I couldn't concentrate on a page five minutes. I often didn't test well. I had trouble paying attention to the test and would get frustrated. Sometimes I would just draw little designs all over the test."

Tell me about your coping skills.

"I always had the ability to take a very small piece of information (hard data), look at it, touch it, hear it, and then turn around and draw a picture of the finished product. One experience I remember was in sixth grade when we had to do oral reports in front of the class. Earlier in the year I had no problems because we could make or draw something, then just get up and talk about what we made. This time the teacher required a written report to get up and share. I never did it because it was very difficult for me to concentrate and focus long enough to get it down in writing. I remember that I memorized all of the data and information and presented the report orally from memory. My teacher was furious. She tore me up one side and down the other."

What memories do you have of secondary school?

"Teachers branded me as a non-achiever. I vividly remember my history teacher in my senior year of high school. In my family there was no question that I would be going to college. Everyone in the family was a college graduate. This teacher did everything in her power to prove that I was not 'college material.' She would exclude me from class and had me sitting in a back room drawing maps for her, instead of letting me participate in class. People say that with time you forget those kinds of experiences, but you don't. I still can feel the anger and animosity toward that teacher."

What advice can you give teachers? What would have made a difference?

"I guess I would tell teachers that there are a thousand roads to roam. Not everyone is going to choose the same path. Everybody has different ways of assimilating data—different filters, different life experiences that affect how they look at things and process information. To be fair, teachers need to first evaluate whether some other method of learning is available to help one child or another to do what he has to do. Some might be adept at reading. Others are like me: If you touch it and feel it, you own it. For me to do my best, put me in a group with three or four people (of whatever aptitude). I get the most from a group structure where there is a lot of verbal interchange."

section

3.2

Multisensory Instruction

As has been discussed in other sections of this book as well, we must make every effort to teach the curriculum through multimodal approaches. Multisensory instruction is necessary to reach the diverse learners in our classrooms. Section 3.1, Reaching Students Through Differentiated Instruction; Section 3.3, Reaching Students Through Their Learning Styles and Multiple Intelligences; Section 2.5, Attention!! Strategies for Engaging, Maintaining, and Regulating Students' Attention; and all of the academic sections address this topic and provide specific multisensory strategies to implement in the classroom.

Learning style statistics show that the majority of students learn best through visual and tactile/kinesthetic input. Far fewer students are stronger auditory learners. This is particularly important for secondary teachers to be aware of. If your teaching style emphasizes lecturing, with *you* doing most of the talking, a high percentage of students are not being reached.

For most of us, the five primary senses do not contribute equally to our learning. We have sensory preferences—favoring one or two senses over the others when gathering information to deal with a complex learning situation. A person can still process with the other senses, but most of us rely more on our preferences when faced with a complex task (Sousa, 2001a).

Studies of sensory preferences in U.S. school children grades three to twelve in the mid-1990s show that nearly half (46 percent) have a visual preference, over one-third (35 percent) have a

tactile-kinesthetic preference, and just under one-fifth (19 percent) have an auditory preference (Sousa, 2001a; Swanson, 1995).

Sousa further shares that retention of information also depends on the type of teaching method used. Studies in the 1960s by the National Training Laboratories of Bethel, Maine (now the NTL Institute of Alexandria, Virginia) provided the enlightening statistics below. Studies on recall of learning twenty-four hours after students were exposed to different teaching methods showed that people on average are able to recall:

Lecture (5 percent)
Reading (10 percent)
Audiovisual (20 percent)
Demonstration (30 percent)
Discussion Group (50 percent)
Practice by Doing (75 percent)
Teach Others/Immediate Use of Learning (90 percent)

The obvious implications are that we need to present lessons with a combination of methods. Students need hands-on experience. They also need the opportunity to verbalize their understanding frequently during the school day. Cooperative learning situations (with partners, triads, groups of four) are very effective for getting students to discuss their learning—to verbalize, share, and teach one another.

Students who have the opportunity to work together and discuss with peers, and who are actively, physically involved and participating in the lesson, will have the most success in learning and retaining the information.

Multisensory Strategies for Learning Multiplication Tables

The following is an example of how to teach multiplication facts and multiples of a number (in this example, times 4) using a multisensory approach.

Auditory

Teach the sequence of skip counting by fours through use of rhythm, melody, song, or rap. There are various tapes and CDs on the market that teach multiplication tables through such techniques. Musically inclined students can be given the assignment of writing their own melody or rap, and teaching it to the class.

Visual and Tactile

Practice the multiples of four on the computer. There are a number of computer programs that have fun drill and practice games.

Practice multiples of four on a calculator. Have students punch in the fact, then write down the answer, or have them fill in a drill sheet and check themselves on the calculator.

"Donut Math"

Using construction paper, make a paper circle (approximately 12 inches in diameter) with the center cut out. On the circle, write the numerals 0 through 9 in random order. Punch a hole along the "donut" and thread string or a piece of yarn through the hole. Tie the ends of the yarn—making a donut necklace. Hang it on a hook over the chalkboard/dry-erase board. Write "× 4" in the center of the circle on the board. Give students practice coming to the board and writing the products along the outside of the circle. This same "donut" can be used for practicing any other math fact by simply erasing the answers

on the outside of the circle and inner circle and writing in a different number or operation in the center of the circle.

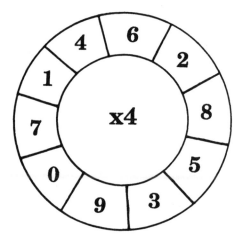

It is recommended that the teacher have a set of a few donuts (each pre-made with 0 to 9 in random order, so that each one looks different). This is particularly useful for playing games. Competitive students enjoy having donut races. Hang a few of the donuts across the board, and write the multiple (× 4 or any other) in the center. Students race to write their answers on the outside of their donut.

Play games by rolling a die and multiplying the number on the die by four. Since students can only practice up to 4 × 6 with the use of one die, the same technique can be used by spinning a spinner that has numerals that go higher. An alternative is to have students first roll two dice of the same color together and add the numbers (for example, 6 + 3 = 9); then multiply that sum by 4 (or whatever math fact is being practiced). For a full review and practice of multiplication facts, after adding together the two dice of the same color, they can roll a third die of a different color and multiply those two numbers.

Use traditional flash cards that students make and color. Triangular flash cards are often best because the same cards can also be used to practice the division fact. For example, there will be a set of triangular flash cards for each of the multiples of 4. The number four will be written on one point of the triangle, and for each of the flash cards 0 to 9 is written on another point. The product for each is written on the third point. Students practice by covering with their hand each of the points of the triangle while reciting, for example: "4 × 3 = 12; 3 × 4 = 12; 12 divided by 3 = 4; 12 divided by 4 = 3."

Make tactile flash cards. This can be done with puff paint or by writing the facts in glue, sprinkling with sand or salt (preferably colored sand/salt), and shaking off the excess when dry. Students then use these flash cards by tracing the numerals with their finger while they say the fact out loud.

Use graph paper and make grids for each of the multiples of four. Students draw a horizontal line that is four boxes in width. They draw a vertical line from the same starting point down to the number of each of the multiples. Connect the lines to make a rectangle for each of the multiples of four and cut them out. Students can write the product in the center of each of the rectangles.

Spatial

Use designs for helping students visualize the pattern and sequence of multiples. The program *Touch Math* has posters and designs for each of the multiples. They use the pattern of "bowling pins" for the multiples of four. Make a poster of this pattern.

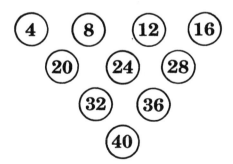

Color the first two single-digit numbers (4 and 8) in yellow. The next two numerals, which have a 1 in the tens place (12 and 16) are colored in orange. The second row of "pins," with numbers in the twenties (20, 24, 28) are colored

red. The next row of pins with numbers in the thirties (32, 36) are colored purple. The numeral 40 is colored blue.

Have students make their own charts/small posters, filling in the numbers in sequence and coloring them.

Make large, laminated colored "pins," shuffle them, and have students lay them out on the floor in proper sequence. Play games such as asking a student to hop on the correct circle (bowling pin) to a prompt, "Jump to the circle that is 4 × 6." This is also a kinesthetic technique involving body movement.

Note: Many students with ADHD (particularly those with co-existing learning disabilities) have significant difficulty memorizing multiplication facts. The "spatial" approach seems to be the answer for some of these children. I have had students who may not be able to ever skip-count, or memorize the sequence of fours—even with repetitive practice. However, with this approach they had been able to visualize and recall where a number is placed spatially in the pattern. With their eyes shut, they could easily visualize and tell you where 4 × 8 or 4 × 3 was placed and the color of the "pin." Many children with learning disabilities who have significant weakness with sequential tasks are gifted spatially.

Use a number chart or matrix of the numerals 1 to 100 and have students count by fours—coloring in each box that is a multiple of four. Seeing the visual pattern that is formed on the matrix helps many students who learn best visually and spatially.

Have students use interlocking plastic cubes that are combined into groups of four, using a different color for each group. As they stack ten groups of four, have students count by fours. This can be done the same way with plastic links or other manipulatives.

The following is another method that is fun for students and helpful for spatial and visually oriented students. Draw a circle and space the numerals 0 through 9 along its circumference

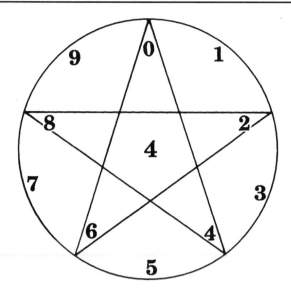

(as shown above). This is a base 10 circle clock. Write a 4 in the center of the circle. Have students write out the multiples of four in sequence (4, 8, 12, 16, 20, 24, 28, 32, 36, 40). Have them begin by putting their pencils on the numeral 4 (4 × 1) on the circle. Draw a straight line from the 4 to the 8 (the next multiple in sequence). From the 8, students draw a straight line to the 2 (which represents **12**), and from the 2 to the 6 (which stands for **16**), then to the 0 (which represents **20**), and continue the pattern. From 0 back to 4 (representing **24**), then to 8 (**28**), to the 2 (**32**), the 6 (**36**), and 0 (**40**). The same digits (4, 8, 2, 6, 0) will be repeated over and over as students continue the sequence (24, 28, 32, 36, 40, 44, 48, and so on). Students love to make these designs. Each of the multiples makes its own unique pattern and design.

Verbal

It is critical, of course, that students understand the concept of multiplication. They should have many opportunities to make up their own word problems to share with the class. One way to do this is to have students brainstorm as a class and generate a class chart that lists "things that come in fours." From this list (which might include wheels on a wagon, quarts in a gallon, quarters in a dollar, legs on a horse, suits in a deck of cards), students then make up problems for their classmates to solve.

Mnemonic (Memory) Devices

Another excellent technique for learning math facts and aiding the memory process is by learning a fact through association with a cartoon and story. A few programs teach math facts this way. One is called *Times Tables the Fun Way*. An example of one of the facts is a picture of a teen in a vehicle driving up a steep hill. On the door is the fact "4 × 4." The teen is saying, "16! At Last!" The picture has the caption: "Remember: When it's 4 × 4, the fours become a 4 by 4 (4 × 4), and you have to be 16 to drive it."

Another program with a similar method of teaching multiplication facts through associations is called Memory Joggers™. The Memory Joggers™ system uses numbers and words that rhyme or are shape-related in order to stimulate memorization. Each number has a corresponding visual object. For example: 0 looks like a mouth that eats up other numbers. 1 sounds like gum and resembles a stick of chewing gum. 1 like gum, sticks to another number and becomes that number. 2 rhymes with shoe. Shoes come in twos (pairs). 3 rhymes with tree. 4 rhymes with door and is shaped like a door, and so on. The story Memory Joggers™ uses for teaching the 4 × 4 fact is as follows:

Once there were twin sisters who had bedroom doors shaped like a 4, next to each other. The doors were half doors so the sisters could talk to each other. The twin sisters were turning 16 and their mother was planning a wonderful "Sweet 16" birthday party for them. But all these twin girls did from their bedroom doors (4), was argue! One of them would say, "I'm sweet 16!" and the other would say, "No! You're mean 16!" They argued so much their parents finally said, "Forget it! No 'Sweet 16' birthday party for either of you until you make up and stop arguing!" Well, the last thing I heard, they were still leaning out their doors (4) × (4) arguing about who was Sweet 16."

Semple Math® is another excellent program that utilizes a network of mnemonic cues (images, songs, rhymes, stories, associations) and multisensory methods for teaching math to students with learning difficulties.

Conceptual

There are hundreds of hands-on games and activities that can help students understand multiplication at the conceptual level. Students need to see the relationship between multiplication and addition (repeated addition of numbers), and the inverse relationship between multiplication and division. Memorizing multiplication facts and solving problems at the symbolic level does not accomplish this.

Multisensory Spelling Strategies and Activities

Children with ADHD and/or LD who are poor spellers need effective spelling instruction. According to the International Dyslexia Association (IDA/Moats, 2000), spelling instruction should emphasize these principles:

* Knowledge of sounds, letter-sound association, patterns, syllables, and meaningful parts
* Multisensory practice
* Systematic, cumulative study of patterns
* Memorizing a few "sight" words at a time
* Writing those words correctly many times
* Using the words in personal writing

The following are a variety of spelling activities and techniques that incorporate all the different senses. Spelling is frequently a difficult skill for many students with ADHD and/or

learning disabilities. Utilizing multisensory strategies is key to their success and provides the motivation necessary to practice spelling skills.

Novelty

Add novelty with fun materials and utilize tactile (feeling) strategies (Rief, 2003). Here are some ideas:

* Dip clean paintbrush in water and write words on a tabletop or chalkboard.
* Write words in the air while sounding them out (sky writing).
* Write words in a flat tray or box of either sand or salt using one or two fingers.
* Write words in glue or liquid starch on pieces of cardboard. Then sprinkle any powdery material, glitter, yarn, beans, macaroni, or sequins over it to create textured, three-dimensional spelling words. Substances such as sand, salt, and glitter are good to use for students who benefit from tracing the words with their fingers.

Note: *The act of tracing with fingers on a texture helps make a sensory imprint on the brain that increases memory and retention.*

* Write words in a sandbox with a stick.
* Pair students and have them write words with their fingers on each other's back.
* While they are sitting on the carpet, have them practice writing the words directly on the carpet with two fingers using large muscle movements.
* Have students practice writing words on individual chalkboards (or dry-erase boards) with colored chalk (or colored dry-erase pens).
* Finger paint words using shaving cream on tabletops; or use pudding, whipped cream, or frosting on paper plates.

* Type each of the words on a computer in a variety of fonts and sizes. Highlight tricky sounds/patterns in different colored fonts.
* Write the words using alphabet manipulatives and tactile letters (for example, magnetic letters, sponge letters, alphabet stamps, alphabet cereal, letter tiles, or linking letter cubes).
* Practice writing words with special pens (glitter pen, neon gel pens) on black paper.
* Use a flashlight in a darkened room to "write" the words on a wall.
* Write words forming the letters with clay or Wikki Stix.™
* Write words vertically in columns.

Song and Movement

Use song and movement to practice spelling words (Rief, 2003). Here are some ideas:

* Pair movement while spelling words aloud (clap to each letter, bounce ball, yo-yo, jump rope, trampoline). Get creative!
* Tap out the sounds or syllables in words (pencil to desk; fingertips to desk or arm; spelling word while tapping with one hand down the other arm, shoulder to hand).
* Use kinesthetic cues for letter/sounds and act out those motions or refer to those cues when segmenting words to spell. See Fetzer and Rief's (2000) book: *Alphabet Learning Center Activities Kit*. This book features the "Holder & Fastie Alphabet," which provides kinesthetic cues and attention to how and where each sound of the alphabet is formed in the mouth.
* Sing spelling words to common tunes/melodies (for example, "Row, Row, Row, Your Boat" or "Old MacDonald").
* Spell words standing up for consonant letters and sitting down for vowels.

Color

Use color to help call attention to letters within the word and to aid memory (Rief, 2003). Here are some ideas:

* Write words using the "rainbow technique" of tracing over each of the words at least three different times in different colored pencils, crayons, chalk, or markers. Then, without looking, write the word from memory.
* Color-code tricky letters (silent letters) in hard-to-spell words.
* Write the words by syllables in different colored markers.
* Write syllable-by-syllable, color coding each one. Vowels are written in red.
* Write the first letter of the word in green, the last letter in red.
* Write silent letters (ghost letters) in white pen.
* After taking a pretest, color the known part of a word (correctly spelled letters) in one color. By the time the word is spelled correctly with further trials, the whole word should be written in color.
* Color consonants in one color, and vowels in another.
* Color-code key elements/features of the word (for example, prefixes/suffixes, final e).

Additional Ideas

Other ways and "choice activities" for students to practice, study, and reinforce spelling words (Rief & Heimburge, 1996) are listed below. Students may choose from a menu of activities such as the following:

* Make a word search on graph paper using all of the words. Include an answer sheet.
* Make a set of flash cards. Study each of the words with a partner (or parent). Leave out the words that were missed. Restudy them.
* Say spelling words into a tape recorder. Spell them correctly into the recorder, and listen to the recording.
* Make a rebus using some of the words. Use syllables and pictures to get ideas across clearly.

* Make a word picture with the spelling words. Lightly draw with pencil a basic shape. In thin black marker, write the words in small lettering around the basic outlined shape. Now erase the pencil marks and the words will form the shape!
* Find letters in magazines or newspapers. Glue down each letter on a paper forming spelling words with a variety of printed letters.
* Make up word skeletons. Give them to a partner, who must figure out the words. Example: _ _ s _ r _ _ e _ t for the word *instrument*. You may need to give a clue if your partner is stumped. Check that your partner has spelled the words correctly.
* Place the words in alphabetical order.
* Write out each of the words. Circle the silent letters and underline the vowels.
* Study with a partner. Take turns dictating words and writing them on a dry-erase board or magic slate.
* Make up rhymes from the spelling words.
* Have someone dictate the words to you. Write your words using the copy, write, cover, check method (CWCC).
* Trace words with a pencil while spelling the word. Then trace with an eraser. Get up and do a brief physical activity (for example, five jumping jacks). Now write the word and check for accuracy.
* Illustrate words and keep a notebook or card file of those words.
* Underline misspelled letters or trouble spots in words.
* Use the "Look, Say, Write" method of practice. Look at the word and trace it with your finger or pencil. Then say the word, spelling it out loud while copying it. Next, write the word without looking and check for accuracy. Fix any errors immediately because it helps with remembering the correct spelling of the word.
* Find as many little words within words as possible (words in sequence only). Examples: *incredulous* (in, red, us); *lieutenant*: (lie, tenant, ten, ant).

Instructional Suggestions for Teachers

In another of my books (Rief, 2003), I presented the following ideas for teachers:

* Introduce words on the overhead projector. As a class, ask students to look at the configuration, little words within the word, and any mnemonic clues that would be helpful in remembering how to spell the word. Write the word in syllables in different colored pens. Discuss the word's meaning and use in context.

* Have readily available several resources for student access, such as dictionaries, electronic spell-checkers, lists of commonly used words, and so forth.
* Use commercial games that teach and reinforce spelling (for example, Scrabble®, Boggle®, Hangman®).

Note: *When playing games in which correct spelling is not a requirement, extra bonus points can be awarded for words that are spelled correctly to add the incentive for spelling accuracy.*

* Have students develop their own personal lists, word banks, word cards attached to a ring, notebooks, card files, and so on, for spelling words they wish to keep and practice. This is particularly useful when these personal spelling words are selected from misspelled words from the student's own written products.
* Teach students to look for patterns in words by using phonograms, word families, onsets, and rimes. Color highlight patterns within the words.
* Provide systematic phonetic training to enable students to become good spellers. It is very important to explicitly teach letter/sound correspondence—the code of the English language. At least 50 percent of

words in the English language are phonetically regular and can be decoded and/or spelled correctly with phonetic knowledge and strategy application.

* In addition to teaching words with different phonetic spelling patterns, teach words from high-frequency word lists. Make it a grade-level priority to teach and reinforce the spelling of a certain number of words from a list of high-frequency vocabulary words.

* The high-frequency words that students are expected to spell correctly in their written work should be posted in a highly visible location. In addition, student desk/notebook copies can be provided for reference.

* Maintain a word wall in the classroom that includes content area words, high-frequency words, and irregular words, as well as other words deemed important listed under each letter of the alphabet.

* Teach students to use every other line when writing rough drafts of papers. When writing, students can circle, put a question mark, or write "sp" above any words they think are probably spelled wrong. This helps them to self-monitor, and they can also apply strategies for checking the spelling of those words.

* Provide daily hands-on opportunities for active exploration of words (referred to as "word study"). Word-sorting activities are key word-study strategies *(see Bear, Invernizzi, Templeton, & Johnston, 1996).*

* Provide students with words on cards, Post-it Notes, or sheets to be cut out and sorted by a pattern, feature, or category; for example, sorting words written with letter combinations: ar/or; ea/ee; ng/nk; ch/sh/th; tion/sion; open syllable/closed syllable words. The word sorts depend on the students' stage of spelling development and skills that need to be practiced and reinforced (for example, sorting by beginning sounds, short vowels/long vowels, prefixes/suffixes).

* Word sorts are helpful in calling the students' attention to features of a word (for example, spin/spine, win/wine, grim/grime) and noting the pattern.

* Use mnemonics whenever possible to help students remember and learn memory strategies to apply in the future. Example: He is a fri**end** to the **end**.

* Use choral, unison techniques for practicing spelling of irregular words—those that are not spelled phonetically (for example, "said," "of," "where"). Chant words or clap out words and use voice inflections to help call attention to certain letters (for example, emphasizing in a louder voice the tricky letters).

* When dictating words, stretch out the word and say it slowly. Model the technique and encourage students to use it when spelling, pulling apart the sounds to hear them more distinctly.

* Provide many peer tutoring and partner spelling opportunities (quizzing, practicing together in fun ways).

* Post models or exemplars of different phonograms for student reference (for example, picture of an eagle or seal for **ea**; picture of a house or mouse for **ou**; a train or snail for **ai**).

Accommodations and Modifications

The point is that all methods do not work for all children, so don't hesitate to modify even further if necessary for special needs students:

* Reduce the number of words required to be learned for spelling tests. Students with reduced lists may be tested only on the predetermined number of words (for example, ten or twelve out of the twenty). But they may try all of the other words on the class test, which would be added bonus points if they answer any correctly.

* Instead of assigning some of the very difficult, low-frequency words on spelling lists, assign high-frequency words that are likely to be used in students' writing.

* Allow and encourage the use of a spell-checking device.

* Increase the amount of practice.

* Grade content and spelling/mechanics separately.

INTERVIEW WITH BRITA
(37 Years Old, California)

Brita was diagnosed as an adult with learning disabilities and ADHD (inattentive type).

What are your memories of elementary school?

"My family was one of avid readers. I grew up surrounded by books. I loved to be around books, but I couldn't read them. I remember how much I loved hearing my teacher read *Charlotte's Web* to the class in third grade. Hearing the stories was so powerful. My biggest frustration was not being able to get further in my reading."

Tell me how your attention difficulties affected you in school.

"One of the pitfalls with ADD is that I would have my good days and my bad days. I never knew when the trap door would open and I'd lose my train of thought. For example, in class I would want to ask a question. I would raise my hand and repeat in my head over and over the question I wanted to ask, so I wouldn't forget. In the meantime, I would miss everything in between the waiting and getting called on. I lost a lot, and it was very frustrating. I spent hours on homework. Reading and writing were very difficult for me."

What about junior high and high school?

"One of my survival skills was being 'Miss Goody Two Shoes.' I wasn't popular, but that didn't matter much to me. Friends came second to my wanting to do well. Teachers always liked me. I would always tune in to what the instructors wanted and do what I could to please them.

"I had some very good teachers. A lot of my trauma was self-inflicted. I used to have teachers so fooled. I fooled everybody, but in fooling people (for example, hiding that I couldn't read), I thought I was cheating. In speaking with a lot of other adults who have learning disabilities, many of us felt that we were cheating by not doing what was expected of us the traditional way. We might have squeaked through the system, but we had to find our own methods. Most of us knew when we were very young that something was wrong, but we didn't know what.

"In junior high I remember being the last to get started. I would sit down to write something, but I just couldn't get started. I would get so frustrated, and my anxiety level would go up and up, making it worse. I often felt that my body and I were separate. My body was next to me. My brain and body weren't coordinated with each other."

How did you cope with your difficulties?

"I had trouble coping. In fact, I went through periods of serious depression. I saw psychiatrists when I lived back East. No one ever figured out that I couldn't read. I have learned how to accommodate myself. In class I sit up front, close to the teacher and do as much one-to-one with the teacher as possible. In college I never missed a single class. I am a very disorganized person, but I have an office that I am responsible for organizing. I can do this successfully by setting up visual cues for myself. I set things up in neat little boxes and color code them all. I use electronic tools to help me compensate, and I take advantage of Recordings for the Blind and Dyslexic, which will record books and texts on tape for individuals with learning disabilities. If I can't reach the top shelf, I can with a ladder. So what if you need aids to compensate! I can do a lot of things that others can't do. I'm very creative. I'm learning to pat myself on the back now, so I don't go back into that black hole I was in for thirty years."

3.3

Reaching Students Through Their Learning Styles and Multiple Intelligences

*H*ow do children learn that it is all right to be different—to learn, think, approach problems in different ways? How do children come to accept others and recognize that we all have strengths in some areas, weaknesses in others? Children learn that we all have our unique differences—which are to be respected, appreciated, and celebrated—by what we (significant adults in their lives) model, communicate, and teach about diversity. This may indeed be one of the most important lessons parents and teachers can ever teach, if we hope our children will grow up to be tolerant, empathic adults who are capable of developing positive relationships in their lives and working successfully in a global society.

One of the best ways to instill this understanding in our students is to teach them that we each have our own uniqueness, comprised of (among many other things) varying learning styles and multiple intelligences (Rief & Heimburge, 1996). Students need to be developing understanding that we all learn differently, that there is no right or wrong way to learn. It is helpful if, from the first week of school, teachers communicate to their students something like, "Each of us has our own unique way of learning, and may need some different kinds of help in order to do our best at school. Therefore, I will probably treat each of you differently throughout the year—to make sure you all get what you need to be successful in this class." This kind of statement also addresses the common concerns teachers have about "fairness issues" when they provide accommodations (academic or behavioral) for individual students or do something for one student that is not typically done for the rest of the class. Fairness is not treating everyone the same, but providing the support and help each individual needs in order to have an equal chance to achieve success.

We all have different learning styles that affect our ways of thinking, how we behave and approach learning, and the ways we process information. Through learning style training, teachers first go through a self-awareness process. A variety of instruments may be used for learning style assessments. First, teachers take a close look at their own functioning as learners—their own propensities, strengths, weaknesses, and preferences, and how that is transferred into the classroom they teach. It is enlightening to see the variety of styles among us, to better understand ourselves and our colleagues. This awareness and sensitivity to learning styles helps us become better equipped to teach all kinds of learners, especially those students who struggle academically, emotionally,

181

and behaviorally in the classroom (Rief & Heimburge, 1996).

Teachers who are committed to differentiating instruction (Section 3.1, Reaching Students Through Differentiated Instruction) employ many methods in order to reach and teach all students in the classroom. Differentiated instructional practices require use of numerous strategies to engage the attention, interest, and active participation of students (Section 2.5, Attention!! Strategies for Engaging, Maintaining, and Regulating Students' Attention). It involves skill in flexible grouping of students with a focus on cooperative learning (Section 3.4, The Advantages of Cooperative Learning for Students with ADHD). Differentiated instructional strategies are multisensory in nature—involving all of the senses (Section 3.2, Multisensory Instruction). Another key component of differentiated instruction is attention to students' diverse learning styles and their multiple intelligences—teaching through and building on students' strengths and making accommodations and adaptations to support in areas of weakness.

We all benefit from being exposed to a variety of strategies. It is a wonderful discovery that there are many ways to do things, not one "right" way. Teachers who offer their students a balance of instructional methods, groupings, structures, and environmental adaptations that take into account the diversity of learning styles in their classroom will be most effective in reaching all of their students (Rief & Heimburge, 1996).

Learning Styles

A number of definitions of learning styles exist. Dr. Rita Dunn (1988) defines them as "the way in which each learner begins to concentrate on, process, and retain new and difficult information." Learning styles have also been described as how one deals with ideas and day-to-day situations, one's learning preferences and propensities, how one approaches thinking, and how one best perceives and processes information.

As pointed out in Section 3.2, Multisensory Instruction, by far the majority of students prefer and perform better with visual and tactile-kinesthetic techniques. Yet, in many classrooms—particularly at the secondary level—the primary mode of instruction is through lecture (auditory means).

Modality (Sensory) Preferences and Instructional Strategies

Not everyone learns in the same way. Our "learning styles" encompass a number of factors, such as cognitive styles and sensory modality preferences (visual, auditory, tactile-kinesthetic). Modality preferences are the sensory channels through which it may be easier for a person to learn and process information. It does not mean that one has an impairment or weakness in the other modalities/channels, but that one *favors* a particular means of receiving information (input) or in showing his or her understanding (output).

The following (Rief, 2003) describes what it means to be an "auditory learner," "visual learner," or "tactile-kinesthetic learner." Most people learn through a combination of all of the above. It is important for teachers to recognize the different types of learners, as well as the need to use a variety of teaching strategies that address students' diverse learning styles, and draw on their different strengths.

Visual Learners

These types of students learn best by:

* Seeing, watching, observing, viewing, and reading
* Visual stimulation: pictures, images, graphics, and printed words

Support visual learners by providing and encouraging the use of

* Graphic organizers
* Written directions (including pictures)
* Maps, charts, diagrams

* Handouts
* Flash cards
* Films, videos/CDs/DVDs, multimedia presentations
* Advance organizers, framed outlines
* Modeling, demonstrating, illustrating
* Color-highlighted materials
* Overhead projector
* Dry-erase, flannel, and magnetic boards
* Clustering, webbing, diagramming
* Strategic use of color (organizing and highlighting important information to remember)
* Letter cards (arrange into words), word cards (arrange into sentences), and sentence strips (arrange into paragraphs)
* Circling, underlining, drawing boxes, and using visual symbols next to important information
* Outlining the configuration of word shapes and color-coding structural elements (for example, prefixes, syllables, suffixes, vowels) to aid visual learners with word recognition and spelling
* Visual cues to alert, get attention, and remind student (for example, taping a picture cue or key word of target behavior card on the child's desk, pointing to a visual prompt of routine or expectation)
* Prompting students visually: "Can you see what I mean?" "Look at this . . ."

Auditory Learners

These types of students learn best by:

* Verbalizing, listening, explaining, and discussing
* Asking and answering questions
* Studying with a partner or small group
* Thinking out loud/self-talk

Support auditory learners by providing and encouraging the use of

* Music (rhythm, beat, and melody) to reinforce learning of information
* Rhyming/verse/song

* Drama
* Stories
* Speeches
* Debates
* Books on tape/access to listening post
* Brainstorming
* Oral reports
* Word games
* Paraphrasing
* Verbal repetition
* Spelling bees
* Audiotapes
* Phonics
* Readers' theater
* Cooperative learning (work with partners or small groups)
* Think-pair-shares
* Discussions
* Study groups
* Reciprocal teaching
* Auditory cues to alert, get attention, and remind student (for example, use of a brief verbal message such as, "Listen . . . this is important," and nonverbal auditory signals such as chimes, a bell)

Tactile-Kinesthetic Learners

These types of students learn best by:

* Touching, doing, moving (physical activities)
* Hands-on learning

Support tactile-kinesthetic learners by providing and encouraging the use of

* Frequent movement opportunities
* Learning games
* Experiential learning
* Field trips
* Project-oriented, active learning
* Objects to touch/manipulatives
* Lab experiences
* Performances, role playing, simulations
* Crafts, construction
* Various arts/crafts
* Computers and other technology

* Concrete examples for abstract concepts (for example, arm wrestling to demonstrate the conflict between protagonists and antagonists in a story)
* Tracing with fingers on sandpaper, carpet, and other textures/surfaces
* Studying information by reciting, rehearsing, and, if possible, by reading while in motion (for example, walking, riding a bike, jumping rope, bouncing a ball, jotting down notes, or other active means)
* Tactile-kinesthetic cues (for example, hand on shoulder) to alert, get attention, and remind student

Cognitive Style Preferences

Learning styles also are comprised of cognitive styles, which include analytic-global learners and left-right hemisphere preferences. The terms left-brain or left-hemisphere dominant/right-brain or right-hemisphere dominant, analytic/global, and inductive/deductive have been used in the literature over the past several years to describe individuals' learning styles.

In most cases, the left cerebral hemisphere of the brain controls the functions of language, sequential thinking, literal thinking, logical/rational thinking, reasoning, and analysis. Reading, writing, and speaking, as well as time awareness/orientation are generally left hemisphere functions. Basically analytic, inductive, and "left-hemisphere dominant" individuals are the kind of learner who tend to have the following characteristics, according to Rief & Heimburge (1996):

Analytic, left-hemisphere dominant learners tend to be logical, sequential, linear processors who learn best by:

* Working from parts to whole
* Making lists
* Using words/language to process information
* Following written directions
* Following schedules
* Following step-by-step in a process

Global, right-hemisphere dominant learners tend to be simultaneous, holistic processors of information who learn best by:

* Seeing the "big picture" (given examples of the end product)
* Focusing on the whole or main concepts first, and then tackling the details
* Clustering, webbing, mind mapping, and other such techniques
* Seeing patterns
* Using images/graphics
* Discussing the relevance and making connections (particularly at an emotional level)

In most cases the right cerebral hemisphere controls the following functions: simultaneous processing, imagination, sense of color, musical abilities, pattern thinking, spatial tasks, and intuition. This is the creative and emotional side of the brain. These individuals tend to be spontaneous, intuitive, creative, and random, and typically have visual, tactile-kinesthetic learning styles.

Although research supports that the left and right hemispheres of the human brain have specialized functions—processing and storing information differently—both usually work together when learning as an integrated whole. Also, specialization does not mean exclusivity. These functions are not always exclusive to only one hemisphere. Research shows that most people have a preferred hemisphere and that this preference affects personality, abilities, and learning style. The preference runs the gamut from neutral (no preference) to strongly left or right. Once again, preference for either hemisphere does not mean that we do not use both hemispheres. In doing a simple task, we use the hemisphere that will accomplish it more efficiently. When we are faced with a task that is more complex, the preferred hemisphere will take the lead, although the non-preferred hemisphere will likely be involved, as well (Weisman & Banich, 2000).

Learning Style Elements

Among the leaders in "learning styles" are Drs. Rita and Kenneth Dunn. Both are professors and researchers who developed a well-known model of learning style elements. The Dunn and Dunn Learning Style Model (which can be viewed in its graphic form on the website of the Learning-Styles Network (www.learning styles.net), describes twenty-one specific elements that comprise a person's individual learning style.

According to the Dunns, there are

* *Environmental elements*—an individual's preference regarding *sound, light, temperature,* and *design* in the learning environment
* *Emotional elements*—a person's level and/or type of *motivation* for learning (for example, intrinsic/extrinsic), *persistence* on a learning/instructional task, *responsibility* (independent worker/needing supervision or feedback), and need for *structure*
* *Sociological elements*—how an individual prefers to work on a learning task (for example, working by *self,* in *pairs,* in *small groups, teams,* with *adults,* or *varied*)
* *Physiological elements*—*perceptual* modality preferences, *intake* (need to eat, drink, or chew while engaged in learning activities), *time* (preference for time of day to work on tasks requiring high concentration/effort), *mobility* (need to move while involved in concentration)
* *Psychological elements*—including *global-analytic* preferences in learning, *hemispheric* preferences, and *impulsive-reflective* style

Of the emotional elements, students with ADHD typically have difficulty with the elements of motivation and persistence to task. They need far more extrinsic motivation (for example, rewards/incentives) than the average child in the class. They also need more supervision, feedback, and structure from adults than other students that age/grade usually require. Teacher supports and ingenuity in creating lessons and learning activities that will be engaging (increasing their motivation to begin the task and persist until completion) are necessary.

As will be discussed in Section 3.4, cooperative group learning is an important structure for the classroom—with great benefits for all students. However, students with ADHD may struggle being productive, cooperative workers in a group situation, and often do best working with a good, focused and supportive partner. Sometimes, it is best to work alone, and students may be more productive and attentive to task. Adult supervision/monitoring/feedback almost always needs to be increased significantly for students with ADHD. So basically, of the sociological elements, varied approaches may work best, with an emphasis on optimizing partner work opportunities for students with ADHD.

Of the physiological factors, for students who have ADHD, the elements of intake, time, and mobility should be considered as relevant. Keep in mind that students who are on stimulant medications may not be hungry in the morning. In spite of parents' efforts to get them to eat breakfast or the availability of breakfast programs at schools, some children on stimulant medication may just not have the appetite to eat. That may be a factor as the morning wears on and they get hungry, if they had no breakfast. Consider having a stash of something nutritious available for any students who need a little snack and didn't have one with them from home. Also, water intake is important. We need to drink water for our brains to function optimally. Many teachers permit students to bring a water bottle with them to class (especially on hot days).

Time is certainly an element that is relevant for students with ADHD. They commonly have difficulty with time awareness and time management. Also, be aware of the factor of time when children are taking medications.

Children who take a short-acting stimulant prescription need to get their second dosage on time (usually around lunch time), or there will be a negative effect on the child's learning and behavioral performance when the morning dosage wears off. It cannot be left to the child to remember to go to the office for his or her second dose without some kind of reminder, because of the difficulty they usually have with memory and time awareness. Fortunately, there are long-acting formulas of medication for treating ADHD, which have eliminated the problem of needing a dosage of medication provided at school and which steadily maintain the positive effects on reducing symptoms throughout the school hours. Keep in mind the time factor when scheduling activities, classes, and so forth and try to schedule for optimal alertness and performance.

Mobility is another key element. We know that our students with ADHD physiologically *need* to move. Teachers must try to structure lessons and build frequent opportunities for movement into instruction, in order to address the needs of students who learn best kinesthetically.

Of the psychological elements, many students with ADHD tend to be more global (big picture) learners. Any kind of visual or real models to show what is expected help. Any examples of final products that have the elements required for "at standard" or "above standard" criteria are important for all students (very important for those with ADHD) to see, in order to better plan how to produce to that standard or performance level.

Finally, because children with ADHD are so impulsive, we must make a concerted effort to teach them how to be more reflective. Teach self-monitoring techniques. Use self-evaluations after completing an assignment or project (such as forms, rubrics, journal entries, and so forth), requiring them to reflect and self-assess how well they performed. Identify things they are particularly proud of and what they can do better next time.

Environmental Adaptations and Accommodations

Environmental factors are another element of learning style. The following are a number of strategies (Rief, 1998) that are essential to effective classroom management and preventing behavioral problems. They also address the needs of diverse learners, and accommodating individual learning styles

Seating

Seating is a big environmental factor for students with ADHD. Providing preferential seating is an important accommodation. In most cases, a preferred choice of seating for a student with ADHD would be

* Within close proximity to the teacher and the center of instruction
* Within easy access for cueing, prompting, monitoring, supervising
* With the desk positioned so teacher can easily and frequently make eye contact with student
* Surrounded by well-focused, tolerant, and supportive peers (if possible)
* Away from (whenever possible) distracting locations or high-traffic areas such as doors, windows, learning centers, pencil sharpeners, heating/air-conditioning units

Disruptive and/or distracted students often do better in individual desks rather than at group tables. Physically arrange the classroom with options for seating. For example, single desk options as opposed to two-person desks/tables for those students who need more buffer space.

Typically, for students with ADHD, table formations where desks are clustered with four to six students per group and facing each other is not recommended (although commonly used in most elementary classrooms). More optimal desk formations are

* U-shaped/horseshoes
* E-shaped
* Straight rows
* Staggered rows (for example, groups of four students per row in the center; and slanted groups of two students per row on the peripheries)

The key to furniture arrangement is the ability of the teacher to easily access (with as few steps as possible) each student without obstruction. The best classroom management strategy is teacher proximity—moving among the students, monitoring, cueing, and giving feedback. (See Section 2.1, Classroom Management and Positive Discipline Practices, for more information on this topic.)

If you are able to have some flexibility (providing choices and options as to where and how students do their work), it is very helpful for students with ADHD. Many children with ADHD have a difficult time working in their seats at their desks. Here are some options that have been found helpful and can increase student productivity and on-task behavior:

* For children who have discomfort and trouble sitting in their seats, try seat cushions. Two recommended cushions are Movin' Sit Jr. and Disc O'Sit Jr. Both are inflatable "dynamic" seat cushions that accommodate a child's need for squirming and wiggling in the chair.
* There are a number of other options to sitting in one's seat to work. For example, allowing a child to sit on a beanbag chair with paper attached to a clipboard may increase productivity and motivation.
* Attach paper to an easel and allow student to stand and write.
* A round therapeutic ball, a T-stool, or the kind of computer seat that is meant to be knelt on are sometimes helpful alternatives to sitting and working at a desk and hard chair.

* Allow ADHD students an alternative desk or chair in the room (two-seat method).
* Permit the student(s) who cannot sit for very long to stand near the desk while working at certain times (if productive).

In addition:

* Be open, flexible, and willing to make changes in seating when needed. Be responsive to student complaints about their seating, and honor reasonable requests to move.
* Have variation in desks, seats, and tables (single and double desks, rounds), and allow some students more desktop space.
* Be sure desks are adjusted (raised or lowered) so that each student can sit at a desk and chair of the appropriate height. Make sure furniture is stable, not wobbly (which can be quite a distraction for a student with ADHD).
* Allow students to move to a quiet corner or designated area of the room if needed.
* Be sure desks and tables are positioned so that all students can see the board and overhead screen, or at least are able to move their chairs easily to do so.
* Provide "office areas" or "study carrels" for seating options during certain times of the day as needed (Rief, 2003).

Structure to Reduce Auditory and Visual Distractions

Permit students to use earphones to block out noise during seatwork, test taking, or other times of the day. Some teachers purchase sets of earphones to be used for this purpose or allow a child to bring to school his or her own earphones. It is encouraged that *all* students experiment with and be allowed to use these tools (not just students with special needs).

One of the best environmental modifications for students at the elementary level with attention difficulties is provision of study carrels or office areas. It is very helpful to have two or

three "office areas" in the classroom for optimal use during seatwork/concentration time (particularly test-taking). By making these desirable areas and available for anyone who requests them, you are preventing them from being viewed by the class as areas of punishment.

Purchase or construct privacy boards to place on tables while taking tests, or to block visual distractions and limit the visual field at other times of the day. Construct desk-size, collapsible privacy boards with three pieces of heavy chipboard and duct tape.

In addition:

* Reduce the clutter and unnecessary writing and visual overload in the classroom.
* Keep a portion of the room free from distracters. Do not seat a student with ADHD under mobiles or other hanging objects.
* If the room is not carpeted, it helps to insert old tennis balls on the tips of each chair leg to reduce the noise level.

* Allow students to move to a quiet corner or designated area of the room if needed.
* Establish rules and procedures for movement within the classroom: when it is okay to get up, get a drink, sharpen pencils, and so on, to reduce distractions in the environment.
* Have designated quiet times of the day.

Add Organization and Structure to Materials and Space in the Environment

* Designate physical boundaries with colored masking tape on the carpet, floor, or tables.
* Define areas of the room concretely.
* Have informal areas of the classroom (for example, carpet area, soft cushions, beanbag chairs).
* Provide desk organizers to help children easily locate materials.
* Store materials in clearly labeled bins, shelves, tubs, trays, and/or folders.
* Use furniture, shelves, and partitions to divide space.
* Provide some students extra workspace and/or storage space.
* Remove any unnecessary furniture from the classroom, creating additional free space.

Add More Visual and Auditory Cues to the Environment

* Use colored signals (red, yellow, green cards) to indicate the noise level permitted in the class at that time. For example, "red zone" means it must be silent (for example, for test-taking). "Green zone" may mean quiet, inside voices permitted.
* A similar visual cue can be used to indicate the degree of movement permitted, for example, must be in seats; quiet, purposeful movement around the room is permitted.
* Use private visual cues—look at me, time to listen, no talking.
* Post all schedules, calendars, and assignments.

* Have pictures and/or a list of rules and daily routine.
* Provide a lot of visual prompts, models, and displays for student reference (including visual depictions of procedures, routines, and rules).
* Use tools such as timers (various kinds), bells, and so forth for signaling changes of activity. The visual CD *Time Timer* available at www.timetimer.com and the overhead timer *TeachTimer*™ by Stokes Publishing Company, www.stokespublishing.com, are highly recommended.

Use of Music

The use of music in the classroom is another environmental consideration. Music can be used during transitions, to calm and settle a class, particularly after recess, P.E., lunch. Music can be played quietly during work periods. For some students with and without ADHD, music increases productivity. Music can be used for arousal and activating (when the class needs energizing—particularly in the afternoon). Many students enjoy and benefit from having music in the classroom. Others do not, and cannot tolerate it. Make provisions for those who can and cannot.

Experiment with background music at different times of the day and for various activities/purposes (for example, to calm and relax, motivate, and stimulate thinking). Try a variety of instrumental cassettes/CDs, including environmental sounds (for example, rain forest), Baroque music, classical, jazz, show tunes, and so on. (See Section 6.2, Music for Relaxation, Transitions, Energizing, and Visualization, for recommended musical selections.)

Address Physical and Sensory Needs

Be sensitive to the physical needs of students that may interfere with learning: need for a drink of water, snacks, use of restroom. As mentioned earlier, consider allowing students to bring bottles of water to school. Teachers may want to keep a stash of some healthy snack food available, if needed.

Provide for students (particularly ADHD students) who have a physiological need for mobility. Build in many movement opportunities throughout instruction. Be aware of their need to exercise, and avoid using loss of recess time as a consequence for misbehavior or incomplete work. Allow exercise breaks, running the track, and doing errands for the teacher that enable children to leave the classroom (for example, to take something to the office). Build in stretch breaks or exercise breaks after sitting any length of time (Rief, 2003).

Other Sensory Input in the Environment

Certain aromas are sometimes used that have various effects. There has been research in aromatherapy regarding the use of scent to create or change behavior. The following are scents that apparently are good for alertness or attention: peppermint, wintergreen, pine, lemon, eucalyptus, and spearmint. Aromatherapists say the fragrances of chamomile, jasmine, lavender, sandalwood, marjoram, and honeysuckle have positive effects on relaxation or reflection (Karges-Bone, 1996).

Note: *Because of individual sensitivities to different scents or possible allergies, teachers would have to use them very cautiously in the classroom. However, parents may wish to experiment, for example, with one of the mint fragrances in the homework area.*

Colors are known to have various effects on behavior. Teachers may want to consider use of certain colors for specific purposes. For example, orange, purple, and red raise levels of alertness. For relaxation, pale blue or green, light pink, lavender, peach, or rose are recommended. In general, cool hues such as blue are relaxing (Karges-Bone, 1996).

Multiple Intelligences

"Multiple Intelligence (MI) theory proposes that people use at least seven relatively autonomous intellectual capacities—each with its own distinctive mode of thinking—to approach problems and create products. Every normal individual possesses varying degrees of each of these intelligences, but the ways in which intelligences combine and blend are as varied as the faces and the personalities of individuals." (Gardner & Blythe, 1990)

Dr. Howard Gardner, professor of education at Harvard University, developed the theory of multiple intelligences (MI). In his book *Frames of Mind* (1983), he posed the theory that there are at least seven distinct intelligences and corresponding styles of learning. Since then, Dr. Gardner added an eighth intelligence and is researching at least one other at this time.

Gardner's Eight Multiple Intelligences

Linguistic Learner. Word smart: These individuals are adept in verbal and language skills (reading, writing, speaking). Lawyers, journalists, broadcasters, and novelists are some professionals who require this aptitude. Linguistic learners are able to appreciate and use metaphors, analogies, various forms of humor, and play with language (word games, tongue twisters, puns). People with strength in this intelligence are often good at playing games such as Scrabble®, Wheel of Fortune®, hangman, and crossword puzzles. They may be skilled in debating, learning foreign languages, and any forms of oral or written communication. They generally do well in school, as they learn and can express themselves best through oral and written language (Kagan, Kagan, & Kagan, 2000; Rief & Heimburge, 1996).

Logical Mathematical Learner. Number smart: These individuals are skilled at manipulating numbers, problem solving, and analytical reasoning and are good at interpreting data, figuring things out, and exploring abstract patterns and relationships. Mathematicians, scientists, and engineers are some professionals who require this aptitude. These individuals learn best through the opportunity to experiment, search for patterns, and make their own discoveries. They typically enjoy games of strategy such as various card games, Rummikub®, Battleship®, and so forth (Rief & Heimburge, 1996).

Spatial Learner. Art smart: These individuals are skilled at visualizing, perceiving, and recreating aspects of the spatial world. They use their mind's eye, making mental pictures, and are adept with drawing, constructing, designing, creating, building, painting, and imagining. Sculptors, painters, navigators, architects, and interior designers are some professionals who require this aptitude. These individuals learn best through visual presentation (use of images, color, pictures, graphics) and opportunity to engage in artistic activities. Games such as Pictionary® address this intelligence (Rief & Heimburge, 1996).

Bodily-Kinesthetic Learner. Body smart: These individuals are adept in physical activities and executing goal-oriented movements with their bodies (for example, surgeons, athletes, dancers, actors, craftspeople, mechanics). They learn best by doing—through active learning, movement, and hands-on activities. Bodily-kinesthetic learners often report that they need to be in movement to process new information (walking/pacing, acting out a concept, manipulating objects). Various sports, crafts, and games such as charades address this intelligence (Rief & Heimburge, 1996).

Musical Learner. Music smart: These individuals appreciate, recognize, and are attuned to rhythm, melody, pitch, and tone. Musicians, singers, instrument makers, conductors, and composers are professionals who require this aptitude. They should have the opportunity to listen and respond to, produce, and express through music. They learn best through music (for example, melody, rhythm, and songs that teach). They often seek background music when they work (Rief & Heimburge, 1996).

Interpersonal Learner. People smart: These individuals are sensitive and attuned to others' feelings, moods, and desires and motivations. They are empathic and understanding of other people's needs and often are the mediators of conflicts and leaders. Therapists, clergy, teachers, social workers, salespeople, and politicians are some professionals who require this aptitude. These individuals enjoy and learn best through interaction with others (for example, cooperative learning and games with partners/groups) (Rief & Heimburge, 1996).

Intrapersonal Learner. Self smart: These individuals understand and know themselves well. They are introspective, often dreamers, and are able to recognize and pursue their own interests and goals. This important intelligence enables a person to utilize self-knowledge to guide actions and make decisions. Philosophers and theologians have strength in this intelligence. These people often like to work alone, be independent, have time for reflection and introspection, and often learn best working at their own pace, in their own space, on individualized projects (Rief & Heimburge, 1996).

Naturalist Learner. Nature smart: These individuals appreciate, recognize, and understand flora, fauna, rocks, clouds, and other natural phenomena. They enjoy collecting, analyzing, studying, and caring for plants, animals, and environments. They are sensitive to interdependence within ecologies and to environmental

issues. Ecologists, farmers, biologists, zoologists, landscapers, and botanists are some professionals who require this aptitude (Kagan, Kagan, & Kagan, 2000; Nicolson-Nelson, 1998).

Everyone has abilities in all of the above multiple intelligences. However, most people excel in only one or two areas. A recommended activity in our book *How to Reach & Teach All Students in the Inclusive Classroom* (Rief & Heimburge, 1996) is entitled "100 Percent Smart." It involves students identifying how they perceive their own distribution of strengths and weaknesses. They make a pie graph of "I Am 100-percent Smart" using Gardner's multiple intelligences.

Student Learning Style/Interest Interview

When teachers are trying to learn more about their students' learning style preferences, interests, and motivators, one of the best ways to find out is to *ask* them. The following are some sample questions teachers may wish to ask students in one-to-one interviews. It is very rewarding to find the time to meet with students individually, talk with them, and get their input (as to how they learn best and what they enjoy doing in and out of school). A great deal of information can be learned in this interview format. Also, students typically appreciate their teacher's attention and interest in learning more about them as unique individuals.

A number of surveys, questionnaires, inventories, and learning style assessments are available. They can provide valuable insight as to how one learns best. This is useful for teachers wishing to address individual learning differences and for the child/teen in his or her development of most effective study skills and learning strategies.

The following is an example of interview questions (from Rief, 1998) that incorporate many of the learning style elements, such as those described throughout this section.

Note: Teachers choosing to interview students will need to record responses either in direct notes, on a tape recorder, or a combination of both.

Learning Style Interview

1. Think back over the past few years of school. Whose class did you feel most comfortable in? Tell me a little about your favorite classes—ones you felt successful in. What did you particularly like about those classes or teachers?

2. What are some of the best school projects you remember doing? Is there any project you did or activity that you participated in that you are especially proud of?

3. Do you prefer working in a classroom that is warmer or cooler in temperature?

4. When you are trying to concentrate in class or read silently, do you need the room to be completely quiet? Do you mind some amount of noise and activity during these times when you are trying to concentrate, study, or read silently? Do you think it would help to use earphones or earplugs to block the noise? Would it help to have some music in the background, or would it distract you?

Note: More questions may be asked regarding music preferences/dislikes.

5. I want you to imagine that you can set up the perfect classroom any way you want. Think about it and tell me or draw for me how you would like the classroom to be arranged. Would you like the tables or desks in rows? Tables/desks in clusters? Tell me (show me) where you would choose to sit in order to learn best in this room. Where would you want the teacher to be standing when giving instructions?

6. Do you like to do school projects alone, or would you prefer to work with others?

7. When you have to study for a test, do you prefer to study alone? With a friend? Small group? With a parent or teacher helping you?

8. In your classroom, if you had a study carrel (private office area or partition) available, would you choose to do your seatwork in it if some other students in your class were also using them?

9. When do you feel you are able to do your best work and concentrate best? In the morning before recess? After recess but before lunch? After lunch in the afternoon?

10. Do you usually get hungry and start wishing you could have a snack during the school day? What time of day do you usually start feeling hungry?

11. If your teacher assigned a big project, giving you choices of how to do it, would you prefer to:
    — Make an oral presentation in front of the class?
    — Tape record something?
    — Act it out/drama?
    — Build something (for example, from clay or wood)?
    — Draw something?
    — Write something/type it (or have someone else type it)?

12. Do you think you are good at building things? Taking things apart and putting them back together?

13. Do you like listening to stories?

14. Are you good at learning words to songs?

15. Do you like to read? Write stories? Do math? Do science experiments? Do art projects? Sing? Dance? Play an instrument? Play sports? Which ones? Use the computer?

16. What school subjects and activities do you usually do best in? What do you like about those subjects/activities?

17. What are the subjects/activities that you usually have the hardest time doing at school? What don't you like about those subjects/activities?

18. What kind of school assignments do you dread or hate having to do?

19. Tell me what you think you are really good at. What do you think you are not so good at?

20. Do you ever feel you cannot concentrate in class and have problems paying attention? What kinds of things distract you?

21. How is it easier for you to learn: when someone explains something carefully to you or when someone shows you?

22. If you have to give directions to somewhere or instructions for how to do something, is it easier for you to explain and tell that person or is it easier for you to draw a map or write it down for them?

23. When do you concentrate best and prefer to do your homework: soon after you get home from school? Have a break (play first) after getting home from school, but do it before dinner? Do it after dinner?

24. What are your favorite things to do at home?

25. If you had a chance, what would you love to learn to do? For example, if you could take special lessons or have someone work with you to teach you, what would you really want to learn how to do?

26. At home, where do you usually do your homework? If you had your choice, in what place in the house would you like to do your homework/study?

27. Pretend that your parents would build you or buy whatever you needed in your home for a good study space. What would it look like and have in it?

28. Do you like to be alone or with someone else around when studying/doing homework? Do you need it to be really quiet? Do you like having some music or background noise when studying?

29. At school (in this classroom) name five people you prefer to work with in partner activities. Don't name your best friends; give me names of students with whom you can productively get work done well.

30. If you were to work toward earning a special privilege, activity, or other reward at school, name some things you would like to be able to earn.

31. What do you think is important for your teacher to know about you?

32. If you were promised a trip to Hawaii with your family and also $1,000 for spending money only if you got an "A" on a very difficult test (for example, a social studies test covering four chapters, with lots of information and stuff to memorize and learn):
    — How would you want your teacher to teach it to you?
    — Tell me exactly what you would like your teacher to do in class so that you can learn the information.
    — How would you go about memorizing all the information you were taught?
    — How would you need to study at home?
    — What kind of help would you want your parents to give you?
    — Do you want to study alone? With someone? Tell me as much as you can.

INTERVIEW WITH AMY
(17 Years Old, California)

Amy was diagnosed at a young age with ADHD (inattentive type) and learning disabilities.

Tell me about your favorite teachers in school.

"My best teacher was in second grade. She expected so much of you and she made learning fun. She wasn't mean, but she was firm. She gave me individual time, had me come up to the board, and really talked to me. When I had trouble concentrating, she had me sit at a table with walls around it, but it wasn't a punishment. It was just so I could work without distractions. It was a very supportive classroom.

"My history teacher last year was very understanding. You were supposed to read a whole chapter at a time, and at the end of each section, answer the questions. I worked really hard but couldn't get it done in time. Then I told my teacher that I have a learning disability. I am dyslexic. He gave me all the time I needed. I was never frustrated or nervous in his class."

How about your worst classes?

"In tenth grade my math class was so difficult for me. I would raise my hand for ten minutes and the teacher always ignored me. He would walk right by me and never listen to me or help."

What is your advice to teachers?

"Teachers should be understanding of the child's needs. If the kid says, 'I just need a little more time on this,' the teacher should say, 'Okay. Would you like more time tomorrow? Do you want to take it home or do it in the Learning Center?' Sometimes teachers are so difficult, you just want to cry. You get so frustrated!"

3.4

The Advantages of Cooperative Learning for Students with ADHD

The crux of differentiated instruction (see Section 3.1) requires teachers to employ methods and strategies that enable *all* students, with their diverse learning abilities and differences, to be able to master the curriculum and content/performance standards. This is achieved through instruction, assessment, and learning activities that are meaningful and engaging. Cooperative learning is one of the best means of doing so, with decades of research that validates its efficacy. All teachers should be trained in best practices for implementing cooperative learning in the classroom. Teachers may mistakenly believe they are using cooperative learning when they simply have students working together in groups. This is not cooperative learning. In fact, students (particularly those with ADHD) often have difficulty learning and functioning productively in unstructured group work. Cooperative learning involves a high degree of careful planning and structuring, and as such it is an excellent format for students to learn, including those with ADHD. When students are taught how to work as a team, and given the opportunity to learn and produce cooperatively with peers supporting one another in their learning, significant gains (academic and social) can be made by all.

Dr. Roger T. Johnson and Dr. David W. Johnson—researchers, professors, and co-directors of the Cooperative Learning Center at the University of Minnesota, Minneapolis, are national authorities and leaders on cooperative learning. They explain that all learning situations can be structured so that students either *compete* with each other ("I swim, you sink; I sink, you swim"), *ignore* each other and work independently ("We are each in this alone"), or *work cooperatively* ("We sink or swim together").

With *individualization* there is no correlation among goal attainments. Students work by themselves to accomplish learning goals unrelated to those of other individuals. With *competition* there is a negative correlation among goal attainments. Individuals work against each other to achieve a goal only one or a few can attain. Through *cooperation* there is a positive correlation among goal attainment. Individuals in the group work together to achieve shared goals and maximize their own and each other's learning. Cooperative learning is supported by a vast amount of research as the most beneficial structure in the classroom. Much of the information presented in this section is summarized from *Cooperation in the Classroom* (Johnson, Johnson, & Holubec, 1998), and used with their permission.

The Five Elements of Cooperative Learning

Johnson, Johnson, and Holubec discuss the following five elements of cooperative learning:

1. *Positive Interdependence.* This is the most important element—when group members perceive that they need each other to complete the task and cannot succeed unless everyone in the group is successful. To structure positive interdependence, the teacher must establish and include mutual goals, joint rewards, shared resources, and assigned roles.

2. *Individual Accountability.* Each member of the group must be accountable for contributing his or her share of the work. The teacher must assess the performance of each individual in the group and give the results to the individual and the group. There are various ways to provide for individual accountability that may include giving each group member an individual exam, observing, and recording the frequency of each member's contribution, randomly calling on one member to answer questions or present his or her group's work to the teacher/whole class.

3. *Face-to-Face Promotive Interaction.* A few children (usually three or four) are grouped together, arranged facing each other (eye to eye, knee to knee). Team members promote each other's productivity by helping, sharing, and encouraging each other's efforts to produce and learn. This facilitates the building of personal commitment to each other, as well as to their mutual goals.

4. *Interpersonal and Small Group Skills.* Students do not come to school with all the social skills they need to collaborate effectively. Teachers must teach teamwork skills as purposefully and precisely as they teach academic skills.

5. *Group Processing.* Group members need to discuss how well they are achieving their goals and maintaining effective working relationships. Give time and procedures for students to evaluate how well their group is functioning. For example, after each session have groups answer: "What did we do well in working together today? What could we do even better tomorrow?" In addition, teachers monitor groups, providing feedback on how well they are working together.

Many students without proper structure and management have difficulty working cooperatively. Students with ADHD tend to struggle the most in such group situations. Teachers need to take particular care in planning for students who have difficulty inhibiting their behavior and attending to task so that they will be successful academically and socially within the cooperative learning situation. Children with ADHD should be placed in groups when possible with peers who are supportive, relatively tolerant, and positive role models. If the cooperative learning assignment provides for students with ADHD (as well as all students) to assume a role of responsibility in the group and to contribute to the assigned task in ways that draw on their strengths and interests, most are motivated and successful in the cooperative group format.

Students with ADHD will likely need more monitoring, prompting (for example, through visual cues and gentle reminders), and rewards. If the child is on an individualized behavioral program (for example, a daily report card or token system), the student's degree of cooperative and productive behavior every X number of minutes of group time can be rewarded—providing extra incentive. If the student is uncooperative, does not comply with cooperative group rules and behaviors (for example, leaves the group to wander around, is disrespectful in words and actions to group members), a punishment or response cost can be applied. At times a student may need to be removed temporarily from the group if highly disruptive or uncooperative (but still be held accountable for the task being done in the group). For the most part, this is a supportive learning situation in which most students like to work (if it is well-structured and supervised and the learning task is interesting and motivating).

Getting Started with Group Work

Here are some ways to use groups in the most productive way:

* Pre-plan instructional decisions about how to structure (group size, roles, materials, room arrangement).
* Establish signals (to move into groups, to quickly get students' attention), and other management strategies before implementing any cooperative learning format.
* Make up groups that are preferably heterogeneous and small in size: pairs, triads, with a maximum whenever possible of four.
* Seat students close to fellow group members (seating conducive to facing each other when speaking and listening, and sharing materials comfortably).
* Think through and plan for each of the five elements of cooperative learning described earlier.
* Plan how to integrate cooperative learning experiences throughout the curriculum.
* Assign each student a role or job to do (for example, reader, recorder, checker for understanding, encourager of participation or cheerleader, materials or resource handler). Roles should be flexible and rotated so that all students have a chance to assume various roles.
* Clearly explain the academic task and criteria for success.
* Explicitly teach critical social skills.
* Make your expectations of group behavior clear: explain, model, role play, and demonstrate.
* Be prepared to spend your time circulating throughout the room, observing and questioning students while they are working.
* Monitor, provide feedback, and reinforce students.
* Be prepared to intervene when necessary to improve a group's task work or teamwork.

Structuring to Achieve Positive Interdependence

Help students realize that they achieve their goals only if all members of the group also attain their goals. This can be achieved by using any of the following structures and techniques from Johnson, Johnson, and Holubec (1998):

* *Structure positive goal interdependence.* For example: "You are responsible for learning the assigned material and making sure that all other members of your group learn the assigned material."
* *Require one answer from the group.* Randomly select or collect only one product that is signed by all (meaning that all contributed, can explain, and defend). This single product represents the group for evaluation.
* *Establish a mastery level required for each member and reward for success.* For example, the group goal is for every member to demonstrate 90 percent mastery (or other criterion) on a particular test. The group is rewarded with extra points if all members attain the goal: "If all members of your group score at least 90 percent (or X percent), each of you will receive five bonus points [or other reward]."
* *The goal is for the overall group score to reach the criterion specified.* Each member's individual scores are added to make a total group score. The total group score must reach a specified criterion for success.
* *Build positive interdependence through regular celebrations of group efforts and success.*
* *Build interdependence by the division of labor*—through different roles necessary to the group dynamics and/or different student

responsibilities (for example, each member being responsible for parts of the task).

* *Provide resources that must be shared* (division of materials), which also helps build positive interdependence.

Teaching Social Skills Through Cooperative Learning

Section 1.7, ADHD and Social Skill Interventions, addressed the social challenges and difficulties with interpersonal relationships that are common among children/teens with ADHD. It was explained that some children have social skill deficits—in which they have not learned how to perform a specific social skill. However, typically children with ADHD do not have a

skill deficit, but a performance deficit. Due to their problems with inhibition and self-control, they know what they are supposed to do, but fail to perform the skill when needed.

Cooperative skills are essential for getting along in life. Whether a child is deficient in social skill awareness or in social skill application, it is vital to be able to learn and practice these skills in order to use them appropriately in daily life. There is no better place or structure for teaching and practicing appropriate social skills than through the context of working in groups together with classmates in real learning situations.

There are different ways to teach what working cooperatively "looks like" and "sounds like." The behaviors must be stated very explicitly. One

DECKER FORREST

way is to develop a *T-chart* together with the students. A specific social skill is selected (for example, reaching agreement). Then behaviors describing what reaching agreement might *look like* are listed, for example, heads together, smiling, shaking hands, thumbs up. Similarly, behaviors are listed under what reaching agreement might *sound like*: "Good idea." "How do you feel about that?" "What do you think?" (Johnson, Johnson, & Holubec, 1998).

Brainstorming the behaviors for the specific social skill and then creating a rubric of observable behaviors demonstrating that skill is another technique teachers may use. Groups can refer to the rubric and score themselves on the criteria after the cooperative activity.

In the context of each cooperative group lesson, incorporate one or more social skill or collaborative skill to teach and practice (along with the instructional and academic tasks). Teach the skill by explaining the need and importance in students' daily lives. Together with students, brainstorm what the skill would look like and sound like to any observer. Model, demonstrate, and role play examples (and non-examples). As students are working, circulate around the room, recording observations of groups' implementation of the targeted social skills. As students are working, positively reinforce pro-social skills; and at the end of the lesson, provide feedback—sharing your observations. In addition, have students self-evaluate their group's performance on the targeted skill(s). (See Section 1.7, ADHD and Social Skill Interventions.)

As discussed in other sections of this book, visual cues in the environment are very important in helping to remind and prompt students about behavioral expectations. Create posters with illustrations and a few brief words depicting the proper social skills/behaviors. A visual cue card of those expected behaviors can be provided at the start of each cooperative group activity to each group (along with other group resources provided). Another strategy is to take photos of students demonstrating the proper cooperative behaviors and using those as cues—either at the groups' working sites or hanging in the room as a visual display.

In addition to Johnson, Johnson, and Holubec, the Kagans (2000) are other leading experts on cooperative learning. Their acronym for what they see as the four basic principles of cooperative learning is PIES: P (positive interdependence), I (individual accountability), E (equal participation), S (simultaneous interaction). They have developed a variety of structures and formats for teachers to use that ensure that all students within the group are active and equal participants. Rather than participate sequentially (one student at a time), the task is structured for simultaneous interactions—significantly increasing the degree of each student's response opportunities and participation. As was discussed in Section 2.5, Attention!! Engaging, Maintaining, and Regulating Students' Attention, high-response opportunities and active participation are vital for the success of students with ADHD.

The Kagans and others have developed a number of structures teachers can choose to implement in cooperative groups to ensure the above principles of cooperative learning are being addressed in each lesson. For example, one strategy the Kagans recommend that equalizes participation during a team open-ended discussion is "Talking Chips." It basically involves providing each member of the group a certain number of plastic chips. Any student on the team can begin the discussion by placing his or her chip in the center of the team's desk and keeping his or her hand on the chip while speaking. When finished, the chip is left in the center of the desk. Other team members do the same when they wish to speak. Teammates continue in this fashion while sharing their ideas (Kagan, Kagan, & Kagan, 2000). This is an excellent strategy to use with students who have ADHD, as it helps them regulate their impulsive talking and provides structured practice in how to take turns appropriately.

There are wonderful resources available on the "how-to's" of implementing cooperative learning in the classroom. It is advisable to integrate cooperative learning as much as possible into daily instruction. There are so many benefits for *all* students, but especially for children who are more difficult to motivate, keep engaged, and desperately need to practice social skills at "the point of performance"—in real situations, it is a very valuable instructional format. Cooperative learning is particularly beneficial for students with ADHD because it allows for high-response opportunities, increased peer interaction in a structured format, and practice of social skills in an authentic setting and context (Rief, 2004).

The following "Social Skill Lesson Plan," "Report Form: Social Skills," and "Ideas for Monitoring and Intervening" are adapted from *Cooperation in the Classroom* (Johnson, Johnson, & Holubec, 1998) and are used with their permission.

Social Skill Lesson Plan

What social skills are you going to teach?

_____

_____

_____

_____

STEP 1: How are you going to communicate the need for social skills?

_____ Utilize room displays, posters, bulletin boards, and so forth.

_____ Tell students why the skills are needed.

_____ Jigsaw materials on the need for the skills.

_____ Have groups work on a cooperative lesson and then ask students to brainstorm what skills are needed to help the group function effectively.

_____ Give bonus points or a separate grade for the competent use of the skills.

_____ Other(s): _____

STEP 2: How are you going to define the skill?

Phrases (list 3):

_____

_____

_____

Behaviors (list 3):

_____

_____

_____

How will you explain and model each social skill?

_____ Demonstrate the skill, explaining each step of engaging in the skill, and then re-demonstrate the skill.

_____ Use a videotape or film to demonstrate and explain the skill.

_____ Ask each group to plan role-play demonstrations of the skill to present to the entire class.

_____ Other(s): _____

Social Skill Lesson Plan, contd.

STEP 3: *How will you ensure that students practice the skill?*

_____ Assign specific roles to group members, ensuring practice of the skills.

_____ Announce that you will observe for the skills.

_____ Have specific practice sessions involving nonacademic tasks.

_____ Other(s): _____

STEP 4: *How will you ensure students receive feedback and process their skill use?*

Teacher Monitoring: **How will you monitor students' use of the skill and give feedback?**

_____ Formally observe with a social skills observation sheet, focusing on each learning group an equal amount of time (30 minutes, 6 groups, each group is observed for 5 minutes) and counting how many times each student uses targeted skill and other needed behaviors.

_____ Informally observe each group: give verbal or written feedback on how well members are working together and using the targeted skill.

_____ Other(s): _____

Teacher Intervening: **How will you prompt groups to use the skill?**

_____ Noticeably give positive feedback to group using the skill to remind surrounding groups to use it.

_____ Supplement positive feedback with a tangible reward to students or groups using the skill.

_____ Give a "secret note" to a group member asking them to use the skill; praise the whole group when the group member does it.

_____ Other(s): _____

Student Observers:

_____ Have one student in each group tally each time a member uses the skill while they continue to participate in the group work.

_____ Teach students to observe using a social skills observation sheet. Students take turns sitting outside the group and observing members' use of the skill.

_____ Provide time for the student observers to give group members feedback.

Processing: **Students need to reflect on their skill use so they can congratulate themselves for improvement as well as devise ways to continuously progress. How will you have students reflect on their use of the skill?**

_____ Ask them to analyze the feedback from you (the teacher), student observers, and their own memories.

_____ Provide questions to help the groups engage in reflective thinking: "How well did you use the skill?" "How well did each group member use the skill?" "What are some things that helped you use the skill?" "What are some things that helped group members use the skill?"

Social Skill Lesson Plan, contd.

_____ Help the students plan for continuous improvement with questions such as: "What are two things you did today to help your group?" "What do you plan to do differently next time to help your group work better?" "What did you learn about being a good group member?"

STEP 5: *How will you ensure that students persevere in practicing the skills until it becomes natural?*

Daily:

_____ Remind them that you will be listening for their use of the skill.

_____ Give feedback on what you heard.

_____ Have them process their use of the skill.

Periodically:

_____ Discuss with the class the stages of learning a skill (awkward, phony, mechanical, and automatic).

_____ Have students or groups rate their level of use and chart progress.

_____ Give class reward if students use their skill a preset number of times.

_____ Have the principal, an aide, a parent, or another teacher observe and give feedback on how frequently the skill is being used.

_____ Tutor or coach target students on the use of the skill.

_____ Have students think of places outside of the class to use the skill, have them do so and report on how it went and what they noticed.

When most students have reached the automatic stage, plan to teach them another skill!

Report Form: Social Skills

Student: _____   **Date:** _____   **Grade:** _____

N = Needs Improvement   *P = Making Progress*   *S = Satisfactory*   *E = Excellent*

Shows Cooperative Attitude (Forming Skills)
____ Moves into Group Quietly
____ Stays with Group; No Wandering
____ Uses Quiet Voice in Group Work
____ Takes Turns
____ Uses Others' Names
____ Respects Rights of Others
____ Positive About Working in Group
____ Is Willing to Help Others
____ Follows Directions
____ Shows Courtesy Toward Others

Leadership (Functioning) Skills
____ Gives Direction to Group's Work
____ Contributes Ideas, Opinions
____ Requests Others' Ideas, Opinions
____ Summarizes, Integrates
____ Encourages Others' Participation
____ Supports; Gives Recognition, Praise
____ Paraphrases
____ Facilitates Communication
____ Relieves Tension
____ Clarifies Goals

Facilitates Understanding (Formulating) Skills
____ Summarizes, Integrates
____ Seeks Accuracy
____ Relates New Learning to Old
____ Helps Group Recall Knowledge
____ Checks for Understanding
____ Makes Covert Reasoning Overt

Intellectual Challenge (Fermenting) Skills
____ Differentiates Members' Ideas
____ Integrates Members' Ideas
____ Asks for Rationale, Justification
____ Extends Others' Reasoning
____ Probes; Asks Complex Questions
____ Criticizes Ideas, Not People

Adapted from *Cooperation in the Classroom,* Interaction Book Company, 7208 Cornelia Drive, Edina, MN 55435.
© Johnson, Johnson, & Holubec.

Ideas for Monitoring and Intervening

CHECK FOR	IF PRESENT	IF ABSENT
Members seated closely together	Good seating.	Draw your chairs closer together.
Group has right materials and are on right page	Good, you are all ready!	Get what you need, I will watch.
Students who are assigned roles are doing them	Good! You're doing your jobs.	Who is supposed to do what?
Groups have started task	Good! You've started.	Let me see you get started. Do you need help?
Cooperative skills being used (in general)	Good group! Keep up good work!	What skills would help here?
A specific cooperative skill being used	Good encouraging! Good paraphrasing!	Who can encourage Kate? Repeat in your own words what Kate just said.
Academic work being done well	You are following the procedure for this assignment. Good group!	You need more extensive answers. Let me explain how to do this again.
Members ensuring individual accountability	You're making sure everyone understands. Good work!	Roger, show me how to do number 1. David, explain why the group chose this answer.
Reluctant students involved	I'm glad to see everyone participating.	I'm going to ask Helen to explain number 4. Get her ready and I will be back.
Members explaining to each other what they are learning and their reasoning processes	Great explanations! Keep it up!	I want each of you to take a problem and explain to me step-by-step how to solve it.
Group cooperating with other groups	I'm glad you're helping the other groups. Great citizenship!	Each of you go to another group and share your answer to number 6.
One member not dominating	Everyone is participating equally. Great group!	Helen, you are the first to answer every time. Could you be accuracy checker?
Groups that have finished	Your work looks good. Now do the activity written on the board.	You are being very thorough. But time is almost up. Let's speed up.
Group working effectively	Your group is working so well. What behaviors are helping you?	Tell me what is wrong in the way this group is working. Let's make three plans to solve the problem.

Adapted from *Cooperation in the Classroom,* Interaction Book Company, 7208 Cornelia Drive, Edina, MN 55435. © Johnson, Johnson, & Holubec.

3.5

Organization, Time Management, and Study Skills

*F*or those with ADHD, most are challenged in their daily lives (from a mild to severe degree) with weaknesses in organization, time management, and study habits. It is common for students with ADHD to be unprepared for class (for example, frequently losing or misplacing papers, leaving needed books/materials and completed homework at home). They are often late. Poor time awareness and time management typically cause students to have incomplete work and fail to meet important deadlines/due dates. This is a direct result of their "executive function" deficits (see Section 1.1), which involve difficulties with:

* Memory/forgetfulness
* Judging and managing time
* Activation (mobilizing and getting started on tasks)

* Sustaining attention, alertness, and effort
* General self-management and ability to work toward future goals

It is no wonder that parents and teachers lament about homework and the work production struggles that plague children and teens with ADHD. Students with an attention deficit disorder (even those who do not have academic difficulties per se in reading, writing, or math) will require parents and teachers to provide assistance and structure in organization and time management. This includes support and training in:

* Organizing their materials and work space
* Recording their assignments consistently
* Utilizing and referring regularly to a planner/agenda

* Planning and prioritizing activities
* Making a schedule and following it
* Planning for short-term assignments
* Breaking down and systematically tackling long-term assignments
* Knowing standards of acceptable work
* Reading and regularly using a calendar
* Reading an analog (as well as digital) clock
* Judging more accurately the amount of time allotted to do a task and time it takes to actually complete it
* Knowing what to take home and leave home daily
* Knowing what to take home and return to school
* Knowing when and where to turn in assignments
* Knowing what materials are needed and expected
* Homework preparation: Having what is needed to do the homework
* Homework monitoring: Making sure the homework is done, brought back to school, and turned in

What Teachers and Parents Can Do to Help Build Organization Skills

Supplies and Materials

It is highly recommended (Rief, 1998, 2003) that schools have a policy requiring all students to carry a bookbag/backpack and specific notebook to and from school daily. Beginning in the third (or perhaps fourth grade), students should be required to use a three-ring binder containing colored subject dividers and a pencil pouch for the notebook (including a few sharpened pencils with erasers and other small supplies/essentials). This notebook should also contain a three-hole punched calendar or agenda for recording assignments. Children in primary grades—beginning at kindergarten—should also begin the habit of carrying a folder to and from school daily in their backpacks. Notebooks or folders for all students should have designated pockets/areas for papers to take home and leave at home and papers to return to school (Archer & Gleason, 2003).

The assignment sheets or calendars/planners for recording assignments should be hole-punched and prominent—located up-front in the notebook. If using a daily or week-at-a-glance calendar for recording assignments, there should also be a month-at-a-glance page within the notebook. Whatever system is used, it must be utilized consistently for recording all classroom assignments. Teachers and parents must model, monitor, and reinforce the daily use of these tools.

Have a consistent location in the notebook for storing homework assignments and other papers categorically. There are a variety of ways for doing so, such as:

* Use colored pocket folders (single pocket or double) that are three-hole punched and inserted into the notebook. For example, a red folder can be labeled "homework" and contain all homework (either one for all subjects placed at the front or back of the notebook, or one red folder behind the tab for each subject). A different colored folder may be labeled for graded and returned papers, or anything to "leave at home."
* Some prefer to use colored folders labeled "to do" and "done/turn in."
* Another option is use of large laminated envelopes that are three-hole punched and inserted into the notebook for homework, assorted project papers, and so forth.
* Jenks recommends paperwork be separated into "do," "doing," and "done" categories (Jenks, 2003).
* Newton suggests colored tabs behind each subject area (for example, "daily work and notes," "tests or quizzes") to further organize within each subject area. She also recommends a three-hole punched expandable file folder with opening toward the

binder rings to hold anything that becomes loose and items that are not three-hole punched, such as index/note cards (Newton, 2003).

Parents and teachers should model and reinforce how papers should be organized by placing them behind the tabs of the appropriate subject section of the notebooks. There should be a supply of clean notebook paper behind a separate tab of the notebook, or within each subject section.

It will also be essential to provide the necessary supplies for homework and to keep them readily accessible. Parents can help their child considerably in cutting down on wasted time spent searching the house for homework supplies and materials. Not only is it a frustrating waste of precious minutes, but it also causes a major break in productivity, pulling children unnecessarily off-task. It is recommended to create a "homework supply kit."

The Homework Supply Kit

The Homework Supply Kit can be stored in anything portable—preferably a lightweight container with a lid. Some children work at their desks; others on kitchen or dining room tables; and others prefer to spread out on their beds or the floor. With this system, it does not matter where your children choose to study. The necessary supplies can accompany them anywhere. Recommended supplies (depending on age of your child) (Rief, 1997):

Plenty of paper	Paper clips
Sharpened pencils with erasers	Single-hole punch
	Three-hole punch
Pencil sharpener	Dictionary
Ruler	Thesaurus
Crayons	Electronic
Paper hole reinforcers	spell-checker
	Self-stick notepads
Glue stick	Highlighter pens
Colored pencils	

Colored pens and markers (thick and thin points)	Index cards
	Calculator
Stapler with box of staples	
Clipboard	

Class, Room, Desk, and Work Areas

Students with ADHD need a desk or table with as much tabletop space as possible, with tools and structuring to limit the clutter. Help children minimize the amount of materials on and in their desks. Some do better with a basket or box on the floor next to the desk/table for keeping needed papers and books easily accessible and visible, but not on the desk or tabletop until needed.

There are many strategies that can be implemented to help structure the work area to make it more organized and manageable.

Teachers

* Organize the classroom with clearly labeled shelves, files, and bins so that you and the students know precisely where things belong and can easily locate them.
* Clearly identify certain places in the room (trays, color-coded folders, or boxes) where students consistently turn in assignments or store unfinished work.
* *Schedule* regular times for students to sort and clean out their desks and notebooks. Students with problems in organization need direct assistance sorting and dumping (recycling) unnecessary papers periodically. Any adult or a peer buddy can be used for this purpose.
* Make sure students have adequate storage space and as few materials to worry about as possible.
* You may want to try an organizational system in your room with tubs or trays labeled "to be checked," "corrected work to return," "needs help." Students know precisely where

to turn in work to be checked. The teacher, student teachers, parent volunteers, cross-age tutors, or other assistants in the classroom can pull assignments from the "needs help" tray and assist individual students.

Parents

* Together with your child, choose a place in the home for homework that has adequate lighting, is comfortable for working, and is as free from distractions as possible.

* Carefully examine your child's workspace. Make sure there is a large working surface (desktop) available that is free from clutter. If your child has a computer, do not place it on the desk, as it considerably cuts down on his or her working surface area. Instead, place the computer on a separate desk or table.

* Have your child clear out desk drawers and shelves of work, projects, and papers that were from different school years. Together, decide on what you would like to keep and store out of the way (in colored boxes, zipper portfolios) in order to make room for current papers and projects.

* Provide your child with a corkboard and pins to hang up important papers.

* Label trays and bins for storing supplies/materials that will remove some of the clutter from the desktop.

* Provide the necessary storage space (shelves, closet space, bins, trays, drawers) for organizing your child's room efficiently.

* Keep a three-hole punch and electric pencil sharpener easily accessible.

Use Visual Cues and Strategic Use of Color

Teachers

* Color-coordinate by subject area to make location of subject materials quicker and easier. For example, the science text is covered in yellow paper or has a yellow adhesive dot on the binding; the science notebook/lab book

or folder is yellow; and the schedule with science class period and room number is highlighted in yellow. So is the tab/divider for science in the three-ring notebook.

* Prepare important notices and handouts on colored paper, preferably color-coded for certain categories, for example: weekly/monthly newsletters in blue, spelling lists in pink, and so on.

* Use brightly colored paper for project assignments, providing details and due dates. Give two copies (one for the notebook, and one to be posted at home).

* Use visual/pictorial cues for showing expected materials, daily routines, and schedule. Encourage students to use "self-stick" notes for reminders to themselves. Have them adhere the notes to book covers, in their lockers, planners, and so forth.

Parents

* Dry-erase boards are helpful to hang in a central location of the home for all phone messages and notes to family members. In addition, hang one in your child's room or his or her bathroom for important reminders and messages.

* Write notes and reminders on colored self-stick notes and place on mirrors, doors, and other places your child is likely to see them.

* Encourage your child to also write himself/herself notes and leave them on the pillow, by the backpack, by car keys, and so forth.

* Use electronic reminders and organizers. (See time management tools later.)

* Provide a file with color-coded folders in which your child can keep papers stored by category.

* Color-code entries on a calendar (for example, school-related, sports, social activities).

More Organizational Tips

Teachers

* Provide handouts to students that are always three-hole punched in advance.

* Attach a pencil to the child's desk (either with string or Velcro).
* To help keep papers stored appropriately in the notebook, provide adhesive hole reinforcers for ripped out papers and plastic sleeves for papers that you do not want to punch.
* Encourage students who need daily reference tools (for example, times tables chart, frequently misspelled words list, or dictionary) to keep these in a section of their notebooks.
* Teach your expectations for materials that students should have with them in class at all times (for example, sharpened pencils with erasers, notebook paper). Allow for natural consequences of not having needed materials. DO NOT reinforce poor study habits and "reward" students who are unprepared by giving or loaning them new, desirable materials/supplies. Instead, if they have to borrow from you, provide less desirable materials as substitutes. Some teachers keep recycled paper and a can of golf pencils and/or old pencils and erasers for this purpose.
* You may want to keep spare supplies available so that time is not wasted with students searching or asking around to borrow from classmates. However, consider "charging" students (for example, they must pay you from their class money/tokens) or fining in some way (points), for not being prepared and having to borrow supplies from you.
* Begin and end each school day with a five- or ten-minute organizational session. The time may be used to clean out tote trays, review materials needed for the day, check folders, ensure that homework assignments have been recorded, and check that homework materials are being taken home (Illes, 2002).
* Provide containers (for example, bins, buckets, organizing trays, baskets) as needed for supplies in or on desks/tables.
* Particularly for younger children, store tote trays near the teacher's desk. This will permit the teacher to monitor the child's tote tray and will prevent the student from being distracted by its contents. Limit the contents of tote trays. Attach a list to the tote tray that specifies what materials are allowed to be stored in it (Illes, 2002).
* Teach and provide models of how to organize papers (for example, headings, margins, spacing).
* Provide exemplars/models of well-organized, projects, science boards, and so forth.
* If the student has trouble remembering to bring books to and from school, provide a second set of books to keep at home.
* Provide direct assistance getting started on homework assignments and projects at school.
* If using a daily assignment sheet or planner, also have students transfer to a monthly calendar any of the due dates for projects, tests, special events such as field trips, or other important dates for the month.
* Require labeling of materials/supplies with students' names.
* Provide bonus points or some reward for improved organization skills, and reward your disorganized students when, upon request, they are able to quickly locate a certain book or paper in their desks/notebooks.
* At the end of the day, check that students have the necessary books/materials in their backpacks to take home.
* Provide in-school help and adult assistance for putting together projects. Many students with ADHD and/or learning disabilities have a hard time laying out the pieces of projects and impulsively glue papers to boards without first planning for the amount of space they have. Help with the little extras (nice lettering on the computer; cutting papers straight with a paper cutter, rather than scissors, and so on), as this will make projects look so much better.

Parents

* Provide the necessary supplies to help your child be organized at school. You will likely

have to replace and replenish supplies often. Have your child take inventory of what needs replacement, or ask the teacher.

* Remove from your child's backpack unnecessary items (for example, toys) that will be a distraction.

* Make the time to help your child clean and organize his or her backpack, notebook, desk, and room.

* Assist your child with cleaning and organizing by at least starting the job together.

* Offer a reward or incentive for straightening and organizing materials, putting away belongings, and so forth.

* If using a token economy system/behavior modification at home, give points or tokens for meeting an organizational/clean-up goal.

* Label all your child's materials and possessions with his or her name.

* Avoid early morning rush and stress by developing the routine of your child getting as much as possible organized and ready for school the night before (for example, clothes/outfit to wear, lunch prepared, everything loaded into the backpack). Shower or bathe in the evening.

* Place the backpack in the same spot every night.

What Teachers and Parents Can Do to Help with Time Management

Time management—making efficient use out of the minutes and hours of our days—is a challenge for many of us. Time management requires a number of skills that involve "executive functions," such as the following (Rief, 1998, 2003):

* Estimating
* Planning ahead
* Prioritizing
* Breaking things down into steps
* Problem solving
* Staying focused on a future goal

For individuals with ADHD, these are areas that pose significant problems. Children and teens with ADHD generally need a great deal of structure and support in order to learn and gain competence in this important "life skill."

Time Awareness

Lack of time perception or awareness is very common among individuals with ADHD. Consequently, they often underestimate how much time they have to complete a task or to arrive somewhere on time. Students with ADHD tend to be oblivious to deadlines and due dates. Remember that this is part of the disorder and not apathy or deliberate misbehavior.

Any opportunity to practice time estimation is very helpful for increasing such awareness. For example, challenge children to estimate how long it takes to walk to the office and back (without running), get dressed in the morning, or any other task. Make a game out of predicting, timing, and checking their time estimates for various activities.

Encourage self-monitoring during homework and independent seatwork time in class by recording the start time on the paper. When the work period is over, have the child record the time (noting, as well, how much work was actually produced). This is helpful documentation, as well, with regard to how well the child is able to stay on-task and work productively.

Assignment Sheets, Calendars, Student Planners/Agendas

Parents and teachers need to communicate and maintain the clear expectation that all assignments are to be recorded on students' assignment calendars, and monitor that this is occurring.

Teachers

* Model the writing of assignments on the calendar using a transparency of the calendar. Take a few moments at the end of the subject period or school day to lead students

in the recording of assignments on their calendars/planners.

* When using an assignment calendar, teach students to write the assignments on the day they are *due*. Walk them through recording on the correct date. Dr. Anita Archer, one of the authors of the popular *Skills for School Success,* points out that *due* dates are when the assignments are to be turned in, not when students are supposed to *"do"* them (Archer & Gleason, 2003).
* Check assignment calendars/planners, as students with ADHD often make careless recording errors, often entering assignments on the wrong date.
* Provide assistance to students who have difficulty recording assignments fully or accurately. Routinely ask table partners or groups seated together to check each other that everything is accurately recorded on calendars.

* Post daily assignments in a prominent, consistent location, as well as maintain a visible, up-to-date monthly calendar of class and school activities.
* If using a daily assignment sheet or weekly agenda, also provide students with a single or double-page monthly calendar for their notebooks. Provide support having students transfer due dates of any projects, tests, class trips, or important activities/events onto their monthly calendars.

An example of a homework assignment log is shown below.

The importance of the planner/assignment calendar cannot be overstated. When the child or teen gets used to recording information into

Homework Assignment Log

Week of: _____

Teacher's signature: _____   Parent's signature: _____

Date: _____   Subject: _____

Assignment _____

    Materials: _____   Due Date: _____

    _____   Date turned in: _____

Assignment _____

    Materials: _____   Due Date: _____

    _____   Date turned in: _____

Assignment _____

    Materials: _____   Due Date: _____

    _____   Date turned in: _____

Assignment _____

    Materials: _____   Due Date: _____

    _____   Date turned in: _____

Assignment _____

    Materials: _____   Due Date: _____

    _____   Date turned in: _____

the planner and referring to it frequently on a daily basis, it will become an indispensable tool for life. Many of us cannot consider managing our lives and myriad responsibilities without our planners/calendars. The sooner we build the habit and routine, the better. The planner/assignment calendar also serves as a powerful means of home/school communication and enables mutual monitoring and reinforcement of school assignments.

Jenks (2003) describes how her school makes use of the planner in additional ways. Students are encouraged to note personal reflections within their planners (for example, "I needed more time with my teacher to clarify her directions"). They also are taught to record estimated (E) time needed for certain assignments and the actual (A) time it took to complete the task. In addition, students are encouraged to prioritize and rank recorded tasks within their planners. For more information, see www.assets-school.net.

Schedules

In other sections of this book (for example, Classroom Management), I discussed the importance for children of establishing a schedule and daily routine in the classroom. Schedules need to be highly visible and referred to frequently. Even kindergarten students should be aware of the schedule, which would be posted in pictures depicting the day's activities in sequence.

Teachers

* Walk through the schedule each day and point out any changes in the daily/weekly routine that will be taking place.
* For students receiving special education/related services, write down their weekly schedules and tape them to their desks. Keep accessible each of your students' special schedules so that you know at all times the days and times they are pulled out of class or when special service providers are coming to the classroom to work with the student.

* Encourage students and parents to carefully plan a weekly schedule, including an established homework/study schedule. Ask parents to first help their son or daughter become aware of how much time he or she spends in a typical day on all activities from school dismissal until bedtime.

Parents

* Help your child create a weekly schedule. Work with your child in the scheduling process by first examining and tracking how he or she spends time during the entire twenty-four-hour day. This obviously includes morning routine before school; hours spent between school dismissal and bedtime; and time spent sleeping.
* After a few days of examining his or her daily schedule, your child should have better awareness of how much time is typically spent on routine activities: meals, sleeping, grooming, walking to class, watching television, talking on the telephone, on the computer, recreational and social activities, and study/homework time.
* Schedule a time for homework. Some children like to come home and immediately get part or all of their homework done and out of the way. Others need a break before tackling any homework. Together with your child, plan a schedule or time for homework that takes into account your child's needs and preferences (best time of day, need for breaks, extracurricular commitments, and family activities). Then do whatever is possible to adhere to the homework schedule as consistently as possible.

Long-Term Projects

Parents and teachers must structure any long-term assignments (for example, book reports, research projects, science fair projects) by breaking them into smaller, manageable increments. The following ideas are from Rief (2003).

Teachers

*   Make sure students have access to needed materials.
*   Assign incremental due dates to help structure the timeline toward project completion. For example, assign separate due dates for stages of the project (getting a topic approved, outline submitted, research notes/resources listed, turning in first draft, and so on).
*   Call close attention to due dates. Post those due dates, refer to them frequently, and remind students and parents in notes home, newsletters, school voice mail, and other ways.
*   Call some parents to make sure they are aware of the projects and have at least one copy of the handout explaining project guidelines, with its timeline and scoring rubric, to keep posted at home.
*   Suggest to parents that they closely monitor timelines and help with pacing (for example, get started promptly on going to the library and gathering resources).
*   Monitor progress by asking to see what the student has accomplished so far, and provide a lot of feedback along the way.
*   Consider providing some of your ADHD students and their parents advanced notice about upcoming projects and reports, enabling them to have a "head start" (especially with planning and research).

Parents

*   Help your child break down longer assignments into smaller, manageable chunks with deadlines marked on the calendar for incremental steps of the project.
*   Pay close attention to due dates (final and incremental steps), and post the project requirements.
*   Together with your child, record on a master calendar the due date of the final project, and plan when to do the steps along the way (for example, going to the library, getting resources and materials).
*   Ask the teacher for feedback. Do not assume your child is working on projects at school, even if he or she is given some time in class to do so.
*   Large and long-term projects can be easily overwhelming and discouraging for your child (and you). Your child will likely need your assistance, as well as help at school, with pacing and monitoring timelines toward project completion.

More Time Management Tips

Parents and teachers need to

*   Assist with prioritization of activities and workload.
*   Teach children how to tell time and read a non-digital clock.
*   Teach children how to read calendars and schedules.
*   Teach and model how to use "things to do" lists (writing down and then crossing off accomplished tasks).
*   Encourage your school to establish a school-wide expectation and organization/study skills program for consistency (for example, *Skills for School Success* [Archer & Gleason, 2003]).
*   Use frequent praise and positive reinforcement, rewards for meeting deadlines, finishing in-school assignments, and so forth.
*   Encourage students who take short-acting medication at school to have a beeper or vibrating watch set for the time they need to go to the nurse's office for their second dosage.

Timers are very useful in providing auditory cues and motivating targeted behaviors within certain time frames.

Note: *See time management tools later for sources of some recommended timers for home and school.*

Teachers

* Provide students with a course outline or syllabus.
* Make sure that *all* assignments, page numbers, due dates, and so forth are presented to students both verbally and visually.
* Post all assignments in a consistent place in the room (for example, corner of the board, separate assignment board).
* Attach a "things to do" list to students' desk, and monitor the practice of crossing off accomplished items.
* Provide enough time during transitions to put material away and get organized for the next activity.
* Set timers for transitions. (First state: "You have five minutes to finish what you are working on and put away your materials." Then set the timer.)
* Teach students how to self-monitor on-task behavior so that they are using class time effectively for finishing their work.
* Include "seated by beginning bell time," or some other behavior, indicating students' punctuality on the home/school monitoring system (for example, daily report card or daily/weekly monitoring form).
* If tardiness is an issue with a student, try an individual contract to motivate the student to improve that behavior.
* Provide extended time as needed, and consider more flexibility with regard to accepting late work.
* Make sure the child is not "circling the task." (Illes, 2002) Children with ADHD often postpone starting a low-interest task by engaging in delay tactics (such as sharpening a pencil or searching the tote tray for some unnecessary materials). Stand next to the student to make sure that the task is begun quickly.

Parents

* Help to plan a "things to do" list when your child comes home from school, scheduling for the evening, and estimating together with your child how long each assignment/ activity should take.
* Let your child choose, but assist in planning what to do first, second, third, and so forth.
* Post a large calendar/wall chart in a central location of the home for scheduling family activities and events. Encourage everyone to refer to it daily. Each family member may have his or her own color of pen for recording on the calendar.
* Expect your child to record assignments (see the teacher for help) and monitor that this is being done. Ask to see your son's or daughter's assignment calendars/sheets/ planners every day.
* Help transfer important extracurricular activities/scheduling onto your child's personal calendar/planner.
* Morning and evening routines/rituals for getting ready for school and preparing to go to bed at night are very helpful. Clear reminders of the routine (for example, through the use of a checklist of sequential tasks to complete) reduce the nagging, rushing around, and negative interactions at these times of the day. Checklists are great tools for time management and staying on schedule.
* With your child, decide on the steps of the routine that he or she is most comfortable with and list in that order. For example: (1) lay out clothes for tomorrow; (2) shower; (3) check master calendar and planner; (4) pack lunch; (5) load backpack.
* Each task that is completed on the list or chart is crossed off (or if it is a permanent chart, a clothespin can be clipped and moved down the steps of the routine as the task is completed.
* Combine the above with a positive reinforcement system. If your child has all items completed and checked off by a certain time, he or she earns extra points or tokens as a reward.

* Use electronic devices with timers to help remember appointments, curfews, and keep on schedule. (See time management tools below.)
* Consider "no phone call" times in the evening, as calls often interfere with staying on schedule.

If organization and time management are areas of weakness for you, as well as your child, seek outside help (for example, consider hiring an organizational coach).

Time Management Tools

In addition to clocks, calendars, and planners/agenda books, there are a number of electronic tools and gadgets that are helpful in time management.

It is recommended that individuals with ADHD get in a habit of wearing a watch. Sports watches are very useful, as many have alarms, countdown timers, and programmable messages. One popular brand of watch for individuals with ADHD is called WatchMinder (www.watchminder.com). It is a vibration watch that has numerous pre-programmed messages (for example, pay attention, do homework, go home) and up to sixteen different vibration alarms. It can be worn on the wrist or attached to a belt with a clip. Individuals with time management difficulties often benefit from wearing or carrying some device that will alert them (either with an audible alarm or vibrator). Cell phone alarms also can serve this purpose, if necessary.

Timers must be a standard tool for the home and classroom. There are various kinds, ranging from inexpensive kitchen timers and sand (hourglass) timers to more sophisticated types. The company Time Timer™ (www.timetimer.com) has timers that are excellent for helping children of all ages easily observe and recognize visually the passage of time (how much time has elapsed and is remaining before the time period ends). Their timers are in the form of an analog clock showing in the color red

the amount of time set for that period, and the red area shrinks as time elapses. Stokes Publishing Company (www.stokespublishing.com) produces a wonderful timer called TeachTimer™ that can also be used on an overhead projector. It has many functions that teachers will find very helpful. When set for a certain amount of time and projected on the overhead in the countdown mode (minutes and seconds), students can see precisely how much time they have remaining before the alarm goes off. Warnings (for example, two-minute) can also be programmed into the timer.

Homework Tips for Parents

Many families have conflicts in their homes over homework. In families of children with ADHD, the challenges and stress surrounding daily homework issues can be very intense—placing an enormous strain on the parent/child relationship.

Dr. Terry Illes (2002) describes how homework is a complex series of subtasks that must be completed in sequential order. In order to complete a homework assignment, the student must:

* Know what the assignment is
* Record the assignment
* Bring the required materials home
* Do the homework
* Return the homework to their bookbag or backpack
* Bring the homework to school

He further explains:

"Children with ADHD have a difficult time maintaining their focus and motivation as they proceed from one subtask to another. They are easily sidetracked and may forget to perform one of the subtasks or simply give up because the process appears to require too much effort. And because ADHD children are unconcerned with future consequences, often the only motivation to perform the homework is to get their teachers or parents off their backs. This explains why students with ADHD commonly complete their assignments and then fail to turn them in. Although adults see the failure to get credit for work completed as being a ridiculous waste of effort, it makes more sense if we understand that receiving credit for the completed homework was never the motivation for completing it. From the ADHD child's point of view, once the homework has been completed, the nagging stopped and playtime resumed, the homework process becomes irrelevant and forgotten." (Illes, 2002)

In addition to strategies suggested for parents and teachers in the organization and time management items of this section, the following are further recommendations to help support children in the homework process:

* Communicate with the teacher(s) early in the year about their homework expectations (for example, how much homework he or she assigns, how long the teacher[s] expect assignments to take). If your child has an IEP or 504 Accommodation Plan, discuss any homework accommodations that may be included within the plan and establish the best way to communicate with each other throughout the year— email, student planner, phone conversations (Hennessy, 2003).
* Establish a routine and schedule for homework (a specific time and place) and adhere to the schedule as closely as possible. Don't allow your child to wait until the evening to start.
* Choose a homework location that is quiet, has low traffic and few distractions, but is accessible and easy for you to be able to monitor homework production.
* Limit distractions in the home during homework hours (reducing unnecessary noise, activity, and phone calls and turning off the TV).

* Assist your child in dividing assignments into smaller parts or segments that are more manageable and less overwhelming (for example, folding a math paper in half or reading to a certain point or page of the book).
* Before starting on homework, provide your child with a snack and bathroom break.
* Assist your child in *getting started* on assignments (for example, reading the directions together, doing the first items together, observing as your child does the next problem/item on his or her own). Then get up and leave. Monitor and give feedback without doing all the work together. You want your child to attempt as much as possible independently.
* Break the homework session into manageable time periods. For example, for children in the lower elementary grades, two ten-minute sessions may be reasonable. For older elementary students, two twenty-minute sessions may be appropriate. For secondary students, perhaps thirty-minute sessions. Use a timer to indicate when each homework session begins and ends. It is recommended to use a digital timer that counts down by seconds (Illes, 2002).
* Praise and compliment your child when he or she puts forth good effort and completes tasks. In a supportive, non-critical manner it is appropriate and helpful to assist in pointing out and making some corrections of errors on the homework. It is not your responsibility to correct all of your child's errors on homework or make him or her complete and turn in a perfect paper.
* Children with ADHD need added incentives to motivate them through the homework process (some kind of reinforcers—such as tokens—as they complete tasks, work productively for X amount of time). Remind them, "When you finish your homework, you can [watch TV, have your friend over, play outside]." Turning in completed homework can also be part of a home/school daily

report card or contract. A larger incentive may be worked out as part of a home/school plan. For example, "If you have no missing or late homework assignments this next week, you will earn . . ." or "If at least 80 percent of assigned homework has been completed this week, you will earn. . . ."

* Let the teacher know your child's frustration and tolerance level in the evening. The teacher needs to be aware of the amount of time it takes your child to complete tasks and what efforts you are making to help at home. If your child's teacher is not willing to make some *reasonable* accommodations, speak with the administrator.

* Help your child study for tests. Study together. Quiz your child in a variety of formats.

* If your child struggles with reading, help by reading the material together or reading it to your son or daughter.

* Work a certain amount of time and then stop working on homework. Don't force your child to spend an excessive and inappropriate amount of time on homework. If you feel your child worked enough for one night, write a note to the teacher attached to the homework.

* If your child is on medication for ADHD during school hours but does not have the benefit of medication during the homework hours of late afternoon/evening, discuss this with your child's doctor. Many families find extended medication coverage through homework hours to be very helpful. An extra dose of short-acting medication or changing to a long-acting formula can make a significant difference.

* It is very common for students with ADHD to fail to turn in their finished work. This is very frustrating to know your child struggled to do the work, and then never gets credit for having done it. Papers seem to mysteriously vanish off the face of the earth! Supervise that completed work is placed in the designated homework folder

and is packed in the backpack the night before. Place the backpack in the same location (for example, by the front door) every evening before going to bed. You may want to arrange with the teacher a system for collecting the work immediately upon arrival at school.

* Many parents find it very difficult to help their own child with school work. Find someone who can. Consider hiring a tutor! Often a junior or senior high school student is ideal, depending on the need and age of your child.

* Make sure your child has the phone number of a study buddy—at least one responsible classmate to call for clarification of homework assignments.

* Parents, the biggest struggle is keeping on top of those dreaded *long-range homework assignments* (reports, projects). This is something you will need to be vigilant about. Ask for a copy of the project requirements. Post at home and go over it together with your child. Write the due date on a master calendar. Then plan how to break down the project into manageable parts, scheduling steps along the way. Get started at once with going to the library, gathering resources, beginning the reading, and so forth (Rief, 1998).

Homework Tips for Teachers

Keep in mind how much longer it typically takes for a student with ADHD to do the work. What takes an average child fifteen or twenty minutes to complete frequently takes three or four times longer for this child!

* Be responsive to parents reporting great frustration surrounding homework. Be willing to make adjustments so that students with ADHD and/or LD spend a reasonable, not excessive, amount of time doing their homework.

* Realize that students with ADHD who receive medication during the school day

(to help them focus and stay on-task) often do not receive medication in the evening. Students with ADHD are in class during their optimal production times, yet will not manage to complete their assigned work. *It is an UNREASONABLE expectation that parents will be able to get their child to produce at home what you were not able to get them to produce all day at school.*

* Many teachers have a practice of sending home unfinished class work. Avoid doing so with ADHD students. Instead, provide the necessary modifications and supports so that in-school work is in-school work, and homework is homework.

* Remember that homework should be a time for reviewing and practicing what students have been taught in class. Don't give assignments involving new information that parents are expected to teach their children.

* Homework should not be "busy work." Make the homework relevant and purposeful—so that time spent isn't on obscure assignments that are not helping to reinforce skills or concepts you have taught.

* Never add on homework as a punishment or consequence for misbehavior at school.

* Make sure you have explained the homework and clarified any questions.

* Supervise students with ADHD before they walk out the door at the end of the day. Make sure they have materials, books, and assignments recorded and in their backpacks.

* Assign a study buddy (or two) to your students with ADHD. They should have one or two classmates who are responsible and willing to answer questions who can be called in the evening about homework if necessary.

* As discussed under time management, one of the most important things you can do to help *all* students (and their parents) keep on top of homework, tests, and long-term projects is to require the use of an assignment calendar/agenda. Then guide, walk through, and monitor the recording of assignments. If this is a daily expectation and routine, it will help everyone.

* With some students, require that parents initial the assignment calendar daily. With this system, it is a good way for you to communicate with parents as well. You may write a few comments or notes to the parent on the assignment sheet and vice versa.

* Modify, modify, modify the homework for students with special needs. Ask yourself: "What is the goal?" "What do I want the students to learn from the assignment?" "Can they get the concepts without having to do all the writing?" "Can they practice the skills in an easier, more motivating format?" "Can they practice the skills doing fewer?"

* Think in terms of shortening and reducing the work load—particularly the amount of written output required.

* Some teachers find having students graph their own homework completion and return rates to be helpful. Improved rates can result in some kind of reinforcement (Warger, 2001).

* Communicate regularly with the parents of students who are falling behind in homework. Work out a system of letting the students and parents know that they are not turning in the homework (for example, monitoring homework chart/form).

* Provide parents with a weekly progress report. A sample weekly progress report is shown on page 221.

* Communicate with other teachers in your team. Students who have several teachers are often assigned a number of tests, large projects, and reading assignments all at the same time from their different classes. Be sensitive to this. Stagger due dates, and coordinate whenever possible with other teachers to avoid the heavy stress of everything being due at once.

Weekly Progress Report

Student's Name _____ Room Number _____ Week Starting _____

Work Habits

____ Worked hard to complete assignments—Great job!

____ Participated and used time effectively most of the week

____ Work completion so-so this week

____ Poor work completion (class and/or homework)

____ Parent/Teacher Conference Needed

Citizenship

____ Excellent Behavior—Tried hard most of the week

____ Acceptable behavior most of the week

____ Behavior so-so this week (some difficulties)

____ Behavioral problems—difficult week

____ Parent/Teacher Conference Needed

Missing assignments listed on back that must be done

Teacher Comments:

Parent Comments:

_____ _____
Teacher's signature   Date

_____ _____
Parent's signature   Date

* Be sure to collect homework and give some feedback. It is very frustrating to students and parents to spend a lot of time on assignments that the teacher never bothers to collect.

* Provide extra copies of texts to lend parents. This avoids problems from leaving needed books at home or school.

* Provide incentives for turning in homework. One wonderful incentive that is being used successfully in classrooms of all grades is called Homeworkopoly® found at www.teachnet.com/homeworkopoly or www.homeworkopoly.com. This website has components teachers can download and use to make, laminate, and hang up in the classroom a game board that looks similar to a Monopoly® game board. Students who turn in their completed homework get to roll a die and move their individual marker that number of spaces along the game board. There are various opportunities along the way to land on special game squares—earning them small prizes or privileges. This is an ongoing game, with students continuing to move around the game board throughout the year. Teachers report that students are highly motivated for the chance to roll the die and move their markers.

* Finally, realize how *critical* it is for students with ADHD and/or learning disabilities to participate in extracurricular activities. They need every opportunity to develop areas of strength (athletics, arts/crafts, music)—which will be their source of self-esteem and motivation. These after-school activities are just as—if not more—important to the child's development as academics. Also keep in mind that many students with learning/attention difficulties work with other professionals in the community (for example, tutors, therapists/counselors) and participate in additional academic training programs outside of school (Rief, 2003).

More Study Skills and Learning Strategies

See Section 3.6 for more information and strategies on study skills, such as memory techniques, reading textbook strategies, test-taking, and note-taking. Also, there are some very useful websites to aid students and teachers. One excellent resource is: www.geocities.com/athens/academy/6617/index6.html.

This is a virtual library for middle school and beyond with excellent links to educational sources for research and homework help.

Learning Strategies and Study Skills

Students with ADHD generally are deficient in their awareness and application of effective skills necessary for learning strategically and studying efficiently. Students with ADHD (as well as those with learning disabilities) may benefit greatly from being taught specific learning and study strategies for school success.

Learning Strategies

Learning strategies are

* Efficient, effective, and organized steps or procedures used when learning, remembering, or performing (Sousa, 2001)
* Thoughts or activities that assist in enhancing learning outcomes (Chamot & O'Malley, 1994)

Chamot & O'Malley (1994) describe learning strategies as encompassing the following types or categories:

* *Metacognitive strategies*—planning for learning, monitoring one's own comprehension and production, and evaluating how well one has achieved a learning objective
* *Metacognitive knowledge*—understanding one's own mental processes and approach to learning, the nature of the learning task, and the strategies that should be effective

* *Cognitive strategies*—manipulating the material to be learned mentally (as in making images or elaborating) or physically (as in grouping items to be learned or taking notes)

Metacognitive Strategies

These are the learning strategies that are often weakest in students with ADHD because of their direct relation to the executive functions. They involve:

* Previewing and planning for how to go about learning or studying the material
* Organizing for the task, getting ready, and setting goals
* Monitoring one's own attention, production, and comprehension
* Self-assessment and evaluation of how well goals were met and learning took place (Rief, 2003)

What is metacognition? It is the explicit awareness in an individual of his or her own unique mental processes. The essence of metacognition is self-knowledge. To be metacognitive is to think about thinking, usually not to solve a problem, but to work out *how* to solve it and then how to generalize from it to a similar problem. So a student faced with an essay to write or physics to learn would articulate the task, plan its solution, monitor and adapt the process, evaluate its success, and bridge from the final solution to other learning or writing tasks (Townend & Turner, 2000).

Metacognitive strategies are self-regulatory—helping students become aware of learning as a process and of what actions will facilitate that process. Students who use metacognitive strategies set goals for learning, coach themselves in positive ways, and use self-instruction to guide themselves through learning problems. They monitor their comprehension or progress and reward themselves for success (Sousa, 2001).

Metacognitive instruction involves providing students with tools to assist them in improving their organizational skills and completing their assignments. It may include a number of different components such as:

* Planning the steps necessary to complete a task
* Ordering those steps into correct sequence
* Monitoring one's progress on those steps

In short, metacognitive instruction helps students think about their assignment, plan the sequence of steps required, and monitor how they are doing on each step (Bender, 2002).

The following are examples of metacognitive learning strategies:

* Previewing the main ideas and concepts of a text
* Organizational planning (figuring out in advance how to accomplish the learning task)
* Planning when, where, and how to study
* Monitoring one's comprehension during listening or reading
* Monitoring one's production (oral or written) while it is taking place
* Monitoring one's thinking while speaking or writing

* Self-assessing how well one has accomplished a learning task
* Keeping a learning log
* Reflecting on what one has learned (Chamot & O'Malley, 1994)

Students applying metacognitive strategies are actively thinking: "How do I learn?" "How can I learn better?" "What plan will I follow?" "How well am I doing?" (Chamot & O'Malley, 1994).

Efficient learners are metacognitive. It is recommended to explicitly teach and practice these metacognitive strategies with all students—but particularly those with ADHD and/or LD, including techniques such as modeling and encouraging students to ask themselves questions such as the following for:

* Self-direction:
  "What is my goal?"
  "What do I need to do?"
  "What will I need?"
  "How will I do this?"
  "How much time will I need?"
* Self-monitoring/self-correction:
  "How am I doing?"
  "Do I need other information/resources?"
  "Do I need more support?"
* Self-evaluation:
  "How did I do?"
  "Did I finish on time?"
  (Hennessy, 2003; Hennessy & Soper, 2003)

There are various metacognitive strategies throughout this book in the sections on organization and time management (Section 3.5), written language (Section 3.9), reading (Section 3.11), and math (Section 3.12); as well as the self-regulation of attention strategies (Section 2.5). Also see strategies that enable students to understand their unique learning style profile and how they learn best (Section 3.3).

The following are a few examples of metacognitive strategies:

Journal Responses

There are a variety of ways to use journals to engage students in thinking, questioning, making associations, and so forth *during* their reading, and responding and reflecting *after* their reading.

* *Double-entry journals*: The paper is divided into two columns. Notes are taken in the left column, citing anything of particular interest to the reader (for example, quote, description, metaphor) along with the page number. In the right-hand column, the reader comments and records personal thoughts, interpretations, connections, and questions triggered by that section of the text.
* *Metacognitive journal / learning log:* The page is divided into two columns. The left column is labeled "What I Learned." The right column is labeled "How I Learned This." This assists students in thinking about and analyzing their own learning process. The right-hand column can state other things, as well, for example: "How this Affects Me" or "Why This was Difficult (or Easy) for Me." The key is reflection and analysis of one's own learning.

Reading Logs

Students can write their feelings, associations, connections, and questions in response to the reading. They may be given specific prompts to guide what is recorded in their logs, for example: "What did you learn?" "How did this make you feel?" "How did this relate to any of your own life experiences?" "What did you like/dislike about the author's style of writing?"

Think Aloud

This approach basically involves externalizing and making overt the thinking processes used when reading—demonstrating what efficient thinking sounds like. Students have a model of what it might sound like to internally grapple with the text.

Note: *For ADHD students with executive functioning weaknesses that may impair their use of inner language, this is an important teaching strategy to model.*

* The teacher orally reads to the students as they generally follow along with the text.
* The teacher models the process of interacting with the text (for example, stopping to guess what will happen next/making predictions, asking questions of self or author, describing what is visualized, working through problems to figure out unknown vocabulary, making connections, and so forth).
* The teacher clearly models how to self-monitor his or her own comprehension by stopping periodically and asking: "Is this making sense to me?"
* Students can then practice some of these strategies with partners (Rief, 2003).

Metacognitive reading strategies involve active monitoring of comprehension while reading by constantly asking oneself questions throughout the reading of the text such as (Townend & Turner, 2000):

* Does this make sense?
* Do I understand this word?
* Do these ideas fit in with previous information?

Cognitive Learning Strategies

Cognitive strategies help a person process and manipulate information to perform tasks such as taking notes or asking questions. They tend to be useful when learning or performing certain specific tasks (Sousa, 2001).

The following are examples of some cognitive strategies (Chamot & O'Malley, 1994):

* *Resourcing:* using reference materials such as dictionaries, encyclopedias, textbooks
* *Grouping/classifying:* words, terminology, quantities, or concepts according to their attributes
* *Note-taking:* writing down key words and concepts in abbreviated verbal, graphic, or numerical form
* *Elaboration of prior knowledge:* relating new to known information and making personal connections
* *Summarizing:* making a mental, oral, or written summary of information gained from listening or reading
* *Deduction/induction:* applying or figuring out rules to understand a concept or complete a learning task
* *Imagery:* using mental or real pictures to learn new information or solve a problem
* *Auditory representation:* replaying mentally a word, phrase, or piece of information
* *Making inferences:* using information in the text to guess meanings of new items or predict upcoming information

The "Strategies Instructional Approach" developed by researchers at the University of Kansas for Research on Learning (Schumaker, Deshler, Nolan, et al., 1981) provide a number of research-validated cognitive learning strategies such as RAP.

RAP

The RAP strategy for paraphrasing involves the following steps:

* *Read* the paragraph.
* *Ask* yourself to identify the main idea and two supporting details.
* *Paraphrase* or *put* the main ideas and details into one's own words.

There are numerous other cognitive learning and study strategies. They are interspersed throughout the academic sections of this book, and also include the following.

SQ3R

This strategy increases comprehension and retention of textbook material (expository or informational) and involves the following steps:

* *Survey*—Briefly look through the reading assignment at the titles, chapter headings, illustrations, charts, and graphs. Skim through the assignment and read the chapter summary and/or end-of-chapter questions.
* *Question*—Turn the headings and subheadings of the text into questions, for example, *producing antibodies* can become: "How do our bodies produce antibodies?" *Organic motor fuels* can become: "What are the different organic motor fuels?"
* *Reading*—Read to find the answers to the questions developed above. Identify the main ideas and jot down any questions, notes, or unknown vocabulary.
* *Recite*—At the end of each chapter section, state the gist of what was read.

Note: *Restating or summarizing into a tape recorder is often very effective.*

* *Review*—Check recall of important information from the reading. To that end, a study guide of some kind may be created.

SQ4R

This is the same as above, but includes an additional step beginning with the /r/ sound—*Write*. The SQ4R procedure is survey, question, read, recite, write, and review. After a brief verbal summary of what the reading passage was about, one must *write* the answers to the questions (in step 2) and then review.

RCRC

This is a strategy involving the steps:

* Read
* Cover

* Recite
* Check

For example, with RCRC, the student first reads a portion of the material. Then the passage is covered up (by hand or paper) and the student restates it in his or her own words. Finally, the student checks for accuracy by looking at the text again.

A number of effective learning strategies involve use of a mnemonic device that assists a student in understanding and completing an academic task, usually by specifying a series of steps to be completed in sequential order (Bender, 2002). Many strategies are summarized in the form of an acronym that the student is expected to memorize and subsequently apply.

For example, the SLANT strategy is part of the Learning Strategies Intervention Model and was designed for the purpose of increasing active participation in class. The acronym SLANT stands for:

* **S**it up.
* **L**ean forward.
* **A**ctivate your thinking (What is this about? What do I need to remember? This is about . . . I need to remember. . .).
* **N**ame key information (answering the teacher's questions, sharing your ideas, addition to other's comment).
* **T**rack the talker. (Bos & Vaughn, 1994; Ellis, 1991)

More learning strategies using acronyms include these examples (Hoover & Patton, 1995; Polloway, Patton, & Serna, 2001; Shannon & Polloway, 1993):

COPS for detecting and correcting common writing errors:

C—capitalization of appropriate letters
O—overall appearance of paper
P—punctuation used correctly
S—spelling accuracy

FIST is a questioning strategy that assists students to actively pursue responses to questions related directly to material being read.

First sentence is read.
Indicate a question based on material in first sentence.
Search for answer to question.
Tie question and answer together through paraphrasing.

PARS for reading includes these items:

Preview.
Ask questions.
Read.
Summarize.

SCORER is a test-taking strategy that assists students to carefully and systematically complete test items (Hoover & Patton, 1995; Polloway, Patton, & Serna, 2001):

Schedule time effectively.
Clue words identified.
Omit difficult items until end.
Read carefully.
Estimate answers requiring calculations.
Review work and responses.

Study Skills

James Madison University's Special Education Program developed a wonderful website with a U.S. Department of Education grant on Steppingstones in Technology Innovation for Students with Disabilities. The website was developed to be responsive to the specific needs of students with learning disabilities and ADHD. Features of the website that respond to these needs include reduced amounts of text for reading; use of graphics to enhance the meaning of the reading material; a consistent structure of accessing the various learning toolbox sites; and elimination of distracting stimuli such as non-purposeful animations and sound effects.

This wonderful, highly recommended, user-friendly website is found at http://coe.jmu.edu/LearningToolbox. It contains over sixty unique learning strategies under the topics of organization, test-taking, study skills, note-taking, reading, writing, math, and advanced thinking. Three examples of their creative strategies include the following.

S2TOP is a study skills strategy to help stay focused when studying:

Set a timer.
See if you are off-task.
Touch the circle (and tally mark inside circle when noticing that you have drifted off the task).
Organize your thoughts.
Proceed again.

FLEAS is a test-taking strategy to help complete tests on time:

First read the directions.
Look over the test.
Easiest questions answered first.
Answer questions that are worth more.
Skip a question.

CHECK is a study skills strategy to help start studying:

Change environments (to one free from distractions).
Have all equipment nearby.
Establish rewards for yourself.
Create a checklist of tasks to be done.
Keep a "worry pad" (if ideas popping into your head are distracting you).
(Learning Toolbox, 2003)

Note: Some of the JMU faculty (Esther Minskoff, David Allsopp, Jerry Minskoff, and Margaret Kyger) along with other faculty, staff, and students, were instrumental in the development of the Learning Toolbox.

Chamot & O'Malley (1994) recommend that learning and study strategies be taught explicitly by:

* Modeling how you use the strategy with a specific academic task by thinking aloud as you work through a task (for example, reading a text or writing a paragraph)
* Giving the strategy a name and referring to it consistently by that name
* Explaining to students how the strategy will help them learn the material
* Describing when, how, and for what kinds of tasks they can use the strategy
* Providing many opportunities for strategy practice

The following are some additional study and learning strategies.

Resource Materials

Use resource and reference materials to locate information (for example, use of dictionary, atlas, encyclopedia, thesaurus, Internet). There are prerequisite skills to using many resource materials: knowing alphabetical order and understanding use of guide words; being able to read and understand the legend of a map; and learning basic research skills.

Note-Taking

This requires listening and simultaneously writing down major ideas and key information in a useful format so the information can later be accessed. There are a variety of note-taking techniques. One example is the Cornell note-taking method (Pauk, 1997), which is considered by many to be the best for lecture and discussion. It involves dividing a piece of paper into two columns:

* The first column—the left margin is about one-fourth to one-third of the width of the paper (about 2.5 inches). This is where key words/terms, main ideas, questions,

additions, and corrections are written after the class period. It is used for recall of important information.

* The second column—which is two-thirds to three-fourths of the page—is where the lecture notes are written (on the front side of the page only).
* Students are to review their notes within twenty-four hours (preferably within three hours) after the lecture. During this time they reread and then fill in key terms, make additions, corrections, and so forth in the left column.
* In addition, space is left at the bottom of each page for a summary. Good note-taking requires learning how to make abbreviations and use symbols (Williams, 2003).

Mind mapping and webbing are other techniques that can be used for note-taking and linking key and subordinate ideas of a topic (from lecture, discussion, information from texts) in graphic formats.

Graphic Organizers and Mapping Strategies
These are described in the other academic sections of this book. For example:

* Using advanced organizers and study guides to help organize thinking about key topics of the lesson
* Using sequence charts, story maps, sentence maps, webs, clusters, flow charts, and Venn diagrams to aid in comprehension of material, pre-planning for writing about a topic, and so forth
* Providing framed outlines for filling in missing words and phrases during instruction

Organization and Time Management Strategies
These are described in Section 3.5.

Test-Taking Strategies

Teach students the distinctions between different kinds (standardized, published, teacher-made) of tests, and specific test-taking tips and procedures for different formats (essay, short answer, multiple choice, matching, true/false). This also involves teaching students strategies for carefully reading and processing test questions, such as reading directions more than once, numbering parts of a multi-part question, circling or underlining key words (for example, <u>most</u>, <u>always</u>, <u>never</u>, <u>define</u>, <u>identify</u>, <u>prove</u>, <u>summarize</u>, <u>describe</u>, <u>defend</u>, <u>contrast</u>, and <u>evaluate</u>). In addition, it is helpful to teach students practical techniques to help them reduce test anxiety, which can sabotage the best of efforts to do well on tests (Casbarro, 2003; Williams, 2003).

Memory Strategies and Accommodations

Difficulties with memory and retention of information are very common for individuals with ADHD. To improve memory skills, it helps to create meaningful links and associations (visual, auditory, conceptual) between bits of information. For example:

* Draw and visualize vivid pictures associated with the information that is supposed to be memorized. Keep in mind that memory is facilitated by exaggeration, emotion, action, color, and absurdity, so the more ridiculous and detailed your image, the better.
* Link a series of events, terms, or facts together through a silly story. The key is utilizing a sequence of funny, outlandish mental images.
* Teach a variety of memory (mnemonic) strategies such as the following:
  — Use first letter mnemonics and acronyms such as: HOMES (The Great Lakes): **H**uron, **O**ntario, **M**ichigan, **E**rie, and **S**uperior; Roy G. Biv (Colors of the rainbow): **R**ed, **o**range, **y**ellow, **G**reen, **B**lue, **i**ndigo, **v**iolet; Dead Monsters Smell Badly (Steps for long division): **D**ivide, **m**ultiply, **s**ubtract, **b**ring down.

* Create acrostics or whole sentences to aid memory, such as: "Every Good Boy Does Fine" in order to recall the sequence of lines in the treble clef (EGBDF).
* Use the "key word mnemonic method" from Mastropieri and Scruggs (1991). They describe three steps involved in the use of the key word mnemonic method:
  — First, students reconstruct the term to be learned into an acoustically similar, familiar, and easily pictured concrete term.
  — Second, they select a key word that relates to the new information in an interactive picture, image, or sentence.
  — Third, students retrieve the appropriate response by thinking of the key word, recalling the interactive picture and what is happening in the picture, and then by stating the information.
  — For example, to help students remember that *barrister* is a lawyer, students create a key word for the unfamiliar word *barrister*. Then they create a picture of that key word and definition interacting together, for example, a picture of a bear that is acting as a lawyer in a courtroom, standing in front of a jury (Kleinheksel & Summy, 2003; Mastropieri & Scruggs, 1991).
* Use peg words for learning basic math facts. These are short words that sound like numbers: Three/Tree; Four/Door; Six/Sticks; Seven/Heaven; Eight/Gate; Nine/Line. Various programs make use of the peg word technique and imagery in memorizing and recalling multiplication facts. See Rodriguez and Rodriguez (1999) and Semple (1986; 2001).
* Check out www.uiowa.edu/~xfacts. This website (which is downloadable) includes various mnemonics. For example, 3 × 3 = 9 is a tree and tree on a line; 7 × 8 = 56 is "heaven on a gate by gifty sticks." Visualize a gate with an association for heaven (for example, smiling cloud) on the gate next to a bundle of sticks tied together with a big bow.
* Learning and remembering the spelling of tricky words can be done through mnemonics such as the following (Suid, 1981):
  — Attendance: *At ten* we'll take *attendance* for the *dance.*
  — Enormous: A th*ou*sand p*ou*nds is an en*o*rm*ou*s am*ou*nt.
  — Because: **B**ig **e**lephants **c**an't **a**lways **u**se **s**mall **e**ntrances.
  — Rhythm: **R**hythm **h**as **y**our **t**wo **h**ips **m**oving.
* Use melody and rhythm to help memorize a series or sequence. There are raps, rhymes, and songs that help in learning multiplication tables and other information (days of week, months of year, presidents of United States). See Wallace (1993) for a number of jump rope rhymes, raps, and chants for memorizing information (for example, states, capitals, continents, oceans).
* Utilize songs that have been created to help students learn and recall key content area information at grade-level standards such as Science Songs Aligned to Fourth Grade Science Content Standards at www. musicallyaligned.com. The company, Musically Aligned, created music and lyrics for teaching the science curriculum at different grade levels. For example, for physical science some songs include "Electromagnets" and "Heat, Light, and Motion." For teaching concepts in life science, songs include "Working Together," "Food Chain Gang," "Decomposers," and so forth.
* Teach and practice attaching information to a familiar melody, as this will facilitate memorization and make learning more fun. Many of us still rely on using the melody we learned years ago for recalling the sequence of the alphabet, months of the year, presidents of the United States, and so forth.
* Use rhymes to remember rules (for example, "i before e except after c").

Also do the following to help students increase their recall and retention of important information:

* Use frequent review, repetition, and practice.
* After instruction, have students *list all they remember, in whatever order, as fast as they can.*

* Ask kids to review during the last five minutes of the lesson and during the first five minutes of the next lesson.
* The best way to remember new information and material is to use it in some way immediately.

INTERVIEW WITH SUSAN
(38 Years Old, California)

Susan has a B.A. in occupational therapy and an M.A. in rehabilitation. She is a rehab counselor who was identified as an adult as having learning disabilities and ADHD.

What is your advice to teachers?

"Help students be aware of their strengths. If we just go after the 'sore teeth,' people give up and leave school. If they work through their strengths, interests, and learning styles, students will be motivated to learn the skills they need and will forget about their 'sore teeth.' Set up an environment that will make them reach out and interact with other people."

What has helped you get through school successfully?

"I've learned to identify my learning style and to compensate for my weaknesses. I am a weak auditory processor. [*Note:* Susan requested a face-to-face interview rather than one conducted over the phone.] I am a strong kinesthetic learner. I take walks a lot. That is how I get my best ideas. When I get bogged down on a project, I go walking and am able to get the whole concept. Then I can move forward. I allow my kinesthetic abilities to help me. For example, my statistics class was extremely difficult for me. I tape recorded lectures and would listen to them a few times at home, but it didn't help much. Then I started walking around the lake while I listened to the lectures. This helped me considerably. I now take frequent breaks, move around a lot, and balance my activities. I don't make myself sit at a desk."

Writing and Reading Challenges for Students with ADHD

It is rare for someone with ADHD not to have some degree of difficulty with regard to writing. Children and teens with attention deficit disorders are often verbal and knowledgeable, but unable to communicate what they know on paper.

Why Writing Is Such a Struggle for Students with ADHD

Weaknesses in written language are very common in those with ADHD because the process is so complex. It involves the integration and often

DECKER FORREST

233

simultaneous use of several skills and brain functions (for example, organization, spelling, fine motor, planning, self-monitoring, memory, language). Writing difficulties are manifested because the process requires:

Pre-Planning and Organization. This requires being able to generate, plan, and organize ideas. This stage of the writing process is often the most challenging and neglected, especially for those who experience difficulties with written expression. When given a written assignment, students with ADHD often get stuck here. They do not know what to write about, how to organize and begin, or how to narrow down and focus on a topic that will be motivating to write about (Rief, 2003).

Memory. Working memory is necessary in order to juggle the many different thoughts that one might want to transcribe onto paper. It involves:

* Keeping ideas in mind long enough to remember what one wants to say
* Maintaining focus on the "train of thought" so the flow of the writing will not veer off course
* Keeping in mind the big picture of what you want to communicate, while manipulating the ideas, details, and wording

The process of writing also requires the retrieval of assorted information from long-term memory (facts, experiences) to share about the writing topic, as well as recall of vocabulary words, spelling, mechanics, and grammatical usage (PBS, 2002).

Spelling. People with attention difficulties are often:

* Inattentive to visual detail, and do not notice or recall the letters, sequence, or visual patterns within words

* Prone to making many careless mistakes
* Often weak in spelling (especially if co-existing LD exists) due to
  — Deficiencies in phonemic awareness and auditory-sequential memory deficits (causing great difficulty learning letter/sound associations, as well as discriminating, remembering, and writing those sounds in the correct order)
  — Poor visual-sequential memory (causing them difficulty recalling the way a word looks and getting it down in the correct order/sequence). This results in misspelling common, high-frequency words (such as *said, they,* or *because)* that cannot be sounded out phonetically and must be recalled by sight (Rief, 2003).

Note: The International Dyslexia Association points out: "The visual memory problems of poor spellers are specific to memory for letters and words. A person may be a very poor speller, but be a very good artist, navigator, or mechanic; those professions require a different kind of visual memory." (IDA, 2000)

Language. Writing requires the ability to express thoughts in a logical and coherent manner. Good writers are able to use a wide vocabulary to express themselves and utilize descriptive sentences while maintaining proper sentence and paragraph structure. Each writing genre (for example, persuasive, response to literature, personal narrative) involves its own structural components. The writer must know the structure and specific language/vocabulary to use in order to persuade/convince an audience, compare/contrast, or whatever is required.

Grapho-Motor Skills. Many children with ADHD and/or learning disabilities have impairments in grapho-motor skills. This affects the physical task of writing and organization of print on the page. They often have trouble:

* Writing neatly on or within the given lines
* Spacing/organizing their writing on the page
* Copying from the board or book onto paper
* With *fine-motor skills,* causing the act of handwriting to be very inefficient, fatiguing, and frustrating (affecting pencil grip, pressure exerted, and legibility)
* Executing print or cursive with precision or speed (Rief, 1998, 2003)

Note: Memory is also involved in fine-motor skills (remembering with automaticity the sequence of fine motor movements required in the formation of each letter) (Richards, 1995). Those with co-existing learning disabilities in visual processing also frequently reverse or invert letters (b/d, p/q, n/u) and form numerals/letters in strange, awkward ways.

Editing. Individuals with ADHD have significant difficulty during the revision and proofreading stages of the writing process. Many students with ADHD want to go directly from the initial draft to the final draft without making revisions, as it is tedious and takes too much effort to do (without the use of assistive technology and other supports). They are typically inattentive to the boring task of finding and correcting errors. It is common to find lack of capitalization, punctuation, and complete sentences, along with numerous spelling errors in their written products (Rief, 2003).

Self-Monitoring. Fluent writing requires:

* Thinking and planning ahead
* Keeping the intended audience in mind and writing to that audience with a clear purpose
* Following and referring back to the specific structure of a writing genre (steps of a complete paragraph, narrative account, persuasive essay, friendly letter, and so forth)

* Knowing how to read one's own work critically in order to make revisions and develop ideas more thoroughly

Speed of Written Output and Production. Some students with ADHD rush through writing assignments, often leading to illegible work with many careless errors. Others with ADHD write excruciatingly *SLOWLY*. Although they know the answers and can verbally express their thoughts and ideas articulately, they are unable to put more than a few words or sentences down on paper. Needless to say, this is extremely frustrating. Part of the problem with speed of output may be due to

* Impairments in impulsivity and inhibition
* Difficulty sustaining attention to task and maintaining the mental energy required in written expression
* Grapho-motor dysfunction (Rief, 2003)

Common Reading Difficulties in Children and Teens with Attention-Deficit Disorders

Because of the inherent difficulties associated with poor executive functioning and sustaining focused attention to task, it is common for individuals with ADHD to have difficulty with recall and comprehension of reading material (Rief, 1998, 2003). Although they may have strong decoding and word recognition skills (if they do not have the co-existing learning disability of dyslexia) and *appear* to be skilled readers, it is still most common to find that individuals with ADHD are generally not strategic readers and have "spotty" comprehension.

The following are common difficulties many children and teens with ADHD and/or learning disabilities experience with reading:

* *Failure to utilize "metacognitive strategies."* This refers to the practice of self-monitoring comprehension while reading the text by

addressing errors in comprehension as soon as they arise. Many people with ADHD (children/teens/adults) have difficulty with this due to executive function weaknesses. In such instances, the reader is not using his or her *internal language* and *self-talk* to actively engage the text, such as asking oneself:

— "What is the main idea?"
— "What is the author trying to say in this paragraph?"
— "What does that remind me of?"
— "What do I predict is going to happen next?"

* Another aspect of executive functioning weaknesses is *poor working memory,* resulting in limited recall of the reading material. Obviously, this also affects comprehension of the text (for example, ability to summarize, retell, and respond to questions related to the reading).
* *Inattention* (being drawn off-task) while reading results in missing words and important details, which consequently, impedes comprehension.
* Silent reading is difficult for many individuals with ADHD. They frequently need to subvocalize or read quietly to themselves in order to hear their voices and maintain attention to what they are reading. If you observe students doing this, permit them to do so. Many students need the auditory input to stay focused, as they struggle to process the text through silent reading.
* Students often *lack a "schema" or structure* to guide them in figuring out the critical elements and main ideas of what they are reading.

Maintaining attention during whole-class instruction is an area of difficulty for many students with ADHD, resulting in the following:

* They often struggle paying attention to stories and text being read out loud in class.
* When one person is orally reading, it is common for students with ADHD to have a hard time following along with the rest of the class.
* They are frequently on the wrong page of the book, and especially struggle to follow the reader if he or she lacks fluency and expression.

In addition:

* A large percentage of individuals with ADHD report having difficulty maintaining their train of thought while reading. Although they may have excellent decoding skills and fluency, their high level of distractibility impedes them from processing the information. This problem is compounded if the student is presented with dry, uninteresting, or difficult material.
* Many have difficulty losing their place when reading, as their attention drifts.

A Few Instructional Tips to Keep in Mind

* It is often more beneficial for the teacher to first read the text with fluency and expression to the entire class, and then have students reread with partners or small groups.
* It is also helpful to first have students read passages along with a partner or a small group, and then reread sections in a large-group setting.
* If possible, seat ADHD students among well-focused students during this part of instruction.
* Metacognitive strategies and techniques such as reciprocal teaching, brief note-taking, summarizing, and self-questioning are helpful strategies to teach students. Any techniques that require active involvement and thinking about/responding to what is being read help maintain focus and attention.
* Numerous strategies can be employed to engage students in the reading process. Many students with ADHD benefit greatly from explicit instruction in various reading comprehension and learning strategies— being taught *how* to be strategic, active

readers/thinkers. (See Section 3.11, Reading Comprehension Strategies and Interventions, and Section 3.6, Learning Strategies and Study Skills.)

Also see Section 3.8 for a host of other written language strategies and interventions, including those to help students: with pre-planning and organizing for writing assignments; spelling, fine-motor/handwriting skills; and a variety of strategies and assistive technology recommendations to bypass and accommodate writing difficulties.

Reading Disabilities/Dyslexia

Roughly 30 to 60 percent of children with ADHD also have specific learning disabilities. Among the various learning disabilities, reading disorders are most common. Some children have specific processing deficiencies (auditory or visual perception, short-term memory, phonological awareness, or receptive/expressive language) that affect their acquisition of reading skills.

Dyslexia is a language-based learning disability. Dyslexia refers to a cluster of symptoms that result in people having difficulties with specific language skills, particularly reading. Students with dyslexia may experience difficulties in other language skills such as spelling, writing, and speaking. Current studies suggest that 15 to 20 percent of the population has a reading disability of some kind. Of those, 85 percent have dyslexia (IDA, 2000).

Note: To determine whether a child/teen has learning disabilities in reading (dyslexia) requires a psycho-educational evaluation.

What Research Tells Us About Learning to Read and Reading Difficulties

Fairly recently, the converging evidence based on thirty years of research into reading has become available. Numerous studies investigated (Rief, 2001, 2003):

1. How children learn to read
2. Why some children struggle in learning how to read
3. What can be done to prevent reading difficulties

One of the main sources of the current information is the National Institute of Child Health and Human Development (NICHD), National Institutes of Health. The high rate of illiteracy and reading difficulties in the United States (roughly 17 to 20 percent of the population) is considered not only an educational problem, but a major public health problem.

To address this issue, the NICHD has supported scientific research continuously since 1965 to understand normal reading development and reading difficulties. NICHD developed a research network consisting of forty-one research sites in North America (and other parts of the world), which conducted numerous studies on thousands of children—many over a period of years.

Note: The findings from this wealth of research were presented as testimony by G. Reid Lyon, Ph.D. (chief of the Child Development and Behavior Branch of the NICHD, National Institutes of Health) to the Committee on Labor and Human Resources, U.S. Senate, in 1998.

In addition, more research findings on this topic come from the Committee on the Prevention of Reading Difficulties in Young Children, National Research Council. This committee was entrusted by the National Academy of Sciences to conduct a study of the effectiveness of interventions for young children who might be predisposed to reading difficulties. This committee reviewed several factors:

* Normal reading development and instruction
* Risk factors useful in identifying groups and individuals at risk of reading failure
* Prevention, intervention, and instructional approaches to ensuring optimal reading outcomes

The results of their research findings are found in *Preventing Reading Difficulties in Young Children* (Snow, Burns, & Griffin, 1998).

The following includes some of what is now known based on the scientific evidence from the above sources:

* Failure to read proficiently is the most likely reason that students drop out, are retained, or are referred to special education.

* Approximately 50 percent of reading difficulties can be prevented if students are provided effective language development in preschool and kindergarten and effective reading instruction in the primary grades.

* There is a very strong association between a child's ability to read and his or her ability to segment words into phonemes (hear and separate a spoken word into its individual sounds, such as "pig" as /p/ /i/ /g/).

* Kindergarten children's phonemic awareness can predict their levels of reading and spelling achievement even years later. It is a more powerful predictor of reading progress than IQ.

* By providing explicit instruction in alphabetic code, sound-spellings, and phonemic awareness, we may prevent many children from needing to enter special education programs. (As many as 80 percent of referrals to special education involve reading difficulties.)

* Learning letter-sound correspondence (necessary for reading and spelling) requires an awareness that spoken language can be analyzed into strings of separable words comprised of sequences of syllables made up of smaller units of sounds (phonemes).

* Most children with severe reading difficulties have substantial weakness in auditory-related skills (for example, phonemic awareness) and associating those sounds with the printed letter (sound-symbol relationships).

* The most frequent characteristic observed among children and adults with reading disabilities is a slow, labored approach to decoding or "sounding out" unknown or unfamiliar words and frequent misidentification of familiar words.

* Children who are most at risk for reading failure enter kindergarten limited in their awareness of sound structure and language pattern, phonemic sensitivity, letter knowledge, and the purposes of reading, and have had little exposure to books and print.

* Effective prevention and early intervention programs can increase the reading skills of 85 to 90 percent of poor readers to average levels. (Lyon, 1998b, 2000; Snow, Burns, & Griffin, 1998)

Dr. Lyon states the following:

"In the initial stages of reading development, learning phoneme awareness and phonics skills and practicing these skills with texts is critical. Children must also acquire fluency and automaticity in decoding and word recognition. Consider that a reader has only so much attention and memory capacity. If beginning readers read the words in a laborious, inefficient manner, they cannot remember what they read, much less relate the ideas to their background knowledge. Thus, the ultimate goal of reading instruction for children—to understand and enjoy what they read—may not be achieved." (Lyon, 2000)

Dr. Louisa Moats, another leader in the field, provides the following abysmal statistics: About 42 percent of fourth graders score below basic in overall reading skill on the National Assessment of Educational Progress (NAEP). In some communities the proportion of students beyond third grade who cannot read well enough to participate in grade-level work is between 60 and 70 percent, depending on the grade and year of assessment (Moats, 2001).

Moats also shares the following:

"Most reading scientists agree that a core linguistic deficit underlies poor reading at all ages (Cattas et al., 1999; Shaywitz et al., 1999). At any age, poor readers as a group exhibit weaknesses in phonological processing and word recognition speed and accuracy, as do younger poor readers (Stanovich & Siegel, 1994; Shankweiler et al., 1995). The older student has not practiced reading and avoids reading because reading is taxing, slow, and frustrating (Ackerman & Dyckman, 1996; Cunningham & Stanovich, 1997). Therein lies the most challenging aspect of teaching older students: they cannot read, so they do not like to read; reading is labored and unsatisfying, so they have little reading experience; and, because they have not read much, they are not familiar with the vocabulary, sentence structure, text organization and concepts of academic 'book' language. Over time, their comprehension skills decline because they do not read, and they also become poor spellers and poor writers. What usually begins as a core phonological and word recognition deficit, often associated with other language weaknesses, becomes a diffuse, debilitating problem with language— spoken and written." (Moats, 2001)

What Is Known About Effective Intervention for Struggling Readers

Dr. Joseph Torgeson, a professor at Florida State University, in his keynote address to the International Dyslexia Association National Conference (Torgeson, 2003), shared the consensus regarding instructional features needed for effective intervention:

* Systematic and explicit instruction on whatever component skills are deficient
* Significant increase in intensity of instruction
* Providing ample opportunity for guided practice of new skills in meaningful contexts
* Appropriate levels of scaffolding as students learn new skills
* Providing systematic cueing of appropriate strategies in context
* Teachers who are relentless

Dr. Kevin Feldman (2001), director of reading and early intervention, Sonoma County Office of Education, Santa Rosa, California, shares how older struggling readers must fill in the holes and build the literacy foundations they have missed, such as:

* Phonological/phonemic awareness
* Grapheme/phoneme matching
* Decoding of single/polysyllabic words
* Reading fluency
* Word structure—syllable complexity, morphology, and so on
* Word study and layers of the English language
* Comprehension and text handling strategies
* Study skills/habits/strategies in content area reading and writing

Written Language Strategies, Accommodations, and Interventions

Pre-Planning / Organizing, Handwriting, Assistive Technology

*P*re-planning is a critical stage of the writing process, involving the generation, planning, and organization of ideas and deciding "what" and "how" to express ideas before actually beginning to write. This is a challenge for many students with ADHD. The following are some *pre-writing* techniques designed to stimulate ideas, topic selection, and effective planning and also provide much needed structure, organization, and motivation to write.

Strategies to Help with Planning/Organizing (Pre-Writing)

Parents can help their children think of possible writing topics by doing the following (Rief, 1998):

* Look through family albums together and reminisce about people and events.
* Talk about happenings in your child's life (humorous incidents, scary moments, milestones) that your son or daughter may not remember.
* Share family stories and discuss current events.
* Ask leading questions that encourage your child to open up and share (for example, feelings, fears, dreams, aspirations, likes/dislikes).

* Provide resources such as books, reference materials, access to the library and the Internet.
* Encourage your child to keep a journal or a file on the computer for jotting down thoughts or questions he or she is pondering; observations; things that happen that cause strong feelings (embarrassment, fear, joy); reactions to events in the news; and connections he or she makes (for example, between movies seen, books read, music heard, and his or her own life). These are all possible topics for future essays, personal narratives, and other writing assignments.

Pre-Writing Techniques in the Classroom

* *Brainstorming*—These sessions are very short and focused (no more than three to five minutes). Given a general theme or topic, students call out whatever comes to mind related to that topic while someone records all responses.
* *Quickwrites*—Give students a few minutes (no more than three or four) to write down everything that they can think of related to a given topic. Model the same uninterrupted writing along with the students at this time.

* *Writing Topic Folders*—Have students maintain a folder, card file, or notebook of possible writing topics for reference purposes. Include hobbies, places visited, jobs they have done, personal interests, interesting/colorful family members, neighbors, friends, pets, special field trips or school assemblies, and so forth.

* *Personal Collage Writing Folder*—Have students use words and pictures cut out from magazines, newspapers, and travel brochures and laminate the folder when done. Students should include lists of their favorites (for example, places, food, sports, hobbies). This can also be created on the computer, along with digital pictures of people, things, or occasions they want to remember; topics found through exploring sites on the Internet that they find interesting; and so forth.

* *Reference Books*—Pass out reference books to groups of students to look through for ideas of writing topics (for example, mysteries of nature, airplanes, music, astronomy, mammals, dinosaurs, sports, fashion).

* *Writing Prompts*—Provide a stimulus such as a poem, story, picture, song, or news item to prompt writing. In addition, keep a file of pictures from magazines, old calendars, postcards, or other sources as stimuli for writing activities. It often helps to offer students a variety of sample topic sentences, story starters, and writing prompts when they are struggling for an idea.

* *Self-Questioning*—Teach students to talk themselves through the planning stage of their writing by asking: "Who am I writing for? Why am I writing this? What do I know? What does my reader need to know?"

* *Telling Personal Stories*—In cooperative groups have students orally respond to prompts by *telling* personal stories, for example, "Tell about a time you or someone you knew got lost." After the oral telling and sharing of stories in small, cooperative groups, have students fill out a graphic organizer, then write rough drafts or outlines of the stories they told.

* *Tape Recorders*—Encourage the use of a tape recorder with some students, so they can first verbalize what they want to say before transcribing ideas onto paper.

Graphic Organizers

These are among the most effective ways to help students generate their ideas, as well as formulate and organize their thoughts. For students with written language difficulties, use of a graphic organizer of some sort is a critical intervention in helping them pre-plan before they begin to actually write.

The following are some examples:

* *Concept Map*—Write the main idea in a box or rectangle in the center of the page and surround the main idea box with bubbles containing all subtopics and supporting ideas.

* *Writing Frames*—Students fill in blanks from a framed outline.

* *Web/Mind Mapping*—A box or circle is drawn in the center of a page. The topic or main idea is written inside the center box/circle; and related ideas are written on lines stemming from the circle (see the example at top of page 243).

* *Diagrams*—For example, Venn diagrams (see the example on page 243) can be used, which are graphics of overlapping circles that show a comparison between two or three items, topics, characters, or books.

* *Compare/Contrast Charts*—This is another way of depicting similarities and differences.

* *Story Maps*—These are used in pre-planning the critical elements to be included when writing a story (setting, characters, problem, action, and resolution).

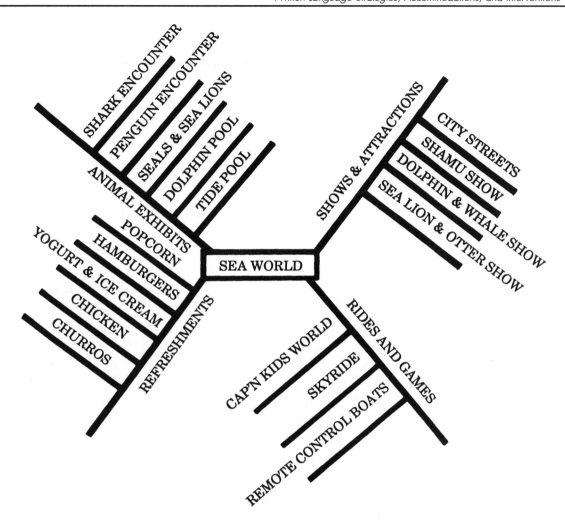

SEA WORLD

- ANIMAL EXHIBITS
  - SHARK ENCOUNTER
  - PENGUIN ENCOUNTER
  - SEALS & SEA LIONS
  - DOLPHIN POOL
  - TIDE POOL
- SHOWS & ATTRACTIONS
  - CITY STREETS
  - SHAMU SHOW
  - DOLPHIN & WHALE SHOW
  - SEA LION & OTTER SHOW
- REFRESHMENTS
  - POPCORN
  - HAMBURGERS
  - YOGURT & ICE CREAM
  - CHICKEN
  - CHURROS
- RIDES AND GAMES
  - CAP'N KIDS WORLD
  - SKYRIDE
  - REMOTE CONTROL BOATS

Charlotte's Web

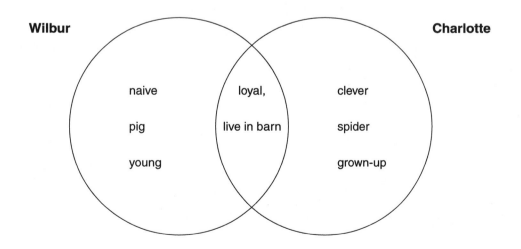

Wilbur   Charlotte

Wilbur	loyal,	Charlotte
naive	live in barn	clever
pig		spider
young		grown-up

Note: *See Section 3.11, Reading Comprehension Strategies and Interventions, for additional graphic organizers. There are numerous resources available, including several sites with free, downloadable graphic organizers on the Internet. Also, the software programs Inspiration™ and Kidspiration™, available through www.inspiration.com, are excellent tools for clustering and visually organizing ideas during the pre-writing stage.*

Additional Pre-Writing Tips (Rief, 2003)

* Model and provide guided instruction in the use of various types of graphic outlines. Have students practice using each format. Post examples of filled-out graphic organizers as reference, and make them readily available for students and parents.
* Students who have difficulty with writing need many models of good writing presented orally and visually. Read examples of written works that demonstrate the skill you are emphasizing (for example, interesting hooks; expanded, descriptive sentences; well-developed paragraphs; and use of metaphors/similes).
* Teach and display steps of the writing process (pre-writing, composing first draft, responding, revising, editing and proofreading, publishing).
* Stop students after a few minutes of writing and ask for student volunteers to share what they have written so far.
* Provide models of papers highlighting important elements (for example, an introduction, body, and conclusion).

Planning and organization are some of the "executive functions," which are areas of weakness in many individuals with ADHD. Therefore, it is very important to provide instruction and support to guide them in the kind of thinking and questioning that is needed to effectively plan and organize before writing. It is valuable to provide a *pre-writing checklist* that lists specific questions students need to ask themselves at this stage of the writing process. When creating a pre-writing checklist, teachers may want to select a few of the questions from the list below:

* Have I brainstormed and written down a number of possible topics?
* Have I selected my favorite topic among those choices, and can I write enough about that topic?
* Have I identified my target audience?
* Which writing genre am I going to use?
* In what style or voice will I write?
* Have I listed several words, ideas, or phrases related to my topic?
* Have I narrowed down my topic?
* Have I researched and collected enough interesting information from a variety of sources (for example, books, newspapers, Internet, magazines)?
* Am I taking sufficient notes from resources to support what I am writing about?
* Have I carefully documented the sources of any research information I might use so I will remember later where I found it and give proper credit?
* What are possible introductions that will excite and grab the attention of my audience?
* What details and examples might I use that will be interesting?

When writing a story, the planning involves asking/recording:

* Who will be the characters, and what will they be like?
* What will my setting be (time, place)?
* What is the main problem going to be?
* What is the plot and action?
* How will the problem be solved?
* What will the ending be?
* Will the main character have changed in some important way? How?

Help with Organization in the Pre-Writing Stage

* Take notes or write ideas on separate index cards. That makes it easier to spread out and group, organize, and sequence those thoughts and ideas.
* Break down notes into subtopics.
* If using *Inspiration*™ software, there is an outlining feature built in. Categories listed in the graphic web format are automatically placed in outline form with the press of a button.

Strategies for Improving Fine Motor, Handwriting, Written Organization, and Legibility

When one struggles with handwriting and written organization, it interferes with production and being able to "show what you know." Paper/pencil tasks are a source of great frustration for many children with ADHD. When the physical act of writing is so tedious and the results of one's efforts are messy and illegible, it is no wonder that children with ADHD often hate to write and resist doing so.

Children with ADHD may be developmentally delayed in their fine-motor skills (the small muscle movements required in writing).

Fine-Motor Skills

The following are some observable behaviors of children with fine-motor difficulties:

* Poor grasp, leading to poor form, fluency, and frequent discomfort when writing
* Difficulty controlling speed of movements, leading to excessive speed and resultant untidy work or work not being completed due to overly slow movements
* Difficulty with precision grip and inaccurate release, and therefore problems with games that involve placement of pieces (for example, dominoes)

* Difficulty with spatial relations, leading to difficulties with design and copying
* Tearing paper and/or breaking pencils due to force-control difficulties
* Difficulty with learning to dress and undress (tying shoes, buttoning, zipping)
* Preference for outdoor activities
* Clumsiness and frustration: spills food; drops objects; breaks objects
* Frustration toward and/or resistant behavior to manipulative and graphic tasks
* Excessive muscular tension when performing fine-motor tasks (Landy & Burridge, 1999)

Many children with ADHD also have the learning disability referred to as "dysgraphia." Signs of dysgraphia include:

* Generally illegible writing despite appropriate time and attention
* Inconsistencies: mixtures of print and cursive; upper and lower case; irregular sizes, shapes, or slants of letters
* Unfinished words or letters, omitted words
* Inconsistent position on page with respect to lines and margins
* Cramped or unusual grip, especially holding the writing instrument very close to the paper or holding the thumb over two fingers and writing from the wrist
* Strange wrist, body, or paper position
* Talking to self while writing, or carefully watching the hand that is writing
* Slow or labored copying or writing even if it is neat and legible
* Content that does not reflect the student's other language skills (Jones, 2003)

Note: *If a child is observed to struggle with the physical task of writing, consult a specialist (occupational therapist or special education teacher). An evaluation, consultation, or direct service from an occupational therapist and/or special education teacher may be needed.*

The following are some activities and tips for building fine-motor skills:

* Do finger warm-up exercises (open/shut, snapping, touch each one at a time to the thumb quickly) and fingerplay activities (for example, "Itsy Bitsy Spider").
* Roll out and form clay or Play-doh® into snakes and other shapes.
* Squeeze a stress or squish ball to build strength in the hand muscles.
* Do activities requiring placement of paper clips, clothespins, or clamps on objects.
* Build things with small Lego® pieces.
* Build with various types of blocks and linking manipulatives.
* Use jigsaw puzzles.
* Do stringing, lacing, and threading activities (for example, making necklaces from stringing beads).
* Teach how to knit or crochet.
* Practice buttoning and opening/closing snaps on clothing.
* Sort small objects (for example, buttons, cereal, shells) into an egg container or ice cube tray by category.
* Pick up small objects with tweezers and tongs. (Rief, 1998, 2003)

Handwriting, Organization, and Legibility

One of the reasons children struggle in writing is because they do not automatically recall the muscle movements and motor planning skills involved in forming strokes (curves, loops, counterclockwise motion), and sequencing the steps involved to form each of the letters. They also may not have formed a clear mental picture of how each letter looks to reproduce from memory and are constantly seeking a visual model.

A number of factors determine whether or not writing appears legible. These include letter formation, slopes of letters and their consistency, size consistency, spacing, individual style, and positioning of letters with regard to lines (Landy & Burridge, 1999).

The following are strategies and tips for teaching handwriting and improving legibility of written work:

* When teaching letters (print or cursive), group them by similarity of formation (for example, l/t/i; a/c/d; v/w). Also introduce those that are more frequently used (for example, s, m, r) before those less commonly found letters in words (for example, j, q, z).
* Point out and discuss similarities and differences in letters.
* Have children trace letters and then write a few independently. Afterwards, have them circle their best ones.
* A highly recommended program for teaching print and cursive to children with writing difficulties is *Handwriting Without Tears*™, developed by an occupational therapist, Jan Olsen. She uses numerous multisensory techniques and mnemonic cues for helping children learn proper letter formation. The program also structures the sequence of letters introduced by clusters. For example, cursive o, w, b, and v are taught together as the "tow-truck letters" because of their special high endings.
* Another recommended handwriting program is the *CASL Handwriting Program*, developed at Vanderbilt University, and research-validated as successful for children with disabilities (Fuchs & Fuchs, 1999; Graham & Harris, 2000).
* Use dots, numbered arrows, highlighters, and other means to provide extra visual cues and supports.
* Teach appropriate grasp of a pencil (pencil grip) in the early grades.
* If the child struggles to hold and manipulate a pencil, there are a variety of pencil grips that can be used to make it easier (for example, triangular plastic, molded clay, and soft foam cushion that the pencil slides through).

* Try self-drying clay to mold a pencil grip to the size/shape of the child's fingers.
* Try mechanical pencils for older students who frequently break their pencil tips from applying too much pressure.
* Use real-life situations to stress the need for legible writing (job applications, filling out checks).
* Stress how studies have proven that teachers tend to give students the benefit of the doubt and grade higher if their papers look good as opposed to being sloppy or hard to read, because neatness and legibility make a positive impression.
* Provide students sufficient time to write in order to avoid time pressures.
* Set realistic, mutually agreed-on expectations for neatness.
* For some students it is easier to write using narrow-ruled paper (shorter line height) than paper that has wider-ruled lines.
* Teach placing of index finger between words (finger spacing) to help students who run their words together without spacing.
* Use special paper with vertical lines to help with spacing letters and words appropriately.
* Remind the child to anchor his or her paper with the non-writing hand or arm to keep it in one place while writing.
* If the student's paper is frequently sliding around, try a clipboard.
* Make sure there is always a sufficient supply of sharpened pencils and erasers on the desk.
* Provide a strip or chart of alphabet letters (manuscript or cursive) on the student's desk for reference of letter formation. Draw directional arrows on the letters the child finds confusing and difficult to write.

Tactile-Kinesthetic Techniques (Rief, 2003)

* Make a "gel bag" by placing some hair gel in a Zip-Loc® bag. With a permanent marker, write each letter for practice on the outside of the bag. While tracing the letter, the student feels the interesting texture of the gel inside of the bag (especially when the gel or ooze bag is refrigerated).
* Color-code the strokes of a letter on the outside of the gel bag. The first phase of the stroke can be one color, the second phase can be another color. Arrows can be drawn indicating the directions of the letter formation as well.
* Practice correct letter formation by tracing letters written on a variety of textures (for example, puff paint, sandpaper).
* Many upper-grade students have not mastered how to form cursive letters and struggle with formation or speed. Provide guided practice for students by modeling on the overhead projector in color while talking them through the steps.
* Model letter formation (print or cursive) in color while writing on paper on an easel, dry-erase board, or overhead projector.
* Trace letters in sand or salt trays, on the carpet, or other textures using two fingers.
* Write letters in the air with large muscle movements while giving a verbal prompt. Holding the child's wrist, write in large strokes in the air while talking through the strokes. For example, with the letter B, give the following instruction:
    — Start at the top.
    — Straight line down.
    — Back to the top.
    — Sideways smile. Sideways smile.
  Then repeat without guiding the child's hand, but observe that the formation is correct (Fetzer & Rief, 2000). (See the author's books: *Alphabet Learning Center Activities Kit* (2000) and *Ready, Start, School* (2001) for several more strategies for teaching letter formation.)
* When teaching the correct relative size of letters and their formations, it is helpful to introduce the graphic of a person with the head reaching the top line (head line), the

trousers' belt at the middle line (belt line), and the feet on the bottom line (foot line). Then, when instructing how to form each letter, refer to those lines by name. See the illustration for an example.

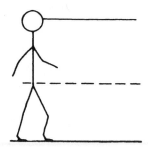

Say: "To make the letter *h*, start at the head line and go straight down to the foot line. Trace back up to the belt line and make a hump that goes back down to the foot line."

Additional Tips

* It is important to provide a lot of practice at home and school when children are learning how to print or write in cursive. Observe carefully as children are practicing, and intervene immediately when you notice errors in letter formation. Gently correct if you observe children making the strokes incorrectly (for example, bottom-to-top rather than top-to-bottom; circles formed clockwise rather than counterclockwise).

* Provide parents with a model of how the letters are being taught in class (for example, arrows indicating steps of letter formation and any verbal prompts) to be consistent.

* Provide prompts for correct letter formation/directionality by placing a green dot indicating where to begin and arrows indicating in which direction to write the strokes of the letter(s).

* Allow for frequent practice and corrective feedback using short trace and copy activities.

* If cursive is a struggle, allow students to print.

* Encourage appropriate sitting, posture, and anchoring of paper when writing.

* Add variety for motivational purposes, using different sizes, shapes, textures, and colors of paper; also experiment with fancy stationery and different writing instruments. Also have students write on individual chalkboards with colored chalk or on dry-erase boards with colored pens.

* Provide students with a slant board (for better wrist position). You can make one by covering an old three-ring notebook completely with Con-Tact® paper. The child then places his or her paper on the slant board when writing.

* Teach and post standards of acceptable work in your classroom, whatever those standards may be (for example, writing on one side of paper only, rough draft papers written on every other line, math papers with two to three line spaces between problems, heading on upper-right section of paper).

* Use a computer and encourage final drafts to be typed, providing assistance as needed.

* Post and provide individual copies of handwriting checklists for students to self-monitor their own written work for legibility. The following are a list of possible questions that may be included on a student handwriting checklist (depending on age/developmental level and grade-level standards):
  — Are my letters resting on the line?
  — Do tall letters reach the top line, and do short letters reach the middle line?
  — Do I have space between words?
  — Are my letters the right size (not too small, not too large)?
  — Am I writing within the lines?
  — Are my words in lower case, unless there is supposed to be a capital?
  — Am I consistent in my letters—all print or all cursive, not mixed?
  — Is my writing neat?
  — Have I stayed within the margins of the paper?

Strategies for Bypassing and Accommodating Writing Difficulties

It will often be necessary to provide various accommodations or modifications to enable struggling writers to work at grade-level standards. The following are possible accommodations and ways to help students bypass some of the obstacles they face in writing (Rief, 2003). Consider the following when writing IEPs and 504 Accommodation Plans to support children and teens who struggle with writing.

Reduce Writing Demands

* Stress quality writing—not volume.
* Reduce the need to copy from the board or book.
* Remember that it takes children with ADHD significantly longer (often two to three times as long) to produce written work as it does their peers. Assign reasonable amounts of homework and writing assignments. Be willing to make adjustments if written output is a struggle, and accept modified homework and reduced written tasks.
* Bypass through other modality strengths and direct assistance.
* Substitute non-written projects for written assignments such as oral reports and demonstrations.
* Give students options and choices that do not require writing, choosing instead to draw on individual strengths. This can be accomplished through hands-on, project-oriented assignments that involve investigating, building, drawing, constructing, creating, simulating, experimenting, researching, telling, singing, dancing, and so on. (See Section 3.3, Reaching Students Through their Learning Styles and Multiple Intelligences, and Section 3.1, Reaching Students Through Differentiated Instruction.)
* Follow written exams with oral exams and average the grades for those students.
* Allow oral responses for assignments/tests when appropriate.
* Permit students to dictate their responses and have someone else transcribe for them.
* Provide note-taking assistance by assigning a buddy who will take notes, share, and compare with the struggling student.
* Provide assistance for typing/printing final drafts of papers.

* Help students get started writing by sitting with them and talking or prompting them through the first few sentences.
* Have the student dictate while an adult writes the first few sentences to get the student started.

Provide

* Worksheets with extra space and enlarge the space for doing written work (math papers, tests, and other projects)
* In-class time to get started on assignments
* Access to a computer and motivating writing programs with a variety of fonts and graphics
* NCR (multiple-copy carbonless paper) for the designated "buddy" note-taker to use (Students, including those with ADHD, should still take notes in the classroom, but be allowed to *supplement* their own notes with the more detailed and organized copies from their buddies.)
* Photocopies of teacher notes or from designated students who take neat, organized notes; share them with students who struggle copying information from the board or taking notes from class lecture
* Increased time for completing written tasks
* Extended time for testing, particularly written assessments (for example, essay questions)

Teach

* Proper keyboarding/typing skills so children learn the proper finger positions (and provide many practice opportunities to increase skills) (See reference listing at the end of Part 3 for software recommendations.)
* Word processing skills, including the use of editing options (for example, cut and paste, spell-check, grammar-check) and various format options

Other

* Permit and encourage subvocalizing or talking out loud while writing, as auditory feedback often helps the students to stay focused and self-monitor.

* Permit students to write in either print or cursive—whichever is easier and more legible.
* Increase the amount of guided practice of handwriting, keyboarding, and other writing skills.
* Grade content and spelling/mechanics separately.

Use of Tools and Assistive Technology

* Provide students with tools such as highlighting tape, paper with wide and narrow lines, various types of pens and pencils (for example, mechanical), and different shapes of pencil grips.
* Allow students to use a tape recorder instead of writing for summarizing learning, responding to questions, planning, and recording ideas.
* Allow the use of a handheld electronic spell-checker.

Use quality software programs to assist in the writing process, such as *Inspiration*™ and *Kidspiration*™ (both available at www.inspiration.com). These are user-friendly, motivational software programs that are research-validated as effective in helping students to develop written expression. Both programs allow students to do the following:

* Create their own graphic organizers (concept maps, webs, flow charts)
* Brainstorm ideas with pictures and words
* Organize and categorize information visually
* Plan and organize ideas prior to writing

For young children, the program *PixWriter* by Slater Software, Inc., is wonderful. It allows the beginning writer to pick pictures or select words supported by pictures.

The company Don Johnston (www.donjohnston.com) is one of the leaders in products for students with reading and writing difficulties. They carry the following recommended products to help struggling and reluctant writers:

* *Write:Outloud*®—This is an easy-to-use talking word processor. This program reads each word out loud as students write and also reads any electronic text. One feature is that it highlights as it reads, connecting the spoken word to the text. Another is that it contains Franklin Dictionary and Homonym Checker (to help writers use expanded vocabulary) and Franklin Spell-Checker (which consistently finds the phonetic errors).
* *Co-Writer 4000*—This is a talking word prediction program that coaches in spelling and grammar, enabling writers to build better sentences.
* *Draft:Builder*™—This helps the student produce a first draft by (1) outlining and mapping; (2) organizing notes that are entered; and (3) building a logically sequenced draft.

Some recommended programs for keyboarding/typing include:

* *Type to Learn* (Sunburst Communication)
* *UltraKey* (Bytes of Learning, Inc.; www.bytesoflearning.com)
* Keyboarding for Individual Achievement (Teachers' Institute for Special Education; http://special-education-soft.com)

Provide or allow use of portable word processors. For example, *AlphaSmart* is a portable keyboard with a four-line display that serves as an inexpensive substitute for laptop computers for individual student use. *AlphaSmart* is user-friendly and allows the student to type and store material until it is later transferred to their personal computer for editing and revising. Brainium Technologies Inc. also produces portable word processors (Dreamwriter), which are excellent for student use. For more information see www.alphasmart.com and www.brainium.com.

Another useful tool is the *QuickLink Pen* (by Wizcom Technologies). This allows students to electronically scan notes from print and transfer this information to computers for use in writing and editing papers. It can be very helpful when doing research.

Speech recognition software can be of great assistance to struggling readers/writers. Two recommended programs are Read & Write Gold® from www.texthelp.com and Naturally Speaking from www.scansoft.com/naturallyspeaking.

Richard Wanderman, a specialist and consultant in technology and learning disabilities, recommends: "The simpler the tool, the more it will get used. The more it gets used, the faster it will fall into the background and real work will get done" (2003).

There are various websites that have excellent information on assistive technology resources, such as www.ldonline.org/ld_indepth/technology/technology.html.

Additional recommended resources and websites to aid struggling writers are listed at the end of Part 3.

Strategies for Building Written Expression and Editing Skills

Written Expression—Strategies and Supports

Written expression is the most common academic area of difficulty among students with ADHD. As discussed in Section 3.7, Writing and Reading Challenges for Students with ADHD, several brain processes are involved and utilized simultaneously (for example, language, attention, memory, sequencing, organization, planning, self-monitoring, and critical thinking) when trying to compose a written piece of work.

Students are expected to meet grade-level expectations and standards in a variety of writing formats and genres. Teachers are expected to differentiate instruction to teach writers of all levels and abilities. The teaching of writing requires knowing how to scaffold the instruction and provide the necessary structures and supports to students who need more help in the writing process. The following are strategies and tips for helping students become more successful writers:

Vocabulary and Sentence Structure

Here are some ideas I've mentioned before (Rief, 2003) for working with ADHD children around vocabulary and sentence structure:

* Have students generate vocabulary lists of words related to a theme or topic. For example, everyone might supply a word related to nature, climate, archaeology, words that make me shiver, words that make me hungry, soft words, angry words, and so forth.
* Teach sentence structure and build on sentence writing skills. Students need to understand that all complete sentences have (1) a *subject* (noun—person, place, or thing) that tells who or what is doing something and (2) *predicate* (which includes a verb and modifiers) telling "what about" the subject.
* Teach students to write more interesting, expanded sentences. Start with a simple "bare" sentence (for example, "The puppy cried."). Have them "dress it up" by adding or replacing with colorful, descriptive adjectives and adverbs, more powerful verbs, and prepositional phrases (When? Where? How? Why?). For example: "The frightened puppy whimpered and whined as it hid shaking under the sofa during the thunderstorm."
* Provide lists and posted words for student reference (for example, powerful verbs, alternatives to "said," transition and linking words/phrases).

* Have students generate a class list of interesting words they find in the books they read. For example, locate ten descriptive adjectives in the chapter.
* Teach descriptive language and the use of figurative language to enhance writing style. Generate class and individual lists of examples found in literature or poetry of metaphors, similes, personification, analogies, onomatopoeia, and so on. Have students create their own figurative language examples. They may even illustrate in pictures, as well, for fun.
  — Metaphors are figures of speech that compare two unlike things but not using the words "like" or "as." Examples include: "The road was a snake coiling around the mountain"; "The theater is a refrigerator"; and "The blasting music was a hammer pounding on my head."
  — Similes are comparisons of unlike things that use the words "like" or "as." Examples include: "angry as a wounded bear"; "as white as milk"; "as hard as flint"; and "sparkled like diamonds."
* Encourage students to find and bring into class good examples of sensory description (how something sounds, looks, smells, tastes, feels).
* Teach students to create a scene and describe it in vivid detail. This can be done with a number of activities such as the following:
  — Have students close their eyes and ask them to visualize a scene (for example, a boy fishing in a stream with his grandfather, a snowstorm, winning the lottery). Then brainstorm as a class what is in their mind's eye, what the scene sounds like, feels like, tastes like, looks like. Then have students write a paragraph about it.
* Teach words that are used to *signal sequence* (for example, First of all, To begin, Furthermore, Meanwhile, Next, Then, Subsequently, Finally). Post these words or provide a student desk copy for reference.

* Teach *transitional words and phrases* (for example, However, Consequently, In addition, Therefore, So, As a result). Post these words for reference or provide a copy for individual student use.
* Point out to students phrases such as, "I suggest. . ." or "I believe. . .", which *signal an author's point of view,* and words/phrases such as "nevertheless" or "on the other hand," which are used *to compare and contrast* two or more things. Provide a reference of such words to aid writing.
* Encourage the use of alternatives to overused words. Generate a class word list or word bank of overused, dull words (1-cent words) that can be substituted for more interesting words (10-cent words, 25-cent words). Use a thesaurus to have students find "more valuable" words. Some examples follow:

1 cent	10 cents	25 cents
run	race	sprint
	dash	scramble
	speed	hasten

Writing Genres

The following are some of the types of expressions and genre that students are expected to write (depending on the grade and developmental level):

* Paragraphs (summary, directional—"How to's," compare/contrast, procedural, descriptive, and narrative) with a clear beginning, middle, and end
* Letters (friendly, business)
* Informational or expository report (includes topic, main ideas, supporting details, and conclusion; often involves research, observations, and analysis)
* Personal narrative (relating ideas, observations, or recollections of an event or experience), presenting information with descriptive details, as well as a beginning, middle, and an end

* Story (with literary story grammar: setting, characters, problem, sequence of events, climax, and resolution)
* Summaries (narrative and expository), including introduction, body, and conclusion
* Persuasive essay (writer tries to change the reader's point of view by presenting facts and opinions and arguing a point)
* Response to literature (demonstrating an understanding of the literary work and supporting judgments with examples from text and prior knowledge)

Self-Monitoring/Metacognition

Written expression requires a great deal of self-monitoring from writers. They need to put themselves in the place of their potential readers and keep asking themselves:

* "Does this make sense?"
* "Is this clear?"
* "Do my ideas flow logically?"
* "Am I using the best choice of words?"

It is important to provide students with a checklist of structural components in every writing form/genre they are assigned. For example, when asking students to write an expository (nonfiction piece), some questions they need to ask themselves in structuring the work and self-monitoring may include:

* How am I introducing the subject or topic?
* What will be the main idea(s) about my subject?
* What kind of hook can I use to capture the reader's attention?
* How am I going to develop my main ideas?
* What details and examples am I going to use?
* What will be my flow and sequence of ideas?
* What will be the final thought or wrap up?
* On what note am I leaving the reader?

Explicitly teach students specific strategies to aid recall of steps and application of the process. One example is the POW strategy by Karen Harris and Steve Graham (2000):

P = Plan what to say.
O = Organize what to say
W = Write and say more.

Harris and Graham, with support from the U.S. Office of Special Education Programs (OSEP), pioneered the Self-Regulated Strategy Development (SRSD) approach, which includes POW and other strategies. With SRSD, students are explicitly taught how to use self-regulation procedures (for example, goal setting, self-monitoring, self-instruction, and self-reinforcement) in the process of writing (ERIC/OSEP Research Connections, 2002; Harris & Graham, 2000). The POW strategy and others are available online at www.vanderbilt.edu/CASL.

With OSEP support, Jeanne Schumaker and Don Deshler (University of Kansas) developed and evaluated four written expression learning strategies: Sentence-Writing Strategy, Paragraph-Writing Strategy, Error-Monitoring Strategy, and Theme-Writing Strategy. For more information on these written expression learning strategies, contact them at University of Kansas, Institute for Research on Learning Disabilities, www.ku-crl.org/contact.html.

Use graphic organizers and displays to structure the planning of each form of writing assignment. The following are a few examples from Kemper, Nathan, and Sebranek (2000):

Parts of a Business Letter
* Heading (sender's address and date)
* Inside address (name and address of person or company)
* Salutation (greeting)
* Body
* Closing
* Signature

Paragraph Structure
* Topic sentence
* At least three supporting detail sentences (answering the 5W's)
* Conclusion or summary statement

More Instructional Recommendations

Writing Components of a Balanced Literacy Block

It is important to provide daily *modeled writing*—direct teacher modeling of the structure and processes involved for each grade level and correct use of writing conventions. *Shared writing* and *interactive writing* are included in this instructional component. *Guided writing* is another essential instructional component, during which the teacher guides students (typically in small group) through writing part of their composition—providing feedback and ideas for improving students' writing.

Students must also be given frequent opportunities for *independent writing,* as well, to build their writing fluency (Fisher & Tucker, 2002).

Even students with significant writing difficulties are often able to meet writing standards when they receive a high degree of explicit teacher modeling of writing skills and guided assistance.

Note: The video Successful Classrooms: Effective Teaching Strategies for Raising Achievement in Reading & Writing *(Fisher, Fetzer, & Rief, 1999) demonstrates these highly effective writing strategies in elementary classrooms.*

Encourage students to frequently ask themselves the 5W questions (who, what, when, where, why—and how) as they write. Answering these questions will help ensure that they have provided enough vivid information for their readers.

Use the *Writers Workshop approach,* which provides class time for students to write on topics of their choice. In Writers Workshop instructors:

* Move through the following stages of the writing process: pre-writing, drafting, revising, editing, and publishing
* Model each stage with students and schedule writing groups to give feedback and suggestions

* Help students interact and assist each other in revising, editing, sharing their writing, and so forth
* Teach mini-lessons as needed on specific skills and strategies

Rubrics

Provide students (when giving the assignment) any scoring guide/rubric that will be used to assess the written product when completed. This significantly helps students with writing difficulties, as it gives them a visual tool for planning, structuring, and self-monitoring their written work. It also helps parents by explaining from the beginning exactly what the teacher expects in the writing assignment, and what is considered proficient performance for the grade level. The table on page 257 provides an example of a writing rubric.

There are numerous rubrics and variations of scales—typically on a 1 to 4 or 1 to 5 scale. Some school districts score students as follows:

1 – Novice
2 – Apprentice
3 – Practitioner
4 – Expert

or

1 – Below standard (below basic)
2 – Approaching standard (basic)
3 – Meets standard (proficient)
4 – Exceeds standard (advanced proficient)

The following is an example of one school's "3–practitioner" criteria for first grade:

I have a beginning, middle, and end.
My writing goes with my picture.
I use at least two descriptive words.
I have three or four complete sentences.
My writing is neat with spaces.
Most of my letters are formed correctly on the line.
I spell most "word wall" words correctly.
I use correct punctuation and capital letters most of the time.

Nonfiction Writing Rubric: Informational Paragraphs on the Life Cycle of a Butterfly

4. Expert   Topic sentence is used to introduce paragraph.

All four stages of the butterfly life cycle are included.

Descriptive details are given for each stage of the life cycle (at least four descriptive words).

All "word wall" words are spelled correctly.

Correct punctuation and capital letters are used all of the time.

3. Practitioner   Topic sentence is used to introduce paragraph.

All four stages of the butterfly life cycle are included.

Descriptive details are used (at least two descriptive words).

Most "word wall" words are spelled correctly.

Correct punctuation and capital letters are used most of the time.

2. Apprentice   Some of the butterfly life cycle stages are included.

There is one descriptive detail.

Some "word wall" words are spelled correctly.

Correct punctuation and capital letters are used some of the time.

1. Novice   The stages of the butterfly life cycle are not included.

There are no descriptive details.

"Word wall" words are not spelled correctly.

There is no use of correct punctuation or capital letters.

Here's an example of another school's fourth grade level 3 (proficient—at standard) criteria:

Uses correct indentation.

Has an opening paragraph that states a clear purpose (opinion or main idea) for the essay.

Has a body that develops the opinion or main idea with supportive details.

Flows from one paragraph to the next using linking words.

Has a conclusion that is linked to the opening paragraph.

Help with Editing Strategies and Other Tips

For students with ADHD, this stage of the writing process (revising, proofreading, and making corrections) is extremely difficult (Rief, 2003).

Understandably, they are often very resistant to making changes, once they have struggled to write the first draft.

Revising work is the step of the writing process that involves adding or deleting information, resequencing the order of sentences and paragraphs, and choosing words that better communicate what one wants to say. Revision requires self-monitoring and critically evaluating one's own work. Students with ADHD need a lot of direct instruction, modeling, and feedback to learn how to do so.

The following are strategies for both teachers and parents to help students in editing and revising their written work:

* Teach students the skills of proofreading and editing. One method is by making transparencies of anonymous students'

unedited work or using teacher samples of writing with errors in capitalization, punctuation, and so on and then editing the piece as a group.

* Have students write rough drafts on every other line. This makes it much easier to edit and make corrections. Provide students with checklists to help self-monitor during the revision process. The following is a list of sample questions that may be included in a self-editing checklist. Select some (not all) of the following questions (Fetzer, 1999; Muschla, 2004) in creating a list appropriate to the age and developmental level of the child:
   — Have I given enough information?
   — Have I identified my audience?
   — Have I written for my audience?
   — Does my introduction capture the attention of my readers?
   — Is my beginning interesting and exciting?
   — Did I develop my ideas logically?
   — Have I left out any important details?
   — Does everything make sense?
   — Did I stick to my topic?
   — Have I presented my ideas clearly?
   — Are the ideas in the right order?
   — Have I given details and examples for each main idea?
   — Have I included enough facts and details to support my subject?
   — Have I given enough information to my readers?
   — Have I used descriptive words to make my writing interesting?
   — Do my paragraphs have a beginning, middle, and end?
   — Have I chosen the right words?
   — Does it read smoothly?
   — Do I need to insert, move around, or delete any ideas?
   — Did I write an interesting, powerful conclusion?
   — Did my conclusion restate the main ideas or refer back to the introduction?
   — Have I satisfied my purpose for writing?
   — Have I said everything I need to say?

More Useful Tips

* Teach students to respond to their own writing. "My best sentence is _____." "A simile or metaphor I used was _____."
* Teach students to self-talk through the editing/revising stage of their writing: "Does everything make sense? Did I include all of my ideas? Do I need to insert, delete, or move ideas?"
* Use peer editing. Have students work with a partner to read their work to each other:
   — The partner listens and reads along as the author reads.
   — The partner tells what he or she liked best.
   — Then the partner questions the author about anything that does not make sense; suggests where more information is needed for clarification; and helps edit when he or she hears or sees run-on or incomplete sentences.
   — Roles are then reversed.
* Conduct teacher-student writing conferences:
   — At that time, the teacher provides feedback, the student reflects on his or her own work, and both share what they like about the piece of writing.
   — The student self-evaluates improvement and the skills to target for continued improvement. "My writing has improved in: [sentence structure, paragraphing, fluency, creativity, organization, capitalization, punctuation, spelling]. I plan to work on . . . ."
* Teach the skills needed to make choice of words more interesting (for example, more descriptive adjectives, adverbs, verbs).
* See vocabulary section above for strategies to help students make better word choices in their revisions.
* Display models and standards for acceptable written work.
* Provide a rubric with all writing assignments and show models of what written work looks like "at standard" and "exceeding standard."

* Display models of proper headings, spacing, and organization of written work.
* Teach how to use the editing tools and options (thesaurus, spell-check, cut and paste) on a word processing program.
* Allow and encourage writing on the computer, which makes editing and revising so much easier. Another benefit is being able to save various draft versions electronically, rather than storing paper, which helps maintain better organization and management of written work.
* Read or listen to the child read his or her writing. Then provide positive feedback, consisting of something you like about the piece of writing and any growth in skills that are apparent. Ask the child when something is confusing or unclear, and more information is needed.

Proofreading for Errors and Polishing the Final Product

* Provide direct instruction and guided practice in the skills of mechanics (punctuation and capitalization). Challenge students to find and correct the errors in capitalization/punctuation in a given sentence.
* Parents should encourage their child to self-edit by circling (or coding in some manner) words he or she thinks were possibly misspelled, and then check the spelling of those words together later.
* Encourage the use of an electronic spell-check device for use at home and school.
* Tell students to add the "Midas touch" to their sentences and paragraphs, making them "golden."

* Teach editing symbols and provide a reference chart (for example, insert, delete, capitalize, new paragraph).
* Provide a self-editing checklist for proofreading work for capitalization, sentence structure, and mechanical errors. The following are possible questions in developing a proofreading self-edit list for students:

> Did I use complete sentences?
> Did I begin all sentences with a capital?
> Did I end my sentences with a final punctuation mark (., ?, !)?
> Have I capitalized all proper nouns?
> Have I checked my spelling for correctness?
> Have I indented my paragraphs?
> Are verb tenses consistent?
> Did I check for run-on sentences?
> Is my paper neat and organized?
> Have I used adequate spacing?
> Have I erased carefully?
> Is my writing legible?

* Teach a mnemonic proofreading strategy to help students recall and apply an effective learning strategy. The COPS strategy developed by researchers Deschler and Schumaker (part of the Strategies Instructional Approach, University of Kansas) includes the steps of self-checking for:

C – Capitalization
O – Overall appearance
P – Punctuation
S – Spelling

Note: *The recommended resources for this section include useful resources and assistive technology to aid in written expression and editing, as well as the other written language components.*

Reading Strategies and Interventions

Building Decoding Skills, Vocabulary, and Fluency

*I*n this section we will address common reading difficulties, particularly among those children with ADHD who also have a co-existing learning disability in reading (are dyslexic as well as ADHD). Recommended literature for children with ADHD (books that have story characters or themes related to having ADHD), as well as research-validated intervention reading programs are included near the end of the section.

The Reading Process: What Good Readers Do

It is recognized that reading is a complex process with the goal to acquire meaning from the printed word. People who are "good readers" are adept at the following (Rief, 1998, 2001, 2003):

* Decoding and recognizing words at a rate that enables them to read with fluency and automaticity
* Using all cueing systems (semantic, syntactic, and grapho-phonic) to figure out unfamiliar words or language
* Understanding and figuring out challenging vocabulary and word meanings
* Knowing how to read for a specific purpose
* Using whatever background or prior knowledge they have about the subject to make inferences and get meaning out of what they are reading
* Making connections as they read the text to other books previously read, to their own life and experiences, and to other information/concepts they know ("This reminds me of . . .")
* Reflecting as they read
* Utilizing effective metacognitive strategies to think about what they are reading and self-monitoring their comprehension and understanding
* Checking for their own comprehension and using self-correction ("fix-up") strategies when realizing they are not getting meaning or making sense out of what is being read
* Constantly predicting and either confirming or changing their predictions as they read
* Understanding organization and structure for different types of text (literary and expository)
* Understanding organization/story structure (characters, setting, problem, action, resolution to problem) to aid comprehension of literary text
* Understanding the structures or schemas for various kinds of expository text
* Visualizing when they are reading (for example, scenes, characters), and making mental images

* Distinguishing main ideas and important information from details and less important information in the text
* Summarizing and paraphrasing after determining the key ideas of material read
* Focusing on the main content
* Recognizing and understanding cause/effect, fact/opinion, and compare/contrast
* Making inferences and drawing conclusions
* Reading from a variety of genres (for example, mystery, historical fiction, folktales, biographies, science fiction, fantasy, and others)
* Self-selecting books of personal interest and finding pleasure in reading books of choice
* Applying a host of strategies in the process of actively reading for meaning

Balanced Literacy Programs

In classrooms throughout the United States there is an effort to teach a "balanced literacy program." The writing components of a balanced literacy curriculum are discussed in Section 3.9, Strategies for Building Written Expression and Editing Skills. The following are reading components of balanced literacy:

* Shared book experiences
* Reading aloud to children
* Phonemic awareness training
* Organized, explicit phonics decoding instruction and practice
* Oral language development and listening experiences
* Systematic vocabulary development
* Guided reading, with attention to comprehension
* Individualized reading lessons, with attention to the construction of meaning
* Sustained silent reading
* Content area reading
* Ongoing diagnosis to ensure skills are acquired (Harwell, 2001)

Reading aloud at all grade levels provides the opportunity for the class to enjoy reading for pleasure, as the teacher demonstrates fluent reading from a variety of genres and authors.

Shared reading provides the opportunity for students to read and reread text, for example, through use of charts, Big Books, transparencies, and multiple copies of books.

Note: *In both read-aloud and shared reading experiences, the teacher is able to model good reading behaviors and effective strategies (for example, activating prior knowledge, predicting and confirming, making personal connections, self-questioning).*

With *guided reading* students have the opportunity to work in small groups reading and discussing their copies of the same book(s) at their common instructional reading level. The teacher provides guidance and coaching.

Independent reading provides the students the opportunity to practice reading at their independent level. Today's classrooms often have an extensive library of books/reading material students may choose from. "Leveled libraries" make it easier to locate suitable books for each individual student. During this time, teachers generally confer individually with students and are able to informally assess each one's reading skills and strategies.

Strategies for Building Word Recognition, Reading Vocabulary, and Fluency (Rief, 1998, 2003; Rief & Heimburge, 1996)

Lack of fluency in reading interferes with comprehension. In order to become a fluent reader, the child must first become skilled at decoding the printed word. Students who struggle to figure out unknown words and have poor word recognition (decoding skills) need direct instruction with strategies and interventions as early as possible.

As many students with ADHD also have the learning disability "dyslexia," they must be identified and provided with specialized instruction designed to build their reading skills. However, certainly not all children who have poor decoding skills and lack fluency are dyslexic. Many students have had minimal phonics and word analysis instruction and have simply not sufficiently been taught these skills and strategies.

Students who receive help in learning how to decode print (in order to become fluent readers) benefit from the following:

* Phonemic awareness (the auditory recognition of individual sounds and the ability to manipulate those sounds)
* Alphabet knowledge
* Letter/sound association for all consonants, vowels, blends (for example, br, sl); consonant digraphs (for example, ch, sh); vowel digraphs and diphthongs (for example, oa, ea, ai, oi, ou); vowel patterns (for example, final e, "r" controlled)
* Word families/onset and rimes (for example, *-ack* words such as black, stack, quack, pack, Jack).

Note: *Onsets are the letters before the vowel (bl, st, qu). Rimes are the vowel and following letters in single-syllable words (ack).*

* Structural analysis of words (awareness of word parts such as root words, compounds, prefixes/suffixes)
* Strategies for decoding multi-syllabic words (for example, first breaking the word into syllables)

Children who struggle to identify words should be taught different strategies and cueing systems to recognize words in print:

* *Semantic clues:* Determining whether the word makes sense in the context of what is being read and being able to self-correct (substitute a different word if it does not make sense)

* *Syntactic clues:* Determining whether the word sounds right grammatically and being able to self-correct (substitute a different word that does grammatically fit in the context of what is being read)
* *Grapho-phonic clues:* Using recognition of the printed letters (graphemes) and their corresponding sounds (phonemes) to figure out a particular word

Phonetic awareness of the sound associations for consonants, vowels, digraphs, and others is critical in word recognition. So is the ability to take isolated sounds and blend them into words.

Children with reading disabilities are generally deficient in one or more of their cueing processes. They typically struggle with graphophonics and need a highly multisensory approach (using all of their senses) that incorporates mnemonic (memory) clues to help them learn and remember the sound/symbol associations.

Note: *There are some excellent programs and multisensory strategies that teach in this format, and have a high success rate with children who have learning disabilities affecting their ability to read and spell. Some of them include the following:*

* *Orton-Gillingham*
* *Lindamood-Bell*
* *Wilson Reading System*
* *Project Read Language Circle—Phonology, Corrective Reading*
* *Language!*
* *Rewards*
* *Stevenson Program*
* *Slingerland*

Most research-validated reading programs for children with reading disabilities in decoding skills incorporate systematic instruction in phonics, direct instruction, and mnemonics (memory devices).

Reading intervention programs/curriculum that are research-based and field tested with good evidence of success for older students include some of the above, as well as:

* Read Naturally—www.readnaturally.com
* Boys Town Reading Program—Boys Town USA
* Read 180—Scholastic
* Corrective Reading/Reading Mastery—SRA (Feldman, 2000)

Many elementary schools use *Reading Recovery,* a research-validated intervention in helping young readers learn and practice the cueing systems to figure out unknown words in the text.

Note: See contact information at the end of the section regarding programs/interventions listed.

Word recognition also involves teaching students the following (Rief, 1998, 2003):

* *Observing word patterns:* Teaching students how words can be grouped by rhyming sound families or visual patterns (rock/stock/flock, right/might/flight/bright) to build proficiency in reading and spelling. These are called "word families" or "onsets and rimes."
* *Structural clues:* Many students are helped by directly teaching them structural analysis (recognition of prefixes, suffixes, base words, and their meanings). Focusing on the visual configuration of the word is a useful strategy for many readers. One might ask: "Does this word look like any other word I know?" Knowing how to break a word down into its component parts and syllables is crucial to word recognition.
* *Sight-word recognition:* To be a fluent reader, some words must be learned and recalled at an automatic level. High frequency words and irregular/sight words (for example, *said, there, they*) are generally learned by a whole word approach and become words that are automatic. Many struggling readers (especially with visual-sequential memory problems) have difficulty

doing so, and do not have a large bank of words they know at the automatic level. Provide frequent practice in motivating game formats, through multisensory strategies and *color* to help lock these words into the memory bank for instant recognition.

"Word sorts" is a popular instructional technique for studying words and focusing on elements that are the same or different. This involves sorting words into two or three categories according to features of the word (for example, sounds within the word: long/short a, br/bl, ou/oi; different pronunciations of "ed" endings—walked, bombed, folded).

In addition, there are numerous strategies for building students' word banks and improving their recognition and understanding of reading vocabulary:

* Label words in the environment.
* Have children maintain their own card files of vocabulary words they are learning or have mastered.
* Use charts, posters, word walls, and as many visual displays as possible to enable children to recognize the printed word and its meaning.

Building Reading Fluency

Fluency is built on four components:

* *Accuracy*—the ability to decode single words correctly with freedom from mistake or error
* *Automaticity*—accurate and effortless word identification at the single-word level
* *Rate*—practice to increase speed while maintaining accuracy and automaticity
* *Prosody*—contextual reading at a smooth and even pace with expression (Avrit & Carlsen, 2003)

So it is important to teach students to be accurate readers, which requires explicit instruction in:

* Sound-symbol relationships
* Blending and segmenting
* Syllable structure
* Word parts
* Irregular words
  (Wilson, 2003)

Barbara Wilson (2003) also shares that the goals of fluency instruction are to

* Develop the student's fluent and rate-appropriate independent reading of connected text for meaning
* Develop a student's oral reading with ease and expression

Strategies for Increasing Fluency and Practicing Oral Reading

The following strategies are from Rief (1998, 2003) and Rief and Heimburge (1996):

Choral Reading

* Everyone in the class or group reads together at the same time. This is an excellent strategy when using a short piece to focus on.
* Make a transparency of a poem or passage from the text (for example, humorous poem).
* First model the oral reading with expression and fluency.
* Then students read it together in unison in different variations (every other verse, line, boys/girls, left/right side of room, and so forth).

Cloze Technique

* Read (or reread) a passage orally to the class, leaving out key words. The students fill in the missing words aloud.

Mirror (Echo) Reading

* Read aloud while students follow along visually (in their books or on overhead transparency).
* After reading a sentence or part of a passage, the students repeat it.

* Stop model reading after a few paragraphs or pages, and students orally reread certain passages.

Repeated Readings

* Provide a short, interesting passage.
* Students read and reread the passage until they achieve a certain level of fluency.
* Students record their progress on a graph, noting the fewer errors they make as they become more fluent in reading the passage.
* It is motivating for students to tape record their improved reading fluency.
* The reading program *Read Naturally* (www.readnaturally.com) is recommended for building fluency in this manner.

Fluency Practice Drills

* Use single words, phrases, or passages of decodable text.
* Reread in a variety of situations.

Note: The process of rereading passages that have already been heard before increases fluency and comprehension and is particularly helpful for students with reading difficulties.

* In response to teacher prompts and questioning, have students locate specific information and orally reread those passages.
* Try rereading in different formats: with partners; individually; in small groups; into a tape recorder; in chorus (unison); or with an adult (teacher, aide, parent volunteer).

Buddy or Partner Reading

* Students read orally with partners, either in unison or alternating between paragraphs or pages.
* Try the following:
  1. Have students share one book that is placed between them.
  2. One reader points to the words while the other is following along.
  3. Roles are then reversed.

4. Partners help each other with words and suggest strategies for figuring out unfamiliar words.

5. Partners question each other, discuss readings, and summarize.

6. Assign questions that each pair of students will answer at the end of the reading assignment to encourage focused attention.

Independent Reading

Rief (2003) and Fetzer and Rief (2000) stress that this is an important component of a balanced literacy program. Rich classroom libraries containing various levels and genres of books are essential for enabling all students to access and select books of choice at each of their independent levels. Independent reading is critical for building fluency, but the book selected must be at an appropriate "independent level."

One method of quickly determining whether a book meets the criteria is the "Five-Finger Check":

* The student reads one page from the book, holding up a finger when coming to a word he or she cannot read.
* If there are more than five fingers up, the book is too hard for independent reading.

Another method is "One in Twenty":

* Select a passage from a child's chosen book to read orally.
* If the child makes fewer than one error in twenty words, the reading material is at the independent level.

During independent reading time, teachers generally have individual reading conferences with some of the students, which involve discussion and asking questions about their books.

Another important strategy for building reading skills is to incorporate a period of uninterrupted time for everyone to be engaged in *silent reading* of self-selected material at his or her independent reading level. In schools, this has a variety of names, including Sustained Silent Reading (SSR) or DEAR (Drop Everything and Read). For those students who cannot read silently, they may be allowed to listen to a book on tape while following along at a listening post.

Oral Reading Strategies

Rief (1998, 2003) and Rief and Heimburge (1996) also discuss oral reading in the classroom as necessary, but sometimes problematic. To discuss a story or text, it is naturally important that all students have read the material. However, "round robin" reading with the students taking individual turns reading aloud to the class is generally not the most effective or productive strategy, especially in a large classroom.

Students who have reading difficulty have a hard time following along and paying attention. These students lose the continuity and flow and, consequently, the meaning of the passage. They may become so fearful of being embarrassed by their poor skills in oral reading that they spend the whole period in panic, trying to predict what will be their portion to read and practicing ahead. Therefore, they are not listening or following along.

Teachers can try the following:

1. Orally read and model for fluency, expression, and interest; students follow along in the text. Perhaps have students orally reread certain passages at prompts. Have students locate information in the passages at your prompts and questioning, and orally reread those passages containing the information.

2. Have students first read silently before the class or group reads orally. Students (particularly older ones) who are uncomfortable reading orally should never be forced to read out loud to the class. They should be able to volunteer when they wish to read in front of the class. *Buddy reading,* or reading in small groups, is a much "safer,"

preferable way for students to practice their oral reading.

3. To use this technique, assign (or let students pick) a reading buddy. After the pairs of children have read their stories silently, explain that the partners will take turns reading orally and listening to each other. Indicate how many lines the children should read before letting their buddies have a turn. Often only one book is used by each pair during this activity; but for distractible children it may be better for each to have a copy of the book.

Sometimes buddy reading is conducted with students sitting in pairs back to back, taking turns or reading in unison. Teachers can assign questions that each pair of students will need to be able to answer. It is important that students be given a lot of space to spread out away from other pairs of students, so they won't be distracted by all the voices reading at different paces.

Note: Many children with ADHD have a difficult time maintaining their focus and paying attention to the words they are reading—especially during silent reading. They may need to hear the words as they read (softly saying the words aloud) to help themselves attend to and process what they are reading. Allowing them to take their books to a quiet corner and read to themselves aloud should be permitted. Another strategy is to provide a curved plastic device that is held to the ear as a receiver and in the other end the child can softly whisper and hear the words amplified. The curved plastic channels the children's voices directly to their ears. Two recommended products are Whisperphone (available through www.linguisystems.com) and Toobaloo (available through www.superduperinc.com).

Vocabulary Enhancement

Some children with ADHD have language disorders as well and may be weak in vocabulary skills and usage. Vocabulary can be taught through the following techniques and methods:

* Using a direct definition
* Explaining through words that are the same (synonyms) or opposite (antonyms)
* Using a description or metaphor
* Teaching the word through examples and non-examples
* Using context clues
* Using vocabulary word walls and word banks
* Instructing students to use a dictionary, glossary, or thesaurus to find the meaning
* Reading to students and providing other language experiences that will expose them to rich vocabulary

According to Dr. Louisa Moats: "Normally progressing students can read most of the words in their listening vocabulary by fourth or fifth grade. From then on, they learn new vocabulary—primarily by reading—at the rate of several thousand new words per year. Many poor readers must overcome a huge vocabulary deficit before they will be able to read successfully beyond the fifth-grade level" (Moats, 2001).

Keep in Mind

* A number of students have difficulty with the language/vocabulary of books at their grade level. However, all children should have the opportunity to hear and discuss literature and expository text that is interesting, motivating, and challenging.
* Although the vocabulary may be difficult, a non-proficient reader can equally participate in reading of grade-level material through shared reading, read-alouds, teacher-guided reading, and the host of reading comprehension strategies in which students collaboratively read the text.

Note: See Section 3.9, Strategies for Building Written Expression and Editing Skills, for a variety of vocabulary-building strategies.

Reading Tips and Strategies for Parents

Try to read *to* and *with* your child every day. You can do "shared reading" in a number of ways (Rief, 1998, 2001):

* Take turns reading the paragraphs or pages. For example, you read the pages on the left of the book, and your child reads the pages on the right.
* Read together in unison with your child, with you as the lead reader running your finger under the words.
* Try the following technique:

    First, read a portion of the text ranging from a sentence or two to an entire paragraph.

    Read at a normal rate while moving your finger smoothly under the words as your son or daughter watches.

    Then read the same sentences or paragraph together while continuing to point to the words.

    Finally, your child reads the same sentence or passage alone, as you listen and support with difficult words, as needed.

When listening to your son or daughter read, do not stop to correct or make your child sound out every single word. Coach your child in using different "cueing strategies." For example, when approaching a tricky word that your child cannot figure out, prompt to pass over that word and read to the end of the sentence. Then see if your child can go back and figure out the unfamiliar word. Ask questions such as:

"Does that make sense?"

"Did that sound right to you?"

"What other word beginning with that sound would make sense here?"

If your child has the tendency to forget to bring books home from school, causing homework problems, consider purchasing or borrowing another set of books for home use.

Distractible children often lose their place easily while reading. It helps to provide a bookmark to help keep their place. Another strategy is to block the page partially by placing a piece of cardboard, paper, or index card over part of the page. A piece of thin, colored transparent plastic that the words can be read through is another option that may hold some children's attention to the page. Some students may benefit from using a "window box" such as the example below. Any number of variations may work.

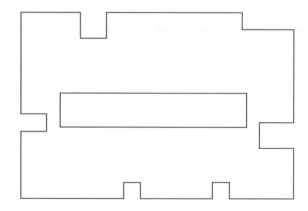

On the sample window box, the notches along the sides of the card are different sizes to accommodate different sized print in the book. Students select an appropriate notch and place it at the beginning of each line (sliding it down the left side of the page). Other children may need to place the window box over the page, blocking out the print except for the words that are exposed in the window. They slide the card across the page to reveal a few words at a time. The window opening in the center of the card can be cut to the length and width desired.

Check out books on tape from your local library. If your child is receiving special education services due to reading disabilities, he or she is entitled to a service of being provided books on tape through Recordings for the Blind and Dyslexic (RFB&D). Contact them directly or ask your local chapter of the Learning Disabilities Association (LDA) for information on how you can apply for this service. (See following text for more information on RFB&D.)

Encourage your son or daughter to read to a younger child and increase the motivation to read by allowing your child to choose material they are interested in.

Struggling readers are easily intimidated by lengthy books with few illustrations. There are wonderful options:

* Picture books that are interesting and appropriate for older children
* Joke and riddle books
* Comic books and magazines
* Reference books with color pictures and short reading passages
* Sheet music with lyrics of favorite songs and poetry

Have your child participate in school book clubs, purchasing inexpensive books of choice on a regular basis. Purchase your child a subscription to a magazine (for example, *Sports Illustrated for Kids, Ranger Rick, Cricket*). Consult with librarians and children's bookstore employees about popular titles and books that tap into your child's interests.

It often helps to photocopy a chapter/unit from your child's textbook to make it easier to study the text. Encourage your child to color-highlight key information and take notes directly on those photocopied pages. For example, important vocabulary and definitions can be highlighted in one color (for example, yellow); the main ideas can be highlighted another color (for example, orange); and so forth (Rief, 1998).

Research-Based Reading Intervention Programs

Some of the programs that are validated by research as effective interventions were mentioned earlier in this section, but contact information is provided below. Additional research-based programs that are effective with children who have reading, writing, and language difficulties are included here as well.

Corrective Reading, by G. Johnson & Z. Engleman (DeSoto, TX: SRA/McGraw-Hill) www.sra4kids.com

The Herman Method for Reversing Reading Failure (Herman Method Reading Institute, 2002) is a multisensory program based on the Orton-Gillingham philosophy and is a remedial program for struggling readers at all grade levels. www.hermanmethod.com

Language! by Jane Fell (Longmont, CO: Sopris West) www.soprswest.com

Lindamood-Bell Learning Processes (San Luis Obispo, CA) www.lindamoodbell.com

Orton-Gillingham Failure Free Reading Program, produced by the Institute for Multi-Sensory Education (ISME, 2002), is based on the Orton-Gillingham method of reading instruction developed by Dr. Samuel T. Orton and educator Anna Gillingham (www.ortongillingham.com). The methodology uses phonetics and emphasizes visual, auditory, and kinesthetic learning styles.

Project Read—Language Circle. This program by Mary Enfield and Victoria Greene (Bloomington, MN: Language Circle Enterprise) has five curriculum strands of phonology, linguistics, reading comprehension report form (expository), reading comprehension story form (narrative), and written expression. Project Read follows the principles of systematic learning, direct concept teaching, and multisensory strategies. www.projectread.com

Read Naturally. (St. Paul, MN: Read Naturally, Inc.) www.readnaturally.com

Reading Mastery by Engleman et al. (DeSoto, TX: SRA McGraw Hill) www.sra4kids.com

Reading Recovery Program, by Marie Clay (Worthington, OH: Reading Recovery Council of North America) www.reading recovery.org

Rewards—Reading Excellence: Word Attack & Rate Development Strategies (2000) by Anita L. Archer, Mary M. Gleason, & Vicky Vachon (Longmont, CO: Sopris West) www.soprswest.com

The Slingerland Approach is an adaptation for classroom use of the Orton-Gillingham method. This structured, sequential, simultaneous, multisensory teaching approach is designed to teach students the integrated skills of speaking, reading, writing, and spelling. (Bellevue, WA: Slingerland Institute for Literacy) www.slingerland.org

Wilson Reading System, by Barbara Wilson (Millbury, MA: Wilson Learning Center) is a research-based reading and writing program that uses a multisensory approach to teach a structured language program. www.wilsonlanguage.com

Other Important Resources

Learning First Alliance. (1998). *Every Child Reading: An Action Plan.* Washington, DC: Learning First Alliance. www.learningfirst.org/publications

Lyon, G. Reid. (1999). "The NICHD Research Program in Reading Development, Reading Disorders and Reading Instruction: A Summary of Research Findings." From *Keys to Successful Learning: A National Summit on Research in Learning Disabilities.* New York: The National Center for Learning Disabilities.

Moats, Louisa. (1999, June). *Teaching Reading Is Rocket Science: What Expert Teachers of Reading Should Know and Be Able to Do.* This report is from the National Federation of Teachers review of the reading research and describes the essential knowledge base for teacher candidates. www.aft.org/edissues

National Institute of Child Health and Human Development. (2000). Report of the National Reading Panel: *Teaching Children to Read: An Evidence-Based Assessment of the Scientific Research Literature on Reading and Its Implications for Reading Instruction.* This final report of the National Institute of Child Health and Human Development (NICHD) assesses the effectiveness of various approaches to teaching children to read. Washington, DC: NICHD. (800-370-2943; www.nichd.nih.gov/publications/nrp/smallbook)

Reading for Blind & Dyslexic—Learning Through Listening. A nonprofit organization, RFB&D is the nation's educational library serving people who cannot read standard print effectively because of a visual impairment, learning disability, or other physical disability. They lend audio books in a broad range of subjects at all educational levels, from kindergarten to post-graduate studies. Nearly 75 percent of the people who use RFB&D's audio textbooks have dyslexia or other reading-based learning disabilities. (800-221-4792; www.rfbd.org)

Some Books for Kids About ADHD

Carpenter, Phillis, and Ford, Marti. (2000). *Sparky's Excellent Misadventures.* (Illustrated by Peter Horjus). Washington, DC: Magination Press.

Spencer—known as "Sparky" for his red hair—is lively, smart, and has a great sense of humor. He also has ADHD. Told in a first-person diary format, Sparky's fun tale includes many valuable insights and ideas that can help kids with ADHD gain more control of their lives.

Corman, Clifford L., Trevino, M.D., & Trevino, Esther. (1996). *Eukee the Jumpy, Jumpy Elephant.* (Illustrated by Richard Dimatteo). Plantation, FL: Specialty Press.

A success story about parents, teachers, and doctors working together to help a child with ADHD.

Galvin, Matthew. (2001). *Otto Learns About His Medicine: A Story About Medicine for Children with ADHD* (3rd ed.). (Illustrated by Sandra Ferraro). Washington, DC: Magination Press.

Teaches children how and why medication can help with hyperactivity.

Gehret, Jeanne. (1996). *Eagle Eyes: A Child's Guide to Paying Attention.* (Illustrated by Susan Covert). Fairport, NY: Verbal Images Press.

Gordon, Michael. (1991). *Jumpin' Johnny Get Back to Work: A Child's Guide to ADHD.* DeWitt, NY: GSI Publications.

Janover, Caroline. (1997). *Zipper, the Kid with ADHD.* (Illustrated by Rick Powell). Bethesda, MD: Woodbine House.
Provides a good description of ADHD and a model for managing behaviors. The book is about a fifth-grade boy with ADHD.

Moss, D. M. (1989). *Shelley, the Hyperactive Turtle.* Bethesda, MD: Woodbine House.
Explains ADHD to preschool or primary-grade youngsters.

Quinn, Patricia, and Stern, Judith. (1991). *Putting on the Brakes: Young People's Guide to Understanding Attention Deficit Hyperactivity Disorder.* New York: Magination Press.

Weiner, Ellen. (1999). *Taking A.D.D. to School.* (Illustrated by Terry Ravanelli). Valley Park, MO: JayJo Books.

Zimmert, Debbie. (2001). *Eddie Enough!* (Illustrated by Charlotte M. Fremaux). Bethesda, MD: Woodbine House.
Third-grade student Eddie is always getting in trouble at school until his ADHD is diagnosed and treated.

Note: *Most of these books are available through* www.addwarehouse.com.

INTERVIEW WITH MALINDA (14 Years Old, California)

Malinda was diagnosed with ADHD and LD.

Which of your classes did you like the most during elementary school?

"I don't remember too much about a lot of my classes. I liked the teachers who made what we were studying a reality. For example, if we were studying something in history, they would explain and discuss what was currently in the news and tie it in to what was happening in the world now."

What is your advice to teachers?

"Teachers need to give students more time to try to understand. You need to explain carefully, see if there are any questions, and take more time to teach it before you move on."

Reading Comprehension Strategies and Interventions

Children and teens with ADHD who do not have co-existing learning disabilities may be fluent readers, who do not struggle with word recognition, decoding skills, or vocabulary. However, it is very common for those with ADHD to still have difficulty with reading comprehension to some degree, due to lack of attention and focus on the text, and retention of the material read. (See Section 3.7 for more information about common reading difficulties associated with ADHD.)

It is vital that students with ADHD be actively engaged in the reading process, or else they will struggle with reading comprehension. They must be taught explicit strategies that develop their use of metacognition, and must be involved in techniques to help them interact with the reading material.

To read for meaning and to gain comprehension, there are a number of strategies that are helpful and effective *prior to* reading, *during* reading, and *after* completing the reading assignment.

The following strategies are from Rief (1998, 2003) and Rief and Heimburge (1996).

Pre-Reading Strategies

Pre-reading strategies are important for activating the reader's prior knowledge about the topic, for building connections and comprehension of the text, and for generating interest and

the motivation to read the material. Here are some of them:

* Prior to reading, relate the story or reading material to the students' experience and background knowledge through: class discussions, brainstorming, and charting prior knowledge ("What do we already know about . . . ?").
* Set the stage and establish the purpose for what students are about to read. For example: "As you read, think about what you would do if . . . ."
* Lead the class through making/listing predictions prior to reading.
* Generate interest and increase students' background knowledge and frame of reference before reading by using concrete objects and audiovisuals related to the topic of study (for example, maps, music, photos, video/DVDs, and other means).
* Give time to students to preview the key information in the text (illustrations, captions, headings, chapter questions) before reading through the chapter/text. Previewing can also involve students listening to passages read aloud first before independently studying and rereading.
* To activate prior knowledge, students can be asked to write down everything they know about the topic in their "learning logs."

* Discuss selected vocabulary that may be challenging for students.
* Link prior knowledge to new concepts and information that will be studied, using advanced organizers, anticipation guides, and other strategies such as KWL and semantic maps (as described later).

During-the-Reading Strategies

During-the-reading strategies should be taught and modeled in order to engage the student in thinking about and interacting with the reading material. This is crucial for comprehension and maintaining focus on text. Some strategies are:

* Teach students how to paraphrase a paragraph, putting into their own words the main idea and significant details. Some students find that paraphrasing each paragraph or passage and stating it into a tape recorder is a very helpful technique.
* Teach textbook structure (significance of bold, italic print, headings, and subheadings).
* Teach how to find introductory paragraphs and summary paragraphs.
* Teach students how to rephrase main ideas and headings into their own words.
* Teach how to find the subject, main ideas, and sift out the key facts and important details from the irrelevant and redundant words/text.
* Provide students with a pad of self-stick notes. As they are reading they can jot down notes, vocabulary words (to clarify), and questions by items they do not understand. The self-stick paper can be placed directly next to key points and main ideas for fast/easy reference.
* Teach story mapping: identifying the setting (time/place), characters, conflicts/problems, action/events, climax, and resolution of conflicts.
* Use any of the instructional strategies involving students with collaborative reading and analysis of the material (for example, Reciprocal Teaching, Literature Circles).

* Encourage students to activate their imaginations and visualize while reading. Having students illustrate the scenes they visualize is a very helpful technique.
* Questioning and self-questioning are most critical while reading. The reader must ask such questions as: "Where does the story take place?" "What is the problem?" "What will the character do next?" "Why did she say that?" "What's the main idea?" "Does this make sense?" "What is the point the author is trying to make?" "I wonder what I would do in that situation."
* Teacher-directed guided reading may involve the following: setting a purpose; sharing prior knowledge; making predictions; having students read silently for a while to answer a question the teacher posed; and then having a discussion, using the text to validate responses.
* Allow students to subvocalize—say the words aloud softly as they are reading. This auditory feedback often helps those who struggle maintaining attention to the reading material when reading silently, allowing them to better focus on the words and what they are reading in the text. (Devices can be used for students to whisper into as they are reading. The words are channeled directly to their ears to provide this auditory input without disturbing others.)
* Schedule breaks to increase motivation and sustained attention during independent reading. For example, encourage the child to set mini-goals in pacing his or her reading. Have the child read to a certain point in the text or to read for a predetermined amount of time. After reading to that point, the child rewards himself or herself by taking a brief break.
* Use partner reading and cooperative learning formats in reading texts.
* Use instructional strategies such as "think-pair-share" and other buddy reading techniques.
* Try using a reading marker or strip of cardboard with students who lose their place in

reading and have difficulty visually focusing on text. The window box shown in Section 3.10 or other such variations are other options.

* Teach clustering, webbing/semantic mapping to pull out the main idea and supporting details from the text.
* Enlarge a page of the book and make a transparency of it. Have students come up to the overhead and locate certain information by underlining it.
* Photocopy chapter pages and have students highlight important information.
* Provide study guides to aid in looking for key information in the text.
* Underline or circle important points in text.
* Color-code a master textbook for lower readers. For example: one color for vocabulary, another color for definitions, and a third color for important facts and topic sentences.
* Tape-record textbooks for individual use or group listening at a listening post. Use a good quality tape and a recorder with counter numbers. For ease in following text, have clear signals on the tape for when to turn the page, or include periodically on the recording the chapter and page number. Pages can be marked with the counter number at the beginning of each chapter.

After-Reading Strategies

After-reading strategies should be utilized to involve the student in deeper thinking and exploration of the reading material:

* Use the information to complete fill-out charts and graphic organizers.
* Have deep discussions about the concepts or events in the text or about character analysis.
* Make connections through related writing activities.
* Do further extension activities related to the theme and content of the reading to apply the learning.

Many of the strategies used *during* reading are also continued or completed *after* the reading. The following are a number of instructional formats and strategies that are research-validated as highly effective in building reading comprehension.

Graphic Organizers (Graphic Outlines or Graphic Aids)

Numerous graphic displays that accompany reading of literature and textbook material aid comprehension. They help students recognize and organize information in the book, and guide critical thinking by creating a graphic representation of the text.

* *Framed outlines*—Students are given copies of a teacher-prepared outline that contains missing information. As the student reads, or later through subsequent discussion, students fill in the missing information. Ideally, this can be modeled on the overhead to teach the skill.
* *Storyboards*—Divide sections on a board or piece of paper and have students draw or write story events in sequence in each box/frame.
* *Story maps*—This graphic includes essential elements of a story (setting, characters, time, place, problem or conflict, actions or happenings, and resolution).
* *Story frames*—These are sentence starters to fill in that provide a skeleton of the story or chapter. For example: "The setting of this chapter takes place. . . . The character faced a problem when. . . . First he _____. Next, _____. Then _____. I predict in the next chapter _____."
* *Timelines*—These are used to help visualize chronological text and sequence of events.
* *Plot charts*—Charts for stories use the following format: Somebody . . . Wanted . . . But . . . And So . . .
* *Prediction charts*—Charts that are modified as the story is being read are called prediction charts. Based on the title and

illustrations, students make initial predictions. As they read, stop and ask them to predict what will happen next. Continue questioning, predicting, and recording. Make clear to students that predictions are best guesses based on the information we know at the time and that good readers are constantly predicting when they are reading.

* *Venn diagrams*—Two overlapping circles are used to display differences and similarities between [characters, books, settings, topics, events]. (See the example comparing two characters from *Charlotte's Web* in Section 3.8.)

* *Comparison chart*—Much like a Venn diagram, these are used to compare and contrast two or more items/events/concepts/characters/themes.

* *Flow chart*—Organizes a series of items or thoughts in logical order (usually with arrows showing the sequence of flow).

* *Cluster maps / semantic maps*—A central concept or main idea is placed in the center of related subtopics; further details extend from each of the subtopic areas. These are used to categorize or identify related information.

* *5W's chart*—After reading an article or excerpt from a text, the student identifies the 5W elements (Who? What? When? Where? Why?) and records that information on the chart.

* *Favorite part graph*—The class identifies a number of scenes or parts of the book that are plotted on the graph. Everyone records his or her favorite part on the bar graph.

* *Character web*—Put the character's name in the center of the web with traits and descriptions stemming from the center (see example).

* *Circle story organizers*—Used for stories that are cyclical, such as *If You Give a Mouse a Cookie* or *The Ox-Cart Man*. Write on the chalkboard all the main events. The whole class decides where they fit on the circle. Then, on individual paper plates

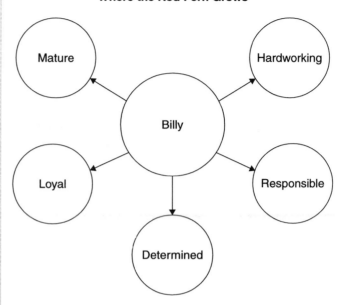

Where the Red Fern Grows

divided into sections, students reproduce the story in sequence (pictures/words) and retell it.

* *Wanted posters*—Students create posters listing identifying characteristics of a character in the book.

There are numerous other graphic organizers for main idea/supporting detail, cause/effect, sequence, classification matrix, and so forth.

Other Reading Comprehension/ Meaning-Making Strategies

Anticipation Guide

An anticipation guide is a series of teacher-generated statements about a topic given to students in advance of the reading. Students individually respond to the statements (for example, true/false) before reading about that topic. Typically, they are asked to discuss their choices briefly with partners or small groups prior to reading the passage. After reading the text material, they again discuss whether their beliefs have changed.

Directed Reading-Thinking Activity (DRTA)

With this technique, students are guided in active reading to make predictions about a passage or story. Then the passage is read (orally or silently) and at predetermined points students are asked to summarize the reading. At these points students are asked to confirm or revise their predictions and to give reasons for their decisions with evidence located and cited from the text. After a certain number of passages or pages are read, the process starts again.

Imagery/Visualization

This is a technique that aids comprehension by creating mental pictures of what is being read. Students are encouraged to create images in their minds as they read. This skill can be taught through a series of guided questioning techniques that elicit from the child vivid detailed pictures as they move through the passage. Examples of guided questions: "What do you see?" "What colors?" "Where is he sitting?" "How does it feel?"

Note: *A good resource for teaching this skill is the program by Nanci Bell entitled* Visualizing and Verbalizing for Language Comprehension and Thinking.

KWL

This is a strategy used prior, during, and after the reading process. It involves a chart divided into three columns:

* The first column (**K**) indicates what is already **known** about the subject/topic. This step activates students' prior knowledge. Ideas are recorded during a class brainstorm.
* The middle column (**W**) is **what** the students want to learn or find out about the subject. This column sets the purpose for reading—to find the answers to those questions.

K	W	L

* The third column (**L**) is filled in on the chart as new information is **learned** from the reading or other teaching. This column is for recording "What We Learned."

KWL Plus is the same as above, except it also adds mapping and summarization to the original KWL strategy. These two tasks incorporate the powerful tools of restructuring text and rewriting to help students process information (Ong, 2000). The information listed on the chart is mapped and organized graphically under categories of topics. Finally, a summary is written based on that graphic organization of ideas.

KWLE is another variation, which is the same as KWL, but adds the additional component and column of E, which stands for *evidence*. This is particularly helpful to guide students in identifying sources of authority for persuasive and argumentative readings/writings (Thompson, 2004).

Question-Answer Relationships

With this technique (QAR), students are taught the different classification of questions: (1) right there, (2) think and search, and (3) on your own.

1. The answers to "right there" questions are stated directly in the text and simply require literal comprehension.

2. The answers to "think and search" questions are not as explicit and easy to locate, but are found somewhere within the text. Answering these questions requires interpretive or inferential comprehension and "reading between the lines." Finding the main idea of a passage is an example of inferential comprehension.

3. "On your own" questions are more abstract, and the answers cannot be found in the text. These questions require reading "beyond the lines" and involve higher-order thinking skills such as analyzing, evaluating, and creative thinking. Examples include comparing and contrasting or answering questions such as: "What do you think caused . . . to happen?" "What other solution can you think of for that problem?" (Raphael, 1982)

Summarizing

Summarizing is one of the most important reading comprehension skills. It always involves identifying the main idea. Sometimes the main idea is explicit and easy to find, and other times it is implied or embedded in the passage. Techniques requiring students to stop at points in the reading to paraphrase in their own words or summarize in one or two sentences provide excellent practice building this skill:

* Students can summarize verbally (for example, "Tell your partner in one sentence what the paragraph was about").
* Summaries can also be done by filling out graphic organizers (with provision of just a couple of lines to record key information only).
* Outlining is another summarizing technique.
* Students can also write a summary sentence or paragraph.
* Students can be asked to monitor their comprehension by responding to these

kinds of prompts: "The main point of this was . . . ." "Overall, this was about . . . ."

Narrative Text Structure

With this technique, students are taught story grammar or story mapping to understand the structure of literary text. This includes setting, characters, problem or conflict, sequence of major events (actions), and the resolution or problem solution. Younger students generally focus on the main characters, setting, and story structure—beginning, middle, and end.

Expository or Informational Text Structure

Students using this technique are taught how to identify the main ideas and supportive details (facts, statistics, examples) in the text. They are explicitly shown that the main ideas are generally found in the chapter titles and headings and that subheadings express the next biggest ideas and points. Learning how to use the glossary, table of contents, index, and tables/graphs, as well as the techniques of scanning and skimming to find the answers, are important teaching points for helping students learn how to read and comprehend expository text.

Note: *The SQ3R and SQ4R techniques described in Section 3.6 are very valuable learning strategies for effectively reading and comprehending informational/expository text.*

Journal Entries

This technique utilizes reflective journals, metacognitive journals, and double-entry journals. A sample outline for each is shown here.

Literature Logs/Journals

To employ this technique, have students record their personal reflections, summaries, and predictions. (See Section 3.6, Learning Strategies and Study Skills, for more information on journaling.)

Reflective Journal

WHAT HAPPENED	HOW I FELT	WHAT I LEARNED

Metacognitive Journal

WHAT I LEARNED	HOW I CAME TO LEARN IT

Double-Entry Journal

Quotation: PHRASE or SENTENCE I ESPECIALLY LIKE	MY THOUGHTS ABOUT THIS QUOTATION

Retelling

Review the literature students have read through storytelling, summarizing, timelines, quick writes and quick-draws, tape recordings, pocket charts with colored sentence strips, plot charts, or any of the graphic organizers.

Hot Seat

Here, a student volunteers to be on "the hot seat," representing a particular character from the story. Students ask him or her questions that must be answered in the way the character would answer them.

Reader's Theater

Work on scripting a piece of literature into dialogue, then read it aloud dramatically.

Other Active Reading/Discussion Formats

Fishbowl

The class is divided into two circles (inner and outer). The inner circle actively engages in discussion about the book (or other topic). The outer circle observes and cannot contribute to the discussion. Their role is to note how well the inner group functioned in critical communication skills (listening to each other's points of view, asking relevant questions, asking for clarification, politely disagreeing, not interrupting). Roles are then reversed, and the outer circle students are the ones participating in the discussion.

Jigsaw

Students are divided into "home" groups, each responsible for reading and understanding the same material. Each member is assigned a number (for example, 1 to 5) that corresponds to a section of the reading assignment. The students with the same number from each home group then meet in their "expert" groups in order to reread and study their sections in depth. Expert groups work together in learning their portions of the material and planning how to teach that information and content to their home group members. Then everyone returns to their home group, and each member teaches his or her content to home group peers (Ong, 2000).

Guided Reading

This is an instructional strategy in which students of approximately the same reading level are in reading groups (usually no more than six per group). The teacher selects books for each group to read together that are new to them and will involve working on strategies that students in that group specifically need to practice. Usually "leveled" books are used for guided reading groups or any selection that is at the students' instructional level.

The teacher coaches students to apply strategies throughout the reading of the selected book with the purpose of teaching them how to read for meaning.

1. The procedure begins with an introduction to the book and "walking through" pages (looking at illustrations, making predictions, providing some background information, and focusing on some of the difficult vocabulary that will be encountered in the book).

2. Students then read *to themselves* as the teacher moves to each individual student and "listens in" as he or she reads (asking students to read aloud softly).

3. The teacher provides prompts and asks questions to guide students in using strategies for figuring out the text and problem-solving challenges they encounter in their reading. For example, "Reread that sentence. Does that make sense? What other word would make sense there that starts with *ch*?" "Are there any little words you recognize in that big word?" "Sound it out."

4. Students are prompted to reread when they finish the initial reading, extending their comprehension and thinking about the book.

5. There are teaching points and strategies taught during and after the reading, depending on what the teacher determines are the needs of the group (Fountas & Pinnell, 1996).

Literature Circles

This is an instructional format in which the class is divided into self-selected groups with students in each group reading a common book (unabridged version). After a period of independent reading, groups meet for deep discussion and analysis of their books. As students do their independent reading prior to meeting in their group, they are responsible for keeping notes and journals/logs. Students are asked to record their responses to the literature, questions that they have, and other comments (for example, connections they make, feelings evoked). When the groups meet, they respond to the literature and the various literary elements.

There are specific roles that individual members of the group may assume (Bender & Larkin, 2003; Daniels, 1994; Vacca, Vacca, Grove, et al., 2003). For example, these may be from among the following (and depend on the size of the group):

* A group leader (discussion director) responsible for asking questions that require higher-order thinking skills

* A literary luminary, who reads aloud important, memorable sections of the text
* The "book connector," who is responsible for making connections between what is read in the current book and other books read
* A vocabulary enricher, who is responsible for locating interesting words and/or finding the meaning of unknown words
* An artist/illustrator
* A summarizer, who highlights key points in and the gist of the day's reading
* A "travel agent," who tracks where the characters have traveled to and so forth
* An investigator/researcher, who provides related background information (for example, about the author, geography, historical events)

GIST

This acronym stands for Generating Interaction between Schemata and Text (Swanson & DeLa-Paz, 1998). This is a strategy used for comprehending informational text and determining the "gist" of the reading material:

1. In cooperative groups, students read sections silently.
2. When done reading a short section, the members of the group work together to write a one-sentence summary.
3. All group members then record that summary sentence.
4. Students continue in this fashion of reading a segment, stopping at logical points, jointly deciding on a summary sentence, and then recording on their own papers.
5. Those papers can then serve as a study guide for the reading material.

Reciprocal Teaching

This approach, originally developed by Palincsar and Brown (1984, 1985), is one of the best-researched strategies available to teachers (Marzano, Pickering, & Pollock, 2001). It involves students working together in cooperative groups taking turns designing and asking questions and leading the group in the process of discussing and working through small portions of the text for comprehension purposes. Research has found that good readers spontaneously use strategies of predicting, questioning, clarifying, and summarizing. Poor readers do not self-monitor or use these strategies that lead to understanding.

In a reciprocal teaching format, the group is led through the process of reading a short section and (1) *questioning* about the content read to identify important information in the passage; (2) *summarizing* questions may be asked such as: "What is this paragraph mostly about?" "What would be a good title for this passage?"; (3) *Clarifying* anything confusing in the reading with questions that might include: "Has anyone heard this expression before? What do you think it means?" "Can anyone explain this?" The process continues with (4) *predicting* what will happen in the next portion of the reading. The students proceed in this format, taking turns in the leader role as they read the next portions of the text.

PASS

This reading comprehension strategy by Deshler, Ellis, and Lenz (1996) is a four-step process (preview, ask, summarize, synthesize). Sousa (2001) describes the steps of this strategy. The teacher guides the students through the four steps.

1. Preview, Review, and Predict
   — Preview by reading the heading and one or two sentences.
   — Review what you already know about this topic.
   — Predict what you think the text or story will be about.
2. Ask and Answer Questions
   — Content-focused questions (Who? What? Why? Where? How does this relate to what I already know?)
   — Monitoring questions (Does this make sense? How is this different from what I thought it was going to be about?)

— Problem-solving questions (Do I need to reread part of it? Can I visualize the information? Does it have too many unknown words?)

3. Summarize
   — Explain what the short passage you read was all about.

4. Synthesize
   — Explain how the short passage fits in with the whole passage.
   — Explain how what you learned fits in with what you knew.

Book Projects/Activities

The following are examples of various book activities or projects that incorporate different learning styles and modalities. Allowing students to choose from a menu of possible projects related to the books they have read is a wonderful means of differentiating instruction and drawing on the interests and strengths of all students in the classroom.

Draw

* A map or diagram of the setting of the story
* A poster advertising the book
* A bookmark with pictures or symbols on one side and a list of important events or summary on the other

Design

* A picture postcard of the setting; on the back, write to a friend as if you were the main character in the book and describe the setting and events happening there
* A T-shirt for your main character that represents attributes of the character's personality or with symbols representing events in the book

Make

* A diorama of the setting
* A literary scrapbook about a character in the book with postcards, pictures, award certificates, report cards, and so forth

* A cube on which you draw the key events of the story
* A word and picture collage of the main events
* A board game based on the book
* A mobile of the plot
* A pop-up book, mini-book, accordion book, or Big Book
* A memory basket with items representing events or themes in the story
* Foods mentioned in the book

Pretend

* You are a TV interviewer and audio- or videotape an interview with a character in the book.
* You are a prosecuting attorney. Put one of the characters in the book on trial for a crime. Prepare your case, giving all your arguments and support them with facts.

Write

* A letter to a friend telling her or him about the most exciting parts of the book
* A letter to the main character suggesting what might have happened if he or she acted in another way
* A new ending or sequel
* A TV commercial advertising your book
* A diary entry by the main character describing a major event in the story
* A travel diary describing the places you have traveled in the story
* A letter to the author

Create

* A book jacket
* A crossword puzzle using words and characters from the story

Perform

* An original song related to the story
* A phone conversation between two or more characters
* A reader's theater scripted from the book

INTERVIEW WITH JOHN
(23 Years Old, a Senior at a University in Colorado)

John was diagnosed with ADHD as an adult.

Tell me what you remember as being difficult for you in elementary school.

"From first grade I felt that I was one of the 'dumb kids.' Teachers always said that I had the ability, but just didn't apply myself. I remember in sixth grade that for a school project I worked very hard and built a solar house all on my own. I didn't have any help from my parents. I knew what I wanted to do, but I didn't have the tools to get it all together. I got a poor grade on the project because it didn't look like I spent much time on it. My teacher said, 'You could have done better than that!'

"In elementary school, storytelling time was difficult for me. I fell asleep. My teacher would ask all the time, 'John, do you feel all right?' because I couldn't listen to her stories. She didn't understand . . . I had to sleep to stay quiet.

"In one of my grades one of the kids in the 'top' group did a project on optical illusions. I remember thinking how her project didn't look like much . . . I know I could have done a better job. But because I was in the lower group, I never had a chance to do all the special projects."

What do you wish could have happened when you were younger?

"If I could go back now, I would like to relearn how to learn. If there were only teachers who really cared and tried to find out what my problem was. For a long time I could hardly read a story. I had to keep rereading it because I was 'off somewhere else,' and not paying attention to what I was reading. I would read a sentence over and over again, and read it out loud, and still not have any idea what I read."

What about junior high (middle school)?

"Most of the problems I had in school were disciplinary, especially in junior high. I started ditching class because algebra was so difficult for me."

What is your advice to teachers?

"The most important thing is to be there for the kids. Those kids who have problems early and are identified are the ones who can be helped!"

Mathematics

Challenges and Strategies

*D*uring the past few years there has been increased demand for higher achievement and proficiency of students in mathematics, which is reflected in today's math standards and curriculum for K–12. Math content is becoming increasingly complex at earlier ages (CEC, 2003).

According to Sousa (2001), about 6 percent of school-aged children have some form of difficulty with processing mathematics. Among those children are frequently students with learning disabilities and/or ADHD. This section will address common mathematical difficulties, current information regarding math standards and expectations in grades K–12, numerous strategies to build math skills and proficiency, as well as various accommodations/modifications for struggling students.

Math Difficulties Associated with ADHD

Many students with ADHD and/or learning disabilities experience academic difficulty with mathematics, due to the multiple processes and brain functions involved in executing math problems. Some math challenges may be specifically related to weaknesses with ADHD (for example, inattention, organization, working memory, self-monitoring). Others may result more directly from a learning disability (for example, sequential learning, perceptual-motor, language). Remember, some children have both ADHD and co-existing learning disabilities.

The following list of impairments is associated with ADHD and LD, and how they negatively impact performance in math is described (from Rief, 2003):

Memory Weaknesses

With math, active working memory is involved, making it a struggle for an ADHD student to hold information in the head long enough to utilize it throughout the steps of the problem. Long-term memory is also involved for the retrieval of processes and math vocabulary learned in the past. Memory weaknesses cause problems with:

* The learning and acquisition of basic math facts
* Being able to recall math facts and retrieve those math facts quickly and accurately
* Computing multi-step problems (forgetful of sequence and recalling where they are in the process)
* Recalling rules, procedures, algorithms, teacher instruction, and directions

Attention Weaknesses

Problems with attention result in numerous careless errors and inconsistent performance—even when the student is skilled at solving math problems. The following are issues related to inattention:

* Noticing processing/operational signs in math problems (for example, being aware that the + sign changes to −)
* Paying attention to other details (for example, decimal points and other symbols)
* Self-correcting and finding own errors in computation
* Ability to sustain the focus and mental effort necessary to complete the problems with accuracy

Sequencing Weaknesses

Sequencing weaknesses can lead to problems in the following areas:

* Ability to do algebra and other step-by-step equations
* The execution of any multi-step procedure
* The ability to do skip counting (for example, 3, 6, 9, 12, 15 . . .) and multiples of other numbers
* Recognition and use of patterns

Perceptual/Visual-Motor/ Fine-Motor/Spatial-Organization Weaknesses

These weaknesses account for the following:

* Copying problems from the board or book onto paper
* Aligning numbers or decimal points accurately on paper
* Writing and computing within the minimal amount of given space on the page; spacing between problems; leaving enough room
* Remembering and using correct directionality for solving math problems (for example, beginning with the column to the right and moving right to left; regrouping accurately)

* Recognizing and not confusing symbols (for example, +, ×, 6/9, 38/83)
* Speed of writing down problems and answers (often either too fast and illegible, or too slow and cannot keep up or complete assignments/tests)
* Difficulties in the above result in numerous errors and need for frequent erasing and correction, causing the student much frustration

Language Weaknesses

Difficulties with language can result in difficulties:

* Understanding and relating to the numerous abstract terms in math
* Solving word problems (interpreting and understanding what is being asked; separating relevant from irrelevant information provided)
* Following directions
* Understanding the complex and confusing language/vocabulary found in many math textbooks

In addition, as writing is infused in all curricular areas in today's classrooms, students are generally expected to write about their thinking processes and how they solved problems. Consequently, a student who may be strong with numbers and mathematical problem solving, but struggles in written expression, may do poorly in math class as a result of language/writing difficulties.

Self-Monitoring/Self-Management Weaknesses

These important executive functions, which involve self-awareness, metacogitive skills, and self-management, cause the following difficulties in math:

* Taking time to plan strategies for solving a problem
* Realizing when something is not working or making sense (for example, answer is

not close to estimate) and readjusting or trying another strategy

* Being aware of time and time-management in pacing and working the problems given
* Maintaining the level of attention and perseverance necessary to complete problems with accuracy
* Being able to check for errors and self-correct (Misunderstood Minds, 2002)

Math Strategies and Interventions

As described in my earlier works, in spite of the challenges with math computation and problem solving, there are a number of ways that teachers and parents can help. The following are strategies to strengthen and build math skills, as well as appropriate modifications and accommodations to support struggling students. Make the abstract more concrete by:

* Providing many kinds of manipulatives to help visualize and work out math problems (cubes, chips, tiles, counters, beans, base-ten blocks, number lines)
* Introducing mathematical concepts with demonstrations using real-life examples and motivating situations. For example, cut a sandwich into five equal parts to share in a small group (1/5 per student); or first count the total and then equally divide a bag of candy among a number of students (32 pieces divided by 5 kids = 6 each with 2 left over).
* Teaching multiplication, relating things that come in sets of a certain number (for example, 4's—quarters in a dollar, legs on a dog; 5's—fingers on a hand, days in a school week)
* Purchasing and using manipulatives that can be projected on the overhead projector, such as clock faces, coins/bills, pattern blocks, base-ten blocks, tangrams, and calculators
* Modeling the use of drawing, diagramming, and labeling in the problem-solving process and encouraging students to use those strategies

* Using concrete references such as the technique in a wonderful program, Semple Math (Semple, 1986), where "Whole Number Street" is used to teach place value, with different houses of numbers (unit house, thousands, millions house, and so on)
  — Semple Math also provides mnemonic associations and spatial anchors, for example, "kids" are referred to as the numbers in the units place, "teens" are numbers in the tens place, and "adults" in the hundreds place.
  — Users of Semple Math quickly can identify which "house" the number lives in and know how to consequently read and write that number.
  — There is also a brick wall symbol on the right side of the paper as a cue, which helps the children remember how to place the numbers in relation to "standing near the wall" (Semple, 1986).
* Giving as many opportunities as possible at home and school for using math in the context of real-life situations (for example, using money, balancing a checkbook, determining mileage on a fantasy road trip, comparison shopping, ordering a meal with tax and tip)

Note: *The author's book* How to Reach & Teach All Students in the Inclusive Classroom *contains a selection of over sixty "Survival Math" activities that are motivating to students.*

Compensate for memory difficulties and increase recall of math facts and procedures through the following methods:

* Use multiplication fact sheets, charts, and tables, and keep them readily available for reference.
* Allow and encourage the use of calculators, and have students use them to check their work. (A calculator that is recommended is Math Explorer, by Texas Instruments, which offers the integer remainder choice, and not just the repeating decimal.) (Cawley, Parmar, Salmon, & Roy, 2001)

* Teach children the "counting up method" on their fingers for a reliable back-up system to memorizing addition and subtraction facts to eighteen.

* Use mnemonic devices (memory clues, images, and associations) to help them remember facts, sequential steps, procedures, and abstract concepts/vocabulary.

* A variety of rhymes, chants, raps, and songs help students memorize the multiplication tables. Students can make up their own or use those commercially available.

* Use mnemonics such as **D**ead **M**onsters **S**mell **B**ad or **D**ear **M**iss **S**ally **B**rown for learning the steps of long division (**d**ivide, **m**ultiply, **s**ubtract, **b**ring down).

* Teach the different "finger tricks" available for learning ×6, ×7, ×8, and ×9 tables. Such tricks can be found in various resources, such as *Taming the Dragons* (Setley, 1995), and others.

* Some mnemonic programs are available that use picture associations and clever stories to help master multiplication facts as well. One such program is *Time Tables the Fun Way: A Picture Method of Learning the Multiplication*. Others are *Memory Joggers* or *Semple Math,* which uses very creative associations and mnemonics.

* Have students practice one sequence of multiples at a time (×2s, ×3s) in a variety of multisensory formats until mastery. (See Section 3.2, Multisensory Instruction, for several recommended strategies to learn multiplication facts.)

* Encourage keeping a card file of specific math skills, concepts, rules, and algorithms taught, along with specific examples of each on the card for reference.

* Practice and review facts in frequent, brief sessions (five minutes per session, a few times each day).

* Daily timings of basic facts can be great practice and motivation *if* students compete against themselves, not their classmates. Have students chart their own progress and mastery. Don't display visually for the whole class to see. This is demoralizing and embarrassing for students who struggle to pass timings.

* Give students a blank multiplication chart (matrix of ×0 through ×9 horizontally and ×0 through ×9 vertically). Have them fill in the facts they know. Look for patterns and shortcuts. First the row of zeros, ones, fives, and tens are easily identified and eliminated from the list of multiplication facts that must be memorized. Once students know multiples of 0-5s, teach ×9s. When students are able to recognize and recall the commutative property of multiplication (for example, $3 \times 7 = 7 \times 3$), it significantly reduces the stress and feeling that there are so many facts to learn. Actually, there will only be twelve more facts left to memorize (4×4, 4×6, 4×7, 4×8, 6×4, 6×6, 6×7, 6×8, 7×4, 7×7, 7×8, 8×8).

* *Touch Math* is a supplementary/compensatory technique for children with difficulties memorizing math facts. Through the use of touch points strategically placed on numerals 1 through 9, students learn to rapidly visualize and accurately compute without having to pull up their fingers. This can be a useful bypass strategy and technique for students who struggle with learning basic facts.

Note: *Poor mastery of basic facts should never prevent students from being taught grade-level math curriculum and higher-level concepts. Provide compensatory tools (for example, math tables/charts) to help them past this hurdle, while continuing to teach, practice, and review math facts on a regular basis.*

Help compensate for spatial organization and perceptual-motor difficulties in the following ways:

* Encourage students to write and solve their computation problems on graph paper rather than notebook paper. Experiment with graph paper of varying square/grid sizes.

* Turn notebook paper sideways (with lines running vertically rather than horizontally). This makes it much easier for students to keep numbers aligned in columns, and reduces careless errors.

* Reduce the requirement of copying problems from the board or book by photocopying the page or writing out the problems on paper for certain students.

* Struggling students may be required to copy from the board/book just the first three or four problems for practice, but then be given a photocopy or assistance recording the remaining problems of the assignment.

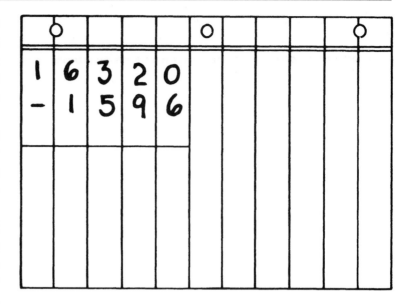

* Remove individual pages from consumable workbooks. Give one page at a time instead of the whole cumbersome workbook.

* Provide a large workspace on tests. If necessary, rewrite test items on other paper, with lots of room for computation.

* Provide scratch paper for student use in computation.

* Provide lots of space on the page between problems and at bottom of the page.

Instructional and Assessment Strategies/Modifications

* Allow extra time on math tests so students are not rushed, leading to careless errors.

* Avoid the anxiety of timed tests and drills (especially those posted for all students in the class to see); and/or extend the amount of time permitted for certain students as "passing."

* Grade by number of correct problems over the number assigned (which could be different for students receiving modified homework/classwork).

* Provide frequent checks for accuracy. Set a certain number of problems to complete (for example, one row only, or four or five problems) and then check before the student is permitted to continue. This reduces the frustration of having to erase and fix a number of problems done incorrectly.

* List steps/procedures to multi-step problems and algorithms. Post clear numbered steps and/or give students a desk copy model of steps to solve problems.

* Cut up a page of problems into strips/rows, and give to students one at a time.

* Have review problems prepared on cards (three to five per card). Students choose a card to complete.

* Give students a choice of computing with a calculator, paper/pencil, or mentally.

* Let students choose problems to do first, or to cross out or eliminate any two or three problems in the assignment they wish.

* When testing long division or multiplication problems that involve using several digits and regrouping, give problems with numbers for which most all students know the math facts. (Example: $6274 \times 52 =$) Most students know the times tables 5s and 2s. This way they are tested on their understanding of the process, and are not penalized because they have poor memory skills.

* Provide models of assignments and criteria for success (rubrics).

* Provide immediate feedback whenever possible. Go over homework assignments the next day, allowing students to comfortably ask questions and work any problems that they did not understand together as a class.

* Encourage students to come for help when needed (before, during, or after class). Do not allow students to remain confused without providing any necessary re-teaching and/or tutorial assistance.
* Keep sample math problems on the board and have students keep them in a notebook for reference.
* Work problems on an overhead projector or dry-erase board, using color to make the steps and processes more visually clear.
* Provide frequent review of skills.
* Instruct with a teaching model of demonstrating, working together (for example, in cooperative groups/partners), working independently, and checking.
* Use choral responses in instruction (for example, chanting in unison: multiples, evens/odds, place value, names of geometric figures).
* Use cooperative learning structures and formats in math instruction (Kagan, Kagan, & Kagan, 2000):

    Partners: Working in pairs, one works a problem while the other coaches. Roles are reversed. Then, after a couple of problems are completed, partners pair up with another set of pairs and compare answers/check one another.

    Groups/teams: Teams of four work a problem together and check each other's understanding on one or more problems. Then the team breaks into two pairs, who continue to work together to solve the next couple of problems. Students then continue independently working similar problems.

* Reduce the number of problems that you assign. There is no need to assign every problem on a page to assess your students' understanding or to provide practice. Allow students to do odds, evens, multiples of. Ten problems required to be written neatly, well-spaced, and with work shown is preferable to requiring thirty problems on a page, which will be done carelessly.

* As mentioned earlier, avoid anxiety of timed tests of basic facts. There are a number of students (ADHD and LD) who have extreme difficulty memorizing basic facts. This is not due to laziness or lack of practice. Even if these students do basically know their facts by memory, they often choke and cannot perform on a timed test. Consider allowing some extra time for students who can't recall facts and write them down rapidly. Give credit for being able to respond orally if writing rapidly is too difficult. If some students have serious difficulty memorizing facts and rely on counting with fingers (or other manipulatives), don't penalize them.
* Use individual dry-erase boards. Have students compute one step of a problem at a time, asking them to hold up their boards upon your signal after each step.

Strategies for Increasing Focus and Attention

* Color-highlight or underline key words and vocabulary in word problems (for example, <u>shared</u>, <u>doubled</u>, <u>product</u>, <u>average</u>, <u>larger</u>, <u>slower</u>, <u>difference</u>, <u>altogether</u>, <u>equal parts</u>).
* Put colored dots by the ones (units) column to remind students the direction of where to begin computation.
* Color-highlight processing signs for students who are inattentive to change in operational signs on a page. For example, color addition signs yellow, subtraction signs pink, and so forth.
* Color-highlight place value. For example, given the number 16,432,781, write the hundreds (781) in green, the thousands (432) in orange, and the millions (16) in blue.
* Reduce the number of problems on a page.
* Block part of the page while working on problems, or fold the paper under to reveal just one or two rows at a time.
* Softly say steps of the problem out loud to keep attention focused.

✽ Allow the child to stand up and stretch or take a break of some kind after a certain number of problems are completed and checked for accuracy.

Increase the Amount of Practice and Review

✽ Review previously learned skills with high frequency.

✽ Make sets of practice/review problems (a few per page) with answers on the back for independent practice.

✽ Use computer software games for drill and practice of math skills. Computer programs can generally be adjusted for speed and level of difficulty. They provide immediate feedback and are fun, non-threatening, and motivating to students. Also, they tend to hold the interest of an ADHD student, as the stimuli is constantly changing.

✽ Pair students to practice and quiz each other on skills taught.

✽ Motivate the practicing of skills through the use of board games, card games, and other class games. Many board games (for example, Uno™, Battleship™) and card games are excellent for building math skills (for example, counting, logic, probability, strategic thinking). Try using as many games as possible that do not have a heavy emphasis on speed of recall, or the type of competition that will discourage struggling students from even trying.

Tips for Parents

✽ Since there is not enough time during a school day for the needed daily practice of math drill and rote memorization, try to spend at least five minutes a day practicing at home in a variety of formats. Do so in a fun, relaxed manner, without pressure or tension.

✽ Many children with ADHD and/or learning disabilities are not proficient with functional math skills (measurement, time concepts, counting money/change). Practice as much as possible at home. These are critical skills that teachers often do not have enough time to teach until mastery. Include your child in activities such as cooking/baking, constructing, sewing, gardening, home improvements, and so on, as these all involve measurement and other functional math skills.

Self-Monitoring and Metacognitive Strategies

✽ Provide direct instruction to help students think about their approach in problem solving.

✽ Help students self-monitor their level of alertness when working, so they maintain attention to task, stay paced, and work problems with accuracy.

✽ Model how to first read problems (particularly word problems) and plan a strategy for solving before beginning the work.

✽ Teach how to work each problem carefully and check for accuracy.

✽ Teach how to estimate and determine whether an answer given is reasonable or not.

✽ Encourage students to stop after completing a few problems and check for accuracy (independently, with a partner or teacher).

✽ Use math portfolios/assessment. Have students keep a journal of their thinking, reasoning, questions, and understanding of math concepts. Also have students write their understanding about mathematical concepts before and after the unit is taught.

✽ Guide through the steps of a problem, modeling what to ask oneself when solving, for example: "Where do you always start?" (ones column). "Read the ones column" (5 minus 9). "Can you do that? Can you have 5 and take away 9?" (No). "So what do we have to do next?" (Regroup, or borrow from the tens column).

✽ Model talking out loud while reasoning out/thinking about a mathematical problem. Encourage students to do the same—externalizing their thinking and verbalizing while solving problems. Listen to students as they think out loud, and correct gaps in their comprehension when possible at this point.

* Teach students to think about what they are being asked to figure out in the problem and state it in their own words.

National Council of Teachers of Mathematics (NCTM) Standards

The NCTM standards (2000) emphasize the need to prepare all students for algebra beginning in kindergarten and progressing through each grade. Gagnon and Maccini (2001) summarize these standards, based on five basic goals for students:

1. Learning to value mathematics
2. Becoming confident in their ability to do mathematics
3. Becoming mathematical problem solvers
4. Learning to communicate mathematically, and
5. Learning to reason mathematically

The Principles and Standards involve a framework of six general principles, five content standards, and five process standards for achieving these goals:

Six General Principles of Mathematics (Gagnon & Maccini, 2001; NCTM, 2000)

1. Equity is the assertion that "mathematics is for all students, regardless of personal characteristics, backgrounds, or physical challenges."
2. Mathematics should be viewed as an integrated whole, as opposed to isolated facts to be learned or memorized.
3. Teachers must display the attributes of (a) a deep understanding of math; (b) an understanding of individual student development and how children learn math; and (c) the ability to select strategies and tasks that promote student learning.

4. The view that students will gain an understanding of mathematics through classes that promote problem solving, thinking, and reasoning.
5. Need for continual assessment of student performance, growth, and understanding via varied techniques (for example, portfolios, mathematical assessment of concepts embedded in real-world problems).
6. Importance of technology (for example, computers, calculators) and the realization that use of these tools may enhance learning by providing opportunities for exploration and concept representation.

Five Content Standards or "Strands" Addressed in the NCTM Standards

1. Number and operations
2. Algebra
3. Geometry
4. Measurement
5. Data analysis and probability

These content strands extend across four grade bands (preK–2, 3–5, 6–8, 9–12) and have different value or weight within each band.

Five Process Standards from the Principles and Standards

1. *Problem-solving*—emphasizes the use of problem-solving contexts to help students build their mathematical knowledge.
2. *Reasoning-and-proof*—involves logical thinking during problem solving and considering whether an answer makes sense.
3. *Communication*—refers to talking about, describing, explaining, and writing about mathematics in a clear and organized manner.
4. *Connections*—refers to relating mathematical ideas to other mathematical ideas, curricular areas, and real-world situations.
5. *Representation*—refers to expressing math ideas/concepts through charts, graphs, symbols, diagrams, and manipulatives.

Note: The current NCTM Principles and Standards for School Mathematics can be found at www.nctm.org.

Drawing on Their Learning Strengths

Students with learning disabilities, attention deficit disorders, and other typically underachieving students often have learning strengths (and are sometimes highly gifted) in spatial awareness, logical thinking/reasoning, and visualization. They may be able to excel in a balanced mathematics curriculum, which emphasizes patterns, geometry, measurement, probability, and logic.

These students are frequently hands-on, visual learners by nature and would benefit greatly from the use of manipulatives (pattern blocks, base-ten blocks, interlocking cubes such as Unifix® cubes, tiles, and others), graphing activities, searching for patterns, and other nontextbook, non-worksheet strategies.

We question the instructional practice of assigning students problem after problem, page after page of tedious computation in isolation from problem-solving situations. The trouble with this still-common practice in many classrooms is that many times students can compute pages of problems without ever understanding the algorithms or knowing how and when to use them. Many adults report using calculators and mental math far more frequently than paper-and-pencil computation in their personal and professional lives. Students need to be trained in, exposed to, and permitted to use all tools and strategies available to solve problems.

Teaching Math Through a Hands-On, Cooperative, Problem-Solving Approach

Mathematical procedures taught should be related to situations in which they are required. This helps children see the connection and relevance to solving real problems in their lives.

Teachers who embrace this approach structure their classroom instruction so that students work together with peers in problem-solving situations. They are encouraged to explore and make discoveries together and to share (with the teacher and classmates) their reasoning and the methods/strategies they chose to solve problems. This is facilitated by teacher questioning such as: "Can you guess about how much the answer will be before doing it?" "Can you draw a picture to show what is happening in the problem?" Students are also asked to frequently write—put their thinking/reasoning on paper, explaining

and illustrating their discoveries. By valuing and sharing individual reasoning and problem-solving strategies, students realize that there are a number of ways that problems can be solved, not just one "right" way.

The benefits of such math programs/approaches for all students, but particularly those with ADHD and/or LD, include:

* High motivation
* Students perceive the relevance and better grasp concepts
* Challenging and non-threatening
* Interactive, cooperative group work ensures that students are participating and attention is engaged
* Promotes higher self-esteem
* Utilizes students' strengths and taps all learning styles
* Students who may not have great skill in arithmetic/computation may very likely excel in other strands. You may be salvaging some future mathematicians, scientists, and discoverers.

Word-Problem-Solving Strategies

* Teach steps needed for solving math problems. Clearly list the steps, and keep a visible chart of various problem-solving strategies.
* Teach and model a number of strategies for solving word problems:
  Read the problem out loud.
  Read at least twice before beginning.
  Restate in own words.
  Look for and color-highlight significant clue words (for example, *altogether, how much more, faster than, part of*).
  Draw pictures, diagrams, and sketches representing the problem.
  Cross out irrelevant information.
  Circle, underline, or color-highlight the numbers that are important.
  Write the kind of answer needed (for example, miles per hour, degrees, dollars/cents).

  Use objects/manipulatives.
  Construct a chart or table.
  Make an organized list.
  Act it out.
  Look for a pattern.
  Make a model.
  Work backwards.
  Eliminate possibilities.
  Guess (estimate) and check.
* Teach how to first estimate and then evaluate the answer to determine if it is reasonable or not.
* Show how to reason whether or not an answer should be larger or smaller than the numbers given.
* Teach important math vocabulary and key words that indicate the process or strategy needed, for example: total, sum, altogether (addition/multiplication); more/less, fewer, difference, what's left? missing? larg**er** than/ fast**er** than/small**er** than—for subtraction; what part of/per unit (indicating division).
* Make up word problems using students' names, situations, and interests.
* Encourage thinking of different ways to solve a problem.
* Talk through the steps of problem solving.
* Let students use their own methods for solving problems (for example, mental, pictorial, fingers, manipulatives, paper/pencil).
* Always build in time during the lesson for students to share how they solved the problem, and emphasize that there are a variety of ways—not just one method.
* Provide many opportunities for students to make up their own word/thought problems to share with the class, and do as a group, whenever possible within the context of the classroom activities. For example, when planning a class party or field trip, the students can work in teams deciding how many cars/drivers are needed, how many bottles of soda need to be bought, how many dozens of cookies are to be baked, and so forth.

More Strategies to Teach Problem Solving

Identify Problem Types

For example, students identify types of problems for addition and subtraction. Once they know the type of problem they are dealing with, they can make the computations to solve it. Three types most often used in addition and subtraction are

* *Change*—A change occurs to the beginning set, which results in change in the end set.
* *Group*—Involves part-whole relationships and knowing that the whole is equal to the sum of its parts.
* *Compare*—One set serves as the comparison set (CEC, 2003).

Jitendra (2002) shared that of these three different problem types, students can be guided in memorizing rules for identifying the total and determining the operation needed to solve the problem. An example follows.

Finding the Total

* "Change" Problem—If the problem ends up with more than it started with, then the ending set is the total. If the problem ends up with less than it started with, then the beginning set is the total.
* "Group" Problem—The larger group set is always the total.
* "Compare" Problem—The larger set (compared or referent) in the comparison or difference statement is the total.

Figuring Out the Operation (Addition or Subtraction)

* When the total is unknown, add to find the total.
* When the total is known, subtract to find the other amount (Jitendra, 2002).

Bassarear (2001) suggests the following four steps for solving problems:*

1. Understanding the Problem
   — Do you understand what the problem is asking for?
   — Can you state the problem in your own words, that is, paraphrase the problem?
   — Have you used all the given information?
   — Can you solve a part of the problem?
2. Devising a Plan
   — For example, guess, check, and revise, keeping track of "guesses" with a table; make an estimate; look for patterns; look to see whether the problem is similar to one already solved
3. Carrying out the plan
   — Are you keeping the problem meaningful or are you just "groping and hoping"?
   — On each step ask what the numbers mean. Label your work.
   — Are you bogged down? Do you need to try another strategy?
4. Looking Back
   — Does your answer make sense? Is the answer reasonable? Is the answer close to your estimate if you made one?
   — Does your answer work when you check it with the given information?
   — Can you use a different method to solve the problem?

*Adapted from Bassarear, 2001

More Recommendations for Math Instruction

* Make a real effort to use computer programs for drill and practice. If your students have access to computers in the classroom or computer lab, make use of the many software programs available that make learning math skills fun for students.
* Use math portfolios/assessment.
* Have students keep journals of their thinking, reasoning, questions, and understanding of math concepts. Encourage PYBOP: "Put your brains on paper." It is interesting to see students' understanding of a concept (through journal entries in their own

words/illustrations) before and after a unit is taught.

* Team teach! If you personally dislike math or feel threatened by it . . . don't teach it (if possible). Take advantage of the many courses, workshops, and training to help you feel more comfortable and enthused about teaching mathematics.

* Try graphing on a regular basis at all grade levels (bar graphs, picture graphs, Venn diagrams, circle graphs, line graphs). Graphing is a way to present and organize data so that relationships in the data are seen easily. In order to interpret and use graphs as a problem-solving tool, students need to make their own first.

* Include many estimation activities in your curriculum.

* Make math instruction hands-on, contextualized, highly interactive, interconnected, systematic, engaging, interesting, and understandable (Cawley & Foley, 2002).

* Computing taxes, negotiating a car purchase from a dealer—all are examples of real-life word problems (Witzel, 2003).

* Incorporate word problems throughout a lesson rather than adding them to the end (Witzel, 2003).

* Analyze the problems that students miss to determine where their understanding breaks down. Then teach those targeted skills.

* Explicitly teach, illustrate, and maintain a word wall of grade-level math vocabulary—particularly any words in math that cause confusion for students.

* Use money (pennies, dimes, dollars) to teach place value.

Researchers have determined that certain components of effective instruction positively influence the mathematical performance of students with learning and behavioral disabilities (Maccini, McNaughton, & Ruhl, 1999). These include:

1. Teaching prerequisite skills, definitions, and strategies

2. Providing direct instruction in problem representation and problem solution

3. Providing direct instruction in self-monitoring procedures

4. Using organizers

5. Incorporating manipulatives

6. Teaching conceptual knowledge

7. Providing effective instruction

Use mnemonics as a learning strategy to recall math processes or procedures. For example: RIDE (from the website of the Special Education Department of James Madison University, www.coe.jmu.edu/learningtoolbox):

Read the problem correctly.

Identify the relevant information.

Determine the operations and unit for expressing the answer.

Enter the correct numbers and calculate, then check.

Another is STAR (Maccini & Hughes, 2000; Maccini & Ruhl, 2000):

Search the word problem (read the problem carefully, write down known/facts).

Translate the words into an equation in picture form.

Answer the problem.

Review the solution (reread the problem, check the reasonableness of the answer).

Math and Writing Connection

The following are possible journal starters that were shared by a teacher in New York City:

Feelings About Math

* My best experience/worst experience with math was when . . . .

* When it comes to math, I find it difficult to . . . .

* Math interests me because . . . .

* I find math challenging because . . . .

* One mathematics activity I really enjoy is . . . because . . . .

Math Journal Starters

* Today I learned about (or how to) . . . .
* The most important ideas I learned today are . . . .
* I am still confused by . . . .
* Next time I . . ., I plan to . . . .
* I discovered that . . . .
* The mathematical rule for this problem is . . . .
* The way I remember (how to) . . . in my head is . . . .
* The tricky part of this problem is . . . .
* The thing you have to remember with this kind of problem is . . . .
* The steps I used to solve this problem were . . . .
* I could use this type of problem solving when . . . .
* I was frustrated with this problem because . . . .

Math and Literature Connection

The following are some examples of literature books that involve mathematical concepts and can be integrated into math instruction:

* *26 Letters and 99 Cents,* by Tana Hoban. (New York: Mulberry Paperback Books, 1995)
* *A Million Fish . . . More or Less,* by Patricia C. McKissack. Illustrated by Dena Schutzer. (New York: Dragonfly Books, 1992)
* *A Remainder of One,* by Elinor J. Pinczes. Illustrated by Bonnie MacKain. (New York: Houghton Mifflin, 1995)
* *Annabelle Swift, Kindergartner,* by Amy Schwartz. (London: Orchard Books, 1988)
* *Anno's Magic Seeds,* by Mitsumasa Anno. (New York: Philomel Books, 1995)
* *Anno's Mysterious Multiplying Jar,* by Mitsumasa Anno. (New York: Philomel Publishing, 1983)
* *Counting on Frank,* by Rod Clement. (Milwaukee, WI: Gareth Stevens Publishing, 1991)

* *Cubes, Cones, Cylinders, and Spheres,* by Tana Hoban. (New York: HarperCollins, 2000)
* *Fly Away Home,* by Eve Bunting. (New York: Clarion Books, 1991)
* *Grandfather Tang's Story,* by Ann Tompert. Illustrated by Robert Andrew Parker. (New York: Crown, 1990)
* *Hannah's Collections,* by Marthe Jocelyn. (New York: Penguin Putnam, 2000)
* *How Much Is a Million?* by David Schwartz. (New York: Mulberry Paperback Books, 1985)
* *If You Made a Million,* by David Schwartz. (New York: Mulberry Paperback Books, 1989)
* *Inchworm and a Half,* by Elinor Pinczes. Illustrated by Randall Enos. (New York: Houghton Mifflin, 2001).
* *Is a Blue Whale the Biggest Thing There Is?* Author and illustrator Robert E. Wells. (Morton Grove, IL: Albert Whitman & Company, 1993)
* *Math Curse,* by Jon Scieszka & Lane Smith. (New York: Viking/Penguin, 1995)
* *One Grain of Rice,* by Demi. (New York: Scholastic Press, 1997)
* *Sadako and the Thousand Paper Cranes,* by Eleanor Coerr. (New York: Dell Yearling, 1993)
* *Sir Cumference and the Knights of the Round Table,* by Jon Scieszka & Lane Smith. (Watertown, MA: Charlesbridge Publishing, 1997)
* *Sir Cumference and the Great Knight of Angleland,* by Jon Scieszka & Lane Smith. (Watertown, MA: Charlesbridge Publishing, 2001)
* *Sir Cumference and the Dragon of Pi,* by Jon Scieszka & Lane Smith. (Watertown, MA: Charlesbridge Publishing, 1999)
* *The Doorbell Rang,* by Pat Hutchins. (New York: Greenwillow Books, 1986)
* *The Giraffe That Walked to Paris,* by Nancy Milton. Illustrated by Roger Roth. (New York: Crown, 1992)

* *The Icky Sticky Trap,* by Calvin Irons. (Melbourne, Australia: Mimosa Publishing, 1998)

* *The King's Chessboard,* by David Birch. Illustrated by Devis Grebu. (New York: Puffin Pied Piper Books, 1988)

* *The Number Devil: A Mathematical Adventure,* by Hans Magnus Enzenberger. (New York: Holt, 1997)

* *The Patchwork Quilt,* by Valerie Flournoy. (New York: Dial Books, 1985)

* *The 329th Friend,* by Marjorie Weinman Sharmat. Illustrated by Cyndy Szekeres. (New Zealand: Four Winds Press, 1979)

* *The Village of Round and Square Houses,* by Ann Grifalconi. (Boston: Little, Brown & Co., 1986)

Part 3: General References

Section 3.1

ASCD. (2002). *At Work in the Differentiated Classroom: Facilitator's Guide.* Alexandria, VA: Association for Supervision and Curriculum Development.

Chapman, C. (2000). *Sail into Differentiated Instruction.* Thomson, GA: Creative Learning Connection.

Gardner, H. (1983). *Frames of Mind: The Theory of Multiple Intelligences.* New York: Basic Books.

Heacox, D. (2002). *Differentiating Instruction in the Regular Classroom.* Minneapolis: Free Spirit Publishing.

Nunley, K. (2001). *Layered Curriculum™.* Kearney, NE: Morris Publishing.

Pettig, K. L. (2000, September). On the Road to Differentiated Practice. *Educational Leadership, 58*(1), 14–18.

Rief, S., & Heimburge, J. (1996). *How to Reach & Teach All Students in the Inclusive Classroom.* San Francisco: Jossey-Bass.

Tomlinson, C. (2000, September). Reconcilable Differences: Standards-Based Teaching and Differentiation. *Educational Leadership, 58*(1), 6–11.

Tomlinson, C. A. (2001). *How to Differentiate Instruction in Mixed-Ability Classroom*s (2nd ed.). Alexandria, VA: Association for Supervision and Curriculum Development.

Section 3.2

Bear, D., Invernizzi, M., Templeton, S., & Johnston, F. (1996). *Words Their Way: Word Study for Phonics, Vocabulary and Spelling Instruction.* Upper Saddle River, NJ: Prentice Hall.

Fetzer, N., & Rief, S. (2000). *Alphabet Learning Center Activities Kit.* Paramus, NJ: The Center for Applied Research in Education.

International Dyslexia Association & Moats, Louisa. (2000, Jan.). Just the Facts. Spelling. Fact Sheet #981-01/00. Baltimore: www.interdys.org.

Liataub, J., & Rodriguez, D. (1999). *Times Tables the Fun Way!* Minneapolis: One Creek Press. www.citycreek.com; 800-585-6059.

Rief, S., & Heimburge, J. (1996). *How to Reach & Teach All Students in the Inclusive Classroom.* San Francisco: Jossey-Bass.

Rief, Sandra. (2003). *The ADHD Book of Lists.* San Francisco: Jossey-Bass.

Semple, J. (1986). *Semple Math.* Attleboro, MA: Stevenson Leaning Skills, Inc. www.stevensonlearning.com; 800-343-1211.

Sousa, D. (2001a). *How the Brain Learns* (2nd ed.). Thousand Oaks, CA: Corwin Press.

Sousa, D. (2001b). *How the Special Needs Brain Learns.* Thousand Oaks, CA: Corwin Press.

Swanson, L. J. (1995, July). Learning Styles: A Review of the Literature. *ERIC Document No. ED 387 067.*

Touch Math®. (1975). Colorado Springs, CO: Innovative Learning Concepts. 800-888-9191.

Wikki Stix®. Phoenix, AZ: Omnicor, Inc. www.wikkistix.com; 800-869-4554.

Yates, D. *Memory Joggers—Multiplication and Division Learning System™.* Irvine, CA: Memory Joggers. www.memoryjoggers.com; 888-854-9400.

Section 3.3

Dunn, R. (1988) Introduction to Learning Styles and Brain Behavior: Suggestions for Practitioners. *The Association for the Advancement of International Education, 15*(46), 6–7.

Dunn, R., & Dunn, K. (2003). *Dunn & Dunn Learning Style Model.* Center for the Study of Learning and Teaching Styles at St. John's University. Retrieved December 17, 2003, from www.learningstyles.net/n3.html.

Gardner, H. (1983). *Frames of Mind: The Theory of Multiple Intelligences.* New York: Basic Books.

Gardner, H., & Blythe, T. (1990, April). A School for All Intelligences. *Educational Leadership, 47*(7), 1–5.

Graser, Nan Stutzman. (1992). *125 Ways to Be a Better Listener.* East Moline, IL: Lingui Systems.

Kagan, S., Kagan, M., & Kagan, L. (2000). *Reaching Standards Through Cooperative Learning—English / Language Arts.* Portchester, NY: National Professional Resources, Inc.

Karges-Bone, L. (1996). *Beyond Hands-On.* Carthage, IL: Teaching & Learning Company.

Movin' Sit Jr. and *Disc O' Sit Jr.* are available through several companies, such as www.theraproducts.com or www.southpaw.com.

Nicolson-Nelson, Kristen. (1998). *Developing Students' Multiple Intelligences.* New York: Scholastic.

Rief, Sandra. (2003). *The ADHD Book of Lists.* San Francisco: Jossey-Bass.

Rief, Sandra. (1998). *The ADD / ADHD Checklist: An Easy Reference for Parents and Teachers.* San Francisco: Jossey-Bass.

Rief, S., & Heimburge, J. (1996). *How to Reach & Teach All Students in the Inclusive Classroom.* San Francisco: Jossey-Bass.

TeachTimer™ by Stokes Publishing Company. www.stokespublishing.com.

Time Timer by www.timetimer.com.

Touch Math®. (1975). Colorado Springs, CO: Innovative Learning Concepts. 800-888-9191.

Weisman, D., & Banich, M. (2000). The Cerebral Hemispheres Cooperate to Perform Complex But Not Simple Tasks. *Neuropsychology, 14,* 41–59.

Section 3.4

Johnson, D., Johnson, R., & Holubec, E. (1998). *Cooperation in the Classroom* (7th ed.). Edina, MN: Interaction Book Company.

Kagan, P., Kagan, M., & Kagan, L. (2000). *Reaching Standards Through Cooperative Learning—Social Studies.* Port Chester, NY: National Professional Resources, Inc.

Rief, Sandra. (2004). *ADHD & LD: Powerful Teaching Strategies & Accommodations.* (Video). San Diego, CA: Educational Resource Specialists. www.sandrarief.com.

Section 3.5

Archer, Anita, & Gleason, Mary. (2003). *Skills for School Success.* North Billerica, MA: Curriculum Associates®, Inc.

Hennessy, Nancy. (2003, Winter). Homework Hints for Parents. The International Dyslexia Association: *PERSPECTIVES, 29*(1), 32–35.

Illes, T. (2002). *Positive Parenting Practices for Attention Deficit Disorder.* Salt Lake City, UT: Jordan School District.

Jenks, Patti. (2003, Winter). Navigating Time Travel. The International Dyslexia Association: *PERSPECTIVES, 29*(1), 7–11.

Rief, Sandra. (2003). *The ADHD Book of Lists.* San Francisco: Jossey-Bass.

Rief, Sandra. (1998). *The ADD/ADHD Checklist.* San Francisco: Jossey-Bass.

Rief, Sandra. (1997). *How to Help Your Child Suceed in School.* (Video). San Diego, CA: Educational Resource Specialists. www.sandrarief.com.

Warger, Cynthia. (2001, March). *Five Homework Strategies for Teaching Students with Disabilities.* ERIC Clearinghouse on Disabilities and Gifted Education. http://ericec.org. Posted Oct. 2, 2002, ERIC/OSEP Digest #E608. Retrieved February 7, 2004, from www.ldonline.org/ld_indepth/teaching_techniques/five_homework_strategies.html.

Section 3.6

Bender, W. N. (2002). *Differentiating Instruction for Students with Learning Disabilities.* Thousand Oaks, CA: Corwin Press & Council for Exceptional Children.

Bos, Candace S., & Vaughn, Sharon. (1994). *Strategies for Teaching Students with Learning & Behavior Problems.* Boston: Allyn & Bacon.

Casbarro, Joseph. (2003). *Test Anxiety & What You Can Do About It.* Port Chester, NY: Dude Publishing.

Chamot, A. U., & O'Malley, J. M. (1994). *The CALLA Handbook: Implementing the Cognitive Academic Language Learning Approach.* Reading, MA: Addison-Wesley.

Ellis, E. (1991). *SLANT: A Starter Strategy for Participation.* Lawrence, KS: Edge Enterprises.

Hennessy, Nancy. (2003, Winter). Homework Hints for Parents. The International Dyslexia Association: *PERSPECTIVES, 29*(1), 32–35.

Hennessy, Nancy, & Soper, Sandi. (2003, November 12–15). Exercising Executive Function for Efficient Learning. Conference session at 54th Annual Conference of the International Dyslexia Association, San Diego, California.

Hoover, J., & Patton, J. (1995). *Teaching Students with Learning Problems to Use Study Skills: A Teacher's Guide* (pp. 107–109). Austin, TX: PRO-ED, Inc.

Kleinheksel, Karen, & Summy, Sarah. (2003, November/December). Enhancing Student Learning and Social Behavior Through Mnemonic Strategies. Council for Exceptional Children: *TEACHING Exceptional Children, 36*(2), 30–35.

Learning Toolbox. (2003). James Madison University Special Education Program website: http://coe.jmu.edu/LearningToolbox.

Liautaud, Judy, & Rodriguez, Dave. (1999). *Times Tables the Fun Way!* Sandy, UT: City Creek Press. www.citycreek.com.

Mastropieri, M. A., & Scruggs, T. E. (1991). *Teaching Students Ways to Remember: Strategies for Learning Mnemonically.* Cambridge, MA: Brookline Books.

Memory Joggers™ (1996). 24 Nuevo, Irvine, CA 92612.

Pauk, W. (1997). *How to Study in College* (6th ed.). Boston: Houghton Mifflin.

Polloway, E A., Patton, J. R., & Serna, L. (2001). *Strategies for Teaching Learners with Special Need* (7th ed.). Upper Saddle River, NJ: Merrill/Prentice-Hall.

Rief, Sandra. (2003). *The ADHD Book of Lists.* San Francisco: Jossey-Bass.

Rodriguez, Dave, & Rodriguez, Judy. (1999). *Times Tables the Fun Way: A Picture Method of Learning the Multiplication Facts.* Sandy, UT: Key Publishers.

Schumaker, J. B., Deshler, D. D., Nolan, S., et al. (1981). *Error Monitoring: A Learning Strategy for Improving Academic Performance of LD Adolescents* (Research Report No. 32). Lawrence: University of Kansas, Institute for Research on Learning Disabilities.

Science Songs Aligned to the 4th Grade Science Content Standards. (2003). Musically Aligned. www.musicallyaligned.com.

Semple, Janice. (2001). *Semple Math—A Basic Mathematics Program for Beginning, High-Risk and/or Remedial Students.* Attleboro, MA: Stevenson Learning Skills, Inc.

Shannon, T. R., and Polloway, E. A. (1993). Promoting Error Monitoring in Middle School Students with LD. *Intervention in School and Clinic, 28,* 160–164.

Sousa, D. A. (2001). *How the Special Needs Brain Learns.* Thousand Oaks, CA: Corwin Press.

Suid, Murra. (1981). *Demonic Mnemonics.* Torrance, CA: Fearon Teacher Aids.

Townend, Janet, & Turner, Martin. (2000). *Dyslexia in Practice—A Guide for Teachers.* New York: Kluwer Academic/Plenum Publishers.

Wallace, Rosella R. (1993). *Smart-Rope Jingles (Jump Rope Rhymes, Raps, and Chants for Active Learning).* Tucson, AZ: Zephyr Press.

Williams, Jamie. (2003, Winter). Study Skills: The Difference Between Pupils and Students. The International Dyslexia Association: *PERSPECTIVES, 29*(1), 12–18.

Section 3.7

Ackerman, P., & Dykman, R. (1996). The Speed Factor and Learning Disabilities: The Toll of Slowness in Adolescents. *Dyslexia, 2,* 1–21.

Cattas, H., Fey, M., Zhang, X., & Tomblin, J. (1999). Language Basis of Reading and Reading Disabilities: Evidence from a Longitudinal Investigation. *Scientific Studies of Reading, 3,* 331–361.

Cunningham, A., & Stanovich, K. (1997). Early Reading Acquisition and Its Relation to Reading Experience and Ability 10 Years Later. *Developmental Psychology, 33,* 934–945.

Feldman, Kevin. (2001, November). *Supporting Struggling Secondary Readers: Decoding, Fluency & Comprehension—What Works?* CEC Annual California State Conference, November 2001. Sonoma County Office of Education. www.scoe.org (reading corner).

International Dyslexia Association. (2000, May). *Just the Facts—Dyslexia Basics.* Fact Sheet #962. Baltimore: The International Dyslexia Association. www.interdys.org.

Lyon, G. R. (1998a). *Overview of Reading and Literacy Initiatives.* Testimony provided to the Committee on Labor and Human Resources, United States Senate. Bethesda, MD: National Institute of Child Health and Human Development.

Lyon, G. Reid. (1998b). Why Reading Is Not a Natural Process. *Educational Leadership, 55*(6), 14–18. Also found in *LDA Newsbriefs* (2000, January/February). Learning Disabilities Association of America, LD Online. www.ldonline.org/ld–indepth/reading/why–reading–is–not.html.

Moats, Louisa. (2001, March). When Older Kids Can't Read. For *Educational Leadership.* Retrieved February 17, 2004, from www.scoe.org (reading corner).

PBS: *Misunderstood Minds. Writing Basics, Difficulties, Responses.* WGBH Educational Foundation, 2002. www.pbs.org/wgbh/misunderstoodminds.

Rief, Sandra. (1998). *The ADD/ADHD Checklist.* San Francisco: Jossey-Bass.

Rief, Sandra. (2001). *Ready, Start, School—Nurturing and Guiding Your Child Through Preschool and Kindergarten.* New York: Penguin Group.

Rief, Sandra. (2003). *The ADHD Book of Lists.* San Francisco: Jossey-Bass.

Richards, Regina G. (1995). *When Writing's a Problem.* Riverside, CA: Richards Educational Therapy Center.

Shankweiler, D., Crane, S., Katz, L., Fowler, A., Liberman, A., Brady, S., Thornton, R., Lindquist, E., Dreyer, L., Fletcher, J., Stuebing, K., Shaywitz, S., & Shaywitz, B. (1995). Cognitive Profiles of Reading—Disabled Children: Comparison of Language Skills in Phonology, Morphology, and Syntax. *Psychological Science, 6,* 149–156.

Shaywitz, S., Fletcher, J., Holahan, J., Shneider, A., Marchione, K., Stuebing, K., Francis, D., Pugh, K., & Shaywitz, B. (1999). Persistence of Dyslexia: The Connecticut Longitudinal Study at Adolescence. *Pediatrics, 104*(6), 1351–1359.

Snow, Catherine E., Burns, Susan M., & Griffin, Peg (Eds.). (1998). *Preventing Reading Difficulties in Young Children.* National Research Council. Washington, DC: National Academy Press.

Stanovich, K., & Siegel, L. (1994). The Phenotypic Profile of Reading-Disabled Children: A Regression-Based Test of the Phonological-Core Variable Difference Model. *Journal of Educational Psychology, 86,* 24–53.

Torgeson, Joseph. (2003, November). San Diego, CA: International Dyslexia Association, 54th Annual Conference. Keynote Address. www.fcrr.org.

Section 3.8

AlphaSmart. www.alphasmart.com.

Bytes of Learning, Inc. www.bytesoflearning.com.

Dreamwriter. Brainium Technologies, Inc. www.brainium.com.

Don Johnston Co. www.donjohnston.com (learning intervention resources).

ERIC/OSEP. (2002, Winter). Instructional Approaches That Improve Written Performance: Integrating Technology with Writing Instruction. ERIC/OSEP: *Research Connections in Special Education, 10,* 2–4.

Fetzer, Nancy. (2003). *The Writing Connections Book.* Murrietta, CA: Nancy Fetzer's Literacy Connections.

Fetzer, Nancy, & Rief, Sandra. (2000). *Alphabet Learning Center Activities Kit.* San Francisco: Jossey-Bass.

Fisher, Linda, Fetzer, Nancy, & Rief, Sandra. (1999). *Successful Classrooms—Effective Teaching Strategies for Raising Achievement in Reading & Writing.* (Video). San Diego: Educational Resource Specialists. www.sandrarief.com.

Fisher, L., & Tucker, H. (2002). *Learning Headquarters' Writing Manual.* San Diego: Grinolds Publishing.

Fuchs, Lynn, & Fuchs, Doug. (1999). CASL (Center on Accelerating Student Learning), Vanderbilt University. www.vanderbilt.edu/CASL/reports.html.

Graham, S., & Harris, K. (2000, Fall). Preventing Writing Difficulties. Nashville, TN: *CASL News,* Vanderbilt University. www.vanderbilt.edu/CASL/reports.html.

www.geocities.com/Athens/Academy/6617 (Middle School Cybrary). This has numerous links to various sites of valuable information and resources to aid in writing (for example, Word Central, The 5 Paragraph Essay).

Inspiration software. www.inspiration.com.

International Dyslexia Association & Moats, Louisa. (2000, January). *Just the Facts. Spelling.* Fact Sheet #981–01/00. Baltimore: www.interdys.org.

Jones, Susan. (2003, Spring). Accommodations for Students with Handwriting Problems. The Inland Empire Branch of the International Dyslexia Association. *The Resource, 18*(1), 6–12. www.dyslexia-ca.org.

Kemper, Dave, Nathan, Ruth, & Sebranek, Patrick. (2000). *Writer's Express.* Wilmington, MA: Great Source Education Group, Inc.

Landy, Joanne M., & Burridge, Keith R. (1999). *Fine Motor Skills & Handwriting Activities for Young Children.* Paramus, NJ: The Center for Applied Research in Education.

Muschla, Gary. (2004). *The Writing Teacher's Book of Lists with Ready-to-Use Activities and Worksheets* (2nd ed.). San Francisco: Jossey-Bass.

Naturally Speaking. www.scansoft.com/naturallyspeaking.

Olsen, Jan Z. (1997). *Handwriting Without Tears*™ Potomac, MD. www.hwtears.com.

Purdue University Online Writing Lab. http://owl.english.purdue.edu/handouts/general/index.html.

Read & Write Gold®. www.texthelp.com.

Rief, Sandra. (1997). *How to Help Your Child Succeed in School—Strategies & Guidance for Parents of Children with ADHD and/or LD.* (Video). San Diego: Educational Resource Specialists. www.sandrarief.com.

Rief, Sandra. (1998). *The ADD/ADHD Checklist: An Easy Reference for Parents and Teachers.* San Francisco: Jossey-Bass.

Rief, Sandra. (2001). *Ready, Start, School.* New York: Penguin Group.

Rief, Sandra. (2003). *The ADHD Book of Lists.* San Francisco: Jossey-Bass.

Rief, Sandra. (2004). *ADHD & LD: Powerful Teaching Strategies & Accommodations.* (Video). San Diego: Educational Resource Specialists.

Rief, Sandra, & Heimburge, Julie. (1996). *How to Reach & Teach All Students in the Inclusive Classroom.* San Francisco: Jossey-Bass.

Richards, Regina G. (1995). *When Writing's a Problem.* Riverside, CA: Richards Educational Therapy Center.

Schumaker, J., & Deshler, D. (n.d.). Center for Research on Learning Effective Instruction: IEI Products. Lawrence: University of Kansas, Institute for Research on Learning Disabilities.

Teachers' Institute for Special Education. (n.d.). *Keyboarding for Individual Achievement.* http://special-education-soft.com.

Wanderman, Richard. (Fall, 2003). Tools and dyslexia: Issues and ideas. IDA: *Perspectives* 29, No. 4, 5–9.

Wizcom Superpen. http://wizcomtech.com.

Section 3.9

ERIC/OSEP. (2002, Winter). Instructional Approaches That Improve Written Performance: Integrating Technology with Writing Instruction. ERIC/OSEP: *Research Connections in Special Education, 10,* 2–4.

Fetzer, Nancy. (1999). *The Writing Program.* San Diego: Fisher and Fetzer Educational Systems.

Fetzer, Nancy. (2003). *Writing Connections—From Oral Language to Written Text.* Murrietta, CA: Nancy Fetzer's Literacy Connections.

Fisher, Linda, Fetzer, Nancy, & Rief, Sandra. (1999). *Successful Classrooms—Effective Teaching Strategies for Raising Achievement in Reading & Writing.* (Video). San Diego: Educational Resource Specialists. www.sandrarief.com. 800-682-3528.

Fisher, Linda, & Tucker, Heidi. (2002). *Learning Headquarters' Writing Manual.* San Diego: Grinsolds Publishing.

Harris, Karen, & Graham, Steve. (2000, Fall). *Preventing Writing Difficulties.* Nashville, TN: Vanderbilt University. www.vanderbiltedu/CASL/reports.html.

Kemper, Dave, Nathan, Ruth, & Sebranek, Patrick. (2000). *Writer's Express.* Wilmington, MA: Great Source Education Group.

Muschla, Gary. (2004). *The Writing Teacher's Book of Lists with Ready-to-Use Activities and Worksheets* (2nd ed.). San Francisco: Jossey-Bass.

Rief, Sandra. (1998). *The ADD/ADHD Checklist: An Easy Reference for Parents and Teachers.* San Francisco: Jossey-Bass.

Rief, Sandra. (2003) *The ADHD Book of Lists.* San Francisco: Jossey-Bass.

Schumaker, J., & Deshler, D. (n.d.). Strategic Instructional Model. Lawrence: University of Kansas Center for Research on Learning Disabilities. www.ku-crl.org/contact.html.

Section 3.10

Avrit, Karen, & Carlsen, Kathleen. (2003). *Closing the Gap in Reading Fluency.* San Diego: The International Dyslexia Association 54th Annual Conference, session presented November 14, 2003.

Feldman, Kevin. (2000). *Ensuring All Students Learn to Read Well: Linking Research to Practice in Effective Reading Programs.* Sonoma County, CA: Sonoma County SELPA.

Fetzer, Nancy, & Rief, Sandra. (2000). *Alphabet Learning Center Activities Kit.* San Francisco: Jossey-Bass.

Harwell, Joan M. (2001). *Complete Learning Disabilities Handbook* (2nd ed.). Paramus, NJ: The Center for Applied Research in Education.

Moats, Louisa. (2001, March). When Older Kids Can't Read. *Educational Leadership.* Retrieved February 17, 2004, from www.scoe.org (reading corner).

Rief, Sandra. (1997). *How to Help Your Child Succeed in School.* (Video). San Diego, CA: Educational Resource Specialists. www.sandrarief.com.

Rief, Sandra. (1998). *The ADD/ADHD Checklist.* San Francisco: Jossey-Bass.

Rief, Sandra. (2001). *Ready, Start, School—Nurturing and Guiding Your Child Through Preschool and Kindergarten.* New York: Penguin Group.

Rief, Sandra. (2003). *The ADHD Book of Lists.* San Francisco: Jossey-Bass.

Rief, Sandra, & Heimburge, Julie. (1996). *How to Reach & Teach All Students in the Inclusive Classroom.* San Francisco: Jossey-Bass.

Wilson, Barbara. (2003). *How to Develop Automaticity, Fluency and Comprehension: Three Keys to a Student's Success.* San Diego: The International Dyslexia Association 54th Annual Conference, session presented November 14, 2003. www.wilsonlanguage.com.

Section 3.11

Bell, Nanci. (1991). *Visualizing and Verbalizing for Language Comprehension and Thinking.* Paso Robles, CA: Academy of Reading Publications.

Bender, William N., & Larkin, Martha J. (2003). *Reading Strategies for Elementary Students with Learning Difficulties.* Thousand Oaks, CA: Corwin Press.

Daniels, H. (1994). *Literature Circles: Voice and Choice in One Student-Centered Classroom.* York, ME: Stenhouse.

Deshler, D., Ellis, E., & Lenz, B. (1996). *Teaching Adolescents with Learning Disabilities: Strategies and Methods.* Denver, CO: Love Publishing.

Fountas, Irene C., & Pinnell, Gay Su. (1996). *Guided Reading.* Portsmouth, NH: Heinemann.

Marzano, Robert, Pickering, Debra, & Pollock, Jane. (2001). *Classroom Instruction That Works: Research-Based Strategies for Increasing Student Achievement.* Alexandria, VA: Association for Supervision & Curriculum Development. www.ascd.org.

Ong, Faye (Ed.). (2000). *Strategic Teaching and Learning: Standards-Based Instruction to Promote Content Literacy in Grades Four Through Twelve.* Sacramento: California Department of Education.

Palincsar, A., & Brown, A. (1984). Reciprocal Teaching of Comprehension Fostering and Comprehension Monitoring Activities. *Cognition and Instruction, 1*(2) 117–175.

Palincsar, A., & Brown, A. (1985). Reciprocal Teaching: Activities to Promote Reading with Your Mind. In T. L. Harris & E. J. Cooper (Eds.), *Reading, Thinking, and Concept Development: Strategies for the Classroom.* New York: The College Board.

Raphael, T. (1982). Questioning-Answering Strategies for Children. *The Reading Teacher, 37,* 377–382.

Rief, Sandra. (1998). *The ADD/ADHD Checklist.* San Francisco: Jossey-Bass.

Rief, Sandra. (2003). *The ADHD Book of Lists.* San Francisco: Jossey-Bass.

Rief, Sandra, & Heimburge, Julie. (1996). *How to Reach & Teach All Students in the Inclusive Classroom.* San Francisco: Jossey-Bass.

Sousa, David. (2001). *How the Special Needs Brain Learns.* Thousand Oaks, CA: Corwin Press.

Swanson, P. N., & DeLaPaz, S. (1998). Teaching Effective Comprehension Strategies to Students with Learning and Reading Disabilities. *Intervention in School and Clinic, 33,* 209–218.

Thompson, Steven. (2004, May). *Cognitive Theory and Evidentiary Support Scaffolding for Emergent Writers and Thinkers.* Paper presented at the meeting of the International Teacher Education Conference, Calgary, Alberta, Canada.

Vacca, J. L., Vacca, R. T., Grove, M. K., Burkey, L., Lenhart, L. A., & McKeon, C. (2003). *Reading and Learning to Read* (5th ed.). Boston: Allyn & Bacon.

Section 3.12

Bassarear, Tom. (2001). *Mathematics for Elementary School Teachers: Explorations* (2nd ed.). Boston: Houghton Mifflin.

Burns, Marilyn. (See any materials by Marilyn Burns—Math Solutions Publications.)

Cawley, John, Parmar, Rene, Salmon, Susan, & Roy, Sharmila. (2001). Arithmetic Performance of Students: Implications for Standards and Programming. The Council for Exceptional Children: *Exceptional Children, 67*(3), 311–328.

Cawley, John, & Foley, Teresa. (2002, March/April). CEC: *TEACHING Exceptional Children, 34*(4), 14–19.

CEC. (2003, January). Teaching Math to Students with Disabilities. *CEC Today, 9*(5), 1–13. www.cec.sped.org.

Coolmath 4 Kids. www.coolmath.com.

Flash Action Software—Addition / Subtraction; Multiplication / Division. Grand Rapids, MI: School Zone Publishing Co.

Gagnon, Joseph C., & Maccini, Paula. (2001, September/October). Preparing Students with Disabilities for Algebra. CEC: *TEACHING Exceptional Children, 34*(1), 8–15.

Great Leaps Math Program. www.GreatLeaps.com.

Hot Math. www.vanderbilt.edu/CASL.

IntelliTools, Inc. This company has spent several years creating a series of educational math programs accessible to all children, particularly those with disabilities. This was made possible through a grant from the National Science Foundation (NSF). They developed programs including: *Exploring Patterns, MathPad, Measure It!, Number Concepts 1,* and *Number Concepts 2.* www.intellitools.com; 800-899-6687.

James Madison University. Special Education Department. www.coe.jmu.edu/learningtoolbox.

Jitendra, Asha. (2002, March/April). Teaching Students Math Problem Solving Through Graphic Representations. CEC: *TEACHING Exceptional Children, 34*(4), 34–38.

Kagan, Spencer, Kagan, Miguel, & Kagan, Laurie. (2000). *Reaching Standards Through Cooperative Learning in Mathematics.* Port Chester, NY: National Professional Resources.

Maccini, P., McNaughton, D., & Ruhl, K. (1999). Algebra Instruction for Students with Learning Disabilities: Implications from a Research Review. *Learning Disability Quarterly, 22,* 113–126.

Maccini, P., & Hughes, C. A. (2000). Effects of a Problem-Solving Strategy on the Introductory Algebra Performance of Secondary Students with Learning Disabilities. *Learning Disabilities Research & Practice, 15,* 10–21.

Maccini, P., & Ruhl, K. L. (2000). Effects of a Graduated Instructional Sequence on the Algebraic Subtraction of Integers by Secondary Students with Learning Disabilities. *Education and Treatment of Children, 23,* 465–489.

Making Math Real™. (A multisensory, structured program). www.makingmathreal.org.

Math Baseball. www.funbrain.com/math.

Math Explorer. (Calculator manufactured by Texas Instruments). www.education.ti.com.

Math Fundamentals Problem of the Week. mathforum.org/funpow.

MathLine™. (Concept-building system). www.howbrite.com.

Math at Work. (Software series). www.quicksilver.com.

Math-U-See. (A multisensory approach to math, involving building with manipulatives, saying, and writing. A manipulative based K–12 curriculum). Misunderstood Minds. 800-454-6284.

National Council of Teachers of Mathematics. (2001). Principles and Standards for School Mathematics Navigations Series, including *Navigating Through Algebra* in Grades Pre-K through Grade 2, in Grades 3 to 5, in Grades 6 to 8, in Grades 9 to 12. Also: *Navigating Through Geometry, Navigating Through Measurement* in Pre-kindergarten to Grade 2, *Navigating Through Probability* in Grades 6 to 8, *Navigating Through Data Analysis* in Grades 6 to 8, in Grades 9 to 12.

National Council of Teachers of Mathematics (NCTM). (2000). *Principles and Standards for School Mathematics.* Reston, VA. www.NCTM.org.

Rief, Sandra. (1998). *The ADD/ADHD Checklist.* San Francisco: Jossey-Bass.

Rief, Sandra. (2003). *The ADHD Book of Lists.* San Francisco: Jossey-Bass.

Rief, Sandra, & Heimburge, Julie. (1996). *How to Reach & Teach All Students in the Inclusive Classroom.* San Francisco: Jossey-Bass.

Rodriguez, Dave, & Rodriguez, Judy. (1999). *Time Tables the Fun Way: A Picture Method of Learning the Multiplication Facts.* Sandy, UT: Key Publishers, Inc. www.citycreek.com. (also has addition/subtraction facts)

Semple, Janice L. (1986). *Semple Math—A Basic Skills Mathematics Program for Beginning, High-Risk and/or Remedial Students.* Attleboro, MA: Stevenson Learning Skills, Inc.

Setley, Susan. (1995). *Taming the Dragons (Real Help for Real School Problems).* St. Louis: Starfish Publishing Company.

Sousa, David. (2001). *How the Special Needs Brain Learns.* Thousand Oaks, CA: Corwin Press.

Think It by Hand. *Math Manipulatives That Work on a Vertical Surface.* www.thinkitbyhand.com.

Touch Math®. Innovative Learning Concepts, 6760 Corporate Drive, Colorado Springs, CO; www.touchmath.com; 888-Touch Math.

Witzel, Brad. (2003, November 14). *Filling the Arithmetic to Algebra Gap: Word Problems—Helping Secondary Students with Word Problems.* IDA 54th Annual Conference, San Diego, California.

Yates, Donnalyn. (1996). *Memory Joggers—Multiplication and Division Learning System.* 24 Nuevo, Irvine, CA 92612; 888-854-9400.

Part 3: Recommended Resources

*T*he following are a variety of recommended resources to build math skills, in addition to those found in the reference section of 3.12. Unfortunately, we cannot list all the great programs out there.

Burns, Marilyn (any materials by Marilyn Burns—Math Solutions Publications).

Coolmath 4 Kids. www.coolmath.com.

ERIC/OSEP. (2002, Winter). Instructional Approaches That Improve Written Performance: Integrating Technology with Writing Instruction. ERIC/OSEP: *Research Connections in Special Education, 10,* 2–4.

Fetzer, Nancy. (2003). *The Writing Connections Book.* Murrietta, CA: Nancy Fetzer's Literacy Connections.

Fisher, Linda, Fetzer, Nancy, & Rief, Sandra. (1999). *Successful Classrooms—Effective Teaching Strategies for Raising Achievement in Reading & Writing.* (Video). San Diego: Educational Resource Specialists. www.sandrarief.com.

Fisher, L., & Tucker, H. (2002). *Learning Headquarters' Writing Manual.* San Diego: Grinolds Publishing.

Flash Action Software—Addition/Subtraction; Multiplication/Division. School Zone Publishing Company.

Great Leaps Math Program. www.GreatLeaps.com.

Handwriting to the Beat. www.therapyshoppe.com.

IntelliTools, Inc., has spent several years creating a series of educational math programs accessible to all children, particularly those with disabilities. This was made possible through a grant from the National Science Foundation (NSF). They developed many programs, including *Exploring Patterns, MathPad, Measure It!, Number Concepts 1,* and *Number Concepts 2.* www.intellitools.com; 800-899-6687.

Kemper, Dave, Nathan, Ruth, & Sebranek, Patrick. (2000). *Writer's Express.* Wilmington, MA: Great Source Education Group, Inc.

Making Math Real™. www.makingmathreal.org (a multisensory, structured program).

Math at Work software series. www.quicksilver.com.

Math Baseball. www.funbrain.com/math.

Math Explorer, a calculator manufactured by Texas Instruments. www.education.ti.com.

Math Fundamentals Problem of the Week. mathforum.org/funpow.

MathLine™ Concept-Building System. www.howbrite.com.

Math-U-See, a multisensory approach to math involving building with manipulatives, saying, and writing. A manipulative-based K–12 curriculum. 1-800-454-6284.

Misunderstood Minds. www.pbs.org/wgbh/misunderstoodminds/mathstrats.html. WGBH 2002, Educational Foundation. WGBH Educational Foundation, Boston. (2002). The Misunderstood Minds project consists of a PBS documentary, first airing March 27, 2002, companion website on PBS online, and the Developing Minds Multimedia Library.

Muschla, Gary. (2004). *The Writing Teacher's Book of Lists with Ready-to-Use Activities and Worksheets* (2nd ed.). San Francisco: Jossey-Bass.

National Council of Teachers of Mathematics. (2001). *Principles and Standards for School Mathematics Navigations Series,* including *Navigating Through Algebra* in Grades Pre–K through Grade 2, in Grades 3 to 5, in Grades 6 to 8, in Grades 9 to 12. Also: *Navigating Through Geometry, Navigating Through Measurement* in Pre-kindergarten to Grade 2, *Navigating Through Probability* in Grades 6 to 8, *Navigating Through Data Analysis* in Grades 6 to 8, and in Grades 9 to 12.

National Council of Teachers of Mathematics. (2000). *Principles and Standards for School Mathematics.* Reston, VA: NCTM. www.NCTM.org.

Naturally Speaking. www.scansoft.com/naturallyspeaking.

Purdue University Online Writing Lab. http://owl.english.purdue.edu/handouts/general/index.html.

Read & Write Gold®. www.texthelp.com.

Rief, Sandra. (1997). *How to Help Your Child Succeed in School—Strategies & Guidance for Parents of Children with ADHD and/or LD.* (Video). San Diego: Educational Resource Specialists. www.sandrarief.com.

Rief, Sandra. (2004). *ADHD & LD: Powerful Teaching Strategies & Accommodations.* (Video). San Diego: Educational Resource Specialists.

Rief, Sandra, & Heimburge, Julie. (1996). *How to Reach & Teach All Students in the Inclusive Classroom.* San Francisco: Jossey-Bass.

Richards, Regina G. (1995). *When Writing's a Problem.* Riverside, CA: Richards Educational Therapy Center.

Schumaker, J., & Deshler, D. (n.d.). Center for Research on Learning Effective Instruction: IEI Products. Lawrence: University of Kansas, Institute for Research on Learning Disabilities.

Semple, Janice. (2001). *Semple Math—Levels I through IV—A Basic Skills Mathematics Program for Beginning, High-Risk and/or Remedial Students.* Attleboro, MA: Stevenson Learning Skills, Inc.

Teachers' Institute for Special Education. (n.d.). *Keyboarding for Individual Achievement.* http://special-education-soft.com.

Think It By Hand. Math manipulatives that work on a vertical surface. www.thinkitbyhand.com.

Touch Math®. Innovative Learning Concepts, 6760 Corporate Drive, Colorado Springs, CO; 888-Touch Math; www.touchmath.com.

Wizcom Superpen. http://wizcomtech.com.

www.geocities.com/Athens/Academy/6617 (Middle School Cybrary). This has numerous links to various sites of valuable information and resources to aid in writing (for example, Word Central, The 5 Paragraph Essay).

www.ldonline.org/ld_indepth/technology/technology.html

www.ldresources.com

www.visualthesaurus.com

Yates, Donnalyn. *Memory Joggers—Multiplication and Division Learning System.* 24 Nuevo, Irvine, CA 92612; 888-854-9400.

Personal Stories and Case Studies

A Parent's Story

What Every Teacher and Clinician Needs to Hear

A very special parent, Mrs. Linda Haughey, has shared the very personal story of her family's journey—of living with the challenges of ADHD, and trying to obtain the proper help from professionals—so necessary for these children's success. This family's story sends a very powerful message to teachers and clinicians. Linda had courageously and generously agreed to write this section for my book, which was published in the 1993 edition. Two of her wonderful sons had been my students in my resource program while in the elementary grades, and I have the greatest respect for this very loving, exceptional family. I have learned so much from Linda, and greatly value her insight, wisdom, support, and friendship over the years. I thank the Haughey family for sharing their story with us.

A Parent's Story*

I imagine that we all have childhood dreams. One of my many dreams was to grow up and marry a handsome prince, who, like me, wanted a dozen little boys. Part of that dream came true. The handsome prince came along (without the official title), and instead of twelve little boys, we have been blessed with five wonderful sons whose ages are now eighteen, seventeen, twins thirteen, and eleven years old. Our bonus package came tied in pink ribbons! Our precious little girl is now five years old.

I can honestly say that we happily and busily balance these many ages and needs in our family today. But, of course, it hasn't always been that way. Like most families who have one or more children with ADHD, each day can be a joyful surprise or a painful disappointment—sometimes both on the same day! One thing is certain, though: each day is not predictable, and we have learned to "go with the flow." We have had no choice! Our seventeen-year-old and our thirteen-year-old twins have all been diagnosed with ADHD. It has been the painful part of our journey that has brought hope and confidence to our family.

*By Linda Haughey (1992)

Many special people have given of themselves to help change the directions of our children's lives, and, yes, the lives of each member of our family. When one person struggles in a family, all members are affected. Likewise, when there is self-esteem and success for one, the others reflect that also.

I can remember the exact moment in which a key unlocked the first of many doors. Each door represented a range of emotions and experiences, beginning with exhaustion, confusion, and plenty of questions. This is where I will begin our story.

We have, as a family, decided to share our story with the hope of helping other families like our own. We know how very difficult life can be on a daily basis. Most of all, we simply want to bring hope and encouragement to those families and the special people involved in their lives. Teachers *can* and *do* set the tone and make a difference in a child's life.

The phone rang as I walked through the front door of our home. Frazzled and frustrated from an attempt to make a brief stop at a local department store with my young children, the last thing I wanted to do was talk on the phone. That phone call, however, was the beginning of a new chapter of our family's life. It was the neuropsychologist who had been reviewing the developmental and psychological evaluations for our five-year-old son, Christopher.

I explained to him that while shopping my son threw himself to the ground and began to sob. He cried, "Mommy, Mommy, get me out of here. I have to go home, Mommy." I felt his pain. He was actually in pain! Not the pain of touching a hot stove, but internal, unexplained torment. This kind of situation was all too familiar to me. It could happen anywhere, depending on the circumstances. While I didn't fully understand why, his little body seemed to be overresponding to the stimuli in the store. I knew that discipline was not the solution.

The memory of that morning eight years ago is etched firmly in my mind. That phone call was the very first time that someone understood what I had just experienced with Chris. He not only understood, but also validated what I had known in my heart for years: Discipline is not the issue here. What was happening to Chris was beyond his control and very much a part of his delicate neurological makeup.

Relieved to know that it wasn't a total lack of parental skills causing these outbursts, I gladly set up an appointment to discuss the evaluation further. "At last," I thought, "there's light at the end of the tunnel." Little did I know how many dark tunnels our family would enter before the bright light!

The follow-up visit became the first of many future evaluations and consultations. Out of a constant need for new coping skills and a better understanding of the challenges we faced, we sought the help of those specialists who we hoped could fill in the blanks.

Our own pediatrician at that time would tell me there was nothing wrong with Chris that some good spankings wouldn't fix. Many of our friends and family members concurred. More often than not, I felt as if I was being judged as an inadequate mother, lacking skill and control over my son.

We had to work exceptionally hard with Chris to help him manage his anger and frustrations. His memory seemed to play tricks on him, and there were times that his interpretations of something we would say seemed to get jumbled when he tried to follow directions or repeat our words. I soon realized that those people who were offering their advice and criticisms had absolutely no idea how hard our job was. Nor did they understand that we were raising a child who required far more insight and coping skills than Dr. Spock offered in his helpful book!

Examinations and observations revealed that Chris was a bright child who had Attention Deficit Disorder with hyperactivity [currently referred to as ADHD-Combined type]. This was accompanied by a history of learning disabilities, auditory and visual processing difficulties, and significant expressive language problems.

All of this meant, of course, that Chris would require much intervention throughout his young life: pediatricians, psychologists, a neurologist, speech therapy, occupational therapists, tutoring, special education, and extra help in the mainstream classroom. The doors of communication had to remain open between home and all of these special people associated with our precious son.

Our highly energetic and demanding child was much more prone to greater mood swings, distractibility, and angry outbursts than our other children were. On the other hand, he was filled with a great sense of humor, consideration, thoughtfulness, and endless curiosity for the world around him.

I am in awe of this child who was born fighting mad and ready to take on the world around him. It was obvious from the day he was born that his temperament would require a lot of patience and love. If his socks didn't fit perfectly across the tops of his toes, he would take them off and start all over. There were particular textures of clothing he refused to wear because he couldn't stand the feel of them next to his body. I later found out this had to do with sensory integration and the effect on his immature nervous system. It was literally painful to him!

Many of his developmental milestones, such as sitting and walking, were within normal range. Speech was significantly delayed, having developed a "twin language" with his brother Phillip. As a toddler, Chris experienced "night terrors": extreme, terrorizing nightmares that were almost impossible to wake him from. This, too, had to do with his immature nervous system. During the same period of his life, we discovered that Chris and Phillip both had obstructive sleep apnea.

When surgery was performed to remove the tonsils and adenoids to help correct the sleep apnea, Chris also had tubes placed in his ears to help drain fluid and to help him hear better. Within a month after the surgeries, Chris was talking in full sentences and sleeping through the night for the first time since his birth two and a half years earlier. We were also dealing with other health problems, such as chronic asthma, croup, allergies, and digestive problems. This is important to mention because many families whose children have ADHD must frequently deal not only with the classic symptoms of ADHD and the behavior problems often associated with it, but also with other chronic health issues.

All of these problems can create a tremendous pressure and burden for the child, the parents' marriage, and the entire family. It can be extremely expensive. Most insurance companies will not cover the cost of evaluations and treatment specifically designed to help the ADHD child. The irony of this is that early detection and intervention are critical.

The reality is that most families cannot afford this out-of-pocket expense. They can be faced with the decision to enter into further debt and create new problems, or suffer the guilt and pain they feel because they are unable to obtain the necessary help.

We gave Chris and his brother Phillip an extra year of growth before placing them in kindergarten. It turned out to be the best decision possible. When the time came, they were eager to begin. The transition seemed to be going very well. Unexpectedly, within a month after kindergarten started, Chris began to have horrendous tantrums in the mornings before school. I had exhausted every reason I could come up with to explain his behavior. All he could do was cry and say he couldn't go to school.

One morning I called ahead to the school counselor. When we arrived, she and Chris's teacher met us at the car and gently persuaded my angry, crying son to come up to the counseling office. We finally detected the problem. Chris was required to sit on a rug in the classroom, surrounded by other children. His personal space was being invaded! We've since discovered this is a very common problem for children with ADHD. Even something as simple as standing in a line to wait can require more endurance than the child may possess. Again, this is because their central nervous systems are so fragile.

What may seem natural and ordinary to most of us may cause great distress and even pain for children like Chris. As curious as that may seem, many children like Chris have an opposite response to similar circumstances. They may be oblivious to what's going on around them. They may also have an unusually high pain threshold.

Considering all he has had to deal with, Chris has done remarkably well in school. We have learned to expect that every new school year there will be difficulty in the adjustment of getting back into school and meeting new changes and classroom expectations. Most years have not been easy. The most difficult year he has had was with a teacher who adamantly demanded that he would learn her way. Her rigid ways became a nightmare for him . . . and for us.

We have found that some flexibility is critical. Predictability and clarity are important in any classroom, and they're a must for ADD/ADHD children. Making changes and "shifting gears" for new projects is very difficult for them under the best of circumstances. Our most trying times in school often come from a lack of these necessary elements. A substitute teacher often represents chaos and behavior problems for a child with ADHD. Expecting a math test and suddenly switching at the last minute to a surprise spelling test can create high anxiety and undue stress for the child.

Consistency in rules and schedules for the classroom invite predictability and more inner calm for the child. They know what to expect and what is expected of them. Flexibility in homework assignments and demanding projects can also make a tremendous difference. It can lighten an already heavy load.

Overall, we have had the privilege of watching Chris become a happy, confident, and responsible child. He is learning to cope and to compensate for the challenges in his life. He loves science, history, cooking, and gardening. Now thirteen, he has a zest for life that's infectious. He does homework and chores without being asked. He is sensitive to the needs of others. Chris seldom has a day go by that he doesn't do something extra nice for someone. The loving words we have spoken to him, he now speaks to us: "Great job, Mom." "Dad, you're the best!"

Miracle child? No. Loved child? Yes. Cared for by some exemplary and very special people who have given of themselves to make life better for Chris. A change of pediatricians many years ago helped to pave a path of greater discovery to meet our challenges. While he hasn't always understood all that we were dealing with, he keeps an open mind, trusts our judgments and intuition, and shows respect for our opinions. He draws Chris into the conversations and shows respect for him as well. He's had the wisdom to be able to help us when we needed it and refer us to other resources when necessary. His pride has never interfered with the health and welfare of our children. He continues to encourage our family and be there for us.

The speech therapists, occupational therapists, and developmental pediatricians, whose hearts were clearly in their work with Chris, also made a significant difference in his life. They've helped him to become more aware of his body and his needs by identifying weaknesses and building on his strengths.

His grandparents, all of whom were mystified by much of what happened in the early years, have always loved and accepted Chris for his differences and qualities. Along with Chris's siblings, they have created a safe haven of acceptance and support.

All of this has been absolutely invaluable. There is, however, one other facet of this multi-modality treatment that has been the core of Chris's success: a school staff dedicated to their work and to helping children. As a parent, I've always acknowledged that much of the responsibility for my child's education falls on me. I have to coordinate and monitor the many elements that have to work in conjunction with one another to get the services he needs.

I am not always sure how to evaluate the programs or even know what's best. I have to remind myself I'm not the only one involved in this effort. It requires teamwork. If I've done my job and found trusted specialists, we can work together to determine what is best for my child. They know the programs; I know my child.

By a very fortunate set of circumstances, that's exactly what we got—an exceptional team consisting of resource specialist, teachers, nurse, and principal. The staff at our elementary school has worked together to create an atmosphere of cooperation designed with the best interests of the children in mind. Emphasis is placed on self-esteem, learning styles, and respecting individual differences. They have an excellent program to teach study skills and organizational techniques that has been extremely helpful.

I cannot stress enough the vital importance of all these factors in working with ADHD children. In order to bring it all together, teachers and other staff must be knowledgeable of the disorder and interested in applying different techniques to help these children. Recognizing the challenge of ADHD and employing tactics to help the child will very likely mean the difference between success and failure. This is a lot of responsibility, and yes, it's one more problem to contend with in the classroom. However, when you weigh the benefits of a whole child versus the tragedy of a broken one, how can we ignore the blatant reality of this problem?

Dealing with the ADHD child is time-consuming and exhausting. Just when you think you've got things under control, you're met with new surprises and challenges. For example, this child who has been turning in his homework on a daily basis for the last week and a half suddenly shuts down and has difficulty turning in anything at all, including communication from home or a signed permission slip. That brings up another interesting point. Much of what is sent home frequently does not *reach* home. I can't begin to estimate the number of important materials I have not received due to our son's forgetfulness or lack of organization. Please believe me when I tell you we have tried everything we can think of to help get those papers to and from school.

The problem is getting better as the children get older, but I have to remember it is not intentional. It is a part of the challenge they face. That is why I work extra hard at home in teaching organizational skills and talking with the children about all of life's topics as much as possible. Most important, I have to listen. In fact, that's usually more important than my talking!

It is important to note, too, that depression and isolation are common for the child and the child's primary caregiver. Because an ADHD child can be demanding and in need of constant attention and direction, he can be unpleasant to be around. I have found that many people who do not have a child like mine don't have the understanding or tolerance to be with them for any length of time. Making new friends may be very easy. Keeping the friendships harmonious is another story! Once a child visits the home of a friend, it may encourage a fast ending to an otherwise promising friendship.

This can be a major factor in the depression and isolation. Since spending time with other families can create further problems for the child and parent, it may limit support and socializing for them. Some of my very closest friends are parents who, like myself, have children with ADHD. I know I can pick up that phone and call on an understanding friend during a time of crisis or happiness! It makes a difference to share with someone who has been where I am. I didn't have that support when my sons were younger. Not much information was available concerning ADHD. The fact that I also had two hyperactive little boys to guide was an additional drain on what energy was left. Today I make it a point to get more rest, exercise, and time out, so that I can be a better mom. In dealing with the constant demands of these children, I believe it is very important that we have to care for ourselves in a healthy way in order to have a healthy attitude!

After all, just dealing with everyday stresses of living, and the added demands of the ADHD child and other family members, can truly become a test of survival. What goes on at home can sometimes be more stressful to deal with than the appearances a child projects at school. This is because a child can "let it all hang out" at home. Usually it's the mom who becomes the target for those pent-up emotions and frustrations.

I have known families who, because of problems in school or maladjustments in the child, have been referred to a school counselor or psychologist. The problems the child is experiencing may be a direct result of ADHD in the child or they may worsen ADHD in the child. Once referred, it is then noticed that the child's parents have marital problems, and someone then assumes that the child's problems are the direct result of the family's problems. The parents then receive treatment.

Meanwhile, the child may be misdiagnosed and has still not received the help he or she needs because someone cannot see the real picture of what is going on with the child and his or her family. The traditional view in child psychiatry has been that most children's problems are the result of the problems of parents or families. If we live with a child whose needs drain our energies, resources, time, and budget, of course we're going to have marital problems. Any good marriage has some problems. Again, getting the right kind of help from the professional field, especially understanding, flexibility, and determination from the child's teachers, is invaluable.

We know first-hand the distinct difference in the life of a child identified and helped in the early years as opposed to a child identified much later. The symptoms of the disorder are usually present at birth—for example, an infant who cries all the time and becomes over-stimulated very quickly. As they grow older, they anger quickly and become more aggressive. Some children, like Chris, are walking advertisements for ADHD. Other children, like Chris's twin brother, Phillip, and older brother, Scott, are seen as anything but your typical ADHD child. That is, until the problem begins to unmask itself.

Experts say that only about half of those afflicted with the disorder have been properly diagnosed, and even fewer receive the comprehensive therapy the condition requires. Many of these youngsters in whom the condition goes unacknowledged are seen as slow, lazy, and undisciplined. Others like our son Scott are labeled as "bad kids" or the product of uninvolved, careless parents. Unsuspecting parents blame themselves or other circumstances such as health problems, a death or divorce in the family, or what they may perceive as their lack of parental skill for their child's poor behavior and performance.

When Phillip was eight months old he became very ill and his little body slowed way down in growth. Today he is a year and a half behind in bone growth development, and we suspected that the reason for his slowness in school was due to the habits he established during that period of time. One teacher remarked that she wanted to "put a stick of dynamite under him." That observation became a clear message that something else was probably going on and needed to be addressed.

This happened during the winter when Phillip was quite ill once again. He'd missed a lot of school and was having a difficult time catching up and staying caught up. With some reservations, we requested testing toward the end of the school year. Dissatisfied with the results of the tests, we requested reassessment to be done in the fall when he was feeling better and starting fresh. The second IQ test resulted in a greater than 30-point difference and clearly identified Phillip as gifted.

Some learning disabilities were discovered, as well as a distinct possibility that Phillip also had ADHD. This puzzled us. So much material had been written on ADHD with hyperactivity. What about the child who appears bright, cooperative, and quiet . . . just maybe a little "spacey" or "slow"? Further outside evaluations confirmed our suspicions. Phillip had ADHD without hyperactivity (what is termed today as the predominantly inattentive type of ADHD). Had he not been given the benefit of the doubt and received further assessment and cooperation from our school team, he would have been mislabeled, misunderstood, and underestimated.

We realize that he clearly has a pace quite different from Chris. He may need extra time to finish projects or even get started. He's very bright and intense. I believe it's quite common to think that because a person is slow, he's not bright. Wrong! It simply means he's slow! Many believe that because a person is diagnosed with learning disabilities that he or she is not bright. Wrong again! Chances are more likely than not that the child is extremely bright. They just need to learn in their own ways. I have to work hard just to keep up with our sons. It seems as though they're usually far ahead of me.

It wouldn't be fair to discuss the success we've had without mentioning the rest of the story! It's necessary to know of all the caring people who were there for us—and those who could have made a positive difference and chose not to.

We were very fortunate to obtain an accurate diagnosis and appropriate intervention for Chris and Phillip. Although it has been a lot of work and a struggle finding the right combination of help, it's been more than worth the effort. Their self-esteem is intact. They both greet each new day with optimism and confidence. They've experienced varying degrees of success and can willingly move on to new challenges.

Our seventeen-year-old son, Scott, was not so fortunate. In retrospect, I can see that, as an infant, many of the signs were there, for example, extreme fussiness and overstimulation. But because he was my first child, I had no way of knowing that all new babies weren't like that! He was an extremely bright child. He reached and passed development milestones quite early. He was confident and handled himself in an unusually mature manner. He was one of those children we all know: three years old, going on thirty!

Because of that, we put him into kindergarten at the age of five, never questioning his abilities and maturity. One more year of growth for Scott could have made a lot of difference then, but we had no way of knowing that. It wasn't a popular practice at the time to "hold children back a year." Kindergarten seemed to progress smoothly. It was in first grade that something began to happen. The "phone calls" (as I refer to the communication between school and home) began at that time. They were always the same: "Your child is so bright, but I just can't get him to turn in his homework." "He can pass a test and get an *A*, but he just won't finish his work in class."

It wasn't until fourth grade that he had a teacher who took a special interest in him and helped change his attitude about school and homework. She encouraged Scott, took time for him, and challenged him. While this made a tremendous difference in the way Scott was viewing things, he still lacked the ability to get work finished on time and stay on-task. At that time Scott was in a private school. We knew he needed more individual attention. Whatever it was that Scott needed (and we didn't know exactly what that was), he wasn't receiving it there. We decided to try public school.

It was in fifth grade that the behavior problems began to manifest themselves. There were more of "the calls." There was more of the inappropriate behavior. Where at least the test scores had been superbly high, they were now becoming lower and lower. Counseling didn't seem to help much. We were still at a loss for Scott's lack of motivation and low self-esteem. We had reasoned that it was caused by a traumatic event in his early years of life. When we ruled that out, we blamed home life and lack of skill. I was doing everything I felt I could do. It never occurred to me that ADHD was the root of our problems. The high test scores threw us off course. The maturity that we saw in Scott as a very young child was deceiving. As we realized much later, he was mature, but not ready for school at age five.

By seventh grade Scott had been in three different schools (including kindergarten). He moved on to seventh grade at our local junior high. That year, without a doubt, was one of the most painful and saddest years in Scott's life. It was there that Scott's self-esteem plunged to the depths of despair. He encountered many new situations he had never experienced before, including racism, personal threats of harm and violence, fights, and displays of weapons at school. The classrooms were overloaded. Conversations with teachers revealed they were overstressed. While in the G.A.T.E. (gifted and talented education) program, Scott had a teacher who called me often to let me know how "lazy" and "disruptive" my son was in her class. She made it clear that she did not have the time or tolerance to deal with him. When was I going to do something about this? This same woman, I found out later, wrote in his school records: "This kid is a big fat zero."

Meanwhile, I had received a multitude of phone calls and met with Scott's teachers. One day his vice principal told me she knew what Scott's problem was. First of all, we weren't disciplining him enough. Second of all, he was obviously (in her opinion) "a classic case of a child with learning disabilities" that had gone undetected. I requested and pursued testing through the school. We were repeatedly denied testing on the basis that Scott was "too bright." In other words, he hadn't met the criteria of falling two full years below grade level. He certainly wasn't performing to the fullest of his ability either. I can't help but ask myself over and over how many of our kids are falling between the cracks because our priorities are such that a child must fully fail before he can be given the tools he needs to fully succeed.

I set up an appointment with yet another outside source to have Scott thoroughly evaluated. Our young son was found to be in a full-blown state of depression. On top of that, he was diagnosed with Attention Deficit Disorder. Scott was placed on medication. Within a short period of time his attitude began to change and he was better able to focus. The suicidal thoughts he once had began to dissipate. The low self-esteem remained.

Self-esteem is the backbone of our children's ability to succeed or fail. When this is gone, all they have left is humiliation, anger, and deep-seated frustration that results in despair. That is when I see kids like Scott giving up. I am convinced that young people like Scott account for the majority of kids who make up the high dropout rate in this country.

In trying to "fit in" and find some place they belong, they pick unsuitable friends and act out destructive behavior patterns. When you combine that with a school setting of administrators and teachers who lack the knowledge and skill to deal with these children, it becomes a devastating, overwhelming problem.

That is exactly what happened to us in eighth and ninth grades, as well. We moved Scott into a private school for eighth grade and on to a four-year high school for ninth grade. In matters of discipline at both schools, administrators chose to humiliate and insult Scott rather than address the issues that created the problems in the first place. We even brought in the psychologist who had been working with us to help mediate between school and home. These children become caught up in a vicious cycle: "I'm no good. I'll fail anyway. Therefore, I won't try, then I'll have an excuse for failing."

In tenth grade I began to hear the words "I want to quit school." My heart sank even deeper. I couldn't blame him for feeling that way. All along I'd been searching for answers. For years I read books, attended conferences and meetings, and shared stories with my good buddy who had a son experiencing the same sort of trauma in another school district. We both knew our greatest obstacle was not our children. It was finding competent schools geared to the challenge and dedication of working with children like ours.

During the first semester of tenth grade, Scott brought home five *F*'s and one *B*. The *B* came from an English teacher who respected Scott's abilities and eccentricities. He lit a fire under Scott. He took the time for him. He challenged him. Scott still talks about him with the utmost regard. Phone calls, conferences, pleas for help, and even punishing Scott didn't make much difference.

Just prior to the second semester I'd heard about a magnet school that was designed to meet the needs of children especially interested in theater and other arts. I visited the school and signed Scott up. It seemed too good to be true. Scott loves music and art, and his greatest strengths have always been in these areas. We had nothing to lose and everything to gain if this worked out.

I will never forget that first semester at our new school. The first phone call home was from Scott's art teacher. She said, "I want to thank you for sending Scott to our school. He brings a ray of sunshine into my classes." Not meaning to be sarcastic, I thought she had the wrong number. *I* knew that he was a ray of sunshine. He was a joy in my life. But his *teacher* saw him as a "ray of sunshine"! How I longed to hear those words. I thanked her with all my heart—and then I cried. At age fifteen and so many teachers later, I knew we'd found a special place for Scott. I shared this with my closest friends and they cried, too. They know as I did that in those simple words came acceptance and hope.

Within a week I met our school principal for the first time. I briefly described our school history. She reached out to me and held my hands. She said, "Let me help you. I can make a difference." By 9:00 a.m. the following day she had Scott's records on her desk and me on the phone. In conversation with Scott, she told him she knew what it was like to have ADHD because some people very close to her also have it. She said the hardest thing for him to do at this point in his life was to find his own niche—and that's exactly what they were going to help him do. By 4:00 p.m. that same day, Scott's teachers had individual consultations with him to make plans for his success. By the end of the semester he was bringing home a *B* average.

In discussions of discipline, Scott is treated with the utmost respect. If there is a problem, I receive a concerned phone call and suggestions for dealing with the problem. Our remarkable principal reviews his progress and report cards, always taking time to jot down a positive note to Scott. His schedule has been changed as needed to work in the classes he needs and to obtain tutoring. His wonderful resource teacher and her staff have become a "home base" where Scott can get a break away from the school pressures and put some of his ability and talent to work helping others.

In conjunction with the phenomenal intervention at the school, we found someone very special to help Scott with medication and a new approach to life. Since the assistance for ADHD children comes in many forms, we sought the most essential help in putting all of this together. Deciding to use medication was truly an agonizing dilemma. After trying three different psychiatrists over a period of a few years, the fourth turned out to be exactly the person to work with Scott. He helped to create an atmosphere of trust and acceptance that has allowed our son to be himself and begin to like it.

Today, Scott is no longer on medication. He has opted for healthy lifestyle changes. He is learning to direct his incredible energy toward positive thoughts and behavior. In a few minutes he can design an art format that looks professional, though he can hardly pay attention in the classroom. In the same way, he can rattle off meaningful lyrics to a song or the emotional words of a poem. Yet, he still has trouble finishing his homework.

I remain eternally grateful to this first art teacher, who has also become a friend and mentor. Although he no longer has a class with her, she still stays in touch with him. They both love animals and art. Her genuine interest and love for her students has become an inspiration. For us, she represents a beacon of hope in a dark sea of near hopelessness.

I love watching the changes take place in this wonderful young man. It's beginning to fall together because of people like the ones I've mentioned who helped make it happen.

It is not my intention to give the impression that once a child gets the appropriate diagnosis and intervention that everything is wonderful. There is some comfort in knowing what the problem is and that we are getting help for it. But this is an ongoing, tedious process that requires constant attention. These children don't outgrow ADHD. The hope is that the older they get, and with each school level they reach, they will be learning new coping skills to allow them to compensate and reach their full potential as capable and competent adults. They will then be ready to share their unique gifts with the world.

It is not just a matter of getting the help, it is the way in which it is given. It is also in the way we speak to our children. This was so beautifully illustrated for us recently when our son brought home a paper that was clearly illegible. His devoted and knowledgeable teacher wrote a note at the top of the page: "Phillip, please write this more neatly so my poor ol' eyes can read it."

There is absolutely no substitute for a teacher who loves his or her job and wants to make a difference in the lives of our children. Trust and believe in your ability to change the future of a child. Dare to make a difference. Celebrate the magnificent gift of uniqueness in every child. A plaque I once saw summed it up this way:

"Teachers affect eternity.
One can never tell where their influence ends."

Follow-Up on the Haughey Family—Twelve Years Later

As in all families, so much occurs in over a decade. There are innumerable events and periods of joy and well-being that evoke positive, happy memories. All families, as well, live through troubling experiences and difficult times.

As a family, the Haugheys had more than their fair share of struggles and painful periods. This wonderful, beautiful family got through those darker times fortified by their deep love and support of each other, and their strong religious faith.

I recently had the chance to get together and have lunch with Linda and some of the "kids." It was such a delight to see them. They are all mature adults, handsome, charming, and fun. I will always hold this family dear to my heart, and I treasure our friendship. As a current update on what's new in their lives, it is with pleasure that I can share the following:

* Scott is the proud father of a beautiful baby boy. He also has his own business, which he loves, and through which he is able to use his artistic talents.
* Phillip is an emergency medical technician in training to become a fireman. He plans to attend paramedic school in the near future.
* Since the age of seventeen, Chris has spent the past years working with, counseling, and helping at-risk youth through a local agency. He helps run a program for homeless and runaway youngsters. Chris's understanding, passion, and skills enable him to give these other children/teens the support and encouragement they so desperately need.

* Stacey, the baby sister in the family (who was in kindergarten at the time Linda wrote this section), is a stunning young lady—an athletic junior in high school. Stacey had also been diagnosed with an attention deficit disorder and learning disabilities. She had been homeschooled (with the exception of three years) until high school. Stacey is happy and doing well in her current school placement.
* Jeff graduated from college with a degree in business/marketing. He is doing very well in applying his skills in the business world.
* Pat is a Ph.D. student in architectural history at MIT.
* Linda and Chuck are so grateful for their family's many blessings, and are thrilled to be new grandparents.

Case Studies and Interventions (Adam and Vincent)

*I*n this section, it is with great pleasure to be able to feature the case studies and intriguing stories of Adam and Vincent—two young men with ADHD (one currently in middle school and the other a senior in high school). I am very grateful to Vincent's and Adam's mothers—friends of mine from different regions of the United States—who have generously and poignantly shared their children's histories, school intervention plans, and valuable insights for this section. Names and other identifying information have been changed to protect their privacy. As in Section 4.1, A Parent's Story, much can be learned through the experiences of these families in seeking and obtaining the diagnosis, proper care, and interventions needed for their sons. There is a wealth of information that can be gleaned from these case studies, and the very personal and powerful details that these mothers were willing to share.

Both Vincent and Adam have had the benefit of multimodal treatments throughout the years; and both have extraordinary, very knowledgeable, wonderful parents—who have been highly involved in learning about ADHD, and who have assumed the important parental role of "team manager" in their care. Over the years, as different issues emerged (both boys have ADHD and co-existing conditions), their parents have steadfastly helped their sons by being vigilant and addressing their needs. They have made every effort to pursue an accurate diagnosis, obtain proper treatment, and communicate and collaborate effectively with the school and clinicians.

These two case studies, as well as the Haughey family story in Section 4.1, are very compelling and illustrate the reality of how difficult it is to find what works for any given child. It takes a great deal of caring, commitment, and effort on the part of all parties (educators, parents, and clinicians), to do what it takes for a child with ADHD to be successful. Interventions and treatments that are needed at different times during the child's life will change. What we plan doesn't always work, or it loses its effectiveness after a period of time. We need to keep monitoring and reviewing the interventions we put in place, and make adjustments and revisions to our plans, accordingly.

Adam (Twelve Years Old, Seventh-Grade Student)
Medical and Developmental History

Adam lives at home with both biological parents and two older siblings (brother one year older, and sister five years older). They are a close family, with no significant issues. Although mother's pregnancy with Adam was uncomplicated, the delivery was complicated by a C-section, and he was in the intensive care unit immediately following birth because of breathing difficulties. Once these resolved, Adam appeared to be a healthy infant. His mother describes him as a somewhat restless and fussy baby who had some difficulty sleeping, but did respond to cuddling. She also describes him as somewhat overly active and irritable as an infant. "From the beginning, Adam was more fragile emotionally and trickier behaviorally than his older sister and brother." Most motor and language developmental milestones were reached at the appropriate ages. There were no difficulties with toilet training or eating problems. In spite of relatively normal language development, he had some articulation difficulties that made him difficult to understand. He did receive speech/language therapy for approximately six months. Adam had a number of ear infections between the ages of two to five ("Five times more than his siblings").

Mother also describes the following:

"Adam has always had extreme *environmental sensitivities,* specifically: *temperature.* As a toddler, he often had ruddy-red cheeks and complained of being too hot. In the middle of winter with snow on the ground, he would overheat in a jacket. *Smell:* His sense of smell is keen—he is bothered by smells that literally no one else can perceive. *Touch:* Clothing tags have always been an ongoing, painful nuisance; they must be removed. *Visual radar:* He has an uncanny ability to sense if something is new or out of place in his environment. For example, he will notice within seconds of walking into the house if an obscure vase has been relocated, or if a new book has been placed on the bookshelf. This radar is a remarkable attribute in that it seems to directly contradict his other identified short-term memory issues.

"Adam also has a history of *inflexibility* and being *rigid.* Making simple choices can be difficult. When he was younger, there were many mornings he would break down and cry at breakfast because he was unable to choose between cereals—Cocoa Puffs or oatmeal? 'I can't decide.' At the same time, it was unacceptable for me to select for him. If I gave him only one choice, he would not eat it. There was one memorable morning when he was six or seven that he adamantly insisted upon having ice cream for breakfast. No amount of reasoning or persuasion could convince him otherwise. After flatly saying 'No' to him, and with both of us in tears, he refused to budge from his seat. It was a complete impasse. Since then, I have learned to pick my battles, and we still talk fondly about the morning we ended up on the floor eating vanilla ice cream together. Adam continues to be inflexible about food—some months he will only eat tuna fish; other months he will only eat peanut butter and jelly sandwiches.

"As a baby he was fussy and often inconsolable. And as a toddler, he would sit and cry for no apparent reason. His year-older brother discovered the most successful way to distract him was by doing some silly 'Three Stooges' routines. Adam would watch his brother's performance over and over and laugh through his tears. His brother is very intuitive; he has always been attuned to Adam's special needs. They share a unique bond, and I have often wondered what they would do without each other.

"In nursery school, Adam's teachers told us he was 'extremely sensitive' and cried easily. In grade school, his teachers said he lacked coping skills."

Initial Diagnosis

Adam received his first multidisciplinary school evaluation at the end of the kindergarten year. Because his parents had ongoing concerns during the school year about Adam's behavior and academic progress, it was agreed that a baseline evaluation would be appropriate.

Summary of School Evaluation (End of Kindergarten)

Adam demonstrated overall cognitive ability in the average range. He had above-average receptive and expressive vocabulary and language skills. Minor articulation errors were noted, but speech/language services were not indicated. Academic difficulties were found in letter identification, letter/sound association, and limited sight word vocabulary. Based on parent and teacher responses to behavioral scales, Adam's problem behavior section fell within the moderate problem range.

Adam was identified as having specific learning disabilities in the areas of visual/auditory integration and recall, affecting reading and writing (letter identification, reading decoding, sound/symbol associations). There was a severe discrepancy between his ability and achievement in reading and writing readiness areas, qualifying Adam for special education.

His parents were willing to look into an ADHD evaluation privately, if indicated. However, the school team felt academic (resource) support would be the most appropriate place to start at that time.

In first grade, after receiving reports from his teacher that Adam was having an exceptionally hard time sitting still in class, his parents pursued an evaluation for ADHD. He was diagnosed with ADHD at that time. To quote his mother: "Working initially with his pediatrician, we began the medication journey soon thereafter. It was a rocky road pharmaceutically from the get-go; and the pediatrician referred us out to a child psychiatrist for more specialized medical care. He was the first in a series of child psychiatrists with whom we've worked over the years."

Since the initial evaluation, Adam has been receiving special education (resource) services. In later grades he had related services (counseling/consultation to teacher) added to his IEP. Adam's IEPs (for example, in fourth grade) indicate: "specific learning disabilities impacting the educational areas/tasks of written expression, task completion, coping skills." IEPs also indicate that Adam experiences considerable anxiety, and goals addressing anxiety-reduction were included in the IEP.

Note: *It is interesting that in none of his IEPs over the years does it mention that Adam also has ADHD, which has been under treatment since the first grade with a myriad of interventions (pharmacological and psychosocial). He is receiving special education under the disability category of "specific learning disabilities." However, he also does qualify for special education and related services under the category of "other health impaired" (due to ADHD). Both the LD and Adam's ADHD cause significant impairment in school functioning, qualifying him for special education, related services, and accommodations/modifications in his educational program.*

In the fourth grade Adam was evaluated privately by a clinical neuropsychologist. His parents requested the evaluation due to his history of ADHD and LD, and to document his current cognitive and educational status, as well as the effectiveness of his current medication. Besides one-to-one evaluation in office visits, the neuropsychologist was able to view three videotapes that were supplied of Adam functioning in the classroom.

Test Results from Private Evaluation (Age 9)

Overall intellectual ability was in the high average range, with visual spatial abilities at the upper end of the high average range and verbal ability at the upper end of the average range. Questionnaire data indicated significant difficulty maintaining the focus of his attention over time at both home and in the classroom. More prominent was his overactivity and impulsivity in both environments.

On tests of executive function, Adam did not appear to have difficulties generating plans, but rather in implementing them and monitoring the execution of them for appropriateness. Adam was found to have visual-motor integration inefficiency, which, combined with his impulsivity, is believed to play a role in his difficulties with writing. A relative weakness was found in his verbal expressive ability when compared to his overall ability, and especially compared to his visual processing ability. Thus, he does experience problems effectively conveying his meaning in pragmatic conversation (spoken language) and this likely affects his written language, as well. (See Section 1.1 for information about executive functions.)

Academic Achievement

Reading decoding and comprehension were average for his age/grade. Mathematical reasoning and conceptualization were at the upper end of average range, with somewhat more difficulty with computation problems. In terms of written language, his performance on an unstructured test of writing that required him to generate a several-paragraph story to go along with a picture was notable for its unusual brevity. Writing was very difficult to decipher. Ability to apply rules of punctuation and spelling in context was in the low average range. Adam did not use as complex language as one would expect from him. The shortness of his story also impacted its organization and plot development. (See Section 3.7, Writing and Reading Challenges for Students with ADHD.)

The evaluator noted that, even on medication, Adam showed clear and pervasive difficulties maintaining the focus of his attention over time. This sustained attention deficit affected his ability to take in oral and visual information, and the effects were particularly notable for verbal memory.

Socioemotional

Parents' and teacher's scales of socioemotional functioning indicated attentional problems, and both viewed him as experiencing feelings of unhappiness and stress. An additional component was his emotional dysregulation, in that he could change moods quickly and sometimes unpredictably—experiencing intense anxiety and frustration at times.

Other clusters of elevated scales included acting in a verbally or physically hostile manner, especially at home, and to a lesser degree at school. Both parents and teacher indicated he consistently argued when not getting his own way or getting what he wanted, suggesting difficulties delaying gratification. The other area that was consistently difficult was Adam's sharply diminished ability to adjust to changes in routine and environments, including shifting from one task to another.

An important feature of all his responses was the lack of hostile action or latent aggressive intent. That is, while he could react impulsively to a situation with anger, there was no evidence that he harbors any deep-seated resentment or anger.

Strengths and Interests

Adam has been described as a warm, caring, hard-working, sincere, and bright boy, who can be very understanding and empathic. He is athletic and enjoys hockey, basketball, and lacrosse. Adam is friendly, inquisitive, and can appreciate humor. In primary grades it was noted that he plays the piano, loves art projects (especially working with clay), and takes gymnastics—at which he is quite good.

Educational History

Adam attended preschool for two and a half years, and has been in public school general education classrooms throughout elementary and now middle school. Since he was found eligible for special education, Adam has been in the Resource Program, with goals and objectives mostly in written language. He has also had related services of counseling (consult with classroom teacher). In addition, he has received various accommodations/modifications to support his success in the classroom.

IEP reports of Adam's levels of performance in second grade included:

* Sometimes has difficulty being flexible when working with others.
* Experiences a great deal of anxiety when faced with new assignments or academic challenges.
* Is an active participant in class and small group sessions. Needs frequent reminders, however, to wait his turn, raise his hand, and to attend to the task at hand.

* Often looks around the room and is easily distracted by those around him.
* Continues to have difficulty with written expression—particularly getting his thoughts down in writing in an organized, timely manner.

The second-grade IEP reports also included that Adam was responding to a reward system to encourage more timely work completion and working on strategies to reduce anxiety (taking a breath, asking for help, rereading directions).

Throughout the grades, Adam has mostly functioned academically within grade-level range in all areas except writing. His ADHD-related behaviors (inattention, impulsivity) have interfered with his school performance—in written language and in social-emotional/behavioral functioning.

Of all his school years, third grade was the most difficult and stressful—due to many challenges in medication changes/titrations and frequent conflicts with his classroom teacher.

Social and Adaptive Behavior Functioning

Adam had many adaptive behaviors of concern in kindergarten/first grade. During that time he complained a lot about superficial aches and pains, displayed frequent impulsive behavior, and became very frustrated if things did not come easily to him. Adam wanted his way, and sometimes had temper tantrums. To get his attention and improve chances of his listening, Mom said she had to hold his face in her hands and say, "Adam, I'm talking to you." He interrupted frequently, and his feelings were easily hurt.

Adam's mother reported in fourth grade that "he had some difficulties interacting appropriately with others and had a diminishing number of lasting friendships. He tended to be somewhat impulsive and bossy. He often had to be first or win to the point of cheating at games or changing the rules to suit him."

Adam's mother currently shares the following (Adam at twelve years old):

"Socially, things have always been a challenge, and frequently heartbreaking. He is on the margins, and friendships seem to be hard to sustain. Although Adam is never inclined to initiate play-dates (only at my prodding), he readily responds whenever someone invites him to play. Sometimes, it's as if an awareness window opens and he will say out of the blue, 'Mom, I just realized I haven't played with a friend in a long time,' or he will call me into his bedroom at night and say tearfully, 'I just realized I don't have any friends.' Heartbreaking. He seems to know that his social skills are lacking, but be unable to control them. And no amount of social coaching (and we've done tons on our own and through therapy) has been completely successful. The worst is when he very carefully and oh-so-casually asks if he's gotten anything in the mail. 'Just wondering,' he says—but usually it turns out that he's overheard about a party and he's not invited. In many ways, he is fortunate to have an older and very social brother whose friends are over all the time. But again, he is on the edge during these times—endured as younger brothers are, but not really a part of things.

"Adam continues to need more nurturing than other children—notably when he's under time pressure or he's required to focus on something. Sometimes, a simple raised voice or criticism will be enough to fragment him. His eyes well up, his head hangs low, his body becomes motionless and unresponsive. The irony is that he can also be extremely insensitive to others; he can bully with the best of them, which makes it difficult for him to receive appropriate sympathy from others when he most needs it." (See Section 1.7, ADHD and Social Skills Interventions.)

Educational Supports and Interventions

Adam has benefited from numerous school interventions: special education and related services, annual (and sometimes biannual) multidisciplinary team meetings, and classroom accommodations/modifications to his educational program. In the fourth grade, the school district's behavioral consultant observed Adam in the classroom on a few occasions (to determine whether a functional behavioral assessment was needed). It was not deemed necessary to conduct a full functional assessment, but the following recommendations were made that were incorporated into his IEP:

Environment

* Adam needs a structured environment—Eliminate as much unstructured time as possible.
* Adam does better when there are a lot of different activities for short periods of time, as well as a lot of movement.
* When Adam needs to copy something, it helps to give him a copy at his desk so he does not have to try and read the information off the board or overhead.
* Provide Adam with a written schedule of his day.

Academic Tasks

* It is important to warn Adam that he needs to be listening before a direction is given.
* Before beginning a new task, have Adam put everything else away and "put his eyes on the teacher."
* It is beneficial to give Adam an overview of what he is going to be expected to do—preview expectations and task requirements.
* Warn Adam about any transitions, so that he has time to complete the task he is working on and prepare for the next activity.
* It helps to break up written work with listening activities, art, and so forth.
* He often needs help getting started with ideas—especially with writing. When he knows what to do, Adam does it well.
* It is important to give Adam choices and structure tasks. He has a hard time with open-ended questions, and needs tasks structured.
* Adam appears to benefit when there are visual cues to support verbal directions.
* When he doesn't understand something, it is important that Adam has it explained again with someone who uses a soft, calm voice and does not engage when he tries to make excuses or explain why he didn't understand the first time.

Behavior

* It is important to tell Adam what he is doing right and encourage him through discussion of things he has done well.
* Using a positive tone of voice when Adam is slightly frustrated or upset seems to help him calm down and stop him from escalating.
* It is important to be firm, but supportive and to give Adam space when he starts to get upset, so he can get himself under control.
* Adam needs someone who is willing to re-explain things and does not discuss with him whether or not he should have been listening.
* Adam seems to redirect easily when positive reinforcements are used.
* Consistently follow-through with rewards and consequences.
* Use nonverbal cues (tap on the shoulder, eye contact) to redirect Adam's attention.
* Allow Adam to move around and break tasks down; he does better with several short tasks than with one long task.

Accommodations/Modifications (Fifth-Grade IEP)

Classroom Activities

* Warn about transitions, new assignments, and expectations for time in which to complete assignments
* Use time extensions as appropriate
* Provide alone space/break space for Adam, as appropriate
* Provide copy of notes for Adam to ease anxiety of writing and processing from board to paper
* Have frequent check-ins from teacher
* Use Alpha Smart/computer for writing
* Redirect him one-on-one outside of classroom (esp. when he is very anxious)

Daily Assignments/Homework Assignments

* Have Adam repeat directions back to ensure understanding
* Use time extensions as appropriate
* Modify lengthy writing assignments to multiple choice, fill in the blank or math to fewer problems, so he is not overwhelmed
* Use prompts to get Adam started

Class Projects and/or Reports

* Break down steps to a task
* Modify lengthy written reports as appropriate

Classroom Quizzes and Tests

* Use time extensions as appropriate
* Use teacher reassurance in order to minimize anxiety
* Dictate written answers to teacher as appropriate
* Modify tests to include multiple choice, fill in the blank, as appropriate
* Use small group testing if appropriate

Other

* Allow Adam to move around frequently—for example, send him on errands, do a classroom job
* Praise accomplishments often—Adam responds positively to praise
* When possible, give Adam choices on what he can write about when asked to write an essay

Adam's mother recalls the following supports provided in school that helped her son with attention, work production, and impulsive behaviors:

* In kindergarten and first grade, the teachers used key words/phrases when the class got out of control. They would say "Milk" and the class would respond in unison "Shake." Or the teacher would say "Burger" and the class would respond "King." This helped all of the kids refocus and snap back to attention.
* For Adam, in second grade, his classroom teacher instituted a personal reward system. He got stickers every day for staying on task or other behaviors, and after a certain number were collected, he earned privileges—such as helping her set up a new bulletin board, or helping her with another project.
* A fifth-grade teacher had a check system in which she quietly wrote a child's name on the chalkboard, adding a check for misbehaviors. Each day that the checks were kept to a certain minimum, the entire class earned a "link." The paper links were connected and hung from the wall. When they reached across the room, the entire class celebrated with a pizza party.
* Assignment notebooks were crucial assists for homework. Each day before he left school, Adam's assignment notebook was checked to make sure his tests, projects, and other homework assignments were accurately listed. In fourth grade, various "buddies" were asked to help Adam write down the assignments since he had great difficulty writing.
* Having a second set of books at home in elementary school proved invaluable as Adam could never remember to bring home the books he needed, or was too disorganized to bring home the correct ones.
* Homework Hotline is a phone-in system available to all students at Adam's middle school. You dial the teacher's extension and he or she dictates the day's homework. It is a valuable resource for all students and parents—but especially for children with ADHD, like Adam. It's just one more way to help ensure more students can succeed. (See Section 3.5, Organization, Time Management, and Study Skills Strategies.)
* Resource—a special class for eligible middle school students who may need help with organization and study skills. It takes the place of one of the "electives" that other students are taking (woodshop, home living, and others). Adam has time in this class to study, prepare, or get tutoring help as needed.

Out-of-School Interventions and Supports

Adam's mother shares the following about the various strategies, supports, and interventions that have been implemented over the years:

Counseling

"We have intermittently taken Adam to outside therapy sessions. Adam is acutely aware that not all kids talk to therapists/counselors, and has not been particularly receptive to the process or the efforts of his therapists. It is likely that we just haven't found as yet someone who is a right match for Adam—with whom there is good rapport, effective communication, and skills/strategies taught that he is willing to implement. One therapist's effort to help him with coping skills when he was getting overly anxious was Cue Cards. Adam wrote down 'Chill Out,' 'Take Deep Breath,' and other cues on cards, and he was supposed to pull them out of his pocket and review as needed. But in reality, he really couldn't remember to do this in the heat of frustration; he also was probably too embarrassed to call attention to himself by doing so. When his middle school counselor sent him a pass to come and talk with him about 'how things are going,' Adam initially complained about having to go. Now, however, he seems to take it in stride, and although he isn't sharing much with me about the sessions, he does go."

Tutoring

"Because of late development in reading and writing skills, we started taking Adam to outside tutoring as a first-grader. We did this for about a year. In third grade, to support math and reading challenges, we enrolled him in another tutoring enrichment program. This effort also lasted about a year. Rewards for completing tutoring assignments were critical—usually the rewards were for favorite snack foods or drinks, or the ability to go outside and play when he was finished. Overall, tutoring by outsiders has been a challenge because of Adam's resentment. We found the best way to get 'buy-in' was to simultaneously (and expensively!) enroll his brother—who, of course, loved these programs. The best tutor for Adam, it turns out, is his older brother, who enjoys helping him solve math and other problems. This seems to benefit both brothers, and there is zero rancor. However, we recognize that his brother won't always be willing or able, and we are receptive to hiring an outside tutor whenever it becomes necessary."

Homework

"Homework is always a challenge for Adam. It requires vigilant monitoring to ensure it gets done, and the time spent is significant. Two- and three-hour study sessions on school nights are the norm. A useful device has been a timer—setting the timer on the kitchen stove seems to help Adam stay on task and complete assignments within reasonable time periods. Of course, he frequently checks the timer, and often needs time extensions after it beeps. It also helps to prioritize wait patiently for their turn to participate). Poor performance in a team sport unfortunately can lead to more ridicule and social rejection for a child with already fragile self-esteem. Children with ADHD often do better in sports such as swimming, track and field, gymnastics, and martial arts.

Michael Shapiro, Ph.D., a child psychologist and certified instructor in Tae Kwon Do, explains the particular benefits of Tae Kwon Do for children with ADHD. These include building physical fitness, self-confidence, discipline, and the ability to protect oneself, if necessary. Students progress at their own pace, and success or failure of an entire team is not dependent on one individual's performance. Tae Kwon Do students are first made to learn the five tenets of their art: courtesy, integrity, perseverance, self-control, and indomitable spirit. They are trained to use nonaggressive methods to resolve disputes and avoid physical confrontation; and when learning to spar, they are taught how to apply their techniques in a highly controlled situation requiring strategy, planning, and a "cool head" (Shapiro, 2002).

Environmental sounds (for example, rain forests, oceans, waterfalls) and baroque music ("Claire de Lune" by Debussy and "Four Seasons" by Vivaldi) have a calming effect. Examples of more contemporary artists whose music is calming include: Kitaro, George Winston, Steven Halpern, Hillary Stagg, Zamfir, and Jim Chappell, among others.

There is evidence that certain kinds of instrumental musical arrangements and rhythmic patterns have therapeutic calming and focusing effects. Some musical resources are listed in the resources for Part 6, including those by Gary Lamb (a variety of arrangements at sixty beats per minute), REI Institute, and OptimaLearning®.

Listening to energizing music can also help children and teens with ADHD when they are cognitively fatigued or have low energy for tasks. *Songs for Self-Regulation* (Alert Program, 1995) is an excellent resource of selections for elementary school teachers, clinicians, and parents.

See Section 6.2, Music for Relaxation, Transitions, Energizing, and Visualization, for numerous musical selections and more on this topic.

Leisure Activities, Recreation, and Hobbies

Nurture a child's interests, and encourage participation in calming leisure activities such as working with clay, knitting, fishing, and drawing. In addition, find recreation and leisure activities to enjoy as a family such as bicycling, hiking, skating, or other physical activities. There is nothing like having fun together as a family to reduce stress and strengthen loving, positive relationships (Lanham, 2001).

A new sport and recreation that friends and families with ADHD report as being great fun and a perfect way to spend a few hours is called *geocaching*. This is a sort of "high-tech treasure hunt," which requires the use of a hand-held GPS (global positioning system). GPS systems at this time range in price from around $40 to well over $1,000 for the sophisticated models. For those with an adventurous spirit who seek the challenge and excitement of this sport, visit the website of www.geocaching.com— a site for cache enthusiasts—and the official global cache hunt site. Geocaches can now be found in over two hundred countries. Such websites print the longitude and latitude coordinates of various hidden caches. One enters the ZIP Code (close to home or wherever he or she may be traveling) and caches in that area are listed. The "cachers" program in the coordinates for a particular nearby cache, read the clues that have been journaled on the web page, and then begin the hunt. They will usually be finding sealed containers, hidden in clever outdoor locations, that contain a logbook and an inexpensive trinket/treasure of some kind. When a cache is found, the cacher signs the logbook and may leave one of his or her own trinkets behind. It is a sport/activity that is fun to do with family and pets—with a chance to explore the outdoors. Cachers log their find on the Internet site, and then take off on new adventures.

Exercise and Sports

It is known that exercise stimulates the central nervous system, increasing blood flow and oxygen to the brain. Some of the benefits of exercise include a boost in mood, and increase in focus, alertness, learning, and memory. For children who have an abundance of energy, it is a healthy, positive way to expend that energy. It is particularly important, therefore, for children/teens with ADHD to exercise regularly. In fact, exercise in the morning (for example, a before-school jogging program or some kind of aerobic workout) may increase a child's academic and behavioral performance. Aerobic exercise increases the enzymes that produce dopamine and enhances the production of stem cells in areas of the brain that are responsible for memory and learning. Exercise also directly increases dopamine, serotonin, and endorphin levels (Putnam, 2002).

Many children with ADHD, due to the core and related symptoms of the disorder, are not successful in baseball, and some other team sports (especially those that require having to homework over sports and social activities: We tell him school comes first, so he must get as much homework done as possible before he can go to football/hockey/or other practice. This is a strong motivator."

Sports

"Adam derives a great deal of pleasure from certain sports. He discovered football this year, and perhaps it's the military/structured mentality of the sport that makes him love it so. Part of it must be that he feels like an integral part of a team—an important and reinforcing feeling for an ADHD kid like Adam. He also has been a hockey goalie for years, and he seems to enjoy not only the responsibility and reflex-physical skills the position entails, but also the pressure. It does seem to fly in the face of anxiety issues—but he embraces the challenge most times. There are still exceptions: after a bad loss, he will come off the ice totally fragmented and in tears, and I wonder if sports are a good thing for him. Ultimately, he always wants to go back for more, though." (See Section 6.1, Stress Reduction, Relaxation Strategies, Leisure Activities, and Exercise.)

Advocates

"One particularly difficult school year we hired an advocate to attend a couple of team meetings with us. We found her to be a great asset because of her professionalism, the insightful questions she asked, and specific follow-up actions she relentlessly requested, that I wouldn't have thought of. Hiring her helped empower us. She was not inexpensive, and I only used her that year, but I wouldn't hesitate to use her again if needed."

Medical Interventions

"Another saga. Who knew finding the right medication could be so difficult for our son? Over the years we worked with our doctors, trying a number of medications (types, dosages, combinations) to 'get it right.' Getting the correct titrations (timing and exact amounts) on these medications has always been difficult in Adam's case. Too much or too little at different times results in major activity and mood swings. This is an ongoing project—we anticipate changes as his body changes, and we have been forewarned that he may rebel entirely against taking medications as he gets older." (See Section 1.4, Medication Treatment and Management.)

Ongoing Communication Between Home/School/Clinicians

Adam's mother has maintained close communication with his schools each year. The following is an example of a letter Adam's mother wrote that was sent to all of his middle school teachers—asking for their help to track his behavior by time of day/different class periods. "The primary goal was to provide feedback to the physician in titration of his medication. The secondary goal was to keep Adam on his teachers' radar screen." (See Section 5.1, Teaming for Success: Communication, Collaboration, and Mutual Support.)

Dear _____ (lists all teachers),

To help us track Adam's in-class behavior, and to ensure he is receiving appropriate medications, would you please be good enough to observe his behavior daily over a week's time and mark your observations on the attached Conners' Scale?

If you would kindly return it in the attached self-addressed stamped envelope, I would be most appreciative. As Adam grows and changes in his new middle school environment, our goal is to help him achieve continued success in your classroom. Many thanks for your cooperation.

Sincerely,

Parent's signature

Cc: Physician

Vincent (Seventeen Years Old, High School Senior)

In the following case study, Vincent's mother is the historian and narrator, and these are her words.

Medical History

Vincent is the older of two children in our family, the result of a planned pregnancy with appropriate prenatal care. He was born full-term, and his weight was within normal limits. As an infant, Vincent received all appropriate medical care and timely immunizations. He suffered from ear infections and upper respiratory infections during infancy, and was treated with numerous rounds of oral antibiotics until P.E. tubes were surgically inserted at age eighteen months, after which his health improved. Sinus infections, allergies, and strep infections were identified and treated in early childhood and the primary grades, with less frequent episodes of upper respiratory continuing into adolescence. Irritable bowel syndrome was identified and treatment with anti-spasmodic medication followed an acute episode when Vincent was about nine years of age. Gastroesophogeal reflux was identified in about the seventh grade. Allergies persisted and Vincent continues to take daily medications to prevent/treat them. Vision and hearing have been tested regularly, and no problems have been identified in those areas. Vincent's academic and behavioral progress is described in the social/educational narrative here.

Social/Educational History (Narrative)

Vincent's behavioral issues were noted first with feeding problems, jaundice, and tremors in early infancy. He began to be able to feed well within a few days; he responded well to phototherapy and the jaundice resolved. A pediatric neurologist who saw Vincent at two months of age stated that the tremors might be what was called "twilight tremors," noted when a baby is waking up, and otherwise, Vincent appeared to be functioning within normal limits. At about eighteen months of age, Vincent began experiencing what is referred to as "night terrors," a sort of "gear-shift problem" in the brain that typically occurs when the child is making the transition from one phase of sleep to another (for example, from deep sleep to lighter sleep phases that include more motoric activity). These "night terrors" went away before Vincent was three years of age.

Vincent achieved all developmental milestones, including toilet training, within normal limits. He did not tantrum at a rate above what would be expected for his age, but he was observed to have great difficulty calming down once he was upset. It was observed that if he could not calm himself within about five minutes, he was unlikely to be able to do so even an hour later without parental intervention such as holding or rocking. Vincent was observed to have a vocabulary that was within normal limits (that is, he was not observed to be precocious in any way), although visitors frequently commented on the clarity of his articulation. Other than his "night terrors" and difficulty with calming down, he appeared to be a "regular kid," but "quirky." That is, if one *only* considered developmental milestones. . . .

Some of Vincent's "quirks" included a tendency to avoid eye contact with people, a resistance to being touched, a tendency not to smile much, a tendency to resist changes in his routine or his environment, overreaction to emotions like joy or anger (for example, if he got "really happy," he'd become so "silly" that he'd hurt himself or others and he appeared not to be able to calm himself down; in fact, it almost appeared that he had to *cry* to get calmed down). These "quirks" became much more pronounced as he got older, and these behaviors became more "discrepant" from his peers' behavior. For example, we could do a lot of "prevention-work" to assure that Vincent would not become overaroused, but the avoidance of eye contact began to be labeled as "attitude" and "disrespect" by his teachers and grandparents and perceived as "aloofness," "coldness," or "haughtiness" by peers.

Another behavior noted at the time was that Vincent was extremely "picky" about the texture of his clothing. He would "chafe" at materials that seemed to "itch" him, and would refuse to wear (or would take off, as soon as he was able) clothing that contained tags, "bumpy" seams, or even button-plackets. Certain socks, for example, or polo shirts that had a few buttons on the chest, would irritate him to the point of distraction. Nowadays, some professionals would suggest that Vincent was suffering from what is referred to as a sensory processing disorder or sensory integration disorder, but information of that type was not readily available at that time. At this time, such disorders are still considered speculative, and there is a need for more scientific study of these behaviors.

At age two, a caregiver remarked that Vincent was particularly "selfish" and "grabby" in his Mother's Day Out program. We replied that it was our understanding that it was developmentally appropriate for children not to "share" until about age three, and that a more reasonable expectation was that a two-year-old could "take turns" (the developmental precursor to "sharing"). However, at age three, four, and five, Vincent was observed across many settings, such as church, school, home, and in public, to have continued difficulty with "taking turns," much less "sharing." Behaviorally, he appeared to have increasing problems with impulsive grabbing, pushing, "bossing," following directions, accepting changes in routine, and hyperactivity. The older he became, the more apparent the social discrepancy between Vincent and his peers became.

Vincent was fortunate to have a remarkable preschool teacher (Ms. JH) who, in addition to excellent communication with us, documented examples of the behaviors that would help our family as we sought diagnostic help in later years. This teacher communicated in meaningful ways to Vincent that he was a valuable human being, and she employed some noteworthy teaching strategies.

Modeling the desired behavior. Each day, Ms. JH gathered the children and then simply and briefly outlined what was going to happen that day. For example, if they were going to be spreading peanut butter on crackers in an "interest center," she demonstrated the proper use of the knife and how to avoid spreading germs, and so forth. This type of modeling not only helped Vincent to adjust to changes, but it helped him (and all the children, for that matter) to know what behavior was expected and how to behave well.

Music. Another particularly effective strategy was her use of song to aid in gaining the children's attention and in easing transitions from one activity to another. While her songs were not typical ones for most classrooms, it was amazing to see how the rhythm of a song like "Johnny Be Good" (made popular by Chuck Berry) could result in the rhythmic picking up of blocks.

While not specifically observed at preschool, Vincent responded fairly well to the following interventions at home:

* *"Broken record" and "rehearsal."* We had to "give ourselves permission" to repeat behavior rules over and over and over, like a broken record. This was rather difficult, at first, as we had grown up with the idea that you should not have to repeat rules that a child of normal intelligence should already know. It became apparent that Vincent did *know* the rules, but he exhibited great difficulty *"retrieving"* them on demand. In other words, he *knew* the rule, he just wasn't *using* the rule to help govern his behavior. The "broken record" or "rehearsal" approach seemed to help him, especially before the event occurred. For example, we would rehearse, "The blocks stay in your hand." If he got excited and threw a block, he was calmly told the rule again (broken record) as an appropriate consequence was applied. In this case, we put away the blocks and tried again on another day.
* *"When/then" statements (also known as Grandma's Rule).* "When you finish your dinner, then you get dessert." Not only did this help with motivation, it helped with making the transition to the next activity.

* *Enjoyable challenges.* He enjoyed a race with himself (not competitive with others), such as racing an egg timer to complete a task.

* *Obstacle course.* Vincent also responded well to "obstacle course," a game that we played to help him learn to keep multi-step commands in his head. We would start with one step, and then increase the number of steps in the command as he became successful with remembering what he was supposed to do. He enjoyed this game immensely, and while we don't have much evidence to prove it, we believe that it helped him with remembering classroom routines (such as "Take off your coat, hang it up, go to your desk, sit down, and get out your pencil."), and much later, when remembering rules to complex math problems!

* *Novelty and complexity.* This strategy sounds strange, but Vincent always acted like he was trying to "feed his brain." That is, he was "hungry" for stimulation. While he'd settle for "good" stimulation or "bad" stimulation (like getting in trouble), he behaved best and "stayed focused" longest when his brain was "fed" with a moderate amount of novelty and complexity. We found if a situation was too familiar ("boring") or too simple (like copying easy words on paper while sitting in a chair), he'd lose interest and behave poorly. On the other hand, if the situation was too novel or too complex (like playing an unfamiliar game with lots of rules), he'd become overwhelmed and quit. However, we could spark his interest and he could maintain appropriate amounts of attention when the task was given "just a twist" of novelty. For example, he did better copying when he did it in sand, on special-shaped paper, standing up at an easel, or other ways like that. Or instead of copying the word, he'd write a word, widely spaced, in the middle of a sheet of paper and then he'd trace around each letter with a series of colored pencils, so that when completed, it looked like a rainbow. It was kind of like the old story of the three bears: not too hot, not too cold, but just right! Of course, because Vincent seemed to need more novelty than other children, we often felt like he was riding on one of those "people-mover" conveyor belts at the airport and we were running alongside him, placing new challenges just in front of him! We had to "keep our running shoes on" with him, but his love of learning made it all worthwhile. It was fun!

* *Simplifying tasks.* If a task was too complex, as we mentioned above, Vincent seemed overwhelmed. Vincent responded best to performing complex tasks, such as cleaning up his room, when the task was broken into smaller interesting parts such as attribute-recognition: "Find all the things with *wheels*" or "Pick up all the blocks that are *long*."

* *Social scripts.* Another type of rehearsal that we called "script rehearsal" was used frequently. He responded fairly well to rehearsal of "scripts" for social situations; for example, we would practice saying "No, thank you" to an offer of asparagus, instead of "Gross, those are slimy!" Please note, however, we are *still* working on that.

In kindergarten, Vincent "touched everything" and was constantly "fiddling." He was in an educational setting that promoted the idea that a child was "self-regulating" and would learn certain things as he became ready to learn them. Later we realized that he was one of a sub-group of children who *don't* self-regulate very easily and for whom certain educational aspects were *not* going to be mastered by "readiness" alone. For example, Vincent avoided any tasks that involved writing, but he did not avoid all fine-motor tasks. Vincent was exceptionally good at puzzles and linking blocks like Legos. Therefore, his writing problems were considered to be "developmental." His teacher described him as "bright, but immature," and recommended that he repeat kindergarten. While we agreed with his very kind teacher, who actually had described him accurately, we chose not to accept that recommendation, for the reason that he seemed "bored" and we were concerned that he would be even more "bored" the following year.

Instead of repeating kindergarten, Vincent was enrolled in a "developmental" first-grade class, which in retrospect was not a good decision for our particular child. He continued to be "bored" and he continued to be labeled "immature." We pursued additional testing in the second half of that year, as Vincent seemed "miserable." It was determined that he was functioning intellectually just fine. His fine-motor skills were technically okay; in other words, he passed developmental and psycho-educational testing. It was noted that Vincent was not reading yet, at age seven, but it was considered to be a "developmental problem," and "time" was offered as the only intervention. In response to our increasing awareness that something was interfering with Vincent's ability to function well, and our concerns about possible ADHD, his developmental first-grade teacher told us, "If Vincent has ADHD, then every other child in my class has ADHD!" We continued to seek information and support for an increasingly unhappy but intelligent child. (See Section 1.8, ADHD in Preschool and Kindergarten.)

Diagnosis, Part I

A diagnosis of ADHD was made by a neurologist in the summer between developmental first grade and first grade, and he was prescribed stimulant medication. We could tell on the first day of the medication trial that Vincent was helped by the medication. It was a tremendous relief. We now had a "name" for what was troubling Vincent, and we could get some help for him. When Vincent calmed down, it seemed like our whole family calmed down. However, that was not the end of our story and, unfortunately, we did not live happily ever after with the aid of modern pharmacology.

Behavioral challenges continued, in spite of a reduction in the symptoms of hyperactivity, distractibility, and fluctuating attention. Eye contact problems and social skills problems persisted. Academically, Vincent seemed to improve dramatically, especially in his reading skills, but he demonstrated significant problems with handwriting, spelling, punctuation, and grammar.

About that time, we joined CHADD, a national support group for children and adults with ADHD and related disorders. (See Section 5.1, Teaming for

Success: Communication, Collaboration, and Mutual Support.) We learned that most people with ADHD respond best when they are supported by three things:

* Up-to-date diagnosis/appropriate medical help
* Appropriate educational supports
* Appropriate emotional support/counseling/therapeutic interventions (See Section 1.3, Multimodal Treatments for ADHD.)

At a CHADD meeting, we heard that appropriate support for a person with ADHD can be compared to a three-legged stool. A three-legged stool cannot stand up if one of the legs is missing. We were fortunate that we had access to all three of those factors, and we have relied on them in varying degrees over the years.

While it would be untrue, in a strict sense, to say that we valued one of the "legs" more than another, it is absolutely true when we say that we relied on educational supports and interventions more often than the other two supports. This statement becomes logical when one considers that Vincent was in school or doing homework for the majority of his waking hours.

In the section below on helpful educational supports, we have combined supports that happen primarily at school with supports that were implemented primarily at home. This is because many of the items were shared at home and at school, or they led from one setting to the other.

First- Through Third-Grade Educational Supports

* *Positive outlook of teacher.* We placed the most difficult-to-define feature of support first in this list because it, by far, has made the most difference for Vincent. After years of partnering with teachers, we can say that those teachers who were able to withhold judgmental behavior and find "something positive" in each child in their classrooms were the teachers who were able to help Vincent find "the positive" in himself. In our case, it wasn't always the kind of positive we'd expect, and in some cases, it was just plain funny! For example, when Vincent was in the second grade, he dictated the caption for a photograph of him showing off a "city" they'd built during a class project. The caption read "I'm *good* with cardboard!"

    We are not saying that a teacher must never get tired or frustrated or dislike a particular child's poor hygiene or always feel happy. That is not realistic; we know that teachers are human beings too. But positive outlook, for us and for Vincent, was communicated as respect for the child as a worthwhile human being, one who has something meaningful to offer the world. For at least one child, "cardboard" is meaningful. Those moments of "positive outlook" have served us as a sort of "booster shot" of self-esteem; they have tided Vincent over many moments of discouragement and doubt. (See Section 1.6, Critical Factors in the Success of Students with ADHD.)

* *Facilitation of medication monitoring.* While this does not sound like an accommodation, our experience has been that teachers have been critical

partners in helping us and his physicians determine the appropriate type, dosage, and timing of Vincent's medication. One morning in first grade, Vincent was accidentally sent to school without having taken his morning medication. His teacher called at about 9:00 a.m., stating, "I don't know what is wrong with Vincent, and he isn't hurting anybody, but he is rolling around on the floor under his desk, giggling." Over the years, we have gained invaluable information from different teachers who were sensitive observers of their students. (See Section 1.4, Medication Treatment and Management.)

* *Allowing Vincent to stand at his desk or lie down to work when appropriate.* We quickly learned that the typical recommendation of positioning the student with ADHD close to the teacher can be difficult to implement if the classroom is set up traditionally, with the teacher at the front of the class and the students in rows of desks. In addition to the likelihood that an average classroom contains more than one student with ADHD, and the difficulty that comes when trying to place all of those students near the teacher, Vincent, being rather tall, would have caused visual disruption to the class if he were allowed to stand. In consulting with the teacher, we learned that he seemed to need to stand or lie down, particularly when working on writing tasks or after fairly long periods of seatwork. So in most cases, the teacher arranged for *everyone* to have that option, so it "normalized" the process and it seemed like everyone was happier. We learned, over the course of time, that it was less important for Vincent to be seated close to the teacher than it was for him to be positioned where he could not be a visual distraction to other students, and that contact and encouragement from the teacher was best facilitated when the teacher moved around the room and provided contact and encouragement to *all* the students. (See Section 2.1, Classroom Management and Positive Discipline Practices, and Section 3.3, Reaching Students Through Their Learning Styles and Multiple Intelligences.)

* *Allowing him to hold things or touch things or chew things that did not make noise.* While this appeared to be allowing "immature" behavior, and one teacher found it to be quite distasteful to her, personally, we advocated that he be allowed to continue this "bad habit." We had found, via generally good home/school communications, that when he wasn't allowed to chew his pencil, he was being more disruptive to the learning environment, such as talking to his neighbor or blurting out anything that came to his mind or tapping on the desk or humming to himself. So in the interest of minimizing classroom disruptions, Vincent was able to hold, touch, or mouth objects as long as they did not make any noise. (See Section 3.3, Reaching Students Through Their Learning Styles and Multiple Intelligences.)

* *Staying by teacher for transitions.* One of the things we learned very quickly with our child was that he tended to have more problems with behavior during the transition from one activity to another or from one place to another (for example, in going to the library or to "specials" like music class). During those times, Vincent did seem to need extra support from the teacher as

to what to do with his hands, his feet, or other items, so having him assist the teacher and stay close to her was extremely helpful. It became clear to the other students that Vincent was "special," and like a child who experienced mobility problems and required special assistance, they quickly realized and accepted the fact that "fair doesn't always mean equal" and were very gracious about the situation. (See Section 2.2, Preventing or Minimizing Behavior Problems During Transitions and Less Structured Times of the School Day, and Section 2.1, Classroom Management and Positive Discipline Practices.)

* *Proactive playground and cafeteria supervision.* After careful observation, it became clear that behavioral problems tended to happen more often when Vincent was in low-supervision situations. Communication with key individuals at the school resulted in subtle changes in monitoring of those settings so that any emerging problems could be "nipped in the bud." (See Section 2.2, Preventing or Minimizing Behavior Problems During Transitions and Less Structured Times of the School Day.)

* *Providing a "homework" folder.* This folder consisted of assignments and notes to come home in one section and things to be completed/returned in the other section. As Vincent got older, a "planner" or "agenda" took its place.

* *Keeping the backpack by the front door.* Our house probably looked a wreck to visitors, but this strategy made all the difference to us. Our efforts to get a child with ADHD up and out the door in the morning resulted in trying out every bit of organizational support that we could find. This really worked for us. After homework time, it went back to the front door.

* *Parent sitting with him to do homework.* While this does not appear to be reasonable or doable for some families, it was critical for us. Early on, Vincent could not stay seated in a chair, much less focus on directions or written assignments.

* *Providing a designated place, time, and stuff for homework.* We stored all necessary/useful items in a portable box, what the author refers to as a "homework survival kit." With a child like ours, we could not afford to have any distractions like getting up to find a stapler or something. If we did, we had to "start over" with the whole process. (See Section 3.5, Organization, Time Management, and Study Skills Strategies.)

* *We made a real commitment not to answer the phone during this time.* This effort was made harder by the negative response of friends, family, and coworkers, but eventually everyone adjusted to this commitment.

* *Reduced written assignments, especially for rote tasks like copying spelling words.* Even with a parent sitting with Vincent, we found that he took about two hours (this is not an exaggeration) to complete what should have been twenty minutes' worth of work. Instead of copying a word three times, he copied it once. (See Section 3.7, Writing and Reading Challenges for Students with ADHD.)

* *If written assignments were not completed within allotted class time, then allow extra time or send them home.* This was a trickier accommodation to

pull off in reality than we expected. In one case, Vincent had a teacher who, for whatever reason, thought that giving him extra time to complete an assignment meant "allowing" him to finish it during recess. To Vincent, and to us, this was perceived as punishment, so we immediately requested that the work be sent home with him. For a child who has significant problems with "production," having work sent home can be an incredible burden on an already-stressed family. As a result, we have become stronger advocates of the "quality, not quantity" theory, in which we ask, "If the child can show you what he knows, why would he need to demonstrate it five times over?" We never did completely solve the "within class time" problem, but we tried to balance the reduction of written work with extra time or bringing the work home. (See Section 3.5, Organization, Time Management, and Study Skills Strategies.)

* *Allowing Vincent to dictate instead of writing, when possible.* At this stage, in the primary grades, this was fairly easy to accomplish. We have learned some lovely things about Vincent's creative mind that we'd never have seen if he'd had to write the words himself. (See Section 3.8, Written Language Strategies, Accommodations, and Interventions: Pre-Planning/Organizing, Spelling, Handwriting, Assistive Technology.)

* *"Earnings" for progress.* "Earnings" were things that Vincent would select, with our help, to reward himself for small successes. This was a strictly voluntary process for our son. For example, Vincent might choose to have a sip of his drink for every three spelling words he copied. Or he might get to put an animal cracker into a cup to eat after his homework was finished. He could see the animal crackers pile up (to five or six) and he would be very pleased with his progress. (This process was carefully set up and monitored and under no circumstances could we take away what he'd earned once he'd earned it, even if his behavior "fell apart" five minutes later. This is a crucial aspect of "earnings," in our opinion, and involves basic respect).

Fourth and Fifth Grades and Diagnosis, Part II

Academically, Vincent struggled with "production problems"; that is, he was clearly bright but he was not able to produce quality written work. His teachers appeared to be very frustrated, and the terms "lazy," "smart, but inconsistent in his work," and "undisciplined" began to creep into communications with us. Vincent became increasingly oppositional and discouraged during this period (fourth grade, in particular), both at home and in school.

In the fifth grade, we began seeking further assessment, suspecting learning disabilities, as Vincent's writing skills appeared to be at about a second-grade level (a three-year discrepancy between his grade level and his performance). The assessments in the fifth grade revealed that Vincent was, indeed, struggling with learning disabilities. We pursued an Individualized Education Plan via the local public schools, and Vincent finished fifth grade with accommodations in place for specific learning disabilities in the area of "written expression."

Sixth Through Twelve Grades

(See Section 1.9, ADHD in Middle School and High School.) Vincent was accepted into one of our city's magnet schools, which included students from sixth through twelfth grade. We were very fearful of the idea of communicating with eight teachers (even more when we counted the special services faculty and therapists and administrators). However, we discovered a few things that relieved our anxiety tremendously and helped us to ensure that Vincent would not flounder at this level of his education.

First, we discovered that Vincent would have a "case manager" who would serve as an excellent point of contact. In our case, Vincent's case manager was a learning disabilities teacher, but we have since come to believe that a great middle school point of contact could be any teacher or staff member who cares about your child and is willing to serve as an informal liaison between home and school. This could be a librarian, a vice principal, or an administrative assistant—anyone who is a good communicator. In other words, a good point of contact, in our opinion, does not always need to be someone in a position of formal authority at the school. Vincent's LD teacher, Ms. B., incidentally, never actually had him in her classroom as he was able to be "mainstreamed" in every subject. Ms. B. became a mentor to Vincent, a communication facilitator, an advocate for him, and served as a "reality check" for us at home if and when we faced difficulties. She was wonderful.

Second, after making several mistakes in communicating with the faculty in his elementary school and after coming to feel that we had slid into an adversarial role with his teachers in the fourth and fifth grades, we knew we needed to adjust our own communication strategies and come up with a better way of advocating for our child. After some real soul-searching, it became evident that we had been saying something to this effect: "*What can* you *do to help our child learn?*" This statement seemed to cause teachers and others to feel defensive and resentful and, more often than not, brought out resistance in teachers rather than the kind of assistance we were seeking. In looking back over some truly awful episodes, we realized that we needed to find non-threatening ways to advocate for Vincent. So we began to ask teachers "*How can* we help you *help Vincent to learn?*"

This seemingly small change in wording became a critical change of strategy for us, and it helped us to re-establish the kind of rapport that we wanted. That is, by asking how we could help the teacher, instead of demanding that the teacher help us, we could all relax and enjoy being united in our concern for Vincent's success in school. "Help for the teacher" was generally interpreted, it appeared, to mean that we respected the difficulty of the teacher's task, that we wanted to support him or her, not drain precious energy or make overwhelming demands. While we were never asked to do anything that was outside of our ability to do, we *were* asked to

* Assist the teacher by providing as much information as we could about Vincent.
* Arrange communication routes that fit the teacher's routine.

✳ Let the teacher know as soon as possible if it appeared that Vincent was beginning to struggle in or outside of class (including things like sleeping problems). (See Section 5.1, Teaming for Success: Communication, Collaboration, and Mutual Support.)

The third thing that made all the difference for us during middle school (and on) was making sure that we had the most effective Individualized Education Plan that we could. (See Section 5.4, Educational Laws and Rights of Students with ADHD.)

Truthfully, this took more work than we expected, given that we were both working full-time and raising two children and dealing with everyday challenges of life in an ADHD household. We attended workshops offered by our local Parent Training Center to learn about the rules and regulations for the different types of plans for which our child might be eligible (each state has at least one office, and they provide support and training for parents at regional sites). We went to a couple of conferences and fairs that had to do with children with special needs (in fact, it was at one such fair that we found out about all the assistive technology that was available, such as specialized computers), and we talked to other parents to find out what had helped their children. We checked books out of the library or borrowed them from our local chapter of CHADD. We tried to anticipate every resource that would help prevent problems or nip them in the bud. Our goal was that Vincent, who was bright but seemed "allergic" to school and homework and even the social demands of school life, would not just "survive," but maybe even thrive in his new school!

The IEP: Vincent's Individualized Education Plan included the following list of symptoms and the relevant accommodations:

1. Works very slowly, cannot finish assignments and tests during time allotted.
   Accommodations: Provide extended time for classroom assignments and tests.
2. Handwriting problems.
   Accommodations: Provide *AlphaSmart* word processor (laptop) for keyboarding in class.
   Accept typed work in lieu of written work.
   Occupational therapy X hours per week.
3. Frequent spelling, grammar, punctuation errors.
   Accommodations: Do not count off for spelling, etc., errors unless specifically being tested on those subjects.
   Allow Vincent to edit in-class work.
4. Disorganization.
   Accommodations: Teacher to provide written back-up notes and assignments.
   Structure activities and transitions to prevent confusion.
5. Problems following directions.
   Accommodations: Give Vincent extra time to process directions or requests.

6. Problems maintaining proper behavior.
   Accommodations: Ignore negative vocalizations unless determined to be abusive.
   Allow extra time for Vincent to attempt to calm himself if upset.
   If unable to calm within two or three minutes, employ "Safety Net" where Vincent leaves class and goes to specified school places/personnel.
   Provide positive reinforcement for his efforts.
   Do not touch Vincent without his permission.
7. Medical problems, for example, irritable bowel syndrome.
   Accommodations: Allow Vincent to discretely notify teacher and leave class to use restroom as needed.

Discipline

We have already mentioned his LD teacher, but it is vital to add that she was the one who helped us put our ideas for Vincent's IEP into appropriate wording and into measurable terms in order to comply with local, state, and federal guidelines. She helped to educate her colleagues about Vincent and his IEP and kept us informed every step of the way. Perhaps most importantly, after the drafting of Vincent's IEP, she also helped Vincent improve his behavior by being gentle but firm about her expectations for him. She became Vincent's "Number One Safety Net"; he was to go to her class first if he became too upset to remain in the classroom. Incidentally, Vincent only needed to employ his Safety Net a few times in all his years at the school, in large part because of this teacher's care and concern. However, she was not Vincent's *only* fantastic teacher. And to be blunt, some of the best teacher-supports came from the teachers we least suspected.

Avoiding Power Struggles

Vincent's seventh-grade history teacher appeared to be the strictest teacher on earth, and Vincent seemed to "butt heads" with this teacher, Mr. C., on the very first day of school. When we visited with Mr. C., we learned that he expected all his students, when responding to a question, to stand at their desks, look at the teacher, and articulate as clearly as they could. Vincent had difficulty making eye contact with the teacher, but Mr. C., with unbelievable wisdom, chose not to confront Vincent about it. Rather than approaching and looming over Vincent, which would have likely resulted in a "fight or flight" response from Vincent, Mr. C. backed up, *away* from Vincent, so that Vincent had to lift his chin and head to even gaze in the general direction of the teacher. By stepping back, Mr. C. could also pretend that he could not hear Vincent; and in order to project his voice better, Vincent had to look up and raise his chin. Mr. C. helped Vincent to begin to communicate better, first, making it a normal expectation for everyone in the class; second, by thinking through how to obtain the desired behavior; and third, by refraining from a power struggle or the use of shame or intimidation. Mr. C. not only had the best-behaved classes in the school, and students who learned to respect each other and respect each other's opinions, but his enthusiasm for history and the self-discipline necessary for scholarship were contagious. We can't say that Vincent quit complaining about doing homework, but he began to express a love of learning that he'd not shared in some time. (See Section 2.3, Individualized Behavior Management, Interventions, and Supports.)

Assistive Technology

We had learned about *AlphaSmart,* a remarkably affordable type of word processor that looks similar to a laptop computer, at a "health fair" for individuals with special needs. There are probably other varieties of this technology, but they likely share the essential feature of allowing students with disabilities to enter information into them and then recover that information at a later time. The *AlphaSmart* was attractive to us because, in addition to it being practically indestructible, it featured (at that time) eight different word processing files that the student could access with the touch of one key. Vincent could have one file for each class. For example, Vincent could open up his English class file at a touch; he could type notes into the file, then bring it home and "dump the data" either to a computer or a printer almost instantaneously. We must admit that when we first asked about it, through Vincent's occupational therapist, she indicated that she did not know what we were talking about! However, we were pleasant but firm about wanting to access this possible resource, and persistent in advocating that the school "go up the ladder" a little bit. We quickly learned that an *AlphaSmart* could be loaned to us by our school district, along with the simple cable that allowed the data to be "dumped." This was to become a real relief to us, once Vincent started using it. At first, he was concerned about "looking different" from the other students, a valid concern, but when he actually began to use it (out of desperation), he found out that it became a status symbol! All the other students wanted one! Overall, this resource turned out to be even better than we expected. (See Section 3.8, Written Language Strategies, Accommodations, and Interventions: Pre-Planning/Organizing, Spelling, Handwriting, Assistive Technology.) Our only regret was that we had to "educate educators" in order to access it. It was disconcerting to find that we, as parents, knew more about some resources for our child than our child's therapist did. We had been "trained" to believe that professionals in a position of authority were experts and should never be questioned. However, the experience taught us to be patient and to consider that we had strong motivation to seek out resources for our particular child. In the meanwhile, teachers and therapists and other professionals were, out of necessity, focused on groups of children, not on one particular child's needs. We learned the importance of sharing our knowledge politely and the importance of not underestimating our own ability to serve as advocates for our child. As a lovely teacher (who was also the parent of a child with ADHD) once reassured us, "If *you* don't advocate for your child, who will?"

Note-Taker in Math

Vincent had a truly challenging time copying off the board, and the assistive technology that was provided for us could not meet his needs in algebra and geometry classes, as he needed to copy mathematical terms and equations. At our request, his teacher discreetly found a capable student who was willing to take the class notes using carbonless paper (one type is called an NCR form), which can be purchased from printing companies or even copy shops like Kinko's. After the student took notes on this special paper, he kept the original and gave Vincent the copy each day. This accommodation worked remarkably well; the only factor that gave us any concern, initially, was confidentiality. However, his teacher was very thoughtful about it and educated the note-taking student about the importance of privacy. The boys became friends.

Drama

Vincent was only mildly interested in this subject at first, but at the recommendation of his counselor, he enrolled in a drama class. Vincent made good, if sporadic, progress socially and in his maturity, under the tutelage of his drama teacher. Because it was a small drama program, he worked with the same teacher for five years. This could have become a problem, because he entered the class in the sixth grade after a couple of years with teachers whom he felt he could not trust. Given the types of activities that usually take place in a drama class, activities that require the student to feel safe and secure in extending himself or herself and "take risks," Ms. MW certainly had her work cut out for her! As Ms. MW taught Vincent, she patiently built trust with him, and she balanced her nurturing with appropriate doses of constructive criticism, challenging him to "stretch" to meet higher and higher levels of performance, understanding, behavior, and teamwork. While Vincent experienced some of his most spectacular social failures in her class, and he suffered tremendous personal agony at those times, he also gained important skills. He learned how to "take direction," become more introspective, take responsibility for his behavior, become a real team player, and how to get back up and dust himself off and try again, even when he made (sometimes humiliating) mistakes. As it turned out, five years with the same teacher was probably not enough! He has gone on to work with two other stellar drama teachers, but he will probably always describe his first drama teacher as one of the most powerfully positive influences in his life.

Creativity, Empathy, Care, and Concern in Teaching

Vincent had another excellent teacher, but as with the other teachers we've mentioned, things started out "rocky." His school required a foreign language early on, and each sixth grader took a course that provided an overview of French, Spanish, and Latin. Vincent decided he'd prefer to take Latin in the seventh grade. We were horrified because we knew that Latin was primarily a written language, and Vincent had trouble writing or spelling or forming proper sentences in English, much less in Latin! We tried to discourage him from pursuing what we considered a suicide course, but he, very logically, stated that if he wanted to become a doctor or a scientist some day, he'd be best served by knowing Latin (and Greek) so that he could understand all the terminology! How could we argue with that? Well, as it turned out, Dr. G., the Latin teacher, was probably more concerned than we were. We went to visit with her, and sensing

Dr. G.'s hesitation to work with Vincent, we tried to take things slowly in an attempt to avoid an adversarial relationship. We asked about her approach to teaching the class, which turned out, to our pleasant surprise, to sound quite inviting! Dr. G.'s use of story, games, and the planned class explorations of cultures and history and architecture sounded wonderful to our ears. She mentioned some of the trips that she and her husband, a well-respected French teacher, took to Europe frequently. As she talked about their experiences in other cultures, she mentioned an expression in France that is loosely interpreted as "being comfortable in one's skin." "That describes Vincent!" we replied. "Only in his case, he has *never* felt 'comfortable in his own skin'!" From that moment on, she seemed to "understand," or at least have empathy for Vincent. Dr. G. had a wry sense of humor that Vincent truly enjoyed, and while he was probably never her best student, with creativity on her part, he was able to master it well enough to earn A's and B's in the subject over the subsequent three years. One of our favorite memories of this period in his life is this: At a school open house one year, Dr. G. quietly remarked that she was informally using some of the accommodations/supports she'd used with Vincent with another student, with great success! While Vincent's original reason for taking Latin may be long forgotten, we reaped the benefits of a teacher whose love of scholarly endeavors was contagious, and whose care and concern for her students extended well beyond what was required by law.

Medication

We feel strongly that Vincent would not have been able to pay a bit of "attention" to any of his teachers or learned any of the important lessons he needed to learn without taking the stimulant medications he was prescribed. See the next item in the list, for an example that convinced us.

Good Communication

In addition to the wonderful Ms. B. (Vincent's case manager/LD teacher), we were impressed with communications in general. Vincent's teachers sandwiched their occasional concerns between so many encouraging comments that we gradually lost our sense of "phone phobia" (that fear of answering the telephone that many parents of children with ADHD develop). Anyhow, toward the winter break of sixth grade, Ms. C., Vincent's English teacher, called, saying that for the previous three weeks, he had failed every quiz and not turned in any assignments! When we questioned Vincent about it, we learned that he had been placing his medication each morning on a little ledge ("lip") under the kitchen table. We discovered precisely fifteen tablets on that ledge! When we assessed the situation with Vincent, he told us that he only wanted to be able to "control himself," since we had been telling him for years that it was his responsibility to control his own behavior. This was a real dilemma, in a tragically funny sort of way, as we attempted to find a balance between the reality that he had a problem in his brain that he could not solve with willpower alone and our stated expectation that he take responsibility for his behavior and that he engage in appropriate self-discipline. After learning that he was "crashing" in his English class, he agreed to begin taking his medication again. Later, he painfully referred to that self-imposed experiment as "The Time of the Very Bad Idea." We prefer to think of that time as an important experience that we'd not have had without good communication with his school. (See Section 1.4, Medication Treatment and Management.)

Behavioral Plan

Vincent's success in school was also supported by a thoughtful behavioral plan. (See Section 2.3, Individualized Behavior Management, Interventions, and Supports.) By the time he entered sixth grade, we knew that he'd never been involved in aggression in which he instigated the problem. Rather, he was observed to be highly reactive to other people's aggressive acts. However, we very quickly learned that, in school, it does not matter who "started the trouble," all participants are guilty and must be punished! We already had a good idea of the situations in which he could get into trouble (see notes from his elementary years as well). His IEP included the following plan: If Vincent began to get upset or too frustrated, he would be given a special card, shaped like a regular business card, which he was to place on his desk if he needed to leave the room to employ his "Safety Net." Vincent's "Safety Net" was a series of places he could go to calm himself down. In his case, his number one place was his home/school liaison, Ms. B.'s class. His number two place, in case Ms. B. was not available, was his history teacher, with whom he had excellent rapport. He had three other steps in his Safety Net, in the event that the first two "steps" were not available. It should be mentioned that while Vincent was in excellent hands, academically, he was attending an inner-city magnet school in a neighborhood very concerned with gang violence and drug/alcohol abuse. As a result, at his school, students were not typically allowed to be unescorted anywhere in the building during class time, so this accommodation was not given lightly.

Naturally, Vincent was expected not to abuse this accommodation by going anywhere except the places he was authorized to go. He was also expected to be the one to monitor his own emotional state and to employ his Safety Net before he got into trouble. This was a big responsibility. As he grew, the "players" in his Safety Net changed a little, but the plan remained unchanged. Over the years, Vincent only needed to employ his Safety Net a few times, and he never needed to employ steps three, four, or five. However, having that plan in place, we believe, gave him the sense that he had safe options when his emotions overcame his ability to function in the classroom.

In addition to having problems with calming down if he became frustrated or upset, and problems with his behavior during transition times, we were aware that he seemed to be "hyper-reactive" to being touched. This was particularly evident when he was touched by surprise (such as someone approaching him from behind and laying a hand on his shoulder or poking him) or when someone got too close to him (such as a person approaching him rapidly, "getting in his face" or shaking a finger in his face). Unfortunately, Vincent would usually respond to those behaviors in a reflexive flash. In the case of being touched or bumped from behind, he'd typically whip around with his arm extended or, if he perceived threat from the front, he'd fling his arms up in a reactive attempt to protect himself. We were afraid that if he responded that way to a teacher or administrator, he could accidentally hit someone and then he'd be accused of assault! In order to prevent those possibilities from becoming horrifying realities, we asked that teachers remain at least three feet away from him and gain his specific permission before touching him. At the same time, we instructed Vincent to place his hands in his pockets whenever he felt "pressed" by another's physical presence and to take literal steps backward if he could. The hands-in-pockets rule was especially effective with peers, and in one isolated occasion, it saved him from real trouble with an administrator who chose not to comply with the behavioral terms of his IEP. The administrator was held accountable, by the way.

Another behavioral aspect of Vincent's plan was handled beautifully, in our opinion. He had been diagnosed with irritable bowel syndrome, which can include bouts of diarrhea. In order to accommodate for this potentially embarrassing problem, all he had to do was put the same Safety Net card on his desk and he was able to leave the room to go to the restroom.

Finally, we knew that Vincent had problems with blurting out impulsive statements, which he'd always want to "take back" the moment he'd considered the wisdom of the statement. While we are confident that his medication has helped him become less impulsive, and we can't imagine how many inappropriate things he'd say if he wasn't taking his medication, he still struggles with this problem. So we asked that his teachers ignore impulsive comments (usually groans or sighs about an assignment, or an under-his-breath muttered complaint that it was boring) unless it was directly abusive. That is, if the statement broke a school rule, such as cursing or threatening, then clearly it should not be ignored. Vincent was never to be allowed to break a school rule, but impulsive groans of discontent were not violations of a rule. They were just annoying.

This was potentially a difficult situation in that Vincent's inappropriate comments could, theoretically, disrupt the learning environment for everyone. We carefully reasoned that if the teacher ignored his impulsive comment (which Vincent would instantly retract anyway), then it would be considerably less likely that his comment could ignite a power struggle between Vincent and the teacher. However, if the teacher responded to Vincent's impulsive statement, it would practically be *guaranteed* to disrupt the learning environment! This line of reasoning was very difficult for some teachers to accept, and a good argument on their behalf was that Vincent's mutterings and "blurtings" could incite other students to behave in the same way. In other words, it could be "contagious."

Our response to this valid concern was that we recognized that most students who had spent any time at all with Vincent would know that he was "special" and they'd not be likely to emulate him. We also indicated that Vincent would continue to work with his counselor on controlling his impulses and that they could look forward to those behaviors becoming increasingly rare over time. As it turned out, our rationale for obtaining the accommodation that teachers ignore his impulsive statements was accurate, and he never caused or experienced discipline problems with his regular classroom teachers again. Truthfully, though, Vincent's "blurtings" did cause some difficulty for a young student teacher one year. As we'd experienced numerous times at this school, excellent communication between home and school provided us the opportunity to meet with this young teacher and his mentor (whom Vincent admired very much). Our good rapport enabled us to learn that Vincent was frustrated by the presence of this student teacher (Mr. H.) because he admired the fabulous teaching skills of the mentor-teacher (Ms. CB) and he missed her and the intellectual stimulation of her presence. Through consultation, we were able to find another way for Vincent to work closely with this fabulous mentor-teacher in after-school activities, and we were able to gain Vincent's resolve that he would work even harder to control his impulses in order to support the very able but inexperienced Mr. H.'s already-fragile sense of control in the classroom. The student teacher ended the year with confidence; he earned the admiration of his new colleagues; he became liked and respected by all his new students (Vincent included); and his career as a teacher looks bright.

High Expectations for Success

The mentor-teacher, Ms. CB, who taught history, mentioned above, and another mentor-teacher, Ms. TD, who taught English (Vincent's hardest subject by far), provide two examples of individuals who believed Vincent could be successful even when he (and we, at times) did not. While not every teacher is recognized for his or her exceptionality (Ms. TD earned State Teacher of the Year when Vincent was in tenth grade), these two teachers, along with a mathematics teacher (Mr. McG.) and all the other teachers we've mentioned so far, did something that his IEP could never mandate. They held out high expectations for Vincent. They expected him to put forth his very best effort for them. They encouraged him to stretch beyond his "comfort zone" and work hard to show people what he knows. These teachers never allowed him to use his ADHD or his learning disability as an excuse for not doing his best. They helped him see that he was capable of being successful and that his input was as valuable as anyone's. He was asked to submit some of his writing to a poetry contest, he entered a piece of artwork in a national competition, and he tried out for all the school plays. Vincent chaired his high school's Junior-Senior Prom committee because Ms. CB said she believed he could do a fine job. And he did.

Therapeutic Interventions

Earlier, we mentioned the importance of a "three-legged-stool" of support for individuals with ADHD. The counseling/therapeutic "leg" of the three-legged stool, in our opinion, has been another important facet in Vincent's life, but we must admit that not all of the people who have been important in supporting Vincent socially and emotionally were clinicians. We defined therapy as *any experience that enabled Vincent to better understand himself and others and that resulted in improved behavior.* Therefore, Vincent could experience therapy in a variety of ways, and he did. (See Section 1.3, Multimodal Treatments for ADHD.)

As far as clinicians go, we worked with a couple of skilled therapists, both of whom have helped Vincent develop more insight into his behavior and feelings; and they have helped him gain more emotional balance in his life. However, one therapist, in particular (Mr. G.), made such a difference for Vincent that we can't imagine what our lives would be like without his caring and sensitive support. He suggested that Vincent consider enrolling in some drama courses or workshops in order to improve his eye contact, increase his ability to pay attention to what people are saying, enhance his understanding of nonverbal social cues (like facial expressions), improve his turn-taking skills, "take direction," and enhance his ability to communicate socially. As a result, Vincent began taking drama classes in the sixth grade. The impact of that suggestion has been remarkable. While Vincent may admit that he still experiences problems with social skills in "un-scripted" situations, his acting skills are noteworthy.

Beyond the important few clinicians with whom we have worked, the majority of the people who have been meaningful supports for Vincent have been teachers who mentored Vincent at different points in his school career. But they were not always teachers! As of this writing, in addition to two new drama teachers and a physics teacher in his life, he feels well supported by the mother of a friend who has become like an "aunt." She can "tell it like it is," and Vincent listens "from the heart."

We have also found that supportive people do not need to have been in Vincent's life for very long or involved in an intensive relationship with Vincent. For example, another key support person for Vincent when he was first entering high school was actually a friend of ours who is a clinical psychologist. Vincent has never "seen" this psychologist (Dr. LP) professionally, but she was introduced to him at a family party. At this party, Dr. LP showed him a couple of card games, played with "regular" cards, that contain the added value of helping to improve attending, impulse control, the remembering of rules, and the social skills involved in winning/losing. Thus, we have found that even brief interactions have resulted in meaningful supports for Vincent. Incidentally, the impact of that experience, not counting the hilarity, resulted in our collaboration with Dr. LP in designing and implementing a Family Game Night in the community, designed to help improve the social skills of school-aged children with ADHD. This helpful community-based intervention is still ongoing, years later, and while the name of the project has changed, it all began with Vincent's therapeutic moment at an informal party.

In addition to the informal therapeutic supports mentioned above, Vincent found that volunteering in the community and (to a lesser extent) through church was therapeutic. His volunteer work provided a sense of purpose, of belonging, and of well-being that he'd not necessarily experienced in other ways. We'd tried to get him involved in volunteering through scouts, community events, and so on, but those avenues never "took." We were worried that he'd never "find his niche" in the community, but eventually Vincent found that volunteering on stage or behind the stage was engaging enough for him to "stick with." He spent two summers volunteering with our local Shakespeare in the Park; another summer volunteering at a nearby town's Community Theatre; and also performed in occasional dramas for our church.

It is important to mention that we are not suggesting that scouts or other leadership-building or service programs are not good for youths with ADHD. We simply want to share the importance of continuing to search for the best "fit" for any one person. What is meaningful to one person may be completely uninspiring to another. Vincent learned that volunteering (or a paid job, for that matter) is not always fun, and we encouraged him not to expect "fun" all the time. Sometimes it was boring, or just plain hard work, but as with most other successful experiences in his life, he found the right combination of novelty and challenge to motivate him, and he had enough fun and gained enough of a sense of mastery and satisfaction to sustain him. (See Section 1.6, Critical Factors in the Success of Students with ADHD.)

The Saga Continues

As of this writing, Vincent is completing his senior year in high school. He recently starred at his school as Macbeth in Shakespeare's play of the same name. He is smart, talented, funny (when you get to know him), "dead sexy" (as his admirers say), shy (hard to believe when you see him on stage), awkward in unplanned social situations, philosophical, moral, loyal, creative, sensitive, and (at times) his own worst critic. We know he wishes he could have done better in many ways, but we also know that he can also look back on his school years with some satisfaction. His senior class ring has become a very meaningful symbol for him, like a badge of honor, because he had to work so much harder than average to earn it.

Vincent is considering college now. He has begun auditioning for college scholarships and was very encouraged when he was offered a generous theatre scholarship on his first try. However, he is concerned, too. He has to write essays for admission to some of the colleges, even the college to which he was offered a scholarship. Will he be accepted? Will he need accommodations at college? What about the living arrangements and the new social demands?

We share those concerns as well. However, we have seen tremendous development in Vincent's ability to take responsibility for himself, manage his time, participate appropriately in class, and in his academic performance. We have witnessed Vincent growing from "getting lost between the kitchen and the bathroom" in the mornings to taking on long-term projects like teaching himself to play guitar or learning complex scripts for a play. We are painfully aware that he will have to work harder than most other people his age to become a successful college student and young adult.

As a gardener might say, we hope that we have "planted seeds" of competence and justice. We hope we have nourished him with balanced amounts of support. We hope we have "pruned" and "weeded" with appropriate discipline so that Vincent will become a functional adult member of society. We hope he will understand that asking for needed help is a sign of strength, not weakness, and that he'll continue to seek out any supports he might require in the future. And we hope that Vincent will be able to show all those who have supported him throughout his school career that their efforts were fruitful.

Also, because a gardener's work is never done, we are not really done either! We failed to mention that Vincent's younger sister, Victoria, was diagnosed with ADHD and learning disabilities in the area of written expression when she was in the third grade. . . .

part 5

Collaborative Efforts and School Responsibilities in Helping Children with ADHD

Section 5.1: Teaming for Success: Communication, Collaboration, and Mutual Support

Section 5.2: The Role of the School's Multidisciplinary Team

Section 5.3: School Documentation and Communication with Medical Providers and Others

Section 5.4: Educational Laws and Rights of Students with ADHD

Section 5.5: Innovative Collaborative Programs for Helping Children with ADHD

Teaming for Success

Communication, Collaboration, and Mutual Support

*T*he success of children and teens with ADHD is dependent on a *team effort* among everyone involved in the care, treatment, and education of that child. Collaboration and communication are critical among all team members (parents/caregivers, teachers and other school personnel, clinicians—medical and mental health professionals, and of course, the child).

The Necessity of a Team Approach

As ADHD is a chronic disorder that is "managed" not cured (such as asthma or diabetes), various supports and treatments (Rief, 1998, 2000) will typically be needed throughout childhood and adolescence. The most effective approach in treating ADHD is multimodal, involving a number of interventions from a variety of different professionals and service providers.

Parents have the key role—as leaders of their child's team. They have the greatest responsibility to try assembling the best team of professionals they can who will be treating, educating, and supporting their child and family and to ensure that team members are communicating with each other and working together on joint goals. From diagnosis to the employment and maintenance of effective interventions, teamwork is required.

The diagnostic process involves a team:

* Parent information is provided (through interviews, rating forms, and questionnaires).
* School information/data is gathered from classroom teachers and other school personnel directly working with the student or observing the child's functioning in various school settings.
* The multidisciplinary assessment (IEP) team may conduct a school-based evaluation of the student (for example, special education teacher/evaluator, school psychologist, speech/language therapist, school nurse).
* A physician or mental health professional evaluates the child for ADHD.

The treatment plan involves a team:

* Treatments outside of school may include counseling for the ADHD child/teen, his or her parents, or the family. Often it involves a combination, with counseling of various types (for example, by clinical psychologists) as needed at different times in the child's life.
* School interventions are generally provided through a variety of school personnel and other resources that may include classroom

teachers, school counselors, social workers, the school nurse, special education teachers, speech-language therapist, adapted P.E., occupational therapist, administrators, tutorial service providers, instructional aides, guidance aides, peer tutors, cross-age tutors, and parent or community volunteers.

* Medical intervention can be provided by different medical doctors (for example, pediatricians, family practitioners, child psychiatrists, neurologists).

* It is important for the child/teen to participate in activities that build on his or her interests and strengths and provide an emotional and/or physical outlet. This may require a variety of the following: coaches, trainers, instructors, youth group leaders, scout leaders, mentors, and others working with the child/teen in extracurricular activities.

* The child may be involved in other treatments to address specific needs (for example, social skills training, private academic tutoring).

* Parent training groups (for example, on behavioral therapy) may be provided by various community professionals/trained facilitators in behavior management and positive discipline strategies.

* The school's SST/504 team should be monitoring and revising, as needed, any intervention plans that have been developed for the student. If the child is in special education, then the school's IEP team/service providers will be involved in the implementation of all aspects of a child's IEP.

* Support groups for parents of children/teens with ADHD will be comprised of a number of people who can serve as resources and support—a very helpful intervention for parents.

It is critical that the diagnostic process, as well as *any* treatment and intervention provided, involve communication among key parties:

home, school, physician, and other service providers in the community.

Most students with ADHD require close monitoring and mutual support between the home and school to be successful.

* Teachers need to keep parents well informed about work assignments; upcoming tests and projects; how the student is performing and keeping up with daily work; as well as behavior and other issues.

* Parents need to communicate with teachers regarding how the child/teen is functioning at home, the child's stress level, and other issues that may be affecting the child's performance. In addition, they need to stay on top of monitoring that homework is being done and follow through with any home/school plans (for example, to aid and reinforce behavior, work production, and organization skills).

Note: *See the example in Section 2.3 of the weekly progress report, which is a useful home/school monitoring form. Daily report cards are other excellent methods of communication about the child's daily school performance (see Section 2.3).*

Also, medical and mental health professionals involved in the care of the youngster must also be monitoring the treatment effects and seeking feedback on the interventions from home and school. Any child/teen taking medication requires regular communication between the teacher(s), school nurse, parents, and the physician.

The Parents' Role in the Collaborative Team Process

As mentioned above, parents of children with ADHD must assume a leadership role—in forming and working with a team of various professionals who will be treating and educating their child. This does not come easily for many. It involves a process of gaining knowledge and understanding about ADHD (becoming an "ADHD expert"), in order to more confidently and competently advocate for the child's needs, and finding the necessary supports in school and the community to facilitate their son's or daughter's success. A parent armed with knowledge about ADHD and effective strategies and interventions can also be a valuable resource to other team members.

Dr. Terry Illes (2002) points out that most children are flexible and resilient and are able to adjust to many different types of situations. However, children with ADHD are much less adaptable and lack the inner resources to overcome an environment that is too challenging. Thus, it is essential to place these children in optimal situations that improve their chances for success—which means parents doing what they can to have their child placed in a good school with the teacher and classroom situation that may be the best match for the child's unique set of needs.

A child with ADHD will have the best chances for a successful school year if parents are able to establish a positive relationship with the teacher—one in which both parties work together on behalf of the student in a spirit of collaboration, cooperation, and mutual respect.

What Parents Can Do to Establish a Positive Working Partnership with Teachers (Rief, 2003)

* At the beginning of the school year, meet with the teacher(s), share information about your child, and establish the best means of communication (for example, phone conferences, email, home/school notes).
* Let teachers know you are interested, available, and accessible, and want to support school efforts.
* Understand the teacher's responsibility to all students in the class.
* Keep in mind what is reasonable when making requests.
* Cooperate in reinforcing appropriate behavior and work production goals.

* Communicate closely, openly, and frequently with classroom teachers. Find out as much as you can about how your child is functioning at school and ways you can support at home.
* Ensure that the child is coming to school "ready to learn" (adequate sleep, prepared with books, materials, homework).
* Treat the teacher with courtesy and respect.
* Often the best way to establish a positive relationship with the school is to be a helpful, involved parent who volunteers time and service to the school. There are countless ways that schools can use the direct or indirect services of parents. All schools are seeking parent involvement in the classroom or various school committees, programs, and projects. Become more involved in the school community and get to know staff members.
* Let teachers or other staff members who are making a strong effort on behalf of your child know that you are appreciative. It is generally the little things that make a difference (for example, thank-you note, a positive comment or message to the teacher or administrator).
* Avoid becoming defensive, aggressive, accusatory, or hostile with school personnel. Try to always remain polite and diplomatic.

Terry Illes (2002) also makes the following excellent suggestions:

* Do not be defensive about your child's behavior problems. Acknowledge past problems and problems at home to help the teacher feel comfortable about discussing them with you. Make sure the teacher understands that you accept your child's limitations.
* Express empathy for the teacher. Let the teacher know that you understand that your child is not going to make the teacher's job any easier and that you will share

responsibility for your child's education. Ask the teacher to inform you if he or she is feeling overwhelmed or frustrated.

* If you have a concern about the teacher or your child's educational program, talk directly with the teacher before going over his or her head (to the principal or district administrators). Involving others unnecessarily will embarrass the teacher and create resentment.

* Offer to provide resources (timers, incentives, organizational tools, and so forth) to the teacher when needed. It often costs teachers out-of-pocket money to purchase additional materials for children with ADHD. Make sure that you, and not the teacher, are absorbing this expense. If possible, ask the teacher if there is anything you can do to lighten his or her load, such as serving as a parent helper.

Supports and Training Parents Need

Parenting a child with ADHD is often far more challenging than it is to parent a child who does not have the disorder. The following are some of the supports and training that may be of benefit to parents of children with ADHD—enabling them to better cope with the challenges and become well-equipped to help their son or daughter (Rief, 1998, 2003):

Learn as Much as You Can

There is a great deal of reliable information about ADHD available. It is recommended that parents obtain as much knowledge and training as they can by attending conferences and seminars, as well as reading books, magazines, and information available on reputable websites. Knowledge about ADHD and the treatments that work will empower parents with the necessary confidence, hope, and skills.

Parents must become educated in the school laws (IDEA and Section 504 of the Rehabilitation Act). Children with ADHD may be eligible for special education, related services, and/or accommodations in the classroom. With awareness of these laws, parents can help their child obtain school supports.

Seek Professional Help

Parents of children with ADHD benefit from learning behavior management skills and specific methods of addressing challenging behaviors that the average parent doesn't need. Parent training in behavior modification and positive discipline are important components of effective treatment. Hopefully, there is such training available and provided by skilled professionals in the community for interested parents.

It is recommended that parents seek counseling to attend to personal problems or family issues, which compound the difficulty in the home. Many families experience marital strife and family crises due to some of the issues surrounding the ADHD child's behavior. Parents need to support each other and do everything they can to function as a team, getting professional help when necessary.

Find Support Systems

Among the best supports for parents are organizations such as CHADD (Children and Adults with Attention Deficit Disorders). It is highly recommended that parents seek information about CHADD in their community and attend a local meeting to learn more. (See information below.) Some communities have other kinds of support groups or regular meetings available for parents of children with ADHD and/or learning disabilities (through schools, agencies, hospitals, and so forth).

Support groups/organizations such as CHADD are very helpful in that parents can network with other parents and learn from each other. Just hearing "You aren't alone" from other parents who are dealing with similar struggles can be reassuring and a great source of help. Parents of children with ADHD are often the best sources for referrals to professionals in the community and in advising how to access support and services for their child at school. In addition, at CHADD meetings (or other groups) there is typically a guest speaker from the community addressing various relevant topics and issues.

It is hard to cope with stress and frustration alone. When feeling physically or emotionally overloaded, it is important to seek assistance:

* Parents need to "share the load" with household responsibilities, as well as all parenting issues such as homework, monitoring, discipline, and so forth.
* Single parents need to find support wherever possible (for example, friends, relatives, neighbors, after-school tutoring programs).
* Providing parents with some respite by volunteering to baby-sit for a while or inviting the child to his or her home for a weekend is a wonderful gift from a relative or good friend.

Parents need various supports from teachers and other school personnel such as:

* Accessibility and willingness to communicate clearly and regularly
* Monitoring the child's daily/weekly performance and providing feedback
* Sensitivity and responsiveness to struggles the child is experiencing (for example, with social difficulties, homework issues)
* Flexibility regarding accommodations/ modifications as needed for their child

Communication and Advocacy Tips for Parents

Parents of children with ADHD will find that they need to learn advocacy strategies to ensure that their child receives the help he or she needs (Rief, 1998, 2003). As a parent, it is your responsibility to step in and intervene on behalf of your child whenever the situation arises that your son or daughter needs more support, intervention, and understanding of his or her disorder.

Parents can be very helpful by providing resources and information about ADHD to teachers, coaches, and other adults directly working with their child on a regular basis. Much of the teacher training and public awareness regarding ADHD is a direct result of parents' strong efforts (for example, individually or through organizations such as CHADD) to educate others about the needs of their children.

They should learn about their child's rights under federal laws to a free, appropriate public education and to accommodations and/or direct special services if the ADHD is affecting the child's ability to learn or perform successfully at school. (See Section 5.4, Educational Laws and Rights of Students with ADHD.)

To be an effective advocate parents must communicate with school staff regarding their son or daughter to a far greater degree than is necessary for most children. The level of involvement with the school significantly increases when one has a child with any disability or special needs.

Many parents feel uncomfortable at school meetings, particularly team meetings that involve several members of the school staff. Here are some tips during team meetings:

* Try to enter meetings with an open mind and cooperative attitude. Be willing to share your opinions, feelings, observations, suggestions, and any information about your child or family that may help with planning and intervention.
* Do not be afraid to ask questions and request that certain language (educational jargon) be explained. Ask for clarification on anything you do not understand.
* At certain meetings, such as IEP meetings, you should receive a copy of any reports or paperwork to which staff members make reference. If not, request a copy.
* Take notes during meetings. In addition, it is helpful if you enter meetings prepared with a few notes to yourself regarding items you wish to share, discuss, or ask about.
* You are welcome to bring someone with you to meetings. It is most helpful if both parents can attend school meetings together—even

if parents are divorced but share custody. Schools are used to working with sensitive family situations and will do what they can to effectively communicate and work with parents and guardians.

* Keep a file on your child that includes all copies of testing, reports, IEPs, report cards, health records, immunization, and other important data.

* Include in a file a log of communication with the school and other professionals working with your child, including dates of doctor appointments and medication logs; summaries of conversations, meetings; notification of disciplinary actions/referrals your child received at school; interventions promised to be put into effect; and so forth. Having this information easily accessible will likely come in handy at some time.

* Prepare for meetings by trying to learn how your child is functioning at school (in classroom and other settings); in what areas your child is struggling (academic, social-emotional, behavioral); and the kinds of supports and accommodations that may be helpful and available.

Parents have a right to have their child's educational needs assessed by the school district. If they wish to have their son or daughter evaluated to determine whether he or she has a disability that qualifies for special education, related services, or accommodations, they should:

* Speak with the classroom teacher, special education teacher, other members of the multidisciplinary team, the principal, or director of special education about pursuing an evaluation.

* Submit to the school a written, dated letter requesting an evaluation, including the reason for the assessment (for example, concern about a child's educational performance). This will begin the IEP process and timeline. The evaluation will determine whether a child qualifies for special education/related services based on an identified area of disability.

* It is generally recommended to first proceed through the SST process to initiate and evaluate effectiveness of pre-referral interventions before requesting formal testing if this process is used at the school site. (See Section 5.2.)

* Read the paperwork the school provides regarding procedures, the assessment plan, and due process rights under the law. If you have any questions, ask.

* Know that you are a key member of the team in this entire process.

It is highly recommended that any professionals with whom parents choose to work (physicians, psychologists, educational therapists) exhibit the following qualities:

* Are knowledgeable about research-validated treatments and keep current in what is known about ADHD

* Have experience and training working with children/families with ADHD

* Have an understanding of family issues with regard to a child/family member who has a disability

* Be familiar with the surrounding issues and common co-existing conditions/disorders with ADHD

* Be aware of and adhere to the AAP Guidelines in diagnosis and treatment

* Possess a firm belief in a multimodal treatment approach

* Have a strong interest in working together as a team (with parents and school personnel) and willingness to communicate on a regular basis

More Tips for Parents

* Be assertive in checking the level of expertise of the professionals you seek out. If you are uncomfortable with their treatment approach, express your concerns. If they do not appear committed to a team approach, you will be better off finding someone else.

* To be an effective advocate for your child, you will need to monitor the plans as well as your child's progress. Request update

meetings or parent/teacher conferences. If something is not working, it can always be changed. Always attempt to solve problems using a cooperative team approach.

* Any plan, formal or informal (for example, 504, IEP), can be reviewed at any point during the school year. If you have concerns, you may always request a review of the plan or any services, programs, or special placements. You do not have to wait until an annual review meeting or a quarterly/semester parent-teacher conference. The best is to continuously remain in close communication to monitor growth and progress and implement changes/modifications as needed.

The Educators' Role in the Collaborative Team Process

What Teachers Can Do to Establish and Nurture a Positive Working Partnership with Parents (Rief, 1998, 2003)

To optimize the success of students with ADHD, educators must make every effort to collaborate closely with parents (as well as clinicians and other service providers involved in their care). Teachers and other school professionals must understand and appreciate how essential it is to reach out to parents—welcoming their involvement, building positive rapport, and communicating effectively.

When a student has behavioral challenges, teachers and other school personnel sometimes view the child and his or her family in a negative light. The overt or subtle message received by many parents of children with ADHD is "What are you going to do about your child and his or her inappropriate behavior?" Such a message can sabotage any efforts for teamwork between home and school. When parents perceive that their child is disliked, misunderstood, or blamed for the disorder (or that their own disciplinary methods and parenting style are being questioned or criticized), an adversarial rather than collaborative, respectful relationship is most likely.

To establish and build a positive relationship with parents, communicate:

* In a manner that is respectful and non-judgmental
* That you welcome their "partnership"
* Your acknowledgment that they are the "experts" on their son or daughter
* That you value their input and any information/insights
* That you truly care about their child and intend to do all you can to ensure a successful school year

Be proactive:

* Call or write notes home communicating positive messages to parents about their child (what you appreciate about the student).
* Make yourself easily accessible and let parents know when and how they can best contact you.
* Reach out to parents by letting them know they are welcome at school and in the classroom.
* Communicate that you are eager to work with parents as a "team" to ensure that their child is successful in your class.

It is much easier to discuss concerns with parents once you have opened the lines of communication in a positive manner. In order to establish rapport with parents, it is important to recognize and speak about their child's areas of strength and competence. Make every effort to learn about the child, identifying his or her individual strengths, interests, and positive characteristics.

Clearly communicate to parents early in the year (first days of school) and on an ongoing basis via weekly/monthly newsletters regarding your classroom goals, policies, expectations, activities, and special events. Always invite and encourage parent participation.

When you have concerns about a student:

* Make the personal contact and explain to parents what you are concerned about.

* Again, try to always indicate something positive as well.
* Describe how the child is functioning (academically/behaviorally).
* State your observations objectively without "labeling" the behavior or child (for example, "lazy," "apathetic," or "bad").
* Communicate your interest in doing everything possible to help the student do well in school.
* Ask parents whether they have noticed any of the difficulties you have described (at home) or if previous teachers ever communicated these concerns in the past.
* Let the parents know what specific strategies and interventions you are currently utilizing and/or will begin to implement to address the areas of concern.
* Solicit parents' input—asking whether they have any additional suggestions or information that can help you meet the student's needs.
* Really take the time to listen to what parents have to say, and communicate your interest and respect for their opinions, feelings, and goals for their child.

Supports and Training Teachers Need

Parents and administrators must realize that teachers frequently have several students in a classroom who need extra assistance, support, and attention including (Rief, 1998, 2003):

* Children with ADHD, learning disabilities, and other neurobiological, developmental, or behavioral disorders
* English-language learners (students who are not yet proficient in the English language)
* Children with social/emotional/behavioral problems due to trauma, instability, or situations in their personal lives
* Students with a wide range of skill and developmental levels

It is by no means an easy job to be an effective teacher and address the diverse needs of students in the classroom. There are high demands/expectations on teachers to be accountable for student achievement. However, there are often shrinking resources and support available to do so.

The following are some of the supports that teachers need in order to address the needs of students with ADHD (and *all* students in the classroom):

Training

* Regarding the special needs of his or her student population, specifically about ADHD
* Awareness training as well as specific skill-building training that is ongoing
* In behavior management strategies and interventions
* In differentiating instruction to reach and teach diverse learners
* Opportunities to attend workshops, seminars, and conferences on ADHD

Teaming with Colleagues

* Most children with ADHD will be educated in general education classrooms. Some will be receiving special education services, and others will not. However, collaboration and consultation between special education and classroom teachers and other school support personnel regarding effective strategies and accommodations is helpful in addressing students' individual needs.
* Teachers who team-teach different subject areas, plan and team as a grade level, or team for special projects and/or disciplinary purposes, often report much greater job satisfaction. In addition, the students benefit from the opportunity to have more than one teacher, especially when teachers are able to enthusiastically share their areas of interest, strength, and expertise with students.
* Buddying with a partner teacher is often helpful to exchange ideas, reenergize each other, and for disciplinary purposes (for example, sending a student for a brief "time-out" in the buddy teacher's class).

Administrative Support

* Providing teachers and support staff with the *time* and *opportunity* (for example, through creative scheduling) in order to meet, plan, team, and collaborate with each other
* Providing teachers with professional development opportunities that are practical and useful to teachers
* Providing assistance for teachers who are overloaded with more than their fair share of "challenging students" (for example, fewer students in the class, more prep time, scheduling preferences, more push-in help from support staff or school aides)
* Allowing/encouraging teachers to "experiment" with various strategies and techniques to find what works for an individual child

Support Team Members Who

* Are knowledgeable about children with ADHD
* Are responsive and helpful when teachers express concerns and seek assistance
* Strategize and help teachers plan appropriate actions/interventions for students
* Follow through and provide timely feedback

Resources Available

* A lending library of materials teachers and parents can access, including books, videotapes/DVDs, and other resources on ADHD

Extra Assistance in the Classroom

* When there are children in need of one-on-one assistance in the classroom, it is helpful to have another person, at times, in the room to provide extra support (for example, instructional aide/assistant, push-in support services, student teacher, parent volunteer, cross-age tutor).
* Parent volunteers who are willing to donate time to assist in the classroom (or work on projects at home that are requested by the teacher) are excellent sources of much needed teacher support.

Other Supports

* Academic interventions that are not part of a special education program (for example, tutorial assistance, extra direct reading instruction) that teachers can access for students in need. Such supports can also serve as pre-referral interventions that teachers can try prior to referring a student for special education.
* It is helpful for teachers to have the opportunity to observe other teachers and have mentor/peer coaching assistance if needed or requested.
* Teachers benefit from periodic opportunities for exchanging and sharing (for example, information, lessons, materials, instructional/behavioral strategies and techniques) with colleagues.
* Teachers need to be cheered on to keep on learning and growing. The best support is being able to associate with positive, upbeat, and enthusiastic colleagues who love to teach, are committed to their students and profession, and want to keep advancing their skills and knowledge.
* Teachers must be treated as professionals whose opinions and input are solicited and listened to for site-based decision making and district policy.
* Being human, we all need to know that our efforts are recognized and appreciated. A thoughtful "thank you" or positive comment from a colleague, parent, administrator, or student means a lot to teachers.

Other Factors Teachers Must Be Aware Of (Rief, 2003)

* Regardless of whether parents are able to attend a meeting (for example, SST initial meeting), they should always be kept well informed, and every effort should be made by the school to include them and receive their input.
* Parents are key members of any team meetings involving their child—a Student Support Team, 504, or IEP team meeting. Realize how intimidating it can be for a

parent to attend any such meeting—sitting around a table with a number of school people discussing their child. Hearing about how one's son or daughter is struggling in school is not easy for any parent; and it often raises one's defenses, anxiety, anger, and fears. It is important to be sensitive and empathetic to what parents may be feeling, and really take the time to listen to what they have to say. We must clearly communicate that the school is committed to working together in any way possible to help their child succeed.

* Teachers and other school personnel need to be aware of the necessity for cultural sensitivity and awareness—especially working with families whose child has a disability or medical/mental health needs.

* Teachers must communicate observations and provide (with parental permission granted in writing) any requested information to clinicians involved in the diagnosis or treatment of the student.

The Clinicians' Role in the Collaborative Team Process

Medical and mental health professionals must communicate closely with and obtain direct information from parents and educators. They must have a clear picture and understanding of the child's issues and challenges and of how the child/teen is functioning at home, school, and other key environments. Clinicians must be available and accessible to other team members in the collaborative team process.

Cultural Sensitivity and Its Impact on Effective Communication and Collaboration

It is very important to be culturally sensitive when working with and making efforts to develop teamwork with parents. Of course, whenever there is a language barrier, all efforts must be made to bridge that barrier, such as provision of translation services, simplifying the language in reports and written communication, and including more charts/graphics to make information clearer (Al-Hassan & Gardner, 2002). Parents with limited English proficiency may not feel confident communicating with school personnel and, in fact, might feel intimidated by highly educated school personnel (Holman, 1997). Further, these parents might not understand the special educational needs and the nature of their child's disability (Thomas, Correa, & Morsink, 2000). For example, they may not be able to read the reports that teachers are sending home—in some cases, even when the report is in their native language (Al-Hassan & Gardner, 2002).

Teachers should not assume they have communicated effectively with parents who have limited English proficiency; they should verify by having the parents communicate back what they have heard (Al-Hassan & Gardner, 2002). Educators and clinicians must also be sensitive to matters pertaining to nonverbal communication (for example, eye contact, facial expression, gestures, proximity, touching, clothing) among diverse cultural groups (Thomas, Correa, & Morsink, 2000). For example, cultural norms vary widely on the type and frequency of touching that occurs during friendly professional interactions. Also, it is important for educators to fully inform immigrant parents about their rights and their role in their child's education (Al-Hassan & Gardner, 2002). Educators can find parental information in various languages through the Federal Regional Resource Center. It also is generally very helpful if the school team (and clinician's office) includes someone from the same ethnicity or culture whenever possible.

Cultural differences are important factors that affect the likelihood of whether or not a child will be evaluated or treated or whether or not a student may receive specialized interventions/supports in the school or community. It is important for educators (and clinicians) to be aware of these cultural factors and take efforts to become more culturally sensitive and aware.

Cultural differences can result in disparate beliefs about disability and the nature of disabilities served through special education services. This disparity may result in differing goals for the child's educational programs (Cloud, 1993; Lamorey, 2002). Perhaps more significantly, cultural beliefs influence the value placed on parent-professional partnerships in decision making, a concept not valued equally across cultures (Dabkowski, 2004; Kalyanpur, Harry, & Skrtic, 2000). For example, cultural beliefs might result in a parent indicating agreement with a team decision out of respect for professional educators rather than conviction. Professional team members need to be aware when such a possibility exists and provide another avenue for a parent's voice to be heard. Here, this might be accomplished through the availability of a parent liaison with a similar cultural background (Dabkowski, 2004).

Understanding and building on a family's cultural interpretations of disability is essential in creating partnerships with parents of children receiving special education services. Parent beliefs about the nature of disability are related to parent beliefs about and participation in treatment and intervention. Optimal outcomes for children with disabilities can only occur when professionals create a bridge from the culture of schooling to parents' multifaceted perceptions of the disability, its cause, its acceptable treatments, and the available resources of formal and informal support (Lamorey, 2002).

Culture is an important buffer in the lives of families who have a child with a disability. Parents and their extended families may have different belief systems relative to the meaning of disability from the typical teachers from middle class Euro American backgrounds who provide educational and support services. There may be some aspects of Western acculturation that families from different cultural backgrounds choose to embrace. Attempting to understand a child's disability, however, may occur more securely within the context of a family's familiar traditional cultural ways and supports. When practitioners can accept parents' beliefs, parents may no longer feel the need to hide traditional beliefs from the practitioners

and possible combinations of intervention approaches can occur in the context of a duality of belief systems (Lamorey, 2002).

There are other cultural barriers to be aware of. For example, the strong mistrust, particularly in African American families, of having their child labeled, placed in special education, or receiving mental health service.

African American parents may resist a diagnosis of ADHD, especially for young male children, because African American males make up 6 percent of the U.S. population, but represent 35 percent of children in special education and 50 percent of the prison population in the United States (Kunjufu, 1982; Taylor-Crawford, Richardson, & Madison-Boyd, 2003). There is evidence that African Americans may be more mistrusting of medical research and treatment than individuals from other ethnic groups. A study done by Harris Interactive, funded by McNeil Consumer and Specialty Pharmaceuticals, called Cultural Attitudes & Perceptions about AD/HD (Samuel, Curtis, Thornell, et al., 1997) "clearly indicated the mistrust African-Americans have for diagnostic accuracy of this disorder along racial/ethnic lines for their children and other children of color." (Taylor-Crawford, Richardson, & Madison-Boyd, 2003).

Final Thoughts on Home/School Collaboration

Coping with a hard-to-manage child both at home and school is stressful, draining, and frustrating for parents and teachers alike. It is helpful for parents to spend time in the classroom to acquire an appreciation of how difficult a teacher's job is—teaching, managing, and caring for thirty or more children and their many special needs. By attending a parent support group meeting, listening carefully to parents, and becoming well informed on ADHD issues that influence the home and social arena, teachers will also gain awareness and greater respect for parents. Once again, it is through the coordination of efforts and mutual support between home and school that we enhance the chances for our children's success.

The Role of the School's Multidisciplinary Team

When concerned about a student's academic or behavioral performance, teachers and parents need to initiate efforts to work together on behalf of the student. The first step should always be a parent-teacher conference to discuss and plan strategies for the student's success. It is recommended that parents always take their concerns directly to the teacher as a first step, as well. This is proper protocol in most schools, and is often communicated to parents at the beginning of the school year by the administration.

Once parent-teacher contact has been made, agreed-on strategies and actions should be implemented. If the problem is not resolved and more intervention is needed, the next step in most schools is to proceed through a multidisciplinary team process, which goes by many different names across the country. Throughout this section (and book) this team will be referred to as the Student Support Team (SST).

The Student Support Team (SST) Process

Most schools have a team process for assisting teachers in devising instructional and behavioral strategies and supports for students experiencing difficulties in general education. This process and team is referred to by many names or acronyms (Rief, 2003, 2004):

* SST can stand for "Student Support Team," "Student Study Team," or "Student Success Team."
* In some districts the team is called the "SAT" (Student Assistance Team), "SIT" (Student Intervention Team), "IST" (Instructional Support Team), or "TAT" (Teacher Assistance Team).
* In others it may be called the "Consultation Team," "Child Guidance Team," "Child Study Team," "Multidisciplinary Intervention Team," and so forth.

SST (or whatever name the district chooses to use) is *NOT* a special education process or procedure, but rather a function of regular/general education to strategize and problem solve about students who are experiencing difficulty (academic, behavioral, social-emotional). The SST process and protocol differ from district to district and school to school, yet usually there are many similarities, as well.

SST is basically a process and forum for teachers to meet with a team typically comprised of some school support personnel, an administrator, and often the parents in order to share input regarding children they have concerns about. For the SST process to be effective, the SST must meet on a regularly scheduled basis. At the SST meeting:

* The team brainstorms possible supports, interventions, and strategies that can be tried to assist the student(s) on the agenda.
* A few of those strategies/interventions are selected to implement for a period of time.
* SST meetings should result in an action plan with a follow-up date to monitor the effectiveness of the plan in addressing the concerns.

Depending on the support personnel available at the school (and their schedules), the members of the team vary. Generally:

* The school psychologist, school counselor, special education teacher (resource teacher/ specialist), school nurse, administrator, and classroom teacher(s) are on the team.
* The speech/language therapist, adapted P.E. teacher, and other special service providers are other members of the team who may perhaps not be in attendance at all team meetings, but participate when the team will be discussing a student with issues involving speech/language, motor skill development, and so forth.
* Some schools have social workers, reading specialists, and others with various areas of expertise who are able to join the team.

Benefits of the SST Process

This process has the potential of being a highly effective method for early intervention, providing much needed support to struggling students and their teachers. The SST process:

* Provides the teacher with access to a group of colleagues who share information and expertise—enabling the teacher to better meet the individual needs of students
* Assists the teacher in problem solving, strategizing, and developing a plan of appropriate classroom interventions

* Facilitates student access to additional school-wide and perhaps community-wide supports and safety nets (as needed)
* Provides teachers with an expanded "toolbox" or repertoire of instructional and behavioral strategies and adaptations/ accommodations useful for students in the general education classroom
* Provides the necessary pre-referral intervention documentation if a formal referral for special education is required
* Provides an appropriate vehicle for making recommendations to parents as a team when a clinical (medical/mental health) referral is indicated
* Enhances the home/school partnership in efforts to collaboratively address student needs

Because there are many schools with a large population or high percentage of students in need of support, a bi-monthly or weekly SST meeting with a single team may not be sufficient. To be effective, schools must be creative in finding ways to meet more frequently and consistently, as well as expand on the resources and personnel in the building who can contribute to and participate in the SST.

Some schools are using very creative models to increase the number of SST meetings to discuss and plan for student needs without overtaxing the members of the school-wide SST. The following are some examples:

* Establishing multiple teams in the building with different members of support staff, administration, and teachers assigned to each team
* Utilizing a layered or tiered SST process/ structure in which students are first discussed and strategies/interventions designed in grade-level teacher teams, cluster teams, or house teams (If problems are not resolved at this level, then a school-wide SST is scheduled with parents and other SST members.)

Note: The author has been very involved in working with schools (especially those with high levels of student needs in urban communities) to establish effective processes / structures as noted above. For more information, contact the author at www.sandrarief.com, and see general references and recommended resources for this section.

What Teachers Are Often Asked to Do Prior to Requesting an SST Meeting

It is very helpful for teachers to follow through on preliminary steps prior to the SST meeting. They would usually:

* Implement some strategies/interventions and document effectiveness
* Communicate with student's previous teachers
* Review the cumulative records and student data
* Collect work samples
* Share concerns and strategies attempted so far with appropriate SST members at the informal level
* Establish communication with parents—notifying them of observations regarding the student (positive as well as concerns), strategies tried/attempts to assist, eliciting their input, and trying to establish a partnership on behalf of the student

Note: With these preliminary steps taken, then the SST meeting is more productive. The team is in a position to recommend "next step" interventions.

Request for SST Meeting

Teachers will be asked to complete a referral/ SST request form prior to meeting. The coordinator/facilitator of the SST generally makes a copy of the completed form to distribute to team members either before or at the time of the meeting. A typical SST request (or referral) form generally asks the teacher to provide the following types of information:

* Student's identifying information (name, address, teacher, grade, parent/guardian name, home phone, and other information)
* Student's strengths
* Checklist of items that appear to describe the student that may be areas of concern under the categories of:

  — Health/physical factors (for example, frequent absences; appears pale, listless, apathetic; extremely active and restless; possible vision or hearing deficit; poor motor control; growth or developmental lag; physical injuries; frequent complaints of health problems)
  — Speech/language factors (for example, limited speaking vocabulary; difficulty relating own ideas; incomplete sentences/poor grammar; responses are inappropriate; difficulty following directions; articulation—mispronunciation of speech sounds; stuttering—speech blocks/breaks/poor rhythm; voice—quality is hoarse/harsh/too soft)
  — Education factors (for example, academic difficulties in reading/math/ written language; poor retention of subject matter; poor handwriting or reversals/messy work; difficulty staying on task/inattentive; difficulty comprehending directions/subject matter; difficulty changing activities; easily discouraged/often frustrated; work completion difficulties—rushed/slow/ fails to finish)
  — Personal/social factors (for example, generally withdrawn/timid/fearful; poor self-control/impulsive; frequently angry/temper outbursts; inappropriate language; poor peer relations—fights/ disturbs others; seems unhappy—moody/cries easily; feelings of inadequacy/low self-concept; fantasizes/ exaggerates/lies; challenges authority—defiant/oppositional; shows little empathy/concern for others)

* Interventions/strategies tried so far (and degree of effectiveness)
* Parent contacts/dates/purpose/outcome

During the SST Meeting

Here are some things the team typically does at the first meeting:

* They examine student records: past report cards, assessment data, portfolio of work collected (if available), current work samples, attendance record, health records/vision and hearing screenings, and so forth. Members of the team share their observations of the student in different settings.
* The team discusses prior strategies and interventions that have been implemented.
* The teacher shares information about the student's performance and observed areas of strength and weakness, and may be asked to identify what he or she has found to be effective in motivating and reinforcing the student.
* There is a designated recorder at the team meeting, even though typically everyone takes his or her own notes.
* One of the team members is responsible for facilitating the meeting, and a timekeeper may be used, as well.
* The team brainstorms possible strategies/ interventions to address areas of concern.
* A plan of action—generally comprised of a targeted goal for improved student outcome and a few strategies/interventions to achieve that goal—is decided on and written on the SST action plan.
* A follow-up date to examine the effectiveness of the strategies and interventions is typically designated in the plan. This may involve either a follow-up SST meeting (for example, scheduled in a specified number of weeks) or a less formal follow-up between the teacher, parents, and one or two members of the team, as appropriate.

SSTs may recommend and form an action plan that involves a number of possible inter-ventions. Often particular team members will leave the meeting with the responsibility for:

* Observing the student in various settings
* Helping the teacher create a behavior modification plan (contracts, charts, reinforcement systems)
* Meeting with parents to further share and discuss concerns
* Employing classroom strategies and modifications (including instructional, behavioral, and environmental)
* Providing small group, one-to-one assistance from available resources

Parents' Participation in the SST Process

The parents' role in the process is described below:

* Parents may or may not be in attendance at SST meetings, as this depends on the school/district protocol.
* Some schools prefer to meet initially without parents (generally for efficiency purposes) in order to discuss more students within the designated amount of time. When parents are in attendance, it is harder to keep to a tight time schedule. Such schools will inform parents prior to a meeting as well as immediately after regarding any plan of action, and then will generally invite parents to attend a follow-up meeting.
* Many schools request that parents attend all SST meetings. Parent input is extremely important and helpful in the problem-solving/strategy-planning process. Generally, parents appreciate being invited to SST meetings, regardless of whether or not they are able to attend.
* In all cases, it is necessary to inform parents when the SST meeting will be taking place, and also to reveal the outcome of the meeting (which usually involves a written plan of action).
* Parents will be asked to share their perceptions of the child's functioning at home

and school, areas of strength/interest, areas of difficulty, needs, and so forth. If behaviors are exhibited at school that are of concern, parents will be asked whether any of these behaviors are observed outside of school.

* Any information that parents are willing to supply which can assist in determining an appropriate plan of action for the child is very helpful. Parents may be asked what they have found to be effective in motivating and reinforcing their child.

* If parents are not attending the SST meeting, it is recommended that the school obtain their input by phone interview or by sending home a parent input form prior to the meeting.

Additional Points About SSTs

* For the SST to be effective, it has to be a priority in the school. Administrators must make all efforts to resolve scheduling issues by taking such measures as providing coverage for classroom teachers if the meetings take place during school hours.

* If it appears that the student may have ADHD, the SST meeting is often the perfect forum to share information and resources with parents and discuss what is involved in an evaluation. A diagnostic evaluation can be initiated at this time if parents are so inclined.

* A good SST action plan for a child with ADHD is often very similar to a 504 Plan. After assessing and determining eligibility, many 504 Plans involve basically rewriting the SST interventions/strategies that are proving to be effective and adding any other agreed-on accommodations, supports, and information onto a district 504 form.

* For an action plan to be effective (whether it is one generated at an SST meeting, a 504 Plan, or an IEP), there must be *follow-up* for accountability. The best of plans fail if we don't revisit the plan and assess how effective it is.

"Safety Nets" and Supports for General Education Students

It is important for schools to provide interventions, special programs, and "safety nets" to students in need among the general education population so that special education is not the *only* means of getting additional assistance.

Schools will do their students a great service and reduce the number of children in need of special education if they are proactive and provide early intervention to their "at-risk" students (including remedial/tutorial help). Proactive schools find the means and resources to establish an array of interventions and safety nets (during the school day and extended hours) to address the various needs of their students. These include such programs and interventions as:

* Homework assistance
* Organization and study skills assistance
* Computer lab for developing research skills, learning to type, and other needs
* Practicing/reinforcing basic skills
* Assistance from peer or cross-age tutors, parents, and community volunteers
* Small group reading programs
* Extra guided reading and writing
* Math lab and tutoring
* Mentor or "special friend" programs
* Activity clubs, service clubs, sports and recreation, creative and performing arts, and other means

SSTs are most effective when they not only help the classroom teacher with designing and implementing effective classroom strategies, but can also offer students additional school supports to address their needs (as part of the general education program).

SSTs and Special Education Referrals

Special education may be required and thus play a role. The following information can be helpful:

* Schools that have effective and efficient SSTs in place can be very proactive in

identifying children with needs and intervening early with various supports, adaptations, and safety nets.

* Most districts advise teachers and other school personnel to first discuss and plan for the child with any general education supports that may be provided before referring a child to special education (for example, beginning the IEP process).
* Most districts require that schools document interventions and strategies that have already been tried as part of the referral process to special education. An SST is a perfect vehicle for doing so.

Special education referrals may come directly from a teacher or parent/guardian requesting that a student be tested to determine whether he or she qualifies for special education and/or related services. This referral process begins a legal timeline during which the designated case manager:

* Prepares paperwork
* Informs parents of legal rights/due process
* Contacts all parties involved to prepare their assessment plan for the parents to agree to (in writing)
* Has a multidisciplinary team assess the student, write their reports, and meet with the parents in an IEP (individualized education plan) meeting.

It is strongly encouraged that teachers and parents refer students through the SST process first (although this is not a requirement). It *is* a requirement that a variety of interventions and modifications be implemented for a period of time and documented before a student is permitted to be assessed for special education. The SST process is an ideal means of gathering resources and putting heads together in an effective, efficient manner to address the needs of students and make this intervention plan. Then, if more help seems warranted to meet the student's needs, it is appropriate to pursue assessment for special education. Any special education referral must include documentation of interventions that have been implemented.

When parents request an evaluation under IDEA or Section 504 of the Rehabilitation Act of 1973, keep the following in mind:

* Parents may be *asked* whether they are willing to first discuss their concerns at an SST meeting (which should be scheduled very quickly and timely).
* Parents cannot be denied the immediate initiation of the IEP process if they choose it and make that request/referral.
* Parents *always* have the right to bypass the SST and directly request a formal assessment for special education and related services under IDEA or Section 504.
* Sometimes schools will initiate the IEP evaluation process and still concurrently schedule the SST meeting to discuss and document what has already been tried and the effectiveness of those strategies/interventions.

It is important to note that a school professional may refer a child to special education without an SST meeting, as they are not required by law. However, schools generally discourage their school staff from doing so and strongly urge that the SST process be followed as a pre-referral intervention.

SSTs are sometimes perceived as the "gatekeeper" to special education, as teachers may view the process as extra "hoops to jump through" before a child is referred. The SST process *should not* significantly delay appropriate referrals for evaluation or special education, when indicated.

If You Suspect a Student Has ADHD

Recommendations and Information for Teachers and Other School Personnel

When you observe a student displaying inattentive, hyperactive, and impulsive behavior in the classroom, you should automatically attempt to deal with those behaviors by using strategies proven to be effective (for example, environmental structuring, cueing and prompting, study skills assistance, behavior modification techniques).

Obviously, this is simply good teaching practice, as all students who display the need should be provided behavioral/academic help and support. School professionals should consider the following when they wish to initiate an evaluation for students suspected of having ADHD (Rief, 1998, 2003):

* Keep records of interventions you are attempting, anecdotal records regarding the student's behaviors and classroom performance, and work samples, as well as any phone contacts/conferences with parents.
* Communicate with the previous year's teacher(s) to see if your areas of concern were also an issue the prior year; and if so, find out what strategies and interventions were used successfully or unsuccessfully by that teacher.
* Consult informally with appropriate support staff (for example, school counselor, school nurse, psychologist, or special education teacher). Always share your concerns and ask for advice and assistance as needed.

In most schools the SST process is the next step teachers should take. At the SST meeting, support staff, the classroom teacher(s), parents, and an administrator generally:

* Review the student's school history and other relevant information
* Share the child's strengths, interests, and areas of difficulty
* Discuss interventions implemented both in the past and currently
* Strategize next-step interventions and develop a plan of action, which may include implementing some more interventions in school (for example, counseling, social skills group, non-special-education academic

supports, behavioral contracts/plans, and so forth)

This initial or follow-up SST meeting is often the time and place (when discussing the child's behaviors and areas of difficulty at school and home) where, if the school suspects ADHD, an evaluation is recommended to parents.

Generally, parents are informed at this time of what the diagnostic process involves and given the options—if interested in doing so—of how to proceed with a clinically based or school-based screening/assessment.

Note: *It is vital that teachers be cautious in the way in which they express to parents their concern that a child might have ADHD, as there are potential liabilities that may be incurred. In fact, some states have legislation restricting what school personnel are permitted to discuss with parents. It is suggested that teachers check the protocol at their school. A team is the best forum for discussing whether the child's behaviors are possibly indicative of ADHD and recommending an evaluation to parents. At a minimum, one other school professional should join the teacher when doing so (for example, school nurse, counselor, psychologist).*

The following are some possible statements to use in communicating with parents:

* "These are the behaviors we have been observing that have been causing your child difficulty at school, and affecting his or her learning (or school performance)."
* "Sometimes there are physiological reasons causing these difficulties (for example, with paying attention, self-control, impulsive behavior, being highly active and restless). Of course, the only way to know that is through an evaluation."
* "You may want to consider [or "We recommend"] sharing these concerns with your child's doctor [or "having your child evaluated"]."

When meeting with parents, teachers should:

* Share objective information and descriptions of the child's performance
* Communicate their concern and caring for the child
* Emphasize the difficulties the *student* is having, not the problems the child is causing the *teacher*
* Be culturally sensitive to differences in values and norms when speaking with parents of a different race, ethnicity, or cultural background

Keep the following points in mind:

* Parents must understand that diagnosing ADHD is not simple; it requires the collection of significant data that must be interpreted to determine whether the child meets the diagnostic criteria for ADHD.
* A school-based evaluation can be conducted *for educational purposes.*
* For a medical/clinical diagnosis of ADHD to be made, the parents will need to have the school supply data to the physician/mental health professional conducting the assessment. Of course, any possible medical conditions that may cause symptoms of ADHD or "look like" ADHD would have to be determined or ruled out by a medical professional, not by school professionals.
* If parents wish to pursue an evaluation (school-based or clinically based), they will be asked to sign permission forms to enable the school to start gathering appropriate information (for example, behavioral rating scales, questionnaires, observation forms, screening devices, informal/formal diagnostic testing).
* If a formal school evaluation is decided on (psycho-educational testing), the procedures and paperwork for an IEP will be initiated.

Caution to Teachers

* Do not tell parents that you think their child has ADHD and should, therefore, be seen by their doctor.

* Do not attempt to diagnose ADHD.
* Do not recommend that the child be placed on medication or discuss medication with parents. If parents bring up the topic and ask you questions, suggest they share such questions with medical professionals.
* Do not share with parents your personal beliefs or biases about ADHD treatment approaches.
* Learn as much as you can about ADHD. Utilize a team approach and make any referrals/suggestions that the child possibly has ADHD through the team.
* Be prepared to let parents know how *you* will help implement strategies and supports to help their child (regardless of any outside treatments the parents may pursue).
* Teachers need to *objectively describe* what they see regarding the child's behavior and performance in the classroom.

The School's Role and Responsibilities in the Diagnosis of ADHD

As described in Section 1.2, the diagnosis of ADHD is dependent on gathering sufficient information to get a clear picture of how ADHD symptoms observed (currently and in previous years) affect the child in key environments. Obviously, the school is a key environment—where the child spends much of his or her life. The school's role is to provide the information and data to enable the evaluator to determine past and present school functioning.

Besides the presence of symptoms, the evaluator must obtain sufficient information in order to determine the degree of impairment the symptoms are causing (for example, academic functioning and productivity, behavioral problems, ability to make and keep friends, social/emotional functioning, and so forth). Teachers and other school personnel who interact and observe the child on a daily basis are in the best position to provide this information.

Parents have a right to expect the school to be supportive and responsive in the diagnostic process. Schools need to provide information requested by the child's physician or mental health professional conducting a clinical evaluation for ADHD. It will be necessary for parents to sign a release of information form before school personnel can communicate with other professionals outside of school or provide documentation and data regarding the child.

See Section 1.2 for data that is valuable to be provided by the school when a child is being evaluated for ADHD. For example:

* A teacher narrative of a paragraph or two indicating how he or she views the child in relation to other students in the classroom (for example, behavior, social skills, work production/output).
* Observing the child in different settings of the school day provides significant information. In addition, school personnel can provide insight and helpful data to the evaluator regarding the child's functioning by making observations in the classroom and other school settings (for example, playground).
* Information indicating the existence of symptoms in previous school years is gathered in the history and review of school records. A great deal of useful data is located in the student's school records/ cumulative file (for example, past report cards, district/state achievement testing, other school evaluations such as perhaps a previous psycho-educational assessment, past and current IEPs).
* Disciplinary referrals (which may be among the records of guidance counselors and/or administrators) may provide information about the student's behavioral problems in school.
* Copies of work samples, particularly written samples and curriculum-based assessment, are also good indicators of a child's level of performance and production. When providing work samples—particularly of writing—it is helpful to also include a scoring guide (rubric) for that product so the evaluator knows how that piece of work compares to grade-level expectations.

It is highly recommended that schools provide the information to the physician in a manner that takes into account the physician's limited time. A one- or two-page summary of the child's school history and current performance is helpful.

Teachers should be willing to speak and confer with whoever is conducting the evaluation. It is very beneficial for the physician (or other evaluator) and teacher to speak directly with each other (for example, phone conference).

Note: *If a child is receiving an outside evaluation for ADHD and the school is NOT requested to send information, and no attempt is made to communicate with or obtain input from the school, it is an* inappropriate *evaluation for ADHD. The evaluator is NOT following recommended diagnostic guidelines by the American Academy of Pediatrics or acquiring sufficient evidence to meet ADHD diagnostic criteria as determined by the American Psychiatric Association.*

Also keep in mind that the school is responsible for:

* Initiating and following through with a comprehensive evaluation if the child is suspected of having ADHD or any other disability impairing educational performance (This includes behavioral, not just academic performance.)
* Determining a student's educational impairment
* Providing supports and services to eligible students under either of the two federal laws, IDEA or Section 504 of the Rehabilitation Act of 1973

School-Based Assessment for ADHD

Some school districts are very proactive and involved in helping to identify, diagnose, and provide effective interventions for students with ADHD. These school districts generally have specified procedures and a process for school-based screening/evaluation of students for ADHD. The following steps or variations are typical in such school-based ADHD screening/assessment (Rief, 2003).

Most school-based screening/evaluation for ADHD begins with the student support team (SST) process, with parents as members of the team. In the case of a child suspected of having ADHD, teachers may be advised to carefully observe the student in comparison to other children in the classroom (for example, degree of off-task behavior, out-of-seat behavior, completion of assignments) and to start documenting or collecting evidence of difficulties in school performance (for example, work samples, anecdotal records of behavioral incidents) in preparation for the SST meeting. During the SST meeting:

* Teacher and parents will be asked to discuss their concerns and observations about the child's behavior, academic performance, social/emotional adjustment and coping skills, organization and study habits, and so forth.
* If the team determines that core symptoms of ADHD (inattention, impulsivity, hyperactivity) are a concern in the school setting, as well as at home, an initial screening for ADHD may be recommended. Parents are generally provided information about steps the school can take in the diagnostic process for possible ADHD.
* A plan of action is developed, including some specific strategies/interventions the teacher agrees to try for a period of time (usually between three and six weeks). The action plan may also involve other school supports.
* Parents are asked to sign a release of information form and give written permission to the school if they wish to proceed further. This begins a period of initial screening, which may involve:
  — Review of cumulative school records (including report card grades and teacher comments, standardized assessment, curriculum-based assessment, work samples)

  — Classroom observation by at least one person other than the classroom teacher
  — Observation, when possible, of the child in other school settings (for example, cafeteria, P.E., playground)
  — Vision and hearing screening
  — Screening scales or rating scales for teacher(s) and parents to fill out indicating existence and degree of symptoms and impairment at home and school
  — Questionnaires or structured parent interview (to gather developmental, health, family, and school history)

Note: *Generally it is the school psychologist who has the primary responsibility for interpreting the data (which can be provided by various team members such as school nurse, counselor, etc.).*

Some districts designate a time frame (for example, six to eight weeks or eight to ten weeks) to complete the following: gather all of the above information; review the data; implement and determine the effectiveness of strategies/interventions tried; and reconvene the SST to decide appropriate next steps. These next steps might include:

* Continuing strategies and interventions proving to be effective
* Choosing a new or revised set of strategies/interventions to implement
* Initiating a medical referral (with summary of above being sent with written parental consent to the child's physician)
* Initiating a referral for special education
* Providing supports, information, training, and referrals for parents
* Any or all of the above

If screening instruments indicate possible ADHD, and classroom interventions are not successful in resolving the student's difficulties, the school will generally recommend a medical and/or special education referral. In some school districts, if the child appears to have ADHD after careful review of the information gathered from screening and data review, their protocol is

* To make a medical referral
* To send the completed packet of information and brief summary page to the physician (with parental permission)
* To obtain a physician's diagnosis and statement in writing that the child has ADHD in order to be considered eligible for special education under "other health impaired" (OHI) criteria

During the school-based screening and evaluation for ADHD, it often becomes apparent that the child is also experiencing problems with learning, speech and language, motor skills, or other areas of need. Remember, there are a number of common co-existing conditions and disorders with ADHD. When this is the case, a referral for special education and assessment of all areas of concern must take place under IDEA (the IEP process).

If the school team (which includes parents) is able to determine that the ADHD symptoms are causing an adverse impact on the student's educational performance, the child is entitled under law to reasonable school accommodations and special education/related services, if needed. As ADHD is on the list of "other health impairments" under special education law (IDEA), a student whose ADHD symptoms are causing significant educational impairment, which the team agrees requires special education intervention, the student would meet the eligibility criteria under OHI—entitling that student to special education and related services. (See Section 5.4, Educational Laws and Rights of Students with ADHD.)

Most districts require a medical diagnosis of ADHD to qualify a student for special education under the category of "other health impaired." However, this is a gray area under IDEA law and varies from state to state, district to district, depending on how OHI eligibility is interpreted. As such, a school-based assessment (without physician statement or medical diagnosis) may or may not be sufficient for qualifying a student under OHI (for educational purposes only).

Services and Supports for Students with ADHD

Students with ADHD whose school performance is significantly impacted by their ADHD may be entitled to services and supports under two federal laws: (1) IDEA and (2) Section 504 of the Rehabilitation Act of 1973. If the team feels that a student may be in need of special education, they should make a referral for an evaluation under IDEA. However, many students with ADHD don't need a special education evaluation or qualify for special education. Instead, they should be considered for a Section 504 Plan evaluation, as described below.

Section 504 of the Rehabilitation Act of 1973

Section 504 of the Rehabilitation Act of 1973 is the civil rights law designed to protect the rights of people with disabilities from discrimination by any agency (for example, schools) that receives federal funding. As mentioned above, children with ADHD are often eligible for reasonable accommodations/supports, and sometimes related services, under Section 504. Students who may have been tested under IDEA and did not qualify for special education are possibly eligible for a 504 Accommodation Plan.

Note: There are no additional funds allocated for supports or services under Section 504. The school or the district office covers all services within existing programs. Again, see Section 5.4, Educational Laws and Rights of Students with ADHD, for more detailed information about IDEA and Section 504.)

SSTs and Section 504

To determine eligibility for accommodations under Section 504 of the Rehabilitation Act of 1973, the school team is also responsible for a 504 assessment. The SST also serves as the 504 team in most schools. The ADHD screening/ assessment procedures described earlier are sufficient for determining whether a child has "a physical or mental condition that significantly limits a major life activity (learning)." If a child meets that criteria under Section 504, then the SST/504 team can write a 504 Accommodation Plan for the student, which contains reasonable accommodations and supports that will be implemented to help the student.

Accommodation Plans

A good SST Action Plan is very similar to a 504 Accommodation Plan. Either might include a few specific strategies or interventions such as the following:

* *Area of difficulty:* Difficulty staying focused and on-task; inconsistent work performance/ completion

* *Actions, strategies, modifications/person(s) responsible:* (a) reduce amount of written work required (teacher); (b) break down assignments into manageable chunks (teacher and parents); (c) teacher prompting and cueing to help keep focused (teacher); (d) use a timer to motivate and increase speed of work production and provide a reward for completed tasks within those timed periods (teacher); and (e) use of a journal to go back and forth between home and school for parent/teacher communication, noting incomplete/missing assignments (parents/teacher)

Note: *Throughout this book are numerous strategies, accommodations, and modifications that can be used when tailoring appropriate interventions for an SST action plan, a 504 Accommodation Plan, or an IEP.*

School Documentation and Communication with Medical Providers and Others

School personnel can provide valuable input (observations, insights, data) regarding a student that is very useful to a clinician in the diagnostic process and in the management of any medical and/or psychosocial treatments initiated. Sections 1.2 and 5.2 describe the type of information that is recommended from teachers and other school staff who work with the student. The following are some examples of school communications to physicians that help inform the clinician about the child's functioning in the school environment and steps that the school has taken so far. These communications are helpful in facilitating a collaborative effort between the school and clinicians.

Note: *No such communication is permitted without first obtaining written consent from parents enabling the school and clinicians to share information about their child.*

Communication with Physicians

In the following example, Steven is a third-grade boy who was evaluated in second grade and found eligible for special education. He has an IEP and is receiving resource services (combination of pull-out and push-in support in his classroom). Behaviors symptomatic of ADHD had been significantly impacting his educational performance since kindergarten. The school team had shared their concern that Steven needs more intervention and recommended that parents pursue a clinical evaluation.

Parents agreed and granted the school permission (in writing) to communicate with Steven's physician and to share school data and information that may be helpful. The school team compiled the following for parents to give to the doctor:

* School testing results (psycho-educational evaluation)
* A copy of Steven's IEP
* A one-page summary of information from the cumulative records that indicated his school history and interventions that had taken place in the past
* A one-paragraph teacher statement of her direct input
* The following letter, written by his special education (resource) teacher

Sample Letter to Steven's Physician Regarding Steven B.

Dear Dr. . . .:   Date:

I am very concerned about Steven's ability to function at school, both in the large classroom and in the small-group settings. It has been my observation that Steven is unable to maintain attention or remain seated for more than a few minutes. His excessive movement and impulsivity (talking out inappropriately in class, frequently falling from his chair, difficulty keeping his hands and feet to himself, doing flips in the class when the teacher turns her back) are extremely disruptive. His behaviors impact his academic performance and also his social success.

His classroom teacher has already moved Steven several times because he is unable to sit near the other children without bothering them constantly. He typically cannot complete assignments without someone sitting directly with him and keeping him on-task and focused. Steven has been given preferential seating in the classroom (right near the teacher for direct instruction). We are also going to try letting Steven use a study carrel (partitioned office area) to help block out distractions and give him more "space" for independent work times of the day. We have recently begun use of a behavioral chart in his classroom for monitoring specific behaviors and communicating with parents on a daily basis. Our school counselor will be assisting the teacher with this, and providing incentives/rewards for successful days.

In the small group setting, I have been using a great deal of structuring and cueing. He is also on an incentive program in the resource room, with positive behaviors earning him points (which are later applied toward a bank of rewards/privileges). Even with these interventions, and only five other students in the group, Steven is having significant difficulty attending to task and controlling his behavior.

Steven is a very likable and affectionate boy. We are willing and eager to do whatever is necessary and possible to help him succeed at our school. We are pleased that Mr. and Mrs. . . . are pursuing a medical evaluation at this time to determine whether Steven has ADHD (in addition to his learning disabilities in visual-motor integration and auditory sequential memory). Enclosed you will find: the results of the psycho-educational evaluation conducted last spring by our school team, Steven's IEP, a couple of current work samples, and a summary of Steven's school history (based on past report cards, prior teacher referrals and SST action plans, and other school records). In addition, we will be happy to provide any other information/data you need for your evaluation.

Our team is committed to working closely with parents and physicians to help coordinate efforts on behalf of the child. Please feel free to contact me at any time.

Sincerely,
Name, Title
School name
School phone
Email address

The following letters are other examples of ones sent to the student's doctor, along with other appropriate documentation, records, and reports.

Sample Letter to Lucas's Doctor

Regarding: Lucas Z.   Date:

To whom it may concern [or Dear Dr. . . .]:

Lucas was referred to our school's Student Support Team in first and second grades. He was also evaluated for special education in first grade, with an IEP held on [date].

Enclosed are copies of his IEP, assessment reports, and referral forms. He was referred for testing in first grade due to academic difficulty in all areas—reading, math, and written language. He displayed poor self-control, having great difficulty settling down, staying on task, and controlling impulsive behaviors. Lucas's first-grade teacher described him as "cooperative, enthusiastic, seems to be bright."

My notes from the SST meeting on [date] include the following comments from Lucas's first-grade teacher: "Lucas is very inconsistent in his attention to task. He seems to have an auditory strength. He is lovable, with an outgoing personality. His behavior is erratic and impulsive. He can settle down, but flits from one idea to the next. He is always blurting out answers and directing everything, but he can't stay still." His kindergarten teacher also described Lucas as needing to "develop self-control."

As a result of this meeting, the team worked with Lucas and the teacher. Recommended strategies were shared with his teacher. Lucas was to continue with small-group instruction from the reading teacher, speech/language services for articulation needs, peer/cross-age tutoring, and working with the counselor on specific behaviors (with contracts, charts, positive reinforcement). Our guidance counselor was to recommend some free or affordable parenting classes to his mother.

Later that year, the school tested Lucas. He did not qualify for special education because he did not meet the eligibility criteria for having a disability. (See psycho-educational testing and reports.)

This year (second grade) Lucas was referred again on [date] to the SST by his teacher, [name]. She was and is still concerned about the same behaviors. He is noted as having a very high activity level, lack of self-control, and impulsive behavior. He is continuing to receive interventions of school counseling, small-group assistance, academic supports/tutoring, and many in-class interventions (change of seating, behavior modification, close communication with teacher and parent, someone working with him and assisting directly for much of the day). The team has met with Lucas's mother and discussed our recommendation that she pursue a medical evaluation for Lucas.

We are very concerned about Lucas. He is still trying hard to please and is very sweet and charming. He continues to receive maximum intervention within general education. His behaviors are continuing to interfere with his success in the classroom. We appreciate your assistance in helping this child.

Please let us know if we can provide any other information that will be helpful. You may contact me at any time at the numbers below, or contact other members of our team, who have known and worked with Lucas for the past few years.

Sincerely,
Name, Title
Contact numbers (home and school)
Email address

Letter to Christina's Doctor

Dear Dr. . . .:   Date:

I am writing this letter regarding Christina T. to provide you with past and current school observations, concerns, and most recent diagnostic information. Christina has attended Parker Elementary School since kindergarten, and is currently in second grade. She was evaluated last year due to her academic difficulties, and was found to have specific learning disabilities in visual processing skills (visual sequential memory, visual perception, and visual-motor integration). Christina was certified into special education and has been receiving services and supports through the resource program for the past year and a half.

Christina is a beautiful, very sweet little girl who tries hard, has a positive attitude, and wants to please. She is motivated and likes school. All teachers working with Christina since kindergarten observe that she is also very distractible, has significant difficulty focusing and attending to task, and has a high activity level. Christina talks/jabbers incessantly, is in constant motion, and has great difficulty remaining in her seat or sitting on the rug (sliding, rolling, tapping hands and feet, and so on). With gentle reminders and cues, she tries to control her behavior, but clearly it is not something she is able to do.

As Christina is one of my students, I work with her in small group daily for forty minutes three times a week (in the resource room), and in the classroom setting twice a week. She has an outstanding classroom teacher, who is very skilled at teaching children with attention and learning difficulties and willingly implements several accommodations to address her special needs. For example: Christina receives in her classroom:

* Preferential seating and many opportunities provided by her flexible teacher for movement
* Prompts/cues/reminders
* Use of timers and incentives/rewards to increase on-task behavior
* Modified/adjusted assignments
* Extra help and support on reading and writing tasks
* Behavior modification approaches

We have requested that Mr. and Mrs. T. bring this to your attention, so you are aware of Christina's school functioning. Our school team will be happy to provide any further information you may need.

Sincerely,
Name, Title
School
Phone number

Communication Between Schools

The following letter is a communication from an elementary school to the "feeder" middle school that will be receiving this particular student the following September. The purpose of this letter is to alert the middle school team of an incoming student with very significant needs. The letter is also a plea for the school to do whatever is possible to keep trying to obtain the needed help for this boy. It also illustrates the frustration and reality that, unfortunately, teachers and schools have to deal with—children with severe needs that we cannot effectively meet because "our hands are tied." Frequently (due to lack of funds), programs don't exist or the child doesn't qualify for them. In this case, the parent did not agree to school recommendations for program placement. Without parental approval, the school cannot act.

Letter Regarding Damien

Student: Damien N.   Date:
Birth date:
Grade:

Dear [name of resource/special education teacher at the middle school],

Having worked intensively with Damien over the past few years, I would like to share my observations and recommendations at this time. Our team's concern for Damien is that he may very likely have a difficult time adjusting and coping next year in middle school. Our hope is that he will receive a great deal of assistance in his transition to the middle school setting, especially with his social and emotional needs.

Damien has been medically diagnosed as having ADHD, as well as having learning disabilities. He displays all of the classic behaviors associated with ADHD, including high activity level/great need for mobility, extreme distractibility and impulsive behavior, difficulty staying seated, always touching and playing with objects around him and invading others' space, very sensitive to noises around him, and oblivious to social cues—resulting in difficulty functioning with adults and peers.

Damien has episodes of out-of-control behavior during which he is unable to remain in the classroom. On these days, he typically has not received his medication upon coming to school. Teachers need to be aware of and sensitive to his needs. Usually, when Damien receives his medication, he is capable of far more self-control, and the above-mentioned behaviors are more manageable.

Damien is a bright, capable boy with a lot of potential. He has a strong interest and aptitude for math and science. We would like to see him have every opportunity to participate and advance in math and the sciences. Damien has always been weak in reading and language skills (writing and oral expression), due to a learning disability in auditory sequential memory skills. In spite of some difficulty, Damien still has the ability to do most of the work at his grade level (with some modification and assistance).

He underachieves in his classes every year. Due to his low tolerance for frustration, Damien often resists or refuses to do work that he perceives as too difficult. Often days go by when he will not produce any work in class or only a minimal amount. Great care has always gone into placing Damien in classes with teachers who are nurturing, sensitive, and skilled in working with children with special needs.

Damien is a kind and affectionate boy. He is very good with younger children and is sweet and warmhearted. He is also quick to anger and is often upset and tearful. Adults who know him well can see beyond his behaviors, which are often disruptive and inappropriate. He is very vulnerable and likely to be "led into trouble" if the opportunity arises.

Our school team has been concerned about the strong social and emotional factors that impede his functioning at school. He is very easily frustrated and "shuts down" frequently in class and in the resource room. When he doesn't feel like working or participating (which occurs frequently and unpredictably), he will not open books, join the rest of the class, or respond when the teacher speaks to him or asks him questions.

Damien is very moody, and it is impossible to predict how he will function on any particular day. His moods and behavior fluctuate drastically. He very rarely smiles or shows signs of being happy at school. He is quiet, soft-spoken, and rather shy. Often he appears sullen and possibly depressed.

Socially, he has a very difficult time and has few friends at school. Other children basically tolerate him but don't seek him out as a friend. Damien does not pick up on social cues (facial expressions, tone of voice, and so forth) as most children do. This causes him trouble and conflict with others. He is often in the middle of a conflict and frequently is not aware of his part in it. Damien is in great need of training in social skills and appropriate responses, as well as control of impulsive behavior. He has received a great deal of counseling in school, including training/assistance in conflict resolution, dealing with anger and frustration appropriately, social skills groups, and so on. However, his needs are such that in-school counseling is not sufficient.

We have spoken to Damien's mother on several occasions regarding the importance of having him see his physician for a medical follow-up. His medication may need to be regulated or changed. We feel he needs outside counseling and more assistance/intervention than we have been able to provide at school to address his behavioral and emotional needs.

As you can see (attached assessments, IEPs, recommendations), our team has been very concerned about Damien for several years. Every school year we have had several team meetings regarding how to best meet his needs. Damien's mother is very difficult to get in touch with and often does not speak to us when we call. We have written and sent certified letters, gone to the home, met his mother at her workplace, and involved a parent facilitator. Damien has had extensive assessment. In addition to annual review meetings, we have conducted a few "review of placement" IEP meetings, as well. Damien has qualified and been eligible for more intensive special education services in smaller class settings that may have better addressed his needs. However, the parent has never agreed to nor permitted a change of placement or followed team recommendations for more intervention.

We hope that Damien will be able to make a smooth transition to middle school, and that you will be successful in helping Damien obtain the appropriate care and assistance he needs. Please feel free to contact me at any time.

Sincerely,
Name, Title
Phone Number
Email Address

Communication with Community Health Providers/Organizations

As discussed earlier, some school districts have been very proactive in developing a protocol that is used throughout the system—facilitating the identification of students who may have ADHD and in working directly and collaboratively with physicians/agencies in the community in the evaluation and treatment process.

One example is SHIP—San Diego County School Health Innovative Programs (a partnership of schools, health plans, and other health organizations). The following description of SHIP and the San Diego Unified School District's protocol for ADHD referrals is summarized from information provided by SHIP/SDUSD (7/98).

I. Background

With increasing numbers of children identified as potentially suffering from ADHD, providers have expressed concerns about:

* Too many inappropriate referrals creating long waits before first visits
* Lack of communication with schools
* Inconsistent response in addressing identified problems
* Academic and psychosocial issues mistakenly identified as ADHD

Schools identified major concerns as:

* Not knowing what medical services are available or who to refer to
* Not receiving information from health plan physicians about children who have been evaluated
* Too many inappropriate referrals for special education/accommodations

II. Purpose

To improve services to children suspected to have ADHD by:

* Reducing inappropriate referrals
* Transmitting information gathered at school site to the provider
* Coordinating follow-up at school site through transmittal of pertinent evaluation findings by the provider back to the school

SHIP and SDUSD Protocol for ADHD Referral

III. Referrals via SST

Some criteria for referrals include:

* Referrals to health plan/providers for ADHD evaluation will come only through the SST. School personnel will refer children having trouble in school to the SST for review of the possible reasons.
* The SST will review already-attempted classroom modifications, as well as possible academic or behavioral issues.
* If ADHD is determined a likely contributor, the child will be referred to his or her health plan/provider using the SHIP Referral Form.
* If the SST determines the attention disorder may be a primary problem, the PARD program will be implemented for classroom management and information gathering. (See Section 5.5, Innovative Collaborative Programs, regarding the PARD project of San Diego, which is a specialized program at San Diego City Schools for classroom management and information gathering.)
* PARD (Project for Attention Related Disorders) data will be transmitted to the child's primary care provider along with the completed SHIP referral form.
* Providers will complete their evaluation and transmit findings back to the school contact person identified on the SST reporting form.

IV. Non-SST Referrals

If providers receive referrals from other than the SST, the child's parent will be instructed to request SST evaluation at the child's school. A letter from the health plan or provider will inform parents of this requirement and direct them to the appropriate school personnel.

The Evolution of SHIP

SHIP originated in 1994 with a grant from the Foundation Consortium for School-Linked Services. The goal was to develop strategies for increasing communication, referral, and case management between school-linked services and Medi-Cal managed-care systems that receive capitated rates for providing healthcare to the same students and families.

Originally, the stakeholders included:

* *Health plans:* Community Health Group, Kaiser Permanente, ProCare (Great American)
* *School district:* San Diego Unified School District
* *Others:* American Academy of Pediatrics (local chapter), California Children's Services, UCSD Community Pediatrics, Children's Hospital, Council of Community Clinics, County Office of Education, County Health Services, County Mental Health Services, UCSD Medical Group/Healthcare Network. Later, other health plans joined SHIP (Sharp Health Plan, Universal Care).

Starting with a few pilot schools, it later expanded to include the entire San Diego Unified School District. The mission of SHIP is to develop systems for quality, resource efficient healthcare for children enrolled in schools and managed-care systems.

It was year three (1996/1997) of SHIP when the ADHD Evaluation Referral Protocol was implemented district-wide. In subsequent years, other health protocols were established (for example, asthma management, CHDP exams, head lice management, TB skin test reading at school site, school health screen referral follow-up).

The guiding principles of SHIP are

* Goals must recognize the separate, overlapping health goals of the major stakeholders. The goal of schools is to have students healthy enough for optimal learning. The goal of health plans is to keep members healthy by delivering care in a cost-effective, coordinated, and accessible manner.
* Assure continuity of care, financial stability and sustainability, and replicability to different populations.

A sample SHIP referral form is shown below.

SHIP Student Referral Form—Concerns of Behavior, Learning, and Attention

Send completed form to the agency or practitioner. Send via parent and/or use mail/fax. Copy form for school records.

Dear Child Professional,

Our observation and discussion with parents suggest there may be a non-educational component to this student's current behavior. Although it is the family's responsibility to follow through with your assessment, we are facilitating this by providing you with school-derived information. Please reach the school for a more complete description of student's current school progress and to respond to our inquiries. Parental consent (below) has been received to allow exchange of pertinent information.

Name of school: _____ Contact/position: _____

Phone number (and extension): _____ Fax number: _____

Best days/hours to reach: _____

Student's Name:_____ Student's Date of Birth: _____

Student's Grade: _____ Today's Date: _____

Student's Health Plan: _____

Name of School: _____

Sent to [professional's name/address/telephone]: _____

_____

Check that SST (student support team meeting) has occurred and PARD Materials are attached.

School checks: _____ important (appointment this week)

_____ crisis (appointment today)

_____ urgent (danger to self or others; transfer now)

Reason for Concern and Referral _____

_____

_____

_____

Results of Testing Performed at School (description below and/or results attached) _____

_____

_____

_____

Student's Current and Past Functioning at School (academic, behavior, social) _____

_____

_____

_____

Include descriptions of school interventions. _____

_____

_____

_____

Health Professional Response to Referral: _____

_____

_____

_____

This student was evaluated on [date]: _____

If the family has already or will soon be receiving an evaluation report, check the following:
_____verbal report _____a written report _____no report

Teacher Documentation

Teacher documentation of specific behaviors exhibited by the student is very helpful to a diagnostician. Examples include emotional/behavioral outbursts, frustration exhibited by tearing up papers, inability to stay on task/work independently as noted by completing only one or two math problems during a twenty-minute independent seatwork period, and so on.

Teachers use a number of systems for jotting down notes to themselves to save as "mind joggers" for documentation, reasons for referrals, parent/teacher conferences, and other purposes.

Some teachers have a ring of index cards with each student's name on a different card. Whenever something occurs in class that the teacher wants to recall, he or she jots down the incident and the date on that student's card. Some teachers carry pads of stick-on notes in their pockets. When they want to write themselves a note regarding a student, they use the stick-on note and place it in their lesson plan book. Later, they transfer all of these notes into a folder that they maintain on each student. These anecdotal records, together with a collection of work samples, are very useful sources of documentation.

Educational Laws and Rights of Students with ADHD

*T*here are two main federal laws protecting students with disabilities—including those with ADHD: (1) Individuals with Disabilities Education Improvement Act (IDEA 2004) and (2) Section 504 of the Rehabilitation Act of 1973. IDEA is a special education law. Section 504 is a civil rights statute prohibiting discrimination on the basis of disabling conditions by programs and activities that receive or benefit from federal financial assistance.

Both laws guarantee to qualifying students a *free and appropriate public education* (FAPE) and instruction in *the least restrictive environment* (LRE), which means education with their non-disabled peers, to the maximum extent appropriate to their needs.

There are differences between Section 504 and IDEA with regard to eligibility criteria, procedures and safeguards, and the services/supports available under both. Therefore, it is important for all parties involved in the care and education of the child (e.g., parents, educators, clinicians) to be aware of the key components of both of these laws, how they differ, as well as the advantages and disadvantages of both in serving students with ADHD.

Individuals with Disabilities Act (IDEA)

At the time of this writing, after three years of development and negotiation, the eagerly-awaited reauthorization of IDEA 1997 has just taken place. On November 19, 2004, the U.S. Congress passed IDEA 2004, with portions of the new law becoming effective upon President Bush's signature, while other provisions become effective on July 1, 2005. The summary below contains what was in existence from the previous IDEA 1997 and continues to be requirements in IDEA 2004, as well as some of the new provisions that have been changed from IDEA 1997 and added into IDEA 2004 (CHADD, 2004; The Council for Exceptional Children, 2004).

Who Is Eligible?

IDEA sets clear eligibility criteria that school districts follow in determining whether or not a child qualifies for special education and related services. The student must be found to meet the criteria of one of 13 different disability categories; and it needs to be determined that the disability is significantly impairing the child's educational performance. This is an IEP team decision based upon the data collected, assessment, and the input of parents, educators, and other team members.

Note: Later in this section, the members of the IEP team are listed.

The thirteen disability categories under IDEA include:

* Autism
* Deaf-blindness

* Deafness
* Emotional disturbance
* Hearing impairment
* Mental retardation
* Multiple disabilities
* Orthopedic impairment
* Other health impairment
* Specific learning disability
* Speech or language impairment
* Traumatic brain injury
* Visual impairment including blindness

At the discretion of the state and the Local Education Agency (LEA), a child ages three through nine may be found eligible for special education and related services if he or she is experiencing *development delays* in one or more of the following areas, and by reason thereof, needs special education and related services (Debettencourt, 2002; Wright & Wright, 2000):

* Physical development
* Cognitive development
* Communication development
* Social or emotional development
* Adaptive development

Under which disability category do children with ADHD most commonly qualify? Some students with ADHD qualify for special education and related services under the category of Specific Learning Disability (SLD), as many children with ADHD also have co-existing learning disabilities. There are some children with ADHD whose emotional needs are to the degree that they may qualify under the category of Emotional Disturbance (ED). However, students with ADHD are most typically eligible for special education and related services under the IDEA disability criteria of "Other Health Impaired" (OHI).

"Other Health Impaired (OHI)" Eligibility Criteria

Eligibility criteria under this category requires that:

* The child *has a chronic or acute health problem* (for example, asthma, ADHD, diabetes)
* Causing *limited* strength, vitality, *or alertness with respect to the educational environment.*

Note: *When applied to ADHD, this includes the child's heightened alertness to environmental stimuli that results in limited alertness to the educational environment.*

* The health problem results in *an adverse effect on the child's educational performance*
* To the degree that *special education is needed.*

Points to be aware of (Rief, 2003)

* Students whose ADHD significantly impairs their educational performance have been able to qualify for special education and related services under the OHI category (if meeting the criteria) for many years. However, many students were never served under this category by their school districts. Not until the final regulations of IDEA '97 were published in 1999 was ADD and ADHD specifically named on the list of chronic health problems.
* In the past, many school districts have refused to consider ADHD in the category of "other health impairment." Fortunately, the 1999 regulations eliminated any ambiguity and excuse for school districts to deny students with attention deficit disorders who have the need for special education to their right to receive services under OHI.
* Most states and school districts require a medical diagnosis of ADHD and a physician's statement of such to qualify a student under OHI. However, this varies from state to state, district to district - depending on how OHI is interpreted.
* Some states/districts do not require a medical diagnosis in determining that a child has an attention deficit disorder for

educational purposes. Check with your local school district regarding specific requirements for OHI.

✷ The adverse effect on educational performance is not limited to academics, but can include impairments in other aspects of school functioning, as well. Proving a negative impact on educational performance does not require failing grades or test scores; it can also involve other aspects of the student's functioning at school (for example, impairments in social/emotional/behavioral functioning, deficient study skills and work production affecting learning).

✷ Children with ADHD do not automatically qualify for special education services under IDEA. It must be determined that the disability or condition significantly impairs a child's educational performance resulting in a need for special education and related services.

Referral and Evaluation

✷ Parents or school personnel may refer a child, requesting an evaluation to determine eligibility for special education and related services.

✷ An assessment plan is developed by the school's multidisciplinary evaluation team, addressing all areas of suspected disability. A variety of assessment tools and strategies must be used to gather relevant functional, developmental, and academic information.

✷ After parents/guardians are informed of their rights, and consent to the assessment plan, the child receives a comprehensive evaluation by the multidisciplinary team of school professionals.

✷ After the evaluation, an IEP meeting is scheduled with the IEP Team, which is composed of: the parents; not fewer than one regular education teacher of the child; not fewer than one special education teacher/provider; an individual who can interpret the instructional implications of evaluation results; a school system representative who is knowledgeable about the general education curriculum, available resources, and qualified to provide or supervise provision of specially designed instruction; the student (when appropriate); and others (at the discretion of the parent or agency) who have knowledge or special expertise regarding the child.

✷ Based on the results of the evaluation, including input provided by parents and others, the team (including the parents) determines whether the child meets eligibility criteria under one of the disability categories defined by IDEA, and the educational needs of the child.

✷ If parents have had their child evaluated by an outside source, the IEP Team must consider (but does not have to agree with) their findings.

✷ An *Individualized Education Program* (IEP) also known as an *Individualized Educational Plan* is developed and written for qualifying students through a collaborative team effort. It is tailored and designed to address the educational needs of the student with disabilities.

✷ At all stages, parents are an integral part of the process and team; and the IEP does not go into effect until parents sign the IEP and agree to the plan.

IDEA has very specific requirements as to the content of the IEP, including some of the following:

✷ Present levels of educational performance (academic and functional)—including how the child's disability affects his/her involvement and progress in the general education curriculum.

✷ A statement of measurable annual goals (academic and functional) designed to enable the child to be involved in and make progress in the general education curriculum, and meet other educational needs resulting from the child's disability.

* A description of how the child's progress toward meeting the annual goals will be measured, and when periodic reports on the child's progress toward goals will be provided.
* A statement of the special education and related services, supplementary aids/ services (based on peer-reviewed research to the extent practicable), and any program modifications or supports to be provided to the child or on behalf of the child (support for school personnel).
* The extent (if any) to which the child will not participate with non-disabled children in the regular class and other school activities.
* A statement of any individual appropriate accommodations that are necessary to measure the academic achievement and functional performance of the child on state and district-wide assessments.
* Dates and places—specifying when, where, how often services and modifications will be provided, and by whom.
* Beginning not later than the first IEP to be in effect when the child is 16, and updated annually thereafter—(a) appropriate measurable postsecondary goals based upon age-appropriate transition assessments related to training, education, employment, and, where appropriate, independent living skills; (b) the transition services (including courses of study) needed to assist the child in reaching those goals.

After the IEP Is Written

* Services are provided. This includes all programs, supplemental aids, services, program modifications, and accommodations.
* Progress is measured and reported to parents. Parents are informed of progress toward IEP goals during the year, and an annual IEP review meeting is required.
* Students are reevaluated at least once every three years (triennial evaluation), unless the parent and the local educational agency agree that a reevaluation is unnecessary.

What Are Related Services?

The following are some related services/benefits a student may receive from special education. Related services, as listed under IDEA, include (but are not limited to):

* Speech-language pathology services
* Transportation
* Occupational therapy
* Orientation and mobility services
* Parent counseling and training
* Physical therapy
* Audiology services
* Counseling services
* Early identification and assessment of disabilities in children
* Medical services
* Psychological services
* Recreation
* Rehabilitation counseling services
* School nurse services that enable a child with a disability to receive a FAPE as described in his or her IEP
* Social work services
* Interpreting services

Note: *The information regarding IDEA throughout this entire section is predominantly summarized from: Office of Special Education & Rehabilitative Services (2000), The Council for Exceptional Children (November 2004), Wright (November 2004), Bill Number H.R. 1350 (2004), and NICHCY (November 2004).*

Section 504

Who Is Eligible?

Students with ADHD may also be protected under Section 504 of the Rehabilitation Act of 1973 (even if they do not meet eligibility criteria under IDEA for special education). Section 504 is a federal civil rights statute that:

* Protects the rights of people with disabilities from discrimination by any agencies

receiving federal funding (including all public schools)

∗ Applies to students with a record of (or who are regarded as having) a physical or mental impairment that substantially limits one or more major life function. These life functions include: learning, caring for oneself, performing manual tasks, working, seeing/hearing, walking, speaking, and breathing. In the case of ADHD, the negative impact of the disorder on *learning* is key.

∗ Is intended to provide students with disabilities equal access to education and commensurate opportunities to learn as their non-disabled peers.

Note: Some districts may ask parents for a letter or some documentation from the medical or mental health provider that confirms the child's diagnosis.

If the school team determines that the child's ADHD does significantly limit his or her learning, the child/teen would be eligible for a 504 Plan designating:

∗ *Reasonable accommodations* in the educational program
∗ Related aids and services, if deemed necessary (for example, counseling, assistive technology)

The implementation of a 504 Plan typically falls under the responsibility of general education, not special education. A few sample classroom accommodations may include:

∗ Tailoring homework assignments
∗ Extended time for testing
∗ Preferential seating
∗ Supplementing verbal instructions with visual instructions
∗ Organizational assistance
∗ Using behavioral management techniques
∗ Modifying test delivery

Although it is often assumed that students served under Section 504 are limited in only being able to receive accommodations and supports within the general education program, that is not the case. Actually, under Section 504 there are no limits on the services provided (for example, counseling and speech both may be included), or where the services may be provided—in general education or special education classrooms. (DeBettencourt, 2002). Basically, the child may receive any services/supports the team decides are necessary.

Evaluation for Section 504 Eligibility

The school may be asked to evaluate and determine whether or not a student is eligible for accommodations and supports under Section 504, if not under IDEA. Parents or school personnel may refer a child by requesting an evaluation to determine if a child is eligible for special education and/or related services, supports, accommodations under IDEA or Section 504. It is best to put this request in writing.

To determine eligibility under Section 504 (the impact of the disability on learning), the school is required to do an assessment. This may be a much less extensive evaluation than that conducted for the IEP process, although the same evaluation required for special education evaluation can also be used to determine Section 504 eligibility. The 504 evaluation draws on information from a variety of sources, as does an evaluation under IDEA. Unlike an evaluation under IDEA, a Section 504 assessment does not require consent of parents, only notification.

What Both Laws Have in Common:

∗ Require school districts to provide FAPE in the LRE
∗ Provide supports (adaptations/accommodations/modifications) to enable the student to participate and learn in the general education program
∗ Provide opportunity for student to participate in extracurricular and non-academic activities

* Nondiscriminatory evaluation by the school district
* Procedural due process (although more procedural safeguards and due process rights exist under IDEA than Section 504)

Which One May Be Better for a Student with ADHD—A 504 Plan or an IEP?

As I point out in another publication (Rief, 2003), this is a decision that the team (parents and school personnel) must make considering eligibility criteria and the specific needs of the individual student. For students with ADHD who have more significant school difficulties, IDEA is usually preferable because:

* IEPs provide more protections (procedural safeguards, monitoring, and regulations) with regard to evaluation, frequency of review, parent participation, disciplinary actions, and other factors.
* Specific measurable goals are a key component of the plan, and regularly monitored for progress
* There is a much wider range of program options, services and supports available.
* IDEA provides funding for programs/services (Section 504 is non-funded).
* IEPs must include positive behavioral supports/interventions for students having behavioral difficulties.

For students who have milder impairments, and don't *need* special education, a 504 Plan is a faster, easier procedure for obtaining accommodations and supports. They can be very effective for those students whose educational needs can be addressed through adjustments, modifications, and accommodations in the general curriculum/classroom.

Remember: A diagnosis of ADHD does not guarantee or automatically qualify a student for services or accommodations under either IDEA

or Section 504. A school-based assessment must determine that the ADHD is adversely affecting the child's learning or educational performance. Under IDEA, that negative impact on the child's functioning at school must be to the degree that the team feels special education is necessary. Under Section 504, the negative effect of ADHD on the child's learning must be evident, but not necessarily to the degree that special education is needed.

Disciplining Students with Disabilities Under Special Education Law

IDEA provides protections for students with disabilities so they are not unfairly disciplined when misbehavior stems from the disability itself. This safeguard is particularly important to students with ADHD whose behavior frequently results in disciplinary action.

Before a student with a disability is suspended for more than ten days (see circumstances below which constitute a "change in placement"), expelled, or placed in another setting due to behavioral issues and violations of school rules, a "Manifestation Determination Review" must be conducted.

What is "Manifestation Determination Review"?

The following describe this review process:

* This is a review that must take place no later than ten school days from the time the school makes the decision to change the placement of a child with a disability because of a violation of a code of student conduct.
* The local educational agency (school), the parent, and relevant members of the IEP Team must review all relevant information in the student's file, including the child's IEP, any teacher observations, and information provided by the parent to determine: (a) if the conduct in question was caused by or

had a direct and substantial relationship to the child's disability, or (b) if the conduct in question was the direct result of the school's failure to implement the IEP.

* If either of the above was the case, then the student's conduct shall be determined to be a manifestation of the child's disability.
* If the IEP Team does make the determination that the conduct was a manifestation of the child's disability, it must:
  — Conduct a functional behavioral assessment (FBA) and implement a behavioral intervention plan (BIP).
  — Review and modify any existing BIP (if one already had been developed for the student), in order to address the child's behaviors.
  — Return the child to the placement from which the child was removed, unless the parent and local educational agency agree to a change of placement as part of the modification of the BIP.
* A Manifestation Determination Review is not required under certain circumstances to exceed the ten-day suspension or change the student's placement. See below regarding those exceptions.

Do These Disciplinary Safeguards Apply Only to Students with an IEP?

A student facing disciplinary action constituting a change of placement may be protected under the provisional safeguards of IDEA if the school district had knowledge that the child/teen was a student with a disability before the behavior that precipitated the disciplinary action occurred, meaning:

* If the parent stated concern in writing to the administrator, teacher, or the supervisor that the child/teen is in need of special education and related services
* If the parent had requested an evaluation
* If the student's teacher or other school personnel expressed specific concerns about a child's pattern of behavior directly to the

director of special education or to other supervisory personnel

Change of Placement

* A "change of placement" with regard to suspensions is defined as more than ten consecutive days of suspension *or* multiple short-term removals/suspensions exceeding ten days during the school year that constitute "a pattern."
* The length (and total amount) of time the student is removed, as well as the type of behaviors and incidents, are considered in determining the existence of a pattern.
* Under IDEA, services must be provided to the student with an IEP after the tenth consecutive day of suspension (or nonconsecutive removals constituting a pattern that exceed ten days) in order to help the child/teen continue to progress in his or her IEP goals and general curriculum.
* Schools can remove a student with disabilities up to forty-five school days without regard to whether the behavior is determined to be a manifestation of the child's disability in cases of: carrying or possessing a weapon; for knowingly using, selling, or soliciting illegal drugs or controlled substances at school or school functions; or inflicting serious bodily injury upon another person while at school, on school premises, or at a school function. These are the only circumstances that a school may exceed the ten-day suspension and place a student in an alternative setting for forty-five school days without an order from a hearing officer.
* Parents have a right to ten days' notice before a school proposes changing the child's placement. They also may request an impartial due process hearing if they disagree with the school's decision.

If the school believes the student presents a danger to self or others, an emergency order can be filed for the student's removal. An impartial hearing officer can order the child/teen to be removed to an Interim Alternative Educational Setting (IAES) for up to forty-five school days if he or she determines:

* There is substantial evidence that the current placement is likely to result in injury to the student or to others.
* The school made reasonable efforts to minimize the risk of harm, including the use of supplementary aids and services.
* The IAES will provide the student the opportunity to continue to participate in the general curriculum with the services and modifications of his or her IEP.

Students with disabilities in alternative settings must continue to receive a free and appropriate education. IDEA regulations include a "stay-put" or "frozen placement" provision, meaning that:

* If either party requests an impartial due process hearing, the child/teen remains in the last agreed upon (then current) placement until all administrative and legal proceedings are resolved.
* The "stay-put" provision applies to suspensions or expulsions that constitute a change of placement. It does not apply to cases involving drugs and weapons, or when the student is deemed a threat to self or others—which enables the school to place the child/teen in the forty-five school day IAES.

If a student engages in behaviors that "impede his or her learning or that of others," then the IEP Team must consider appropriate strategies, including positive behavioral interventions, strategies, and supports to address that behavior.

***Note:** Information for this section on discipline procedures under IDEA is adapted from the U.S. Department of Education (1999, 2000), Wright & Wright (2004), Council for Exceptional Children (2004), and Wright (November, 2004).*

What Are FBA and BIP?

Rief (2003) describes a functional behavioral assessment FBA) as examining the antecedents (conditions that exist or events that may be identified as triggers to the problem behaviors). Antecedents involve any number of factors (e.g., environmental, physical, performance and skill demands, teacher/student interactions) that precede the problem behavior and may be adjusted to prevent or reduce the reoccurrence of the misbehavior in the future.

The FBA also looks at the consequences that occur (positive and negative) as a result of the misbehavior.

***Note:** When problematic behaviors occur repeatedly, something is reinforcing or sustaining that behavior. In other words, the consequences (e.g., teacher interaction with the student, being sent out of the classroom) are actually meeting a function or need of that student (for example, attention, or escaping an unpleasant task).*

By examining these factors in the classroom and/or other school settings, a Behavioral Intervention Plan (BIP) is then developed specific to that student. The BIP is designed with a focus on utilizing proactive strategies and interventions to avoid and reduce the likelihood of problematic behavior, and teaching the student appropriate strategies and skills.

The team also identifies positive reinforcers to use with the student in the implementation of a behavioral plan that are meaningful and motivating to the individual student. Corrective consequences appropriate to the student's disability are included in the plan and need to be implemented by those adults responsible for disciplining the student. (See Section 2.3, Individualized Behavior Management, Interventions, and Supports, for more information on these topics.)

The Value of an FBA and a BIP

A great deal of student misbehavior could be reduced or eliminated if attention was paid to the triggering events/conditions, and if a well-thought-out plan of response to misbehavior and encouragement of positive behavior was developed for the individual child/teen. A proactive plan is generally far more beneficial than focusing on punishments—especially those leading to removal of the student from the classroom or school environment.

I hope more focus on FBAs and BIPs for students with behavioral challenges will become the norm, rather than the exception, as they currently are in most school districts. For this to happen, more resources need to be allocated and intervention teams formed (e.g., to observe, assess, consult, and develop effective behavioral intervention plans with teachers and parents). The good news is that IDEA 2004 emphasizes the importance of FBAs, BIPs, and "Positive Behavioral Supports." Hopefully, the training of school staff and provision of resources will be prioritized to ensure implementation.

The Reauthorization of IDEA

As mentioned earlier, IDEA was just reauthorized (IDEA 2004) at the time of this writing. It is awaiting the president's signature which will then make it the new special education law of the nation. Throughout the past few years during the reauthorization process, there was much input provided to members of the House of Representatives and Senate; and great concern about possible changes to the law. The House of Representatives introduced their bill (H.R. 1350) to reauthorize the IDEA (presented March, 2002). The Senate IDEA reauthorization bill (S.1248) was presented in July, 2003. By far, the House bill proposed the most significant changes to IDEA 1997, which if passed would have significantly weakened the protections of children with disabilities. The Senate bill was much more closely aligned with the position of disability organizations such as CHADD, The Council for Exceptional Children (CEC), and many others. But, there were proposals in that bill, as well, that could have diminished the protections of students with disabilities.

A report entitled "In the Best Interests of All" by the Children's Behavioral Alliance (CBA), a coalition of advocacy organizations organized by CHADD in response to findings of the President's Commission on Excellence in Special Education, the No Child Left Behind (NCLB) Act, and the upcoming reauthorization of IDEA Act Amendments, was endorsed by several of the nation's leading mental health and education advocacy organizations. The CBA's recommendations (CHADD, 2003; CBA, 2003) regarding the proposed new legislation included some of the following, among a number of others:

* Ensure that children with social, emotional, and/or behavioral problems remain covered by existing eligibility categories within IDEA.
* Amend IDEA to ensure that Functional Behavioral Assessments and Behavior Intervention Plans and School-wide Positive Behavioral Supports are used preventively in response to social, emotional, and/or behavioral problems that have not diminished through the use of standard intervention practices.
* Fully fund IDEA at the 40% federal level originally promised by Congress.
* Require periodic behavioral/mental health screening of all children.
* Expand IDEA Part D professional development requirements to ensure that all educational and related services staff receive training in positive behavioral supports, functional behavioral assessments, and behavioral intervention planning, and to assure availability within all districts of support staff with more intensive training in such strategies.
* Amend IDEA to include the "fully-qualified teacher" provisions and timeliness of the NCLB of 2001 in IDEA and apply them to special education.
* Increase funding for integrated services among schools, juvenile courts, child welfare,

and community mental health providers and tie increases in federal funding to coordinated models of service delivery.

IDEA 2004

Disability organizations are for the most part pleased with the final approval of IDEA 2004 and the contents of the new law, and appreciate the efforts of Congress. The information throughout this section incorporated many (not all) of the revisions and updated requirements of the new law, that have so recently been made public. There are a number of other changes, as well. Of course, it will be necessary for parents and everyone involved in the education of students with disabilities to obtain more information from a variety of resources and your local school district as it becomes available, clarifying all of the changes in IDEA 2004 and provisions under the new law.

The following are just some of the points that are new in the law:

* Language has been added giving school personnel authority, on a "case by case basis," to consider unique circumstances when determining whether to order a change of placement for a child with a disability who violates a code of student conduct.
* Special education teachers are now also required to meet standards of a "highly qualified teacher."
* In determining the impact of a disability on a student's educational functioning and educational needs, IDEA 2004 specifically refers to the academic, developmental, and functional needs of children.
* School officials under the new law are explicitly prohibited from forcing parents to medicate children as a condition for attending school.
* Specific learning disability (SLD) eligibility criteria under the new law has also changed. The local educational agency is no longer required to determine that the child

has a severe discrepancy between achievement and intellectual ability (in oral expression, listening comprehension, written expression, basic reading skill, reading comprehension, mathematical calculation, or mathematical reasoning). Now a local educational agency is permitted to use a process that determines if the child responds to scientific, research-based intervention as a part of the required evaluation procedures.
* Benchmarks and short-term objectives written into the IEPs are no longer required for many students, reducing the amount of IEP paperwork.

Note: This is just a brief listing of some of the key changes in IDEA 2004. There is much that will need clarification regarding the changes; and until the final federal regulations are issued, the implications of the changes are unclear.

No Child Left Behind (NCLB)

Another important law that affects all school-age children in public schools throughout the United States is NCLB.

On January 8, 2002, the No Child Left Behind (NCLB) Act was signed into law by President Bush, which reauthorized and replaced the Elementary and Secondary Education Act of 1965, the federal framework for how we provide public education throughout the U.S. The overall aim of NCLB is to have all students performing at proficient levels in the two educational cornerstones, reading and math, by year 2014, while at the same time closing the achievement gaps of certain populations of students (for example, those of minority groups, students who are English language learners, those who are economically disadvantaged, and students who have a disability) (Schrag, 2003).

Key requirements and provisions of the law include:

* Annual proficiency testing of reading and math by all students in grades three through eight (with science being phased in).

* Schools, districts, and states must submit for review and publish report cards including: student achievement data by subgroups, names of schools identified as needing improvement, professional qualifications of teachers, Annual Yearly Progress (AYP), and other data.
* Highly qualified teachers in every classroom (by 2005–2006 school year).
* Research-based instruction.
* Sanctions against schools who fail to make progress in reaching the goal of all students being proficient by 2014.
* Increased parental rights and public school choice. (Ratcliff, 2003; Wright, Wright & Heath, 2004)

States are required to set annual yearly progress (AYP) targets and annual measurable objectives for student progress, and ensure that school districts test at least 95 percent of students. Districts and schools must report their overall progress and progress in educating specific groups of children who are often left behind, including: low-income students, students with disabilities, English language learners (limited English proficient students), and students from racial/ethnic groups. To meet NCLB standard, all student subgroups must make sufficient academic progress so all students are proficient by 2014. The progress of all schools will be evaluated and the results made public (Wright, Wright & Heath, 2004).

Schools are held accountable for student progress. Schools that have not made adequate yearly progress (AYP) in two years will be identified as needing improvement. Parents in those schools are given the option to transfer to a non-failing school in the district. If the school fails to make AYP for three consecutive years, it must provide free, supplemental services to children remaining there (e.g., tutoring, after-school programs). Such supplemental services must be from a state-approved list of service providers with a proven track-record of success. There are increasingly more severe sanctions in future

years if schools fail to make AYP (for example, replacing school staff, school restructuring).

NCLB places a strong emphasis on reading—and providing children early intervention so that all students will read at or above grade level by the third grade. Part B of NCLB addresses Student Reading Skills Improvement Grants. States submit Reading First grant proposals—with goals and a plan to establish high-quality comprehensive reading instruction for children K–3. Reading First funds applied for must be used for research-based reading programs for students K–3 (Ratcliffe, 2003).

Title IV of NCLB is "21st Century Schools." The purposes of Title IV are to create safe, orderly schools; to protect students and teachers, to encourage discipline and personal responsibility, and to combat drugs (Wright, Wright & Heath, 2004).

Part A under Title IV is "Safe and Drug-Free Schools and Communities." The purposes of Part A are:

* To support programs that prevent violence
* To prevent the illegal use of alcohol, tobacco, and drugs
* To involve parents and communities, and
* To support student academic achievement (20 U.S.C. §7102)

Some key provisions of Part A according to Wright, Wright, and Heath (2004) include:

* Funds are available for school drug and violence prevention programs with priority to programs that prevent violence and drug use for at-risk populations (20 U.S.C. §7112).
* Schools must have a comprehensive plan to keep the school safe, including school discipline policies, security procedures, prevention activities, a crisis management plan, and a student code of conduct (20 U.S.C. §7114).
* Funds are available for educational programs that prevent hate crimes and

improve the conflict or dispute resolution skills of students, teachers, and administrators (20 U.S.C. §7133).

Of concern is the mixed messages that schools are receiving between NCLB and IDEA with regard to discipline. This is very important particularly for students with ADHD.

"On the one hand, NCLB empowers teachers to remove violent or persistently disruptive students from the classroom; and in order to receive funding, states must adopt a zero-tolerance policy towards these students. At the same time, many students who demonstrate violent or persistently disruptive behavior have an emotional or other disability, are already identified as needing special services and, according to IDEA, are entitled to functional behavioral assessments to determine the message behind the behavior or manifestation determination to determine whether the behavior is a result of a child's disability. There is a legitimate concern that teachers and administrators may get mixed messages between the two pieces of legislation." (*SpecialEdge—Ensuring Safe Schools,* 2003)

There are many excellent provisions of NCLB that are of benefit to students with ADHD, LD, or other learning/behavioral difficulties. The emphasis on research-based instruction, early intervention, high standards and accountability for schools to enable *all* students to reach standards and succeed is a good thing. The pressure on administrators and teachers to accomplish this goal, can have a negative impact on their willingness to accommodate and welcome students with ADHD and other disabilities in their classrooms/school.

Readers are strongly urged to become very familiar with IDEA 2004 as well as follow any future amendments, regulations, or changes to U.S. educational laws. Recommended sources/websites are listed at the end of Part 5. With regard to how IDEA 2004 impacts students with ADHD, see the educational rights and legal information available on the CHADD website at www.chadd.org and National Resource Center on AD/HD at www.help4adhd.org.

Innovative Collaborative Programs for Helping Children with ADHD

Some unique projects and programs are being implemented with success in the nation that involve collaborative efforts in the community (between clinicians, schools, and parents) to best address the needs of children with ADHD. This section turns the spotlight on three such innovative programs:

1. The Utah Model—Intermountain Health Care's (IHC's) Care Management System for ADHD (Salt Lake City, Utah)
2. The Project for Attention Related Disorders (PARD) of San Diego, California
3. OU Pediatrics/Kendall Whittier Elementary— Collaborative Model of Care in Tulsa, Oklahoma

The Utah Model is taking place in the Salt Lake City area, with involvement and interest by policymakers at the state level. It may very well become the model of care for children with ADHD throughout the state of Utah. The PARD project affects all children with ADHD in a large school district—those attending San Diego City Schools. The project in Tulsa, Oklahoma, is a smaller-scale collaborative involving a targeted school, with a school-based mental health provider and the University of Oklahoma Pediatrics Clinic in Tulsa.

Two of the projects (Utah's and Tulsa's) were part of the National Initiative for Children's Healthcare Quality (NICHQ)—ADHD Initiative. They had both been showcased as successful projects at NICHQ's International Summit Meeting (Orlando, Florida, November 2002). This summit conference brought together healthcare delivery organizations from around the United States and educators to share NICHQ's vision of transforming the healthcare experience and outcomes of children with attention deficit disorders and their families.

I am fortunate to have worked with these teams as a faculty member of NICHQ. In addition, I had the privilege of being invited to speak and train in their communities, and to observe in action the outstanding, innovative work they do that is making such a positive impact on the lives of children with ADHD. For information about this national initiative and on developing collaborative care models in your community, see *The ADHD Book of Lists* (Rief, 2003). Also, visit the NICHQ website at www.nichq.org.

I have also been privileged to be involved with the PARD project in the earlier years, at the time when I was a mentor-teacher in San Diego City Schools. I learned a great deal as a result of my involvement with PARD and its dedicated, knowledgeable leaders, especially

Susie Horn, R.N. (school nurse and PARD project coordinator), and Dr. Dorothy Johnson. I am delighted to showcase all three of these programs.

In all of the programs described, names of some of the key individuals involved are included, to recognize and credit those who were instrumental in the development of their respective programs/projects. Readers wishing to contact or learn more about any of the following may find specific individuals named and contact information provided at this time are subject to change.

The Utah Model—Intermountain Health Care's (IHC's) Care Management System for ADHD

The source of the following information is from the key team members of this care management system/project, which can be found in the reference list for Part 5.

This model of collaborative care taking place in Utah to address the needs of children with ADHD is hailed by many as the "Cadillac" for delivering family-centered, evidence-based care that is closely integrated with the resources of the community, yet sustainable within the care system.

How Was the Model Developed?

The development of the ADHD care management system has been a collaborative effort between Intermountain Health Care (IHC), the Intermountain Pediatric Society (IPS), which is the American Academy of Pediatrics' Utah Chapter, and Children and Adults with Attention Deficit Disorder (CHADD) of Utah. The system includes a Care Process Model (CPM) for physicians, a School Packet, a Parent Guide, and clinical support materials to make care delivery easier. The hope of the development team is to integrate the ADHD Care Management System into routine practice throughout healthcare and school systems.

Why Was the Model Developed?

Project Overview

There has been growing concern throughout the country regarding the quality of care for children diagnosed with ADHD. The results of the landmark Multimodal Treatment Approach (MTA) Study of ADHD done by the National Institute of Mental Health a few years ago (see Section 1.1) helped to reveal some of the problems regarding the community treatment of ADHD. Soon after, the American Academy of Pediatrics (AAP) released clinical practice guidelines for ADHD. Within the Salt Lake City, Utah, community, strategies were sought for meeting these newly established guidelines. To do so, they believed it was necessary to form a project team—coordinating the efforts of the three principal parties involved in the care and treatment of children with ADHD: parents, educators, and the primary care physician.

The makeup of the project team reflects this bias. The team was composed of two physicians (a pediatrician and a child psychiatrist), a school psychologist, and a parent of a child with ADHD who is involved with CHADD of Utah. Thus, the team contained representatives of the medical community, the schools, and the family. These team members included Jeffrey Schmidt, M.D., a pediatrician at the Sandy Health Center; Sam Coates, M.D., a child psychiatrist in Provo; Terry Illes, Ph.D., a school psychologist in the Jordan School District; and Linda Smith, education director of CHADD of Utah and a parent of a child with ADHD.

The primary objective was to provide a practical tool that would help to implement the AAP guidelines, and thus improve the community practice of ADHD within the greater Salt Lake City area. Toward this objective, the team developed a care management system for Intermountain Health Care (IHC), which is the largest HMO in the Salt Lake City area. A unique aspect of the project was the inclusion of a method for uniting the efforts of parents and schools with the treatment provided by physicians. By establishing collaboration links among parents, schools, and physicians, the team hoped to meet the AAP guidelines and achieve a high standard of care for children with ADHD within the state of Utah.

The outcome of this team's efforts was the development of a comprehensive care management system that is the first of its kind in the United States. The system provides practical tools to improve coordination of care for children with ADHD.

The tools are produced by Intermountain Health Care (IHC) and supported by the Intermountain Pediatric Society and its national organization, the American Academy of Pediatrics. It is also supported by the national non-profit organization and the Utah Chapter of Children and Adults with Attention Deficit Disorders.

Goals of the Project

The stated goals are

* To provide accurate information about the evaluation and treatment of ADHD to parents, schools, and physicians
* To establish standardized community procedures regarding the evaluation and treatment of ADHD
* To clarify the roles of parents, schools, and physicians in the care of children with ADHD
* To foster communication among parents, schools, and physicians regarding the treatment of children with ADHD
* To encourage the development of long-term, multimodal treatment plans that recognize ADHD as a chronic health concern
* To increase monitoring of treatment effects (particularly medication)

Project Description

The project team developed three manuals that provide information and tools to parents, schools, and physicians to help direct the care of children with ADHD. An overview of each of the three manuals is provided here.

Physician's Manual (Care Process Manual or CPM)

The physician's manual contains the IHC care process model for the management of ADHD. It is designed to provide physicians with a model of best care based on latest evidence. This manual is distributed to family practitioners and pediatricians within the IHC community and to interested non-IHC doctors in the State of Utah. Training is provided in the form of clinic-based in-services or conferences called Clinical Learning Days, provided throughout the IHC system by the physicians within their project team. The manual contains discussions on topics including:

* The need for a care process model for the treatment of ADHD
* An algorithm to guide the management of ADHD
* Procedures to be conducted during the initial office visit
* Procedures to be conducted during follow-up office visits
* Diagnostic criteria and other diagnostic considerations
* AAP clinical practice guidelines
* An algorithm to guide the medical management of ADHD

Parent's Manual

This manual provides parents with basic information regarding the nature and treatment of ADHD. It is designed to encourage parents to become actively involved in the care of their child's ADHD. The IHC physician gives the manual to parents during the initial office visit, or school personnel provide the manual during their child's school evaluation for ADHD. The parent's manual addresses the following topics:

* Understanding the symptoms and subtypes of ADHD
* The evaluation process for ADHD
* Treatments for ADHD
* Basic information on home and school management of ADHD

In addition to the parent's manual, CHADD of Utah also compiled a booklet of useful information (called "Parent Empowerment Materials") to supplement the manual. These supplemental materials provide parents with more detailed information on parenting a child with ADHD. The empowerment materials also may be distributed to parents by the primary care physicians or by the schools.

School Manual

The school manual may be considered as the care process model for the treatment of ADHD within the Utah public school system. The plan is for the manual to be distributed to every public school within the state, and members of the project team to in-service key school personnel from across the state with information regarding the evaluation and treatment of ADHD within the school setting. The manual also provides four sets of tools that are described below.

Preliminary Assessment Tools. This section contains rating forms that may be used to conduct the preliminary assessment of ADHD. The preliminary assessment is a set of screening procedures that helps to determine:

* Baseline measures of ADHD symptoms
* Baseline measures of levels of impairment
* The further need for a more comprehensive evaluation of ADHD

The information from the preliminary assessment is sent to the family physician on a summary form provided in the manual.

Evaluation Tools. In this section, school personnel are provided with a list of procedures that may be used to conduct a thorough evaluation of ADHD. A structured interview form that may be used to gain background information from the parents is also provided. In addition, a form is included to help school personnel tabulate the presence of ADHD symptoms according to current criteria for ADHD from the *Diagnostic and Statistical Manual of the American Psychiatric Association* (DSM-IV). This information is designed to make the diagnosis of ADHD easier for physicians. The results of the assessment are then sent to the physician on a summary form included in the manual. The summary form also contains a section for identifying specific treatment target goals.

Intervention Tools. This section contains tools that may be used by school personnel to collect behavioral data or to help implement the behavioral management of ADHD.

Follow-Up Tools. The final section of the school manual provides tools to help measure the effectiveness of treatment interventions. It includes a medication monitoring form and suggests the readministration of the rating forms used in the preliminary assessment. This provides a direct comparison of pre- and post-intervention levels of symptoms and impairment levels.

What Is Currently Happening to Encourage Implementation of the IHC Care Management System in the State of Utah?

The IHC Primary Care Clinical Program under the direction of Wayne Cannon, M.D., and Brenda Reiss Brennan, has set up a committee made up of IHC physicians, administrators, and representatives from the Utah State Office of Education, State Mental Health, and CHADD. The committee meets once a month. They have put together a strategic plan to encourage the process of implementing the ADHD Care Management System. The plan includes steps for in-servicing each segment of the principal groups that need education about how to implement the care management system properly. Each month the committee evaluates what has been done and what further steps are needed to facilitate implementation.

McKay Dee Hospital in Ogden, Utah, has taken on the challenge of developing a pilot model for implementing the IHC ADHD care management system as it is set up. The committee, under the direction of Jerry Gardner, M.D., consists of physicians and administrators from McKay Dee Hospital, an administrator from Weber School District, school counselors representing five elementary schools in Weber School District, representatives from McKay Dee Behavioral Health, and Linda Smith as a representative of parents and CHADD.

Their plan is to use the personnel from the five elementary schools, IHC physicians, and parents of children with ADHD at each of the schools to implement all aspects of the IHC ADHD care management system. They are setting up systems for all parties involved to be able to communicate with each other easily via email; and they are designing a curriculum for community-based education classes about ADHD for the parents, educators, and others to attend. All parties (physicians and school personnel) will be trained in how to use the care management system tools. They will also be training a parent mentor (a parent of a child who has already been diagnosed with ADHD) at each school to help the parents of other children diagnosed with ADHD at the school.

Obtaining a Copy of the Manuals

IHC has generously agreed to post the three manuals on the Internet. To access these materials, follow these procedures:

1. Go to www.ihc.com/clinicalprograms.
2. Under "Select a Topic" that appears in the middle of the page, choose ADHD.

Read "Copyright and Terms of Use" page on their website for information about requirements if you wish to reproduce or download any part of the content of these IHC materials. Direct any questions regarding use to Intermountain Health Care.

Access to the CHADD of Utah "Parent Empowerment Materials"

These materials can be found on the CHADD of Utah website. To access these materials, follow these procedures:

1. Go to the CHADD of Utah website at www.members.aol.com/chaddofutah
2. Click on Parent Empowerment Materials.

Project for Attention Related Disorders (PARD) of San Diego, California

PARD addresses problems of access for many children with ADHD to appropriate medical care and increases the knowledge base of professionals by implementing a cost-effective method of providing health education. Through PARD, a systematic approach to identification and management of ADHD in San Diego City Schools has been developed, and PARD's efforts foster cooperation among community organizations, agencies, schools, and families.

PARD's History

PARD originated in 1989 as a result of a three-day conference on ADHD held in San Diego, California. This conference brought to the surface the frustration and concern of school personnel, parents, and community professionals regarding children with attention-related problems accessing appropriate care and intervention. At that time, there was no system-wide approach to identification or intervention when a child displayed symptoms of what could be ADHD. Most school personnel did not have the awareness of or skill to help students with ADHD, and it was difficult to obtain a diagnosis with little or no information from the school being provided when the children visited a physician in the community.

The San Diego Unified School District (also called San Diego City Schools) was fortunate to have Jeff Black, M.D., F.A.A.P., as its consulting pediatrician and Dorothy Davies Johnson, M.D., F.A.A.P., specialist in neurobehavioral disorders and learning disabilities. Together, with an advisory community group from the school and community, they wrote a grant proposal outlining the following goals and objectives of the PARD project:

✱ To improve the physical and mental health and educational outcome of children identified with ADHD by:
   — Increasing the knowledge base of individuals interacting with children who have ADHD (school personnel, parents, physicians, and other community providers)
   — Improving the coordination of school/community services to children with ADHD and their families
   — Establishing an ongoing school-based system for identifying, evaluating, and managing children with ADHD in the San Diego City Schools
   — Developing a protocol for referral to be used in the district that could also be disseminated to other school districts

The Health Services Department in the school district put together an itinerant team of school personnel to serve as consultants to schools. The team consisted of a school nurse practitioner (one day/week), district counselor (one-half day/week), and psychologist (one-half day/week). All the people on the core team came with training and day-to-day experience in dealing with the frustration and joys of having a child with ADHD. Mentor-teachers from the district also lent their ideas and expertise in giving direction to teachers.

Dr. Dorothy Davies Johnson wrote a manual, *School Physician Collaboration for the Student with Attention Difficulties,* which included information, assessment, and follow-up tools and strategies. In addition, the PARD project contracted two community resources with strong experience and existing programs for children and parents.

Education is a major goal and component of the PARD project. School nurses were trained to be the primary coordinators of the assessment-gathering component, responsible for referral to community physicians and ongoing communication regarding the child's progress. Counselors and psychologists in the schools were trained in social skills development and parent support. Teachers and administrators were offered several

workshops and in-services through the school district on ADHD. Sandra Rief, mentor-teacher in San Diego City Schools at that time, wrote a manual of educational strategies that was provided to district teachers entitled *Hard to Reach/Hard to Teach . . . Meeting the Challenge.*

Another valuable service was offered by PARD in the earlier years. Schools were able to request and schedule a day for Dr. Johnson to come to the school. During these scheduled visits, Dr. Johnson spent time observing a few targeted students that the school wanted assistance in helping, and then met with the consultation team (SST) and teachers of those students in a "debriefing session." Later in the day, the full staff received an in-service on ADHD.

Pediatric consultants polled the medical community and enlisted the assistance of approximately seventeen physicians who agreed to see a couple of PARD project participants each month. Physicians were offered in-service opportunities by Dr. Johnson.

Note: The PARD project was originally directed to Medi-Cal and low-income children with medical needs who had previously not had access to care. These were children who qualified for screening under the Child Health and Disability Prevention Program (EPSDT).

Content of the PARD Packet

The PARD packet for data gathering was developed to obtain pertinent information from teachers and parents to support the diagnostic process. Teachers provide student work samples, complete a behavioral checklist, and supply information regarding:

✱ The problems the child is experiencing
✱ A description of the class situation (for example, number of students)
✱ The accommodations/modifications that the child has been receiving
✱ A summary of the child's academic progress in all areas
✱ The help/support teacher(s) would like to see from the evaluation

The parent packet is very extensive. A complete health, developmental, and family history is elicited. Parents are also asked to complete a behavioral checklist. In addition, parents are asked to share information regarding their child's strengths/interests, parenting/discipline strategies they use, how they feel their child is doing currently in school and in the home, and so on.

The PARD Project Now and in the Past

Although the PARD project was initially directed to a targeted group of children (those with less access to appropriate medical care), the process has ultimately been successful for the entire system in terms of diagnosis and treatment. The forms for data gathering and referral (in the PARD packet) are used in the system for any child, regardless of socioeconomic status. Intervention strategies are also taught system-wide, and are not limited to project participants.

The system-wide changes in San Diego that have occurred as a result of PARD are very positive and recognized by all parties. In the school system, there is a greater awareness and sensitivity to children with ADHD-related issues, and the medical community is now more receptive to the school data that is sent to them.

This project is still going strong in San Diego, and the following data assessing the effectiveness of PARD is provided by Susie Horn as of April 2004:

Evaluation

Two hundred seven active project participants were referred to the project. In addition, over 2,000 students were referred using the PARD materials and 2,241 received some type of intervention, including behavior modification, medication, counseling, or some combination. The PARD packet development has been helpful both within the district and to community providers who receive it as part of the referral for evaluation. Difficulty with follow-up and transience hampered ability to follow some of the participants. When a family followed the protocol and continued with medical follow-up, the student's academic progress and behavior improved. The in-service component was a huge success, training over 2,500 individuals and receiving high scores on all evaluations.

Results and Outcomes

The major outcomes of the project include a system approach to evaluate and manage ADHD students. A protocol was developed and is still used to refer children with attentional problems to outside providers for evaluation. The in-service component has been hugely successful and continues to this date. Parent support groups have been established in the community and are supported by the PARD project.

Future Plans and Follow-Up

PARD has been active for the ten years following grant funding. It received a $50,000 grant over two years to continue to improve the knowledge base of the multidisciplinary teams that deal with ADHD children. The district has also supported its efforts through the Section 504 budget, since most of the district's Section 504 Plans are ADHD-related. The plan is to increase the communication and collaboration among school, parents, and the student's medical home. The project plans to emphasize identification and management of the adolescent with ADHD. PARD will be looking at which services or combination of services improve student outcomes and will disseminate materials and knowledge of best practices to other districts in San Diego County.

Type and Amount of Support

This project is easily adaptable to other school districts, especially in light of the federal mandates to provide a free and appropriate education to all children. Development of the program would require a coordinator and expertise from community specialists in both the medical and mental health communities. A training component is essential to expand the knowledge of all professionals who deal with the ADHD child. Another important component of a successful program is to obtain the support of the school administrators.

Note: PARD was also an active member of a community task force made up of major medical providers in San Diego to discuss the referral process, barriers to access, and communication among schools, parents, and the medical provider. See Section 5.3, School Documentation and Communication with Medical Providers and Others, which describes SHIP (San Diego County School Health Innovative Programs—a partnership of schools, health plans, and other health organizations).

For more information about PARD, contact:

Susie Horn
San Diego City Schools
2351 Cardinal Lane
San Diego, California 92123
858-627-7594

OU Pediatrics/Kendall Whittier Elementary—Collaborative Model of Care in Tulsa, Oklahoma

A school and clinical collaborative to establish a comprehensive multimodal program for students with ADHD has been created in Tulsa, Oklahoma. On a much smaller scale than the above two programs, this collaborative involves students, family, and faculty from Kendall-Whittier Elementary School, the OU (University of Oklahoma) Pediatric Clinic, and the direct services provided onsite at the school by a LCSW (licensed clinical social worker). The social worker is not a school employee, but works for a community mental health agency, Family and Children's Services, Inc. (F&CS), which has several programs throughout the Tulsa area.

The agency funds the social worker's position—to address the needs of children with ADHD at the elementary school—and recently expanded to include a middle school, as well. The social worker (Mary Kevin McNamara)

places on her caseload any students with ADHD referred by the school's multidisciplinary team (which they call the "Care Team"). At the present time, Mary Kevin has several groups of students with ADHD in the elementary school and one group in the middle school. At the elementary school, students are grouped by grade level: K/first, second/third, and fourth/fifth. There is more than one group at grade levels in order to keep the group size down to no more than six students per group. A few students are also met with individually, rather than in groups. There are more students currently waiting to join, pending completion of evaluations and visits with a physician. The majority of the families are not hooked up with a medical provider, which is problematic in obtaining timely evaluations and treatment. The collaborative relationship with OU Pediatrics has been extremely helpful in this matter. Parents are generally referred to OU Pediatrics Clinic and other community medical centers by the school when an evaluation is indicated.

Dr. Donald Hamilton and OU Pediatric Clinic have reached out to the school community to form this collaboration with Kendall-Whittier Elementary (the largest and most culturally diverse school in Tulsa). Dr. Hamilton comes to the school weekly for a half day to staff current patients and consult with the school team about other students and their behavior, or other concerns. In addition, he has been a guest speaker at parent support groups; provided a special parent meeting on ADHD, LD, and brain development for the Hispanic families in the school community; has provided teacher training (along with the child psychiatrist from the OU team); and has funded meals, childcare, and facilitators for parenting classes. In addition, OU through Dr. Hamilton has provided flu shots for children, parents, and staff, and other health services. The commitment of OU's team to the community and the expertise of Dr. Hamilton are greatly respected and appreciated by all. So far, these services have been provided without reimbursement.

The procedure with regard to evaluation typically involves:

* The child is referred through the school's Care Team (multidisciplinary team), after the teacher has the initial conversation with the parent(s) about his or her concerns and school strategies/interventions already tried.
* Behavioral scales are provided to parents and teachers.
* If the family needs to apply for medical coverage through the Medicaid program, OU has enabled Mary Kevin to work with their insurance representative to expedite the process.

Once the assessment has been completed, the family is encouraged to follow up with a behavior management group for the child (provided at school by the social worker) and the parent support group for the parent.

Note: The collaborative is now beginning to work with a different mental health provider, as well, that sends therapists to the home for onsite behavior programs.

Services that Mary Kevin (LCSW) provides to support students, families, and their teachers include:

* Bi-weekly behavior management groups to help educate students about ADHD, help them learn coping strategies and social skills, and help them take responsibility for some of their own care and treatment
* Individual time with a therapist for extra support, as needed
* Close, ongoing parent and teacher consultation
* Weekly parent education and support groups
* Consultation with OU Pediatric Clinic regarding medication and medical needs for students
* Attends sessions with OU pediatric residents and helps them with those students involved

in diagnosis/treatment from Kendall-Whittier (and more recently from the middle school)
* Teacher support (behavior plans, case management, in-services)
* Monitoring and reinforcement of students' performance

To enter the program, parents complete an intake process and sign permission slips if interested in having their child receive these services. The intake process is an approximately forty-five-minute interview with the parent(s) to assess their perspective of their child's challenges and strengths. (The children already have a clinical diagnosis of ADHD.) Mary Kevin's notes and paperwork are not included in the student's school records, since she is employed by the agency, not the school district. After obtaining parents' permission, students are then personally invited to join the group.

ADHD School Groups

The middle school group meets with the primary focus of improving organizational/study skills, and classroom strategies. Email communication with the teachers (students to teachers and Mary Kevin with teachers) is vital with this group, since teens tend to minimize any problems. Again, this extension to the middle school has just recently begun.

Elementary group sessions include:

* An "icebreaker activity" to build relationships and teamwork
* One ADHD fact to discuss and add to their "fact sheet" regarding what ADHD is and is not, and issues associated with the disorder
* A focus on their strengths and abilities, with time reserved to recognize and celebrate students' successes and accomplishments
* Students developing and filling out their weekly goal sheet/contract ("My Plan for Success") and developing strategies to achieve them
* Various activities to learn and practice appropriate behavior and social skills

In addition, Mary Kevin is involved in the monitoring of the students' weekly plans during the week and rewarding them for their accomplishments.

Note: *Some of the students in the program (but not all) are also served through special education (IEPs) and 504 Accommodation Plans, as well.*

Sample Group Activities

One activity involves playing "mock games" such as Uno® and using this as a vehicle to teach and practice appropriate social skills. After playing a game for a short period of time, students discuss what they liked about the game and share compliments with each other about the behaviors they demonstrated when playing. Next they talk about "what ifs." What if a student cheated? What if a player threw the cards across the room because he did not win? What if a student bragged and boasted to everyone because she did win?

Another fun activity is having students role play real-life situations such as (a) You discover that you forgot to take your medicine and Mom is already at work; (b) You are really hungry and in line for lunch and three "cool" guys ask to get in front of you; (c) A substitute teacher gives you three assignments to do at a time with only a short time to do them. They also are encouraged to make up their own situations to role play, which Mary Kevin's students enjoy doing and that likely help them think and process through real events in their lives.

Parent Support Group

The weekly parent support group is another key feature of the program. It is held at school, with refreshments and childcare always provided. The following are sample topics of parent support group meetings for the first few months of the school year:

* Let's make this the best school year ever!
* Parents and stress! Children and stress!

* Guest Speaker: Come spend a relaxing time talking to a doctor from the OU Pediatric Clinic
* Understanding learning disabilities
* ADD, ADHD, LD, ODD, CD, PDD? What difference does it make?
* Guest Speaker: Come learn about your child's IEP's, 504's, and OHI
* Bedtime madness and morning chaos!
* The power of special play for you and your child!
* Help! It's the holiday season and the kids will be home for two weeks!

This collaborative partnership hopes to enhance and expand programs at the current elementary and middle school involved—to provide more support services for parents and medical services and evaluation for children. They also want to implement a model ADHD prevention/treatment program in other elementary at-risk schools in the Tulsa community as well (targeting those with large numbers of low-income families who find it harder to obtain assessment and treatment). The greatest challenge at this point is finding sources to fund these efforts.

For more information about this collaborative, contact:

Don Hamilton, M.D.
4502 East 41st Street
Tulsa, Oklahoma 74135
Donald-hamilton@ouhsc.edu

Insights from Dr. Donald Hamilton, OU Pediatrics

Dr. Hamilton shared some of his thoughts and insights regarding the challenges of doing this work, and what can be done to support physicians in their efforts to facilitate the process of collaborative care for children with ADHD.

What should the American Academy of Pediatrics consider doing to improve care and treatment of children with ADHD?

"I think every community and probably school system is going to be a little different, and that makes this a challenge. I feel the AAP could help pediatricians by listing examples and ways of collaborating and working with schools. The beauty of the NICHQ ADHD Collaborative was hearing what worked for some schools and practices, along with sharing our success stories. The success stories that were published in *AAP News* and other publications started this process."

What topics should be addressed?

"HIPAA is a big concern for communication and is still confusing. Just when I was getting a good system of communicating with some teachers and schools by email, the new HIPAA guidelines went into effect. The confusion about sharing information by email has pretty much prohibited me continuing to use this method. I still use a fax with a disclaimer cover sheet, but honestly I feel this is less secure than email in most offices and schools."

What should be done at the national, state, and practice levels?

"We need insurers to recognize that pediatricians are seeing more complex behavioral disorders and this takes time and expertise that needs to be rewarded by appropriate reimbursement. We hired an experienced nurse with a school health and child psychiatry background several months ago. She has already become invaluable to our practice. We also have formed a collaboration with a home-based mental health provider in Tulsa who will place an intake worker onsite at our clinic to set up services for families while they are in the clinic. Having these services onsite is an investment that many practices cannot afford without improved reimbursement. Our national and state leaders will have to educate insurance providers and legislators that improved reimbursement can mean more services being offered.

"On the practice level I feel practices that deal with these problems must have additional staff and office resource help to deal with ADHD and behavior problems. If it's all left up to the physician, then they will burn out quickly or not do a good job. I was pretty close to being at that point about four months ago. The addition of our new nurse has been a boost and helped me with phone calls, prescriptions, and other issues. Also, being involved in the collaborative has given me a more long-term perspective on what we are trying to accomplish, plus how to get there."

More Innovative Programs and Projects for Improving the Lives of Those with ADHD

Featured in the CHADD publication *ATTENTION!* is a section each edition by Mark Katz, Ph.D., entitled "Promising Practices." In addition to the wonderful programs and projects featured in this section, readers may wish to review others featured in *ATTENTION!* at www.chadd.org.

Note: As mentioned earlier, many individuals are named throughout this section to recognize and credit their efforts in their respective projects / programs. Of course, in the future specific people / contact information is subject to change.

Part 5: General References

Section 5.1

Al-Hassan, Suha, & Gardner III, Ralph. (2002). Involving Immigrant Parents of Students with Disabilities in the Educational Process. Council for Exceptional Children: *Teaching Exceptional Children, 34*(5), 52–58.

CHADD (Children and Adults with Attention Deficit Disorders), 8181 Professional Place, Suite 201, Landover, MD 20785; www.chadd.org; 800-233-4050.

Cloud, N. (1993). Language, Culture, and Disability: Implication for Instruction and Teacher Preparation. *Teacher Education and Special Education, 16,* 60–72.

Dabkowski, Diane M. (2004, January/February). Encouraging Active Parent Participation in IEP Team Meetings. Council for Exceptional Children: *Teaching Exceptional Children, 36*(3), 34–39.

Holman, L. J. (1997). Meeting the Needs of Hispanic Immigrants. *Educational Leadership, 54*(7), 37–38.

Illes, T. (2002). *Positive Parenting Practices for Attention Deficit Disorder.* Salt Lake City, UT: Jordan School District.

Kalyanpur, M., Harry, B., & Skrtic, T. (2000). Equity and Advocacy Expectations of Culturally Diverse Families' Participation in Special Education. *International Journal of Disability, Development and Education, 47,* 119–136.

Kunjufu, Jawanza. (1982). *Countering the Conspiracy to Destroy Black Boys.* Chicago: African American Images Press.

Lamorey, Suzanne. (2002, May/June). The Effects of Culture on Special Education Services. Council for Exceptional Children: *Teaching Exceptional Children, 34*(5), 67–71.

Regional Resource and Federal Centers (RRFC) Network. www.dssc.org/frc/rrfc.htm.

Rief, Sandra. (1998). *The ADD/ADHD Checklist: An Easy Reference for Parents and Teachers.* San Francisco: Jossey-Bass.

Rief, Sandra. (2003). *The ADHD Book of Lists.* San Francisco: Jossey-Bass.

Samuel, V. J., Curtis, S., Thornell, A., George, P., Taylor, A., Ridley-Brome, D., & Faraone, S. (1997). The Unexplored Void of ADHD and African American Research: A Review of the Literature. *Journal of Attention Disorders, 1,* 197–207.

Taylor-Crawford, Karen, Richardson, Jerome, & Madison-Boyd, Sybil. (2003, June). AD/HD: Cultural Attitudes & Perceptions. CHADD: *ATTENTION!, 9*(6), 38–45; Attention@chadd.org.

Thomas, C., Correa, V., & Morsink, C. (2000). *Interactive Teaming* (3rd ed.). Upper Saddle River, NJ: Prentice Hall/Merrill.

Section 5.2

Rief, Sandra. (1998). *The ADD/ADHD Checklist.* San Francisco: Jossey-Bass.

Rief, Sandra. (2003). *The ADHD Book of Lists.* San Francisco: Jossey-Bass.

Rief, Sandra. (2004). *Instructional Support Team Manual.* San Diego: Educational Resource Specialists. (For information, contact author at www.sandrarief.com.)

Section 5.4

Bill Number H.R. 1350 for the 108th Congress, 7th version. (November 2004). Individuals with Disabilities Education Improvement Act of 2004, As Agreed to or Passed by Both the House and Senate. http://thomas.loc.gov.

Boundy, Kathleen B. (2003). Center for Law and Education. www.cleweb.org. Letter by Boundy (co-director) to Senator Gregg and Senator Kennedy, August 3, 2003.

CHADD. (2003, January 29). Mental Health and Education Consortium Endorses Paper Citing Critical Need for Enhanced Services within IDEA. Landover, MD: *CHADD News, 3*(9). chaddnews@lists.chadd.org.

CHADD. (2004, November 23). CHADD Applauds Congress for Final Approval of IDEA 2004. Landover, MD: *CHADD News, 3*(33). chaddnews@lists.chadd.org.

Children's Behavioral Alliance. (2003, January). *In the Best Interests of All.* A position paper of the CBA. Retrieved February 25, 2004, from www.chadd.org/pdfs/inthebestinterestsofall.pdf.

The Council for Exceptional Children. (November 2004). The New IDEA: CEC's Summary of Significant Issues. Retrieved November 28, 2004, from www.cec.sped.org/pp/IDEA_/12304.pdf.

DeBettencourt, Laurie U. (2002). Understanding the Differences Between IDEA and Section 504. Council for Exceptional Children: *Teaching Exceptional Children, 34*(3), 16–23.

Gregg, Soleil. (1996–2004). IDEA, *The Final Regulations, and Children with ADHD.* Landover, MD: CHADD. Retrieved September 17, 2003, from www.chadd.org/WEBPAGE.CFM?CAT_ID=5&SUBCAT_ID=21&SEC_ID=0.

IDEA Talking Points. (2003, September 3). Retrieved September 11, 2003, from www.wrightslaw.co/news/2003/idea.talk.pts.0903.htm.

NICHCY. (November 22, 2004). The Latest Scoop on IDEA Reathorization. Retrieved November 28, 2004, from http://www.nichcy.org/reauth/scoop.htm.

No Child Left Behind Act of 2001 is cited as 20 U.S.C.§ 6301 et. seq.

Office of Special Education and Rehabilitative Services. (2000, July). *A Guide to the Individualized Education Program.* Washington, DC: U.S. Department of Education. Retrieved September 2002, from www.ed.gov/pubs/edspubs.html. Also at www.ed.gov/offices/OSERS.

Ratcliff, Dolores. (2003, Spring). No Child Left Behind: Questions and Answers. The Inland Empire Branch of the International Dyslexia Association: *The Resource, 18*(1), 1–5.

Rief, Sandra. (1998). *The ADD/ADHD Checklist.* San Francisco: Jossey-Bass.

Rief, Sandra. (2003). *The ADHD Book of Lists.* San Francisco: Jossey-Bass.

Schrag, Judy. (2003, Spring). No Child Left Behind and Its Implications for Students with Disabilities. *The Special Edge, 16*(2), 1–12.

Special Edge. (2003, Spring). Ensuring Safe Schools. *The Special Edge, 16*(2), 5–6.

U.S. Department of Education. (1999a, March). *Discipline Procedures—Changes from Proposed Rules—Topic Brief.* www.edgov/policy/speced/leg/idea/brief5.html.

U.S. Department of Education, OSEP. (1999b). *IDEA '97 Final Regulations Discipline for Children with Disabilities—Some Key Changes in the Regulations Regarding Discipline for Children with Disabilities.* www.ed.gov/policy/speced/guid/idea/omip.html?exp=0

Wright, Peter W.D. (November 2004). IDEA 2004 Update: Changes in Key Statutes by Pete Wright. Retrieved November 28, 2004, from www.wrightslaw.com. 20 U.S.C. Sections 1401, 1412, 1415.

Wright, Peter W. D., & Wright, Pamela Darr. (2000). *Wrightslaw: Special Education Law.* Hartfield, VA: Harbor House Law Press.

Wright, Peter W. D., Wright, Pamela D., & Heath, Suzanne, W. (2004). *Wrightslaw: No Child Left Behind.* Hartfield, VA: Harbor House Law Press.

Wrightslaw. www.wrightslaw.com/news/2003/idea.talk.pts.0903.htm.

Section 5.5

Smith, L., Illes, T., & Vayo, T. (2002–2003). ADHD Care Management: Unifying the Efforts of Parents, Educators, and Physicians. *Utah State University Parent News: Center for Persons with Disabilities, 26*(4).

Part 5: Recommended Resources

Section 5.1

CHADD (Children and Adults with Attention Deficit Disorders), 8181 Professional Place, Suite 201, Landover, MD 20785; 800-233-4050; www.chadd.org.

With over 22,000 members in 225 affiliates nationwide, CHADD is the nation's leading nonprofit organization serving individuals with ADHD. Through collaborative leadership, advocacy, research, education, and support, CHADD provides science-based, evidence-based information about ADHD to the parents, educators, professionals, the media, and the general public. The CHADD website (www.chadd.org) can be counted on as a source of accurate and reputable research-validated information.

Regional Resource and Federal Centers (RRFC) Network. www.dssc.org/frc/rrfc.htm.

The Regional Resource and Federal Center and the six regional resource centers for special education may have translated materials you need. These centers are specially funded to assist state education agencies in the systematic improvement of education programs, practices, and policies that affect children and youth with disabilities.

Section 5.2

Sandra Rief, Linda Fisher, & Nancy Fetzer. (Video). *Successful Schools—How to Raise Achievement and Support "At-Risk" Students.* Educational Resource Specialists; www.sandrarief.com; 800-682-3528.

Section 5.4

Children & Adults with Attention Deficit Disorders (CHADD). www.chadd.org.

EDLAW Center. www.edlaw.net.

Federal Resource Center for Special Education. www.dssc.org/frc.

Glossary of Special Education and Legal Terms. www.fetaweb.com/06/glossasry.sped.legal.htm.

IDEA Partnerships. www.ideapolicy.org.

IDEA Practices. www.ideapractices.org.

Learning Disabilities Online. www.ldonline.org.

National Association of Protection and Advocacy Systems (NAPSA). www.protectionandadvocacy.com.

National Association of School Psychologists. www.naspweb.org.

National Center on Education, Disability, and Juvenile Justice. www.edjj.org.

National Information Clearinghouse on Children and Youth with Disabilities. www.nichcy.org.

National Resource Center on AD/HD. www.help4adhd.org/en/education/rights.

Parent Advocacy Coalition for Educational Rights (PACER). www.pacer.org/idea/idea.htm.

Parents' Guide to No Child Left Behind. www.nochildleftbehind.gov.

U.S. Dept. of Education. (2000). *22nd Annual Report to Congress on the Implementation of IDEA.* www.ed.gov/offices/OSERS/OSEP/OSEP2000AnlRpt.

U.S. Dept. of Education. www.ed.gov/offices/osers/idea.

U.S. Department of Education in cooperation with the Council for Exceptional Children. www.ed.gov/offices/OSERS/OSEP.

Wrightslaw. www.wrightslaw.com/info.

Section 5.5

Intermountain Health Care (IHC), Care Management System for ADHD. www.ihc.com/clinicalprograms.

National Initiative for Children's Healthcare Quality—ADHD Initiative. www.nichq.org.

part
6

Additional Supports and Strategies

Section 6.1: Stress Reduction, Relaxation Strategies, Leisure Activities, and Exercise

Section 6.2: Music for Relaxation, Transitions, Energizing, and Visualization

Stress Reduction, Relaxation Strategies, Leisure Activities, and Exercise

Students with ADHD are often in a state of stress from trying to cope with the challenges and daily struggles in their lives. When one is hyperactive, emotionally over-reactive, and/or anxious, it helps to learn relaxation and stress-reduction strategies, as well as find positive outlets to channel one's energy. It is therapeutic to teach children ways to calm their minds and bodies and release inner tension, which can also empower them with a feeling of self-control. The ideas discussed here have health and psychological benefits that are good for all of us, but may be of particular importance for youngsters with ADHD.

Fun and Laughter

Laughter is one of the best ways to release stress and feel good. The chemicals released in the body through laughter reduce pain and tension. So there is probably no substitute for finding ways to have fun and to laugh with our children.

Breathing Techniques

Many of us know the positive effects of controlled breathing through our training in Lamaze or other natural childbirth classes. Controlled, conscious breathing has the benefit of relaxing muscles and reducing stress. Many believe it is useful in the management of some physical ailments and disease, as well.

Teach children how to take conscious, deep breaths to relax, while listening to the sound of the air coming in and out. Show them how to inhale deeply (preferably through the nose) and *slowly* exhale through the mouth. When inhaling, the abdomen rises and expands. Students can do relaxation breathing in their chairs, seated on the floor cross-legged with eyes closed, lying down, or even standing. There are different breathing (pranayama) exercises in yoga that can be taught to children, such as wave breathing, balloon breathing, up and down the mountain, straw breathing, bee breathing (Singleton, 2004).

Teach progressive muscle relaxation by isolating different body parts, tightening and then relaxing them. For example, while they are lying on the floor, instruct children to tighten or squeeze their toes on the left foot while taking a deep breath in, and then relax the toes with a slow breath out. Now tighten and relax muscles in the left lower leg (calf muscles), then the left knee and upper leg (contracting muscles while breathing in, and relaxing on the slow exhale). Proceed in this fashion to the right side of the lower body, to the abdomen and upper body, each arm, hands/fingers, chest, neck, jaws, and face.

Teach children that when their bodies are relaxed, they are better able to think and plan. Help them understand that when they are nervous, stressed, and angry, there is a tensing of certain body parts that they should be able to feel. Once they learn to recognize when their fists clench, jaws tighten, and stomachs harden, there are ways to help themselves relax and gain control. Children can be taught how to begin to breathe deeply and "send" their breaths consciously to relax body parts. For example, a child can learn to send breaths to his or her hands, while silently self-prompting to relax the hands (until the fists are released and fingers are loose).

Help guide children to visualize that with each breath they take in, their body becomes filled slowly with a soothing color, aroma, sound, light, warmth, or other pleasant, comfortable feeling. Ask students to think of a color that makes them feel very comfortable, peaceful, and relaxed. Then have them practice, with closed eyes, breathing in that color and "sending" it (blowing it) throughout the body. If a child, for example, chooses "turquoise," guide him or her to visualize the turquoise going down his or her throat, into the neck and chest, down to the stomach, and so on until the child is filled with the beautiful, peaceful, wonderful turquoise . . . and is relaxed and in control.

Yoga and Slow Movement Exercises

Yoga has many health and psychological benefits—among which are stress reduction and heightening one's focus and awareness. There are a number of yoga postures and slow movement games and exercises that are fun and appropriate for children. The following examples are from a wonderful book (apparently no longer in print at this time), that was written by Holly Young Huth, a relaxation consultant and teacher specializing in early childhood education. This book, *Centerplay: Focusing Your Child's Energy* (Huth, 1984), teaches back, stomach, and sitting postures through pretending to be a rag doll, scarecrow, popped balloon, candle, plow, bike, fish, bridge, snake, bow, boat, flower, crocodile, and others.

During these "postures" the children are told that quiet time is beginning and that if they need to talk, it must be very softly. Children spread out (if they want, with their blankets, carpet squares, mats) and are guided by the teacher. "It's time for us to become . . . ." Through the game of pretending, the teacher guides students to make slow, controlled movements that help calm them, as well as engage their imagery skills and creative expression. Some of the movements shared in *Centerplay* include:

* Carrying a very fragile gift to someone
* Pretending to be a peacock
* Swimming through air
* Scaling through space
* Climbing a pyramid
* Being a wave or the wind

Singleton, in *Yoga for You and Your Child* (2004), teaches the postures of rocking the boat, rocking chair, dead bug, tiptoe tree, windy tree, helicopter, puppet, and others. This is a wonderful book designed for parents to teach and practice yoga together with their child. He shares, for example, the following:

"Eagle: This is a challenging balancing posture that develops concentration and focus. It strengthens the joints and muscles in your legs and gets rid of any stiffness in the shoulders and upper back.

1. Stand up straight with your feet together. Become as still, steady, and firm as you can. Find a point on the wall in front of you and gaze at it softly. Raise your left arm in front of you, palm up. Bring your right arm underneath, so that your arms cross at the elbows.
2. Bend your left arm so that your forearm is vertical with the palm facing to

the right. Then bend your right arm and entwine it around your left arm. Try to join your palms together.

3. Keeping your arms entwined, bend your knees and wrap your right leg around the front of your left leg. Your right foot should hook around the inside of your left ankle. Now unwind your arms and your legs and repeat the pose on the other side." (Singleton, 2004) [Note: Photos are provided in Singleton's book to demonstrate the movements.]

Visualization and Guided Imagery

The ability to visualize colorful, vivid images with rich imagination and detailed action are natural skills of childhood. These same skills have been found to be useful in empowering people to help overcome obstacles in their lives. Visualization techniques are used to improve memory, enhance learning, facilitate healing, and increase other important skills (for example, study, social, coping, creative expression).

As a learning strategy to enhance memory and retention, visualization techniques are powerful. In fact many adults have taken classes (for example, Kevin Trudeau's *Mega Memory*™) that incorporate visualization strategies.

Visualization is thought to have medical/healing benefits, as well. For example, some cancer patients are taught how to use their power of visualization in the effort to help stop the spread of cancer cells in their bodies. One cancer patient who leads a support group in her community explained how she mentally prepares herself for treatments and has found success in battling her cancer through visualization. Through music and relaxation techniques, she first brings herself to a state in which she is prepared for "battle." Then she clearly, vividly imagines her army of "good cells" attacking her "bad cells." The cells come in living colors, equipped with uniforms and battle gear. Beginning at the top of her head, she clearly visualizes how her "good cells" outnumber, overpower, and destroy all of the "bad cells" as they march methodically from one organ and body part to the next.

Huth shares several guided imagery activities that are part of yoga/meditation routines such as the following, which is in the form of a riddle. In others, children are guided through similar journeys—pretending to be a feather, leaf, cloud floating through the air, and so on.

Preparation: "Lie down on your blanket (pillow, mat, etc.) in your most comfortable position . . . just the way you do when you go to bed at night. Move around a little until you find the place that is familiar and cozy. Feel your whole body sinking down into the floor. Take a deep breath through your nose—or, if you like, through your mouth—and let it out. Take another deep breath and just begin to notice your breath swaying you softly, helping you rest. Close your eyes. Try to close your eyes, because that way you can imagine better what I'm going to tell you. You can forget everything else and really be here. Now we are ready to go on a fantasy together. If you want to come with me, to imagine with me, that's up to you. If you don't want to, just rest quietly."
(Sailboat): "You are floating in the water, rocking back and forth, back and forth. Feel your whole body relax in the warm water. The gentle waves come and go against you. You are sturdy and strong. The sun shines and warms the wood that you are made of. The wind comes and blows you softly in the sea. Your big cloth billows and moves you slowly in the breeze. What are you?" (Huth, 1984)

Note: *The teacher goes around to individual children and they whisper what they think is the answer to the riddle.*

Singleton also shares various meditations that involve visualization, such as "Chasing Away the Clouds":

"Imagine a huge blue sky in front, behind, and above and below you. This place is always peaceful and, because it's inside you, you can return to it at any time. Picture any negative feelings as clouds passing across your sky." (They are guided to observe the clouds carefully for a while.) "Remember that no matter how big and dark the clouds that pass across it, the sky never gets damaged. In the same way, strong feelings such as doubt, anger, sadness, and fear cannot hurt us. When you feel ready to let your 'thought-clouds' go, say 'goodbye' and imagine them dispersing and disappearing each time you breathe out. Gradually, your sky becomes bright and blue again and you feel well, happy and free of negative emotions." (Singleton, 2004)

There are a variety of resources available that utilize these techniques for self-help and management. One such CD/cassette recommended for children is *Imagery for Kids—Discovering Your Special Place,* which combines gentle music and a guided journey (Reznick, 1995).

Teach students to visualize themselves in situations where they are achieving and being successful. For example, prior to taking a test, they can visualize themselves in detail—focused, well-prepared, and working diligently taking the test. Encourage them to see themselves persistently and carefully reading each item, pacing themselves, and confidently answering questions. Imagine feeling relaxed—not nervous or anxious. Have students picture themselves finishing the test, then going back and checking for careless errors. In addition, playing a motivational song, such as the theme song from the movie *Rocky,* can set a positive mood and help build confidence.

Music

Music can be very helpful for relaxation, as a pre-visualization activity, to soothe away worries and distractions, and to bring a sense of inner peace. Music also stimulates the brain in ways besides relaxation. Many people find that they are better able to focus and are more productive and motivated when listening to the radio or some of their favorite music.

Many teachers find that playing CDs/cassettes of classical music (particularly baroque), soothing environmental sounds, and instrumental arrangements are very beneficial in the classroom. Different forms of music have been found to be effective in increasing the ability to focus, soothe, and relax and to enhance learning, creativity, and critical-thinking skills. Music therapy draws on the beneficial effects of music for different situations.

6.2

Music for Relaxation, Transitions, Energizing, and Visualization

Music can be a powerful means for creating a mood (calming, energizing), motivating, and inspiring. It is also a useful strategy for alerting, signaling, and transitioning. Music has therapeutic effects and can enhance learning—with numerous benefits in the classroom, home, and other settings (for example, hospitals, therapists' offices). Through music, children can improve their abilities in critical and analytical listening skills, focusing/concentration, and responding to specific directions and prompts. Some examples of using music during transitional times may include:

* "When you hear the drum for the first time, Table 3 may get up and return their books to the bookshelf."
* "When you hear the birds in this song start chirping, come quietly to the rug."

Students can be trained in critical listening through activities such as:

* "Count the number of times you heard the theme repeat itself in this selection" (for example, "Bolero" by Ravel).

Visualization activities in response to listening to musical selections can be integrated with writing, drawing, and oral activities. Many of the recordings listed in this section are useful for visualization activities (for example, "Bydllo"— visualizing an ox pulling a cart far off in the distance, moving closer and closer as the music gradually becomes louder). Teachers can play any of the recordings and allow for creative student interpretation. For example, ask students:

* "What does this music make you think of?"
* "Can you see pictures in your mind when you hear this music? Tell us what you see."

A creative teacher will find countless ways to use music in the curriculum, to establish an environment that promotes individual learning styles, as well as to introduce and enhance music education and appreciation.

Music that gets you from one place to another (for example, marches) is excellent for teaching children the discipline of moving their bodies appropriately. It requires focusing and counting.

Bertha Young, a retired music specialist from San Diego City Schools with a great deal of experience teaching grades K–8, as well as in curriculum development and music writing, provided most of the recommended musical selections that follow. The selected choices of music Mrs. Young carefully compiled include different instruments (trumpet, tuba, bells, guitar, piano, flute, as well as the human voice), and different musical periods (baroque, classical, romantic, modern, and contemporary). A variety of composers from several ethnic and cultural backgrounds are represented from these periods, and the examples of contemporary performers of differing ethnic backgrounds may serve as role models for students.

Music for a Calming Effect

These selections are especially useful after recess, P.E., and other more active times of the day:

* Barber, Samuel. "Adagio for Strings" from String Quartet no. 1, op. 11
* Beethoven, Ludwig. "Für Elise" (piano, approximately three minutes)
* Bizet, Georges. "Berceuse" from *Children's Games (Jeux d'Enfants)*
* Copland, Aaron. "Appalachian. Spring Suite," Sections 1, 6, 7, 8 only (*Note:* Section 7 is "Variations on Simple Gifts"), Time-Life, Inc. ©1967, Robert Irving, conductor. (Available in other recordings with other conductors.)
* Debussy, Claude. "Clair de Lune" (stringed instruments, approximately three minutes)
* Delibes, Leo. "Waltz" from *Coppelia* (stringed instruments, approximately two minutes)
* Halpern, Steve. *Spectrum Suite* (fourteen different color-themed songs each approximately three to five minutes long)
* Holst, Gustav. "Jupiter" from *The Planets* (stringed section, approximately one minute)
* Mendelssohn, Felix. "Nocturne" from *Midsummer Night's Dream*
* Mozart, Wolfgang Amadeus. "Adagio for Glass Harmonica"
* Mussorgsky, Modest. "Bydllo" ("The Oxcart" excerpt from *Pictures at an Exhibition*)
* Offenbach, Jacques. "Barcarolle" from *Tales of Hoffman* (approximately three and one half minutes)
* Puccini, Giacomo. "The Humming Chorus" from *Madama Butterfly*

* Ravel, Maurice. "Bolero" (first half only)
* Rimsky-Korsakov, Nikolai. "The Sea and Sindbad's Ship" from *Scheherazade,* Op. 35 Movement 1 (theme only)
* Saint-Saëns, Camille. "The Aquarium" from *Carnival of the Animals* (approximately two minutes)
* Saint-Saëns, Camille. "The Swan" from *Carnival of the Animals* (approximately three minutes)
* "Sakura," a traditional Japanese folk song (performed on koto, approximately one minute)
* Smetana, Bedrich. "The Moldau" (approximately eleven and one half minutes)
* Wagner, Richard. "The Pilgrim's Chorus" from *Tannhäuser* (trombone section)

Additional Recommendations for Calming and Relaxing

* "Four Seasons" by Vivaldi
* "Water Music" by Handel
* "Brandenburg Concertos" by Bach
* "Wind Shadows" by Kim Robertson
* "Music for Relaxation" by Chapman and Miles

Nontraditional Music for Calming and Relaxing

* *Environments:* set of CDs by Syntonic Research Inc., including The Psychologically Ultimate Seashore; Optimum Aviary; Ultimate Thunderstorm; Gentle Rain in a Pine Forest; Intonation (Om chant, good for meditation); Summer Cornfield (sounds of crickets and other insects); Wood-Masted Sailboat; A Country Stream; Pacific Ocean; Caribbean Lagoon
* *Music for Relaxation:* sets of CDs, including Song of the Dolphins, Soothing Waterfalls, Summer Evening Serenade, Thundering Rainstorm (all enhanced with music), Entertainment Media Partners, 2002
* *Sounds of Tropical Rain Forest,* Gentle Persuasion, SPJ Music, 1999

Artists for Relaxing/Calming (Jensen, 1998)

* David Arkenstone
* Keola Beamer
* Jim Chappell
* Kenny G
* Adam Geiger
* Nicholas Gunn
* Steven Halpern
* Georgia Kelly
* Kitaro
* Mars Lasar
* Hillary Stagg
* George Winston
* Zamfir

Music for Moving from Here to There

Moving from out of classroom, back to classroom (for example, returning from an assembly in auditorium to the classroom):

* Berlin, Irving. "Alexander's Ragtime Band"
* Chopin, Frederick. "Polonaise" in A-Flat Major
* Elgar, Sir Edward. "Pomp and Circumstance," March no. 1 in D major
* Gould, Morton. "American Salute"
* Herbert, Victor. "March of the Toys" from *Babes in Toyland*
* Rodgers, Richard, and Hammerstein, Oscar. "Oklahoma—Finale" from *Oklahoma*
* Sousa, John Phillip. Any of his marches
* Verdi, Giuseppe. "Grand March" from *Aida*

Moving from "here to there" within the classroom (for example, as from a reading circle to seatwork):

* Bolling, Claude. Bolling Suite for Cello, "Galop" only, performed by Yo Yo Ma
* Saint-Saëns, Camille. "The Elephant" from *Carnival of the Animals*
* Satie, Erik. "The Hunt" from *Sports et Divertissements*

* Tchaikovsky, Peter Ilyich. "Dance of the Reed Flutes" from *The Nutcracker Suite*
* Thomson, Virgil. "The Walking Song" (Acadian Songs and Dances) from *Louisiana Story Orchestral Suite* (approximately two minutes)

Music for Transitional Times

Use these selections to signal change from one activity to another, such as math to reading or from science to recess preparation:

* Any concerto (baroque or classical) music for trumpet(s) performed by Wynton Marsalis (largo, adagio, or andante movements only)
* Bach, J. S. "Air"
* Copland, Aaron. "Fanfare for the Common Man" (approximately three minutes)
* Denver, John. "Annie's Song"
* Telemann, Georg Philipp. "Overture in D Major for Oboe and Trumpet" from Fifth Movement, "Adagio" only
* Torelli, Giuseppe. "Concerto in D Major for Trumpet, Strings, and Basso Continuo" from Movements 1, 2, and 3, only the "Adagio" sections
* Vivaldi, Antonio. "Andante" from *Concerto in D Minor for Two Mandolins*
* Williams, John. "Star Wars Suite" (theme from the movie *Star Wars*)

Note: A teacher may wish to dismiss students for recess, lunch, or other transitional times with music that has a repetitive theme. For example, Duke Ellington / B. Strayhorn's recording (or other recording artists') for "Take the A Train" has a main theme that repeats at least six different times. Students can be taught to listen to the music, identifying each time the theme repeats itself. The teacher may assign as follows: "Group 1 may line up the third time you hear the theme. Group 2 may line up the fifth time you hear the theme," and so on.

More Transition Time or "High-Energy Movers" (Jensen, 1998)

* *Hooked on Classics* by Philadelphia Harmonics
* *1812 Overture* by Tchaikovsky
* *William Tell Overture* by Rossini
* Theme from TV's "Rawhide"
* *Peanuts Theme* by Giraldi or Benoit

Highly Energetic Music Selections (Jensen, 1998)

* "C'Mon N'Ride It" by Quad City D.J.s
* "Macarena" by Los Del Mar
* "Hawaii Five-O" theme
* "I Like to Move It" by Reel 2 Reel
* "Miami Vice" theme by Jan Hammer
* *Raiders of the Lost Ark* theme
* "Another Night" by Real McCoy
* "O-Bla-Di-O-Bla-Da" by the Beatles
* "Where Do You Go" by No Mercy
* "Tell It to My Heart" by Taylor Dayne
* "Steelbands of Trinidad and Tobago"
* "Heart of Steel" by Flying Fish
* "Mission Impossible" theme
* *Rocky* theme
* "Eye of the Tiger" by Survivor

Additional Suggestions for Active Learning by LifeSounds

* *Music for Creative Dance* by Chappelle
* *Earth Tribe Rhythms* by Brent Lewis
* "A Tisket a Tasket, A Rhythm Basket"

For Break Times, Recommended by DePorter, Reardon, and Singer-Nourie (1999)

* Movie soundtracks
* Hit collections from the 1960s–1990s,
* Contemporary jazz

Any upbeat music is good for break times (music by Santana, Gypsy Kings).

The following websites may be of interest:

* Essential Musical Intelligence (EMI). www.essentialmusicalintelligence.com.
* American Music Therapy Association. www.musictherapy.org.
* National Association for Music Therapy. www.namt.com.
* National Association of Music Merchants. www.namm.com.
* LifeSounds—Music for Learning (an excellent resource). Get their catalog by calling: 406-755-4875.
* Advanced Brain Technologies. www.advancedbrain.com.
* TV Tunes Online. www.tvtunesonline.com/.

The following are some tips for a "musical prescription" for ADHD recommended by Wyatt (2001):

* Since the brain craves change, listen (or have child listen) to music that contains alterations of rhythm, volume, and pitch. Eighty-five percent of our primary auditory cortex (where all sound is initially processed) exhibits a phenomenon known as "habituation." Any unrelenting sound causes us to deafen to it. (Notice how your attention is drawn to the cessation of sound from a noisy refrigerator or the times when crickets abruptly stop their chanting.)
* Many composers provoke curative benefits, from the Beatles to Duke Ellington's orchestra to Ravi Shankar, Ravel and Debussy, the rags of Scott Joplin, Gershwin, and Berlin songs. Don't limit your choices; find your own sound and then expand on it.
* Earphones may focus attention on the music being listened to, but it also separates the listener from his or her environment. Decide why you may want to withdraw from your milieu before escaping it.

Effect of Music on Mood

Some general guidelines on the human response to various aspects of music are presented by Howard (2000):

INTERVIEW WITH BRUCE
(37 Years Old)

Bruce is a very successful entrepreneur living in Manhattan. He was identified with ADHD and learning disabilities early in elementary school.

Memories of His Childhood

Bruce shares that he basically blocked out his memories of childhood and cannot recall specifics. He does remember the feelings of anger and rage. "I tried so hard and everyone kept putting me down." Bruce describes himself as a survivor and recalls feeling that he was always hiding. "Secrecy was my safety. It protected me."

Bruce got through college by "studying morning, noon, and night." Mathematics and anything mechanical always came easily for him. Reading and writing are still very difficult and tedious tasks.

What have you learned that helps you now as an adult?

"I've learned that I have to exercise every day or I don't feel well. I also learned how to meditate. Learning to relax, calm myself, and control my mind and thoughts were some of the best things that ever happened to me."

---

* The higher the pitch, the more positive the effect generated.
* Slower, minor keys warm the brain, which fosters both cortical and limbic alertness.
* Faster, major keys cool the brain, which fosters better moods.

DePorter, Reardon, and Singer-Nourie, in their book, *Quantum Teaching* (1999), share the following information and recommendations:

* Upper register instruments (flutes, violins) bring a lighter tone, which you may find useful during early morning and afternoon learning.
* To relax students after stressful situations, experiment with the sound of piano, cellos, and violas.
* Music also helps to mask "white noise" (the hum of lights, voices in an adjacent room). Set the music's volume at a level that is just perceptible when there is silence in the room.

* In general, all musical selections for the classroom will be instrumentals. Only music for breaks and special effects will contain lyrics.
* Research shows that learning is easier and quicker when the learner is in a relaxed, receptive state. The heartbeat of a relaxed individual is sixty to eighty beats per minute. Much of baroque music closely matches the relaxed heartbeat of a human being in an optimal learning condition. Baroque's melodic chord structures and instrumentation assist the body in accessing an alert yet relaxed state (Schuster & Gritton, 1986).

Another popular artist is Gary Lamb. See his website at www.garylamb.com. Many of his musical compositions are based on a tempo of approximately sixty beats per minute, the same tempo as a resting heart rate. This tempo centers and calms us, promoting focused thinking, relaxed alertness, the flow state, and learning.

David Sousa, in his book *How the Brain Learns* (2001), suggests the following:

* If you are using music as background to facilitate student work, choose music that plays at about sixty beats per minute. If the music is accompanying a fast-paced activity, choose eighty to ninety beats per minute. To calm down a noisy group, choose music at forty to fifty beats per minute.

* Music played at the beginning or end of class can contain lyrics because the main purpose is to set a mood, not get focus. But if students are working on a learning task, lyrics become a distraction.

* Familiar music is fine when setting a mood. However, when working on a specific assignment, you may wish to use music that is unfamiliar, such as classical or new age music.

Part 6: General References

Section 6.1

Alert Program. (1995). (CD). *Songs for Self-Regulation* (part of program developed by Mary S. Williams & Sherry Shellenberger). Music by The Belle Curvians. Published by Therapy Works, Inc. www.alertprogram.com.

Huth, Holly Y. (1984). *Centerplay: Focusing Your Child's Energy.* New York: Simon & Schuster.

Lanham, Geoff. (2001, June). Leisure as a Positive Experience for Children with AD/HD. CHADD: *ATTENTION, 7*(6), 28–33. Attention@chadd.org.

Putnam, Stephen C. (2002, June). Keeping Up the Motivation to Exercise. CHADD: *ATTENTION, 8*(6), 21–33. Attention@chadd.org.

Rief, Sandra. (2003). *The ADHD Book of Lists.* San Francisco: Jossey-Bass.

Shapiro, Michael. (2002, August). Tae Kwon Do. CHADD: *ATTENTION, 9*(1), 36–39. Attention@chadd.org.

Singleton, Mark. (2004). *Yoga for You and Your Child.* New York: Barnes & Noble Books.

Section 6.2

DePorter, Bobbi, Reardon, Mark, & Singer-Nourie, Sarah. (1999). *Quantum Teaching.* Boston: Allyn & Bacon.

Jensen, Eric. (1998). *Trainer's Bonanza.* San Diego: The Brain Store. www.thebrainstore.com.

Howard, Pierce. (2000). *The Owner's Manual for the Brain* (2nd ed.). Austin, TX: Bard Press.

Schuster, Don, & Gritton, Charles. (1986). Suggestive Accelerative Learning Techniques. New York: Gordon and Breach Science Publishers.

Sousa, David. (2001). *How the Brain Learns* (2nd ed.). Thousand Oaks, CA: Corwin Press.

Wyatt, Robert. (2001, December). A Spoonful of Music. CHADD: *ATTENTION, 8*(3), 18–21. Attention@chadd.org.

Part 6: Recommended Resources

Section 6.1

Geocaching www.geocaching.com

Lamb, Gary. Gary Lamb Music. San Clemente, CA: Kagan Publishing. www.garylamb.com; 800-772-7701.

OptimaLearning®. *Baroque Music*. Available at www.thebrainstore.com.

REI Institute, Inc. (CDs). Including: *Calming Rhythms, Calm Your Mind, Rhythms for Learning*. www.reinstitute.com; 800-659-6644.

Reznick, Charlotte. *Imagery for Kids—Discovering Your Special Place* (CD/audiocassette). www.imageryforkids.com; 310-889-7859.

Trudeau, Kevin. (1989). *Mega Memory*™. American Memory Institute. Available through Amazon.com.

Section 6.2

Cheatum, Billye A. & Hammond, Allison A. (2000). *Physical Activities for Improving Children's Learning and Behavior*. Champaign, IL: Human Kinetics.

Kranowitz, Carol S. (1995). *101 Activities for Kids in Tight Spaces*. New York: Skylight Press.

Putnam, Stephen C. (2001). *Nature's Ritalin for the Marathon Mind—Nurturing Your ADHD Child with Exercise*. Hinesburg, VT: Upper Access, Inc. Book Publishers.

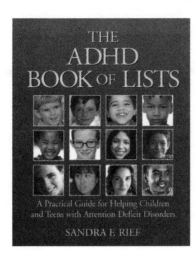

The ADHD Book of Lists: A Practical Guide for Helping Children and Teens with Attention Deficit Disorders

Sandra F. Rief, M.A.

Paper   ISBN: 0-7879-6591-X

www.josseybass.com

"Educating ADHD kids can be a real challenge for everyone involved. *The ADHD Book of Lists* combines Sandra Rief's classroom-proven techniques with current information about this condition and should be required reading for all teachers and parents of ADHD children."

—Harlan R. Gephart, M.D., Center for ADHD,
Bellevue, Washington

The ADHD Book of Lists is a comprehensive, reliable source of answers, practical strategies, and tools written in a convenient list format. Created for teachers (K–12), parents, school psychologists, medical and mental health professionals, counselors, and other school personnel, this important resource contains the most current information about Attention Deficit/ Hyperactivity Disorder (ADHD). It is filled with the strategies, supports, and interventions that have been found to be the most effective in minimizing the problems and optimizing the success of children and teens with ADHD. The book contains a wealth of information to guide in the management of ADHD in school and at home. In addition, *The ADHD Book of Lists'* 8/12" × 11" lay flat format is filled with reproducible checklists, forms, tools, and resources.

ADHD & LD: Powerful Teaching Strategies and Accommodations

Sandra F. Rief, M.A.

Video   ISBN: 0-7879-7472-2
www.josseybass.com

This video, perfect for in-service or pre-service teacher training, provides a thorough, non-technical introduction to ADD and ADHD, complete with intervention strategies and troubleshooting. Designed to be a companion to *The ADHD Book of Lists,* the video offers hundreds of practical instructional and behavioral strategies from culturally diverse elementary and middle school classrooms across the United States.

Learn powerful strategies for student success with this training tool!

Video Outline and Contents

Part 1: Instructional Strategies for Engaging Attention & Active Participation (approximately 20 minutes)—Engaging Students' Attention and Interest; Active Learning/High Response Opportunities; Differentiating Instruction

Part 2: Classroom Management and Behavioral Interventions (approximately 20 minutes)—Creating the Climate and Structure for Success; Individualized Behavioral Supports and Interventions

Part 3: Academic Strategies and Accommodations (approximately 15 minutes)—Organization and Study Skills; Written Language

Part 4: Collaboration and Teaming for Success (approximately 5 minutes)

The ADD/ADHD Checklist

Sandra F. Rief, M.A.

Paper   ISBN: 0-13-762395-X
www.josseybass.com

This complete resource is like having an expert at your side to answer virtually any question on how to reach and teach children with ADD/ADHD! Written by a nationally known educator with two decades of experience, this checklist is packed with up-to-date facts, findings, and proven strategies and techniques for understanding and helping children and adolescents with attention deficit problems and hyperactivity—all in a handy list format. Its comprehensive, but simple, format provides that 'extra understanding' that parents and educators need to help children achieve successful outcomes.

"Sandy Rief's vast knowledge of youngsters with ADD/ADHD is readily apparent in her impressive new book. In a refreshingly concise, easy-to-read style, she provides a wealth of information about ADD/ADHD that will serve as a wonderful resource for parents, teachers, and other professionals. The recommendations she offers for both the home and school environment are clear, practical, and achievable and based on a belief in the child's ability to succeed."

—Robert Brooks, Ph.D., author of *The Self-Esteem Teacher* and on the faculty of Harvard Medical School

How to Reach & Teach All Students in the Inclusive Classroom: Ready-to-Use Strategies, Lessons and Activities for Teaching Students with Diverse Learning Needs

Sandra F. Rief, M.A. and Julie A. Heimburge

Paper   ISBN: 0-87628-399-7
www.josseybass.com

For all classroom teachers, special educators, administrators, and parents, here is a remarkable resource packed with ready-to-use strategies, lessons, and activities for helping students with diverse learning styles, ability levels, skills, and behaviors in today's inclusive classroom.

Focusing on the "whole child" and a team approach that lets you guide a varied group of students toward academic as well as social and emotional success, the book shows you:

- How to reach all students through their multiple intelligences and learning styles
- How to create and run a developmental classroom using portfolios, interest and instructional centers, thematic teaching units and more
- How to promote home/school communication and parent involvement with school outreach efforts
- How to manage behaviors and use positive discipline to reduce and prevent problems
- How to get students organized for learning success
- How to use specific programs and strategies to foster students' self-esteem
- How to reach all of your students with special needs
- How to use interventions and adaptations for accommodating special needs
- How to build positive relationships, social skills, and conflict resolution skills
- How to team with other teachers to better meet your own and their students' needs
- How to apply effective questioning techniques in the classroom
- How to hook reluctant readers/writers through the use of poetry, comic strips, and other motivational materials
- How to make oral language come alive using "Quick-Talks" and other techniques
- How to motivate kids to be successful mathematicians with creative strategies such as "Consumer Math Field Trip" and "Classroom Math Centers"
- How to rev up research skills with the "Mini-Research Project" and the "Learning Fair"
- How to get the most out of students through scientific investigation
- How to capitalize on music in the classroom through "Multicultural Music" and more
- How to reach students through the arts with drawing and other expressive forms

Julie A. Heimburge (B.A., San Diego; M.A., United States International University) has been an elementary teacher in the San Diego schools for the past 25 years.

Alphabet Learning Center Activities Kit

Nancy Fetzer and Sandra F. Rief, M.A.

Paper   ISBN: 0-13-044977-6
www.josseybass.com

Enable young children to hear and feel the letter sounds with modeled reading and writing strategies that help children identify and spell words with ease! You'll find easy-to-follow, illustrated steps for presenting each of the 26 letters of the alphabet using multisensory cues and charts, plus detailed directions and reproducible patterns. Developed and tested successfully in classrooms just like your own, this remarkable resource gives you step-by-step guidelines, ready-to-use learning center activities, and over 200 reproducibles for teaching letter-sound connections and beginning reading and writing skills.

With *Alphabet Learning* you'll teach your students:

- Phonemic Awareness in acquiring knowledge about the complex sounds of our language.

- The "Holder & Fastie" Alphabet that provides auditory and visual cues which help children learn how and where sounds are produced and felt.

- Alphabet "Tubbing" Activities with over 30 hands-on alphabet activities for independent, partner, and small group use . . . and more!

Nancy Fetzer is a District Literacy Trainer and Title One Facilitator for the Naranca School District (El Cajon, CA). She has an extensive background in general and special education, including reading recovery teacher and resource specialist. She has co-authored and co-produced two educational videos: *Successful Classrooms* and *Successful Schools*.